AGAINST EXCESS

AGAINST EXCESS

Drug Policy for Results

MARK A.R. KLEIMAN

BasicBooks
A Division of HarperCollinsPublishers

AME 9436-1/1

Library of Congress Cataloging-in-Publication Data
Kleiman, Mark.
  Against excess : drug policy for results / Mark A. R. Kleiman.
    p. cm.
  Includes bibliographical references and index.
  ISBN 0-465-01103-9
  1. Narcotics, Control of–United States. I. Title.
HV5825.K54 1992
363.4'5'0973–dc20

91-55459
CIP

Designed by Ellen Levine

92 93 94 95 PS/HC 9 8 7 6 5 4 3 2 1

To my teachers
and my students.

Nothing too much.

—Inscription at Delphi

Genug ist genug. (Enough is enough.)

—Yiddish proverb

Contents

IV. DRUGS 201

V. RECAPITULATION AND CONCLUSION 383

Acknowledgments

This book is less a collective effort than a folk song is, but only barely. In addition to all I have learned from those who were paid to teach me and those whom I was paid to teach, and from the practitioners of drug abuse control with whom I have worked over the years, I have a long list of specific debts to acknowledge.

Thomas C. Schelling and James Q. Wilson provided encouragement and practical guidance while the book was in its earliest planning stages. Martin Kessler of Basic Books was generous with his advice and patient with my work habits, as were David Haproff and Susan Zurn, in their successive roles as volume editors. Otto Sonntag offered a masterly copy edit of a manuscript that (not "which") badly needed it.

Douglas Anglin, Eugene Bardach, Don Des Jarlais, Richard Doblin, Francis Hartmann, Lowry Heussler, Herbert Kleber, Herman Leonard, Robert Millman, John Pinney, Daniel Polsby, Peter Reuter, Aaron Saiger, Ernesto Savona, Lewis Seiden, Cathy Shine, Severin Soresen, Eric Sterling, Zachary Tumin, and Franklin Zimring read the manuscript in whole or part and offered, in various proportions, helpful suggestions and equally helpful encouragement. Jonathan Caulkins, Michael Montagne, Mark Moore, and my parents, Jeanette and Allen Kleiman, read it especially attentively, critically, and often.

Andrew Chalsma, Evan Cohen, Andrew Curry Green, Patricia Gorton, Sandy Kendall, Stefan LoBuglio, Amy Lockwood, Sarah Madsen, Lucy Marcus, Lisa Moore, David Osborne, Jenny Rudolph, Kerry Smith, Shirley Stallings, and David Woodruff searched databases, typed, puzzled over sources and over my handwriting, and argued with me about facts, interpretations, and phrasing. All of them made great contributions; those who worked the night through to get the final manuscript ready have my undying gratitude. As usual, Gary Emmett, Merle Frank, and Lesley Friedman came through when I needed them.

Gordon Black, David Boyum, Lisa Brauer, Paul Goldstein, Henrick Harwood, Jack Henningfield, Arthur Houghton, Bruce Johnson, Karyn Model, Joel Schwartz, Javier Trevino-Cantú, and Joe Tye unstintingly shared information.

My colleagues at the Program in Criminal Justice Policy and Management of the Kennedy School cheerfully tolerated two years of "Sorry, I've got to get this book done." What my colleagues at BOTEC Analysis Corporation tolerated, no human tongue can tell.

The Criminal Justice Policy Foundation, supported by grants from the John M. Olin Foundation and the Ford Foundation, provided invaluable financial help. Eric Sterling, William Voegeli, and Anne Kubisch have been the ideal project officers: warmly supportive and scrupulously nondirective.

Research on an earlier version of Chapter 5, "Markets," was supported by a grant, under the title "Modelling Drug Markets," from the National Institute of Justice to Harvard University. Bernard Gropper served ably as monitor for that project; neither he, the National Institute of Justice, nor my other sponsors should be held responsible for my views.

Preface and Warning

WHAT THIS BOOK TRIES TO DO

This book has three intended audiences: people who make and carry out drug policies as elected representatives, public officials, or employees of private organizations; people who influence drug policy from the supreme office of citizen and voter; and scholars and journalists who work on drugs and crime as substantive topics and on policy analysis, economics, and law as disciplines of thought. The members of these audiences are interested in the management of the drug problem as a public affair. But my experience as a lecturer and dinner-table guest over the past decade has taught me that the book will perforce have a fourth audience as well: people who are concerned about the management of their own drug taking or their children's.

That makes me profoundly uncomfortable. This is not a self-help book, and it deliberately takes a nonhortatory tone. It offers a theory with applications about public policy toward drugs. I am not an expert in the techniques of self-mastery either in theory or in practice, so I would be only partially qualified to offer personal advice even if I wanted to. Moreover, I have not deeply meditated on the possible effect of each sentence or paragraph on actual or potential drug takers having every possible set of personal characteristics and facing the entire range of possible situations.

If the book happens to help in that regard, so much the better. I can imagine a reader who starts out thinking of drugs as intrinsically no different from other consumer goods and believing that they have been subjected to needless regulation out of mere superstition and puritanical pleasure-hatred. If he were to learn from this book that drug taking is a treacherous practice, difficult to manage even for those with adequate self-command in other domains, and that it ought to be approached cautiously and undertaken, if at all, vigilantly and under the protection of rigid and conservative personal rules, that would make me happy. If someone previously unaware of one or another aspect of drug-related risk learns something about that risk, that too would be a good result. Informed and thoughtful advice is not so easy to come by that I would willingly neglect the opportunity to offer it.

But someone starting with the belief that all cocaine smoking leads to instant addiction, madness, and death might also learn from this book that only some cocaine smokers get into serious trouble. If she drew from that the inference that she, a reasonably self-disciplined sort, could safely try it just once, that would make me profoundly unhappy; maybe she is right, but it is very easy and horribly expensive to be wrong. I hope to make the reader more familiar with drugs and their dangers, but I greatly fear that familiarity will breed not only contempt for the dangers, but curiosity about the drugs.

This volume is intended to supply the information and analysis needed to substitute careful reasoning about likely consequences for reflex and taboo as the basis for making public policy about drugs. But it does not provide enough information, or information in the right form, to serve as a safe basis for personal decision making about drug taking. Like rubbing alcohol, this book should be labeled: *Warning: Not for Internal Consumption*.

It should also carry another caution label: *Opinions Subject to Change Without Notice*. Some of the specific views expressed here are certainly wrong, and some (not necessarily the same ones) I will come to reject sometime in the future. Sometimes the argument behind a recommendation seems, to me, conclusive; at other points, a modestly revised predictive model, a new fact, or a somewhat different evaluation of the relative importance of two competing objectives would turn the scales. I have tried to indicate how sure I am about the various conclusions, and to make explicit the weights I assign to various competing considerations, so that the reader whose opinions or value weightings differ from mine can adjust appropriately.

I have also attempted to indicate in footnotes where my current views differ substantially from those I formerly espoused. I do this not because I believe that my intellectual autobiography is of intrinsic interest but because I want to alert the reader to the sources of what later seem to be bad policy judgments: inaccurate data, inaccurate or incomplete reasoning about cause-and-effect relationships, changes in the relative importance assigned to various outcome dimensions, and the surprises that the Universe, with its extraordinary sense of humor, uses to keep us on our toes.

TOPICS OMITTED

As a comprehensive discussion of drug problems, this book has three glaring omissions; it seems prudent to point them out here rather than waiting for reviewers to do so.

The Foreign Experience

It draws its arguments and examples almost entirely from the United States and implicitly makes its recommendations largely to U.S. policy makers. Much of the material is quite general in form and potentially transnational in application, but that application should be done by someone who speaks more languages than I do. If this book is a reasonably accurate and comprehensive statement of a general theory of drug policy as applied to the United States, perhaps it will be more helpful to those thinking through the problems of Japan, Mexico, or Czechoslovakia than would any attempt on my part to guess what those problems might be. As Machiavelli tells his Prince, whoever has learned one terrain thoroughly from a strategic viewpoint has also learned how to learn about others.[1]

For similar reasons, I have been hesitant to draw lessons from overseas successes and failures, both because it is hard for a foreigner to determine what actually happened and, why, when Zurich set up a "needle park" or Malaysia started to execute drug dealers and because the social and institutional settings are so different as to invalidate the idea that we can somehow import our drug policies, as we do most of our illicit drugs, from abroad.[2]

The Benefits of Drug Use

The book focuses almost entirely on what might be thought of as the cost side of the drug equation—the damage drugs do to their users and to others—and makes only the most cursory exploration of their benefits. In particular, it largely ignores claims that some of the psychedelics (and the hard-to-classify MDMA) can, under

the right circumstances, facilitate creative work, psychological heal-
ing, insight, personal relationships, and even mystical and religious
experience.[3] Nor will it examine the prospects for the development
of new performance-enhancing psychoactives, particularly drugs to
improve memory and other cognitive functions.[4]

This is a substantial omission, whose importance can only grow
over time. Despite the drug-related catastrophes of the past generation, and even if none of the currently known drugs has benefits sufficient to outweigh its harms and risks, it seems virtually certain that
the joint progress of pharmacology and neuroscience will eventually
produce new substances with greater immediate benefits and smaller
immediate risks. Personal management and public policy alike will be
far more complicated in a world where such "steroids for the brain"
are a reality.

We are far from ready, as individuals or as a government, to deal
with drugs that are neither "therapeutic" (because they are used,
not to cure disease, but to improve normal performance) nor "recreational." Any performance-boosting drug will almost certainly have
unwanted side effects and risks, at the very least the risk of overuse
under the pressure of academic and professional competition. Those
side effects and risks are likely to be imperfectly understood, and
probably underestimated, early in the history of any drug.

Painful experience with previous drugs hailed as performance
enhancers—psychedelics in the 1960s and cocaine in the 1880s and
again in the 1980s—will help to generate personal and governmental
caution about drugs designed as cognitive boosters. The result may
even be to stifle their development entirely. If a legitimate performance enhancer does reach the market, it is likely to change social
attitudes toward drug taking of all kinds, complicating the problem
of drug abuse prevention.

An interesting book could be written on the management of beneficial drugs. For now, however, understanding the cost side of the
drug-policy ledger seems a sufficient task.

Race, Poverty, and Social Disadvantage

While the book acknowledges some of the interconnections between
drug use on the one hand and poverty, racial and ethnic divisions,
and the world of deprivation referred to as "the underclass" on the
other, it offers no comprehensive account of the life of the downtrodden, ways to improve it, or even the reasons that poor and otherwise

downtrodden people and heavy drug use so often occupy the same social space.*

One point of view holds that the drug problem as such is barely worth thinking about, because it is merely one side effect of poverty and other deprivations. In this account, drug abuse will vanish almost automatically once the broader problems of class and race are solved and cannot be more than slightly ameliorated while they endure. This seems wrong, twice.

If all of the residents of the United States had the opportunities and resources now available to the white upper-middle class, some of them would continue to develop drug habits they could not control and to damage themselves and other people in connection with their drug use. Whoever is willing to look past crack and heroin will find that drug abuse and drug-related harm are not exclusively, or even predominantly, associated with any one social group. As recently as 10 years ago, cocaine smoking—then, as now, a viciously destructive habit—was concentrated among the moderately young and extremely affluent. Alcohol takes its toll up and down the income distribution. White high school students are four times as likely as their black counterparts to be frequent drinkers.[5] Whites are 70 percent more likely than blacks to smoke a pack or more of cigarettes per day.[6] Thus the premise that any conceivable social transformation would by itself eliminate the drug problem is probably wrong.

Moreover, heavy drug use and drug dealing are causes as well as effects of poverty, other forms of deprivation, and social tensions. Drug policy is therefore an inescapable part of any larger program to improve the lot of the poor and socially disadvantaged.

I do not want to pretend that better management of our drug problems would of itself constitute an adequate social policy. A child spared exposure to cocaine or alcohol in the womb still needs nutrition, parental care, and education, and all of these are currently in short supply for the children of poverty. A youth who avoids entrapment in drug dealing and is not shot in a drive-by shooting is not thereby magically guaranteed a legitimate career or a successful transition to adulthood. Even if a drug-free America were attainable, it would not be a problem-free America.

---

* Regarding this last puzzle, part of the explanation must be that rundown neighborhoods are more likely than others to be the sites of open drug selling, for the same reasons that they are more likely to be the sites of mugging: because the mechanics of law enforcement make virtually any illegal activity safer for its perpetrators where the victims and neighbors are poor.

But progress on drug abuse control would have valuable results in itself, and would contribute something to progress on other, even more intractable issues. Lacking the expertise (and the courage) for an extended discussion of this country's deepest wounds—most of all, the wounds of race—I will restrict myself to a set of problems about which I may have something valuable to say. If we postpone all other business until those wounds are healed, we will have a long wait.

PLAN OF THE VOLUME

Part I, "Preliminaries," argues that drug policy inevitably has multiple goals and is likely to be ill-served by simple policies expressed in bumper-sticker slogans.

Part II, "Problems," explores the characteristics of drugs that set them apart from other consumer goods and make them appropriate subjects of special public policy attention. Chapter 2, "Drug Abuse and Other Bad Habits," is about why some users keep hurting themselves; Chapter 3, "The Other Victims of Drug Abuse," is about how they hurt others.

Part III, "Policies," develops the vocabulary of public actions—laws and programs—to control drug problems. The laws—taxes, regulations, and prohibitions—are the topic of Chapter 4. Chapter 5 considers the black markets that are likely to arise from drug laws. Chapter 6 examines programs to enforce the laws; Chapter 7 looks at programs to influence drug-taking behavior by persuasion and to provide help for, and impose control on, problem drug users.

Part IV, "Drugs," applies the analysis developed in the first three parts to five drugs: alcohol, marijuana, cocaine, tobacco, and heroin.

Part V is a recapitulation.

AGAINST EXCESS

I

PRELIMINARIES

Introduction: How to Stop Losing the War on Drugs

Fanaticism consists in redoubling your efforts when you have lost sight of your aim. —Santayana

This is a book without a clarion call.

It has been said that in the 1960s America fought a war on poverty, and poverty won. At times, the war on drugs seems headed for a similar result. This does not mean that drug abuse or poverty is beyond the reach of deliberate intervention by public authority. It does mean that war is a poor metaphor for social policy.

Thomas Schelling, the economist and game theorist, once remarked of generals and armchair generals who liken war to chess that "One can only hope that it is chess they misunderstand." Similarly, when politicians demand a "war on drugs," one can only hope that they misunderstand war. War has a beginning, an end, an opponent, and a maxim: "There is no substitute for victory." War is chaotic and wasteful of lives and property. It is conducted under rules remote from the rules of civil life. In none of these particulars is social policy like war.

It is, of course, possible to wage domestic war, war against a part of the population: Phillip II's war on the Protestants of Holland, Cromwell's war on the Catholics of Ireland, Stalin's war on the kulaks. Then the military metaphors of battle, casualties taken and inflicted, victory and defeat, advance, retreat, and surrender become fully appropriate. It is possible to imagine a real "war on drugs"—a war of extirpation directed at drug users and drug dealers. Fleeing in horror from that imagined war, we should leave the military metaphor behind with the rest of the abandoned baggage.

The metaphor of problem and solution is not much better. Whenever anyone asks me, "How are we going to solve the drug problem?" I think about the story of the two old men in a retirement community, one still playing competitive tennis, the other with a chronic heart condition. The cardiac patient asked his friend, "Why were you so lucky?" The tennis player replied, "It wasn't luck; I started every day of my life with a five-mile run." "Oh, now I understand," said the other. "You had shin splints *instead* of heart problems."

Heart problems or shin splints: that's the story of drug abuse control. Either we have the problems associated with drug abuse, or we have the problems associated with trying to control it—or we can choose some of each. Interventions without unwanted side effects are few and far between. Some problems have no solutions, only outcomes. So with drugs. The proponents of a "drug-free America" miss this point; they want no heart disease and no exercise either. That something-for-nothing promise may make good stump speeches, but it makes bad policy.

Other advocates of what they call a "common sense" or "regulatory" approach to drug policy—what their opponents call "legalization" or "surrender in the war on drugs"—also miss the point, but not in the same way. They argue, correctly, that for most currently illicit drugs the problems that grow out of drug abuse control efforts (the shin splints) are worse than the problems of drug abuse itself (the heart problems).[1] But they ignore the fact that this situation is a result of the success of prohibition in limiting abuse. It implies little about how bad abuse might be under another, less restrictive control regime. Consider alcohol and tobacco, which combine small control problems with very large abuse problems. Alcohol almost certainly accounts for more violent crime, and more drug abuse deaths, than does cocaine.[2] Tobacco kills more Americans than all other drugs combined.[3] Is it not strange to use those facts as arguments for treating other drugs as we now treat alcohol and tobacco?

THE GOALS OF DRUG
ABUSE CONTROL POLICY

A spirit of fanaticism is evident in much of what is now done publicly and privately to combat the menace of drug abuse: more and more extreme efforts with less and less clarity about why they are undertaken or what benefits they are expected to produce. Reporters scurry around, writing stories on the panacea-of-the-month: using the army, random drug testing, legalization, the death penalty for drug dealers, boot camps, getting tough with source countries, treatment on demand. Areas and institutions of all sizes and purposes are proclaimed "drug-free."

In the face of all this, it may seem superfluous to ask why drug-taking ought to be a matter for public, rather than only private, concern. But once the question is asked, the answer is not immediately obvious. The general rule in a liberal, free-market society is not to interfere in adults' considered decisions about the management of their own affairs, as long as those decisions do not impinge on the rights of others.[4] Why, then, should public authority directly intervene in decisions about ingesting psychoactive chemicals?

One way to answer this question is to look at all the varieties of harm—behavioral, physical, and economic—that drugs can do to their users. Many drug users look back with regret on their decision to begin taking one or another psychoactive substance. While many decisions include an element of risk—the decision to drive an automobile also often leads to regret—the sheer magnitude and prevalence of harm suffered by drug users is enough to challenge the assumption that drug-taking is an area in which individuals are good stewards of their own welfare.

A close examination of the decision to take drugs raises additional doubts about the applicability of theories of rational consumer choice. Many drug takers, especially first-time drug takers, are not adults but children and adolescents, who are not fully ready to act as their own guardians. For them, the law can supplement, or support, parental authority. Nor is it always plausible to describe even adult drug taking as purely the product of rational choice, even of choice under "bounded rationality." By acting directly on the brain's own pleasure mechanisms, by supplanting the body's internal production of important neurochemicals, and simply by clouding judgment, drugs challenge in fact the personal autonomy on which rational-actor models rely in theory.

Even if one were not persuaded on paternalistic grounds that the harms various drugs do to their users warrant public control, the question of the harms drug users do to others would remain. Some drug users, as a result of their drug use, behave badly, spread disease, and impoverish themselves, thereby imposing predictable burdens on others. The clearest examples of such external harms are crimes and accidents arising from intoxication. Saying "Punish the crimes and require reparation for the accidents" does not solve the problem, because the criminal law and the tort liability system are imperfect and expensive ways of discouraging undesirable behavior. The frequency of automotive accidents due to drunkenness will therefore tend to increase with the frequency of drunkenness.

It is therefore less obvious than the libertarians would have it that the prevalence of drunkenness (and its cognate states for other intoxicants) should be a matter of social indifference, like the prevalence of jogging or bird watching. Intoxication threatens, or at least seems to threaten, the virtue of self-control, the capacity to defer gratification, and even the rational enterprise of making sense of the world. The citizens of a liberal republic rely on one another to regulate their own behavior within the bounds of others' rights (refraining from negligence, assault, and theft); to carry out their responsibilities in their private roles as neighbors, employees, and parents; and to be capable of joining in public deliberation on matters of public concern. Whatever threatens self-rule threatens liberal society. This does not mean that all intoxication is evil, only that its frequency and circumstances are not a matter of social indifference.

Any debate about how much intoxication is too much is likely to arouse passions and inflame social divisions.* The variety of intoxicants makes the problem worse; the argument about which substances to control can too easily become an argument as to which ethnic or generational groups are to be treated as deviant. Many of the participants in such a debate will have no personal experience of the drugs in question, and scientific evidence tends to be more illuminating about tissue damage than about the quality and consequences of the drug experience. Inevitably, then, these debates will have a high ratio of emotion to information.

Thomas Szasz, the psychiatrist, likens the desire of some to forbid to others whatever intoxicants they do not themselves use to religious intolerance. In his view, this proves that drug laws are as unwarranted as heresy laws.[5] But Szasz's comparison only points up the profundity of the social divisions that mind-altering drugs can engender; it does not answer the question about the best way to handle those divisions.

ALCOHOL AND TOBACCO AS EXAMPLES

The attentive reader will by now have noticed that this book assumes that alcohol and tobacco are drugs and that how to control them is

---

* See Shakespeare's *Twelfth Night*.

part of the topic of drug control policy. This assumption is not fully conventional, and thus deserves some justification.

The legal distinction between licit and illicit drugs is sometimes treated as if it had pharmacological significance. Vendors of licit drugs and proponents of a "drug-free society" share an interest in convincing tobacco smokers and alcohol drinkers that smoking and drinking are radically different from "drug use." But a nicotine addict can be just as hooked as a heroin addict,[6] and the victim of an alcohol overdose is just as dead as the victim of a cocaine overdose. The use and abuse of licit drugs is both similar to and entwined with the use and abuse of controlled substances, and much more widespread. A discussion of drug policy that omits only tobacco and alcohol is about as useful as a discussion of naval strategy that omits only the Atlantic and the Pacific.

Of course alcohol and tobacco (more precisely, nicotine) are psychoactive drugs; they are substances taken into the body that influence mood, behavior, and perception, other than by satisfying hunger and supplying nutritional energy. That does not mean that they are evil; caffeine and the other xanthines in chocolate are psychoactive drugs too, if it comes to that.

But alcohol and tobacco also have some of the characteristics associated with problem drugs: alcohol (but not nicotine) is a powerful intoxicant with moderately frequent undesirable behavioral side effects;[7] nicotine (and to a lesser extent alcohol) frequently induces patterns of habitual heavy use, use that continues despite users' conscious desire to suppress it and in the face of bad consequences;[8] both can create severe and lasting health damage. In addition, use of alcohol and tobacco, particularly by the young, is strongly correlated (perhaps causally, perhaps not) with use of illicit drugs.[9]

Once we include alcohol and tobacco on the list of drugs, alcohol and tobacco problems loom large among all drug problems, both in terms of health damage to users and in terms of harms inflicted by users on others. Because they are legal and their use is widespread, they are good sources of data and instances to illuminate the choices we face with respect to currently illicit drugs. For both of these reasons, the following pages will dwell on alcohol and nicotine at some length.

There is another, equally powerful reason to use alcohol and tobacco as examples when thinking about drug policy. Doing so allows us to think about ourselves and our own family and friends as we think about drug use, drug abuse, and drug habituation. Rela-

tively few of the readers of this book will have been users of heroin or
smokers of cocaine or had kin or close friends who were heroin
addicts or crackheads. But most will be at least occasional drinkers
and will have at least one friend or close relative who faces a chronic
battle with alcohol or has died of a nicotine-related disease. This
gives a valuable perspective.

One of the valued weapons in the current war on drugs is intolerance, even "zero tolerance." William Bennett, the former drug "czar,"
has cited the willingness of virtually everyone who does not use illicit drugs to punish those who do as evidence of progress against
the drug problem.[10] A measured intolerance of socially disruptive
and self-destructive behavior can indeed be a powerful resource in
controlling such behavior.

But intolerance can easily get out of hand, particularly as use of the
illicit drugs becomes more and more confined to the young and the
socially marginal. An essay on employee drug testing with the title
"Never Trust Anyone under 40"[11] may say more about the cultural
fears of its author and its intended readers than it does about a
sensible direction for drug abuse control. As Lincoln pointed out to
the temperance crusaders of his day, a war on drugs that turns into a
cultural holy war can be as destructive as one of the Four Horsemen
of the Apocalypse; empathy, charity, and humility are operational as
well as theological virtues.[12]

Thinking about the familiar drugs—how they are used, how they
are abused, what helps control their abuse—will help us understand
the more exotic ones and their users. To understand all is not, in this
case, to forgive all. A crime is a crime, and failure of responsibility
is a dereliction of duty, whether drug induced or not. Once we have
put away our superstitious fears about drugs and drug users, we will
have plenty of rational fear left.

TOWARD A BETTER DRUG POLICY

Our current policies, driven in part by the illusion that a complete
solution exists and in part by professional self-seeking and political
blather, do far more damage than they need to and far less good
than they might. We can do better.

Wisdom in this area, as in so many others, consists in abandoning
the search for the Philosopher's Stone and settling down to the choice
between a bad result and a somewhat less bad result. Some sample
conclusions give the flavor of this thinking.

1. Alcohol and nicotine, the two licit drugs of abuse, are far too readily and cheaply available. Their use should be discouraged not only by higher taxes and "negative advertising," but also by regulations aimed at who may use them, under what circumstances, and how much. They should be treated not as routine items of commerce but as grudgingly tolerated vices. The consumption of alcohol should be a privilege subject to a license, like driving, not an irrevocable right of adulthood. The best reason for not banning cigarettes immediately is the problem of the current user base. In the long run, we may want to ban cigarette sales to all but registered nicotine addicts.

2. For the most widely consumed of the currently illicit drugs, marijuana, a system of high taxes and tight regulation (like the one proposed here for the other mass-market intoxicant, alcohol) might be as effective in controlling damage as the current total prohibition, while costing less and producing fewer unwanted side effects. Such a system is easier to imagine vaguely than it is to specify in detail and much easier to specify in concept than to establish in practice, but a successful design and implementation do not seem impossible.

3. It is much harder to conceive of a workable regulatory regime for either heroin or cocaine. Thus the costs of prohibition must be borne, and the grubby and unpleasant tasks of enforcing that prohibition must be faced.

4. The most vulnerable point in the drug distribution system is the sale to the retail customer. Availability—the time and inconvenience involved in purchase—is probably more important than price (within the range of variation that enforcement can bring about) in determining drug consumption, and availability depends on the number, location, and behavior of retail dealers. Therefore, retail-level enforcement, which drug enforcement professionals often dismiss as "making garbage cases," is more important than high-level, "quality-case" enforcement directed at "drug kingpins," "major money launderers," and other glamorous targets.

5. Drug enforcement can easily swallow the criminal justice system in big cities. (In Washington, D.C., drug cases constituted more than half of all adult felony convictions in each year from 1986 through 1989.[13]) As a result, progressively more serious forms of theft and assault have been effectively decriminalized. That must be prevented, even at the cost of trying fewer crack-dealing cases. Enforcement tactics that do not rely on arrests, trials, and

imprisonment but instead create inconvenience for buyers and sellers and thus slow the pace of transactions are therefore particularly attractive.

6. The U.S. law enforcement system is bankrupt: unable to meet its obligations to deliver the punishments provided by statute. The spread of drug dealing both worsens that situation and is made worse by it. There is a strong case for spending substantially more: at least $20 billion more per year. Without such an increase, the choice between enforcing the drug laws and enforcing all other laws will be intolerably hard.

7. Diversion of prescription drugs for nontherapeutic use causes enormous and largely preventable harm. One way to reduce the harm is to insist that doctors and pharmacies keep and submit to regulatory authorities records of who gets highly abusable drugs and how often. Such "triple-prescription" programs seem to work in the few states that have them, though too little is known about their costs, particularly in the form of undermedication or substitution of less appropriate drugs. Either "triple-scrip" or some better system to control diversion should be made national.

8. Marijuana has substantial therapeutic potential and ought to be licensed for that purpose, even if it remains illicit for nonmedical use. The effect on marijuana abuse would be trivial.

9. Every incarcerated drug-involved offender who wants treatment should get it; even a small reduction in future drug-involved criminality will easily pay for the cost.

10. Drug-involved offenders not behind bars should be required to abstain from drug use as a condition of bail, probation, or parole. (That includes drunken drivers and drunken wife-beaters.) Abstinence should be verified by chemical testing, and missed or "dirty" tests should lead to progressively more severe sanctions, up to time in jail.

11. Many problem drug users can benefit from skilled help. The test of a drug treatment program is not whether it makes its clients lastingly drug-free, but how much and for how long it improves their condition and behavior. Methadone maintenance is not as good as abstinence, but it is a great deal better than heroin addiction, both for addicts and for their families and neighbors.

12. The search for a maintenance substitute for cocaine—based on the analogy with methadone for heroin—is probably futile, because the drugs and the kinds of compulsive use they generate are so dissimilar.

13. In cities where some drug treatment programs have long waiting lists, others have vacant slots. There is no incentive for programs to make referrals to one another, and no central registry of vacant slots and waiting clients. Nor is there any system for matching clients to the programs most appropriate for them. Changing that situation would require changing the way drug treatment is financed.

14. The effort to persuade current and potential drug users to abstain entirely or use in moderation—called, not entirely accurately, "education"—should focus less on facts about drugs and more on the skills of self-management.

These suggestions will be developed and further defended in the pages that follow. Few readers are likely to agree in detail with all of them, which is probably just as well. The goal of the book is to help generate and sustain a serious debate, not to dictate its outcome.

1

Thinking About Drug Policy

A temperate temperance is best.   —Mark Twain

THE GOALS OF DRUG POLICY

Drugs sometimes create damage. Good drug policy limits that damage, doing as little harm as possible in the process.

Drugs are harmful to some of their users. They can lead to injury, even death, from acute bad reactions or from chronic heavy use; to accidents or misbehavior due to intoxication; to poor performance in economic or social roles due either to excessive time spent "under the influence" or to the post-intoxication side effects of drug use; and to the formation of bad drug-use habits that are hard to break.

Drugs can also be harmful to those who do not use them. The victims of intoxication-related accidents or crimes are the most obvious instances, but not necessarily the most important ones. The families of those harmed by drugs also suffer, both because they care about the welfare of their injured kinfolk and because they are likely to have to share the economic and other burdens of drug-damaged lives. Friends, neighbors, coworkers, and fellow citizens bear smaller shares of the sympathetic suffering and the material losses.

Much of the mechanism of contemporary society serves to spread risks from individuals and families to groups. All those who share risks with me, by contributing to common pools of resources to be drawn on by those of us in need, will bear part of the cost if my drug use puts my well-being at hazard. The Social Security Trust Fund, the police force, the ambulance service, and the willingness of passersby to stop and render aid are all such common-property resources. Insurance, "social insurance," and taxation help pass the costs of drug use on to total strangers. If those who harm themselves with drugs put extra burdens on those systems, their problems are not theirs alone.

The primary goal of drug policy, then, is to limit the harms drug users do to themselves and the resulting harms to others and drains on common-property resources. But that primary goal is only half of the story, and an exclusive concentration on it is one major problem with the "war on drugs."

Any public policy has costs. In the case of drug control policy, only some of those costs will be in the direct expenditure of public dollars; the less obvious but not necessarily less important costs will take the form of interference with the harmless pleasures of those for whom drug use is not a problem, but a recreation, a solace, or even a therapy. "Prohibition," said Archy the cockroach, "makes you want to cry into your beer and denies you the beer to cry into."[1]

Any public policy more complicated than planting flowers by the roadside also has unwanted side effects, and controlling drug use is considerably more complicated than planting flowers. Taxes, regulations, and prohibitions generate evasions, violations, and black markets, and thus the need for enforcement. Black markets create adulterated and misbranded products, violence among buyers and sellers (both to settle disputes and because those engaged in lucrative illegality are well worth robbing and unlikely to complain to the police), the flaunting of illicitly gained wealth, and attempts, sometimes successful, to corrupt the machinery of the law.

The great secondary goal of drug policy, then, is to control its own costs and unwanted side effects. Sometimes cost control means adding one law or program to compensate for another, as bribery statutes and police internal affairs divisions act to limit corruption. Sometimes it means choosing policies to minimize side effects; for example, the exemption of drugs prescribed for medical use from drug prohibition preserves some of the benefits of those drugs even as the general prohibition acts to control some of their harms. And sometimes cost control means regretfully deciding that a policy goal desirable in itself—for example, the immediate elimination of cigarette smoking—is simply not attainable under current conditions without unacceptable costs and side effects, and that it is therefore necessary to settle for some second best. Always cost control means counting, weighing, and balancing, which strike some warriors as very unwarlike actions.

Policies intended to protect users can harm them by accident. For instance, the use of nicotine by adolescents has been linked to the use of other drugs later in life.[2] This suggests that making nicotine illicit might reduce the incidence of, say, cocaine use. But tobacco prohibition could also help familiarize some juvenile tobacco users with illicit transactions and lead others to switch from nicotine to other, more dangerous substances. The value of any such policy depends on the relative sizes of its good and bad effects.

Other drug policies harm users by design, in order to make drug use less attractive. At some point, protecting people from themselves involves damaging those who refuse to be protected. Once public action focuses on reducing consumption, it is hard to make distinctions between users whose consumption is harmful to themselves and others and users whose consumption is relatively benign. Even those who themselves do no harm and suffer none still help to maintain the black market.

In the extreme, this line of argument can lead to treating users as the enemy in the war on drugs. Damaging the remaining drug users can become a goal independent of reducing the harms of drug abuse, just as punishing criminals is seen as an objective separate from preventing crime. This tendency is not a new one; Abraham Lincoln warned of it in the temperance movement of the 1840s.[3] To maintain a drug policy consistent with our other institutions, we must remember what Lincoln told the Temperance Society: drug users, considered simply as users, are not the enemy, but fellow citizens and fellow sinners. This puts limits on our rhetorical and practical efforts to deter drug use.

Any drug policy beyond simple persuasion entails an attempt to make a class of people—drug users and potential drug users—better off by limiting their range of personal choices. Being thus coerced for their own good is supposed to make them more responsible citizens and neighbors. Described so baldly, drug control is revealed for what it is: a particularly tricky piece of social engineering. Its wide acceptance among those who otherwise abhor the policies they call "social engineering" should not blind us to the fact that drug control is subject to the frailties of its kind, including a propensity for unexpected and unwanted side effects. Using coercion in a free society is not for the faint of heart.

One of these side effects has already been mentioned. Vice control confronts a paradox: it tends to make those who resist control worse off, and more dangerous to others, than they would otherwise be.

Many states ban hypodermic syringes as a means of reducing heroin use; this may encourage heroin users to share needles and thus to spread AIDS and other blood-borne diseases.[4] Deprived of protective government regulation, users of illegal drugs risk damage from adulterated goods, as when a packet sold as marijuana turns out to be oregano sprayed with PCP.

If the vice involves a commodity, as drug use does, vice control also creates the potential for a black market. Black markets are good for criminals and bad for the rest of us. Already scarce enforcement resources must be used to suppress them. Enforcement creates additional opportunities for corruption. Black-market participants often quarrel with firearms. Open-air retail drug bazaars impose enormous costs on the neighborhoods where they are located.

Furthermore, black markets in drugs are hard to suppress. Drug dealing differs from the common-law "predatory" crimes—all the varieties of theft and assault—in two ways. It requires less in the way of special skills or tastes, so the number of potential criminals is much larger, and it yields a far steadier and more generous income. "The wages of sin," it has been said, "are well below the legal minimum." The typical street robber or household burglar risks years in prison for a "take" unlikely to exceed a few hundred dollars.[5] (The value of property lost by victims is greater, but "fences" are not generous.) Even given the current, rather ineffectual, attempts of criminal justice agencies to apprehend and punish "common-law" criminals, only a fool or someone with a short time horizon or poor self-control would choose a career as a thief: in the long run McDonald's pays better.[6]

Not so for drug dealing, particularly in big cities.[7] The substantial incomes to be made explain why drug dealers quarrel, and even kill, over "territory." Enforcement will not easily drive the herds of dealers from such green pastures. Suppressing drug dealing with arrests and punishments, if the drug in question enjoys a mass market, is likely to swallow enforcement resources—police, prosecutor, courtroom, and prison time—in great, greedy gulps. Raising the risk-to-reward ratio in retail crack dealing to the level faced by unskilled burglars and robbers might require more resources than the existing system can deliver.

It is the unenviable task of drug policy analysts to attempt to design public actions that will serve the three often incompatible goals of protecting users, protecting others, and controlling costs. The key question in any such analysis is, How much? How much will cocaine

use shrink if street-dealing arrests double? How much will the burglary rate rise as a result of the diversion of resources from burglary
cases to dealing cases? How much harm, to users and others, will
more crack arrests prevent? These questions are easier to ask than
to answer.

The total damage users do themselves and others presumably
varies with the number of users and the average quantity consumed.
But the shape of that relationship is unclear, and surely varies from
drug to drug. For most drugs, the bulk of the consumption and visible harm is concentrated among a relatively small number of users;
the three great exceptions are nicotine, heroin, and cocaine in smokable form. This seems to point to a "problem user" strategy that tries
to suppress consumption and misbehavior among the heaviest users.
U.S. alcohol policy since Repeal has been based largely on this model.

But the "problem user" idea can mislead in two ways. Damage and
misbehavior may be more evenly distributed among users than consumption itself; even an infrequent drinker can be a problem drinker
if he gets into a fight every time he drinks. And the number of heavy
drinkers may be closely related to the drinking behavior of the population as a whole, both because any drug user has some probability
of becoming a heavy user and because people adjust their own behavior to the behavior they see around them.[8] Again, this appears
to be true for alcohol, since the per-capita alcohol consumption in a
country predicts quite closely its rate of death from cirrhosis.[9] Under
these circumstances, a "problem user" strategy can miss a large part
of the problem.

Even the total harm done by any drug is more a matter of speculation than of measurement. Some of the direct physical harms are
relatively easy to discern, but social and behavioral effects are much
trickier. Researchers can compare a sample of users to a sample of
non-users, but which way does the arrow of causation point? From
drug use to some undesirable condition such as crime, unemployment, or dropping out of school? From the undesirable condition
to drug use? Both ways at once? Or from some third factor such as
impulsiveness or social disadvantage that causes both?

Finally, there is the problem of substitution or complementarity
among drugs. To what extent does restricting access to one drug
increase or decrease use of another? If schoolchildren kept away from
marijuana are consequently less likely to try cocaine, they, and we,
come out way ahead. If they sniff gasoline or paint instead, they, and
we, come out way behind. Here again, the evidence is almost always
ambiguous; a drug policy analyst without a tolerance for ambiguity
is a very unhappy person.

CHOOSING A DRUG PROBLEM: POLICIES AND OUTCOMES

In 1929, Chicago was wracked by the "Beer Wars." Nationwide, several hundred Americans died in the struggle among rival alcohol-distribution gangs, and 8400 died of cirrhosis of the liver. Ten years later, after Repeal, the Beer Wars were gone, but 10,900 died of cirrhosis of the liver.[10] Was that an improvement?

In 1988, Los Angeles was wracked by crack wars. Nationwide, gunfire related to cocaine dealing claimed several thousand lives. Hundreds or thousands more died of the medical consequences of cocaine use.[11] No doubt, legalizing cocaine would end the crack wars. But how many more would die from taking cocaine?

Alcohol-induced cirrhosis is a drug problem, a bad effect that the drug alcohol has on the human body.[12] The Beer Wars were a drug *policy* problem, a bad side effect of a public action—Prohibition—intended to control the drug problem. Assaults by intoxicated drug users are part of the drug problem; thefts committed to get money to buy expensive illegal drugs are part of the drug policy problem.

The failure to distinguish between the bad effects of drug abuse and the bad effects of drug abuse control sometimes reduces public discourse about drugs to gibberish. Alcohol causes crime because it reduces self-control; heroin causes crime because it is illegal. (Pharmacologically, heroin makes users docile rather than aggressive.) Therefore, controlling alcohol-related crime calls for different measures than controlling heroin-related crime.

Some aspects of the drug problem defy division into results of pharmacology and results of legislation. Chronic heroin users tend to be poor, sick, and miserable, both because long-term opiate addiction is an unhealthy practice and because the drug's illegality keeps prices high, gets users in trouble with the law, and leads them to spread disease by sharing needles. They are victims—participating victims—of both drug abuse and drug abuse control.

Varieties of Drug Policy

For all the complexity of the drug problem, a small number of actions constitute the basic repertoire of drug abuse control. There are laws (taxes, regulations, and prohibitions) and programs (enforcement, persuasion, and providing help and control to problem users). Each of these actions has its own costs, benefits, effects, and side effects. Each may impair, or enhance, the effectiveness of the others.

Laws

Statutory control regimes matter. They determine who, if anyone, may legally use each drug, where and when it may be sold, and (via taxation) at what price.

At one extreme is flat prohibition, under which manufacture, distribution, and possession are all subject to prosecution. A weaker form of prohibition is "decriminalization," under which possession for use is licit, or only mildly punished, but sale is prohibited. (Confusingly, the policy called Prohibition when applied to alcohol was identical to what is called decriminalization when applied to currently illicit drugs.)

Prohibition gives the black market maximum scope by sparing it any legal competition. It saddles the public with the costs of punishing users and the users with the punishments inflicted. Decriminalization attempts to achieve the supply-control benefits of prohibition without the burdens of enforcement against users, but its likely effect is to boost demand (though perhaps only slightly) thereby enriching criminals, who maintain their monopoly on supply. The choice between the two thus trades off black-market and consumption-reduction goals against enforcement burdens.

A disadvantage of total prohibition of psychoactives is that some of them have therapeutic value: the opiates against pain,[13] marijuana against nausea,[14] the barbiturates against epilepsy.[15] Making otherwise prohibited drugs available by prescription tries to preserve those therapeutic benefits, at some cost to drug abuse control. How large that cost is depends on the vigilance of the regulators and the capacity of the black market to produce the drug in question. The use of cocaine as a local anesthetic in eye surgery contributes next to nothing to the huge illicit supply; in the absence of black-market manufacturers, virtually all of the abuse of diazepam (Valium) stems from sloppy doctoring or from the diversion of licit supplies into illicit channels.[16]

Even fully licit drugs need not be ordinary articles of commerce. Alcohol and tobacco, for example, are subject to discriminatory taxation and at least nominally forbidden to minors. Alcohol is also restricted in that it can be sold only by establishments with special licenses, a rule that both restricts the number of outlets and helps enforce other restrictions by giving licensees an incentive for compliance. The effectiveness of taxation in reducing abuse depends on the size of the tax and on the market for the drug: the responsiveness of demand to price and the availability of substitutes. The effectiveness of age restrictions varies with the vigor of enforcement and the willingness of adults to sell or give age-restricted goods to their underage acquaintances.

The distinction between allowed and prohibited drugs is conventional rather than natural. After all, different societies forbid and permit different drugs: the Koran forbids wine but not hashish; the Controlled Substances Act, hashish but not wine; the prohibitions in the Book of Mormon are taken to preclude both, along with nicotine and caffeine. Even within any one society, the rules change over time: in the United States in 1930 marijuana was legal and alcohol was not, but by 1940 the positions had reversed. Nevertheless there is a strong tendency to treat the legal distinctions as if they were natural ones and even to deny that licit psychoactives are drugs at all.

Thus the rhetoric of commerce and the rhetoric of the war on drugs combine to obscure the actual situation: the various legal statuses, from complete availability to complete prohibition, form a continuum, and the practical policy decisions regarding a particular drug involve who should be allowed to use it, under what circumstances, for what purposes, with what restrictions, and what sanctions are to be applied to violations of those rules, rather than simply whether the drug should be called "licit" or "illicit."

It is comfortable to think of the distinctions among drugs as yes-or-no: either a drug is allowed or it is forbidden. That clean distinction is particularly valued in a society that places a premium on individual freedom from government interference. If something is evil, abnormal, or just plain bad, then of course the government ought to forbid it. That isn't "excessive government regulation," it's just common sense and a reaffirmation of common values. But if it isn't all bad—if, like almost all actual drugs, it has some harmless uses but poses some danger of misuse—then the justification for public intervention is weaker. And if the intervention is anything more complicated than simple prohibition, it is likely to involve citizens' applying to officials for permissions: that is, the "bureaucracy" and "paperwork" that Americans love to hate.

Flat prohibition thus seems less intrusive than any sort of regulation. The opponents of alcoholic excess, faced with the difficulty of creating a workably tight regulatory regime, found it easier to assert that all alcohol consumption was excessive, that "temperance" as applied to alcohol use meant no use at all, and that the entire nation ought to be required by law to become temperate in that sense. This understandable tendency is nonetheless undesirable. It leads to both too much prohibition and the under-regulation of whatever is not prohibited. America needs a new social and legal category of "grudgingly tolerated vices": items not strictly prohibited, but forbidden—enforceably forbidden—to minors and to adults who have shown an inability to consume them responsibly, and subject to discriminatory taxation, "negative advertising," and restrictions on promotion.

Programs: Enforcement

The outline of the drug problem is largely determined by the laws pertaining to various drugs. Alcohol is widely abused, and the alcohol industry is peaceful, because the drug is legal. Cocaine use is more confined, but its distribution is more violent, because the drug is illegal.

Law enforcement shapes the details. Laws do not enforce themselves. Where there is prohibition, there will be rum-runners. Where there are taxes, there will be moonshiners. Variation in the vigor and form of enforcement activity influence the behavior of the black-market sellers and buyers and thus drug prices, drug availability, and black-market violence and disorder.

Intense enforcement renders a drug more expensive and less available but can also tend to make it more potent, more likely to be adulterated, and more lucrative for criminal enterprise. Worse, the users of an expensive illegal drug are likely to be poorer, sicker, and more criminally active than they would be if it were cheaper. In addition, vigorous enforcement tends to make it more rewarding for dealers to use violence and corruption. Enforcement tends to weed out less well armed dealing organizations and thereby put the trade in the hands of the most dangerous criminals.[17] Less intense enforcement avoids these problems, but at the expense of greater openness in dealing, more consumption, higher sales volumes for dealers, and reduced public confidence in law enforcement.

Decisions regarding enforcement strategy and tactics also help shape the problem. Choices of enforcement targets—areas, offenders, organizations, offender types—make a difference. So does the choice between tactics designed to yield arrests and tactics designed to seize drugs. These are, or ought to be, largely practical questions rather than ideological ones. Hopeless confusion ensues when enforcement strategies come to be debated and decided on the basis of their symbolism instead of their results, as when any acknowledgement of the fact that no available enforcement activity will reduce drug abuse to zero is taken as undermining the moral force of drug prohibition.

Decisions about which drugs to concentrate enforcement resources on, by contrast, tend to be made on excessively technical grounds. A drug whose use is rising rapidly tends to command a comparably rising share of enforcement attention. This can be wise or foolish, depending on the drug's harmfulness and the prospects for halting the growth of the market; but such strategic thinking is rare among drug enforcement agencies.

Enforcement policy involves choosing stages of the traffic as well as drugs. Crops growing overseas, bulk drugs on their way to the United States, large-scale distributors, "kingpins" of local distribution networks, middlemen, street dealers, and users compete for enforcement attention. The price of illicit drugs is determined largely by enforcement directed at importers and wholesalers; conditions at the retail level determine "search time" and thus how hard it is for drug users to find drugs to start or continue their habits.[18] Longer search times may be more effective than higher prices in reducing drug-related harm. But going after the importers involves more glory and a smaller caseload. This creates an enforcement bias in favor of large cases, a bias that may not make for good policy.[19]

Programs: Persuasion, Help and Control

Laws and law enforcement attempt to compel abstinence from, or reduced consumption of, drugs. Public agencies can also encourage and facilitate voluntary abstinence or reduced consumption, by persuasion directed at those whose drug-related behavior is within their conscious, rational control and by therapy and coercive measures directed at those who have lost control of their habits.

These prevention and treatment programs are sometimes thought of as attacking the "demand side" of the drug problem, while enforcement is described as working on the "supply side."[20] This distinction conceals almost as much as it reveals. Arresting users is an enforcement activity, but it affects demand rather than supply. Giving a heroin-using retail heroin dealer—a "juggler"—access to methadone is likely to reduce his drug sales and thus reduce the effective supply of heroin.[21]

The arguments about supply-side versus demand-side strategy mask the divergent bureaucratic interests, ideological perspectives, and social-class identifications of police officers, on the one hand, and teachers and treatment providers, on the other. The actual relationships between instruments and results are more complex than the slogans suggest. For example, because supply-side efforts are undertaken by police officers, they are often identified with crime fighting. But drug law enforcement is as likely to increase predatory crime by dealers and users as to decrease it.[22] Prevention and drug treatment, by contrast, are unambiguously crime reducing, because they lower consumption without raising price.[23]

Most "prevention" efforts involve persuasion, packaged either as classroom instruction or as advertising. These programs have costs, but they create fewer unwanted side effects than enforcement programs do. Their chief drawback is that their effectiveness may be fundamentally limited, in extent and in social reach: members of the middle class, whether children or adults, are far easier to persuade than the very poor and the socially marginal.[24]

Some unfortunate experiences in the early 1970s tended to discredit persuasion as a strategy, but both advertising and classroom activity have been making a comeback recently. The new enthusiasm is only partially matched by improved knowledge about what works. There is some reason to believe that anti-drug programs are most likely to be successful if they focus on more than drugs. The best programs emphasize a broader health-consciousness and skills for personal decision making.[25] A recent study in Kansas City revealed that an integrated (and expensive) school, home, and media program can have significant results in reducing, or at least postponing, cigarette, alcohol, and marijuana use among seventh graders.[26]

Statute, enforcement, and education all strive to persuade users not to start to harm themselves with drugs. This leaves the problem of those who have become heavy drug users before they decide, on their own or with prodding from criminal justice agencies, to get their drug use under control. For these people, not abusing drugs means recovering from a drug habit: alone, in a self-help group, or with professional assistance.

Treatment programs are difficult both to design and to evaluate. Just as it is hard to tell whether a given bad effect is a consequence or only an accidental correlate of drug use, it is not obvious whether people quit drug use because they go through treatment or whether they go through treatment when they are ready to quit drug use.[27] (This question applies with equal force to low-cost self-help groups such as Alcoholics Anonymous and to high-cost therapeutic communities such as Phoenix House.)

Most paid treatment programs are expensive, if measured in dollars per "cure." Relapse is so frequent, as anyone who has tried to quit smoking can well imagine, that many users require treatment more than once. The cost of three or four courses of drug treatment can look like a lot of money to spend on one user. It is appealing to imagine that such funds could be used to nip a number of new habits in the bud rather than to (attempt to) uproot one habit that is already well planted.

Still, the cost of some forms of drug abuse to users and their neigh-bors is high enough to make even expensive treatment seem cheap: if building a therapeutic community on the grounds of a prison reduces the personal crime rates of heroin-using muggers by 20 percent, it will be well worth its substantial cost.[28] Education for prevention, by contrast, spends most of its resources on those who would never have become abusers anyway, so the cost per prevented abuser may be quite high even if the cost per audience member is low.

Uncertainty about costs and benefits is a difficulty that treatment has in common with other strategies for controlling drug abuse. Treatment programs and enforcement efforts alike are sometimes condemned for their failure to render a certain population of ad-dicts or a given area completely drug-free. No real-world policy can satisfy such fantasy criteria. Instead, the questions worth asking about enforcement should be applied to treatment as well: How much has it reduced the harm done by drugs? At what cost? Does the benefit justify the cost?

Asking these questions about both treatment and enforcement points up the differences in the harms they reduce and the costs they create. Enforcement tries to reduce harm to whole populations, but with predictable unwanted side effects. Treatment, on the other hand, concentrates on individuals. Its side effects are less worrisome, but it offers little to the majority of users who are not its clients. This limits its impact.

DIFFERENT DRUGS, DIFFERENT USERS, DIFFERENT PROBLEMS

All potential interventions—statutory regimes, enforcement policy, and treatment and prevention—must be evaluated in terms of their application to a very complex drug problem. Or perhaps one should say drug *problems*, for there are at least as many problems as there are varieties of drugs and drug users.

Drugs differ in their impacts. A street kid smoking marijuana does not have the same drug problem as a street kid smoking crack. A sub-stantial proportion of all heroin users steal or deal drugs for profit; the vast majority of marijuana users do neither. Users, too, differ in their vulnerability and the threats they pose to others: a stockbroker smoking crack does not have the same drug problem as a street kid smoking crack.

Drugs differ in their consumption patterns. Most heroin use takes place in a few poor neighborhoods in a few cities; marijuana use is spread across the nation and up and down the social spectrum. The two forms of cocaine are somewhere in between, with powder, which is snorted, lying closer to marijuana, and crack (rock, freebase), which is smoked, closer to heroin.

Drugs differ in their distribution patterns. Heroin and crack users tend to buy at most a day's supply at a time; marijuana users often buy for a month or more; powder cocaine users are in between. Most heroin and crack is sold outdoors or in specialized dealing locations, and almost always by professional dealers; powder cocaine and marijuana are more likely to change hands in multiple-use indoor locations (bars, office buildings, living rooms), and dealing may not be the retail dealer's main source of income.

These rather obvious facts are worth reciting only because so much drug-policy rhetoric ignores them, treating "drug abuse" as a single issue to be addressed by a single set of policies, all designed around the theme of reducing drug consumption.* The balance of this book will offer a more complex and differentiated view.

---

* Two national commissions provide the classic examples. The Attorney General's Task Force on Violent Crime recited the facts linking heroin to violent crime and concluded that preventing the importation of marijuana would prevent violence. The AIDS Commission used the link between heroin use and transmission of the AIDS virus as an argument for "drug-free" schools and workplaces. *Final Report of the Attorney General's Task Force on Violent Crime* (Washington, D.C.: Department of Justice, 1981); *Report of the Presidential Commission on the Human Immunodeficiency Virus Epidemic* (Washington, D.C.: US Government Printing Office, 1988), 103–104.

II

PROBLEMS

2

Drug Abuse and Other Bad Habits

I can resist anything except temptation.
—Oscar Wilde

Quitting smoking is easy. I have done so myself, upwards of a thousand times. —Mark Twain

Drugs differ from other commodities in that drug consumers may be less capable than other consumers of protecting their own interests.

Drugs can be dangerous in at least two ways. They are toxic: capable, if taken in sufficient doses and frequencies, of disrupting the functions of the body and the brain and damaging their tissues. They are also behaviorally risky: in drug-induced states of reduced motor skill and impulse control, users sometimes do unfortunate things, ranging from stumbling and falling to killing their spouses. Drugs are also costly, in money and in the time spent under their influence.

If drugs were only dangerous and costly, they would do far less damage to their users and to others than they actually do. What is puzzling and frightening about drugs is a third danger: the loss of self-control over drug taking itself. Some users keep coming back for more after the costs and risks have become all too apparent in their lives. "The burnt child," it is said, "fears the fire." But many who have been repeatedly and severely burned by their own drug use do not behave as if they had learned to fear. People who appear to be able to take care of themselves in other domains have trouble managing their own drug taking.

Drug taking is frequently carried to excess. All of the widely used drugs—including heroin and cocaine, even smoked cocaine—can be used safely if they are used in small and infrequent doses and at times and places where an intoxicated person is unlikely to do or suffer injury. But many users—the proportion varies from drug to drug—get into patterns of heavy chronic use, which they did not anticipate and would prefer not to continue. Excess is not, of course, restricted to drugs,[1] but it appears to be a greater menace with drug taking than with most other activities.

The assumption of self-control, of rationally purposive action, is central to our social organization. It might be said to define modernity vis-à-vis more traditional ways of life. "Of the voluntary acts of every man," says Hobbes, "the object is some good to himself."[2] The assumption that people are capable of doing what is good for themselves underlies Mill's defense of individual liberty[3] and the legal maxim that no person is injured by what he consents to: *Volenti non fit injuria.*[4] All the lovely theorems of elementary welfare economics— the proofs that, under the right conditions, the market equilibrium is in some sense an optimum—start by assuming a consumer capable of making choices for his own good, "maximizing utility subject to constraints."[5] We expect our (adult, healthy) fellow citizens to be good stewards of their own welfare; under no other assumption does either the market economy or personal liberty make sense as a way of securing good results for individuals or the social group.

Even when the governments of liberal societies interfere in personal choices, their strategies for doing so are built largely on the premise that human behavior can be changed through a careful manipulation of incentives: that is, of the costs and benefits to the actor of alternative courses of action. The use of taxes and subsidies in place of prohibitions and commands is one illustration of incentive manipulation as a strategy of ruling.[6] But even prohibitions and commands rely on the efficacy of threats—potential future undesired consequences—in shaping behavior.[7] Pure physical compulsion is perhaps the rarest form of social control: a police officer's "come-along" hold and the straitjacket that confines a violent schizophrenic in a mental hospital are two examples of it, but one is very temporary and the other applies to very few. The officer who arrests a suspect by pointing a gun at him is relying on the suspect's willingness to obey in order to avoid being shot. Controlling someone who is not moved by threats is difficult and dangerous.

There are a number of ways to define rational action, but all of them have to cover the following points:

- A rational actor takes the future into account and is able to make reasonable, even if imperfect, calculations about the impact of current choices on future results.

- A rational person is in control of herself and is therefore able to follow through on the choices she makes.
- A rational person knows what she wants and is able to use her tastes and preferences to choose among alternatives.

Thus, while a person rational in this sense may decide to do something that is bad for others, or something that others may perceive as harmful to her, she will not systematically choose what appears to herself to be bad for herself. The rational-actor model can accommodate the drinker who drinks up the money that should have bought food for his kids: he prefers his own being drunk to their being fed, which may make him a scoundrel but doesn't prove he's irrational. It can also accommodate the drinker who drinks up the money that would have bought his own dinner: he prefers being drunk to being fed which may be a bad choice but is still a choice. But the drinker who smashes his whiskey bottle in disgust in the morning, swearing never to drink again, and buys another in the afternoon—and did the same last month and will do the same again next month—is not acting according to a consistent understanding of his own welfare.

The model of the autonomous, perfectly self-controlled, perfectly rational, perfectly informed consumer is, in several obvious respects, an abstraction from the way human beings actually act. It is even further removed from the way some people behave in regard to drugs. The more drug-using behavior departs from these rational-actor assumptions, the more our drug policies may need to depart from our policies regarding other consumer goods, even dangerous ones.

We are tempted every day to do things we know we should not: watch too much television, buy gadgets we will never use, or finish off that pint of ice cream in the freezer.[8] A wide variety of social institutions are designed in part to protect us from our impulses.[9] If perverse impulses to take drugs are more common than perverse impulses to buy cars, some people who make good decisions about buying cars will make bad decisions about taking drugs.

There is nothing new or mysterious about the problem of self-command. If Homer's Odysseus, who had himself tied to the mast to hear the Sirens' song so that he might resist the temptation to dive in and drown, was the first character in literature to treat his own behavior in the face of temptation as a problem to be solved with outside help, he was not the last.[10]

The vast literature on theories of drug addiction tends to focus on how to explain why some people and not others get in trouble with drugs.[11] This difficult question is of great scientific interest to students of human behavior and of great practical use to those who attempt to prevent or treat drug abuse.* But to understand what special public policies ought to be applied to drug taking, we need to answer a different question: why people get in trouble with drugs rather than with something else.

It is possible to identify at least five separate concepts that help explain why drugs are frequently involved with failures of self-command: intoxication, addiction, distorted risk preference, routine, and the tyranny of fashion, this last supported by a systematic bias in information-gathering about drugs. Only the first two relate directly to the chemical basis of drug taking, but although the others are potential problems for a wide range of pleasurable activities, drug taking has special characteristics likely to make deviations from rationality particularly frequent and large.

INTOXICATION

Drugs affect decisions. It is a commonplace that people behave differently "under the influence" than they do sober. Some drugs, particularly depressants such as alcohol, opiates, and the barbiturates, measurably reduce the speed and accuracy of information processing.[12] Others, including marijuana and the psychedelics, distort mental processes in more complex ways.[13] A wide range of drugs also reduce inhibitions and increase impulsiveness.[14] If we take the sober mind as the reference point, choices made while under the influence of a drug tend to be inaccurate and need to be reviewed in the cold gray light of dawn.

Sometimes, of course, dawn comes too late, as anyone who has ever awakened with a headache, an empty wallet, and a new tattoo can testify. If folk songs are to be believed, English recruiting sergeants seem to have discovered this principle no later than the seventeenth

---

* One suggestive finding concerns the general tendency to take risks and try new things. The 30 percent of adolescents in one large sample who identified this tendency as their dominant personality trait included 94 percent of the crack smokers. Personal communication with Gordon S. Black, based on data from Gordon S. Black Corporation, *Partnership Attitude Tracking Study: A Summary of the Fourth Year Results* (Rochester, N.Y.: Gordon S. Black Corporation, 1991). This result, coupled with the great value placed on risk taking and innovation within the dominant culture of the United States, may help explain why use and abuse of illicit drugs, but not alcohol, is more prevalent here than elsewhere, particularly if the practice of drug use tends to spread from "product pioneers" to their less adventuresome friends.

century, and seducers even earlier. One good reason for requiring a waiting period before a wedding is to give both partners a chance to sober up.

One class of decisions made under the burden of intoxication is the decision to "have another round." Thus one explanation for bad choices concerning drug use is that they are drugged choices. Binge behavior, in which someone keeps using a drug until either his money or his body is exhausted, owes something to such drug-induced lapses of judgment. So does the dangerous practice of mixing drugs. Since some drugs can continue to influence behavior even after the user no longer feels intoxicated, some chronic heavy users probably make almost all their drug-use decisions in a drug-induced haze.

However, for most drug takers the decision to start any given drug-use session is made while sober. Intoxication can account for excess once use has started, but it cannot explain starting too often or why the (sober) decision to start does not correctly allow for the possibility of an intoxicated decision to continue too long. Other explanations are needed.

ADDICTION

The most commonly offered explanation for recurrent drug abuse is also the least helpful. "Drugs are addictive," we are told. But once we recall that *addictive* just means *habit-forming*, then using addiction as an explanation for habitual drug abuse seems less helpful, like Molière's doctor's explanation that morphine induces sleep because of its dormative property. Defining drug addiction behaviorally, in terms of continued use despite adverse consequences, begs the question of *why* drug use continues.[15]

There is, however, a more restricted meaning of *addiction*: the fact that, for some users of some drugs, cessation is physically painful. The classical model of addiction, defined as physical dependency plus tolerance, is based largely on experiences with opiates.[16] After a period of use, cessation causes physical and psychic distress: the withdrawal syndrome. Changes at the cellular and tissue levels have made the body at least temporarily unable to function normally without the drug.[17] These same cellular and tissue changes, along with higher-level learning phenomena, also account for tolerance, the process by which a given dosage has less and less effect on the user (or, equivalently, larger and larger doses are required to achieve the same effect).[18]

The physiological effects of withdrawal are real, and are experienced not only by opiate users but also by some users of barbiturates, alcohol, tranquilizers, and nicotine.[19] Heroin addicts report withdrawal symptoms not unlike those associated with a bad case of the flu: fever, sweating, nausea, diarrhea, aches, and cramps.[20] Chronic alcohol or barbiturate users may have even more severe, sometimes fatal, reactions to a sudden cessation.[21]

Physical dependency certainly helps maintain drug habits.[22] Because cessation is painful, continuing is "rewarded" and quitting is "punished." Those who do not quit may be making what for them is a rational decision. Cessation of drug use will almost certainly bring discomfort; continuation will at worst postpone the discomfort and at best provide pleasure. Dependency creates a barrier of pain between the addict and abstinence. Imagine that you have the flu and that there is a bottle of pills sitting next to your bed that will both stop the symptoms for twelve hours and make you feel better than you felt before the flu, but at the price of postponing your recovery. To be cured, you have to refrain from taking a pill for two consecutive weeks. Could you resist the temptation for every minute of those two weeks? I'm not sure I could.[23]

Chronic drug addiction based on physical dependency has been recognized since shortly after the introduction of morphine in medical practice.[24] More recently, a different form of addictive behavior has come to the fore: what might be called "acute addiction" to short-acting stimulants, particularly smokable cocaine (freebase or crack).[25]

Smoking cocaine, among other effects, increases the rate of peripheral and central nervous activity (sensation and thought) and can produce intense feelings of well-being.[26] But as the effect wears off, nervous activity goes from being artificially elevated to being artificially depressed.[27] The result is a very unpleasant period—the dreaded "crash"—whose duration and intensity of which depend on the length of the drug-use session.[28] The user can forestall the crash by taking another dose. (As the George Carlin routine has it, "Cocaine made me feel like a new man. The first thing the new man wanted was more cocaine.") The result, too frequently, is binge behavior.

In one important sense, these two forms of addiction are opposites. A physically dependent opiate user (human or laboratory mouse) wants his first dose very badly indeed; it keeps him from feeling sick. Subsequent doses are welcome, but the effort he will expend for subsequent doses is less and less.[29] A compulsive crack smoker wants his second pipe more than his first, and his third more than his second.[30] While heroin satisfies the desire for heroin, crack sometimes stimulates the desire for crack. It is as if there were a food that made one hungrier (and kept one awake to experience that hunger).

In either kind of addiction, the desire is strong. The assertion that a heroin addict "chooses" to continue heroin use or that a crack smoker on a binge "chooses" to take another pipe is only half true; one could as well say that a hives victim "chooses" to scratch because he "prefers" to have immediate relief at the cost of more future itching. These are not freely made choices. The failure to stop is regrettable but not puzzling.

It is harder to understand why users who have been through a phase of compulsive use start a new phase. Outside the bounds of a single-use session, cocaine rarely creates a physiological dependency; a crack smoker does not typically go into withdrawal if kept away from his pipe, and most very heavy crack users use the drug episodically rather than daily.[31] The fear of the crash can maintain a crack binge, but it cannot start one. Starting looks like a deliberate act.

Much the same is true of heroin users, though the periods of use and non-use occur at intervals of months rather than days. Interruptions are normal features of heroin-use careers. A user may quit because he goes to prison, because his regular supplier goes out of business, or because the pressures of the life and the burden of a habit swollen by increasing drug tolerance become too heavy to bear.[32] Two weeks of detoxification—either "cold turkey" or with the aid of decreasing doses of methadone—will leave virtually any heroin user unhooked in the sense that he will be free of withdrawal symptoms. Nor is medical supervision essential; many users successfully detoxify themselves, alone or with the help of friends.[33]

If every crack user went through only one binge, and if every heroin user went through only one "run" and one drying-out, those two drugs would present only minor problems. In fact, many users, no longer in their drug's grip in any obvious sense and having experienced its pains as well as its pleasures, start again, and again and again, in ways that look irrational to outside observers and that the users themselves dread in advance and regret afterward.[34] Part of the explanation may be—in the case of the opiates, probably is—that a period of heavy use of some drugs can generate lasting neurochemical changes that make the user no longer able to feel "normal" without them. As part of the homeostatic mechanism of the nervous system, the presence of large quantities of externally supplied opiate over a long period seems to cause a reduction in the brain's internal capacity to produce the endorphins whose pleasure-giving and pain-relieving actions the opiates mimic.[35] There is now some evidence that the same receptor system is involved in some forms of compulsive alcohol use.[36] Similarly, heavy chronic cocaine use can cause changes in the dopamine system that make life without the drug unpleasant to the point of clinical depression.[37] Nicotine, too, may be the source of lasting neurochemical deficits, though they have yet to be identified.[38]

Even with the extended notion of addiction as operating through long-term neurochemical deficits, much actual drug-use behavior remains to be explained, including binge use and the role of "cues" in generating cravings. Clearly, there is more to drug habits than the creation of an artificial appetite in the form of physical dependency.[39]

The preoccupation with addiction as a drug problem—the tendency to treat "addictive" as a synonym for "evil"—has sown endless confusion and done untold damage. People dying of cancer and other diseases continue to suffer needlessly because of their physicians' fear of addicting them (or their own fear of becoming addicted) to opiate painkillers.[40]

The proposition "nicotine is addictive," which is only a little less self-evident than "water is wet" to anyone who has ever been or known a cigarette smoker or read the laboratory studies,[41] has been made artificially controversial because it implies (correctly) that most smokers are, in literal fact, drug addicts. It thus seems to imply (incorrectly) that they are degraded and dangerous. When former drug czar William Bennett said, in reference to his continuing nicotine habit, "I haven't done any drive-by shootings lately,"[42] it is from this social meaning of addiction that he was trying to separate himself.

The recent history of beliefs about cocaine illustrates the power of the addiction idea to mislead. The substantially correct assertion "Cocaine is not addictive" (where "addictive" meant "tending to create a chronic physical dependency resembling that of the opiates") was taken by many policymakers, and probably by many users and potential users, to mean that cocaine is not dangerous. (It is only fair to recall that these studies involved snorting cocaine powder rather than smoking crack.[43]) Then, once the persistence of crack-smoking behavior became obvious, some people concluded that crack must be addictive in the same way heroin is and that we should therefore search for a maintenance substitute analogous to methadone, regardless of the strong disanalogies between a heroin addict's steady drug taking and a crack smoker's repeated bingeing.[44]

Chronic and acute drug addiction make a chilling and gripping narrative, a fairy-tale nightmare of the loss of self-control to an external force. They are also important stories to tell in making sense of the pattern of drug abuse. But they are a long way from being the whole story.

TEMPORAL MYOPIA AND RISK-RELATED IRRATIONALITY

"Let us eat and drink, for tomorrow we shall die" may be a rational policy for a person sure to die on the morrow. Anyone else ought to take the future into account in making current choices. In a world full of chance events, it is also necessary to take uncertainty into account and to manage risk. Decisions across time and subject to uncertainty are complicated; it is easy to blunder when dealing with the factors of time and chance. Since the successful management of one's own drug-taking behavior places heavy demands on the ability to balance risk against reward and the present against the future, it is not surprising that otherwise sensible people make disastrous errors in trying to do so. They may need protection from themselves.

Time

Saving sacrifices current benefits for future resources; borrowing spends future resources on current benefits. Not all such transactions involve money. Working hard to get ahead in one's profession is a form of saving; damaging one's health through overwork is a form of borrowing.

Economists have worked out a general normative theory of "trading off" the present against the future on the saving-and-borrowing analogy. This theory has as its central concept the rate of time preference, or discount rate.[45] Since banks give interest on savings and charge interest on borrowing, it is always possible to have a greater total by choosing to have more tomorrow and less today. But any creature with current needs and a finite lifetime will have some preference for the present: he will accept future benefits only at some discount.

The key to being rational over time lies in applying the same discount rate to all decisions (not borrowing at 20 percent and lending at 8 percent by holding a savings account while owing money on credit cards). Otherwise, by saving less in one way and more in another, it will be possible to have more today and more tomorrow. Having inconsistent rates of time preference is strictly irrational.

This implies, among other things, that one's choice between two benefits at different dates should depend on how far apart the dates are and not when the first one occurs. At a discount rate of 10 percent per year, $100 today is better than $108 a year from now and not as good as $112 a year from now. The same is true if the $100 is available six months from now and the larger sum a year later than that. The choice should be essentially independent of when it is made.

But for almost everyone, the subjective distance between now and tomorrow is much greater than the subjective distance between a month from now and five weeks from now. The closer a possible gratification comes, the harder it is to defer it. This leads to attempts at saving that are then expensively undone as the moment approaches. A ten-year-old child given a choice today between one candy bar in a month and two candy bars in five weeks will probably choose the latter. But faced on the thirtieth day with the choice between half a candy bar right now and two candy bars after five long days, only a very well disciplined or well-fed child will be able to hold out. Grownups behave in comparable fashion. Schelling points out that people eat fewer desserts at lunch if they choose their luncheon menus at the beginning of the day.

This phenomenon, demonstrable in the laboratory and visible in the nursery and the shopping mall, is known in the literature as *temporal myopia*,[46] though *temporal false perspective* would be slightly more accurate. Temporal myopia is ubiquitous and, in the aggregate, enormously expensive; for example, much procrastination stems from overvaluing current leisure as compared with (slightly) deferred leisure. Thrift is counted among the virtues, not because it is always desirable to choose the future over the present, but because most people find it difficult to be as thrifty in the moment as they plan to be in advance or wish they had been afterwards. Teaching children to delay gratification is simply teaching them to be able to act as they would plan to act, or as they would act if they were acting for another.

Recreational drug taking has most of its benefits in a very immediate present. The costs (other than money) all come later; often not very much later, from an outside perspective, but enough later to make the difference. The drink is now, the hangover tomorrow. For anyone with difficulty in deferring gratification, then, drugs are a special trap. Surely temporal myopia is a big part of the explanation for relapses by people who have painfully freed themselves of dependence on heroin, alcohol, or nicotine.

In addition, intoxication reduces forethought. So people who, sober, are quite good at balancing present and future, even with respect to drug taking, must reckon with the possibility that they will be irrationally present-oriented and unable to defer gratification once they have "had a few."

Risk

Drug taking is risky. There is uncertainty about the effect of the drug, even for experienced users, and there is uncertainty about the consequences of behavior under its influence. Since risk management is an area where actual behavior departs radically from normative rationality, it is unsurprising that some drug taking defies rational explanation.

Economists have worked out detailed theories of how a rational actor takes risk into account in making choices. She evaluates each risk by its magnitude and probability. The product of magnitude and probability is called the *expected value*: a one-in-one-hundred chance of a thousand-dollar loss has an expected value of (negative) ten dollars.[47]

In general, a rational actor should try to avoid risk by accepting a somewhat smaller certain reward rather than a chance at a large prize with the same expected value and by taking a small certain loss rather than the equivalent risk of a large uncertain one. Fire insurance on one's home constitutes the classic example: I would rather pay $1,000 per year than accept a one-in-two-hundred chance of losing $100,000, because the insurance premium involves no great sacrifice while larger loss would require cutting back on some very high-priority budget items. Thus risk aversion—the willingness to sacrifice expected value to reduce uncertainty—follows from the law of diminishing (marginal) returns as applied to income.

The rate of risk aversion, like the rate of time preference, should obey some rules of consistency across decisions; otherwise, the result will be both less expected value and more risk than might be obtained by making rational choices.

Alas, the behavior of empirical human beings confronting risk deviates systematically and substantially from that of theoretical rational actors.[48] Most people overvalue very small chances of very large gains or losses; that is how lotteries stay in business. They also undervalue small but important probabilities of substantial gains or losses, treating events with a 5 percent probability as if they were virtually impossible; that is why so few breadwinners carry adequate disability insurance. Less-than-rational behavior regarding risk also explains how companies make money selling flight and cancer insurance, and why some people who unplug their television sets during thunderstorms do not wear seat belts and neglect to change the batteries in their smoke detectors. Thus decisions about drug taking are less likely to be accurate than decisions about activities involving less risk.

ROUTINE

In a complex world, the capacity to acquire and process information—to fit choices to values and circumstances—is always scarce. This limits the validity of pure rational-actor models even as prescriptions. If calculation is itself subjected to a benefit-cost test, it will seldom seem worthwhile to find the exact solution, to make the precisely optimal choice, instead of settling for an approximation close enough that the next dollar's worth of figuring will yield less than a dollar's worth of improved results. Imagine calculating the optimal driving speed for your next vacation trip by finding the derivative with respect to velocity of total travel cost—fuel cost, accident risk, travel time evaluated at your marginal willingness-to-pay for hours at the vacation site, risk of getting a ticket—and finding the point at which the derivative is zero and the second derivative positive, which must therefore be the minimum. Your vacation will be over before you have finished the calculation.

Calculating how much to calculate will lead to an infinite regress unless it is guided by heuristics, rules of thumb.[49] Thinking power can be further economized, once an approximate solution has been worked out for a class of problems, by developing routines, standard responses to standard situations, that can be executed without conscious thought.

For many activities requiring quick execution—playing the violin, catching a baseball, riding a bicycle—routine, automatic reactions are essential. Learning these activities consists largely of developing appropriate unthinking responses to frequently encountered stimuli. Social skills are analogous: in order to arrive at work appropriately dressed before the business day is over, one must have internalized an enormous array of implicit rules about what to wear, so as to be able to act unthinkingly in accordance with them. We must be creatures of habit in order to survive.

While some habits are deliberately cultivated, most are not. They emerge from a complex set of interactions between organism and environment. The mechanisms of habit formation evolved over hundreds of millions of years to help animals incapable of explicit calculation stay alive without it. Behavioral psychology can be understood as a theory of this natural process of forming habit; crudely speaking, the more often a behavior is followed by pleasure and the less often it is followed by pain, the more likely it is to become habitual.[50]

This can be seen as an experiential, trial-and-error approximation to a benefit-cost rule. But obviousness and proximity in time plays—must play—a far stronger role in shaping behavior by trial-and-error behavioral processes than it would if habits were deliberately chosen and mechanically adjusted like a thermostat. A rational choice of habits would attempt to pay attention to indirect, hidden, and delayed effects that the simple reward-and-punishment mechanism necessarily discounts or ignores. (This may help explain temporal myopia.) Learning to manage one's own process of habit development—to bring habitual behavior more closely in line with rational action—is part of the process of growing up. No one does it perfectly or without effort.

Because the frequency and immediacy of rewards enhance the reinforcing power of a behavior, the chance of developing unwanted habits and the difficulty in breaking them are greatest when they involve frequently repeated behaviors that give quick, short-lived pleasures.[51] Cigarette smoking, for example, is a habit easy to acquire and hard to break because the act of taking a puff is so often repeated and its mildly pleasant effects are so quick to arrive. For many smokers, the practice gradually exceeds the bounds of mere bad habit and becomes a compulsion that even the deliberate application of willpower cannot control or can control only with great psychic discomfort.[52] (Since that psychic discomfort can manifest itself as physical discomfort, the distinction between a "physical dependency" based on neurochemical change and a "psychological dependency" based on a reinforcement-generated compulsion is by no means as clear-cut as it is sometimes made to sound.) When rapid reinforcement and frequent repetition are combined with intense pleasure, as in cocaine smoking, the compulsion can become overwhelming.[53]

Naturally as well as deliberately acquired habits are difficult to override or modify. In this way, individuals resemble organizations, which must act more quickly than their members can consult and which cannot afford to decide each new problem afresh.[54] For an organization, the solution is the development of standard operating procedures: rules and norms that establish a mutually recognizable pattern of activity.[55] A volleyball team, for instance, practices a set of responses, "plays," which can then be used in competition. Once the routine is established, it is no longer either necessary or possible for each player to decide for herself which move to make from one moment to the next. The organizational rules establish the player's range of choices and mandate a choice from within that range based on the cues offered by the situation. If none of the available routines is adequate to the situation, or if deception by the opposition triggers the wrong response, the team loses the point. No playbook is perfect.

So too with individual routines. Any habit is a deviation from perfectly rational behavior, because something done routinely is not done thoughtfully or in full contemplation of its consequences. That routine is unavoidable does not make it less dangerous. Routines save us from the "paralysis of analysis" and give us workable second-best answers only at the cost of deviating more or less from the "first-best" optimum in any actual situation.[56]

In addition to the losses generated by the differences between actual situations and the ideal situation to which the habitual response is optimal, habit harbors a deeper problem. "Habit is second nature." Following one's habits is gratifying, and breaking them is painful. Once a behavior becomes habitual, it is costly to reassert conscious control over it, either to override it in some particular situation to which it provides the wrong reaction or to replace it with a new habit in response to changing circumstances or after experience or analysis has revealed defects in the old one. For example, reading the newspaper every morning at breakfast is a reasonable way to combine nutrition with low-intensity information gathering in the morning fog. But I, for one, now find it very difficult to leave the house without having read the paper, even when I know that lingering over the comic page will make me late for class. When your mother told you that bad habits were hard to break, she knew what she was talking about.

If rewards come irregularly or as a culmination to a complex chain of behavior, the resulting habit once formed will be particularly persistent.[57] Thus the very complexity introduced into the life-styles of heavy drug users by the illegality of their drugs may help reinforce their drug habits. Hustling for drugs, which has been described as "a long sequence of complex behavior that is rewarded only intermittently," thus has much in common with the reinforcement regimes that produce the most persistent behavior in the laboratory.[58]

Through Pavlovian conditioning, the pleasure of drug use can come to be associated with the act of drug taking rather than the somewhat later time when the molecules reach the brain. Once the habit is formed, it may persist even after the process of tolerance formation has depleted the actual pleasure involved.[59]

Over time drug use may have bad effects: physical, psychological, and social. The user may recognize that some or all of these changes are due to drug taking. But that conscious knowledge does not translate directly into changes in routine. The process of thought that allows a user to make the connection between drug use and harm is separate from the largely unconscious process that initiates and maintains habits. The bad effects of drug use—the hangover, the crash, the angry spouse or boss—appear not when the drug is taken, but afterwards. The reinforcement process may effectively associate them not with the drug taking but with its cessation, particularly if additional drug taking defers them. That is why drinking to cure a hangover is one of the signs of incipient alcohol addiction. Drugs can thus "fool" the reinforcement system and develop powerful bad habits that are broken only with great effort, especially if the user continues to be exposed to the behavioral stimuli—the cues—that are associated with drug taking.[60]

Thus the assertion that "anyone who *really* wants to quit can quit," if it is not a tautology, is simply false. In the struggle between calculation and habit, calculation is not always the side with the big battalions.* Any person taking his first dose of any psychoactive substance faces some risk of losing control of his drug taking for some period of time. Those risks vary from use to use and from drug to drug.

Some evidence about what might be thought of as *capture ratios* for various drugs—the proportion of their users who go on to compulsive use—comes from the surveys conducted by the Gordon S. Black Corporation. Respondents were asked both whether they had ever tried a given drug and whether they had ever "felt 'hooked' on" that drug. Nicotine was the outlier: 59 percent of those who had ever smoked a cigarette reported that they had been dependent at one

* This analysis cuts across the sharp distinction between "voluntary" and "involuntary" actions on which the philosopher Joel Feinberg relies so heavily in criticizing "paternalistic" drug laws. Joel Feinberg, *Moral Limits of the Criminal Law:* Volume 3, *Harm to Self* (Oxford: Oxford University Press, 1986), 127-134. Habitual action, even short of addiction, is neither fully voluntary—in the sense that it does not reflect the actor's considered view of what is in her best interest—nor completely involuntary. Nor is there a bright line between "voluntary enough" and "not voluntary enough" (p. 118).

time or another. The only other form of drug taking with a capture ratio greater than 1 in 5 was smoking cocaine (22 percent). The ratios for the other three powerful mass-market drugs were remarkably close together: 17.1 percent for alcohol, 16.6 percent for powder cocaine, and 13.7 percent for marijuana.[61] It is important not to take these numbers too literally; they are subject to several kinds of errors. Self-reports about feeling dependent are not objective measures of problem use (and, in fact, many crack smokers who did not regard themselves as dependent seemed to be using the drug with remarkable frequency). The probability of having had a problem up to the point of the interview is an underestimate of the lifetime probability, simply because some subjects will encounter problems later. These results say nothing about the consequences of compulsive use or the difficulty of quitting, which are likely to vary from drug to drug, and they provide only indirect evidence concerning the related question of what proportion of all users regret, on balance, having tried each drug. But the fact that all of the ratios are well above 10 percent suggests that the problem of losing control of one's drug habits is not restricted to any one class of drugs or to a small group of people with "addictive personalities." Developing bad habits around drug use is a characteristic risk of taking drugs, as tendonitis is a characteristic risk of playing tennis.

FASHION EFFECTS AND INFORMATION DISTORTION

The rational-actor model assumes that consumers choose goods on the basis of their value in use. Retailers know better. As long as people care about the opinion of others and as long as those others use consumption choices as cues about the possession of socially desirable characteristics (wealth, status, and socially approved preferences, or "good taste"), it will be rational for individuals to make consumption choices based in part on the inferences they want others to draw about them.[62]

Following fashion is also a way of economizing on information gathering. In choosing a restaurant in a strange town, it is wise to choose a busy one, not because crowding is pleasant, but because the locals know more than you do about where to get a good meal. The heuristic "In the absence of special information, do as others do" is sufficiently useful in a wide enough variety of situations that it can easily be internalized as habit.

In addition, there are distinct costs of not following the fashions of whatever social sphere one wants to inhabit. In every milieu, the excessively different is suspect. It has been observed that all the non-conformists read the same magazines and wear the same clothes. To make choices different from those of one's companions can be easily understood, or misunderstood, as an implicit criticism of the choices they have made. It would be as gauche to order a shot-and-a-beer in the Faculty Club as to order a Perrier in a blue-collar bar.

Taking the right drugs can be as important a part of fashionable behavior as living in the right neighborhood, wearing the right clothes, or listening to the right music. Drug-related behavior is often a key element in defining social status, and advertisements for the licit drugs are heavy with status appeals: "Good taste is always an asset." The greater the fashion-driven element in any area of behavior, the harder it is to claim that (legally) unrestricted choice frees individuals to do what they want to do; following fashion is not the same as acting on one's own preferences.

The use of a new drug spreads through a population according to a pattern that introduces a bias favorable to drug use into the decision-making process of potential users.[63] The pleasures of drug taking tend to be greatest, and its evident harms the least, in the weeks and months immediately following first use. Habituation, in particular, takes time to develop. When a drug is new in a particular social setting it has few long-time users, and, if it is spreading rapidly, many new users. A potential user, therefore, inquiring among her social circle about the drug's costs and benefits, will receive information that, no matter how accurately reported, tends to mislead.

This phenomenon helps explain the growth and decay of drug fashions. When a drug is new, its word-of-mouth reputation is favorable. Good word-of-mouth publicity attracts more new, and at least temporarily satisfied, customers. The force of fashion may serve to silence those who do not enjoy the drug's effects. However, since no one remains a new user forever, the ratio of long-time users to new users must rise over time. Some of the long-timers fall into easily recognized patterns of destructive use; others have bad experiences to report or have been injured or even killed by acute overdose, chronic excess, or intoxicated misadventure. The drug's reputation begins to suffer, which helps the number of new users to shrink, as it must anyway due to the effects of saturation in a finite population. That shrinkage increases the ratio of long-time users to novices, further worsening the mix of good and bad experiences about which novices hear. At some point, initiation may dry up almost entirely, and those current users not caught in patterns of compulsive use will tend to cut back their use or quit. From being fashionable, at least within its social setting, the drug becomes unfashionable. That was the story of heroin in the late 1960s and early 1970s, of powder and freebase cocaine among the wealthy in the late 1970s and early 1980s, and of crack among the poor from 1982 to 1990. Wisdom came, but for many it came too late.[64]

This bias applies almost as much to the scientific literature as to popular rumor, with an additional lag created by journals' publication schedules. Aside from fifty-year-old clinical reports (notoriously unreliable) and experiments on animals (notoriously hard to interpret), it would have been hard in 1975, or even 1978, to find much in the way of evidence—as opposed to conjecture—that cocaine use among the wealthy was going to get many of them into serious trouble.

In the case of drugs whose use is already endemic, the phenomenon of information distortion is less extreme, but not entirely absent. True, a potential cigarette smoker or alcohol drinker could in principle observe an unbiased sample of novice and long-time users. But since age and length of use are associated and since acquaintances tend to sort by age, potential new users even of long-established drugs are likely to get a disproportionate, and disproportionately influential, share of their vicarious experience of it from recent, rather than long-time, users, and thus to overestimate the pleasures and underestimate the risks and pains it offers.

The same distortion emerges in a different form at the individual level. It is widely known among potential drug users that individuals differ in their reactions to any given drug: some are far more vulnerable than others to acute bad reactions, intoxicated misbehavior, and habituation. It is also widely understood that drugs themselves vary in their riskiness, that there are differences of opinion about particular drugs, and that neither drug purveyors nor the distributors of anti-drug messages are disinterested or completely reliable sources of information. The pleasures of drug taking are subjective and widely variable, and claims about drug-induced insight or drug-enhanced performance are notoriously hard to verify.

Confronted with both uncertainty about the costs and benefits of a given drug to the average individual, and with uncertainty about his own position with respect to that average, a potential user who concludes that there is no substitute for personal experiment is not making a mistake in logic. But the results of such experiments are likely to be systematically misinterpreted, because the perceived benefits of the first several uses are apt to be greater, and the perceived costs less, than the true benefits and costs over a longer period.

Thus neither asking nor trying is likely to be a reliable way to find out whether one should use a given drug, and drug use is likely to continue to rise and fall, like hemlines, for reasons far removed from rational decision making. Actual drug-taking behavior cannot be taken as a perfect, or even a very good, indicator of what drug takers believe to be their own long-term interests.[65]

POLICY IN THE PRESENCE OF BAD HABITS

That drug taking is not under perfect rational control does not, of course, prove that all drug taking is irrational or that drugs on balance do their users more harm than good. It does help explain why some people who can manage the rest of their affairs without interference do things with respect to drug taking that do not make sense to their friends, or even to themselves.

The demand for drugs therefore does not bear the same relationship to consumers' considered judgments of what is in their own interest as does the demand for apricots. It is not at all unreasonable for a society that makes most of its regulations about consumer choice on the basis of rational-actor assumptions to be somewhat more paternalistic when it comes to choices about drug use.

Even so, if the only victims of drugs were the drug users themselves, there would be a serious argument against using strongly coercive policies in response. There are limits to how far any government can usefully go in improving its citizens against their will. But drug users do not bear all of the costs of their mistakes, and under no recognizable set of social institutions could they be made to do so. What their bad habits cost the rest of us—what our bad habits cost one another—is our next topic.

3

The Other Victims of Drug Abuse

No man is an island, entire of itself.
—John Donne

An innkeeper loves a drunkard, but not for a son-in-law.
—Sholom Aleichem

If drug users were the sole sufferers from their bad habits, the case for controlling drug use by public policy would reduce itself to the case for governmental paternalism in general. The preceding chapter argued that individuals' actual behavior respecting drug use is likely to diverge more frequently and more significantly from the behavior they would thoughtfully choose for themselves than does their behavior in other respects. If so, paternalistic interference with drug taking has a better chance of being successful in improving individuals' welfare than does interference in other areas of personal choice.

Whether, given the complexity of drug use and the distance that politics and bureaucracy put between ideal policies on the one hand and actual laws and programs on the other, a "better" chance is a "good enough" chance—whether, that is, the average net effect of such interventions would turn out to be beneficial or harmful—is an interesting, if empirically unanswerable, question. But that is not the sole question relevant to making drug policy, because drug use sometimes creates damage that extends beyond the user. Even if public intervention cannot on balance improve the lot of drug users, it may be justified to protect others. The costs that drug users impose on others, like the damage they do to themselves, is likely to be greater, per dose, in a world where the laws make drugs expensive or forbid their sale than it would be in a world where drugs were left cheap and easy to get. In considering alternative laws and programs, we should therefore divide the natural costs of drug abuse from the artificial ones created by the laws themselves. Let us then start by considering the burdens drug use would place on non-users if there were no drug laws, and later consider the harms that may be added by taxes and prohibitions.

CRIME

The two great deterrents to crime are the bite of conscience and the fear of punishment, including both punishments inflicted by the force of law and the more frequent informal sanctions ranging from being glared at by a stranger, through being fired, to being disowned by one's parents. Whatever quiets conscience and dims foresight will therefore tend to increase the frequency of "predatory" crimes: theft and assault in all their forms and mixtures.[1] Intoxication notoriously does both; "Dutch courage," or bravery in a bottle, has been a byword since the seventeenth century. (On the other hand, profound intoxication, particularly with depressants, may actually prevent criminal activity by preventing activity of any kind.) In addition, intoxication provides a built-in plea in mitigation both for the court of conscience and for more public forums: "I didn't mean it, I couldn't help it, I was drunk (stoned, tripping, coked up) at the time."

Some drugs used in some social settings with some expectations on the part of their users can provoke, or at least unleash, aggressive emotions and actions. The most dramatic of these effects are limited to the period of intoxication, but some drug-use patterns can also create aggressive behavior during withdrawal or even generate a general tendency to aggression unrelated to current drug status, as in the stimulant psychosis observed among some chronic cocaine smokers and some intravenous amphetamine users ("speed freaks").[2]

Talk, it is said, is cheap; whiskey costs money. Some consumers would steal to buy drugs even if taxes and prohibitions did not drive drug prices up. Moreover, if drug use reduces some users' ability or willingness to earn an honest living, their resulting impoverishment may also stimulate income-producing crime. But as most economic crime by users is a consequence of the drug laws,[3] discussion of it is best postponed.

We cannot judge the extent to which drugs would be "criminogenic" in the absence of drug laws by observing the behavior of

drug users in the presence of drug laws. Not only do the laws themselves create additional pressures for users of illicit drugs to commit
nondrug crimes, but users of prohibited drugs are by definition lawbreakers. This makes them more likely than non-users to break other
rules for reasons both of self-selection and of habituation. Not only
will the drug laws tend to filter out those potential drug users who
are law-abiding, but breaking the drug laws may help habituate users
to breaking laws in general. The psychological mechanism known as
cognitive dissonance leads those who repeatedly undertake any action
to regard it as less blameworthy than they otherwise would.[4] It is as if
they reasoned, "I break the law. I'm not a terrible person. Therefore
lawbreaking is not terrible."

The self-reinforcing character of lawbreaking is a good reason not
to enact laws that will be widely broken. It is also one reason to believe
that the observed rate of nondrug lawbreaking among users of currently illicit drugs overestimates the effects of the drugs themselves
on lawbreaking. Even for the licit drugs, not all of the difference
between the crime rates of heavy users and those of the rest of the
population is caused by drugs. Just because alcohol is involved in
60 percent of all homicides and 40 percent of sexual assaults[5] does
not imply that getting rid of alcohol would decrease homicide and
sexual assault by comparable amounts. If poor self-command, difficulty in deferring gratification, and carelessness about the effects of
one's actions on others create predispositions both toward drinking
to excess and toward theft and assault, we would expect to observe
a disproportionate amount of heavy drinking among a sample of
predatory offenders even if alcohol had no independent tendency to
cause crime. So too for other drugs.

DERELICTIONS OF DUTY

The world is full of duties: duties to act and duties to forbear, duties
imposed by law and duties voluntarily undertaken, duties for the
dereliction of which there are civil or criminal penalties and duties
enforced only by conscience or informal social pressure. Some duties are clearly marked out, at least in outline: drivers owe other
drivers and pedestrians a duty of reasonable care; parents have
duties both to care for their children and to prevent them from
behaving badly; workers have legally specified duties to employers,
workmates, and customers. Other duties are vague, unenforceable,
and open to widely varying interpretation: there is no legal obligation to give to charity, to vote, to join the PTA, or to offer or summon

help in the case of fire, accident, or crime. But widespread failure to do any of these things carries enormous social costs, particularly under a political and economic regime that reflects a reluctance to resort to coercion, including coerced taking of resources in the form of taxation, to get things done.[6]

Since liberal society is workable only if a large proportion of its members voluntarily do what the state does not compel and refrain from what it does not forbid, the liberal regime is not consistent with every possible distribution of dispositions among the population. If the inclination to be a good citizen becomes too rare, it will become necessary to find new institutions that do not rely on a degree of public spirit that is not in fact present. The relationship between "virtue" and liberty is a commonplace of classical and early modern political theory: Machiavelli treated it as an axiom that a "corrupt" (that is, selfish) people cannot maintain a republic and will eventually get the despotic rule it needs and deserves; Rousseau held that tyranny grows from lack of self-control: "our passions forge our chains"; John Adams predicted that the desire of the French revolutionaries for an American constitution would be frustrated by "a lack of Americans."

Chronic heavy use of drugs that dim foresight and hush the voice of conscience tends to make derelictions of duty more frequent. Driving under the influence is a crime because intoxication is held to interfere with the required degree of reasonable care in operating a dangerous vehicle, both by slowing reaction time and by inducing carelessness. Even a chronically intoxicated person can avoid drunken driving by not driving, if drunkenness does not make him forget that one should not drive drunk. But how can a chronically intoxicated parent fulfill the duties of parenthood?

Drugs may also compete with duties for time and money. In this they are not, of course, alone; opera-going and scuba-diving also are profligate of time and money that might instead go to improving the world. The distinction is one of quantity, frequency, and circumstance; the problem involves excess and bad timing, rather than intoxication in itself. But we observe with licit and illicit drugs alike that drug use is frequently carried to excess.

NUISANCE

We all have a duty not to make nuisances of ourselves.[7] The more closely we crowd together, as in cities, the more essential the acceptance of this duty is to a tolerable life.[8] To some extent, the duty not to be a nuisance (for example, by making excessive noise at un-reasonable hours) is defined and enforced by law, but neither the definition nor the enforcement is something that the legal system handles cheaply or well. Here again, the social looseness we value depends on a widespread willingness to stay within ill-defined limits.

Intoxication is likely to reduce both one's ability to behave inof-fensively and one's level of concern about giving offense. Anything that tends to cause people to be loud, rude, and clumsy makes them less welcome inhabitants of public spaces: thus the laws against be-ing "drunk and disorderly" and the fact that bars and liquor stores are almost universally regarded as undesirable neighbors. In partic-ular, drugs that cause some of their users to pass out in public leave passersby two unpleasant options: to walk past, or over, helpless peo-ple who may be in urgent need of attention or to engage again and again in attempts to help that are usually unwelcome, fruitless, and unpleasant, and occasionally dangerous. Putting such a burden on what ought to be routine Good Samaritan behavior eats away at the roots of social solidarity.

The burden of drug-induced nuisance behavior is widely dis-tributed, but it hits the poor particularly hard because they tend to live in crowded neighborhoods and because they rely on spaces and institutions—public parks, public sidewalks, public transporta-tion systems, public housing projects—that lack gatekeepers and from which the obnoxious can be excluded only after clumsy and expensive due process.

Drugs vary greatly in their tendencies to cause users to make nui-sances of themselves. Drunks are notoriously guilty of more than their share of obnoxious behavior; heroin users (even setting aside their propensity for theft, which is not linked to their intoxication) have at least as bad a reputation. In each case, passing out is a signif-icant part of the problem. Tobacco and caffeine, on the other hand, create virtually no such problems; in the case of tobacco the smoke is offensive, not the smoker. In any discussion of changing the le-gal status of marijuana, the stimulants (cocaine, methamphetamine), or the psychedelics, the potential problem of obnoxious intoxicated behavior among users would deserve substantial weight.

HEALTH DAMAGE:
INVOLUNTARY DRUG EXPOSURE

While drugs damage their users' health in a dizzying variety of ways, their impacts on non-users' health are easier to catalog. Sometimes non-users are involuntarily exposed to drugs or drug by-products, and sometimes users acquire and spread infectious diseases in using their drugs or earning money to buy them, or because drug use or drug-related impoverishment has lowered their resistance.

Involuntary exposure is the simpler case because it is substantially independent of the laws. The air around a tobacco smoker, and as far as the air-circulation system carries it, is filled with nicotine, tars, carbon monoxide, and particulates. The effects of these pollutants can range from mild discomfort to serious disease, depending on the closeness of the area, the duration of the exposure, and the sensitivity of the passive smokers. Smokers' children and spouses have demonstrably more respiratory disease than they otherwise would.[9] Health damage in workplaces is harder to measure, partly because employees change workmates and workplaces more frequently than children change parents. But there is no reason to doubt that passive smoke in the workplace causes disease as well as annoyance.[10]

The problem of second-hand tobacco smoke is aggravated by the sheer frequency with which smokers light up and by the time required to smoke a cigarette, which together complicate any attempt at separating smoking from nonsmokers. Moreover, because forcing a nicotine addict not to smoke can cause severe discomfort, something more than the exercise of ordinary tact and consideration is required to reconcile the interests of smokers and nonsmokers. If marijuana became widely used, it would pose some of the same problems, though in much less severe form because marijuana smokers light up less frequently. It would also create some risk of involuntary intoxication, particularly in very confined spaces such as elevators; the same would be true of smoking opium or heroin.

But the problem of passive smoke is straightforward compared with that of drug use among pregnant women. That maternal drug use can damage fetuses and newborns is now well established: fetal alcohol syndrome is now the most frequent demonstrable cause of mental retardation in newborns, even more frequent than Downs Syndrome.[11] What to do about such damage is more puzzling.

Drugs differ widely in how much fetal damage they can cause.[12] The damage also varies over the stages of pregnancy, in ways as yet only poorly understood. The greater the variety of drugs in widespread use among women of childbearing age, the more complicated the problem of their drug-taking behavior once they become pregnant. With some drugs, the damage may begin even before the pregnancy becomes known. With others, habituation will make sudden changes in drug taking difficult to manage; many women succeed in quitting smoking when they know they are pregnant, but many others try and fail.[13]

There are many ways in which pregnant women can help or harm their future children, and knowledge and opinion about them are in flux. No one proposes to require all women to pursue the current vision of best prenatal practice in every detail, so if the damage done by prenatal drug exposure *in utero* were small, it would not create a serious argument against the free availability of drugs. But maternal drug use is a substantial and apparently growing part of the problem of unhealthy newborns.[14]

The direct victim of such passive drug taking is the child, but there are indirect victims too. Drug-damaged children put burdens on already strained systems of pediatric health care and public education. Some of the forms of damage, particularly to cognitive function and impulse control, will tend to increase crime rates when the children become adolescents and young adults.[15] The damaged child's future schoolmates, workmates, and neighbors will all bear some of the cost.

In addition, it seems hard to deny that the community has an independent interest in the well-being of its future members and an obligation to protect them: the same sort of interest and obligation that leads to laws against postnatal abuse and neglect. How to defend that interest is, however, anything but obvious.

A few local prosecutors have tried accusing drug-using pregnant women of "distributing" illicit drugs to their future children,* and there is some movement among legislatures to create explicit statutory authority for what otherwise seems a rather tortured interpretation of the law. Such prosecutions may discourage drug-using women from seeking prenatal medical care (though one could avoid this objection by making the receipt of such care an affirmative defense).[16] Other jurisdictions are threatening to declare drug-using mothers "unfit parents" and to deprive them of the guardianship of their newborns.[17] Whether the adoption and foster-care systems can

---

* Such a prosecution was upheld on appeal in Florida, despite the general legal principle that forbids "creative" application of criminal statutes beyond the instances to which they unambiguously apply. *Johnson v. State,* No. 89-1765 (Fla. 5th DCA, 18 April 1991), No. 77,831 (Fla. 5th DCA, 21 April 1991). (Case still on appeal.) See Tamar Lewin, "Guilt Upheld for Drug Delivery by Umbilical Cord," *New York Times* (20 April 1991). But Michigan courts rejected an analogous case. *State v. Hardy,* No. 128458 (Mich Ct. App., 1 April 1991): See also *Commonwealth v. Pelligrini,* No. 87-970, Slip op. (Mass. Superior Ct., 15 October 1990) (indictment dismissed); *State v. Inzar,* No. 90 crs. 6960, 6961 (North Carolina Gen'l Ct. Justice, Superior Ct. Div., Robeson Cty., 9 April 1991) (charges of delivery of controlled substance and assault with a deadly weapon dismissed).

offer better lives to the children, whether those systems can stand the strain of increased case loads, and whether the mere threat of losing their babies will deter mothers from taking drugs, all remain to be seen.[18]

All of this legal activity centers on the illicit drugs, particularly cocaine. But alcohol, the drug that causes the most widespread *in utero* damage, has so far been exempt. A California law requiring that the teratogenic properties of alcohol be advertised prominently in bars, surely a rather minimal effort in this direction, has been attacked on the grounds that it would deprive women of childbearing age of the right to drink. There is a hard choice here for those who would make more drugs available for regulated recreational use; would they prefer to accept the fetal damage involved or to expand the range of legal restrictions imposed on pregnant women but not on others?

It is, alas, impossible to discuss this subject without raising the question of the legal status of abortion. To some on each side of that controversy, prenatal drug exposure and abortion seem to be linked. If a woman has a right to terminate a pregnancy, it is argued, by what logic can any less drastic interference with fetal health be legally proscribed? Surely there is a fallacy here somewhere. Whether a woman decides to carry a pregnancy to term is not obviously a matter of public concern, but whether children who will be born alive will be born healthy clearly is. Indeed, the need to regulate drug use by pregnant women more strictly than drug use by other persons can be seen as an argument for the unrestricted right to an abortion; the greater the legal disabilities and restrictions that surround the status of pregnancy, the stronger the case against requiring women to maintain that status any longer than they choose to.

DRAINS ON COMMON RESOURCES

In the private economy, we get what we pay for, and the existence of a paying market means that shifts in demand can be accommodated for by shifts in the quantity supplied. That makes my demand for market-supplied goods and services largely a matter of indifference to you (pollution and congestion aside); if marijuana smokers eat more than their share of chocolate-chip cookies, there will not be any fewer chocolate-chip cookies left for the rest of us.

But not all needs are met by the market; some are supplied by government. The supply of services paid for out of public budgets is far less responsive to demand, at least in the short term, than the supply of market goods and services paid for by consumers. If the police have to visit my neighbor's apartment twice a week because he gets drunk and beats up his wife, that will leave less police protection for me. The extra money and teacher-hours the public schools expend on children who have learning disabilities because they were born damaged by their mothers' cocaine smoking do subtract from the money and teacher-hours available for teaching the other children. Emergency rescue, courts, publicly paid health care: all are finite common resources, and intemperate drug users are more likely to put demands on all of them than are moderate users or non-users.

The same is true of needs met by philanthropy, in all its varieties from the work of massive institutions with office buildings and corporate sponsors to the quiet efforts of neighbors who help neighbors in need and strangers who stop to give, or at least to call for, emergency assistance. Those made homeless by drug abuse compete for shelter space with those made homeless by economic dislocation, family breakup, or fire. The more frequently pedestrians encounter drug users recumbent on the sidewalk, staggering around, or making semi-articulate noises, the less likely they are to help, or even pay attention to, victims—particularly shabby-looking victims—of the acute phases of epilepsy, diabetes, or heart disease.

RISK SPREADING AND CROSS-SUBSIDY

The quest for security in modern society is a frequent target of attack by nostalgic moralists who long for an imagined past when risk was cheerfully accepted. No doubt, there can be a neurotic craving for an unattainable perfect security, and risk-reducing and risk-spreading measures are sometimes pursued beyond the point where additional efforts cause more accidents than they prevent.[19]

Still, the desire to reduce risk—the band of uncertainty around the expected outcome—is by no means irrational. It follows with mathematical certainty from the ability of rational consumers to manage their personal budgets by filling their most pressing wants first.

Consider a starving man with five dollars in his pocket standing outside a grocery store. He can't afford a feast, but he needn't go to bed hungry. With an additional five dollars, he could eat more, or eat better, or both. But the gain from the second five dollars is not nearly as large as the gain from the first five. The man would be foolish to risk losing the money he has for a 50/50 chance, or even a much better than 50/50 chance, of having twice as much.

Suppose, instead, that the same man has a lottery ticket in his pocket, with a 50/50 chance of paying either ten dollars or nothing. (He can find out, and collect his prize if there is one, inside the store.) By the reasoning above, he should be happy to sell the ticket for its expected value of five dollars, or even somewhat less; the certainty of a four-dollar meal is better than an even chance at a ten-dollar feast. He ought, that is, to be willing to sacrifice some of his expected value to reduce his risk, as measured by the uncertainty of the outcome.

Thus, in the language of the economists, the diminishing marginal utility of income—the fact that each dollar serves a need slightly less pressing than the previous one—gives rise to risk aversion, the willingness to sacrifice expected value to reduce variance.[20] (This is a prescriptive conclusion, a theorem about rational behavior, not an assertion about how people actually behave.)

One way to reduce risk is to spread it around, as insurance does. If a large number of individuals, any one of whom has a small but noticeable chance of dying early and leaving his survivors short of money, or wrecking his car, or needing expensive surgery, agree to contribute to a common fund that will make payments to the small minority of participants who actually suffer a loss in any given year, then a catastrophic risk is converted into a certain, but manageable, payment. The arrangement yields a net gain because those who suffer losses are, until they are recompensed, suddenly much poorer than they were before, and therefore each benefit dollar has a greater marginal utility to the beneficiary than did his average premium dollar.

In addition to limiting risk—redistributing money to those who unexpectedly become needy—risk sharing also relieves anxiety. The very possibility of, for example, facing a large medical bill and being unable to pay can cause sleepless nights among many for whom the possibility will never become actual. Anything that limits the feasibility of risk sharing thus increases not only the rare incidence of catastrophic loss but the far more widespread incidence of fruitless worry.

But once a risk-sharing arrangement is in place, the participants have a mutual interest in one another's probability of incurring a loss. Anything that raises the frequency of loss within a group will raise insurance premiums. As soon as you and I are covered by the same fire insurance underwriter, your habit of smoking in bed starts to cost me money.

If insurers could distinguish high-risk insurance buyers from low-risk ones accurately and without cost, and if regulators allowed them to act accordingly, they could adjust premiums to match risks. Smokers would pay higher life insurance premiums, heavy drinkers higher auto insurance premiums, and so on. In effect, such "classification" schemes divide different classes of insurance buyers into separate insurance pools and thus avoid forcing low-risk members of insurance pools to subsidize high-risk members.

Unfortunately, it costs insurance companies money and effort to determine what sort of risk each applicant presents. If an auto insurance company attempted to sell a discount policy for teetotalers only, how could its agents tell who was eligible? The insurance buyer will always know more about himself than the insurance seller can afford to find out. Thus some degree of cross-subsidy is inseparable from risk sharing; the good risks—those with low probability of loss—subsidize the bad risks.[21]

Two additional effects make this problem even more serious. First, if the number of high-risk individuals in the pool is large enough, and the difference between high-risk and low-risk groups great enough, some low-risk individuals will decide that the premiums are too high and go without insurance entirely. Not only does this leave them without the benefits of risk spreading; it also increases the premiums for those who are left. At worst, this process of "adverse selection" can snowball, with each premium increase driving out more low-risk participants, until the arrangement falls apart entirely.[22] Second, since those with insurance all know that they will not have to bear all the losses they incur, the existence of insurance will tend to increase the frequency of risky behavior: insured small boats sink more than uninsured small boats. (The insurance literature quaintly calls this effect *moral hazard*.)

These imperfections in the insurance markets we all use—cross-subsidy, complicated by adverse selection and moral hazard—help spread the burden of drug abuse beyond the ranks of the drug abusers themselves. On average, the cross-subsidy from non-users to users can be compensated for by taxing those drugs whose use tends to increase losses covered by insurance. But the adverse selection problem will remain.

Some risks cannot be shared at all through private markets. Examples include the risk of being laid off from one's job (because too many losses occur at the same time) and the risk of being born with mental or physical disabilities or simply born into poverty (because the outcome is known before a contract can be signed). If these results are to be insured against at all, it must be by a public, compulsory program,[23] or by a system that ties the sale of insurance to a much larger financial decision, typically employment. (The sick and the healthy alike are covered by medical insurance acquired at work.)

Public "social" insurance plans eliminate adverse selection by eliminating selection: everyone must participate and everyone must pay. But this merely reinforces the importance of cross-subsidy and moral hazard. If my drug use makes me sick and unemployed and thus eligible for income support and publicly paid medical care, I do not pay all of the costs, which may make me more careless, and you pay some of them, which makes my drug problem partly your business.

Even if there were no programs designed specifically as social insurance, fellow citizens would still have a mutual interest in one another's incomes via the tax system that supports education, defense, law enforcement, environmental protection, and so forth. Virtually any tax except a flat per-capita levy (poll tax) will take more dollars from the average affluent person than from the average poor person. (A progressive tax system goes further by taking a higher proportion of large incomes than it does of small ones.) Whatever reduces my work effort increases the taxes you must pay to support any given level of public services.

For all these reasons the financial impacts of any risky activity, including drug taking, will spread even more widely than its behavioral impacts. Even seemingly private habits thus affect the public interest. This reasoning does not directly challenge the principle that individuals ought to be allowed to regulate their own lives in matters not touching the interests of others, but it does limit the range of activities to which that principle applies.

THE EPIDEMIOLOGY OF DRUG TAKING

Finally, my drug use can affect you by encouraging your drug use. This effect may be good or bad for you; if it is bad it constitutes a peculiar kind of "external harm."

Some policies that would not be justified to protect any one individual from the consequences of his own drug use may be justified by their effects in reducing such "contagion" effects (assuming always the prior judgment that the drug taking involved produces more harm than good). In particular, while a threatened punishment more damaging than the behavior to be deterred is hard to justify on grounds of individual paternalism, the same limit might not apply to "group paternalism."[24]

There exists a vast literature about the effects of drug use by others on the probability that any given individual will use any given drug and on how heavily he uses it: the *epidemiology* of drug consumption. One set of models treats drug use as a contagious condition, spreading from person to person by direct contact. These models pay attention to the factors influencing the number and "infectiousness" of current users and the "susceptibility" of those who are in contact with them but who are not yet users.[25]

That the spread of drug use can be studied using models designed to describe the spread of disease does not, of course, imply that all drug use is an undesirable or pathological state. Drug use, like skiing, is an activity that new participants are encouraged and helped to engage in by friends and acquaintances who are already participants. Drug use carries some risk of disease and injury, just as skiing carries some risk of broken bones. If one were interested in the epidemiology of traumatic injury, the spread of skiing from current skiers to new skiers would be of interest, but that does not mean that skiing is (always) pathological behavior. One could equally well build a epidemiological model of jogging, or of smoking cessation.

One objection to the epidemic metaphor is that it ignores the extent to which drug use is chosen behavior, to be explained at least in part by its perceived costs and benefits. Models of product diffusion developed by students of consumer-goods marketing and models of innovation diffusion developed by students of the history of technology can more easily accommodate the role of choice in the spread of a practice such as drug use. Those models tend to stress the role of "pioneers" in diffusing the use of a newly introduced good or practice.[26]

Another approach treats the quantity of a given drug used by each member of a population as a random variable and studies the characteristic distributions of those variables. These models suggest a close connection between total use in any population and heavy use in that population on the principle that the extremes stand in some predictable relationship to the center.[27]

What all these models have in common is that they take seriously the influence the members of any social group have on one another's drug taking. As long as human beings are social animals, any attempt to describe their behavior, or make policy about it, as if they were unattached individuals will be doomed to failure.

NOTIONAL DAMAGE

So far we have been considering the more or less measurable, or at least observable, forms of damage that drug users inflict on non-users. But suppose that, without claiming any such damage to me or mine, I simply dislike the fact that you spend your Saturday evening intoxicated (or intoxicated on some particular drug). I find it an offense against reason and against humanity, an offense to the community and to God, and believe that the state should protect you against the degradation involved in your drug use, even if you prefer not to be so protected.

To what extent is this sort of argument a valid basis for public policy? Is the offense that drug use gives to non-users—over and above the direct and indirect personal and social damage it does—to be counted among its harms for the purposes of making policy? There are moral, practical, and political reasons why the answer to this question ought to be no.

The list of activities that are in fact offensive to at least a substantial minority and for which a plausible case can be made that they are degrading to the human spirit, contrary to the good life, hated of the Lord, or just plain disgusting is too long, and the hope that even sophisticated policymakers will be able to distance themselves from the prejudices of their social group is too forlorn, to make abstract judgments about what is or is not fitting behavior the bases of legal proscriptions. I once heard the ancient joke about why Baptists don't make love standing up* from someone who had just spent half an hour furiously denouncing hunting and professional football. Do I hear someone in the back saying, "But drugs are different"? Of course drugs are different. So are sex, violence, impiety, and anything else someone is likely to get upset enough about to want to legislate against. "The difference that makes a difference" needs to be some form of actual damage to some person.

To employ the force of the state to ban voluntary behavior that is not demonstrably harmful is to legitimize the use of democratic politics to wage cultural holy wars. To be sure, the good citizen of a liberal regime has an obligation not to give unnecessary offense

* A: Because they're afraid it might lead to dancing.

to others; good manners are a part of good citizenship. But without a correlative duty not unnecessarily to take offense, such a rule puts us all at the mercy of the most sensitive.[28]

The social world includes enough real problems without admitting imaginary ones as appropriate subjects of governmental remedies. When assessing whether some activity is harmful for the purpose of making policy, we should insist on some evidence of substantial, even if indirect, damage to someone. (In this restricted and modified form, I believe that Mill's principle of noninterference with "self-regarding" actions deserves our assent.) If there are drugs whose demonstrable harms are not great enough to justify prohibition, or can be adequately controlled by regulation and taxation, this rule would not forbid those who oppose the use of those drugs to continue the campaign against them; it would only withhold from that campaign the coercive authority of the state.

DAMAGE UNDER CONDITIONS OF ILLEGALITY

Whatever damage drug use does when the drug in question is freely available, it almost certainly does more damage per dose when it is illegal or heavily taxed. Thus the justification for the laws must be the hope that prohibition or taxation will lead to so great a reduction in the number of doses that the net effect is positive. With some drugs, the damage to non-users, particularly in the form of crime, would be rather small if the drugs were legal; that may well be true of heroin. When that is so, the drug laws themselves will on balance be a cause of predatory crime and will need to be justified by their benefits in the form of preventing harm to users and noncriminal damage to others.[29] But once the laws are in place and we are considering how to enforce them, whether use would be criminogenic if the drugs were legal is largely irrelevant. Even if the drug laws on balance create predatory crime, suppressing use may still suppress crime.

The same is true of communicable disease. If crack were legal and consequently inexpensive, there would be less crack-induced prostitution and thus less sexually transmitted disease. But that does not make it any less true that the spread of crack dealing to a new city is likely to increase the rate of syphilis transmission within that city. Indeed, with some drugs such as crack and heroin, poorly enforced drug laws may be the worst of all possible worlds from the viewpoint

of non-users: illegality creates the conditions for drug use to be criminogenic and disease-spreading, and lax enforcement permits it to be
widespread as well.

Drugs and Crime

Aside from their pharmacological effects on aggression and impulsiveness, drugs are linked to crime because they are bought and sold
in illicit markets. Obviously, drug dealing is a crime by definition once
the drug is prohibited. There is much fruitless debate over whether
violations of the drug laws (as opposed to the violence linked to
illicit drug dealing) ought to be thought of as "victimless" and excluded from the reckoning when crime rates are calculated or crime-
prevention measures considered. If anyone who is damaged by the
violation of a law is the victim of a crime, there are clearly victims of
drug selling, including some users and some non-users; therefore,
if "victimless" is taken to mean "harmless," selling drugs is anything
but victimless. Still, drug dealing can usefully be distinguished from
"predatory" crimes (variations in the themes of assault and theft) in
two significant ways.

The first is purely technical, in the realm of law enforcement:
most drug-sales crimes lack a complainant for the police and a vic-
tim/witness for the court. This enormously complicates the problem
of making arrests and securing convictions. By contrast, an assault
or a robbery tends to create both a victim to call the police and an
eyewitness to testify.

The second difference between predatory crimes, such as theft,
and consensual crimes, such as drug dealing, is implied by the eco-
logical metaphor of predator and prey. Muggers have victims who
try to avoid being mugged; drug dealers have customers who are
looking to "score." Other things held equal, the more muggers there
are on a block the fewer victims will walk by. By contrast, drug buyers
flock to locations where there are many drug sellers. It is a maxim of
ecology that predators do not travel in herds; if they did, they would
soon exhaust the stock of prey.

Thus drug dealing is not subject to the natural limits that constrain theft. Although drug dealers compete for customers and may
eventually grow numerous enough to saturate the market and eat
away at trade margins, they also help build and maintain customer
bases for one another by making it easier to become and remain a
drug user. That explains why a crime such as cocaine dealing can

multiply tenfold in a decade, while rates of predatory crime tend to be far less variable over time.[30]

The customers in illicit drug markets may, if the drug is expensive enough, commit income-producing crimes to pay for their purchases. Designing drug-law enforcement to reduce this "economic" crime is not simple; enforcement can just as easily increase crime by increasing drug prices and thus drug buyers' need for money. Until a decade ago, the dominant image of drug-induced crime was of heroin users stealing to pay for their habits.

More recently, the spread of crack dealing has focused attention on the violence generated by the drug trade itself. Illicit markets engender violence because those who buy and sell in them cannot ask the police or the courts to protect them from predators or to resolve their disputes. Firms in the illicit drug industry may turn to violence to collect debts, sanction employee dishonesty, punish suppliers for defective raw materials, enforce cartel agreements, and defend their property from robbers.[31]

There are clear disadvantages to being, or even being perceived as, the least heavily armed drug dealer or drug-dealing organization in an area. This creates the potential for arms races among drug dealers. More and more powerful weapons may not increase the frequency of violent disputes, but they will tend to increase the lethality of those disputes and the casualty rate among bystanders. Nor do armed drug dealers restrict the use of their weapons to business purposes alone. An argument between two teenage boys about a slight by one of them to the other's girlfriend may lead to a fatal shooting instead of a bloody nose if either one carries a weapon to protect himself in the crack trade. Dealing may also finance the purchase by those already armed of more expensive and lethal weapons; the difference between a teenager carrying a .22 caliber "Saturday night special" and the same teenager carrying a .357 or a semiautomatic rifle may be literally a matter of life and death.

The other major source of drug-market violence is the enforcement process itself. One way to avoid being arrested is to shoot the police officer. One way to avoid being convicted is to shoot the witness, often a customer or confederate who has himself been arrested and has decided to make a deal with the prosecutor. The more vigorous the enforcement effort, and the more severe the sentences for drug dealing compared with those for violent crimes, the greater the incentive dealing organizations have to use violence to build up their ability to withstand enforcement.[32]

The Nuisance Effects of Illicit Markets

Points of retail sale, even for a licit intoxicant, can create problems for those around them, as the attendance at liquor license hearings attests. But the ill-effects can be magnified manyfold when the retail drug commerce is illicit.

The nuisance impact is conceptually distinct from, though not unrelated to, predatory crime by users and violence among dealers. Open drug dealing, either on street corners and in parks or from fixed dealing locations such as apartments or abandoned buildings, is a neighborhood blight of the worst kind. Even if one could be sure of not being the victim of a predatory crime, who would want to live in the middle of a black-market bazaar?

The fear of crime in a neighborhood is generated as much by the visible signs of disorder—broken windows, abandoned cars, unruly groups of adolescents—as by the actual frequency of serious victimization. This is not the sort of merely irrational fear that could be dispelled by better information; there is some evidence that potential victimizers use the presence of such visible disorder to identify places where crimes are likely to go unpunished.[33] Flagrant drug dealing is about as serious a form of disorder as a community can suffer.

Health: Communicable Disease

When drug users spread infectious diseases (for example, AIDS, syphilis, gonorrhea, chlamydia, and hepatitis B) to one another, they damage third parties in two ways. First, they put additional strains on limited health-care systems and on the antibiotic supply (limited by the development of resistant strains of disease organisms). Second, they put at risk their sexual partners, their health-care providers, and their unborn or nursing children. Drug use can spread infectious diseases by encouraging users to engage in promiscuous unprotected sex; pharmacology may play some role in this, but economics—the exchange of sex for drugs or money to buy drugs—appears to play a far larger one.[34]

Drug injection with shared equipment can also spread disease, particularly AIDS and hepatitis B.[35] The expense of illicit drugs encourages the practice of injection, which is by far the most efficient and thus the most economical method of delivering drug molecules to the brain. Formal and informal restrictions on the distribution of needles, also designed as measures of drug-abuse control, create an artificial scarcity that encourages needle sharing.[36] Thus the main links between drugs and communicable disease are forged by the drug laws. But with disease as with crime, once the laws are in place the frequency of violation helps determine the frequency of side effects.

Like other income-producing crimes, prostitution, with its associated sexually transmitted diseases, may either increase or decrease if enforcement succeeds in raising the prices of drugs; the effect depends on how much the price increase reduces drug consumption. But with rare exceptions—most notably arrests of users for possessing needles—more vigorous and effective drug-law enforcement will tend to reduce the rate of infectious disease transmission via needle sharing, since fewer injections create fewer opportunities for transmission whether the price of drugs is high or low.[37]

PROTECTING THE OTHER
VICTIMS OF DRUG ABUSE

Some of the burdens created by the use of drugs, whether legal or illegal, are sure to fall on non-users. Even a strict libertarian, who abhors governmental paternalism and who would never support coercive intervention to protect users from themselves, could still acknowledge some role for public policies dealing with drug sales, drug use, and their aftermath to reduce the burdens on others. Those whose libertarianism is less thoroughgoing, and who value the free choice of consumers as a way of serving their welfare and not as a matter of abstract right, will also acknowledge the need for special policies to protect actual and potential drug consumers from the consequences of their own ill-chosen behavior. In either case, understanding the necessity of having some drug policies is only a prologue, albeit a necessary one, to deciding what they should be. We thus turn to the problem of policy design.

III

POLICIES

4

Laws

Law is an ordinance of reason for the common good.
—Aquinas

Whoever likes laws or sausages shouldn't watch them being made.
—Bismarck

Public actions to control drug consumption and its related harms can be divided into laws and programs. Laws tax, regulate, or prohibit consumption, distribution, and ancillary activities. Programs enforce the laws, persuade users and potential users to practice abstinence, moderation, or more responsible consumption, and deliver services or incentives to those whose drug use is a problem for themselves or others.

That a society based on free choices and free markets needs any laws at all specifically concerning drugs is not obvious in the abstract. It might seem that general laws governing the advertising and labeling of potentially unsafe products and restricting their sale to minors would be sufficient to protect drug users from drug sellers, while the criminal law and the civil law of torts could, between them, bring home to drug users any harms they impose on others.

But the preceding two chapters argue that drugs differ from other consumer goods in ways relevant to legislation. Our general confidence that well-informed adult consumers will not, on average, damage themselves with their choices will be more frequently disappointed with respect to drugs than with respect to wristwatches. Nor are the criminal and civil courts anything like adequate substitutes for the self-control and public spirit requisite to the successful functioning of any complex society, most of all a liberal society.

On the contrary, those formal social controls rely for their effectiveness on personal characteristics—conscientious attention to duty and the ability to shape one's current behavior with regard to future consequences—that some patterns of drug taking tend to diminish, both acutely and chronically.

If certain kinds of drug taking tend to make actual citizens less like the citizens assumed by liberal theory—spontaneously good stewards of their own welfare and the welfare of their children and willing, under appropriate incentives, to accommodate their behavior to interests of their neighbors, coworkers, and fellow citizens—then a well-designed liberal society will be less "liberal" about drug taking than it is about golf playing. Perhaps a liberal society will need to be even stricter about its citizens' drug use than will other social systems that allow less scope for personal autonomy and thus place smaller demands on their subjects' capacity for self-control.

But to say that some drug laws are necessary and not in fundamental conflict with the rest of the assumptions on which we run our collective life is not to say that any actual system of drug laws is well-designed or that its benefits exceed its costs. For the costs, both of compliance and of noncompliance, are likely to be substantial.

Any legal restriction on a drug tends to interfere with its beneficial, as well as its harmful, uses. To mention "benefit" and "drug use" in the same sentence is taken in some quarters as treason in the war on drugs, but, as a logical matter, the fact that some users of a given drug damage themselves by it, or damage others because of it, does not mean that its use has no benefits. Even putting aside strictly medical applications and the possibility that some nonmedical drug taking will create measurable improvements, immediate or lasting, in functioning or well-being, there remains pleasure.

The market economy uses consumers' willingness to pay for things as a measure of the value of the activities that produce them. That drugs are frequently associated with lapses in self-command ought to make us skeptical about taking a heroin addict's willingness to pay for his next fix, or a nicotine addict's willingness to pay for her next cigarette, as an accurate measure of the value of that fix or cigarette. But surely it would carry skepticism too far to deny altogether the pleasures of drug taking. "Wine maketh glad the heart of man," says the Book of Psalms,[1] and gladness is a benefit.

The other costs of drug laws arise out of attempts, legal and illegal, to get around them. Unless the pressure exerted by the laws is almost imperceptible, counterpressure will develop naturally. The simplest counterpressure takes the form of substitution. Drunkards faced with heavy taxes on whiskey may substitute untaxed rubbing alcohol. Poor kids who find illegal marijuana too expensive may switch to sniffing gasoline.[2]

The other way people deal with a law restricting their behavior is to defy it. Where there are taxes, there is evasion. Where there are regulations, there are violations. Where there are prohibitions, there are black markets. Beyond reducing the efficacy of law in limiting drug-related harms, violations produce evils of their own. Black-market violence and corruption, and the costs of related law enforcement, are obvious. The spread of disrespect for laws in general is less obvious but also important, as is the damage done by mislabeled and adulterated black-market drugs.[3]

Least obvious of all is the damage coercion can do to individual and collective powers of self-control. It is widely believed (though never, I think, demonstrated) that during Prohibition drunkenness became more "normal" among those who continued to drink in speakeasies than it had been among habitués of legal drinking establishments.[4] Whether or not that instance is accurate, the principle it illustrates is likely to be broadly valid. If some drug users lack self-control in regard to their drug use, it is easy to imagine a way to make them better off by restricting the range of choices available to them. It is harder to imagine that doing so will improve their capacity for self-control, with respect to drug use or anything else. The growth of norms and customs of responsible drug use is more apt to be retarded than advanced by external coercive measures.[5]

None of this is to say that drug laws are bad in themselves, only that they are likely to replace some of the evils they regulate with evils of their own. The problem is to design a set of laws that, with appropriate programs, will make the sum of those evils as small as possible. The balance of this chapter will discuss the varieties of possible drug laws: first taxation, then regulation, then prohibition.

TAXATION

The most straightforward way to reduce the consumption of a commodity is to increase the price consumers must pay for it, without increasing the inducements for producers to supply it. Governments do this through excise taxation.

Compared with other policy instruments, excise taxes have a number of highly desirable features. Taxes are continuous rather than yes-or-no. Insofar as making wise choices about drug policies involves balancing reductions in the costs of abuse against increases in the costs of control, taxation allows more precise adjustments than does regulation or prohibition. Excise taxes are simple in concept—so many dollars per gram or per gallon—and therefore tend to be inexpensive to collect.* Taxes require no officious prying into the lives of drug users; no official is asked to distinguish among consumers or occasions. No one is forbidden something that may be, for him, a harmless pleasure or even a benefit. Occasional and moderate users are likely to be only very mildly inconvenienced; as an advertisement for premium Scotch once proclaimed, "If the price difference bothers you, you're drinking too much." Taxes paid are revenue to the government, and thus a benefit either to those helped by the programs it finances or to other taxpayers.

Computing Optimal Drug Taxes

Taxes raise the prices paid by consumers; higher prices induce consumers to buy less. To be sure, high price can serve as a lure, both by implying high value and by identifying consumption with wealth and luxury. But it has never been seriously asserted that the net effect of taxation is to increase consumption. How much less consumers will buy depends on the shape of the demand curve: the quantitative relationship between price and quantity consumed.

A consumer confronted with a price increase must choose some mix of three responses: she can cut down on consumption of the affected good (doing without or finding a substitute), cut down on something else, or earn more or save less. To the extent that a good is important in a consumer's life, unimportant in her budget, and without close substitutes, consumption is likely to be quite insensitive (economists say "inelastic") to changes in price. (How much less toothpaste would you use if the price of toothpaste doubled?)

Economists have a useful measure of the sensitivity of consumption to price: the ratio of the percentage change in quantity to the percentage change in price. This ratio is called the *price elasticity of*

---

* In 1989 the Bureau of Alcohol, Tobacco, and Firearms spent just over $50 million on tobacco and alcohol-related compliance and enforcement operations. That same year, the BATF collected more than $10 billion in revenues in taxes on those two drugs; collection costs were thus about 1/2 of 1 percent. *Budget of the United States Government, Fiscal Year 1991* (Washington, D.C.: US Government Printing Office, 1990), A-975. See also Internal Revenue Service, *Statistics of Income Bulletin* (Winter 1989–1990), 120.

demand. If a 1 percent increase in price yields a 2 percent decrease in quantity purchased, the price elasticity of demand is (negative) 2 and demand for the commodity is said to be "relatively elastic." If a 1 percent increase in price yields a 1 percent decrease in quantity purchased, the price elasticity of demand is (negative) 1 and demand for the commodity is said to be "unit elastic." If a 1 percent increase in price yields only a 0.5 percent decrease in quantity purchased, the price elasticity of demand is (negative) 0.5 and demand for the commodity is said to be "relatively inelastic."* In the extreme case, where quantity does not change at all with price, demand is said to be "perfectly inelastic."

Since the total expenditure on a good is the price multiplied by the quantity, simple algebra shows that the total amount of money spent on a good with unit price elasticity of demand will remain constant as price changes. If demand is relatively inelastic—if the change in quantity is smaller, in percentage terms, than the change in price—then a price increase will produce an increase in total spending. (This is most obvious in the extreme case of perfectly inelastic demand where quantity remains constant as the price rises: clearly total spending must rise.) If demand is relatively elastic, less total money will be spent at higher prices than at lower prices. (Again, in the extreme, any price increase that reduces the quantity to zero will clearly reduce rather than increase total spending.) If we know the price elasticity of demand for some drug we can calculate the effect of a tax on consumption and on consumers' budgets.[6]

The price elasticity of demand for a good is not a single, immutable number. It varies with current prices, the size of the price change (what if toothpaste cost a thousand dollars a tube?), and the time consumers have to adjust to new conditions. Given time, consumers can change their habits, invest in conservation technologies, and find substitutes, with the result that the long-run price elasticity of demand is likely to be much higher than the short-run price elasticity of demand. The gasoline price increases of the 1970s provide an illustration. At first, very large price increases produced modest decreases in consumption (estimated elasticities of about 0.2). But in time people formed carpools, bought more fuel-efficient cars, and lived closer to their workplaces, either by moving or by changing jobs. As a result, over the long run, demand for gasoline proved to be about unit elastic.[7]

* The minus signs come from the fact that the relation between price and quantity demanded is negative; use goes down as price goes up.

Drug taking, like driving, is easier to cut back over time than it is immediately. In the case of habituating drugs, the major impacts of price (and thus of taxation) on consumption are likely to be through initiation and, to a lesser extent, desistance. Established habits are hard to change, but new users have a clean slate on which to write. For current users, quitting entirely may be easier than cutting back. Since the effects of reduced initiation and increased quitting are cumulative over time, the long-run demand for a drug may be quite elastic in the long run even if it is quite inelastic in the short run.

For the currently licit drugs, short-run inelasticity of demand is not altogether a bad thing; it is likely to increase the political practicability of raising taxes. Legislatures are far more apt to raise taxes of any kind because they need the money than in deference to arguments about the beneficial effects of a tax on some unwanted behavior.* If drugs have relatively inelastic demand in the short run, raising drug taxes will be an effective way of increasing next year's revenues, because the new, higher tax rate will be collected on almost the old volume. In the longer run, the consumption-suppressing benefits of higher drug taxation will compromise its revenue-raising benefits, but the longer run is, fortunately, much longer than a fiscal year.

If the damage any drug does to its users and to others were strictly proportional to the amount consumed, taxation could be a virtually complete approach to drug regulation. The greater the harm, the greater the optimal tax. Virtually any given level of reduction in consumption could be achieved—up to the limits imposed by tax evasion—by a sufficiently high tax.

Indeed, if harm were strictly proportional to use, and if all we cared about was the damage that drug use does to non-users (what economists call the "external costs"), then the problem of drug taxation would bear a close analogy to the problem of taxation on pollution, on the production of solid waste, or on other "bads." The applicable principles are well understood: each action that creates external costs should be taxed so that the actor pays an additional dollar in taxes for every additional dollar's worth of damage imposed on other people. (In economists' language, the marginal tax should be equal to the marginal external cost.) In effect, such a tax requires those who participate in externally costly activities to consider those costs in making their decisions, just as the ordinary working of the

---

* For example, note the very slow spread of pollution taxes in the face of rising concern about the environment. Perhaps this is in part because taxation does not function well as an expression of public outrage, whether the evil involved is drug use or environmental pollution.

price system forces them to consider the resources required to produce the goods they consume.[8]

But this well worked-out and intellectually elegant approach is only partially applicable to the taxation of drugs. Consumption and harm do not stand in a simple linear relationship. Not all doses of a given drug impose the same external cost: think of the difference between a cigarette smoked alone outdoors and one smoked in an airplane. What sense does it make to "charge" a social drinker who has never engaged in drunken violence for her pro-rata share of the damage done by drunken hooligans? Worse, with those drugs that do much of their harm through the impoverishment of some users and the resort by others to illicit means of obtaining funds, raising the price by taxation may have the perverse effect of increasing the harm per dose; in such cases, the aggregate harm may rise, instead of falling, when taxation is applied.

Moreover, much of the damage done by drugs, and particularly by the licit widely used drugs to which taxation now applies, is damage to users. For commodities other than drugs, we expect consumers to weigh their own costs and benefits and ask the state to step in only to protect third parties. But if a sixteen-year-old considering her first cigarette does not know or does not care about the bronchial cough of the sixty-year-old she will become, or if a chronic drunkard finds it difficult to control his own drinking behavior, or if a crack user in the middle of a binge loses track of just how bad the ensuing crash is likely to be, their unregulated actions will not coincide with their own interests. In that case, taxation only high enough to match the costs to others will be too low. The tax-induced price should serve as an accurate signal of the total costs of drug use, so that independently acting consumers will choose a level of drug use such that the harm done by the last dose—to the consumer and to others, now and in the future—is exactly equivalent to its benefits. When ignorance or temporal myopia is the problem, taxation provides an elegant solution, for the tax is both obvious and immediate. Even where the problem is impulse control, taxation is likely to be useful both in shaping choices and in limiting the damage someone with any given amount of money can do to himself.

As a practical matter, determining that ideal level of taxation would require heroic feats of measurement, since it would be necessary to compare, for example, the pleasures of a beer at lunch with the catastrophe of a traffic fatality. But everyone who has ever considered buying a sports car has implicitly faced a computation no less complex. For actual taxes to improve matters, it is not necessary to be able to compute the hypothetical optimal tax precisely: all that is required is a rough sense of what would be too little or too much.[9]

Unfortunately, while taxes are the same for all, consumers differ, both in the actual costs they will incur for themselves and others by taking one more dose and in their ability to take into account the costs that fall to their share. Any given level of taxation must under-deter the young, the vulnerable, the wealthy, and the thoughtless, or overdeter the old, the poor, and the foresighted.

This over- or underdeterrence, like any other distortion in the price system, will lead to systematic waste: the actual choices made will not be those that would provide the maximum of net human satisfaction from the available resources. Although the world is full of minor price distortions, including those created by taxation to raise revenue, adding a new one is nothing to be proud of. But insofar as drug use has external costs and unreckoned internal costs, untaxed use also faces the "wrong" price. The problem is to use taxation to create the most nearly appropriate set of prices—to reflect to the consumer both the costs his drug use imposes on others and the extent to which his behavior implicitly underestimates the damage drug use does to himself—recognizing that perfection is not among the available options.

Limitations, Disadvantages, and Complexities of Taxation

While taxes have some very attractive characteristics compared to other drug abuse control measures, they also have limitations and disadvantages. Like all control policies, they have unwanted side effects. Moreover, the very simplicity of taxation as a policy instrument makes it an imperfect device for managing the complex problem of drug abuse.

Evasion

While modest taxes tend to be easy to collect, the incentives for dealers and consumers to evade the tax rise with the tax level. Not only does the traffic in untaxed goods cheat the public treasury, it also diminishes the effectiveness of taxation in controlling consumption. Markets in untaxed goods resemble other illicit markets, with substantial enforcement costs, violence, corruption, and the adulteration or misbranding of goods. At sufficiently high levels, taxation is virtually indistinguishable from prohibition, and no easier to administer.[10] The possibility of evasion thus tends to put an upper limit on the practicable level of taxation.* This in turn limits the ability of taxes by themselves to control drug-related harm; the highest practicable tax on smokable cocaine might be much lower than the marginal damage per dose.

Enforceability

The enforceability of a tax depends in part on the technical characteristics of the good involved. If production facilities are cheap, small, and mobile and the drug itself has a high ratio of potency to bulk, evasion is easy. If production must take place in large factories and the drug itself is bulky, evasion is harder. The fact that a kilogram of crack contains more than ten thousand dosage units (rocks) while a kilogram of even the most concentrated alcohol preparation (a one-liter bottle of whiskey) contains only about two dozen dosage units (drinks) would greatly complicate the administration of a cocaine tax unless the tax were so modest as to have little effect on consumption.

Brand loyalty among licit drug users eases the problem of tax collection. Makers and sellers of untaxed contraband find it hard to compete with the cachet of established brands, while trademark owners tend to be too big and too public to easily engage in tax evasion.

Border Effects

Taxes are imposed by governments, and governments have boundaries. Wherever a tax is higher on one side of a boundary than on the other, people will cross from the high-tax to the low-tax side to buy in the cheaper market. Rules against such transborder shopping are sure to be evaded.[11]

This phenomenon gives rise to three distinct classes of bad effects. First, it involves waste, as real resources are expended to take advantage of imaginary boundary lines. Some of that waste effort will take the form of violations of the law, with many of the bad side effects characteristic of illicit markets. Second, "tax shopping" reduces the effectiveness of taxation as a means of drug abuse control in the higher-taxed jurisdiction (an unfortunate effect unless the tax there

---

* Current U.S. taxes on alcohol and tobacco remain at a respectful distance from that limit.

is excessive). Third, the jurisdiction with the higher tax will lose both tax revenue and economic activity to the jurisdiction with the lower tax, thus creating a disincentive for legislators to set drug taxes as high as they should.

The importance of such border effects depends on the size of the tax differential and on the proportion of the population of the high-tax jurisdiction that lives close to the border. This argues for imposing such taxes on as wide a jurisdiction as possible or for cross-jurisdiction negotiation to establish uniform tax rates. Thus federal alcohol and tobacco taxation, perhaps under some revenue-sharing formula, is to be preferred to state taxation.

Impoverishment of Users

Another major worry about using taxation as a primary means of drug abuse control is that it will tend to (further) impoverish those very heavy drug users who are unable or unwilling to reduce their drug consumption. Insofar as they reduce instead their spending on food, clothing, and shelter, taxation makes them worse off. To the extent that they attempt instead to increase their income by crime, taxation makes their neighbors worse off. A few years ago, San Diego conducted an inadvertent and unfortunate natural experiment on this topic by requiring former heroin addicts in publicly supported methadone maintenance programs to begin to pay for their treatment (a matter of some $200 per month). This policy—in effect, a tax on methadone—had two objectives: to help cover the cost of the program and to encourage methadone clients to become drug-free. The results appear to have been to encourage income-producing crimes by some methadone clients and to lead others to switch back to heroin.[12]

Regressivity

Even when it does not impoverish particular users, taxation may worsen the distribution of income. At least with widely used drugs such as alcohol and nicotine, consumption is more equally distributed across the social classes than is income, and thus a larger share of the income of the poor than of the affluent is spent on these drugs. In such circumstances a drug tax is regressive: that is, it takes more from the poor and less from the well-off than would a flat-rate tax on incomes.[13]

Now, to those who believe—as I believe—that, starting from the current position in the United States, a more equal distribution of income could greatly improve the sum of human satisfactions, regressive taxation is an abomination. The alcohol and tobacco industries have been anything but shy about using the cry of regressiveness against proposals to raise taxes on their products. But a little reflection and calculation shows that this objection is almost entirely spurious.

To take the most obvious point first: drug excises provide, and would provide even if they were substantially increased, a modest share of total tax revenues. In 1986, tax collections by federal, state, and local governments in the United States totaled $1.5 trillion. Of that sum, only $21.5 billion—less than 1.5 percent of the total—came from taxes on alcohol and tobacco.[14] Thus, even if the taxes involved were highly regressive, increasing them would not greatly change the overall picture of who pays what to the tax man.

Moreover, the structure of the markets for tobacco and alcohol limits the regressive effect of raising taxes on those goods. In the tobacco market, strong brand loyalty has allowed cigarette companies with established brands to charge prices substantially unrelated to their costs, leading to some of the highest returns on equity to be found in any industry.[15] Cigarette prices are limited less by competition than by the demand curve: what the traffic will bear. Under such circumstances, a portion of any increase in tax revenues will come at the expense of stockholders rather than smokers, because not all of the tax increase will be passed on to consumers: the companies will absorb some of it in reduced profit margins to avoid driving too many smokers away. In effect, the tax allows the government to capture a share of the tobacco companies' oligopoly rents (the excess profits they derive from being in a less-than-perfectly competitive industry). The progressivity of a tax on capital helps offset the regressivity of a tax on smoking. The same analysis applies to beer.

In the case of alcohol, poor people are actually more likely than others to be abstainers, at least in part because of the strength among the U.S. poor of religious traditions hostile to alcohol. Average alcohol consumption rises with, though not as fast as, income. (The major source of regressivity in alcohol taxation is the low rate charged on alcohol as wine compared to the higher rate charged on alcohol as whiskey.) Higher taxes on alcohol would tend to increase this tilt by reducing drinking more among the poor than among the wealthy.

Even insofar as higher alcohol and tobacco taxation would move the tax system in a regressive direction, it is not hard to find balancing tax reductions (particularly in taxes on the wages of low-wage earners) to move it back in the other direction. How progressive the entire tax system is on balance and how much of our revenue comes from drug excise taxes are almost entirely separable questions.[16]

Other than cutting regressive taxes, there are two ways to suppress drug abuse by taxation without redistributing income in the wrong direction. Both are superficially attractive but flawed. One way is to spend the revenues on programs to benefit the poor. Another is to earmark the revenues of drug taxes for drug treatment and prevention programs. This would, in effect, rebate the tax not merely to a particular income class but to the same group that paid the most of it.

These ideas suffer from two problems, one conceptual and one practical. Conceptually, money is all the same color, so it makes little sense to say that we are spending money from some particular source on some particular object. Practically, the question of how high to set the tax is altogether distinct from the question of how much to spend on drug treatment and prevention or on programs to benefit the poor. The optimal tax might bring in more money that could usefully be spent on prevention and treatment, or it might leave them pitifully underfunded.

But the chief objection to spending the money on particular programs is that it conflicts with the idea of using it to reduce other taxes that bear hard on the poor. Whatever is spent cannot also be given back. Since it is possible to fight drug abuse with taxes without increasing the overall amount of money the tax-gatherer takes from the needy, we should do so and not allow ourselves to be diverted by charming irrelevancies.

Even if it were not possible to tax drugs without taking more from the poor, there would still be a strong case for raising drug taxes. Progressivity in taxation is a means, not an end in itself. The end in view is improving the lives of those who are poor, not reducing their share of tax payments. If poor people smoke and die of smoking-related diseases, the cost falls on them and their (poor) families and friends. If poor people get drunk and commit mayhem with guns, knives, or automobiles, or beat their children, most of the victims are likely to be poor as well. If the social benefits of reduced drug abuse fall at the same points on the income distribution as the taxes paid to reduce it, it is hard to see why the overall distribution of well-being should not become more equal as drug taxes rise, or why the well-being of the poor should not increase along with their share of taxes paid.

Taxation of the Same Drug in Various Forms

Nicotine is contained in pipe tobacco, cigars, cigarettes, chewing to-bacco, and snuff. Alcohol is found in wine, beer, and hard liquor. The main active ingredient in marijuana, THC, is also available in more concentrated form as hashish or "hashish oil," or in pure chemical form. Cocaine can be taken by chewing coca leaves, drinking coca tea, snorting or injecting cocaine powder, or smoking freebase or crack. Heroin and methamphetamine also come in both snortable, injectable, and smokeable forms. Finding the right formula for taxing these different forms is not simple.

The most straightforward approach is to base the tax entirely on the quantity of the underlying drug, regardless of form. This plan can claim both simplicity of conception and ease of administration. But it will be ideal only if the damage done for any given quantity of the underlying drug is roughly constant among its various forms. The more the forms vary in the amount of harm done, the less appropriate a constant per-unit tax will be. If cocaine were to be legalized, it would be a mistake to tax the cocaine in weak solutions such as coca tea or the pre-1900 Coca-Cola at the same rate per milligram as the cocaine in crack, because the damage done by a given quantity of cocaine will be less in a dilute oral administration than in a concentrated inhaled one.

Attributing to each form of a drug anything resembling its precise share of the harm done by that drug can be a monstrously complex task. Consider an adult who, as an adolescent, was introduced to alcohol in the form of wine coolers. If he drinks half a pint of Scotch and wraps his car around a tree, should we attribute the damage to the Scotch or the wine coolers? Even in the case of a drug as widely used and as well studied as nicotine, no one has any very precise idea about the relative harmfulness of a cigarette, a cigar, and a pinch of chewing tobacco. All the varieties of social prejudice are likely to complicate the problem. The ideal tax system would make distinctions among the various forms of a single drug according to their relative tendencies to cause harm, including the harm involved in starting someone on what proves to be a bad habit. But it may be doubted how much any actual system that can be devised and implemented will improve on a simple per-unit tax on the underlying drug.

Taxation is a grossly underutilized mechanism for controlling the currently licit drugs, and an essential element in any possible regulatory regime less stringent than prohibition for some of the currently illicit ones. Using it wisely will require the framers of tax policies to think explicitly and seriously about taxation as a means of shaping behavior and not only as a means of raising revenue.

REGULATION

Whether or not the tax system discriminates among different forms of the same drug, it cannot be made to discriminate in any direct way among different users or different occasions, if only because taxes are collected from sellers rather than from buyers. But just such discrimination is likely to be called for, because some users and occasions are socially much more costly than others. Even the highest practicable tax may not cover the costs of the next drink of a chronic drunken driver. Thus the effort to manage drug use, if it stops short of prohibition, needs regulations as well as taxes.

Regulations are more complicated than taxes and thus can be more precisely crafted. However, they are also more difficult to design and, on the whole, more difficult to enforce. It is easier to determine whether a tax has been paid than whether a regulation has been complied with. Taxation and regulation are not alternatives; in the more usual case, they are complements, neither adequate without the other.

Regulating Intoxicated Behavior

Some people misbehave under the influence of drugs. Merely punishing the misbehavior and ignoring the drugs is not always a sufficient response, in part because the misbehavior may be difficult to detect and to prove. In the case of drunken driving, for example, we could in principle ignore the drunkenness and punish reckless driving, speeding, driving on the wrong side of the road, and so forth. But it is impossible, short of constant video surveillance of all street traffic, to detect and prove a sufficient proportion of the instances of bad driving to create an adequate deterrent or to keep a substantial number of chronic bad drivers off the road. Whether someone was driving badly is partly a matter of opinion; whether he was legally drunk can be tested chemically. Doubtless, many people drive more safely drunk than I do stone-cold sober, and it is in some degree unjust to punish their drunkenness and leave my clumsiness and chronic inattention unpunished. But it is hard to doubt that there would be more deaths and injuries in a world without drunken-driving laws than in a world with such laws.

The same reasoning applies to public intoxication. Public drunkenness is unpleasant to others who must share the street: drunks are more likely than others to insult passersby, sing loudly and off-key, stumble and fall, vomit, or lose consciousness, all of which we would prefer our fellow pedestrians not to do. But to have laws against stumbling, vomiting, or passing out would be patently unjust, because they are not voluntary acts. Laws against insult or bad singing would be virtually impossible to enforce, because abuse and disharmony are matters of opinion. Such laws would also be undesirable, because the liberty to speak one's mind freely and to sing, even badly, is valuable. It makes far more sense to forbid the voluntary act of going out in public after having voluntarily made oneself more likely to be a public nuisance than to try to regulate directly the only partially voluntary actions that constitute the nuisance. (The practicalities of enforcement tend to convert such laws into hybrids, since intoxication in itself is not observable at a distance; only the dangerous and offensive behaviors are apt to attract the attention of the police.)

The other step to be taken in regulating intoxicated behavior is purely negative, but no less important for that. We need to stop accepting intoxication as an excuse. Intent is often an important factor in establishing the extent, or even the presence, of liability for wrongdoing, not only in formal criminal and civil prosecutions but also in the discipline administered in families, schools, and workplaces. Intention matters partly for moral reasons (a person is more fully responsible for something done intentionally than for something done inadvertently) and partly for practical ones (deliberate acts may be easier to deter and may be better predictors of future similar acts). Since intoxication is well known to diminish the connection between what one consciously intends to do and what one actually does, the fact of intoxication will frequently be used to suggest that the intoxicated wrongdoer should not be held fully responsible. In most U.S. jurisdictions, as a matter of law, voluntary intoxication may not be offered as part of such a "diminished capacity" defense. But as a matter of fact, prosecutors, judges, and juries, along with parents, principals, spouses, and bosses, are likely to think that intoxicated behavior is not fully typical of a person's character.

Nor are they wrong to think so, except to the extent that intoxication itself is characteristic. But the practice of punishing intoxicated misbehavior less harshly creates two distinct sets of undesirable incentives. First, it encourages persons who wish to engage in forbidden behavior to become intoxicated first.* Second, it deprives inebriates of one of the social props supporting their drug-threatened self-command.

To reduce the damage done by drug use, we would be better off treating intoxication as an aggravation rather than a mitigation of responsibility, as we do now for drunken reckless driving. Such, it is said, was the practice of the classical Greeks, who reckoned it a double offense for a citizen first to become so intoxicated by wine as to forget his obedience to the laws and then actually to violate them. To that moral argument one could add a social-scientific one: if intoxication weakens self-command, then it will require the threat of a greater punishment to deter someone who is drunk than to deter someone who is sober.

Regulation of Commerce

Rules directed at intoxicated behavior will never carry as much of the burden of drug abuse control as rules regarding the conditions of purchase, sale, and consumption. These can be divided into regulations that apply directly to the buyer and regulations covering only the seller, but the division is not precise. Regulations of all kinds will be enforced primarily on sellers, both because there are fewer of them and because the threat to suspend or revoke a license to sell provides valuable enforcement leverage.

Limits on Potency and Form

The effects of a drug on the user's body and mind depend not only on the pharmacology of the drug but also on the dosage taken and the speed with which it reaches the brain. Since "snorting" a drug is faster acting than swallowing it, injection faster than snorting, and smoking faster than injection, the route of administration also matters. In addition, some drug forms help limit dosage. Beer, for example, is so dilute a solution of alcohol that some users run out of thirst or capacity to hold liquids before they are as drunk as they would otherwise become. The alcohol in whiskey, by contrast, is so

---

* It has been said that one of the functions of after-business drinking among work groups in Japan is to allow subordinates to express their true feelings about their superiors in a setting in which the latter are neither required nor allowed to take offense. Such a custom may be very valuable, but only if the aggression involved is merely verbal.

concentrated that an inexperienced user can easily take too much. Cocaine leaches out of chewed coca leaves so slowly that users do not seem to experience much subjective intoxication; by contrast, smoked crack or freebase cocaine enters the brain in seconds. Injection is a special case because it poses special risks of disease transmission largely absent from other modes of drug taking.

Differential taxation is one way to deal with these differences. Another is to make some forms and potencies, and not others, legally available. Such regulations, if tight enough, may be tantamount to prohibition: the Volstead Act, for example, exempted "near beer" containing less than 0.5 percent alcohol by weight, and yet no one thought of that enactment as creating a "regulatory regime" for drinking.

A threshold question here is how easily such a regulation can be evaded. If a drug is easy to convert from one form to another (as powder cocaine, which is snorted, can be converted into smokable crack), the regulation may have little effect unless backed with further regulations to limit the opportunities for conversion. Regulations regarding form can also have perverse effects: since snorting and injection both use the water-soluble form of cocaine, a regulation forbidding the smokable form could contribute to the spread of injection and thus of AIDS and hepatitis B.

But the pitfalls surrounding the attempt to regulate form and potency should not blind us to its possibilities. Simply because a given molecule is relatively safe in one form does not mean that it will not generate enormous problems in another, and vice versa. Are the differences between coca-leaf "tea," with its stimulant dose of cocaine, and coffee, with its stimulant dose of caffeine, really worth fighting a drug war over? But what would prevent the conversion of coca leaves sold for "tea" into pure cocaine? If we were to make cannabis available for nonmedical use by adults, does it immediately follow that we should allow hashish as well as marijuana? There is no difference in principle between permitting one form of a drug while forbidding other forms and permitting the use of some drugs but not others. The problems here are practical, not conceptual; sometimes, as a practical matter, it will be desirable to discriminate among different forms of the same drug.

Limits on Commercial Behavior

Limits on Persuasion. Sellers attempt to encourage buyers. To mainstream economists, these efforts have never seemed to clash with the theory of consumer sovereignty, though a few radicals from Thorstein Veblen to John Kenneth Galbraith and Herbert Gintis have regarded seller-induced wants as less self-evidently worthy of being satisfied than those that arise from natural desires or from social processes not deliberately manipulated for profit.[17] However one views that general debate, a good case can be made for restricting advertising that promotes desires whose satisfaction threatens to be individually or socially harmful. Surely it is better and less intrusive to restrict deliberate attempts to increase an individual's desire for something harmful than to erect regulatory barriers to frustrate that desire once it has been induced.

At their most modest, restrictions on advertising would consist only in forbidding the making of demonstrably false claims or of factual claims that cannot be substantiated. This is merely to apply to drug advertising the rules that the statutes against fraud and the Federal Trade Commission's rules against "unfair trade practices" apply to all goods. Alas, the rules permit "mere puffery" and the making of claims so vague that no substantiation is possible: "Alive with pleasure," for example, or "Things go better with Coke."

A further step would be to require advertisers to warn potential customers about (some of) the dangers of their products.[18] Traditionally, this has involved requiring warnings in advertising or on packaging. But, at least in the case of cigarettes, advertisers have succeeded in designing displays that deliver the required warnings so subtly that a casual observer might not notice them. An alternative approach would be to require that a fraction of the cost of each advertisement be contributed to a fund to sponsor anti-advertisements. (For these and other purposes, corporate sponsorship of sports teams, sports events, music festivals, and the like ought to be treated as forms of advertising.)

But even if the facts are made available to buyers, the emotional content of advertising—its attempt to endow the advertised product with glamour both in the consumer's eyes and in the eyes of those whom he wishes to impress—remains. This, too, can be countered by anti-advertising, as in the anti-tobacco spot that featured the adolescent Brooke Shields making fun of smokers' imagined sophistication. Or emotional appeals could be banned from promotional advertising, which would then be restricted to simple statements of product characteristics, price, and place of availability, after the manner of the "tombstone" advertising to which the Securities and Exchange Commission limits the underwriters of stocks and bonds.

The effectiveness of advertising bans is a subject of legitimate debate; the historical evidence is mixed.[19] One point sometimes forgotten in that debate is that advertisers can and do exercise influence over the editorial content of the programs and publications they sponsor. Magazines heavily supported by tobacco advertising have been notably reticent about the health risks of smoking;[20] an issue of *Newsweek* with a cover story on the evils of smoking carried no cigarette advertising, though tobacco ads are normally a financial mainstay of the magazine industry.[21]

Some combination of an anti-advertising fund and a version of the "tombstone" regulation could probably do as much as or more than a flat advertising ban to reduce consumption and, particularly, the recruitment of new users.[22] It would also avoid the two great disadvantages of a total advertising ban: the virtual elimination of product innovation, including safety-enhancing innovation, and the weakening of competition by lack of information about relative prices and new brands, which allows retailers and the manufacturers of established brands to collect large oligopoly rents at the expense of consumers.*

Limits on Times and Places of Sale. Restricting the times of sale and on-premises consumption of drugs can serve two purposes. It decreases the total quantity consumed: closing the bars at midnight limits the number of drinking hours after work; closing the liquor stores at midnight reduces impulse purchases by the sleepless. It also decreases the undesirable neighborhood effects both of transactions and of consumption that takes place close to the point of purchase; closing the bars at midnight allows the neighbors to get some sleep.

Regulating the places of sale, for example, by licensing bars and liquor stores, can serve those same two purposes. A limit on the number of bars, even if it does not change the total quantity of alcohol consumed, can reduce the number of rowdy street corners. More important, if the number of licensees is kept below the number of outlets that would exist in the absence of regulation, the licenses themselves will acquire scarcity value and regulators will be able to use the threat of revocation or suspension to enforce other restrictions, such as those on the age of the customers. Limiting the number of places also assists the regulatory process by reducing the workload of the regulatory bodies and their inspectors.

Licensing places of sale has three great disadvantages to set off against these advantages. It creates local oligopolies, to the disad-

---

* True, higher prices discourage consumption, but there is no reason to award the resulting revenues to merchants of hazardous commodities in preference to the public treasury.

vantage of the consumers; it generates opportunities for corruption in the distribution of the licenses; and it opens a market niche for unlicensed, and therefore unregulated, establishments such as "after-hours" clubs. A good argument might be made for treating the location of bars and liquor stores as merely a zoning matter and requiring sellers to post bonds for good behavior as a condition of doing business. This would maintain leverage (since regulators could assess fines against the bonds) without leaving quite so much room for corruption. There is no evidence that limiting the number of outlets has a significant effect on the quantity consumed. (The extreme case might be different; eliminating storefront outlets entirely and restricting all sales to mail-order might be effective in reducing impulse purchases.)

Sellers' Responsibility

The market system encourages sellers of drugs, like sellers of other goods and services, to provide what their customers want. Transactions provide both information and incentive for sellers to act in accordance with customers' desires. But the market provides much less information, and much weaker incentives, for sellers to be concerned about the hidden and long-term costs of drug use to the users, still less about the damage that users do to others. While taxation can be designed to bring the average level of such costs to the attention of buyers and sellers, it cannot easily deal with the heterogeneity either of the buyers or of the conditions of purchase and use.

Regulations can plug some of this gap by restricting or forbidding sales under especially hazardous circumstances or denying access to those potential users who seem unusually apt to harm themselves or others. But sellers, particularly retail sellers, have access to detailed and immediate information about their customers, as well as some influence on the conditions of consumption.[23] Instead of, or in addition to, instructing sellers about the specifics of how to conduct their business, the government can make them responsible, by means of financial penalties or the threat of suspension or revocation of licenses, for the frequency and severity of bad conduct by, or bad results among, their customers. This puts the responsibility where the control is.

The only important current application of this principle is to tavernkeepers, whose licenses are, at least in principle, hostage to their ability to maintain some level of order on their premises. They are required to enforce the minimum drinking age. They are required to refuse to serve a customer who has visibly had his fill. In some states, they are financially liable for damage caused by drunken driving on the part of those leaving their establishments. Perhaps this rule should be extended to the other acute ill-effects of intoxication, by making tavernkeepers liable for the costs their customers generate for police, for hospital emergency rooms, and for "drying-out" facilities. In principle, one could also allow the customers to sue the tavernkeepers for their own losses resulting from intoxication, although this would tend to reduce users' incentives to moderate their own drinking and to behave safely under the influence. There is also a movement to extend some of these same responsibilities to those who distribute alcohol to their guests at parties.

But two factors limit the potential of sellers' responsibility as a regulatory device. There are great difficulties, both as a matter of justice and as a matter of administration, in assessing sellers for the subtle or deferred consequences of drug use, particularly since a long-term user rarely sticks with a single retailer. In addition, sellers who provide drugs for off-premises consumption do not usually have the detailed information or the means of control that would make assigning liability to them either just or effective. If the owner of a package-liquor store sells a bottle of whiskey to someone of legal age who is not intoxicated at the time of sale, what sense does it make to hold him responsible for the fact that, a week later, the buyer drinks that bottle and beats his child? (On the other hand, skid-row liquor stores that specialize in cheap fortified wines and half-bottles of rotgut whiskey know who their customers are and what drinking does to them.)

The distinction between sale for on-premises consumption and sale for use elsewhere is an important one in American liquor regulation, and there are still places where "liquor by the drink" is the subject of controversy. But the idea that bars (or their cognates: opium dens, crack houses) are somehow more dangerous than places that sell drugs for consumption elsewhere is not obviously correct. The opposite may be true, or might be made to be true.

Tavernkeepers are special among drug-sellers because they provide a setting for consumption as well as the drug itself. Not only does this make it easier to hold them responsible, it might enable them to help reduce the frequency of bad results, for drinkers and others, of the drinking that taverns facilitate. However, although customers are required to remain on the premises while they drink, they are not required to remain on the premises as long as they are drunk. If bars were required to keep their patrons inside and safe until they were sober enough not to be a threat to themselves or others, the status of bars as neighborhood nuisances might be greatly abated, and they might easily turn out to have lower damage-to-drink ratios than liquor stores do. But this would require different architecture, different personnel, and different operating styles from those of a present-day bar.

Clearly, applying such a rule to alcohol is not a practical possibility given the social role of alcohol in the United States today. The resulting system would be at once too expensive and too confining. But there may well be drugs (some of the milder psychedelics, for example) too dangerous to be sold for unsupervised use but safe enough for use in a controlled setting with trained supervision, and sufficiently valuable or pleasurable that some users would be willing to pay for temporary custodial care along with the chemicals.

Limits on the Purpose of Use: Prescription

Perhaps the most familiar form of drug regulation is the one that limits the use of a particular drug to medical purposes. Some drugs are used medically in ways that do not engage their psychoactivity at all: cocaine as a local anesthetic and vasoconstrictor for surgery on the eye and nose, for example. Others, in particular the opiate and opioid analgesics, can be legitimately administered to take advantage of one of their psychoactive properties—diminution of sensitivity to pain—while the property for which they are used "recreationally"—their ability to produce euphoria—is not a recognized medical application. Still others, particularly the "minor" tranquilizers and sedative-hypnotics, are given therapeutically for the same effects for which they are taken recreationally: to transform anxiety and unhappiness into calm and contentment.

In the case of cocaine, there is virtually no conceptual or practical connection between the permitted medical use and the forbidden recreational use, any more than there is between the use of alcohol as a disinfectant and its use as an intoxicant. By contrast, for the opiates and tranquilizers, medical and nonmedical users alike are fundamentally taking a drug in order to feel better. Permitted uses are distinguished from forbidden ones by the presence in the user of a diagnosed abnormal state and by the fact that the drugs are obtained and used at the direction of a physician, who is himself a licensee of the government and who wields, in effect, delegated regulatory powers over those who wish to use the drug. This form of regulation encounters three kinds of problems: underprescription out of excessive caution, over- or misprescription because of error by the physician or deception by the patient, and leakage of drugs from licit into illicit channels.

Ever since the post–Civil War outbreak of morphine addiction among veterans who had been given morphine for pain relief, physicians have been extremely—sometimes unduly—concerned about the risk of *iatrogenic* (treatment-induced) drug addiction. Consequently they have tended to be sparing in their use of opiate and opioid pain relievers even when the pain involved is extreme and even when the patient's short life expectancy, as in the common case of terminal cancer patients, makes addiction a largely notional problem.[24] More recent cohorts of physicians tend to be less afraid of prescribing too much pain-killer than their older colleagues, but no one doubts that excessive caution on this point continues to cause needless suffering.

A related point, less widely discussed, is the extent to which mood-altering drugs are appropriate to help patients deal with the emotional anguish, not amounting to mental disease, that comes from the knowledge that death is imminent. The advocates of the use of psychedelic drugs (primarily psilocybin, LSD, and MDMA) in psychotherapy claim successes in helping people deal with their own dying.[25] Whether this claim is true or not—and such investigations are notoriously difficult methodologically—at least the risks involved are much smaller and much easier to gauge in terminal patients than in those with normal life expectancies. Acute damage is measurable, and chronic damage is hardly an issue.

The other side of the same coin is overprescription. Physicians, encouraged by drug manufacturers, have in the past overprescribed amphetamines for weight reduction, barbiturates for sleeplessness, benzodiazepines (the family including Valium) for anxiety, oxycodone (under trade names such as Percodan and Percocet) and propoxyphene (Darvon) for relief of moderate pain, without adequate regard to their risks of acute side effects, suicide, or habituation.[26] In each case, as the evidence of damage has mounted, a combination of professional concern and regulatory action has served to tighten up prescription practices, but it is to be doubted whether most physicians have internalized any general message of caution. Most practicing physicians are not experts in psychopharmacology: they form their impressions about the benefits and risks of drugs largely on the basis of manufacturers' literature, sales pitches by manufacturers' representatives, informal conversations with colleagues, and their own clinical experience. These may not be sufficiently sensitive screens for the presence of subtle or only moderately frequent bad results. One way to control overprescription would be to require special training and continuing education in psychopharmacology as a condition of a physician's maintaining her license to prescribe some or all of the psychoactive pharmaceuticals.

The above discussion assumes that the users of prescription-only psychoactives enter the system as sick people visiting their doctors. But there are also people who simply want access to mood-altering drugs. Would-be recreational users of legitimate pharmaceuticals can get them in any of several ways: they can deceive physicians into prescribing them, deceive pharmacists with forged prescriptions, deal with corrupt physicians or pharmacists, steal drugs from pharmacies or hospital supply rooms, or buy drugs illicitly from those who have obtained them in any of these ways.

It is at this point that the regulated drug-distribution process touches the black market. Regulations regarding prescription psychoactives, unlike regulations regarding prescription antihypertensives, need to be drawn with an eye to their enforceability in the face of economic pressures for evasion. Manufacturing quotas, multiple-part prescriptions to detect corruption and complicate forgery, computer screening to identify doctor-shopping patients, and expedited license suspension and revocation for misbehaving physicians and pharmacists are all ways to make the delegated regulation system more effective. Unfortunately, physicians, pharmacists, and pharmaceutical manufacturers are all likely to regard strict regulation and strict enforcement as adverse to their financial interest and professional independence, and there are also concerns about patient confidentiality and the substitution of other, perhaps more dangerous drugs, for those that happen to be marked out for close scrutiny. Thus despite the spectacular success of some triple-prescription programs—diazepam (Valium) prescriptions paid by Medicaid in New York State plunged by 65 percent when it was added to the triple-prescription list[27]—they have been slow to spread.

With sufficiently tight controls, a prescription-only system can keep the medical misuse and recreational use of prescribed drugs, and the flow of prescribed or diverted drugs into illicit markets, down to arbitrarily low levels. But the tighter the regulation, the greater the cost and inconvenience imposed on manufacturers, physicians, pharmacists, and patients. Cost and inconvenience will not only annoy those who continue to produce, prescribe, dispense, and use a variety of valuable medications, they will also act as disincentives to production, prescription, dispensing, and use. If there are less abusable equivalents, that may not be a bad result; otherwise, the authors of regulations must balance the risks of misuse and diversion against the loss of therapeutic benefit from underprescription and the dangers of the substitutes. There is reason to doubt that moving physicians away from prescribing the familiar diazepam toward more recently introduced tranquilizers such as alprazolam (Xanax) creates a net improvement.

The potential for strictly illicit supply via illicit manufacture puts a limit on the capacity of prescription regulation to reduce the availability of drugs for recreational use. In the late 1960s, regulatory laxity and outrageous behavior by some drug manufacturers, pharmacists, and physicians created a huge black market in licitly produced amphetamines (in addition to their medical misuse as diet aids). Tighter regulation and bad publicity combined to create changes that dried up the supply of diverted amphetamine pills, probably with some substantial benefits in reduced consumption.[28] (As always, it is hard to tell precisely how substantial; other factors were influencing amphetamine consumption at the same time.) But since methamphetamine was fairly easy to make in quantity from available precursor chemicals, one result of squeezing the market for diverted stimulants was to create a market for illicitly manufactured stimulants.[29] Further tightening up the regulation of prescription amphetamines would have only a negligible impact on the total supply of amphetamines to the illicit market.

Similarly, whatever cocaine may leak from licit channels into the black market is a drop in the ocean; tightening up on cocaine's medical uses, or even banning the drug entirely, would be a futile gesture. So too with marijuana; if the drug is ever approved for medical use, as its active ingredient, THC, already has been, any contribution diversion might make to the illicit supply simply will not be worth worrying about.

The sheer volume of damage to users from prescription drugs creates a presumption in favor of stricter regulation.[30] But the potential for illicit manufacture puts a limit on how tight those regulations can usefully be, and concerns about undermedication, substitution, and violations of confidentiality suggest that the optimal degree of strictness will be less than the maximum. We can have some of the benefits of prescription availability and some of the benefits of prohibition, but we cannot have both.

Prescription Drugs for Drug Dependency

A special case of regulation by prescription involves the use of controlled doses of a drug, or a close chemical analogue, in the treatment of drug abuse or drug dependency. This can take either of two forms. Given the dangers of black-market acquisition and the unknown quality of black-market supplies, it is doubtless healthier for someone who has been buying a drug illicitly to receive it under a physician's care than to continue to buy it on the black market. A regular dose of a substance of known potency and purity, obtained and used under hygienic conditions, can allow a user to maintain his habit while stabilizing his life. More ambitiously, a physician can attempt, by prescribing steadily decreasing doses of the drug, to "wean" the patient from dependency with less discomfort (and, for some drugs, less risk of severe injury) than "cold turkey" withdrawal. In practice, however, the distinction between "drug maintenance" and "drug-assisted detoxification" is likely to be a blurry one.[31]

There are many good arguments for allowing those who have already become dependent on a drug to have licit access to it under medical supervision. It is too late to prevent them from trying the drug and progressing to heavy chronic use. If it were possible to force them to desist, abstinence might be better than maintenance for them and for those around them, but they are probably even more strongly motivated to find illicit supplies and more skilled at finding them than they were when they succeeded in acquiring their current habits in the first place. If they continue to use their drug, it is certainly better that they get it cleanly and cheaply and without contributing to the revenues of the illicit market. If they are unhealthy, as persons impoverished by the expense of illicit drug use and exposed to its other health risks often are, a prescription system is likely to provide some medical advice along with the drugs. Indeed, the physician may be placed under regulatory requirement to provide something more comprehensive than a maintenance supply, though any such regulation will increase the cost of the system and probably decrease its attractiveness to drug users by increasing the perceived "hassle" of being in treatment.

In some circumstances, a maintenance program may even reduce access to illicit drugs for new users by taking away addicts as customers (and employees) of drug dealers. At least the law enforcement effort will have a smaller number of buyers and sellers to work against if some of the heavy chronic users are removed from the market.

The disadvantages of maintenance are equally obvious. In effect, it makes "drug addict" a legally privileged status: the prize for proving your skill at acquiring drugs illegally is that you get to have them legally. Whether the effect of such a program on the demand for drugs by new users is large or small is hard to guess, but it will certainly not reduce that demand. As for those who enter the programs, some were probably getting ready to desist from illicit drug buying anyway, for one reason or another; desistance is a frequent incident in "addiction careers."[32] Maintenance seems much less attractive as a policy if it substitutes for desistance rather than for continued illicit use. Worse, maintenance may simply help tide an addict over a period when getting drugs is difficult—for example, when his regular dealer leaves the business—thus losing an opportunity to turn a short-term interruption into a more permanent cessation.

Moreover, licitly provided drugs, unless supplied in unlimited quantities, may supplement illicitly purchased ones rather than substituting for them. The more stringent the physician is in limiting the doses, the more tempted the patient will be to buy a little extra on the side (and then perhaps ask for a larger maintenance dose to support a larger habit). On the other hand, if the dosage is liberal, the patient has a ready source of income from selling his extra on the black market to eager new users. No one becomes dependent on an illicit drug without a great willingness to violate rules, and only the wealthy can maintain such a habit without frequent recourse to unlawful ways of making money. Deviousness may or may not be characteristic of those inclined to excess with drugs, but it is certainly characteristic of those who succeed over time in indulging that inclination in the face of contrary laws.

Thus maintenance schemes are likely to be susceptible to leakage. Regulators may find that they need to insist on monitoring the behavior of recipients of maintenance prescriptions and to enlist treatment providers as monitors and as the administrators of sanctions for misbehavior. Such rules will be seen, correctly, as compromising the relationship of physician and patient. All this does not prove that prescription maintenance programs are unworkable, only that designing them properly is difficult and that at their best they are unlikely to work as well in practice as in their proponents' dreams.[33]

The Supreme Court ruled in 1921 that the use of a drug to treat its own abuse syndrome was not "medical use" within the meaning of the Harrison Narcotics Act, the ancestor of the current Controlled Substances Act. Therefore American physicians may not, for example, provide heroin to heroin addicts. Instead, however, Congress in the 1960s approved the use of methadone, a synthetic opioid, for the treatment of heroin dependency.

Methadone is not identical to heroin; it is far longer-acting, so a single daily dose can prevent withdrawal symptoms. It is thus practical to require methadone recipients to take their dose where they receive it, to reduce the incidence of resale. Methadone users, spared the up-and-down rollercoaster ride of the shorter-acting heroin, are also better able to work and to maintain a steady level of drug intake.[34] Pharmacologically, though, the similarities between the two drugs are far more striking than their differences. Methadone finds a ready illicit market, and leakage of various kinds has created an illicit supply in virtually every city with a methadone clinic.[35] The greatest single advantage of methadone over heroin is that it is not called heroin, and one can therefore support its licit distribution without supporting the "legalization" of heroin.

There is more to say about methadone as a mode of drug treatment. For our current purpose it suffices to note that methadone is the one working example of a prescription maintenance system for drug addicts, and it has proven to be neither a disaster nor a panacea. How different its results would be, for good or ill, if the drug prescribed were heroin itself rather than a substitute is open to debate. But surely the question involved is purely practical rather than abstract and moral.

Regulations on Purchasers

Taxes and regulations on the conditions of sale tend to treat all buyers alike. But buyers vary markedly in the relative risks and benefits their drug use creates for themselves and for others. Sick people, who may be able to benefit from various drugs in ways that overwhelm the risks involved, are an obvious instance: thus the prescription system. But even among nonmedical users, the range of variation is wide. It therefore makes sense to have some regulations directed not at commerce in general but at specific categories of consumers. As with taxation, there are large unexploited opportunities to use this sort of regulation to limit the damage done by the currently licit drugs. Detailed regulations about who can use which drugs in what quantities could also be important elements of the post-prohibition regime if any of the currently controlled drugs were to be made licitly available for nonmedical use. There may be some drugs that it would make sense to "legalize" if, and only if, an enforceable set of user regulations were part of the package. Alcohol may be among them.

Minors

A wide variety of commodities and activities are commonly considered appropriate for adults but not for minors. Without endorsing all of the legal restrictions imposed on minors "for their own good," it is possible to identify two characteristics that make age a sensible dimension along which to discriminate.

With youth goes vulnerability; rapidly growing tissues and rapidly changing personalities are more sensitive to damage. In addition, young people have, on average, longer still to live than older people. This magnifies the importance of possible lasting damage when compared with fleeting pleasure, and it gives harmful processes that take place over many years (notably carcinogenesis) longer to work. One peculiar form of chronic damage—the progression to higher and higher levels of use of any given drug and to use of more and more powerful drugs—characteristically takes place, at least under U.S. conditions, in adolescence and early adulthood. Delaying the average age of initiation for the most widely used drugs—nicotine, alcohol, and marijuana—may be a good way to reduce the fraction of the population that eventually progresses to problem use of those drugs or others.

Minors also tend to be less knowledgeable, less aware of consequences, less self-controlled—in a word, less mature—than their elders. They are therefore more likely to make mistakes, especially when current pleasures must be balanced against deferred pains. For this and other reasons, they are not held fully responsible for their misconduct, particularly under the criminal law. (In many states, even above the age of juvenile jurisdiction there is a category of "youthful offenders" eligible for reduced sentences or for deferred prosecution under various labels.) Such special treatment is likely to take place informally even if the law does not explicitly prescribe it. This reduced criminal liability increases the importance of keeping minors away from substances that tend to induce crime.

Every state now forbids the sale of alcohol to those under twenty-one, and almost all states also limit tobacco sales, though with various age limits. But these bans have been markedly and notoriously unsuccessful; minors, and particularly girls, constitute a large and growing share of the market for tobacco products,[36] and young males are more frequently drunk than any other demographic group (a staggering 39 percent of male high school seniors report having had five or more drinks at a sitting at least once in the past month).[37]

Since they cannot buy these products legally, how is it that so many adolescents use them so often? Some of the leakage, particularly of tobacco, takes the form of direct sales from legitimate retail dealers who deliberately or inadvertently violate the law by selling to those below the legal age.[38] In addition, cigarette vending machines give minors easy access to tobacco.

But when it comes to alcohol, the risks to retailers, and in particular to bar owners, from selling to adolescents are sufficiently high to limit this form of leakage, though minors who carry false identification documents with inflated ages can frustrate even serious attempts to keep them from purchasing alcohol or tobacco. The main form in which alcohol leaks across the age barrier, and a significant form in which tobacco leaks, is in transfers from those old enough to buy to those not old enough: parents buying for children, older siblings buying for younger siblings, older friends for younger friends, even to some extent strangers for younger strangers (sometimes with a fee for the illicit brokerage). Once the goods have crossed the age barrier, they are likely to be shared, so one cooperative older brother can supply beer to an entire group of thirsty adolescents.

Commercial leakage could be reduced, to almost any desired extent, merely by adding enforcement resources and increasing penalties. This is somewhat easier in the case of bars and package stores, which have valuable licenses to lose, than in the case of cigarette retailers, but given the will and the money the job could be done. Since the number of retailers is finite and since most retail transactions are stranger-to-stranger, high enough penalties and vigorous enough investigative efforts could render forbidden sales unprofitable (and, where necessary, force persistent sellers-to-minors out of business). In the case of tobacco, it would also be necessary to ban cigarette vending machines, at least from places where minors might have access to them.

Noncommercial leakage poses a much less tractable problem. The number of potential violators is as large as the number of adults. Most of the transactions involve persons known to one another, so undercover investigation—sending out legions of agents posing as underage buyers—is largely impracticable. Even if violators could be caught and convicted, it would be hard to convince a judge to impose serious penalties on the twenty-two-year-old who buys a six-pack for his nineteen-year-old brother. (The noncommercial reseller, not being in business, is not a licensee of the state and is therefore immune to administrative sanctions.) It would therefore be almost impossible to convince buyers and sellers that such resale was unacceptably risky. At the same time, the evident arbitrariness of the age restriction makes it at least equally difficult to convince them that it is seriously wrong. It does little good to convince a minority, or even a small majority; we would need to convince so many adults that a significant number of juveniles would be unable to find *any* adult willing to help them get alcohol or tobacco.

Regulations governing drug availability according to age would be more consistent with common sense, and so more enforceable, if they created a smoother transition from completely forbidden to completely permitted, as the institution of a learner's permit does for driving. But it is difficult to imagine a workable scheme for making that transition. Perhaps eighteen-to-twenty-one-year-olds should have licit access to alcohol only in supervised settings, which they would not be permitted to leave until fully sober. But how many would take advantage of such restricted legal opportunities as long as illegal access remains so easy?

The difficulty of enforcing age restrictions poses a substantial problem for all regulatory approaches to controlling drug abuse. Insofar as it remains unsolved, legalizing a drug for adults will mean effectively expanding access to it for adolescents.[39] (A partial exception here would be marijuana, to which adolescents already have easy access.[40]) In the case of newly legalized drugs, it might be easier to treat distribution to minors as a serious crime than it is when only alcohol and tobacco are involved, but no drug will remain newly legalized forever.

Problem Users

The average minor may be more likely than the average adult to suffer damage from drug use or to inflict damage on someone else while under the influence of drugs, but there are others whose problems can be identified not statistically but individually: those who have been physically injured by their own drug use, whose drug habits are no longer fully under their voluntary control, who have committed crimes under the influence, who have operated dangerous equipment (primarily, but not exclusively, automobiles) while impaired, who have been intoxicated and disorderly in public, who have shown up for work unfit for duty because of their drug use. It makes sense to distinguish such identified problem users from the rest of the adult population in formulating rules regarding access to drugs.

Limiting or forbidding access to drugs by problem users can have two distinct benefits. It can reduce the rate of future damage to or by those individuals, and it can give those not yet identified as problem users an incentive to keep their intoxication, or at least their intoxicated behavior, within limits. The threat of immediate suspension of drinking privileges may be a far more effective deterrent to a potential drunken driver, drunken brawler, or drunken wife beater than any plausible threat of criminal punishment.

The problem with restrictions on access to drugs for problem users is how to enforce them. We could simply impose a legal disability and attempt to enforce it by punishing the possession of drugs by ineligible users, as federal law punishes convicted felons caught in possession of firearms. But that gets us back to the slow, expensive, and uncertain processes of the criminal law, and relies on those with poor impulse control to control themselves. The alternative is to ask sellers to enforce the restrictions, as they do now for the restriction on age. But how are they to know who is eligible to buy and who is not? One approach to this problem is to require individuals to obtain licenses to use drugs and threaten them with license revocation as a consequence of intoxicated misconduct.

Personal Drug Licenses. The fact that drivers' licenses have birth dates on them makes them ideal documents for sellers to use in verifying age eligibility to buy drugs. To enforce non-age restrictions, we would need a similar document: in effect, a drug license. It could actually be the same document as the driver's license, with a data field or simply a difference of background color indicating whether the bearer is licensed to drink (or to buy some other drug) as well as drive. (Most state motor vehicle registries already issue "non-drivers' licenses" to those who do not want to drive but need proof of age to buy liquor.)

The simplest way to handle the issuance of drug licenses would be to issue them automatically; a normal driver's license would—if the holder were of legal age—also be a drinker's (or other drug-user's) license. But that license could be defaced (for example, by a keypunch) or exchanged for a license with different markings or colors, were the license-holder to forfeit his drug privileges for misconduct or give them up voluntarily as a condition of employment or as an aid to self-control. A license with a blue background would be a driver's license only; one with an orange background would also be a drug license. (The system would have to be a little more complex to handle multiple drugs.) This would be a purely "negative" system; everyone of age would have a license unless it had been revoked, suspended, or voluntarily surrendered.

For driving, by contrast, we employ "positive" licensure. Since driving is a dangerous activity, we do not hand out driving licenses at random to all who reach the legal minimum age. Instead, we require applicants for licenses to demonstrate their knowledge and skill on written and practical tests. In most states, the written test is designed not to screen out the unfit but merely to force new drivers to memorize a few facts and a few laws, knowledge of which is held to make them safer drivers. In some states, applicants just above the minimum age are also required to undergo a course of formal instruction. All of these principles—except, perhaps, the practical examination—might usefully be applied to the process of obtaining a drug-user's license. A little solemnity, a small reminder that a bottle or a joint can be as dangerous as a car, would not be wasted, particularly on the young. It would remind them that using drugs is a choice, not an integral component of adult life.[41]

Whether the license system is positive or negative, there will be some unlicensed adults. Since drivers' licenses are routinely displayed as personal identification, it is worth expending a little bit of worry about the extent to which putting drug status information on the license would create a stigmatized class.

For a drug used by the majority—alcohol, in the United States—the problem would be the stigmatization of the nonholder of a drinking license, particularly under a negative licensure system. What did you do to earn the blue background that marks you as ineligible to buy a drink? But even under negative licensure, nondrinkers' licenses would not be confined to those who had misbehaved. Some persons with moral or religious objections to drink would ask for blue licenses, both to express their sentiments and to safeguard themselves against temptation. So would some of those trying to break patterns of excessive or uncontrolled use, for whom turning in their drug license would be a more effective version of tearing up their cigarettes or pouring their liquor down the drain. (The laws should make the step of surrendering one's drug license easy to take and slightly inconvenient to reverse.) In addition, some employers—airlines, for example—might require some or all employees not to be licensed for some or all drugs. (Legislation might be needed to regulate such requirements.) Finally, in the case of drugs whose users tend to make more insurance claims than do non-users, insurers might offer discounts to those not licensed; it would be far easier for insurers to determine which of their policyholders were not licensed to drink or smoke than it would today to determine which policyholders actually refrain from those largely invisible behaviors. Given that ease of administration, nonsmokers might get substantial discounts on life insurance, and nondrinkers (particularly young males) on automobile insurance. Those discounts would in effect put a privately administered tax on drug privileges, and some would choose not to pay that tax.[42]

All of this should create a sufficient number of nonstigmatizing reasons to carry a nondrinker's license. In the case of drugs used only by a minority—the newly legalized drugs, if there were to be any—the problem of stigma would run the other way. If that problem proved sufficiently severe, it would be possible, at some extra expense, to issue a separate document representing the right to buy drugs other than alcohol.

Quantity Limits. Intoxicated misbehavior is one problem. Excessive use—whether chronic heavy use or occasional binges—is another. A licensing system can remove identified excessive users, but by itself it will not prevent excessive use. However, it would be possible to use drug licenses to administer a system of quantity limits.

Such a system would limit purchases to a fixed amount per week or month. Its administration would be similar to the system that ensures that credit-card holders stay within their lines of credit. Sellers would have to verify with some central data registry that the sale they were about to make did not carry the buyer over his quota; that verification would serve to update the system on the current purchase. As the credit-card process demonstrates, such a system is technically feasible and not very inconvenient or expensive. (The administrative problems would be greatly simplified if purchase were restricted to mail-order only. This might make sense in the case of tobacco.)

The chief problem with such a system, other than its obvious intrusiveness and the need to maintain confidentiality, would be how to treat the distribution of drugs at parties. Two dinner parties for twelve could easily exceed a reasonable monthly personal alcohol quota, and a cocktail party for fifty would be completely out of the question. The simplest solution would be to let guests and hosts solve the problem, making "bring your own bottle" part of ordinary etiquette (and avoiding the problem of having hosts "card" their guests). Or hosts could buy ahead, saving up alcohol rations for their parties.

The great virtue of a quantity-limitation system, other than cutting down on individual excess, would be the suppression of leakage. Any personal license system would help stem the flow of the drug involved from adults to minors by threatening the adults involved with loss of their drug-buying privileges. But it would also create a problem of leakage from licensed adults to unlicensed adults. If one licensed buyer could "feed" arbitrarily many unlicensed buyers, the problem would be significant, and it is easy to foresee the development of a commercial black market. Even a fairly generous quantity limitation—cutting off only the upper 5 percent of personal consumption volumes—would greatly mitigate that problem, which could otherwise largely frustrate the purposes of personal licensure. Intermediate between a rigid quantity limitation and none at all would be a system to record sales and identify a small proportion of very heavy buyers for investigation as possible resellers.

Personal drug licensure, particularly with quantity limitations, seems to represent a wild, even Orwellian, extension of government meddling in private life if we apply it to alcohol or tobacco. By contrast, as applied to currently illicit drugs such a system looks like a virtually complete legalization. This demonstrates the width of the gap between the tightest regulation now in place and the mildest prohibition now in place. It hardly seems plausible that there is no drug in the world too dangerous to be managed by the control regime now applied to alcohol yet safe enough under some conditions that a complete ban on all nonmedical use is unnecessary.

PROHIBITION, LEGALIZATION, AND DECRIMINALIZATION

The above analysis is intended to show that the great ideological debate over drug prohibition and drug legalization is largely without meaning.[43] Except for the hortatory function of branding a given substance and its users as evil, prohibition is not practically distinguishable from very high taxes or very tight regulations. The search for a bright line separating safe molecules from dangerous ones, which we can write into law as a distinction between permitted and prohibited substances, is futile.

But it is not such theoretical arguments that have generated an anti-prohibitionist movement in reaction to the "war on drugs." The great argument of the anti-prohibitionists is a practical one: "Prohibition doesn't work."[44]

Of course prohibition does not work perfectly. Prohibition leaves us with a drug problem (and creates a black-market problem). How bad those problems are depends on the drug, the market, and the enforcement effort. But compared with unrestricted availability or loose regulation, even a badly enforced prohibition is apt to substantially reduce the level of drug consumption and thus of those drug problems that relate directly to the consumption level. The Volstead Act, perhaps the most hated and most flagrantly ignored statute in the history of the American commonwealth, seems, despite an enforcement effort that suffered from small resources, great incompetence, and systematic corruption, to have reduced the quantity of alcohol consumed, and the number of persons dying of chronic alcohol abuse, by between one-third and two-thirds.[45]

Whether the mix of alcohol problems was less bad under Prohibition than before and after Prohibition, or whether it was worse, is not obvious. Framing a sound judgment on that question would require a large number of facts, many of them not available, and an evaluation system that could balance cirrhosis deaths against forgone pleasures, machine-gun battles against drunken brawls.[46] But that the ban on selling alcohol actually reduced the volume of alcohol consumed is not open to serious debate.[47] The right question to ask about Prohibition is not whether it "worked" but whether another set of rules would have produced a better mix of outcomes than Prohibition, and whether some new set of rules regarding alcohol would produce a better mix of outcomes than the current policy of virtually free availability. The same questions should be asked about other drugs, currently licit and currently illicit alike.

Some hold out decriminalization of drug use as a sensible middle ground between permission and prohibition.[48] Decriminalization is an odd hybrid, sparing buyers the risk of arrest but leaving sales in the hands of criminals. Of all policies, it seems best calculated to swell the revenues of the black market. Against this disadvantage, it has the advantage of leaving those who would use the drug even if it were flatly prohibited on the right side of the law, thereby making them better off (and probably less prone to break other laws) and saving enforcement resources. The relative importance of these advantages and disadvantages varies from drug to drug. In some instances, it might be better to impose effective decriminalization administratively, by not devoting enforcement resources to users, than to formally legalize the use of a substance that remains illegal to produce or sell.[49]

GRUDGING TOLERATION

The advocates of decriminalization make an important point: current public policy recognizes no middle ground between legalization and prohibition. Our thinking about the legal status of drugs needs a new category.

Currently we assume that any drug not completely forbidden is available to all adults in unlimited quantities and subject to only modest taxes. Our laws provide for no compromise between "Do as you like" and "Go to jail. Go directly to jail." But these do not exhaust the logical possibilities, and they probably do not exhaust the practical ones. We should recognize a category of grudgingly tolerated vices, where the law's message would be "We think this stuff is potential trouble. If you want to use it, within certain limits, we won't stop you, unless and until you make trouble for somebody else or get in obvious trouble yourself." This substitutes an entire gray scale for a simple choice between black and white. A small tax on caffeine: a very light gray. Permission for adults to go away for a weekend and try MDMA under expert supervision: a very dark gray. Limited, heavily taxed quantities of alcohol for adult licensed drinkers: a medium shade of gray.

Creating this category does not mean we should put everything in it. Given a drug such as crack, with a strong tendency to lead to excess, where excess is likely to be dangerous, and where a quantity-limited licit market would be likely to create too many customers for an unlimited-quantity black market, the best regulation is probably prohibition. But that is not because crack is a drug and beer is a beverage, or because crack is addictive and tobacco is not, or because crack is dangerous and caffeine is safe. It is simply because we cannot design a scheme of regulations and taxes for cocaine that seems likely in practice to provide a better mix of advantages and disadvantages than flat prohibition.

Whatever the law, its practical effect depends on the extent to which it is obeyed. In the case of prohibitions and virtual prohibitions, disobedience to drug laws takes the form of illicit market activity. The nature of those markets is our next topic.

5

The Markets for Illicit Drugs

The most powerful drug law is the law of supply and demand. —Anonymous

Prohibitions create illicit markets. Illicit-market transactions make forbidden goods available and thus partially frustrate the purpose of the prohibition. The markets also create problems of their own: violence, corruption, and disorder.

In many ways, illicit drug markets resemble other markets. They are characterized by buyers in search of high quality, low prices, and convenient availability and by sellers driven by greed, wary of risk, and limited by competition. But the drug markets also have some very peculiar features, most of which derive from the legal status and the other peculiarities of their customers and products. To start with the most obvious example, prices are extraordinarily high by licit-market standards. A gram of cocaine that a dentist can buy for $5 has a black-market value of about $100.[1] A marijuana cigarette costs 10 to 100 times as much as a tobacco cigarette or a tea bag,[2] though all three consist of a gram, more or less, of slightly processed vegetable matter in a simple package. Pills diverted from licit- to black-market trade undergo comparable price inflation.[3] Other peculiar features of these markets include dilution and adulteration of the product, long searches by buyers for sellers, rapid changes in prices and volumes, and the geographic concentration of retail activity. A theory of the drug markets is an attempt to explain these phenomena.

TOWARDS A GENERAL
THEORY OF ILLICIT MARKETS

Transactions involving certain goods and services are prohibited in every advanced society, though the list of prohibited items varies. The purchase and sale of foreign currencies and precious metals, sexual services, the labor of children and of certain classes of aliens, babies for adoption, contingent claims of various kinds (particularly those involving the outcome of sporting contests), human organs for transplant, loans not dischargeable by bankruptcy or carrying more than a legally specified rate of interest, methods of preventing or terminating pregnancy, and votes have all been banned at one time and place or another. The production and distribution for nonmedical use of a long list of psychoactive substances are now prohibited almost universally by domestic law and international treaty.[4]

The reasons for the prohibitions are almost as various as the prohibitions themselves. Usury laws are designed to protect borrowers (buyers). Child labor laws are designed to protect the underage workers (sellers). Prohibitions on bribing citizens and lawmakers are designed to protect the political process. Laws about selling sexual services, babies, and organs for transplant seem to be designed to insulate important social institutions from market forces. Currency laws try to maintain the control of the state over the economy.

A special category of prohibited transactions involves items and activities believed to be vices. A vice, in this usage, is a practice likely to have bad effects on the health, welfare, and character of those who engage in it, or who engage in it to excess. By altering the dispositions of their partakers, vices can damage both them and others, particularly if the vicious behavior carries within it a tendency to excess with respect either to frequency or intensity. Laws restricting gambling, prostitution, and drug transactions are all justified in part on vice-control grounds.

The very existence of a prohibition suggests that in its absence there would be a market for the forbidden item: that some consumers would be willing to pay enough for it to induce some producers to provide it. Prohibition does not eliminate that potential market, but, like taxation, it inserts a "wedge" between the price (in money and nonmoney terms) the consumer pays and the price (net of enforcement risk) the producer receives.

If the prohibition is perfectly enforced, that wedge will be of effectively infinite size: the would-be seller will find no buyer and the would-be buyer no seller, at any price. In the more general case, enforcement is imperfect, and the wedge of finite size, so that some buyers and sellers remain in the market and some transactions take place. Illicit-market economics is the study of those transactions and of the attempts to prevent them.

Prohibited transactions take place, in general, at higher money prices than would be true if the transactions were permitted, thus reducing the consumers' surplus as evaluated by the consumers' tastes and opinions at the moment of the transaction. In addition, the nature of illicit transactions imposes costs of other kinds on consumers: risk of apprehension and punishment, uncertainty and variability in product characteristics (for example, adulterated or mis-labeled drugs), lack of legal recourse for fraud or injury, and diffi-culty in obtaining market information, leading both to inability to comparison-shop and to the expenditure of time and other resources in the search for a seller. Putting to one side any psychic benefit the consumer might receive from violating the law, his perceived gain from each completed transaction is thus smaller than it would be if the market were a licit one.

Not all of this loss to the consumer is gain to the producer: thus the wedge. Only the higher money price benefits the producer; the rest is deadweight loss. Moreover, some of the money price represents the additional cost of production and distribution in illicit markets, including not only the inconveniences incident to being unable to advertise, to enter into legally enforceable contracts, and so on, but also the costs of either evading enforcement efforts or suffering the penalties of the law. Consequently, the volume of illicit production and consumption will in general be smaller than would be the case in the absence of prohibition.

If one accepts the judgment that underlies a vice prohibition— that transactions in the commodity involved generate net losses when the real interests of producers, consumers, and third parties are all considered—this reduction in the volume of transactions should be considered as a benefit of prohibition. The capacity of even weakly enforced prohibitions to produce such reductions is demonstrated by the history of American alcohol prohibition.[5]

The efficacy of any given prohibition in reducing the transactions it forbids depends on the interaction of three factors: the strength of demand and its elasticity to price and to nonprice conditions of availability; the individual dispositions and organizational capacities of actual and potential illicit producers; and the vigor and skill of the enforcement effort. Thus the most obvious purpose of enforcement is the support it lends to the purpose underlying the prohibition: in the case of drug law enforcement, the reduction in the volume of drug consumption and its related harms to users and others.

But that is not the only, or even necessarily the most important, purpose of vice enforcement. The arrest and punishment of vice producers and consumers reflects and reinforces public disapproval of the activity involved and helps maintain the normative and deterrent force of other legal prohibitions. Since black-market dealing can threaten a wide variety of important institutions—neighborhoods, workplaces, schools, and families—the enforcement of vice laws can also help maintain the capacity of those institutions to perform their social functions.[6] Insofar as black-market buyers and sellers are disproportionately represented among the perpetrators and victims of predatory crimes (all the varieties of theft, fraud, and assault), and insofar as the disorder incident to black-market dealing creates criminogenic conditions, vice law enforcement can also serve to control crimes other than those defined by the vice laws themselves.[7]

Thus the enforcement of vice laws ought to be designed both to effectuate the underlying purposes of those laws and to limit their unwanted side effects in the form of the social costs imposed by black-market activity. These goals are sometimes complementary, sometimes competing. In particular, price-mediated reductions in vice consumption may be accompanied by increases in black-market side effects. For example, higher heroin prices may lead to short-run increases in theft activity by heroin addicts as they struggle to maintain their habits.[8] Whether this is so will depend in large part on the price elasticity of demand for the vice and the substitution behavior around it.

By far the largest illicit markets are those for drugs.[9] The economic analysis of drug markets can proceed in either or both of two directions: by observing actual market behavior, noting the peculiar features that distinguish drug markets from more conventional markets, and then seeking explanations for those peculiarities either in the illicit nature of the business or the special characteristics of drugs as consumer commodities; or by reasoning from general principles of economic analysis, combined with a few stylized facts about drug dealing (the transactions are illicit; buyers may diverge from ideal utility-maximizing consumers due to physical dependency, habituation, or binge cycles), to propositions about how the drug markets should be expected to behave.

The central questions for drug-market economics are

- At what prices do various drugs trade, and how do those prices vary with transaction volumes? What determines those prices?
- What is the total quantity purchased by final users? What is the relationship between quantity and price?
- What are the revenues of drug-dealing organizations and the earnings of their principals and employees?
- In addition to wages and entrepreneurial earnings, what are the costs of being in the drug-dealing business? What is the relationship between enforcement activity and the costs faced by drug dealers?[10]

OBSERVATIONAL CHARACTERISTICS OF DRUG MARKETS

Drug markets have at least seven peculiarities as compared with other markets. To the theorist, they are phenomena to be explained. To the policy planner, they are circumstances to be manipulated.

High Prices

Illicit drugs are far more expensive than comparable licit commodities, or than the same drugs sold in licit channels. Even if there were little or no enforcement, illicit goods would be more expensive than their licit counterparts because prohibition complicates doing business. Producers who cannot advertise, borrow from banks, sell securities, sign enforceable contracts, patent their inventions, or register their trademarks will have to find clumsier, more expensive substitutes for these business methods, which licit enterprises take for granted. In addition, the lack of advertising and trademarks makes it harder for customers to comparison-shop. (In addition, illegality by itself tends to suppress consumption, independent of its effect on price, both because some consumers are reluctant to disobey the law and because illegal products are harder to find and less reliable as to quality and labeling than legal ones.)*

---

* Peter Reuter, the doyen of illicit-market economists, has referred to this complex of effects as "structural consequences of product illegality." The costs imposed on the illicit industry by the efforts of enforcement agencies are additional.

High Money Incomes

Drug sellers earn higher money incomes than their skills would command as employees of licit, or most illicit, businesses. While their wealth has no doubt been exaggerated in popular and journalistic mythology, there is clearly good money to be made even at the lower end of the traffic. It appears that low-level cocaine sellers in Washington, D.C., have average cash earnings of about $30 per hour, plus whatever drugs they use from their dealing stock; the same individuals earn less than $10 per hour in their licit-market jobs.[11] Not all of the difference is pure gain; against the cash earnings one must set substantial risks of imprisonment, injury in the course of business or business disputes, and the formation of unwanted and uncontrolled personal drug use habits.

Dilution

For some drugs, the actual composition of a retail package is highly variable and only imperfectly known to the buyer. Changes in effective price are likely to take the form of, and be masked by, changes in purity, as changes in the effective price of the chocolate in a candy bar take the form of changes in the weight of the bar.

The heroin content of a retail bag of "street heroin" through the 1970s and early 1980s averaged about 4 percent (even ignoring those instances where the customer was cheated by being sold a mixture not containing heroin at all).[12] Heroin purity has been on the rise since 1986 as the wholesale price of heroin has fallen.[13] In the late 1970s, retail cocaine tended to be about one-eighth cocaine and the rest diluents; since then, purity on the street seems to have risen (to an estimated 70 percent in 1988) and then fallen, with the fall and subsequent rise of wholesale prices.[14] In the absence of regulations on packaging and labeling, the drug buyer has no assurance about the content of his purchase except the word of the seller; even after he has taken the drug, he may be unable to judge its quality with any precision. Since price and quantity are directly observable and purity is not, dealers have an incentive for misrepresentation. Some heroin packagers use trademarks as a means of being able to build and benefit from a reputation for high quality.[15] However, this tactic has had only partial success: the trademarks are not legally protected against competitors who substitute inferior goods for the genuine "Black Star" or "Murder One" brand.

The fact of cutting is well established, and some of its logic is clear. For example, if the dosages are small, dilution may make the drugs easier to handle. Rising wholesale prices increase the short-term benefits to sellers of diluting their product. Selling at above-average purity represents an investment by a dealer in his future reputation; thus the longer he expects to be in business, the greater incentive he has to start out selling a high-quality product. However, no student of the drug markets has ever produced anything like a convincing theory to explain how changes in market conditions cause changes in average purities over time or from market to market.

Bilateral Monopoly and Conventional Pricing

Drug sellers and drug buyers share an interest in maintaining established business relationships, because dealing with a smaller number of transaction partners reduces the risk of enforcement action. As a fictional drug dealer put it: "We only do business with the people we do business with."[16] To the seller, an established customer is less likely to be gathering evidence for the police; to the buyer, his regular "connection" is less likely to cheat him (as well as easier to find and less reluctant to make a sale). Particularly when the heat is on the street, the buyer is grateful to have an established source and the seller to have a (relatively) safe outlet for his goods. In conventional-market economics, such situations go under the label of *bilateral monopoly*. This phenomenon tends to transform simple price competition into something more complicated, because buyer and seller alike have something to lose if the deal falls through.[17]

Buyers and sellers also have a mutual interest in getting business done quickly, especially if they are dealing out-of-doors where they both face the risk of arrest if the police spot the transaction. Haggling and making change tend to slow things down. In addition, the bilateral-monopoly aspect of the situation means that neither the buyer nor the seller is eager to walk away from the deal altogether. Therefore drugs almost always trade at round-number prices conventional in each market. Conventional prices help make sense of variations in purity: dealers use purity changes to adjust effective prices without changing dollar amounts. In some heroin markets, for example, a "dime bag" ($10 package) of heroin, roughly a tenth of a gram (100 milligrams) of white powder, always costs ten dollars, but its heroin content might be as little as 4 mg or as much as 25 mg depending on the price of wholesale heroin and other market conditions. Mediating price changes through purity changes thus helps grease the wheels of illicit commerce.

Geographic Concentration

Drug transactions are highly concentrated geographically—almost certainly more concentrated than consumption—with a strong bias toward poor and socially disadvantaged neighborhoods. Why the markets are so concentrated, and why they are concentrated where they are, begs for explanation.

At the wholesale level, drug markets tend to be regional or even national in scope; for a period of several years, the largest cocaine distribution organization serving the Washington, D.C. market—the network headed by Rayful Edmonds—was receiving its cocaine shipments via Los Angeles, for no better reason than that Mr. Edmonds had a connection there.[18] The costs of transportation, even with the precautions that enforcement makes necessary, are so small compared with the value of wholesale lots of drugs that large differences in prices among major markets are likely to attract arbitrageurs: businesspeople who attempt to profit from such price differences and in so doing help shrink them. (Arbitrage is most difficult for marijuana, which is bulky compared to its value.)

At the retail level, by contrast, relatively small differences in travel time, convenience, and perceived safety are likely to overwhelm price differences from the viewpoint of the user. The extreme example of this is provided by the heroin market in Manhattan. For more than a decade, the purity-adjusted price of heroin in Central Harlem was roughly twice its price in "Alphabet City" on the Lower East Side, half an hour away by subway. Yet Central Harlem buyers, for many of whom heroin was the single largest item in their personal budgets, continued to buy close to home. Any attempt at arbitrage—buying in Alphabet City for resale in Harlem—would presumably have met with a violent reaction from the established uptown street-dealing organizations.[19]

The desire of buyers to buy where they live should tend to spread retail drug dealing around, as it spreads convenience-store operations around. But working against this are the advantages of concentration. For the buyer, a street corner with many dealers is a better place to seek drugs than a street corner with a few, because the search time is likely to be less. For the seller, the picture is more complicated. On the one hand, competition is likely to drain away business. On the other, once a corner is known as a dealing corner, it will attract new buyers and have a better chance of maintaining its existing ones. Being a dealer on a busy corner is like being a physician in a group practice: going away for a week doesn't mean leaving your clientele hanging. But the great advantage of concentration, for buyers and sellers alike, comes from decreased enforcement risk. Sellers cluster for the same reasons fish shoal and birds flock: protection from natural enemies, in this case the police. Since police routines tend to create a distribution of officers that is more uniform than the distribution of illicit activity, being the sole dealer on a corner is far riskier than being one of twenty. Buyers, too, insofar as they face enforcement risk, face much less of it in a crowd than they would alone.[20]

Search Behavior

Since drug dealers do not advertise and have to be at least somewhat discreet about making their whereabouts known to prospective buyers, the process of buying drugs often involves considerable searching on the part of the buyer, far more than is typical of licit markets. The search time for drugs—which varies from buyer to buyer, from market to market, and from time to time—is a measure of what enforcement officials call "availability": the longer the search time, the less available the drug is. But the term *availability* suggests a characteristic that is either present or absent, rather than a quantity that may be higher or lower. At any given money price, some buyers who would pay that price if drugs were easily available will not expend the effort and incur the risk involved in looking for them (and the possibility of searching unsuccessfully). The higher the search time— again, at any given money price—the lower the quantity consumed. Search time thus acts as a second sort of price that users pay for their drugs.[21]

Critics of enforcement efforts sometimes argue that such efforts are doomed to failure because "Anyone who really wants drugs can get them." Strictly speaking, this is true: at some price, after some amount of searching, any commodity that exists can (probably) be procured, and if one defines "really wanting" as being willing to go to any expense and inconvenience, then anyone who really wants any good can and will get it. The effectiveness of drug policy in reducing consumption depends on the sensitivity of the demand for drugs to money price and search time, the capacity of laws and various enforcement approaches to increase one or the other, and the prospects for reducing the willingness of buyers to spend time and money on drugs.

Increases in the money prices of illicit drugs will do both good and harm, in proportions that vary with the responsiveness of demand to price. Higher money prices will help suppress consumption. How much consumption falls as price rises (the price elasticity of demand) depends on how attached various users are to the drug, what substitutes are available, and how large a role drug purchases play in their personal budgets. If demand is highly elastic to price—if users purchase much less as prices rise—then black-market price increases will generate substantial drug abuse control benefits. If the percentage change in quantity is greater than the percentage change in price (that is, if the absolute value of the price elasticity of demand is greater than one), total spending on drugs will fall as prices rise. Not only will this leave users and former users with more money to spend on food, clothing, shelter, and the support of their dependents, it will shrink the revenues of illicit-market dealers. Higher prices for drugs that are in very elastic demand thus do good all around.

For drugs in relatively inelastic demand, the results of price increases will be less happy, at least in the short run. Consumption, and thus abuse, will shrink less than in the former case. Users will be somewhat less drugged than they would have been at lower prices but will be poorer as their total expenditure on drugs rises. Those users who finance their drug purchases by theft or illicit transactions (drug dealing or prostitution) may increase their criminal activity: "The drug squad makes work for the burglary squad."[22] The revenues of drug dealers, and thus their capacity to pay for corruption and violence, will rise. If the frequency and seriousness of disputes among drug dealers are roughly proportional to the total dollars involved, dealing-related bloodshed is likely to increase.

Longer search times for retail drug purchases, like higher prices, reduce drug consumption. But long search times are free of the potential unwanted side effects of high prices. Greater difficulty in buying drugs will lead to a smaller number of completed transactions, while leaving money prices unchanged. This will decrease both drug consumption and drug expenditures, leaving users with more money to spend on other goods and reducing their incentive to commit income-producing crimes. A heroin-using burglar or a crack-using prostitute facing a drug price increase can maintain his or her previous level of drug consumption by breaking into more houses or servicing more customers. But that strategy will not help in the face of an increase in search time, which makes it harder to turn dollars, including illicitly earned dollars, into drugs. Because smaller expenditures for the user are also smaller revenues for the dealer, rising search times are unambiguously beneficial in controlling black-market corruption and violence as well.

Frequent Small-Quantity Purchases

Given the very great gaps between prices at retail and prices only one step removed from the street, the large role of drug purchases in some buyers' personal budgets, and the discomfort some users face when they run out, we would expect consumers to attempt to buy in bulk and maintain personal inventories. This is widely true of marijuana users, but heavy users of heroin and crack rarely hold stockpiles.[23] Lack of ready cash and the risk of losing drugs to thieves or the police are only part of the reason. Some drug users may find it impossible to maintain personal "stashes" simply because they lack the self-command to save any drugs. The most common reason for ending a crack-use session appears to be simply running out of crack, and strongly addicted heroin users reportedly resort to playing tricks on themselves to maintain enough for a "wake-up" shot. Even those users who are also retail dealers seem to have great difficulty in keeping themselves from dipping into inventory for personal use.[24]

How much this phenomenon relates to the nature of the drugs and how much to the nature of the people who become heavy drug users under conditions of prohibition, it is impossible to tell. It is not reported as characteristic either of marijuana or of the psychedelics. In any case, the result is that purchase units for heroin and crack are smaller, and transaction frequencies greater, than they would otherwise be. That magnifies the importance of relatively small increases in retail search time. If a marijuana smoker who buys a month's supply at a time finds that she has to search a few hours longer to find a seller, the pressure on her to reduce marijuana consumption is fairly small. For the crack smoker who buys on as many days as he uses, or even several times in the same day, a change from a five-minute search to a forty-five minute search may make a substantial difference.

SPECIAL THEORETICAL CONSIDERATIONS ABOUT ILLICIT MARKETS

Buyers and sellers in illicit markets face the risk of enforcement action. They also lack legal protection against broken contracts, thefts, and assaults. Enforcement action, victimization, and precautions taken to avoid them contribute to costs. Since any illicit transaction exposes its participants to enforcement risks and the risk of violence or fraud, transactions costs tend to be large, which helps to explain large markups from one distribution stage to the next.[25]

The combination of enforcement risks and the lack of legal recourse create high information costs for buyers and sellers. Not only is it difficult to find a potential transaction partner, but the cost of doing business with that person depends strongly on one's evaluation of his sincerity (that is, his not being an undercover policeman or an informant) and integrity (paying for what is delivered, delivering what is paid for).

The inability to enter into contracts enforceable at law increases what economists call *agency losses*: that is, the costs created by dishonesty in various forms (including goofing off while the boss is not looking) and by measures to discourage dishonesty.[26] Loan transactions are particularly problematic: the risk of the disruption of business by arrest and the seizure of assets increases uncertainty about the borrower's ability to repay, as the lack of legal compulsion raises the costs of ensuring that the borrower will repay even if he can.

Deprived of the coercive power of the state, illicit businesspeople seek alternative means of resolving disputes. But without "a common power to keep them all in awe,"[27] it is difficult to make a dispute-resolution mechanism effective. Individuals and organizations with a reputation for coercive power and for the willingness to use it to enforce their decisions are therefore able to do business as dispute resolvers.[28]

BEHAVIORAL PHARMACOLOGY AND THE ECONOMICS OF DRUGS

An economic theory of the drug markets must take seriously the behavioral pharmacology and sociology of drug use: both the commonalities across drugs and the drug-to-drug variation.

Drug use is learned behavior for the individual, and drug-use practices are communicated within social groups. For most drugs other than the stimulants, the drug effect is perceived as pleasurable only after some experience in use,[29] and the most likely source of that experience is a friend, relative, or acquaintance who is already a user of the same drug.[30] Higher drug consumption in one period and for one individual tends, other things being equal, to increase consumption in future periods and for related individuals. Thus a decrease in price today will, by increasing current consumption, tend to increase demand in the future. These tendencies are common to many classes of consumer goods but seem to be particularly marked for drugs, licit and illicit. Tolerance and dependency—addiction in its classical sense—magnify the interrelationship between past consumption and present demand. Addicted users, even if they constitute a small proportion of all users, may consume the preponderance of the total supply.

The effects of addiction on aggregate consumption are complicated. Logically, someone addicted to an inexpensive drug with no close substitutes should have a very low price elasticity of demand for that drug, and much discussion of the behavior of drug users in general assumes that their drug taking is determined entirely by their habit and not at all by price. Studies of cigarette smoking confirm that consumption by current users changes much less in the face of tax increases than consumption by new users.[31]

If, on the other hand, the drug is so expensive and the habit so large that it consumes a large proportion of the user's budget, effective demand may become somewhat elastic simply due to the budget constraint. Moreover, the status of being addicted can be deliberately altered, at the cost of some discomfort, and there is some evidence that heroin users deliberately detoxify themselves when their habits get too expensive.[32] Thus if price changes influence the frequencies of initiation, quitting, and relapse in drug use, they may create a significant change in the aggregate demand for highly addictive substances even if they have only small effects on those current heavy users who do not quit entirely.[33]

Moreover, the knowledge that a drug is addictive may act as a deterrent to trying it. The higher the price, the greater that deterrent ought to be. A rational person considering whether or not to take an addictive drug should be more strongly influenced by a change in its price than he would be if the drug were not addictive, because the effect of the drug's price on his lifetime budget is greater.[34]

How closely actual drug-taking behavior follows such "rational addiction" models[35] remains an open question, but some drug-taking behavior is clearly irrational. Persons who find themselves losing self-command with respect to drug taking sometimes seek to control their own behavior by removing themselves from drug-taking environments, by joining self-help groups, or by calling in professional help. It is hard to reconcile much of this behavior with the concept of a unitary rational actor maximizing satisfactions over a fixed preference ordering.

A major unresolved question about the behavioral pharmacology of drugs involves the relationships of substitution and complementarity among them. Whether making one drug less available will, in the long run, increase or decrease the consumption of other drugs is crucial to making sound drug policy. The answer is probably different for different drug pairs. This is an issue on which economic theory is largely silent; more empirical investigation is needed.[36]

GENERAL ECONOMIC PRINCIPLES

Economists have deduced a small number of theorems of great generality regarding markets in which there are many buyers and many sellers and in which information flows freely. How, and to what extent, these theorems apply to illicit markets is a central question.

The first of these principles is sometimes referred to as *the law of one price*. It holds that identical commodities will trade at (almost) identical prices; to be precise, that the difference in prices between two markets for the same commodity will not exceed the cost of moving the goods from one market to the other.

The justification for this principle in ordinary markets is straightforward. If sellers prefer to earn as much as they can, and buyers to pay as little as they can, then price differentials will generate behavior that will cause them to shrink. Goods will be carried from markets in which they are cheap to markets in which they are dear, whereas buyers will move in the other direction. Thus in the cheap market the supply will shrink and the demand will expand (driving the price up), and in the expensive market the supply will grow and the demand will shrink (driving the price down). The greatest sustainable price difference, then, will be the cost of the transaction (including the costs of learning about the price difference and finding persons from whom to buy and sell). It is not necessary, for this "law" to hold, that all participants be perfectly rational, or even that they all know of the existence of multiple markets, because of the possibility of "arbitrage" behavior: trading on the price differential by purchasing in the cheap market and selling in the expensive one.

Another general principle of market behavior is the *zero pure profit* theorem. Competition prevents price gouging by driving prices down to the level at which no resource owner can make more money by moving resources into an industry than he could by applying the same resources to another opportunity. While firms in an industry have a common interest in higher prices, an agreement among them to raise prices will fail unless they have a way to enforce the agreement among themselves and have a way of keeping new players out of the game.

The zero pure profit theorem implies that, over the long run, the total paid by the consumers of a good is equal to the total cost of producing that good. In the absence of special circumstances, such as barriers to entry or economies of scale (that is, a situation in which the average cost of producing a unit of some good falls as the total quantity produced by a single firm rises), the total revenue received by an industry will tend to equal its total costs: raw materials, wages, payments for special skills and resources, and the cost of capital, including both the rate of interest on risk-free loans and a premium reflecting the risks to the providers of capital.

As with the law of one price, the zero long-run pure profit theorem is supported by the observation that any deviation from it would allow someone to benefit himself, and that in the process of doing so he would tend to reduce the deviation. If prices in a competitive industry were such that long-run pure profits were available, the factors of production (such as labor and capital) would tend to flow into that industry to share in the supranormal returns, thus expanding supply and tending to reduce price. If prices were so low that costs were not being covered—if the long-run pure profits were negative—productive resources would tend to flow out of that industry into other industries where they were better compensated, thus contracting supply and increasing price. Thus in a competitive industry long-run price equals long-run cost, and whatever increases cost for the producer eventually increases price to the consumer.

The actual process by which market participants adjust themselves to external changes is a complicated one, which goes under the names *dynamics* or *disequilibrium behavior*. But economists have gotten considerable mileage out of reasoning about the way markets will look once the dynamics have settled out and equilibrium is restored. The law of one price and the zero long-run pure profit theorem are both aspects of this idealized world, which goes under the name of *comparative statics* because its method is to compare the resting states of markets under alternative assumptions about external conditions.

COMPARATIVE STATICS AND THE EVALUATION OF DRUG LAW ENFORCEMENT PROGRAMS

If the drug markets obeyed the rule that long-run pure profits must be zero, the market's total revenues would equal its total costs. In particular, the direct and indirect costs imposed by law enforcement would all be passed through to consumers. That would allow a fairly straightforward evaluation of at least that part of the law enforcement effort designed to decrease consumption through increasing prices: the important evaluative dimension would be (marginal) dollars of cost imposed per (marginal) enforcement dollar spent.[37]

Monetizing Enforcement-Generated Costs

The chief difficulty in actually performing such an evaluation would be in assigning dollar values to the four major components of cost imposition: drugs seized, assets seized, prison time, and the costs of avoiding these (precautions, bribes, lawyers' fees, and so on). Evaluating each of these poses conceptual as well as practical problems.[38]

Cash, which accounts for the bulk of nondrug asset seizures, is easy to evaluate. Drugs and other nonmonetary assets are trickier. As a theoretical guideline, seizures ought to be evaluated at the traffickers' cost of replacing them. This applies alike to seizures of drugs and of nondrug assets. In the case of hard nondrug assets such as boats, traffickers' replacement cost may be greater than the sum the government realizes from an auction sale. In the case of drugs, replacement cost will in general be far less than the final retail or "street" value often cited by the press; the further "up the chain" the transaction occurs, the smaller the per-unit replacement value. (An attempt to compare various enforcement efforts in terms of drug volumes seized per dollar spent has been vigorously criticized on this point.[39])

Prison time is even more difficult to evaluate. Conceptually, the question to be asked is, "How does the overall distribution of prison terms among drug dealers influence the price of drugs?" It does so, presumably, through the behavior of those threatened with prison; employees will demand higher wages, and entrepreneurs higher proprietary earnings, as the threat of imprisonment rises.

The Comparative-Statics Challenge to Interdiction

Despite the difficulties outlined above, it is not very difficult to assign rough monetary values to a variety of enforcement activities. Data from undercover transactions and negotiations provide a reasonably clear picture of the replacement cost of seized drugs. The resulting calculations of costs imposed on the illicit industry tend to place a much smaller value on bulk seizures of drugs in smuggling vessels or container freight than is assigned to that activity in the popular imagination, or reflected in the share that interdiction programs take in federal drug enforcement spending.[40]

A shipment of cocaine seized in transit from its source country to the United States, or at the U.S. port of entry, is certainly worth less to the traffickers who own it than they would be able to sell it for once it had been safely landed, but more than it could be replaced for in its source country, since time and money have been expended on its transportation north. With per-kilogram prices in U.S. cocaine-trafficking centers hovering near $20,000 and export prices at about one-quarter of that, assigning a replacement cost of $10,000 per kilogram to a cocaine seizure would seem generous.[41]

Total interdiction seizures of cocaine in the years 1988 to 1990 averaged about 85 metric tons (thousands of kilograms),[42] which is a respectable fraction of the roughly 200 metric tons estimated to be consumed per year in the United States; between a quarter and a third of all drugs shipped are intercepted at or before the border. If one had the view that bulk drugs at export were scarce, and that seized shipments were not replaced, the interdiction effort would appear to be substantially reducing the cocaine problem in the United States compared to what it would otherwise be.

But evaluated as a means of imposing costs on the illicit industry interdiction is far less impressive. Even at $10,000 per kilogram, and even if 100 tons per year were consistently taken, the total impact on the illicit industry would be $1 billion, out of estimated retail revenues of $17.5 billion.[43] Thus the comparative-statics analysis tends to be quite discouraging about the proposition that interdiction efforts can substantially raise the prices of imported drugs.

If in fact the effect of interdiction on price is small and if (as seems beyond dispute) supplies of bulk drugs in source countries are no constraint on the traffic, the effect of interdiction on consumption will be correspondingly small. This in turn implies that the total amount of cocaine shipped from source countries to the United States will tend to rise along with the success of the interdiction effort, as source-country suppliers sell enough to meet the (largely unaffected) final retail demand plus the "demand" represented by seizure. Since it is the export demand that determines the political threat drug trafficking poses to source countries and the environmental damage done there by cocaine growing and refining, an increase in export demand is disadvantageous to source countries.[44] Thus if the comparative-statics or "risks and prices" view of the drug markets is substantially correct, interdiction has small benefits for the United States and imposes substantial costs on source countries.

The Multiplicative Pass-Through Model

The observation that drug prices at export and import are a small proportion of final retail prices does not immediately entail the conclusion that changes in prices at those levels have only a small effect on retail prices. If, for example, the price of heroin at retail were ten times the price at the kilogram level and if that relationship continued to hold true regardless of changes in kilogram prices, a dollar added to the cost of doing business at the kilogram level would cause a $10 increase in the aggregate retail-level revenues of the heroin industry.

The ratio of retail to wholesale cocaine prices remained remarkably constant during the 1980s even as the prices themselves fell dramatically,[45] lending support to the idea that wholesale price changes are passed through multiplicatively, rather than additively, at retail. This is plausible because some of the costs of retail dealing, including all of the costs associated with the risk of losing inventories, and perhaps dealers' urges as well, tend to rise in step with wholesale prices.[46]

However, another interpretation is also available: that both wholesale and retail prices fell due to the same cause. Until the end of the decade, the physical volume of the cocaine traffic seems to have grown considerably more quickly than did the enforcement resources directed at it; this was true at all levels of the traffic. A falling ratio of enforcement effort to physical volume would be expected to lead to falling prices.[47] Thus retail prices might have fallen *along with* wholesale prices without falling *because* wholesale prices were falling.

Nothing less than the value of a large part of the federal government's drug law enforcement effort is at stake in this debate over whether the relationship of retail price to wholesale price is almost additive (with a small multiplicative term) or almost multiplicative (with a small additive term). Unless the relationship between wholesale and retail prices is primarily multiplicative, interdiction cannot contribute much to drug abuse control. To date, the question remains open, with arguments and evidence on both sides.

Another View of Enforcement
Effectiveness: Destroying Capacity

So far, we have implicitly assumed that drug enforcement reduces drug consumption primarily by making drug dealing more expensive. An alternative view, strongly held by many law enforcement professionals, is that enforcement works by destroying dealing organizations and thus reducing the capacity of the drug-distribution system. If so, the evidence of enforcement success would be severe and sustained drug shortages marked either by complete unavailability of drugs at any price or by extraordinary price increases.

Theoretically, this strategy seems unlikely to work unless there is something about the organization destroyed that cannot be replaced. Empirically, the only plausible example of such a shortage is the heroin market in the wake of the destruction of the "French Connection."*

On the other hand, if established drug-dealing organizations experience lower costs than do new entrants into the market and if enforcement fails to put enough of them out of business, the result may be a sudden price collapse as low-cost suppliers fight for market shares. This seems to have been part of the story of cocaine in the early 1980s.[48] Thus even if putting large dealing organizations out of business cannot create shortages, it may serve the important objective of preventing dramatic price decreases.

INDUSTRY-WIDE ECONOMIES OF SCALE
AND POSITIVE FEEDBACK EFFECTS

The enforcement risk faced in the course of any one drug transaction will fall as the number of transactions rises, simply because the police cannot arrest everyone at once. As a result, an increase in the volume handled by any one dealing organization will reduce the per-unit costs of all competing organizations, an effect economists call *industry-wide external economies of scale*.

Industry-wide economies of scale will tend to reinforce upward and downward movements in drug volumes. Larger volumes today will lead to lower costs of dealing and thus lower prices. Lower prices will induce increased consumption. Increased consumption today will

---

* It is also possible that the marijuana price increase of the late 1980s resulted partly from a shrinkage of production and distribution capacity and the consequent ability of remaining producers to extract oligopoly rents, rather than simply from enforcement-imposed cost increases.

lead to increased shipments, and thus still lower prices, and so on. The same mechanisms will be in force as a market shrinks.

This analysis has little to say about the relative value of interdiction and other high-level enforcement activity measured against competing uses of the same resources. But it raises questions about the allocation of enforcement resources across drugs, suggesting that it would be desirable for enforcement resources to lead, rather than lag, trends in physical volume. From this perspective, the massive resources applied to enforcing the cocaine laws in the latter half of the 1980s would have been far more effective had they arrived earlier, when marijuana and heroin continued to dominate enforcement attention as cocaine prices fell and volume swelled. Today, attention to positive-feedback effects would tend to support arguments for the rapid movement of enforcement resources into the heroin market, which appears to be in a resurgence.

THE PERSISTENCE OF THE MARKETS FOR ILLICIT GOODS

Drug markets have both inertia of rest and inertia of motion. Both current levels and current trends tend to perpetuate themselves. This is so for at least six different reasons.

First, current demand is a function of past consumption. Reinforcement, tolerance, and dependency help explain this relationship. In addition, the enjoyment of drug taking seems to be largely learned rather than innate; experience in drug taking therefore tends to increase the associated pleasure and thus the demand. In economist's terms, drug takers form *consumption capital*, a phenomenon that drug taking has in common with such other acquired tastes as exotic food and "difficult" music and art.[49]

Second, current supply is a function of past sales. Individuals and organizations build the inclination to deal in drugs and the skill to do so successfully. Cocaine money may build as much tolerance and dependency as does cocaine itself.

Third, as drug users learn to use drugs and drug sellers learn to sell them, they also learn to do business with one another. Over time, dealers learn to whom to sell, buyers from whom to buy. The relational capital among them—their experience of dealing with one another and the existence of a drug-dealing community within which reputations can be earned and lost—is a common-property resource for the entire industry, and it tends to grow with time and volume.

Fourth, some of the important transaction costs of the drug business—labor time and inventory holding time for dealers, search time for buyers—tend to fall as the number of transactions rises and the experience of buyers and sellers grows. The more buyers and sellers, the shorter the search required to find one or the other. The reduction in transaction costs reduces both components of users' "effective price" (money and search time) and thus increases volume.

Fifth, as enforcement resources are spread over more and more transactions, the enforcement risk of consummating any one transaction falls.

Sixth, since recently initiated drug users are most likely to be excited about the perceived benefits of drug use and least likely to show its ill effects, they are the most potent sources of positive word-of-mouth information and the most likely to initiate their friends. A growing drug market is likely to have many recently initiated users, and they will help it continue to grow; a shrinking market will have few.

Against these six factors creating persistence in the short run are two that create counterpressures over the longer term. As the number of persons who have been using a given drug for a long time grows, so does the number who are feeling and showing its negative effects. Not only are they no longer highly motivated or persuasive recruiters of new users, they actively discourage new use by their bad example, whether observed directly or communicated through the mass media. A few years after a beginning of boom market in a particular drug, its reputation tends to sour. This reduces the number of new users, thus further reducing the number of proselytizers.

Growing drug markets also attract additional enforcement resources, due both to the purely professional desire of drug agents to make big cases and to pressure from the public to "do something." Enforcement resources are likely to continue to grow even after the market itself has peaked. This tends to accelerate the downward trend in volumes by further increasing the enforcement-to-transaction ratio.

The combination of short-term positive feedback and long-term negative feedback tends to create a multiyear cycle of boom and bust. There is evidence that the cocaine market may have reached its peak for this cycle in the past year or two.

VOLUME DETERMINATION AND THE IMPORTANCE OF RETAIL CONDITIONS

All politics, it has been said, is local. Ultimately, all drug dealing is retail. The entire superstructure of international production, transport, distribution, and money laundering is supported by a base of retail sellers doing business with retail buyers. Conditions of retail sale play an important role in determining drug volumes. It is also retail drug dealing that creates the disruptive conditions that make open drug markets so devastating to the neighborhoods in which they appear and a large proportion of the violence associated with the drug trade.

For some purposes, where and how drug dealing takes place may be as important as, or even more important than, the number of users or the quantity consumed. The attempt to influence retail conditions engages a different set of enforcement tactics than the attempt to influence wholesale prices.[50] In some instances, concentrated retail-level enforcement activity has substantially improved the local quality of life.[51]

The nonmonetary costs of drug purchase to the user—primarily the search time required to find a seller—depend on the number, geographic and social location, and aggressiveness of retail sellers. The number, location, and behavior of retailers are not directly influenced by changes in wholesale prices brought about by interdiction or high-level drug law enforcement. It is therefore primarily retail-level enforcement that influences search time and restores or fails to restore order to neighborhoods disordered by retail drug markets.[52]

In local markets as well as national ones, transactions (unwillingly) compete for scarce enforcement attention, thus creating external economies of scale. Further external economies are created by the fact that concentration of participants reduces search times. Thus retail markets tend to concentrate and to remain where they are in the absence of large external forces. There may be a critical level of enforcement effort, continued over time, required to force a market below its minimum viable size. This implies that retail enforcement efforts should be concentrated rather than being dispersed.[53]

Retail transactions can be divided into "flagrant" transactions, which take place in the open or in dedicated drug-dealing locations, and (relatively) discreet transactions, which take place in multipurpose indoor locations. Flagrant transactions are easier to interfere with, and create larger external burdens, than discreet transactions.[54] The last several years have seen the development of a large array of approaches for both officials and citizens to use to disrupt the conduct of flagrant retail drug markets.[55]

One approach to designing such tactics starts with an analysis of the conditions that make a retail drug market viable. It requires a place—a venue—in which buyers and sellers can meet to do business. The buyers need convenient access to that venue, the desire to buy the drugs sold there, income to turn that desire into market demand, and a sense that they can buy with (at least relative) impunity. The sellers need operating scope within the venue, a supply of labor (perhaps their own), attractive ways to spend or save the proceeds to maintain their incentive, a supply of drugs, and again a sense of impunity. Note that on this analysis all interdiction and high-level enforcement is encompassed within one factor (drug supply) out of ten.

Anything that interferes with any of these "factors of production" will reduce the volume of transactions. Tactics that do not involve arrests and trials (for example, changing traffic patterns, noting license numbers of cars cruising to buy drugs and sending postcards to their owners, boarding up drug-dealing locations as public nuisances or for code violations) may not run into the system capacity constraints that have frustrated more conventional enforcement efforts.[56]

6

Enforcement

You don't understand, Doc.
We aren't here to solve the drug problem.
We're here to put bad guys in jail.
—Veteran DEA agent
to academic drug-policy expert

Legislation—bidding and forbidding, regulating, and taxing—is only one half of drug policy. Governments also act on the drug problem by spending money: to hire civil servants, to buy goods and services, and to stimulate private activity by means of contracts and grants, incentives, and subsidies.

These activities—generically, programs—can be divided into three categories: enforcement, persuasion, and helping and controlling problem users. The laws—taxes, regulations, and prohibitions alike—need to be enforced, by preventing some violations and by investigating, adjudicating, and punishing others. Current and potential users can be persuaded to abstain, or to moderate use and exercise appropriate caution about circumstances. The damage done to and by problem users—those with established patterns of immoderate or inappropriate use—can be reduced by offering to help them and by coercing them to change their behavior.

THE GOALS OF DRUG LAW ENFORCEMENT

Whenever there are drug laws there will be illicit markets, which frustrate the intent of the laws by supporting forbidden consumption and which also generate violence, corruption, and disorder. From the viewpoint of drug abuse control, the immediate goal of enforcement is to interfere with black-market activity, raising prices and increasing the difficulty of purchase. Adding more enforcement resources will shrink any existing market somewhat, though the remaining consumption may do more damage per dose to drug users and others than it would have under less vigorous enforcement; higher drug prices, in particular, can make users worse off and increase their predatory criminal activity.

The other practical goal of enforcement is to limit black-market side effects: crime, violence, and corruption. Here, again, more is not necessarily better: enforcement can accentuate the undesirable tendencies of the black markets on which it operates by increasing both the source of money involved and the incentives for violence and corruption. The general problem of drug law enforcement policymaking, then, is to minimize the sum of two kinds of direct harm—the harm done by consumption and the harm done by black markets—plus the indirect harm done by the diversion of enforcement resources from other uses.

It might seem that supporting the original purpose underlying the drug laws—reducing drug consumption—deserves priority over merely limiting the laws' side effects. Not necessarily. Much if not most of the consumption-reducing benefit available from any prohibition is achieved by prohibition itself, backed with just enough enforcement to prevent its becoming a dead letter like the statutes prohibiting fornication. If enforcement can maintain the benefits of prohibition in the form of reduced availability and increased price while holding its disadvantages—black-market violence, user crime, and neighborhood disruption—down to a tolerable level, that may be as much as can reasonably be asked.

But law enforcement is almost never a purely practical enterprise. Questions of justice are always relevant. While a policy analyst can analyze drug law enforcement as "effective regulation of an illicit market,"[1] police, prosecutors, and judges do not and cannot think of themselves primarily as regulators. Part of their mission is to carry out the law and punish guilty persons in a manner proportionate to their guilt. Justice and regulation do not always point in the same direction.

Law enforcement includes anything done by public authority to identify lawbreakers, collect evidence of their crimes, demonstrate those crimes to a judge or some other official authorized to impose a penalty, and actually carry out that penalty.* But although the legally

---

* In addition, the police carry out a variety of social service and order maintenance activities only indirectly connected with punishing crime.

imposed penalty comes at the end of the process, and then only in some cases, the entire process involves punishing—inflicting damage on—lawbreakers (and sometimes others). Being investigated, arrested, and tried, being required to post bail or to remain confined in the absence of bail, and being required to hire a lawyer are all costly or unpleasant. So are the techniques of concealment and evasion that illicit businessmen adopt to avoid enforcement.

The prospect of these costs and pains discourages some potential lawbreakers; this is *deterrence,* either *specific* (involving a potential offender's own previous brushes with the law) or *general* (involving the effect on one potential offender of the punishment suffered by another). Actually undergoing punishment—spending time in prison, losing one's pharmacy license—reduces the ability of some lawbreakers to repeat their offenses, at least for a time; this is *incapacitation.* These are the two ways in which enforcement can reduce the incidence of lawbreaking, and the entire process can be thought of as a way to produce, allocate, and deliver punishments for the purpose of deterrence and incapacitation.*

In the case of drug law enforcement, there are two conceptually distinct, though empirically overlapping, sets of offenders to be deterred and incapacitated: sellers and buyers. The volume of transactions can be reduced either by raising sellers' costs of doing business and giving them incentives to be more cautious in their sales methods, thus increasing prices and search times for buyers, or by making buyers more cautious about buying, thus reducing their effective demand. Deterring users, like increasing search time, reduces the volume of drug consumption without raising money prices, and therefore reduces the total revenues of the drug-dealing industry.

As a purely logical matter, questions of law enforcement strategy and tactics can be discussed independently of the debate over what sorts of drug laws ought to be passed in the first place. Just as laws have advantages and disadvantages, so too do enforcement efforts. It is not at all logically inconsistent to believe both that a given drug ought to be prohibited entirely for nonmedical use and that, once prohibited, it deserves only modest enforcement efforts. There might be more important enforcement targets, or the costs and side effects

---

* Enforcement is also sometimes thought to reduce lawbreaking by reinforcing social disapproval of the acts punished and by improving the moral character of those punished (rehabilitation). These effects, even if they are real and not merely imagined, are not sufficiently well understood to be a firm basis for choosing policies. Law enforcement and punishment also serve the individual and social demands for retribution and the moral demand for justice, but retribution is not in itself a means of crime control.

of increased enforcement might outweigh the good it would do in suppressing consumption. This is a plausible view, for example, about marijuana.[2] By the same token, it is possible to believe that a drug such as heroin should not have been prohibited in the first place but that, once it has been made illegal, every effort ought to be made to drive the black market virtually out of existence. If one were prepared to ignore the damage done to users and concentrate entirely on protecting non-users, there would be a strong case for legalizing heroin; users of licit heroin might be virtually harmless, except to themselves, while users (and sellers) of illicit heroin are a heavy burden on the rest of us. But given the illegality of heroin, there is a clear case for vigorous enforcement as a means of reducing the number of those burdensome users and sellers.

This logical viewpoint is not, however, the viewpoint of practical politics or of ideological warfare. As long as the drug laws themselves are controversial, advocates of continued prohibition and of legalization will use the debates about enforcement tactics as occasions for scoring points in that controversy. Optimism about the effectiveness of enforcement is held to be "pro-war," while pessimism about its effects and serious attention to its costs are held to be "pro-legalization." All remarks about enforcement tactics are likely to be taken by both sides as coded messages about the laws themselves. I disclaim any such intention with respect to the following pages.

Four questions need to be asked about enforcement. How should enforcement activity be distributed among the various illicit drugs? Where in the chain of production and distribution should enforcement activity be concentrated: that is, should the focus be on retailing, on large-scale domestic distribution and manufacture, on importing, or on foreign production and processing? What mix of tactics and resources ought to be employed? How should law enforcement attention be distributed between drug dealing and other crimes? The first of these questions will be touched on in the chapters on specific drugs; the balance of this chapter will discuss the other three.

DECIDING WHERE IN THE CHAIN TO INTERVENE

Drugs pass through many hands on their way from the farmer's field or the underground chemist's laboratory to the consumer. For drugs that start as crops grown abroad, there are farmers, processors, and exporters in the source countries, smugglers of various types who get the refined product into the United States, and importers who receive it, as well as the full array of middlemen between the importer and the retailer. Enforcement can aim at the original producer, the final consumer, or any of the people in between, or at ancillary service providers such as money launderers. As the drugs approach the final user ("the street"), the quantities involved in any one deal, and the amounts of money to be made by any one dealer, tend to shrink. It is thus conventional to call retail or near-retail transactions and organizations "low level," and enforcement directed at them "low-level enforcement"; activity further "up the chain" is "high level."

Source-Country Activities

The ultimate high-level enforcement is stopping drugs at the source, either by eradicating crops in the field or by disrupting foreign-based trafficking groups. The State Department spends a relatively small amount of money helping and a relatively large amount of effort pressuring foreign governments to destroy crops and to arrest and then try to extradite major dealers.[3] Those efforts, which command almost universal political support in the United States, tend to be much less popular abroad, where the spectacle of U.S. drug agents exercising virtual police powers and U.S. military "advisers" attacking fields of drug crops raises hackles.[4]

Drug issues are a persistent irritant in U.S.-Mexican relations. There are strong feelings on the Mexican side that Mexico is being asked to bear too much of the burden of what is primarily a U.S. domestic problem. Mexican officials and scholars also argue that some of Washington's arm-twisting on the issue (particularly threats of economic sanctions if Mexico fails to comply in various ways) reflects both ingratitude for rather substantial Mexican enforcement efforts and inadequate respect for Mexican sovereignty.[5]

The diplomatic situation with respect to Colombia is similar, though somewhat less acrimonious. Colombia has taken heavy casualties, and suffered enormous institutional damage, for its part of the drug war: politicians, judges, and journalists literally live in fear of their lives if they displease major cocaine dealers by their votes, decisions, and articles.[6]

In diplomatic exchanges on the subject, much is made of burden sharing, symmetry, and mutual respect. For example, a widely expressed view south of the Rio Grande is that the United States ought to eradicate its domestic marijuana crop to show its solidarity with

Latin American crop-eradication efforts. Unfortunately, there is less focus on the practically more significant question of what effect foreign drug policies have on the U.S. problem and what effects U.S. domestic policies have on the problems of the source countries.

Drug crops are so plentiful, so cheap, and so little restricted by geography that it is hard to see how any plausible set of crop-eradication efforts abroad could make any difference to the availability of drugs at home. Overseas law enforcement directed at major trafficking groups may be able to put a sizable dent in the market, at least for a while, but only in extraordinary and probably temporary circumstances, when processing and export activities are concentrated in one region and in one or a few organizations.

Four examples are illuminating here: two apparent successes, a failure, and one in between. One success was the destruction of the Turkey-Marseilles-New York heroin trade (the "French connection"). Poppies grown in Turkey, refined into heroin in Marseilles, and shipped into New York constituted a large share of the U.S. heroin supply in the late 1960s. Two roughly simultaneous events—the ban on poppy growing imposed by the Turkish government and a major series of convictions—led to a substantial increase in heroin prices domestically, until increased imports from Mexico and Southeast Asia picked up the slack, and heroin remained expensive and impure for two decades.*

The failure was the spraying of the defoliant paraquat on the Mexican marijuana crop in the early 1970s, which virtually eliminated imports of Mexican marijuana (by scaring consumers about the potential for contaminated crops rather than by eliminating production). The result, however, was to shift the source of supply to Colombia, a shift that happened within a matter of months. It is possible, though not certain, that by opening up Colombian-U.S. drug-smuggling routes, the Mexican spraying program contributed indirectly to the development of the cocaine trade later in the decade; what is certain is that it had almost no impact on U.S. marijuana consumption.[7] By contrast, the increase in anti-smuggling enforcement during the 1980s seems to have roughly doubled marijuana prices, which must be counted as at least a tactical success.

An intermediate case was impact on the U.S. cocaine market of the virtual civil war between the Colombian government and Medellín trafficking organization. The flow of exports was temporarily dis-

---

* Even this instance, treasured by proponents of overseas activity, has been challenged. See Peter Reuter, "Eternal Hope: America's International Drug Control Efforts," *The Public Interest* (Spring 1985).

rupted and prices of coca leaf in South America fell due to lack of demand at the refinery level, while in the United States wholesale prices rose and retail purity fell.[8] But it took less than a year for new supplies to emerge and prices to resume their downward trend.

Overseas enforcement policy should take into account the effects of drug dealing and of anti-drug activities on the source countries as well as their impact on the U.S. market. In a few instances—Bolivia, for example—earnings from drug exports are so important economically that even the social and political impacts of illicit business may be outweighed by the sheer need for export earnings. But in the more typical cases—Mexico, Colombia, Thailand—the drug trade, while clearly beneficial to a few drug merchants and a larger but still relatively small number of peasant farmers, is a national burden, and shrinking it is a goal of national policy for the source country.

Exports can be reduced by in-country enforcement against growing, processing, and exporting. But if such enforcement is directed at major dealers with great wealth and easy access to foreign-made weapons, it puts heavy burdens on poorly developed law enforcement systems; both corruption and anti-enforcement violence are likely to pose significant problems. That has been the case in Colombia.[9] Enforcement aimed at poor farmers is likely to have substantial political costs and can require the use of large military and police forces; that has been the case in Mexico. Law enforcement cooperation with U. S. agencies raises concerns about national sovereignty, most of all when it involves the extradition of source-country citizens for trial under foreign jurisdiction.

Since both drug dealing and drug enforcement create problems, it is to the benefit of most source countries if demand for their drug exports drops. That will happen if the quantity demanded by the consumers decreases, either because of reduced desire for drugs or because of enforcement efforts that raise drug prices or search times. Insistence by source-country officials that the United States "do something" on the demand side are as familiar an element of the international dialogue on drug control as insistence by the United States that source countries do more to control supply.

While demand reduction reduces the flow of foreign-grown drugs, U.S. law enforcement against domestic drug producers can increase the demand for drug exports from source countries. Domestic marijuana is a substitute for imported marijuana; domestically produced methamphetamine is a less perfect substitute, but still a substitute, for imported cocaine. Domestic crop eradication—frequently demanded by Latin Americans and offered by U.S. officials as evidence that the United States is carrying its share of the international drug control burden—actually makes the problems of Mexico, Jamaica, and other marijuana-exporting countries worse by reducing the supply of substitutes for their crops.[10]

Since it is much easier to seize a ton of cocaine all at once at the border than to seize it as a thousand individual kilogram lots or as twenty million vials of crack, the vision of the war on drugs as a war on the chemicals themselves focuses our attention on high-level enforcement, particularly in source countries, on the high seas, and at the border.[11] But an economic analysis suggests that "interdiction"—seizures of bulk drugs—is of only limited usefulness, since the drugs that are cheap for the government to seize are also cheap for the dealers to replace.[12] At an apparent ratio of several enforcement dollars spent per dollar of cost imposed on the illicit drug industry, interdiction does not appear to be a winning strategy.

Drug seizures also boost demand for drugs from source countries. The more cocaine seized in transit from Colombia to the United States, the more that must be produced in Colombia to meet any level of actual cocaine consumption. From the viewpoint of the exporters, a ton seized is almost as good as a ton consumed.[13] Only if the seizure level rises so high that smuggling becomes unprofitable—as seems to have happened with marijuana from Colombia—will interdiction reduce export demand.

The effect on export demand of U.S. domestic enforcement aimed at the distribution of imported drugs is more complicated than the effect of enforcement aimed at U.S. domestic production. On the one hand, seized drugs have to be replaced, creating a larger market for exporters. On the other, the costs imposed on the illicit industry by enforcement efforts—the costs of replacing the lost drugs, adopting more expensive smuggling techniques to avoid interception, losing forfeited nondrug assets, and paying the higher wages demanded by dealers facing greater prison risks—all add to the final retail price of the drugs. The reduction in the quantity finally consumed as a result of those higher prices represents a loss of market for the exporters. The same is true if enforcement increases consumers' search time for drug purchases.

How much drug seizures cost the illicit industry depends on where in the distribution chain they take place. While newspaper accounts and enforcement-agency press releases often assess drug seizures at retail or "street value," the actual cost to the traffickers is only the cost of replacing the lost shipment with a fresh one. One kilogram of cocaine seized from retail dealers costs as much as ten kilograms seized at the border.[14]

The net effect of enforcement on export demand thus depends on the balance between drug seizures, which increase export demand, and on enforcement-induced costs, which decrease it. Interdiction, which generates large-volume drug seizures close to the source where they are cheap to replace, is probably a net contributor to export demand. In 1989 about one-quarter of all the cocaine shipped to the United States was "consumed" in seizures by law enforcement agencies, primarily the Customs Service and the Coast Guard. Domestic enforcement, particularly at the retail level, results in a much smaller quantity of drugs seized per enforcement dollar spent,[15] but the drugs seized are far more valuable and traffickers are more likely to suffer imprisonment and loss of nondrug assets.

The interests of source countries in reducing their export traffic would be best served if the U. S. government concentrated on demand reduction and on enforcement efforts other than crop eradication and interdiction, especially retail-level enforcement, which increases prices and search times without seizing significant quantities of drugs. But the appeal of symmetry is a powerful one, and the international clamor for U.S. crop-eradication efforts is not likely to diminish.

Domestic Law Enforcement

The question of how to allocate domestic enforcement resources across different levels of the traffic requires less attention than it deserves. The actual allocation is determined far more by organizational and intergovernmental politics than by any careful consideration of where additional enforcement dollars would do the most good.

Federal law enforcement efforts represent a larger share of total drug enforcement than is true for most other categories of crime. For the predatory crimes, state and local governments dominate the law enforcement picture; the federal effort is restricted to its special territorial jurisdictions (public lands, Indian reservations) and to a few special topics such as bank robbery, interstate fraud, and the war on the Mafia. The federal government spends only about one-eighth of all law enforcement dollars and holds no more than one-twelfth of the million or so persons confined in American prisons and jails.[16]

Drug law enforcement is an exception: the federal effort constitutes about one-third of the total as measured in dollars, perhaps one-sixth as measured in prisoners (precise numbers are not available).[17] Federal agencies have, naturally, taken the international and interstate aspects of the traffic—which is to say, its higher levels, further from the final sale—as their special province. Thus the federal government's $8 billion-per-year drug enforcement budget represents a commitment to high-level enforcement, and federal agencies have developed an ideology stressing the importance of keeping drugs out of the country (a goal emphasized by the Customs Service) and of disrupting major trafficking organizations (the specialty of the Drug Enforcement Administration and the FBI).

The belief that high-level enforcement is the real drug war, and that enforcement nearer the street is merely a series of holding actions, is also common among state police forces and the elite special narcotics units of some big-city police departments.[18] It is supported by two notions without much theoretical or empirical support, but with powerful emotional appeal: that drug dealing is a vast conspiracy, in which lower-level dealers are mere tools of the shadowy drug lords, and that the goal of drug enforcement is to interrupt the flow of drugs.

Three observations suggest that many of the practical advantages lie with repetitive and routine street-level enforcement activity and not with the exciting and dramatic pursuit of "Mr. Big." First, it is the end user who suffers and causes drug-related damage and who supplies all of the money that feeds the illicit industry; all of the higher-level buying and selling is of no importance, and cannot long continue, unless it eventually results in retail sales.

Second, in the cases of heroin and cocaine, most of the price paid by the final buyer (and thus most of the illicit earnings) represents the markups ("value added") in the last two or three transactions. The further from the final transaction, the smaller the value of the drugs and the smaller the aggregate (as opposed to the percentage) markup.[19] Thus, if dealers at each level pass through wholesale price increases dollar-for-dollar to the next level down, the prospects for bringing about a significant retail price increase by enforcement aimed at high-level dealers are dim.

On the other hand, there is some reason to believe that wholesale price increases tend to pass through on a percentage basis rather than just dollar-for-dollar; if so, doubling the high-level price would lead to an approximate doubling of the retail price. Over time, the price ratios seem to remain relatively unchanged, even as the price levels rise and fall.[20] The practice of dilution suggests that the cost of bulk drugs is significant to retailers; otherwise they would have no reason to cut back on purity when wholesale prices rise. The puzzle has been to understand why high-level prices multiply themselves on the way down the chain. A recent analysis has identified three ways in which increases in wholesale prices tend to increase operating costs, and thus markups, farther down the chain: by adding to the costs of protecting inventories from the police and from thieves and the value of inventory losses when they occur, by increasing the cost of the drugs given as "wages in kind" to employees of dealing organizations, and by pushing up cash wages as employers attempt to secure employee honesty against the increasing temptation to abscond with increasingly valuable drugs.[21] The possibility that the markets are not fully competitive in the short run further complicates the analysis.[22]

The effect of wholesale prices on retail prices, and thus of high-level enforcement on the prices and quantities at the street, is an unresolved issue. The facts may well vary from drug to drug, and from one era to another. The most that can be said now is that no one knows the relative value of an additional dollar spent on high-level enforcement compared to an additional dollar spent on retail-level enforcement as alternative means of increasing retail drug prices.

But the retail price in dollars is only one of the factors that influence the volume of drug consumption and the revenues of the illicit market. Consumption is also affected by availability (search time) and by consumers' fears of enforcement action directed against them.

Search times, like retail prices, vary widely from area to area and from buyer to buyer. The distribution of search times—in particular, the number of potential buyers for whom finding a ready seller poses no substantial problem—depends entirely on the number of retail sellers, how they are spread across geographic and social space, and how openly they offer their wares for sale, especially to strangers. Doubtless, wholesale conditions exert some influence here: the cheaper the drugs, the easier it will be for a retailer to find enough customers to repay the time and risk of setting up in business. But enforcement conditions at the retail level surely play the major role in determining where the sellers are and how open they are. If drugs are to be made harder to find, rather than merely more expensive, and if buyers are to be threatened with penalties, that must be done on or near the street, not at the border.

There is much to be said for concentrating on enforcement tactics that increase search time rather than price. Raising price decreases consumption, but it has other, less desirable consequences as well, particularly if demand for the drug in question responds only weakly to changes in its price: higher prices can make the remaining users worse off and more dangerous and can increase the revenues of the illicit industry. Since the value of increasing retail prices depends on the price elasticity of demand, it varies from drug to drug. In the case of a drug such as heroin, where the myth of an addict with a fixed drug habit has some basis in reality, an increase in price causes more problems than an equivalent increase in search time. With crack, by contrast, where heavy consumption tends to come in binges that end when the crack or the money has run out, higher prices probably translate directly into fewer and shorter binges as well as the recruitment of fewer new users. If higher retail price shows up as lower retail purity, a user's first rock (of the day or of a lifetime) will be less rewarding, less likely to be repeated, and less likely to start a binge.

Raising search time, by contrast, reduces consumption without raising prices: it thus leaves consumers both less drug-involved and better off financially (and thus less prone to become sick, deprive their families, or turn to crime), while depressing the earnings of drug dealers.

The great problem with low-level enforcement directed at drugs with established mass markets is sheer scale. Making retail-level drug arrests is relatively easy; there is perhaps no other police activity so "productive" as measured in arrests per officer-hour. But productivity for police is workload for prosecutors and courts, and a crowding crisis for the prisons and jails. A diligent retail-level enforcement program can all too easily bring the rest of the criminal justice system to a screeching halt, or (to avoid that) be virtually nullified by the failure of that system to enforce substantial punishment on the dealers arrested.[23]

The most powerful argument made for high-level enforcement and against street-level enforcement is an argument not of consequences but of justice. Police, prosecutors, and courts exist, after all, not to manipulate illicit markets but to punish wrongdoers. Since wealthy high-level drug dealers are obviously more important wrongdoers than street-level dealers, focusing enforcement on the streets seems like persecuting Oliver Twist while leaving Fagin alone. User-dealers, in particular, command sympathy as victims of the drug distribution system they serve.

Even accepting, for the sake of argument, that high-level dealers are clearly perpetrators while low-level dealers are quasi-victims, it is anything but clear that increasing high-level enforcement is the best way to create disadvantages for "drug kingpins." More vigorous enforcement tends to raise prices, thereby enriching those major dealers whose own operations do not fall victim to it. Every high-level dealer tries to keep the enforcement spotlight from shining on himself but benefits when it shines on his competitors; that is one reason dealers inform on one another to the police.

The ironic fact is that operators of successful established drug organizations and the drug enforcement agencies have a common interest in high prices maintained by tough enforcement.[24] But enforcement aimed at the lower levels of the traffic, and particularly at retailing, cuts at the economic root of the entire industry. If there were a high-level cocaine dealers' lobby in Washington or in the state capitals, it would be ambivalent about high-level enforcement, but would vigorously oppose not only legalization but retail-level enforcement as the two great threats to its members' economic well-being. Thus the argument that justice demands vigorous enforcement against major dealers is a curious one; it makes those dealers' greater culpability a reason for doing what will hurt some of them while benefiting others, rather than doing what will hurt them all.

THE CHOICE OF ENFORCEMENT TACTICS AND RESOURCES

Enforcement aims to reduce the volume of transactions in the illicit markets and to reduce the undesired side effects of black-market dealing. Reductions in volume can be achieved either by forcing price increases or by interfering with the process of retail dealing so that would-be buyers face increased search times. Other things being equal, smaller markets tend to create less violence, corruption, neighborhood disruption, and user crime, but enforcement tactics can be designed specifically to minimize those side effects or can accidentally magnify them.

Tactics Designed to Increase Prices

In a market that is, roughly speaking, competitive in the long run, whatever increases the costs of illicit transactions will eventually increase consumer prices. Enforcement imposes costs on drug dealers by seizing their drugs, by confiscating their nondrug assets (primarily vehicles, real estate, and money), and by putting them in prison, thus raising the wages and owners' incomes required to attract and retain drug-dealing labor. It also imposes costs indirectly by forcing drug dealers to use more expensive but safer techniques in place of cheaper but riskier ones and to pay bribes, defense lawyers' fees, and other expenses of staying out of prison.

Since the cost of drug seizures is the dealers' replacement cost and not the retail or street value, it is difficult to make drugs seized an important item in drug firms' profit-and-loss statements. In 1989, for example, the replacement cost of all the cocaine seized by federal, state, and local enforcement agencies in the United States and in international transit was about $1 billion, compared with a total retail volume of about $20 billion.[25] Seizures of nondrug assets were of about the same magnitude. The volume of bribes and lawyers' fees is unknown but must be trivial by these standards. There is no easy way to estimate the operational costs of adopting smuggling and dealing techniques less vulnerable to enforcement; too little is known about the actual mechanics and economics of drug dealing. But the primary operational cost is the time of drug dealers, and their time— as opposed to their risk—is probably not very expensive.

Drugs are expensive primarily because drug dealers are able to demand high wages, and those wages in turn are maintained by the risks drug dealers face of spending time in prison or of being shot by employers or competitors. No one has ever surveyed drug dealers to learn how they think about trade-offs between risk and reward, but crude calculations suggest that the incarceration of cocaine dealers adds about $5 billion to $10 billion per year to the price of cocaine in the United States.* Note that the sum of the enforcement-generated costs seems well short of the total revenues of the industry. Some of the difference is the cost of raw materials and operations, some reflects such nonenforcement personal risks as being shot by rivals or becoming a compulsive crack smoker, some reflects the cost of living with anxiety. There may also be some pure profit created by market imperfections.

The conclusion that prison time makes the major enforcement contribution to drug prices is a discouraging one, because it is also the scarcest resource in the enforcement system. Drug seizures are more attractive because they leave cells available for other purposes. Asset seizures are even better, because they contribute to the pub-

---

* There are approximately 200,000 cocaine dealers in prison or jail at any one time; thus cocaine dealers serve roughly 200,000 prison-years per year. What a potential cocaine dealer needs to be paid to incur a prison risk equivalent to the certainty of a year in prison is anyone's guess; it is likely to vary widely depending on the dealer's alternatives outside the industry, but $25,000 to $50,000 per year seems to be a reasonable range (roughly equal to a 1 percent chance of sudden death). Multiplying 200,000 prison-years by $25,000 per prison-year gives $5 billion. Since the cost of maintaining a prisoner for a year is about $25,000, this suggests that it costs the government about a dollar to add a dollar to the aggregate price of cocaine via additional imprisonment. For a more extended discussion, see Peter Reuter and Mark A. R. Kleiman, "Risks and Prices: An Economic Analysis of Drug Enforcement," in Michael Tonry and Norval Morris, eds., *Crime and Justice: An Annual Review of Research* (Chicago: University of Chicago Press, 1986); and Kleiman, "Dead Wrong," *The New Republic* (September 26, 1988).

lic treasury rather than burdening it, but the prospects for making either seizures or asset forfeitures a major cost of doing illicit drug business are not bright. (The question of asset forfeiture is not to be confused with the question of using the techniques of financial investigation—following the money trail—to make criminal cases.)

Most current investigative approaches to catching major drug dealers focus on the movements of the drugs themselves and on conversations and meetings among drug dealers devoted to handling and exchanging the drugs. The basic undercover operation remains the undercover purchase, or "buy and bust": agents pose as dealers eager to purchase drugs from higher-level dealers.

A variation on that theme, quite rare until about a decade ago but increasingly common since, is called the "reverse sting" or "sell and bust": agents pose as higher-level dealers looking to sell rather than as lower-level dealers looking to buy. Reverse undercover operations have three great advantages: they can start at a higher level of the traffic, they introduce an additional category of risk into the illicit trade by making dealers fearful of their suppliers as well as of their customers, and they employ drugs, of which enforcement agencies have a superfluity, rather than cash, which is always scarce. The great fear of agents involved in reverse undercover operations is that the drugs provided by the government will not be recaptured and will eventually reach consumers. Fear of letting the drugs "hit the street" tends to limit the duration of reverse undercover operations, while operations involving buying sometimes go on for months.

This scrupulousness about tactics may carry a high operational price; additional sell-and-bust activity might substantially complicate the development of new retail-level dealing organizations by making it riskier to find sources of drugs. Given the fluidity of the market, it matters very little from the consumer point of view whether the rock of cocaine the retailer offers was at one time in the government's possession, but enforcement agencies continue to be worried about the public-relations risks (and possible civil liability) of making it appear that the government is in the drug-supply business.

The alternative to following the drugs is following the money. A tightening net of regulations about depositing cash, withdrawing cash, buying things for cash, or transporting cash out of the country[26] has made it hard for major dealers to turn their dealing earnings into spendable or savable wealth. More financial investigations—which would mean more financially trained agents within drug enforcement agencies or additional cooperation with agencies such as the IRS that already have such agents on board—might make it harder.

Many outside observers of the drug enforcement enterprise, and some insiders, regard criminal financial investigation as the most important underexploited investigative tool in the field. The issue of following the money is often confused with that of seizing the money, but while criminal financial investigations are more likely than others to lead to major asset forfeitures, forfeiture as a goal is logically distinct from financial investigation as a means. There is no doubt that financial investigations sometimes yield spectacular results at modest costs; the unanswered question is whether the cost to dealers of handling their money could be made to contribute significantly to the total costs of drug dealing and thus to drug prices.

However a case is made—whether it starts from an undercover operation, from a money-laundering investigation, from a tip from a paid informant or a competitor, from the "controlled delivery" of drugs detected in transit, or from human or electronic surveillance and searching—when made it is likely to lead to additional cases as the threat of long prison terms compels persons already caught to "cooperate with the government." Cooperation can range from providing intelligence information not to be used in court, through providing testimony and physical evidence, up to acting as a "confidential informant" (a euphemism for *agent provocateur*). The importance of this practice lies less in the additional cases it yields than in the distrust it spreads among drug dealers. There is some evidence that major dealers, once caught, are unlikely to return to the trade, in part because none of their old business connections will trust them. But the threat of coerced betrayal applies with almost equal force before someone is caught; everyone knows that everyone else may soon have to play "Let's Make a Deal" with the prosecutors.

Only the prospect of heavy sentences leads dealers to inform on one another. If such sentences are not forthcoming in the absence of cooperation, either because the statutes do not provide for them or because judges, faced with crowded prisons, do not impose them, dealers will tend to "stand up." Long sentences also serve two other purposes: they create costs for the industry and they satisfy the public demand that major dealers be severely punished.

Legislators have been eager to make long sentences not only possible, but mandatory. No contemporary piece of anti-drug legislation is deemed complete without additional mandatory minimum sentences.[27] At the federal level, "mandatories" were once provided only for the most serious charges, under the Continuing Criminal Enterprise ("drug kingpin") statute.[28] Now involvement in a transaction for five kilograms of cocaine (about $100,000 worth)—a transaction in which the defendant need not even be a principal—generates a mandatory sentence of ten years in prison, without the possibility of parole.[29] Comparable legislation has passed in many states: the Supreme Court recently upheld a sentence of life in prison without parole under Michigan law for a man with no prior criminal history who participated in a cocaine deal involving about two-thirds of a kilo.[30]

Despite their political appeal, the proliferation of very long mandatory minimum sentences for drug offenses is a bad idea. Mandatories tie up the courts by removing the incentive for plea-bargaining; unless carefully drafted, they can even interfere with incentives for "cooperation." They also eliminate any deterrent to violence that might be created by sentence enhancements: under current laws, a large-scale dealer may be no worse off if he shoots the witness and stands trial for murder. They also fill the prisons with drug dealers serving long sentences, a very inefficient way to use scarce prison cells. It would be far better to spread some of those ten-year terms around among the many convicted drug dealers who now serve no prison time at all. Applying long mandatory sentences to even routine drug-dealing offenses, but not to a wide range of violent crimes, seems to reflect an odd sense of relative values.

It is important not to overestimate the ability of enforcement to drive up the prices of drugs with established mass markets, or to underestimate the costs of trying to do so. Drug prices do influence consumption, and enforcement resources and tactics can influence drug prices. A careful consideration of the likely effects of different programs might improve the performance of the system in making drugs more expensive for their end users. Still, the observation that, a decade into an enforcement-centered "war on drugs," cocaine prices are near their all-time low point suggests the difficulty of boosting the prices of mass-market drugs. It will never be easy to get between millions of consumers with billions of dollars to spend and the high-level dealers willing to take risks to provide them with drugs.

Enforcement Designed to Decrease Retail Availability

Interfering with the process of retail drug dealing presents a different set of challenges. The tactical situations are as variable as the neighborhoods involved, the drugs being traded, and the operating styles of local dealing organizations.

Retail dealing tends to be geographically concentrated so that buyers and sellers can take advantage of both the enforcement swamping and the reduced search times that go with greater transaction density.

That suggests that breaking up such concentration ought to be a goal of retail enforcement activity. Organizing police to increase enforcement response quickly as market activity grows, to maintain that increased effort long enough to ensure that the market is dead and not merely dormant, and then to move on to the next area of concentration poses a massive operational, organizational, and even political challenge for police management.[31]

Both the decisions about where to apply police efforts and the choice of enforcement tactics ought to be based on an understanding of local drug-dealing activity as a market process that enforcement aims to retard. Chiefs of narcotics squads ought to be asking questions such as "What is the annual dollar volume of the crack trade in the city?" and thinking about how particular police tactics can interfere with the traffic in specific drug market areas.[32]

Answering such questions would require information that police do not routinely gather. Some of it could be obtained from drug treatment and other health-care workers; doing so would require surmounting the barriers of distrust between them and the police. The shortage of police work-hours and the lack of officers with appropriate analytical training create additional hurdles. Even in cities such as New York, with active "street epidemiology" research organizations, little of what those units learn is integrated into police decision making.

Police can also learn about drug markets from offenders, particularly those who are arrested for nondrug crimes but have drugs in their system at the time of arrest. They clearly know where and how drugs are bought and sold; at least some of them could be induced to tell. The goal of talking with them would not be to develop informants, though that might occasionally happen, but to produce an intelligence base to support enforcement decision making.

Conditions other than the pressure of drug law enforcement can make a given area more or less vulnerable to retail dealing, and some of them can be deliberately manipulated. Abandoned buildings used for dealing can be boarded up or torn down. Overgrown vegetation in parks and vacant lots that provides cover for drug sales can be cut back. Streets can be rerouted and parking regulations tightened or more vigorously enforced to inconvenience drug buyers. Building owners who allow their properties to be used for dealing can be threatened with confiscation, and tenants who use their apartments or allow them to be used as dealing locations can be threatened with eviction.[33] Drug-dealing premises can be closed down on the basis of a wide variety of legal powers wielded by local governments, including health, fire, and safety regulation and the authority to abate public nuisances. In publicly owned apartments, physical structures, the presence of doorkeepers, and tenant selection policies designed to exclude drug dealers can all make a difference.[34]

The hostility of neighbors to dealing activity is also a potential resource. That hostility can be expressed quietly in telephone calls conveying information about dealing activity to a designated "hot line," or openly in demonstrations at known dealing locations and shouted warnings to potential drug buyers and sellers that their activities are under observation. Police can help elicit such activity, shape their own tactics to take advantage of the information provided, and where necessary protect community anti-drug activists against dealers. Recent years have seen a largely spontaneous upsurge in citizen direct action against local drug dealing.[35]

For a wide variety of crimes, the police have found that conventional police work—focused on making prosecutable arrests—is not the most effective means of crime control. Using police resources to generate crime resistance within neighborhoods can produce much greater results. As a political issue, this idea of "community policing" is sometimes vulgarized into simply the restoration of foot patrols: the famous "cop on the beat." Its actual strategies are much more complicated. Community policing involves not only active engagement of citizens in police decision-making processes but also tapping the resources of other public agencies to deal with crime-creating situations.[36] The QUAD program in Tampa has demonstrated the potential of such programs to shut down retail drug markets.[37]

Finally, enforcement directed at sellers can and should be supplemented with enforcement directed at buyers. Such tactics are becoming more widespread; Phoenix has made anti-buyer enforcement the cornerstone of its drug enforcement effort. Inner-city markets with many suburban buyers driving through are particularly vulnerable to such enforcement, since such buyers are both more conspicuous and less willing and able to wait around until the coast is clear than buyers who live nearby. Suburban buyers may also be especially sensitive to the prospect of arrest and conviction and unusually willing to plead guilty quickly in return for a verdict and a sentence that leave them without a permanent criminal record. Even so, the sheer number of buyers makes such anti-buyer enforcement a potential threat to the ability of the courts to process the resulting cases (as well as the rest of their case load).

But there are ways to make buyers feel unwelcome without arresting and trying them. Undercover police can sell them inert substances at illicit-drug prices or sell them real drugs and then confiscate their automobiles, as instrumentalities of the crime of possession of controlled

substances, as they drive away.[38] Several communities are experi-
menting with a tactic first tried against prostitution customers in Los
Angeles. Police (or volunteer citizens) record the license-plate numbers of out-of-town automobiles cruising through street markets or
parked briefly in front of known drug houses. The plate numbers are
then checked with the motor vehicle registry, and postcards (not letters) are sent to the registered owners, saying roughly, "Dear Driver:
Your automobile, plate #ABC 123, was seen at 8:15 P.M. on Tuesday
9/15 in an area known as a center of drug dealing. Vehicles used to
transport controlled substances are subject to seizure and forfeiture
under state and federal laws." In Los Angeles, traffic died down after
the first week; it remains to be seen whether drug customers are as
sensitive as prostitution customers or how suburban parents react to
the notice that Junior drove the family BMW down to the local crack
market.

Even for those users and low-level dealers who are arrested, tried,
and convicted, corrections capacity in the form of prisons and jails
is, and will probably continue to be, the limiting ingredient in the
law enforcement mix.

Formal punishments—those allocated by judicial sentence after a
conviction or its equivalent, as distinct from the costs imposed by
the process of arrest and trial—fall into two categories: incarceration
and everything else. Nonincarcerative sentences—variously referred
to as "intermediate sanctions," "alternatives to incarceration," and
"community corrections"—include fines, punitive work ("community
service"), and all the varieties of "conditional release" administered
by probation and parole authorities.* Probationers and parolees differ from ordinary citizens in having additional restrictions on their
behavior, in being subject to more intrusive monitoring and investi-

---

* The primary distinction between probation and parole is that probation is imposed
by a judge instead of a term of confinement (or after a specified, usually brief, term)
whereas parole applies to those who have served part of a prison term and are then
released before the expiration of that term, either at the discretion of a board or
under a formula. Administratively, in most states parole supervision is part of an
executive-branch department, while probation supervision is handled by an agency
responsible to the court system. Generally, parolees have committed more serious
offenses than probationers, are more closely monitored (that is, the caseloads of
parole officers are far smaller than those of probation officers), and are more likely
to be found in violation of the conditions of their release (colloquially, "violated")
and sent back to a cell. On intermediate sanctions, see Michael Tonry and Norval
Morris, *Between Prison and Probation: Intermediate Punishments in a Rational Sentencing
System* (New York: Oxford University Press, 1990). See also Douglas C. McDonald,
Punishment Without Walls: Community Service Sentences in New York City (New Brunswick,
N.J.: Rutgers University Press, 1986).

gation, and in being subject to incarceration or reincarceration under procedures quicker and less formal than those of a full criminal trial.

How significant these distinctions are, and therefore how successful probation and parole can be in substituting for prisons as means of deterrence and incapacitation (and perhaps rehabilitation and retribution as well), depends on the nature of the restrictions, the intensity of the supervision, and the willingness and capacity of the authorities to punish violations of the terms of conditional release or the commission of new crimes. (That punishment need not, though it usually does, take the form of a term of confinement). Unsupervised probation, or "supervision" by a probation officer with a caseload of three hundred offenders, may be barely distinguishable from complete freedom. By contrast, intensively supervised probation programs where two officers supervise twenty-five offenders who are required to perform punitive work, observe personal curfews, and present themselves for random drug tests can be so restrictive that substantial numbers of offenders choose an immediate term of several months in jail to a longer period of supervised release.[39]

Nonincarcerative sanctions have attracted considerable attention among law enforcement policymakers in recent years largely as a result of the pressure that increasing numbers of sentences have put on growing, but still crowded, prison systems. There is also concern about the nation's very high rate of incarceration per capita (about 4 U.S. residents per 1,000 are in prison or jail at any one time, a far higher rate than that of any other industrialized democracy) and the extraordinarily high rates among young African-American adult males, particularly in some inner-city neighborhoods.

The case for increasing the extent of social control over offenders not behind bars—for devising ways of punishing people without paying for their room and board—seems strong. Nonviolent low-level drug sellers without extensive records of predatory crime may be particularly attractive candidates for such punishments. But whether increasing the stock of nonprison punishments will allow a reduction in the number of prisoners is an open question, given the need for prison cells as a backup sanction for those who will not or cannot comply with the terms of conditional release.*

---

* In some states, a majority of those entering prison are doing so pursuant to a probation or parole violation rather than a new criminal conviction. For the mathematics of nonprison punishments when each person punished has some probability of being found in violation then confined, see David P. Cavanagh and Mark A. R. Kleiman, "A Cost-Benefit Analysis of Prison Cell Construction and Alternative Sanctions" (Cambridge, Mass: BOTEC Analysis Corp, May 1990).

In many ways the most attractive of the intermediate sanctions is unpaid punitive labor, which unfortunately has been saddled with the euphemism "community service." Making hard work one of the consequences of income-producing crime, rather than an alternative to it, serves both deterrence and justice. The two central problems in managing punitive-labor programs are securing adequate supplies of supervisory labor and providing swift and unpleasant consequences for skipping work or shirking. Both of these problems can be eased by including only docile, low-risk offenders in the program, and accordingly many "community service" programs exclude those with histories of violent crime or drug dealing. But that solution sacrifices the end to the means, restricting what could be the single largest new source of punishment capacity to crimes and criminals that were not much of a problem, or very likely to fill a jail cell, in the first place.

The better solution is to provide a quantity and quality of supervision adequate to handle harder-to-manage workers and to reserve enough cells to ensure that those who refuse to comply find themselves behind bars. One potential source of additional supervisory labor is the same concerned citizens who are forming themselves into community anti-drug organizations; they could spend some of their time watching groups of (preferably local) offenders clear vacant lots, landscape parks, scrape graffiti, and pick up litter in their own neighborhoods, at sites the community groups helped identify.

The supply of supervisory labor could also be expanded if there were new money to pay for it. The obvious sources of such money are the beneficiaries of the labor performed. As long as a team of offender-workers can produce enough value in an hour to pay for an hour of its supervisor's time, there is no reason for "community service" programs to be a net budget burden. While renting out convict labor to ordinary business enterprises would risk severe abuses and meet vigorous opposition, both public agencies and the voluntary nonprofit sector—hospitals, churches, low-income housing ventures, businessmen's and neighborhood-improvement organizations—could be looked to both for projects needing unskilled labor and for funds to cover the costs. Alternatively the money for supervision could be paid for out of public budgets, as prisons and jails are. The problem is not economic, but organizational: the agencies that manage "inpatient" corrections have much larger budgets than the ones that manage "outpatient" corrections.

Retail drug enforcement tests the capacity of the criminal justice system, the ingenuity and persistence of its officials, and the courage and public spirit of the citizenry. Its failures are far more obvious than its successes, simply because the presence of a thriving market is more manifest than its absence. But the importance of retail drug markets in feeding drug abuse, and the devastation their operations can wreak on the neighborhoods where they occur, will continue to create public demand for law enforcement action to break them up. It would be helpful to replace the widespread belief among local police that retail-level enforcement is only a holding action—that the real front in the drug war is in the classroom or in Colombia—with a more lively understanding of the extent to which local drug market conditions are locally determined.

Enforcement Designed to Reduce
Black-Market Side Effects

Enforcement does more than generate costs for drug-dealing enterprises. It also shapes their conduct by creating incentives for them to transact business in one way rather than another. Their conduct, in turn, determines the side effects of dealing in the form of violence and neighborhood disruption.

New organizations are more likely than their competitors to fall prey to enforcement activity. Established organizations can even use enforcement agencies to suppress competition by funnelling information about their rivals to the police. As a result, enforcement is apt to cartelize drug markets.[40] This is not a bad thing in terms of suppressing consumption: cartels tend to raise prices and thus to reduce volume.[41] But it may be a very bad thing indeed when it comes to the side effects of dealing. The growth of wealthy and powerful criminal organizations is undesirable in itself, and it may create additional problems if the organizational capacity built up in the drug trade is then employed in other illicit enterprises, as the Mafia families that grew during Prohibition continued to pose a major social problem long after Repeal. With respect to violence, cartelization may not be so bad: the implicit, threatened violence of a dominant organization may be socially preferable to the active violence of vigorous criminal competition.[42]

These unwanted side effects of enforcement are not inevitable. Enforcement can be designed to pursue particularly undesirable forms of drug dealing with special vigor—in St. Louis, for example, a policy of priority prosecution for drug dealers arrested with weapons seems to have succeeded in keeping the local drug trade largely peaceful— or to select a few very noxious organizations for special, even exclusive, attention. The Federal Organized Crime Strike Forces, until their recent dismemberment, were devoted almost exclusively to the crusade against the Mafia and paid no attention to gambling, loansharking, labor racketeering, or drug dealing by non-Mafia groups. Partly as a result, the Mafia families found themselves struggling for survival and virtually unable to compete for a share of the huge cocaine market of the 1980s. The Central Tactical Units (CENTACs) of the Drug Enforcement Administration were short-term operations aimed at unravelling specific target groups; like the strike forces, the CENTACs had great success until they fell victim to organizational infighting. On the local level, the CRASH anti-gang unit of the Los Angeles Police Department is interested only in crack dealing by the loose confederations of street gangs known as the Crips and the Bloods; it ignores the activities of their unaffiliated competitors.

Enforcement can also try to relocate dealing to areas where it does the least damage, or at least away from areas where it does the most damage. Special penalties for dealing in "Drug-Free School Zones" illustrate the principle, though their effectiveness has not been demonstrated. In cities where open drug dealing is too widespread to make its substantial suppression a realistic goal, police can try to drive it from residential neighborhoods into industrial and warehouse districts, or from the streets into less public areas.

HOW MUCH ENFORCEMENT?

Enforcement, by making prohibited drugs more expensive and harder for consumers to find, decreases consumption and the size of the market as measured by the number of transactions and the physical volume of drugs sold. The decrease in physical volume involves both the number of users and the quantities consumed by the remaining users. These reductions tend to lessen the damage that the drug in question does to users and to others. Enforcement also helps control some of the evils, such as neighborhood disruption, that go with black markets. More enforcement has more of these effects; however, the effectiveness of increasing drug law enforcement is limited by the ability of the dealers and users to adapt to it.

Dealers can modify their locations, their organizations, and their operating styles to adapt to new enforcement efforts. One predictable consequence of concentrated drug enforcement activity is the move-

ment of drug-dealing activity: geographic displacement.[43] It is sometimes asserted, against logic and without evidence, that such displacement is automatic and complete.[44] That would be true only if all locations were equally convenient for dealers and retail buyers, which
is not the case. At a minimum, since buyers and sellers alike benefit
from the clustering of illicit transactions and since coordination is
difficult in a clandestine activity, displacement is likely to take some
time. Still, the local benefits of any drug enforcement activity tend
to be partly offset by the growth of new problems elsewhere.

Even if the actual volume of transactions does not shrink, displacement of drug dealing from residential neighborhoods and public spaces can contribute to the quality of life. Even forcing dealers
to adopt less flagrant operating styles can make a difference in the
perceived level of disorder in an area. This observation suggests a
general rule for a drug enforcement strategy: design enforcement
efforts so that buyers and sellers, in adapting to them, will reduce
the social burden imposed by their activities.

Users can react to increasing enforcement in another way: they
can switch from the drug receiving more enforcement attention to
one that receives less attention, or to a licit drug. This substitution is
no more likely to be immediate or complete than is displacement—
perhaps less so, because not everyone who enjoys cocaine, for instance, will also enjoy heroin or alcohol. Even if the amount of drug
experience (as measured, for example, by the total number of hours
"under the influence" for all drugs combined) were by some magic
a fixed quantity, invariant to changes in enforcement effort, substitution would not make enforcement worthless as long as there is
some congruence between the legal status and enforcement priority of drugs and their actual danger to users and others. Caffeine
presumably substitutes for cocaine, since both are stimulants; but if
the result of an increasing cocaine price were more cups of coffee
or even bottles of No-Doz, that substitution would not substantially
decrease the social benefits of a decrease in cocaine abuse.

Increasing enforcement activity, in addition to the limits on its
effectiveness drawn by displacement and substitution, has some active disadvantages. First, drug enforcement, applied to a drug that
already has a mass market, can be remarkably profligate of enforcement resources. A comparison with enforcement directed at predatory crimes helps illustrate why.

Consider casual commercial or residential burglary. (Carefully
planned warehouse or bank-vault break-ins fall into a different category, requiring a different set of skills.) It is a remarkably unattractive

way to make a dishonest living. The take, once the stolen goods are resold through a fence, is likely to be only a few hundred dollars.[45] Averaged over time and across offenders, the risk of arrest is about one in ten per burglary, and the risk of a felony conviction and a prison sentence (averaging a little less than two years actually served) about one in four per burglary arrest.[46] That nets out to about ten dollars earned per day served in prison, a poor enough return even ignoring the chance of being injured on the job. Only the illusion that one is less likely than average to be caught and punished (an illusion encouraged by the randomness of the criminal justice process) and the fact that the rewards are so much more immediate than the punishments make the crime attractive at all. It is not surprising that burglars and similar predatory criminals tend to have lower-than-average measured IQs;[47] it takes only moderate smarts to figure out that working at McDonald's pays better in the long run than minor-league burglary. (Juveniles face lesser punishments and also have poorer prospects in the legitimate job market; this helps explain why they account for such a large share of burglary.[48]) Even an inadequate enforcement system can deter most potential offenders from so poorly rewarded a crime.

Better yet from the viewpoint of law enforcement, a relatively small number of people commit a large proportion of all burglaries.[49] Thus, simply locking up some of the most active burglars can noticeably reduce the volume of activity. Taking some high-rate burglars out of circulation does very little to improve the rewards of burglary for current or new burglars (except to the extent that it causes householders and shop owners to buy fewer locks and alarms).[50] There is some prospect, then, that raising the "price" of burglary (in terms of expected punishment) by increasing the chances of arrest, the chances of conviction and imprisonment given arrest, or the average length of the sentence could discourage some current and potential burglars without attracting new ones. It is thus reasonable to think that deterrence and incapacitation can combine to reduce the number of burglaries.*

* The evidence of experience is consistent with the efficacy of enforcement to deter predatory crime, but in the nature of things cannot be conclusive. See Alfred Blumstein, Jacqueline Cohen, and Daniel Nagin, *Deterrence and Incapacitation: Estimating the Effects of Criminal Sanctions on Crime Rates* (Washington, D.C.: National Academy of Sciences, 1978); Mark A. R. Kleiman, Kerry D. Smith, Richard A. Rogers, and David P. Cavanagh, "Imprisonment-to-Offense Ratios," Bureau of Justice Statistics *Discussion Paper* (15 November 1988).

Minor-league retail drug dealing is a trade open to many of the same people who commit minor-league burglaries. It has similar occupational requirements, demanding little but indifference to the prospect of injury or legal punishment. Although it requires more hours of effort per dollar of illicit income than burglary, it subjects its perpetrator to smaller risks of prison time per dollar earned. According to a recent study, retail cocaine (largely crack) dealers in Washington, D.C., earned about $30 per hour in cash, plus additional compensation in drugs. For each day spent in prison, retail cocaine dealers earned about $250; to put it another way, someone who worked full-time as a retail dealer would, on average, take home about $35,000 per year in cash earnings and spend about four months per year in prison.[51]

Even given the nontrivial chances of being shot in a drug deal or acquiring an uncontrolled crack habit, these are much more favorable job prospects than housebreaking offers. In consequence, the same study found that cocaine selling was far more widespread among a sample of young male probationers in Washington than any other crime for gain; a staggering 79 percent had sold cocaine at one time or another.[52] Most of the dealers in the sample held legitimate jobs as well;[53] their dealing activity seemed to be limited not by their fear of the law but by the lack of opportunities, as represented by customers. This creates a dim prospect for deterring young men in places like Washington from cocaine dealing by increasing the risks of punishment: at current wages and risks, they are crowding into the field.[54] Incapacitation—getting some of them off the street—would only create new opportunities for those currently dealing part-time.

If we assume that total enforcement resources are fixed, whatever is spent enforcing the drug laws cannot be spent enforcing the laws against other kinds of crime. In effect, much of the increase in local drug law enforcement during the 1980s came at the expense of other law enforcement efforts. At their peak, drug cases accounted for as much as half of all felony cases in some big-city jurisdictions.[55] As a result, certain kinds of property crime are treated as unworthy of investigation or prosecution: the notorious example is automobile break-ins in New York. More recently, the wave of drug enforcement seems to have fallen back in some places as the tide of drug dealing has started to recede.[56] Still, local police departments face the question of whether the effective decriminalization of increasingly serious kinds of predatory crime is an acceptable price to pay for maintaining or increasing local drug law enforcement.

THE CASE FOR MORE LAW
ENFORCEMENT OF ALL KINDS

One way to relax the tension between drug law enforcement and enforcement directed at predatory crimes would be to add to the total law enforcement budget in order to have more of both.

Two facts about crime and law enforcement in the contemporary United States stand out. First, citizens believe, with a good show of reason, that crime (including drug dealing) is a major social problem, and citizens, officials, and expert observers agree that the mechanisms to deal with lawbreaking are inadequate, particularly in the poor sections of big cities where crime is most rampant. But, second, actual public expenditures on law enforcement are not very large compared either with the overall economy or other government programs.

Total expenditures on investigation, adjudication, and corrections—the entire law enforcement system except for privately paid defense counsel—appear to have been about $60 billion in 1989.[57] That represents a little more than 1 percent of the Gross National Product for that year ($5.2 trillion). It constituted about 2 percent of the total expenditures of all levels of government including about 4 percent of "exhaustive" government spending (hiring people and buying things, as opposed to "transfer payments," writing checks to individuals). Public expenditures on education and on defense each exceeded $300 billion, six times as much as the law enforcement budget. Public spending on health care was $250 billion, out of a total health-care bill of more than $600 billion.[58]

These figures mean that a substantial percentage increase in law enforcement effort would cost far less than a comparable percentage increase in, for example, education. There seems to be widespread agreement that if a 10 percent increase in educational expenditure would close a noticeable fraction of the gap that now separates the educational performance of American schoolchildren from that of Japanese or European schoolchildren, the money would be well spent; educational policy is controversial largely because there is no consensus on how to spend more money to achieve better results. But a 10 percent increase in education spending would cost about $30 billion, enough to finance a 50 percent increase in law enforcement spending. The same is true of publicly paid health care, save that the benefits of spending more, except on perinatal care, are far less clear. The relatively small current base of law enforcement spending provides greater leverage for any given number of new dollars. If more law enforcement would actually work to reduce crime, it shares (with programs of health care and education for pregnant women and their newborns) the distinction of offering the chance for substantial social improvement, and particularly improvement in the lives of the poor, on the cheap.

Crime and drug dealing hit the poor, and especially the minority poor, hardest. This is in part because the law enforcement system is most inadequate where poor people live and least likely to take seriously crimes against them or occurring in their neighborhoods.[59] Of all the basic social services, protection against crime is the most unequally distributed by class and race.* The minority poor pay for crime in their personal victimization and in the fear it engenders; in higher prices, shorter hours, and poorer selections of goods in the stores they patronize; in the virtual absence from their neighborhoods of some kinds of establishments, such as banks; and in diminished job opportunities in retailing, office work, and manufacturing as businesses relocate to lower-crime areas.[60]

They also pay in the most precious coin of all: the future of their children. Growing up in a high-crime, low-enforcement-capacity area—experiencing and witnessing unretributed victimization, knowing relatively many career criminals and relatively few legitimate jobholders, learning that one is surrounded with low-risk victims—increases an adolescent's chances of turning to crime himself. This is one natural, powerful, and largely ignored explanation for the difference in criminal activity between African-American adolescents and young adults and others, a difference that persists even when factors such as income are taken into account.[61]

The social facts of lawbreaking and law enforcement suggest that expansion and relocation of law enforcement expenditure ought to be a central demand of the elected and self-appointed tribunes of the urban poor and minorities. The inequities in school funding that cause the school districts where poor people live to spend fewer dollars per pupil than the school districts where rich people live are regarded as a political grievance, even a Constitutional infringement.[62] Why does it not seem equally outrageous that, for the same reasons, the burglary of a poor family's apartment receives less police attention and is less likely to result in a prison sentence for its perpetrator than the burglary of a rich family's house? Public opinion polling suggests that poor people, and particularly minorities, tend to be more concerned about crime and more willing to increase spending

* Poor big-city residents consume more than their share of law enforcement per capita, but this still leaves them with insufficient law enforcement per crime.

on law enforcement than the population at large.[63] How urban crime control, which might logically rank with education on the agenda of the liberal left, became instead a shibboleth of the conservative right—which has nonetheless been more eager to fight it with slogans, statutes, and symbols than with resources—is a story for another place.

The serious imbalance in the current allocation of resources within the criminal-justice system magnifies the opportunity for low-cost improvement. Policing makes up about one-half of the budget, adjudication (judges, their clerks, prosecutors, and publicly paid defense counsel) about one-quarter, and corrections the last quarter (more than 90 percent of that for prisons and jails, with the rest going for nonincarcerative corrections under the administrative categories of probation and parole).[64] Nor is this distribution, with its tilt toward policing, unpopular; when the public demands more law enforcement, it is thinking of more police.

Yet current police efforts, inadequate as they are compared to the level of lawbreaking in high-crime jurisdictions, yield far more arrests than the courts and their attendant lawyers can fairly and expeditiously process by trial—or even by a few trials and a large mass of negotiated pleas—and that overwhelmed court system still produces far more convictions than the corrections system has the capacity to punish. Despite the prison-building boom of the last fifteen years, the most common sentence after conviction is probation, which in high-crime jurisdictions means being assigned to the "supervision" of a probation officer with a case load of between 100 and 300 other offenders. The same crowding that makes a judge reluctant to sentence an offender to prison in the first place also makes her reluctant to remand him to prison for violation of the terms of probation, further reducing the ability of the probation system to function as a serious alternative to incarceration, either to punish or to control. The "intermediate" sanctions are still far more widely discussed than practiced, largely because they rely on the budgets and administrative capacities of probation departments, which are always at the bottom of the pecking order among criminal justice agencies. Thus the value of new law enforcement money would be greatest if it were added to the downstream parts of the system.

The value of adding more punishment capacity is defined by the cost of the crimes that capacity could prevent. Despite the high annual cost per prisoner, there is reason to think that the benefits to potential victims of confining the average predatory criminal are even higher.* A fifty percent increase in the number of prison and jail inmates would cost about $8 billion per year. For half that sum, probation could be converted from a joke into a serious inconvenience for those prepared to comply with its rules and a swift ticket to prison for those not prepared to comply.

Even smaller sums would suffice to substantially improve the speed, accuracy, and dignity with which the courts convict the guilty and acquit the innocent. Here the problem is how to use additional resources to create organizational change and liberate the courts from their quill-pen standards of efficiency and productivity.

With those expansions, and some automation of police paperwork functions, the competition for resources between drug law enforcement and other law enforcement could be eased; we could have more of both. If all new resources were applied to drug enforcement, the total cost of doubling our effective capacity to catch, convict, and punish drug dealers would not exceed $10 billion per year. Contrary to Everett Dirksen's famous remark about "a billion here and a billion there," in a $5 trillion economy $10 billion per year—or about 10 cents per citizen per day—isn't "real money" to spend on fixing a basic social problem. Even $30 billion could be found without substantial economic pain; the problems are political and managerial.

One argument offered against increasing spending for law enforcement, and particularly for punishment capacity, is that a growing law enforcement enterprise threatens civil liberty. But liberty can be threatened by forces other than the state: ask the people who stay indoors in sweltering apartments in the summer because they are afraid to go outside on their own front stoops or the public streets. The argument against increasing the already large proportion of poor male African-American adolescents and young adults under correctional supervision is strong—if one disregards the possibility that their current high rates of criminal activity are partly due

---

* The first attempt to compare the value of the benefits produced by adding prison cells with the costs of doing so was made by Edwin Zedlewski, who for his pains was subjected to a remarkable amount of abuse. See Edwin Zedlewski, *Making Confinement Decisions,* The National Institute of Justice (Washington, D.C., 1987); Franklin Zimring and Gordon Hawkins, "The New Mathematics of Imprisonment," *Crime and Delinquency* 34 (4 [October 1988]): 425–436; John P. Conrad, "Dr. Zedlewski Still Rides," *Federal Probation* (June 1987: 65–66); John Irwin and James Austin, *It's About Time: Solving America's Prison Crowding Crisis,* National Council on Crime and Delinquency (1987). But Zedlewski's qualitative conclusions appear to survive reanalysis. See David P. Cavanagh and Mark A. R. Kleiman, "A Cost-Benefit Analysis of Prison Cell Construction and Alternative Sanctions" (Cambridge, Mass.: BOTEC Analysis Corp., May 1990).

to their contempt for the inadequate law enforcement system they face, and that raising their chances of being caught and punished would reduce their criminal activity—but the argument against continuing to subject poor African-Americans (and others) of all ages and both genders to current levels of crime and drug dealing seems even stronger.

The more serious argument against expanding enforcement capacity is that neither drug law enforcement nor enforcement directed at predatory crimes obviously "works" in the sense that there is a demonstrable relationship between increased enforcement and decreased crime or drug dealing. Even if one could specify an enforcement program certain to succeed, simply giving more money to existing agencies would not reliably produce that program. More likely, it would produce more of the same. Here the resemblance to the education problem is strong: in neither case is pouring more money through existing institutions a very attractive prospect. And while hiring more teachers at worst wastes money, building more prisons, unless it reduces crime, causes fruitless suffering to those imprisoned and to their families, and may even further weaken the social fabric of the neighborhoods from which they are drawn.

In sum, then, the competition for resources between drug law enforcement and other law enforcement counts as a serious problem given the current size of the law enforcement system, but the dollar costs involved are modest compared to the costs of crime and drug dealing. The more important cost is the human and social cost of increasing prison populations. Whether or not that cost is worth bearing depends largely on whether enforcement can be made to work and whether we can make punishment without walls a program rather than a slogan.

THE OTHER DISADVANTAGES
OF MORE ENFORCEMENT

One of the consequences of increased enforcement—indeed, one of its goals—is to make drugs more expensive and thereby discourage their use. But a price increase for an illicit drug is not an unmixed blessing; it has two distinct classes of disadvantages.

First, for those users whose demand for the drug is relatively inelastic—who respond to a given percentage price increase with a less-than-proportionate decrease in consumption—higher prices will lead to greater spending on the drug in question. This will make them effectively poorer, and thus worse off. They will have less money left, after their drug purchases, to buy food, clothing, and shelter, or to meet their family obligations. Some who currently earn part of their drug money in illicit ways will increase their criminal activity to meet their increasing need for income; others may turn to crime for the first time.

If all drug users resembled the mythical addict with a fixed "habit" of so many milligrams a day—if, that is, drug consumption were perfectly inelastic to price—price increases would have only bad effects. In fact, however, drug habits are subject to rises and falls, periods of abstinence and periods of relapse.[65] For most drugs, the using population is subject to relatively rapid turnover as new, younger users replace the older ones who quit. There is thus no reason to believe that any drug has perfectly inelastic demand (a price elasticity of zero). Even for drugs such as heroin and nicotine, where cutting back from established consumption levels is painful for most users, the long-run effect of price on consumption, primarily through effects on initiation, quitting, and relapse is probably substantial. Still, it is likely that increased drug enforcement that causes increased drug prices will have the disadvantage of making some users worse off and more dangerous to others. There is evidence that, in the short run, heroin prices and property-crime rates tend to move in the same direction.[66]

If the overall demand for a drug is relatively inelastic to price, the total amount spent on that drug—the total revenues of its dealers—rises along with its price. This may or may not leave dealers as a class better off, once one considers their losses to enforcement in the form of drugs, other assets, and time spent in prison. But it does increase the dollar size of the illicit industry, and thus its capacity to finance corruption and violence.

Although increased enforcement may reduce the overall number of persons or organizations engaged in the drug trade, this reduction does not take place evenly over the spectrum of market participants. Being arrested is not entirely a matter of luck. While harming the average seller, heavy enforcement actually helps those individuals and groups who are the most skilled at evading enforcement through cunning, violence, and corruption. The removal of "softer" competitors improves the market position of the more skilled and ruthless.*

---

* Peter Reuter points out that as a logical matter increased enforcement might instead favor the quiet and discreet. In the absence of a deliberate attempt to design drug enforcement tactics for that purpose, however, enforcement is likely to favor the tough.

Not only does this aggravate the tendencies of existing drug organizations to employ violence and corruption, it will also lead to criminals and criminal organizations already skilled at the violence and corruption into the drug business,[67] increasing their overall wealth and power. Thus drug enforcement can indirectly contribute to the organized-crime problem.

The last great disadvantage of increasing enforcement effort is that it causes suffering among those punished. In a fairy tale, the punishment of the wicked witch or the cruel stepmother is an enjoyable way to end the story. In the actual world, punishment—harm inflicted by public authority for violation of the laws—is neither a source of enjoyment nor the end of anything. Few law-abiding citizens derive any substantial satisfaction from the thought that lawbreakers in the abstract are serving time in prison; moreover, unlike muggers, drug dealers rarely have identifiable victims. That may explain why the public is eager to add police and happy to support longer statutory sentences but is reluctant to pay for more prisons. Nor does punishment provide more than a temporary respite in the interaction between the lawbreaker, whose term of confinement will eventually end, and the rest of us; the popular movement for capital punishment represents in part an emotional reaction against that fact.

Both for lawbreakers and for their neighbors, it would be a good thing if the result of punishment were an improvement in character (a decrease, for example, in impulsiveness) that left those punished better off and less inclined to offend again. Thus "rehabilitation" is almost always listed among the goals of punishment. But, as Plato and George Bernard Shaw both said, injury tends to damage character rather than improving it, and punishment is injury. Empirical investigation does not provide much support either for the proposition that punishment by law as currently administered in the United States helps wrongdoers to reform or for the opposite proposition that prisons are "schools of crime" and that offenders emerge from them "hardened" and more dangerous than ever.*

* See Alfred Blumstein et al., eds., *Criminal Careers and "Career Criminals"* (Washington, D.C.: National Academy Press, 1986), p. 28; D. Lipton, R. Martinson, and J. Wilks, *The Effectiveness of Correctional Treatment: A Survey of Treatment Evaluation Studies* (New York: Praeger, 1975); L. Sechrest et al., eds., *The Rehabilitation of Criminal Offenders: Problems and Prospects*, Panel on Research on Rehabilitative Techniques, Committee on Research on Law Enforcement and Criminal Justice, Assembly of Behavioral and Social Sciences, National Research Council (Washington, D.C.: National Academy Press, 1979). James Q. Wilson has proposed that the prisons do teach crime, but no more successfully than the grade schools teach arithmetic.

Some suffering on the part of the person punished is inseparable from the objective of deterrence; no one fears what is pleasant. And while incapacitation does not in principle imply suffering, in practice those steps that make persons less able to commit crimes will tend also to reduce their enjoyment of life. The suffering of those who undergo punishment, and that of their families and friends, must be counted as a cost of enforcement, which must be weighed against its benefits in deciding how much of it to undertake.

One way to ease the conflict between crime control and the desire to limit the amount of suffering inflicted by law would be to find punishments that are in fact rehabilitative. The finding that, on the average, those punished wind up neither better nor worse may conceal a situation in which some forms of punishment improve some offenders, while others harden other offenders. If that is true, changing the current mix of punishments or their allocation among offenders might produce a system that was rehabilitative on balance. Combining more incapacitation with less suffering would require improving conditions in the prisons, or learning how to incapacitate without imprisoning. Programs of "home confinement" represent attempts in the latter direction.

The hardest challenge would seem to be to combine limited suffering with high deterrence. But even that problem is not insoluble in principle. If deterrence succeeds in reducing lawbreaking, then it will be possible to combine a substantial threat of punishment with relatively little actual punishment. Starting from a high rate of lawbreaking, it will be necessary to inflict considerable suffering to accomplish the transition to a low rate of lawbreaking, but once that transition is accomplished there will be smooth sailing. This analysis suggests that the right way to increase enforcement levels is quickly, to have a large impact all at once, rather than gradually. How much punishment it will be necessary to inflict will depend on how long it takes for offenders to understand that the price of committing crimes, in terms of the expected punishment suffered, has gone up, and how much that change in perceived risk influences their behavior. There is considerable evidence that the announcement of increased enforcement can have a significant short-term impact on violation rates but that the effects fade as violators notice the gap between promise and performance.[68]

Three insights from elementary behavioral psychology point the way toward getting as much deterrence as possible from any given amount of suffering inflicted. First, a high probability of a small penalty exerts a more powerful deterrent effect than a small probability of a drastic penalty (holding the expected value of the punishment constant). Thus the more equally punishments are allocated across offenses, the smaller the total quantity of punishment will be required to produce any desired level of deterrence. Second, the deterrent power of a punishment is strongly related to the proximity in time between the forbidden act and the punishment. Therefore, the more quickly the justice system acts, the less severely it needs to punish to achieve any given level of crime suppression. Third, first impressions are lasting: punishments experienced after early instances of a behavior are more effective in discouraging it than punishments experienced after the pattern is well established.[69]

Alas, the actual system of criminal justice in the United States, particularly in high-crime areas where the court dockets are crowded and the prisons full, is not built to take advantage of the power of certain, speedy, and early punishment. Our punishment resources are concentrated in the prison system. This leaves very little supervision capacity for offenders not incarcerated. In particular, first-time offenders are likely to be let off with a sentence of probation that differs little from a mere warning. Except for those held in jail pending trial—who are in legal theory not being penalized at all, since they are still presumed innocent—crimes and punishments are likely to be separated by long delays.[70] It would be hard to devise a system to achieve less deterrence for a given level of punishment than the one that actually operates in our more crime-ridden jurisdictions.

One reason that deterring drug dealing is hard—that is, expensive in punishment resources and in the suffering of lawbreakers—is that black-market prices will tend to adjust themselves to the punishment risks imposed by law enforcement. If an increase in enforcement leads to a price increase for cocaine—a good thing insofar as it discourages buyers—it will also help maintain the supply of dealers willing to take increased risks of punishment for increased financial rewards. Thus tougher enforcement will divide those who attempt a life of drug dealing into those who never receive a stiff sentence, who are better off, because richer, than they would have been under a looser regime, and those who eventually take a hard fall, who are worse off than they would have been.

Insofar as drug dealers choose their line of work in full knowledge of its risks, it is hard at first blush to see how increased enforcement could make them, as a class, worse off; wages should adjust to meet added risks. But drug dealers, like other lawbreakers, tend to be impulsive and short-sighted. For such people, a system of justice with low-probability, almost random punishment, and long delays acts as a trap, encouraging them to deal in haste and suffer at leisure.

The analysis is simpler with respect to enforcement directed at users. If all of them are very stubborn about drug use—if the demand for drugs is inelastic to their punishment price—increased enforcement will increase their suffering from punishment without decreasing their suffering from drugs: clearly a bad deal for them and for the rest of us. By contrast, if they are very sensitive to the threat of punishment or if the probability of even mild punishment can be made sufficiently high to deter all but the most foolhardy, then increased anti-user enforcement will be able to reduce significantly their drug activity, and its attendant harms, without using much actual punishment capacity or inflicting much actual damage.

For those already identified as problem users, a high probability of detection can be achieved with frequent random urine testing. If they have already been convicted of crimes, then the probation system provides a possible way to administer quick sanctions as well. But for the general, nonoffender population of drug users, it is virtually impossible to design an enforcement program starting with arrest and working through conviction to punishment that could generate a high enough probability of punishment to be a credible deterrent, simply because the numbers are so large and the cost of formal criminal justice processing is so high. Less formal, and therefore less laborious, ways of discouraging drug buying—ways that do not require a criminal conviction—are thus essential to enforcement aimed directly at drug buyers.*

---

* Using such techniques, of which forfeiture is the most prominent example, demands that the police and the administrative adjudicators practice a degree of restraint and care that can substitute for the court process in protecting the wrongly accused. Such restraint and care are not always on display. See the catalogue of wrongs reported in Andrew Schneider and Mary Pat Flaherty, "Presumed Guilty: The Law's Victims in the War on Drugs," *The Pittsburgh Press* (11–16 August 1991).

7

Persuasion, Help, and Control

*Q. How many drug counselors does it take to
change a light bulb?
A. Just one, but the light bulb has to really* want
to change.

Laws and their enforcement are not the only items in the drug-policy
toolkit. Programs can also influence the preferences and incentives
of current and potential drug buyers. These programs are conventionally thought of as constituting the "demand side" of drug policy,
although legislation and enforcement influence demand as well as
supply. Demand-side efforts attempt to change drug-related attitudes
and behavior in the mass of the population by delivering messages
and to change the drug-related behavior of those who have already
developed personal drug problems by delivering some mixture of
messages, services, and threats.

Enforcement efforts are identified in the public mind with the police, though in fact they engage prosecutors, judges, and corrections
officers as well. Demand-side efforts, by contrast, are largely the
province of teachers and of a mix of physicians, other health-care
workers, and social workers of various kinds: persons engaged in
what are called the "helping professions" (a category rarely con-
strued to include police or probation officers). Much of what passes
for debate about the relative merits of programs to reduce supply
and programs to reduce demand is in fact little more than a reflection
of the ideological, professional, social-class, and even ethnic tensions
between the police on the one hand and physicians, schoolteachers,
social workers, and treatment-program employees (often addicts in

recovery) on the other. This chapter is in part an attempt to demystify that debate.

PERSUASION

The Value, Strategy, and Limits of Persuasion Programs

The harm a drug engenders can be reduced by persuading current and potential users not to try it, to use it less frequently, or to restrict its use to relatively safe times, circumstances, and quantities. In addition to its direct benefits in preventing harm to users, successful persuasion also shrinks illicit markets and their side effects and makes enforcement easier.

These efforts at persuasion are sometimes lumped together as "education," but not all of them take place within institutions labelled "educational." Nor are the goals and methods of these efforts particularly close to those of education; advertising, political campaigning, and religious proselytization all offer equally apt analogies. Those who design, administer, and evaluate anti-drug persuasion efforts conventionally think of and measure success or failure in terms of the programs' impact on the drug-related attitudes and behavior of the target audiences, rather than, for example, how much factual information or analytic material the members of those audiences have absorbed.[1] It is also conventional to describe these persuasion efforts as "prevention," but that ducks the question of what it is they are designed to prevent—use, abuse, or damage—and it begs the question of what role persuasion has, and what role laws and their enforcement have, in preventing drug use and its unwanted consequences.

The enthusiasm for persuasion efforts is pervasive; enforcement professionals and agencies tend to be particularly strong believers in the power of persuasion to shrink the drug markets by drying up the pool of customers.[2] Successful persuasion would indeed be a boon; given two proposed public programs, one relying on persuasion and the other on enforcement, costing similar amounts of public money and preventing approximately equivalent amounts of drug-related harm, there would be strong reasons to prefer persuasion to enforcement. Enforcement involves, as the word suggests, the use or at least the threat of force; persuasion does not. Neither teacher nor student risks being killed in a drug education class; every enforcement operation poses some risk both to the police and to their targets. To the extent that persuasion efforts are successful, they reduce the wealth and power of criminal drug-dealing organizations by depriving them of customers; the effects of enforcement, as we have seen, are more ambiguous. Properly designed persuasion can foster the capacities of their audiences to control their own behavior; enforcement, which always aims at restricting the range of choice available to potential drug users, is as likely to weaken those capacities instead. By reducing the potential size of the market, persuasion can increase the effectiveness and decrease the unwanted side effects of enforcement efforts.

But persuasion efforts have their own problems and limitations. Research into a wide range of attempts to improve health-related behavior via "education" has produced a mix of results: some programs were, on balance, positive; some were neutral; and some were actually counterproductive.[3] Nor is this surprising. Insofar as drug abuse is the product of mistakes, they are not primarily the kinds of mistakes that additional information is apt to prevent: the links between knowledge and behavior are more complex than that.

The Problem of Design

Consider the simplest model of drug abuse prevention through education: tell potential users the facts about drugs, and you will persuade them not to use (or abuse) drugs. That model implicitly assumes several things: that the information given will be believed; that believing that information will be enough to convince potential users that using drugs would be unwise; and that they will have the will and the skill to act on that conviction when confronting the most typical drug-initiation situation: an offer to share made by a friend or acquaintance. While each of these assumptions is true to some extent for each potential user, one or more of them is likely to be substantially false for much of the target audience. Some will not believe what they are told; some will not value the negative consequences of drug use as highly as their teachers hope; some will act on impulse or in response to social pressure in ways inconsistent with their considered judgments.[4]

Worse, some who in the absence of drug education might be scared by unknown and ill-defined risks may in fact be reassured, rather than deterred, by what they are told. Not only do they know more about the risks than they did before, they are also more competent to handle them. In effect, drug education can make them better-informed and more self-confident drug consumers. Some of them will be able to use what they have learned to stay out of trouble, but others will surely illustrate the danger of a little learning. Others, who had never seriously considered drug use as a personal option, may be led by the mere fact of the discussion to think about it. Drug education can increase drug-related damage among its subjects (just as high school driver education increases automotive deaths among its subjects[5]) if the program does more to increase the number of people who engage in the risky activity under consideration than it does to decrease the risk.[6]

Moreover, the benefits of information-based education are limited by the fact that those most open to rational persuasion—those who can absorb new information, integrate it into their decision making, and act on their considered judgment in the face of social pressure—are probably those least likely to go from experimentation to self-destructive, chronic, heavy drug use. For the ones most likely to get into trouble—the present-oriented, impulsive, and reckless— accurate information may not help much, because the probabilities may not be sufficiently frightening; no drug currently in widespread use possesses a large risk of great or irreversible damage to someone who uses it once, and only nicotine is more likely than not to turn an experimenter into a compulsive user.

Drugs are risky rather than always deadly, and those risks are concentrated in the future, months or years after initiation. Assume hypothetically (there is no way to know accurately) that trying one's first dose of crack incurs a one-in-six risk of becoming a long-term compulsive crack smoker. To the reader of this book, that should seem an intolerable risk: the same odds as Russian roulette, with sufficiently appalling, albeit less drastic, consequences should the chamber turn out to be full. To a seventeen-year-old convinced of his own invulnerability, however, five chances in six of avoiding serious trouble may seem quite generous odds, particularly if he attributes the difficulties of problem users to their idiosyncratic weakness rather than to the inherent risks of the drug itself. (Nor can it be said that this attribution is incorrect; rather, the adolescent may be underestimating the probability that he will prove to be the weak or unfortunate one rather than one of the strong or fortunate five.)

There is some evidence that those who identify themselves as "venturesome" or "risk-taking" are much more likely than others to use drugs, particularly illicit drugs.[7] Part of the difference between U.S. and foreign rates of illicit drug use may stem from the high value Americans place on trying new things. This suggests a need to design anti-drug messages that will appeal to the risk takers. These messages could either be delivered as part of general classroom or media efforts or aimed specifically to those identified (perhaps simply by questionnaire) as being of adventuresome disposition.

Perhaps persuasion programs should do more to stress the intrinsic disadvantages of drug use, particularly use to excess, and of intoxication. Oscar Wilde once said, "As long as war is regarded as wicked, it will always have its fascination. When it is looked upon as vulgar, it will cease to be popular."[8] Similarly, there may be less to gain from convincing teenagers that drunkenness is risky than from convincing them that it is uncool.

Most persuasion efforts in the classroom and the mass media tend to be broadcast and scattershot. At best, they are designed for the average of a subgroup: say, suburban sixth-grade boys. At worst, they go to the entire population, as in mass-media advertising.[9] But the heterogeneity of the audience necessarily makes whatever message is delivered inappropriate, or at least irrelevant, to some of those who receive it. For example, a "Don't try it," "Just say no" message may be effective with those who have yet to start drug use. For those who have started already, however, threats of dire consequences following any use are likely to be disbelieved and to weaken the credibility of warnings about sources of elevated risk, such as the use of more dangerous substances, binge use, daily use, and mixing drugs. Predictions of an inevitable degeneration from experimentation to chronic abuse can also do active harm by demoralizing users in their efforts to maintain control.

An alternative to designing messages for teachers or media outlets to deliver directly to potential drug users is to aim persuasion efforts at authority figures and opinion leaders. Professional athletes and movie stars are less important in this regard than health-care workers, coaches, and others involved in leading athletic activity, and similar figures to whom potential drug takers, particularly adolescents, might turn for personal advice. Making people who already have the trust and respect of the target audience more sophisticated and persuasive sources of good advice about drugs, and persuading them that giving it is part of their professional responsibility, could pay large dividends. One model to examine is the effort to encourage physicians to deliver anti-smoking messages to their patients.[10]

Designers of persuasion campaigns also need to worry about how their messages will affect those who continue to use drugs and those trying to quit. Anything that makes people afraid of becoming drug users also tends to make them afraid of those who are drug users. To make the population at large even more afraid of drug users is not

obviously desirable. Decreasing social tolerance for drug use generally, for use of particular drugs, or for heavy chronic use can presumably lessen the attractiveness of those activities. But decreasing
tolerance also reduces the social and economic opportunities available to users and ex-users; "hating the sin but loving the sinner"
requires a disposition more saintly than we can reasonably expect as
a social norm.

Since the most common pattern of illicit drug use is occasional
marijuana smoking,[11] and since there is no evidence that occasional
marijuana smokers as a group are worse neighbors, coworkers, or
fellow students than non-users, generating additional social hostility
toward drug users in general is not manifestly wise or just. Even
for heavy users of more dangerous drugs, who clearly tend to impose costs on the rest of us, the current level of hostility may be more
than adequate: it is easier to find sites for prisons than for drug treatment centers. One good argument for stressing alcohol and tobacco
in anti-drug messages is to avoid making drug use an issue of "us
versus them." But much of the political impetus behind anti-drug
advertising is precisely that of a cultural holy war, pitting the decent
normal people who smoke and drink against the hated and despised
"drug users."

One of the great accomplishments of Alcoholics Anonymous has
been to lessen social hostility toward chronic heavy drinkers. The definition of alcoholism as a disease—whatever its theoretical merits—
does a great deal to deflect animus from the drinker or ex-drinker. As
a consequence, many AA members are eager to help others down
the path to recovery: this is the "Twelfth Step." Ex-users of illicit
drugs, by contrast, even those in twelve-step programs, tend to be
much more wary of letting anyone know about their status.[12]

In a classroom setting, some of these issues can be finessed. Even
within a set curriculum, teachers can tailor messages to fit their students. They can even attempt to communicate some of the complexity of drug use: that it always carries some risks, but fewer if carefully
managed. Mass-media campaigns of necessity allow for less variety
and less subtlety.

The problem of the choice of messages raises the complicated question of the goal of drug abuse education and of drug abuse prevention generally: should they aim to prevent any use of any drug, any
use of a specific list of drugs, or only excessive or inappropriate use?
This is a question both of ultimate ends and of tactics.

All persuasion efforts that concentrate on drug use itself, as opposed to more abstract attempts to teach personal responsibility,

decision-making skills, and resistance to social pressure, are pulled in two directions by the tension between preaching abstinence and preaching moderation. Knowledge of pharmacology—of drugs and dosages, effects and side effects—is essential to moderate use but may be dangerous to the cause of abstinence. To know that one drug is more dangerous than another is to know that the other is relatively safe. To know how much is too much is to know how much is enough. Learning enough about drugs to be a responsible, moderate user is likely to excite curiosity and to generate feelings of competence and a desire to try out newly acquired knowledge in practice. "The young," said Lord Chesterfield, "are as apt to think themselves wise enough, as the drunken to consider themselves sober enough."[13]

On the other hand, the "Just say no" message suggests that drug use cannot be rule-governed behavior. This leaves those who do not "say no" without any model of when or how to "say when." To the extent that personal rules about moderate drug use need the support of social norms and patterns,[14] abstinence campaigns may be counterproductive if they drive those who would have been moderate users to abstinence and thereby create a population of drug users dominated by those with a tendency toward excess.

Persuasion campaigns that address themselves to the specifics of drug taking, as opposed to more general character development, also face the problem of how to treat licit drugs: what to say about them and how much emphasis to give them. The introduction of the wine cooler has made alcohol an issue for junior high and even elementary school pupils; the early teens are also prime years for the initiation of smoking. Those who administer school-based programs (at least outside the tobacco-growing states) are apt to favor a "Just say no" approach to cigarettes, particularly given the rarity of noncompulsive use of nicotine in that form. But alcohol is trickier; complete abstinence is not the norm in mainstream American society, nor is there any mass movement to make it the norm. But teaching minors about responsible drinking is certain to be controversial, particularly since it is illegal for them to buy or possess alcohol. Conveying the message that alcohol is for adults only—an approach that might be summarized as "Just say later"—would be consistent with the law, but identifying alcohol use as adult behavior might only enhance its appeal to adolescents eager to grow up.

On the other hand, it seems unwise to ignore alcohol and tobacco entirely. Not only are they live issues for more of the population—and vastly more of the schoolchildren—than any of the illicit drugs, but to say nothing about them would be to suggest that they are somehow not really drugs at all. Silence about alcohol and tobacco is a very loud silence, one unlikely to go unheard. It would be a bitter irony if anti-drug campaigns had the net effect of encouraging adolescents to smoke and drink.

Persuasion campaigns aimed at licit drugs run into the political clout of the industries that have grown up around the production and distribution of alcohol and tobacco. The largest of the current media-based programs, for example, is run by a consortium of advertising agencies, virtually all of which derive a substantial proportion of their revenues from advertising alcohol and tobacco. The Media Partnership for a Drug-Free America has had nothing to say about the perils of smoking or of the Demon Rum.

The limited body of empirical research on classroom-based prevention programs strongly suggests that success depends on offering students specific reasons not to do whatever the program is trying to prevent.[15] It is not enough for those reasons to be valid for the teachers; they must be persuasive to the students, for whom the present looms much larger than the future and certainties overwhelm moderate risks. In the case of smoking, for example, stained teeth and foul breath today may be a far stronger deterrent to adolescents than the possibility of emphysema in forty years.

This poses a problem for anti-drug education on the "Just say no" model. There is simply no evidence that occasional use of alcohol or marijuana at moderate dosage damages a majority of users, or even a large minority of them. In fact, some evidence suggests that moderate users are, on average, better off in various ways than non-users (which may, of course, mean that well-being leads to moderate use rather than the converse).[16] This lack of factual ammunition creates an unpleasant choice for "Just say no" teachers: stress the virtue of obeying the law (doubtfully efficacious), stress the risk of going from moderate use to excess use (but the risks, for most drugs, are not very high), or misrepresent the facts. That any purchase of illicit drugs helps maintain the black market, with all the damage it does, is surely a good reason not to buy them (though low-dose, occasional use contributes little to criminal coffers), but that argument seems unlikely to have much weight in the decision making of adolescents.[17]

If the majority of the audiences for anti-drug advertising would become drug abusers in its absence, then messages could hardly do harm, just as a brand of mouthwash currently consumed by 1 percent of the population can gain sales from an advertising campaign that attracts attention even if it repels three-quarters of its viewers. But in fact drug abuse is rare, and chronic drug abuse with lasting bad consequences very rare.[18] To be beneficial on balance, a persuasion campaign must both improve the status of those who would otherwise get into serious trouble and not arouse unhealthy curiosity in any substantial proportion of the rest. That this problem is more than theoretical is illustrated by the school-based anti-drug education campaigns of the late 1960s and early 1970s, which aimed either to instill fear of drugs in general or to provide accurate and impartial information. Evaluations showed that both types of programs on balance increased the drug abuse problem among their youthful audiences. The scare messages were not believed by those who needed them most, and the information served as consumer education for the drug markets.[19]

If the goal is to minimize the number of people who get into serious trouble with a drug rather than the total number of users, the best way to reach that goal depends on which of two plausible models best describes the relationship between the overall use of a given drug in a given population and its problem use.

One model is based on a chain of "transition probabilities."[20] This model assumes that anyone who experiments with a drug faces some probability of proceeding to regular use, and anyone who uses a drug regularly faces some probability of proceeding to heavy chronic use or repeated binge use. Regular users confront some probability, and abusers a higher one, of getting hurt. All of these probabilities are higher for persons starting at younger ages. Unless one or more of these probabilities is greatly malleable by educational intervention, the best way to reduce the number of people who get hurt is to reduce the number of people who experiment, or the variety of drugs with which they experiment, or to retard the age of first use as much as possible. This suggests stressing the distinction between use and non-use and downplaying the distinctions among drugs and between use and abuse.

The alternative view is that virtually everyone will experiment with drugs (including alcohol). On this view, the probabilities of proceeding to regular use or to abuse are variables influenced by personal and social characteristics: norms and customs about drug use, the individual's knowledge about the relative dangers of various drug-use practices, and his capacity to make sensible personal decisions and ability to act on those decisions in the face of social pressure or temptation to excess. If this view is correct, drug education should aim at establishing controlled drug-use patterns, give considerable information about the characteristics of different drugs, and teach strategies for managing one's own drug habits.[21]

Since both the chain-of-probabilities model and the responsible-use-versus-abuse model are likely to capture parts of the truth, designers of persuasion programs aimed directly at drug-related behavior are in a quandary. Designing a single program that accommodates both viewpoints seems close to impossible, and appropriately targeting different messages at different audiences seems only slightly easier.

The only apparent escape from this box is to focus attention away from drugs as a topic and toward moderation and self-command as ideals to be cherished and skills to be developed. Making the young aware that their own behavior under temptation or social pressure is a potential problem that they need to learn to manage, and giving them guidance and exercise in managing it, may properly be called an educational mission. It addresses a problem not of a minority but of virtually everyone, and its applications go well beyond drug use. Strategies for developing and observing personal rules, identifying and resisting impulses and social pressures to transgress those rules, recognizing an offer as the occasion for a decision, and analyzing the issues at stake in that decision are relevant to the management of one's sexual, nutritional, automotive, academic, or television-watching behavior as well as one's drug-use behavior.

In a program of education and training for self-command or moderation, drugs would enter in two ways, both important but neither central. First, drug consumption would appear as an example: an area in which individuals often behave in ways not congruent with their own interests. Temporal myopia and the failure to defer gratification, ignorance about or neglect of risk, failure to identify choice points, and social pressure could all be identified as contributors to bad choices. Second, intoxication itself would appear as an independent contributor to distorted decision making and unanalyzed behavior.

Project DARE, the most widespread of the school-based anti-drug programs, is not primarily about drugs. Only three of the thirteen lessons in the original DARE curriculum address drug use; the rest are a mix of exercises in values clarification, material about personal decision making, and skill-building activities featuring role-playing.[22] If DARE were not sponsored and operated by police departments, it might have elicited the same complaints from parents and clergy that have dogged other values-clarification programs, particularly those dealing with sexual behavior.

Given what we know about advertising and classroom education, expecting televised or blackboard "moderation education" to greatly improve the capacity of the rising generation for temperance in its most general sense would be unduly optimistic. But intemperance— not only the intemperate use of drugs—is so costly a problem that even small gains would repay substantial investments.

The Problem of Evaluation

If it were easy to measure the effects of persuasion programs, the theoretical problems about designing and implementing them would be relatively unimportant; trial and error would be sufficient to develop programs that worked, even if no one could quite explain why. Unfortunately, the measurement problem is even more subtle and profound than the design problem.

The frequency of drug abuse is hard to measure, because drug abuse is hard to observe: self-reports are unreliable, and official records (such as criminal histories) are often incomplete and hard to get at for research purposes. Small uncertainties about the frequency of drug abuse matter greatly in the process of evaluation, because the frequency itself is so low. A persuasion program that actually reduced the lifetime prevalence of cocaine abuse in a given population from 5 percent to 4 percent would have to be counted a great success for having eliminated a fifth of the problem without arresting anybody. In practice, though, no one will be able to say for sure whether the rate of abuse before the intervention was really 5 percent rather than 4 percent, or whether the rate after the intervention was really 4 percent rather than 5 percent, and the research reports are likely to conclude that "the intervention did not have a statistically significant effect on the target variable." The element of time further complicates things; six years must pass before we can start to measure the effects of a program aimed at sixth-graders on their drug-use status at graduation from high school. Six years is a long time to wait between the first trial and the first results, and a long time in the history of schools and drugs. The knowledge that Program X was a good program six years ago is only mildly helpful in determining its usefulness today; the kids have changed, the schools have changed, and the drug scene has changed.

Evaluations of the wave of school-based drug-prevention programs during the 1980s have now begun to come in. Some are quite encouraging. It is apparently easier to discourage marijuana use than tobacco use, and tobacco use than alcohol use.[23] However, virtually all of these studies rely on self-reports about attitudes toward drugs or about the prevalence of drug use (not abuse), measured one or two years after the intervention. One carefully designed and carefully evaluated program, aimed at inner-city sixth-graders and including both school-based and community-based elements, seems to have reduced the frequency of alcohol, tobacco, and marijuana use— all around 10 percent in the control group—by about one-third: a very impressive performance.[24] If the self-reports are accurate, and if those abstaining because of the program included one-third of those who would otherwise have gone on to serious drug problems, and if early drug use is an independent risk factor for developing problem use rather than simply a marker for it (or if, alternatively, the program succeeded in shifting the entire population toward less drug use), then that program must be judged a success and, despite its substantial costs, well worth replicating in other, similar populations. We should know by sometime in the mid-1990s. DARE, the most widely implemented program, has shown somewhat disappointing results in evaluations performed so far, but the data are still coming in.[25]

The methodological problems in evaluating media-based campaigns are even more daunting; just separating the "experimentals" (those who have received the messages) from the "controls" (those who have not) is anything but simple. If one effect of anti-drug advertising is to decrease social tolerance for drug use, one likely result will be to reduce the willingness of those who continue to use drugs to say so when surveyed. Self-reports are always tricky to interpret; programs that tend to make them even less reliable are therefore especially hard to evaluate except by following the life histories of large samples of participants and nonparticipants. (Measurement is somewhat simpler for the licit drugs, whose consumption is accurately measured for tax purposes and sufficiently widespread that relatively small changes show up clearly.)

Most evaluations of mass-media anti-drug campaigns have shown no measurable results.[26] An exception was the series of anti-tobacco television advertisements aired under the FCC's Fairness Doctrine before cigarette commercials were banned from television. Even at only 20 to 25 percent of the frequency of positive advertising, the negative commercials appear to have been quite effective: so effective, in fact, that the advertising ban seems to have actually increased smoking.[27] The fact that smoking was (and is) more common than the use of any illicit drug gave the anti-smoking advertisements a larger target to shoot at than anti-drug commercials have, and the accumulating evidence of the health hazards of smoking gave them powerful ammunition. It would be much easier to repeat that success with beer than with cocaine, because beer is more widely used and less widely feared.

The largest current media-based anti-drug campaign has been that conducted by the Media Partnership for a Drug-Free America. Its promoters claim to be using $1 billion per year's worth of space in newspapers and magazines and time on television and radio, all of it donated. An evaluation of that program shows that variations in the intensity of the campaign among otherwise similar areas produced substantial effects as gauged by the self-reported attitudes of a sample of visitors to such "central areas" as downtown business districts and shopping malls.[28] These results were sufficiently interesting to deserve follow-up by other methods, such as panel studies and measurements of adverse drug consequences. The Media Partnership campaign has been the subject of several criticisms focused on its methods: many of its "facts"—including those used in its frank appeal to employers to fire their illicit drug–using employees—appear to have been invented or misquoted, and some of its appeals to children are as likely to produce anxiety as to reduce drug use. As noted, its advertising-agency sponsorship and its reliance on donated print space and broadcast time virtually forces it to ignore alcohol and tobacco.

Thinking about these fundamental problems, and about the mixed evaluation results from other programs designed to promote healthier behavior, ought to modify the enthusiasm of those who believe, or assert, that well-designed education could render legal restrictions unnecessary, or at least allow a substantial reduction in enforcement efforts.[29] Thus the demand that enforcement be cut back to pay for expanded persuasion efforts, or that funding be "balanced" between the two approaches, can hardly be based on a careful calculation that the decrease in desire for drugs resulting from an additional dollar of persuasion will more than compensate for the increase in availability resulting from a dollar not spent on enforcement. Open drug dealing also sends a message: how much of the value of a drug-resistance class is lost if its pupils have to walk past crack dealers on their way home? The widespread faith in prevention through persuasion seems to rest on the feeling that persuasion would be wonderful if it worked, rather than a well-founded conviction that we know how to make it work.

HELPING AND CONTROLLING PROBLEM USERS

Under any system of laws, enforcement efforts, and persuasion programs, there will be some users who get themselves into patterns of drug use that are a menace to their well-being or the well-being of others.

A very small proportion of the drug-using population accounts for a very large proportion of the harm done to, and by, the users of virtually all drugs. (Nicotine in the form of tobacco is an exception.) Most of the benefits of controlling drug use come from controlling problem use: excessive use, use under inappropriate circumstances, and use by those who are unusually apt to behave badly under the influence.

Most laws and programs are blunt instruments; they hit equally at problem and nonproblem users. Prohibitions and taxes make no distinctions among users. While regulations might attempt to distinguish "problem" from other users by making drug use a licensed activity, we have no working model of such a policy. Enforcement, whether directed at sellers or buyers, is naturally undiscriminating. Persuasion efforts, whether in the mass media or in the schools, are addressed to the entire population, or at best to large subgroups, not specifically to the few who are or may become problem users.

Programs directed specifically at helping and controlling problem users have the advantages and the disadvantages of concentrated remedial programs in comparison with broad-based programs of prevention. The relationship between treatment and prevention is the same as that between performing coronary bypass surgery on those with advanced artery disease and encouraging citizens at large to watch their weight and exercise more. Remediation costs more than prevention on a per-subject basis, but it needs to be applied only to a relative few. Which sort of program generates more good per additional dollar spent—in the language of policy analysis, which is more cost-effective at the margin—depends on the available technologies and on the population sizes. A generic debate about the merits of remediation versus prevention (whether by persuasion or by legal restriction and enforcement) seems largely fruitless.

Efforts to deal with problem users are frequently lumped together as "drug treatment." But this assumes that there is a disease (or cluster of disease states) properly called "drug abuse" and that someone knows how to make it better.[30] Since the ethics of therapy put the patient's interest first, calling the process of dealing with problem users "treatment" also implies that the welfare of problem users is or ought to be its paramount concern. At least in the case of drug-involved offenders, this may well be false. The "treatment" label also raises complicated questions about the right to refuse treatment, now recognized as a basic right of the mentally and physically ill.

The actual process of picking up the pieces once drug-taking consumption has gotten the better of someone is substantially more complicated, with respect to means, ends, and rights, than the word "treatment" implies. A sensible approach to problem users would blend attempts to help with attempts to exert social control. The right mix for each individual depends both on how much damage his problem does to other people and on whether the user desires (at some level) to adopt a different behavior pattern. The actual mix of service and coercion delivered to any given user under any given set of programs and policies depends partly on these factors, partly on the social and economic status of the user, and partly on how the problem comes to the attention of the system. A convicted burglar sentenced to drug treatment in lieu of prison can be threatened with referral back to court for failure to comply with its rules, while a treatment client who enters voluntarily can, at most, be expelled from the program.

Many efforts to help and control problem drug users do not address themselves to the problem of drug use at all. Setting the broken arm of someone who fell down the stairs drunk is no different from setting the broken arm of someone who fell down the stairs sober. A year in prison for a burglary committed to buy a bag of heroin is the same as a year in prison for a burglary committed to buy a meal. For now, we will restrict ourselves to those measures of help and control that directly address the drug-related aspects of the user's behavior.

Therapy

The literature on drug treatment is full of ambiguities and equivocal results. The data are sketchy and the methodological problems daunting. Since most of the research is old, much more is known about treating heroin than about treating cocaine, and about treating men than about treating women.[31]

Just making sense of the variety of drug treatment programs is no simple task. One way to start is with taxonomy.[32] The universe can be divided first between programs requiring paid staff, and which therefore cost money, and individual or group self-help, which is effectively free. Resource-using programs can be further classified using three dichotomies: residential (inpatient) or nonresidential (outpatient), short-term or long-term, and drug-assisted or drug-free.

Individual self-help is the most widely practiced, but the least discussed, of the treatment options. That some drug users cannot manage their own habits and need outside help is sometimes taken to imply that being helped is the primary, or even the only, approach to revising one's drug-taking behavior. But a glance at the most widely used drugs suggests how untrue that is. Approximately one-quarter of all current drinkers—more than twenty million Americans—report having had difficulty managing their drinking at some time during their lives, but fewer than 10 percent report having such problems currently.[33] The balance—several times as many people as have ever attended an Alcoholics Anonymous meeting, let alone sought professional help—presumably have brought their problems under control on their own or with a little help from their friends. The arithmetic for marijuana is similar; millions of people who used to be daily marijuana smokers are no longer, yet only a tiny fraction of that number of people have received any kind of treatment for marijuana abuse.[34] Surveys of former smokers suggest that more than 90 percent quit entirely independently, and that in fact those who have sought formal help have a lower success rate than those who have relied on themselves (presumably because those who sought help were poorer bets to start with, most of them having failed on their own).[35]

Current drug abuse control policies do not reflect the importance, or even the possibility, of unassisted desistance. "Telling people to quit" is not the name of a program, except in the case of tobacco smoking. (The Media Partnership, for example, has directed its messages to potential users and to the employers, parents, spouses, and children of current users, but rarely directly appeals to users to quit.) Population sizes are part of the reason: compulsive cigarette smoking is much more common than compulsive drinking, and enormously more common than compulsive use of any illicit drug. Therefore a poster that says "Quit smoking" will be relevant to a far higher proportion of those who see it than a poster that says "Stop shooting up." But since most drug desistance is informal, more attention could be given to increasing the frequency of unassisted quitting.

Group self-help is the second most widely used mode of drug treatment. The twelve-step programs—Alcoholics Anonymous and its offspring—are by far the biggest of the group self-help efforts. They require no resources other than a meeting room and some literature. Their success rate among those who join and remain active is apparently very high. Fewer than half of those who join remain active, however; the chances of success seem to rise with a member's education and social status.[36] Amazingly little is known about the effects of AA on problem drinking, and even less about Narcotics Anonymous or Cocaine Anonymous.[37] The most recent comprehensive study of drug treatment dismissed group self-help as a "quasi-treatment modality."[38]

Since discussions of drug treatment tend to be dominated by employees of the industry that provides paid treatment, the tendency to downplay the role and value of individual and group self-help is natural. Still that tendency is unfortunate; since professional help is expensive, most long-term care for those with drug problems will have to be of the self-help variety. One way to think of the role of short-term formal treatment programs, particularly residential detoxification and "chemical dependency" programs, is as a way of getting their patients ready to join and succeed in group self-help programs. That is in fact the acknowledged goal of many short-term alcohol treatment efforts.[39]

Residential programs, because they provide both 24-hour staffing and room and board, are far too expensive for long-term use by large numbers of patients. But short-term residential programs, both the 5-to-7-day variety called *detoxification* and the 28-day variety called *chemical dependency treatment*, aim to break the current cycle of daily use or repeated binge use, ease the symptoms of withdrawal by providing care and reducing temptation, and prepare their clients for reentry into the world with strategies for avoiding relapse, including referrals to group self-help programs.

One way to manage the detoxification process is to give drugs. Some of those involved are from the general psychiatric armamentarium and are not drugs of abuse. There is some indication that antidepressants can help heavy cocaine users get through the sluggishness and inability to experience pleasure that characterize the period following discontinuation of heavy cocaine use.[40] But the drug user can also be "treated" with his favorite drug or a close substitute. Patients with histories of long-term heavy drinking are sometimes encouraged not to quit suddenly, because the effects of sudden with-drawal from alcohol can be severe, even life-threatening. Instead, they are given decreasing doses from day to day.[41] Heroin addicts can be helped through the withdrawal process with decreasing doses of methadone. Cigarette smokers can phase down their frequency or switch to another form of nicotine intake, such as chewing nicotine gum, on the way to abstinence. With these three exceptions, the drug laws do not allow for gradual withdrawal strategies.

Residential detoxification is delivered almost entirely in hospitals, serves mostly heroin and cocaine users, is paid for largely from pub-lic funds, and focuses on tending its clients through the immediate discomfort of cessation. Since the symptoms of withdrawal from most drugs are not, medically speaking, very serious, it is not obvious that detoxification needs to be conducted on a residential, let alone a hospital inpatient, basis.[42] Outpatient detox is possible; that is, some people who have severe enough drug problems to need help with the short-term pains of kicking the habit nonetheless have enough willpower and social support to break their old habits while remain-ing in their old settings. But that group does not include everyone who could benefit from detoxification. Removing someone temporar-ily from the scenes and companions associated with drug taking can be both a symbol of, and a practical aid to, the resolution to "get clean." Those in especially bad trouble, or with especially slender private resources, are apt to need a period of residential treatment.

Yet "detox" has a poor reputation; an Institute of Medicine study panel summarized the conventional wisdom: "...researchers have found no effects from detoxification that are discernibly superior to those achieved by untreated withdrawal..." and concluded that "...detoxification is not a treatment."[43] The most likely result of any single detoxification episode is a relapse into drug use and a return to detoxification; "treatment recidivism" for detox programs has been estimated as high as 80 percent.[44]

But this glass could usefully be seen as 20 percent full rather than 80 percent empty. Given the personal and social damage associated with a heroin or crack habit, $2500 or so seems a very modest price to pay for a one-in-five chance of a lasting cure.[45] Even a detoxification that eventuates in a relapse produces a period of abstinence and a longer period of reduced drug use and crime as compared with the behavior of the same user if he does not try to quit. If the chances of success are cumulative, as they appear to be for smoking—the best single predictor of success in quitting cigarettes is the number of attempts to quit [46]—even repeated detoxifications may be worth the price. Again, one should factor in the possibility that some of those who are successfully and lastingly detoxified in a hospital would have succeeded on their own, but the question to ask is not whether detox outperforms unassisted desistance, but whether the availability of a comfortable setting and some palliative care increases the number of attempts to quit. The observation that more than 80 percent of coupons for free detox passed out to heroin users in New Jersey as part of an AIDS-control project were used suggests that there is an unmet demand for this service.[47] The benefit-to-cost ratio of detox programs could be even better if it were administratively feasible—as it is certainly clinically possible—to cut costs per day and thus finance more attempts or longer stays, by using nonhospital facilities.[48]

Long-term residential programs pursue more ambitious goals. They seek to transform their clients' personalities and render them more or less permanently drug-free. Most of them work on the "therapeutic community" (TC) model pioneered for heroin users by Synanon, Daytop Village, and Phoenix House: group living under strict rules, confrontational group-encounter sessions, staff recruited largely from among ex-clients. While less expensive per day than detoxification programs, TCs more than make up for the difference in duration: they cost about $13,000 to $20,000 per client per year, and nine months is considered the minimum desirable length of stay, with up to two years not uncommon.[49] Like the self-help groups, TCs claim very impressive success rates among those who come and stay but suffer very high rates of voluntary or involuntary separation, particularly in the first few months. Only 15 to 25 percent of TC entrants stay the course.[50] While therapeutic-community members often have even more powerful reasons to succeed than AA members, the demands of these programs are considerably greater; they are virtually total institutions.[51]

Detoxification and outpatient counseling share a problem: they do little or nothing to change the daily environments their clients face and in which they acquired the habits they are trying to break. Therapeutic communities attempt to solve this problem by creating an artificial environment that is designed to rebuild and to reshape the personality of the member. Some persons seeking treatment seem to need, and to be willing to accept, the discipline of such an institution, including the temporary sacrifice of most of their outside interests and connections. Others, however—most of those who enter—find that the demands are greater than they are willing to tolerate.

This suggests the need for a treatment modality that does more to alter a user's environment than detoxification or outpatient counseling but is less all-embracing than a therapeutic community. The Oxford House movement represents an attempt to fill that gap. An Oxford House is a cooperative living arrangement for persons trying to change their drug (including alcohol) use habits. Many are also members of twelve-step groups. The members share rent and chores and support themselves with ordinary jobs. The rules, developed and administered by each house unit, tend to be simple. Members stay as long as they like; since the arrangement is largely unsubsidized, they face no pressure to move out to make room for new members. The movement has grown as long-time members of established houses become the nuclei of new ones.[52]

The Oxford Houses presume a far greater degree of personal and economic self-reliance on the part of their members than do the therapeutic communities, and in fact seem to serve a more affluent and better-educated clientele who have fewer major personality disorders and shorter criminal histories than many TC clients. They also need and receive far less public money, though small subsidies have recently been made available to fund the start-up costs of new houses. It is possible that they will develop into a substantial drug-treatment resource, particularly as a follow-up to short-term detoxification or chemical dependency treatment.

It may be the case that additional financial encouragement could quicken the growth of the Oxford Houses. But the important scarcity at the moment appears to be, not money, but experienced members ready to form the leadership of new establishments. How far the Oxford House model can be adapted to serve very poor drug users and drug users with other personal problems on top of their drug habits remains to be seen; to date, there is no formal evaluation of the Oxford House movement even for its current membership.

Long-term nonresidential programs come in two basic varieties. One, outpatient counseling, provides advice support services for a drug-free life. For those with private health insurance, this can mean psychotherapy, intensive family counseling, and a range of other activities, cheap compared with inpatient treatment but still likely to run into the thousands of dollars per year. For the uninsured, it is likely to mean an hour a week of group therapy and a little social work. There is evidence that those who stick with such programs reduce their drug use and improve their lives, though it is hard to tell whether this means that those who stay tend to get better or that those who get better tend to stay.[53] In many cases, fewer than 20 percent of outpatient nonmethadone clients complete a course of treatment, a discouraging finding given that they tend to be less badly off to start with than, for example, entrants into therapeutic communities.[54] The sheer variety of such programs and their clients precludes drawing any precise conclusions about them; probably some programs are good for some of their clients, but no one knows which programs or which clients.

The other kind of long-term outpatient treatment is methadone maintenance for heroin users. Methadone is a synthetic drug closely related to heroin. Pharmacologically, the chief difference is that methadone is longer-acting. It substitutes for heroin in staving off the withdrawal symptoms of opiate dependency. Its long-acting nature means that a single daily dose is sufficient, and users can therefore hold normal jobs.

Methadone does not prevent heroin users from getting high, though it may reduce the subjective thrill of any given dose of heroin by competing for receptor sites. (There is a drug, naloxone, that does prevent heroin intoxication by blocking opiate receptor sites; not surprisingly, there is little demand for naloxone among heroin addicts.) Indeed, methadone produces a high of its own, and is in great demand as a street drug, the sources being clinic patients and staff.[55] But because methadone is given to clinic patients orally rather than by needle, they do not experience the euphoric "rush" that heroin users achieve. This, and the limits that clinics put on the amount of methadone they distribute, tempts methadone clients to supplement their methadone supply with black-market heroin. They also often use other black-market drugs.[56] Clinics discourage this practice by administering urine tests to their clients and sometimes sanctioning them by deprivation of "take-home" privileges, reduced dosages, or even expulsion from the program for repeatedly positive tests.

Perhaps the best-established fact in the drug treatment literature is that methadone works. Methadone clients use substantially less heroin and commit substantially fewer crimes than they would if they were not on methadone, and methadone maintenance has the highest retention rates among all treatment modalities.[57] Costs are significant but not prohibitive: about $300 per month, which means that the entire estimated heroin population could be maintained on methadone for between $1 and $2 billion per year.

That methadone works is not surprising. It gives heroin addicts some of what they want, legally, reliably, and usually free of charge. Assuming that their alternative was to continue as users of heroin, this leaves them better off and reduces their incentive to commit crimes for money. Predictably, when free public programs are terminated and methadone clients are forced to pay for their treatment, their condition deteriorates and their crime rates increase.[58]

Treatment by methadone does not "cure" addiction; it substitutes a legal addictive drug for an illegal one. The advantages of methadone maintenance as practiced in the United States over heroin maintenance as once practiced in Britain are partly operational (once-daily administration, ability to work, less of a tendency to steadily escalating dosage, somewhat less of a problem with illicit resale of maintenance supplies) and partly symbolic (the drug being given out is not called heroin).

Nor does methadone turn heroin addicts into model citizens; few of them were model citizens before they became heroin addicts, and years of street hustling do nothing to improve either one's character or one's legitimate economic opportunities. But it does convert some people who would otherwise be very badly off and represent a major social headache into people who are only somewhat badly off and represent a minor social headache. That is not a bad result for only $300 per person per month.

The one serious objection to methadone maintenance is that it traps some former heroin users who would otherwise have quit into daily opiate use. Despite its mythology, heroin use is not a permanent condition.[59] There is no way to tell how many successful methadone clients would otherwise be successful ex-addicts. In the case of clients entering treatment voluntarily, the advantages of methadone in attracting and retaining them seem overwhelming. The case for giving methadone to offender/addicts who are forced into treatment by the criminal-justice system and who are liable to more coercion to quit seems weaker.

The success of methadone in managing the lives of heroin addicts has led to calls for the development of an analogous chemical to treat compulsive cocaine use. But methadone manages a dependency syndrome by averting withdrawal symptoms. It seems doubtful that the reinforcement-based compulsion typical of heavy cocaine users could be managed by maintenance with a substitute. Any stimulant is a partial substitute for cocaine, and although the drugstores are full of licit nonprescription stimulants in the form of caffeine "stay-awake" pills, there is no evidence to date that cocaine users have any interest in them.

Publicly funded voluntary drug treatment could be expanded either quantitatively, by accepting more clients into existing programs, or qualitatively, by enriching the content of the programs or moving clients from lower- to higher-resource programs. While it seems logical that any treatment is better than none and that more is better than less, even those weak claims are only weakly supported by evidence, except in the case of methadone treatment for heroin users. The question of magnitude—of how much improvement could be expected from the next million or billion dollars of annual expenditure for more or better treatment—is even more wide open.* The conviction of treatment advocates that moving resources from drug law enforcement to drug treatment would decrease the total harm associated with drug taking may be correct, but on current evidence it remains what Mark Twain called "a vagrant opinion, without visible means of support."

Balancing Treatment and Enforcement

Much has been said and written about the appropriate "balance" between treatment spending and spending on enforcement. But the facts of the case are not easy to determine, and the appropriate basis for making such a judgment is far from obvious.

The only federal money explicitly allocated for drug treatment consists of money granted to state departments of substance abuse treatment, which get about half of their funds from federal block grants. Federal support for those agencies amounts to about $1 billion per year,[60] which is indeed a far cry from the $15 billion to $20 billion spent annually on drug law enforcement, including both the budgets of drug enforcement agencies and expenditures on drug enforcement by general police, prosecution, and corrections agencies. Moreover, while the overwhelming bulk of drug law enforcement is aimed at the illicit drugs—since enforcement of the terms of liquor licenses by alcoholic beverages control authorities is cheap, and there is almost no attempt to enforce the ban on noncommercial transfers of alcohol to minors—much of the public substance abuse treatment money appears to be spent on the treatment of alcohol abuse.

Thus if we could compare enforcement spending with spending on publicly financed treatment for the illicit drugs alone, the imbalance about which treatment advocates complain so bitterly would look

---

* For a brave attempt from pre-cocaine days, see Henrick J. Harwood, "Economic Costs to Society of Alcohol and Drug Abuse and Mental Illness: 1980." Submitted to Alcohol, Drug Abuse, and Mental Health Administration (Research Triangle Park, N.C.: Research Triangle Institute, June 1984). Harwood's calculations are based on data from the treatment outcome perspective study (TOPS).

even more extreme than it now does. But not all public funds that pay for drug treatment go through "drug treatment" budget lines. Community-based mental health clinics are never counted as part of the "drug treatment" budget, but a substantial proportion of their client base presents them with substance abuse problems. The same is true of drug-abuse treatment provided by the Veterans Administration or the Bureau of Indian Affairs, and of the government-paid health care or health insurance provided to public employees (including the military) and their families; that money is budgeted as part of other activities and considered by treatment recipients as part of their entitlement to health care. In some states, Medicaid programs cover some forms of drug treatment.[61]

The biggest single source of public funds for drug treatment, if one could tally it all up, would probably turn out to be the tax subsidy to employer-paid health insurance and to corporate "employee assistance" programs. Employers' vigorous efforts to tighten the rules governing alcohol and drug treatment provided under employee group health plans suggests that the cost of such treatment is a noticeable part of the more than $200 billion per year in employer-paid health care, all of which is tax-deductible expense to the employer and tax-free income to the employee.[62] Thus a simple comparison of public enforcement spending with public treatment spending is misleading, and debates about the allocation of drug money between enforcement and treatment may be less important in determining how much treatment is actually provided than are rules about the eligibility of substance abuse treatment for financing by health insurance (including Medicaid and Medicare). Indeed, health insurance coverage may be the most sensible context in which to debate the question of how much money to spend on treatment, because drug treatment can be compared with other health-care measures as alternative means of improving the well-being of individuals. Whether treatment can actually serve the other purposes that drug law enforcement serves is far less clear.

The great, largely unspoken argument for drug treatment instead of enforcement as the primary tool of drug policy is that treatment expresses compassion for users while enforcement expresses only anger. To the moderate left ("liberals" in the current rather than the classical sense), this is a powerful appeal.*

---

* In addition, as Jonathan Caulkins of Carnegie-Mellon University has pointed out, there is an implicit false syllogism of the form: "Enforcement doesn't work, but something must work, therefore, treatment works."

But as Machiavelli pointed out, compassion in action may hurt the visible few.[63] If drugs are traps for many users—and otherwise what is the point of offering treatment?—is it, in the end, more compassionate to let people walk into the trap and then help them make the painful climb back out, or to build a high, ugly fence around the trap in the form of drug law enforcement?

At its best, treatment is only a partial substitute for prevention, for the same reasons that hospital trauma units are only partial substitutes for safer cars. By definition, treatment intervenes only after a person has established a pattern of drug use that causes problems for that person and others and is no longer fully under voluntary control. Changing such a pattern is virtually always painful and apt to leave some lasting disability, including vulnerability to future episodes of abuse. Someone who has never had a problem is, on average, better off than a problem user "in recovery." If, then, we imagine two alternate sets of programs, one, weighted toward preventative measures of enforcement and persuasion that allowed a thousand bad drug habits to develop and treated none of them, and the other, weighted toward treatment, that allowed two thousand bad habits to form and treated half of them successfully, the first would be preferred.

Treatment as Social Control

All treatment programs mix the delivery of service with the imposition of control, but the mix varies. No program will tolerate a client who is repeatedly disruptive or abusive or who repeatedly arrives on the premises visibly under the influence. All will use the moral authority of the service provider or self-help group to encourage the behavior patterns—chiefly abstinence from drugs—they aim to produce. Some programs go much further. Therapeutic communities, whose clients are surrounded by rules and under unremitting pressure from the staff and from one another both to conform and to demonstrate their commitment to the goals of the organization, are the clearest examples. But many outpatient programs require strict adherence to schedules and even routinely test their clients' urine to determine whether they are continuing to buy and use black-market drugs. Urine testing is very common among methadone programs, and even required by some states' methadone-treatment rules.

There is good evidence that strong controls contribute to good treatment outcomes.[64] But they have two great disadvantages: they cost money (or staff time, which comes to the same thing) and they tend to drive away clients.

One consequence of the growth in demand for methadone maintenance that followed the rise of AIDS—growth not matched either by increased funding or by the training of additional staff—was a steady decrease in the level of control efforts. Many methadone clinics became little more than drug-distribution centers, partly to cope with increasing workloads and partly because, in the face of the AIDS threat, the importance of keeping clients in some sort of treatment seemed too overwhelming to make expulsion for repeated use of illicit drugs a credible threat. One result of decreased control at the clinics seems to have been worse outcomes for the clients; a study by the General Accounting Office found that in some New York City clinics as many as 40 percent of all methadone recipients were using cocaine.[65]

Most clients enter drug treatment voluntarily. For them, the operators of treatment programs need to worry about "marketing" issues: factors leading to recruitment and retention. Clearly, those who never enter a program cannot benefit from it; since the length of stay in treatment is an important factor in its success, those who enter but are quickly repelled or expelled also do not gain much. These considerations tend to push programs away from making strong demands on their clients. Methadone programs, which have a drug to give out, can be more demanding without having their clientele drift away (unless there is a less-demanding methadone program across the street or across town). The trade-offs are clear: a low-control, low-hassle treatment system can attract and retain more clients and serve them for less money, but a high-control system can achieve better results with those it does serve.

The issues are different for the large minority of drug-treatment clients who are there involuntarily, having been caught committing a crime—perhaps only that of buying or possessing drugs—and sentenced to treatment in addition to, or more commonly in lieu of, other punishment.* Recruiting them is no problem, and retaining them, while not assured—since they can always choose not to go to treatment and face the legal consequences—is at least a smaller problem than with voluntary clients. Moreover, the benefit to others of controlling the behavior of a drug user who is also an offender, especially if the offense is some form of theft, assault, or drug dealing,

---

* In some cities, this is managed under an administrative structure known as TASC: Treatment Alternatives to Street Crime.

is apt to be much stronger than the benefit to others of controlling a drug user who enters treatment under his own steam. The potential value of using treatment programs to control and monitor the behavior of drug-using offenders is enormous; the extent to which potential is realized depends on the willingness and capacity of treatment providers to monitor aggressively and report violations back to the criminal-justice agencies that made the initial referrals and on the willingness and capacity of the agencies to punish repeated violations and thus give meaning to treatment-program rules.

There are two considerations about the use of treatment as a mechanism of punishment and control: how well it comparts with the ethics and mechanics of therapy, and whether the treatment component adds enough to the monitoring process to justify requiring it for the unwilling. The availability of mandated and monitored abstinence as a sentencing option seems to challenge the need for mandated treatment.

It might be better to require abstinence and make therapy optional. Even if those offenders who chose therapy continued to have their urine tests (or whatever) done at the treatment site, it would be clear that those tests were being administered for, and by the authority of, the court or the probation department, that the therapist had no discretion about reporting the results, and that a decision by the client or the program to terminate therapy would have no direct effect on the client's legal situation. This would uncomplicate the responsibilities of the treatment providers, reduce the incentives for clients to try to con their therapists, and relieve clients and staff alike by getting the unwilling out of the way of the willing. Some mandatory treatment programs, particularly the commercial "education" programs that judges in some states impose on drunken-driving convicts, amount to little more than punishment by boredom and humiliation. Worse, there is probably a limit on how many of the attendees of a twelve-step meeting can be there involuntarily without substantially compromising the value of the group for themselves and their colleagues.

However, these conceptual advantages may or may not be outweighed by practical disadvantages. It may be that therapy, or at least therapy of some kinds, even if unwillingly undergone, yields enough additional reduction in future drug use and crime to justify imposing it on those who have made their drug use a problem for the rest of us. They may not, after all, be the best judges of how to quit; merely telling them to quit, without more specific instruction, may be ineffective. Much might be learned from a few random-assignment experiments, comparing testing and sanctions plus mandatory treatment, testing and sanctions plus voluntary treatment, and testing and sanctions alone.

ALLOCATING AND MANAGING TREATMENT RESOURCES

The best-known symptom of the inadequacy of current support for publicly funded drug treatment services is the existence of waiting lists. Since the desire to quit may be intermittent, telling someone who wants to desist from drug use to wait in line is obviously a bad idea, even worse than "rationing by queueing" for other medical services. This has led the proponents of increased treatment funding to formulate a slogan: "Treatment on demand."[66]

A closer look at the treatment system reveals a more complicated pattern than simple scarcity; while some programs have waiting lists, others have unfilled slots. Sometimes there is a complete mismatch between the services available and the services a client needs; sometimes the mismatch is between a client without private resources or insurance and a program not geared to taking public funds.[67] But it can also happen that the same city has both waiting lists for methadone maintenance and empty methadone slots. In general there is no system to match clients and slots, not even a simple database of vacancies.

The simplest step toward a more coherent treatment system would be the creation of an agency or agencies that could provide for those seeking treatment the type of service travel agencies provide to those seeking intercity transportation: up-to-date information about what is available at what price and the ability to make a reservation for any vacant capacity. A variety of individuals and agencies now provide treatment information and referral, but in the absence of a central database or standard compensation mechanism any one referral service tends to work with only a few of the possible providers.

A "travel agency" system would be a considerable advance over the current chaos. But more could be asked for. First, clients could reasonably want access to information about programs' processes and records of success, independently gathered, or at least audited, and in some standardized form to facilitate program-to-program comparisons. Even at the level of program types, currently available data are grossly inadequate;[68] at the level of individual programs, they are virtually nonexistent.

More ambitiously, one could ask the referral service or services to serve as "gatekeepers" to the entire treatment system, assigning clients to treatments on the basis of need and appropriateness, with due regard to cost-effectiveness. Such "utilization-management" for publicly paid treatment is a central recommendation of the Institute of Medicine study panel.[69] In addition to providing cost control, an agency with utilization-management authority could insist on the collection of data and create incentives for programs to compile good records of success, as well as eliminating potentially destructive competition for clients (for example, among methadone programs) on the basis of lax controls on client behavior. It is possible that drug-treatment clients, whose problem by definition includes difficulties in self-management, may not be the best judges of what treatment programs will be able to help them.

On the other hand, in the absence of clear evidence about "what works" or even a consensus about what success means, it is not obvious that the criteria built in to any given system of utilization management would do better at matching clients to programs than the current quasi-market. Utilization management presupposes, and cannot be made to substitute for, a clear set of judgments about what programs work with which clients.

On the privately paid side of the system, utilization management is handled by health insurers and Health Maintenance Organizations. Treatment providers and treatment seekers complain that "managed care" pays too much attention to cost-saving and not enough to therapeutic effectiveness. It probably does; in the absence of effectiveness data such a bias is understandable and perhaps inevitable.

Treatment clients want help (without too much hassle). Providers want to pursue their therapeutic missions (and pay their bills). Third-party payers, whether state agencies or health insurers, want to stretch their treatment dollars as far as they will go (or save them if possible). All agree that the current situation could be improved on. If there were a consensus, or even clear evidence, about the direction in which improvement lay, there might be enough political pressure to force movement in that direction even against whatever economic interests and therepeutic concepts happened to come out behind in the process. In the meanwhile, getting from where we are to a functioning travel-agency system would represent considerable progress.

COERCIVE CONTROL OF PROBLEM USERS

Within the relatively small group of drug users whose habits are a problem for themselves and for their intimates, there is an even smaller group whose drug use chronically harms or threatens strangers, by leading them to act irresponsibly under the influence or to commit crimes (including drug selling) to obtain money for drug purchases. Some of the irresponsible behavior is criminal in itself: assault, for example, or disorderly conduct. Much of the rest is made criminal by special statutes making it a crime to engage in specific activities (driving is the most familiar example) while intoxicated, whether or not any direct harm results.

These user/offenders are the problem drug users most worth controlling, at least from the viewpoint of their neighbors. They are also in some ways the easiest to control, because repeated criminal activity eventually leads to arrest and conviction, and those who have been convicted can be subjected to legal restrictions and to intensive means of investigation that cannot be applied to the general population.

Chronic drug-involved offenders thus present an attractive target for intervention. They do enough damage to others that the cost of even quite expensive programs can be covered by relatively modest changes in their behavior. Many of them are easy to identify, because they are repeatedly arrested; discovering which frequent arrestees are also drug users requires only cheap and simple chemical tests. And the complicated ethical and legal questions about coerced therapy are vastly simplified when the subjects have been convicted of, or pleaded guilty to, crimes and when restrictions are imposed as part of a sentence or a formal agreement in lieu of criminal processing.

Mandatory Abstinence, Testing, and Sanctions

Anyone who commits a crime under the influence of an intoxicant or in order to get money to buy one should be required to abstain from the use of any intoxicant for a period of time equal to the maximum prison term that can be imposed for the crime, and that requirement should be supported by frequent chemical tests to ensure compliance and by swift and predictable sanctions for noncompliance (including failure to appear for scheduled tests). If such a principle were accepted and put into practice, chronic drug-involved offenders would no longer be able to maintain their chosen life-style. Even if this had only a modest impact on the volume of drug sales—and the impact might be substantial for crack and heroin—it would at least reduce the frequency of predatory crime.

An abstinence requirement would be a good general deterrent, a good specific deterrent, and an aid to incapacitation. Making the effective loss of drug-use privileges a consequence of committing crimes would be a means of punishment, and thus of deterrence: those who enjoy using drugs would have to be careful not to get caught committing crimes. Compared to other deterrent punishments, drug deprivation has attractive characteristics: it is unpleasant without being damaging (if anything, it may be therapeutic); unlike prison, it does not interfere with the ability of the person undergoing punishment to hold a job, go to school, maintain family ties, or pay restitution to his victim; and it economizes on scarce prison space. Thus it offers a good way to discourage crimes by the entire class of heavy drug users.

In order for such a program to work, it is not necessary that the drug be criminogenic for all of its users, that all of the offenders' criminal activity be directly related to their drug taking, that the requirement for abstinence be perfectly complied with, or that all deviations from abstinence be detected and punished. Much less will do. It is necessary only that there be a causal relationship between drug use and offending for some offender/users and that the system of testing and sanctions be sufficient to reduce drug use among them.

Mandatory abstinence would also help prevent future crimes, by deterring continued drug use among those assigned to it.[70] This specific deterrence would work better for some subjects than for others; as with any nonincarceration sanction, some will comply and some will not. But those who do not comply are those most likely to continue committing other crimes, and thus most worth locking up. Mandatory drug abstinence with monitoring can thus help ensure that scarce prison space is occupied by those who will commit the most crimes if not incarcerated; unlike other programs aimed at such "selective incapacitation," it need not rely on statistical prediction to isolate high-rate offenders but can allow them to identify themselves by means of missed or positive ("dirty") drug tests. In effect, this plan substitutes drug tests for judges' guesses in selecting candidates for prison cells.[71]

It is an ordinary condition of probation or parole that the offender refrain from any lawbreaking during the probation or parole term. Since drug use implies possession, and since the possession of controlled substances is a violation of law, abstinence from illicit drugs is already in principle required of those on conditional release, and probation and parole officers in most jurisdictions have widespread authority to order urine tests to verify that abstinence and to sanction violations by referring the offender back to the court for revocation of conditional-release status and incarceration or reincarceration.

But the current actual system falls short of what is proposed here in several ways. Some offenders are not given probation terms, are given only short terms, or are assigned to "summary" probation, which means that they receive virtually no supervision. Alcohol, since it is not illicit, is not automatically included in the ban, even in the case of those convicted of drunken driving or drunken assault. Arrestees are not routinely screened for the presence of drugs in their systems; absent some other indication in the record, supervisors have no easy way to separate drug-involved offenders from others. Tests are generally administered only "for cause," rather than randomly; there is solid evidence that probation and parole officers are not very accurate at guessing which of their charges are using drugs.[72]

Finally, in most cases the only formal sanction available is the drastic one of referral back to court for possible incarceration. Given the paperwork demands on overworked probation and parole officers and the prison-crowding situation, this sanction is too expensive to be a credible threat; even if supervisors were willing to punish violations with prison time, most judges are not. Consequently, even known drug-involved offenders sentenced to "intensive-supervision" probation are only occasionally punished for continued drug use.[73]

A better system would screen all arrestees for the presence of drugs and assign all drug-involved offenders to mandatory abstinence and testing. (Some research and development would be required before alcohol could effectively be included in chemical monitoring, since ethanol is a simple molecule with no distinctive metabolites.) Testing would start out on a random, once-a-week basis: each offender would call in once a day to find out whether his turn had come. There would be a set of predetermined, progressively serious, administrative sanctions for missed or dirty tests, starting with increased test frequency and moving up through fines and hours of unpaid labor, personal curfews, brief periods of incarceration, and, finally, referral back to court. The sanctions should be predetermined both to allow for speedy processing and to maximize deterrence through certainty. The goal of such a program would be to convince most offenders that continued drug use is simply more trouble than it is worth. At least one such program has generated very high levels of compliance and measurable decreases in jurisdiction-wide rates of property crimes, despite a shortage of drug treatment programs; the negative incentive provided by testing was apparently a sufficient aid to willpower even among long-time heroin users.[74]

The converse of progressive discipline for violations is the promise of rewards, in the form of reduced testing frequency, for consistent compliance. This can both encourage those who are doing well and economize on testing capacity and expense: weekly testing costs about $1500 per offender per year, not much compared to the cost of imprisonment or continued criminal activity but a substantial sum compared with the per-offender budgets of probation departments.

Mandated, monitored abstinence might be extended to those arrested and released on bail; the District of Columbia has pioneered in this area. Whether there is adequate legal basis for testing and sanctioning persons who have not yet been convicted of a crime remains an open question. Since most of the offenders we are most concerned with are arrested frequently, the issue of pretrial testing would be relatively unimportant if all convicted drug-involved offenders were automatically assigned long periods of mandatory abstinence.

A program that depended largely on post-arrest screening to identify drug-involved offenders would be imperfect. It would miss some users, and it would identify some who had drugs in them at the time of arrest but whose crimes were not causally related to their drug use. Marijuana, the drug most widely used, most easily detected, and least clearly linked to user crime, probably ought to be excluded from programs for adults, as it is from the D.C. pretrial program, both because its use is so widespread that including marijuana would generate many violations, thus straining the capacity to sanction violators, and because its economics and pharmacology do not suggest any strong link between marijuana smoking and predatory crime. Excluding marijuana however, might attract criticism as an implicit invitation to continue illicit drug taking. Fortunately, a perfect design is not required; only some improvement over the current system, which virtually ignores the link between continued drug use and continued crime.

A serious national program of drug testing and sanctions for offenders who are users of illicit drugs could be mounted for approximately $5 billion a year in testing and sanctions costs. The cost could be less if marijuana were excluded, both from the initial classification of drug-involved offenders and from the ongoing monitoring. Including alcohol-using offenders, and testing for alcohol, would raise the costs. Such sums do not seem too much to pay to establish some measure of control over the drug users whose habits make the most trouble for the rest of us.

The same analysis applies, *a fortiori*, to drug-involved offenders serving time. That it is possible to emerge from a prison term still a drug addict testifies to prison administrators' reluctance to face up to the problem. More intensive searches of staff, visitors, and prisoners returning from the outside to detect drug smuggling are likely to prove futile. Frequent random testing with loss of privileges for positive tests and follow-up investigation into the source of the drugs could dramatically reduce the scope of the problem in the prisons, but only at the cost of demonstrating how large the problem is, disrupting the informal prisoner economy, straining the capacity of the prison-discipline system, and in some systems generating substantial turnover in the prison staff, including some transfers to the inmate population. Still, a relatively drug-free prison does not seem an excessively grandiose goal. Here again, there is no legal or even administrative problem with drug testing in the abstract; the difficulty is simply that systematic programs are not in place.

The notion of "civil commitment" for addict/offenders—assigning them to residential drug treatment programs that they are not free to leave—was once hailed as a cure-all for the addict crime problem. It has since lost some of its luster, but there is still evidence that well-designed and managed civil commitment can outperform prison in reducing the subsequent drug use and criminal behavior of those committed. It is not often possible to turn persistent drug-using burglars into members of the Kiwanis Club, but if it is possible to turn them into somewhat less active burglars, that more modest goal is well worth achieving. One careful study of the subject concludes that the differences, in terms of future drug use and crime, between civil commitment and unsupervised release are large enough in favor of commitment to justify its costs.[75] Nor is the difference between the daily life of someone under civil commitment and that of a prison inmate such as to suggest that civil commitment sacrifices deterrence to incapacitation; the prisoner may well be doing easier time.

Some states have created therapeutic communities as separate living units within the walls of their prisons. Unlike the civil-commitment programs, participation in prison TCs is voluntary, but the alternative—the consequence of quitting or being expelled from the therapeutic community—is being back on a cell block. The additional cost of keeping a prisoner in such a community, over and above the cost of having him in prison in the first place, is only a few thousand dollars a year.[76] Once again, it is impossible to measure the benefits of such a program by comparing the recidivism rates of its graduates with those of the general population, because the TC graduates are likely to be self-selected to succeed on the outside. Still, the differences are great enough and the cost (compared to the cost to the state of further imprisonment or the cost to crime victims of further crimes) small enough to suggest that such programs should be much more widespread. One study comparing prison TC alumni with prisoners from the same facility who applied for TC admission but never made it off the waiting list suggests noticeably better outcomes for the TC group; other studies are less encouraging.[77]

SUMMARY

Opponents of the "war on drugs" sometimes argue that improved education and treatment can control the drug problem more effectively, and with fewer unwanted side effects, than prohibition and enforcement. While it is certain that programs of persuasion directed at potential drug users, and an offer of therapy to those struggling to manage their drug habits, can produce benefits in the form of reduced demand, it is much less clear how great those benefits can be with current techniques of persuasion and therapy. Whether any practicable program of "demand reduction" could work well enough to prevent major increases in consumption and drug-related harm in the face of the substantial reductions in price and search time that would follow a drastic cutback in drug law enforcement is unknown. That such a program could prevent increased drug abuse damage if the changes were from prohibition to free legal availability seems highly improbable. Nor is it obvious that drug treatment should be thought of as competing with drug law enforcement for a share of the drug abuse control budget rather than with other health-care programs for a share of the $600 billion per year spent on health care in the United States.

Mass-media persuasion efforts should focus on mass-market drugs, especially alcohol and tobacco; there is still lots of bad news to deliver about those drugs, and a substantial body of positive messages to counteract. School-based campaigns should stress the development of decision-making and resistance skills.

Among the established voluntary treatment modalities, the ones most obviously worth expanding are methadone maintenance for heroin users and therapeutic communities for prison inmates. More resources for methadone should mean not only more clients but better-staffed programs, able to exert more control over their clients' drug use. Detoxification, whether drug-assisted or drug-free, may also be worth expanding, particularly if it can be delivered cheaply in non-hospital settings and linked to forms of follow-up care: counseling, self-help through twelve-step programs, or Oxford Houses.

Those drug users who frequently commit crimes, other than the crime of buying drugs, can and should be compelled to give up their drug use, both as part of their punishment and to reduce their future criminality. Treatment may be a useful adjunct to that process, and the result may well be therapeutic, but its primary mechanism is coercion: quit or else. Under sufficient pressure, most drug users can and will quit, or at least drastically reduce their drug use. The goal of the program should be to make the life-style of a drug-using criminal no longer sustainable.

IV

DRUGS

8

Alcohol

Whisky, you're the devil, you're leading me astray.
Whisky, you're my darling, drunk or sober.
                                        —Irish folk song

If the current cocaine situation demonstrates the social damage that can accrue from an incompletely successful attempt to control a problem drug by prohibition, the current alcohol situation shows the costs of an incompletely successful attempt to control a problem drug without prohibiting it, using regulations, taxes, and programs. Instead of dealer violence and economically induced user crime we have user violence in barrooms, bedrooms, and nurseries. (The reportedly dramatic decrease in discipline problems when half a million U.S. troops were assigned to "dry" Saudi Arabia was a dramatic reminder of the largely hidden day-to-day costs of alcohol-induced misbehavior.[1]) Instead of occasionally and spectacularly corrupt drug law enforcement, we have frequently but discreetly corrupt liquor regulation. Instead of crack-house sex, we have the use of alcohol in seduction, so routine as to be a cliché. Instead of poor adolescents, especially males, becoming trapped in drug dealing, we have adolescents of all social classes, especially males, participating in ritualized binge drinking with alcohol diverted from the licit trade. Instead of a few thousand overdose deaths, mostly among the young, we have tens of thousands of chronic-disease deaths, mostly later in life. Instead of the disorder of street dealing, we have the disorder of public drunkenness. Both drugs produce accidents, poor employee performance, drains on the health-care system, damaged newborns, and failures to fulfill family and neighborhood responsibilities, but the total damage in every one of these categories is clearly greater for alcohol than for cocaine.

Alcohol is beyond comparison the most widely used intoxicating drug in the world. In the United States, about two-thirds of all adults use alcohol at least occasionally, and about one-third drink regularly: weekly or more.[2] Americans spend approximately $90 billion per year on alcoholic beverages, more than twice as much as they spend on all illicit drugs combined. They consume about 105 billion drinks per year: 60 billion cans of beer, 33 billion shots of whisky, and 12 billion glasses of wine.[3] Daily use, considered one of the stigmata of dependency for any other intoxicant, is not unusual when the drug is alcohol. Even by this relaxed standard, perhaps a third of the regular drinkers, about 16 percent of all drinkers, are reported to have a "drinking problem."[4] Of these, between a quarter and a half—a few percent of all drinkers, which is to say a few million Americans— drink so heavily, or drink at such inappropriate times and places, or behave so badly under the influence, that their drinking has begun to dominate their lives.[5] Presumably, some of the people whose lives appear from the outside to have been wrecked by alcohol like it that way, but most appear to feel that their drinking is beyond their voluntary control. Many of them have made repeated attempts to quit or to moderate their intake, without lasting success. Some number are demonstrably addicted to alcohol and will undergo a ferociously unpleasant and even life-threatening withdrawal if they try to quit abruptly. Others, without the physical addiction, are no less caught in behavioral compulsion. In addition to the millions of current chronic serious problem drinkers, there are millions more living out their recovery from alcohol "one day at a time."

Most drinkers, of course, are not problem drinkers. Alcohol was the drug for which the distinction between use and abuse was first invented, and with good reason. Even daily use need not be, and frequently is not, problematic. As anyone who has used alcohol is aware, not all drinking leads to drunkenness: it is possible to be a daily drinker without ever having been "the worse for liquor" in the sense of no longer being capable of responsible behavior. The frequency of intoxication, and of problem drinking, varies enormously from one social setting to another. The northern European countries whose inhabitants drink beer and distilled spirits have far more alcohol problems than do the Mediterranean countries whose inhabitants drink wine with meals, and this pattern seems to carry over to immigrant-descended populations in the United States.[6]

But equally of course, intoxication is a matter of degree. As anyone who has ever been a nondrinker among a group of drinkers is aware, the effects of drink are often far more obvious to an observer than to a user, at least in part because alcohol can suppress the critical faculties even faster than it does the clarity of speech, the coherence of thought, and the sense of balance. In addition, organic damage can occur even when intoxication does not: alcohol beyond very moderate doses is a toxin to the liver and kidneys and a carcinogen.* The people of Italy and France, who despite consuming huge quantities of alcohol are rarely drunk, at least as they recognize drunkenness, and engage in little drinking-related violence, nonetheless suffer gravely from liver disease.[7]

Since even nonintoxicating use puts a strain on the body, and since occasional intoxication, or even consumption short of intoxication, creates additional risks of accidents and irresponsible behavior, by no means all of the problems caused by alcohol are caused by anything recognizable as "problem drinking." The costs of alcohol are nearly as widespread as its benefits.

Those benefits, let us not forget, are far from negligible. True, as with all other drugs, some of the demand for alcohol can be traced to physical dependency, psychological compulsion, binge cycles, the influence of the previous five drinks, social pressure to conform, fantasies about its powers as an aphrodisiac for oneself or a love-philter for one's partner, or inaccurate beliefs about its contribution to other forms of sociability or to work. Of course, for alcohol as for other heavily marketed consumer goods, some of the demand for alcohol can be traced to the efforts of producers to create attitudes and opinions favorable to its use, including the glamour and sophistication that consumers are encouraged to believe is attached to using alcohol, at least under the proper brand names. In addition— and here the demand for alcohol is unlike the demand for most other

---

* A finding several years ago that moderate drinking was actually better for the heart than complete abstinence received considerable attention. See, for example, L. O. Lange and P. M. Kinnunen, "Cardiovascular Effects of Alcohol," *Advances in Alcohol Substance Abuse,* 6 (3 [1987]): 47-52; and R. D. Moore and T. A. Pearson, "Moderate Alcohol Consumption and Coronary Artery Disease: A Review," *Medicine* 65 (4 [1986]): 242-267. It is interesting to speculate how the popular and scientific press, and the government's drug education machinery, would have handled the same finding about one of the currently illicit drugs. Against the value of moderate drinking in preventing heart disease, one must set the additional risk of cancer, which rises steadily with the amount of alcohol consumed. The curve of aggregate mortality risk apparently finds its low point somewhere around one drink per week. (I owe the data on cancer risk, and the aggregate mortality calculation, to as yet unpublished work by Joel Schwartz of the Environmental Protection Agency.)

goods—some of the demand derives from its place in social rituals, ranging from wine as part of a formal or festive meal to champagne for the champions or the wedding party, and from settling the deal over a drink to a bottle of whisky for the building superintendent at Christmas.

But much of the demand simply reflects a willingness to pay for the sense of relaxation and well-being provided by alcohol's effects on the nervous system and for the well-demonstrated value of those effects as social lubrication. Literary testimony to the joys and comforts of alcohol use is nearly coextensive with literature itself, across cultures and centuries. The fact that alcohol demand among current drinkers who are not addicted tends to be relatively inelastic, reflecting a willingness on their part to pay far more than they currently pay, means that at current prices they are deriving a substantial net benefit, a consumers' surplus, from the availability of their drug.

It is possible to analyze the "need" for alcohol as evidence of individual and social pathology, and to believe that healthy persons in a healthy society would not want to use it. We could dismiss alcohol, as a prominent drug warrior once dismissed marijuana, as "a drug to make you stupider"[8] and ask why drinkers are not satisfied with their own natural stupidity without wanting to take more from a bottle. One could even claim that all of the perceived benefits of alcohol use (past the one drink a day that apparently helps prevent heart attack) are illusions of one kind or another, derived from myths, placebo effects, and the failure to account for deferred costs. The temperance movement made all of these arguments in one form or another. But in the absence of convincing evidence, a liberal society ought to give great weight to the opinions of consumers about what they think they like, and a majority of the people on the planet think they like an occasional drink, or even more than one.

If alcohol were a newly developed "designer drug" just emerging from an underground chemist's lab, its intoxicating and addictive properties would lead to its scheduling under the Controlled Substances Act. As a carcinogen even at low doses, it could not be approved as a routine preventive medicine, and it has no current use in clinical medicine, so it would be classified in Schedule I: that is, completely banned except for tightly regulated research. Its recreational and social benefits would simply not enter into the decision.

But that says as much about the deficiencies of a regulatory scheme focused entirely on clinical applications and the control of abuse as it does about the design of a wise alcohol policy. The benefits of alcohol use would constitute a strong argument against a return to Prohibition, even if the memory of the previous experience and the daunting prospect of enforcing a ban on so popular a commodity did not make such a return almost unthinkable.

The serious question regarding alcohol policy is whether we can construct and implement a regime that protects the benefits of alcohol use while better controlling the associated harms to drinkers and others. If the alcohol legalization system we now have is in some respects unsatisfactory, it is not necessary to abandon legalization entirely; we might instead try to find a better set of taxes, regulations, and programs.

Present-day American public policies toward alcohol are built around three primary objectives, which can be stated as maxims: "Kids shouldn't drink." "Alcoholics shouldn't drink." "No one should drive drunk." Alcohol use in itself is not treated as a problem: no one points with pride or views with alarm as the number of drinkers, or the total volume of alcohol consumed, falls or rises.

The obvious problem with current policies is their failure to achieve these simple objectives. The less obvious problem is that the objectives themselves are too modest. The alcohol problem is much larger than underage drinking, alcoholism (or problem alcohol use defined as chronic heavy drinking or binge drinking), and drunken driving. A more sensible alcohol policy would be built around a longer list of concerns: alcohol-related violence (including domestic violence and child abuse) and suicide; the public nuisance of inebriated behavior; alcohol-related accidents not involving automobiles; drinking (even short of drunkenness) before work; the use of alcohol in combination with other drugs; the role of alcohol in teenage sexual activity, sexually transmitted disease, and unwanted pregnancy; and the impact of drinking on the health of users and their newborn children.

That is roughly the same list one would draw up for any other toxic, intoxicating, and potentially habit-forming drug. Making better public policy toward alcohol would involve treating it as part of the drug problem. The conception of alcohol policy as a special case of drug policy is resisted for many reasons, good and bad. The alcohol industry resists it for obvious commercial reasons. Drinkers resist it because they have been taught to believe that drug users are bad people and do not want to think of themselves, or be thought of by others, in those terms. Drug warriors resist it because it would not be possible to maintain the current level of hostility toward "taking drugs" if that term were extended to include a behavior engaged in by two-thirds of all American adults. If alcohol is a drug, and yet use can be distinguished from abuse, then what becomes of "Just say no" as applied to the controlled substances?

There would be great benefit in convincing drinkers that alcohol is a somewhat toxic, quite dangerous, and enormously abusable drug. It would make them less casual about quantities, frequencies, times, and places and perhaps less eager to press alcohol on their friends and guests. Drinkers might be encouraged to approach alcohol the way drivers, hunters, boaters, and mountain climbers are encouraged to approach their dangerous diversions: with care, even ritualized care, about the risks to themselves and others.

But there would also be great potential losses from treating alcohol as a drug, if people who now successfully manage their alcohol use concluded incorrectly that they could therefore manage the use of any other drug. Other things equal, making consumers understand that alcohol is a drug should be expected to push alcohol consumption down and consumption of the currently illicit drugs up. The strategy being pursued by the drug warriors—the parents' movement, the Media Partnership, and the drug czar's office (formally the Office of National Drug Control Policy, or ONDCP)—might be thought of as creating a social firebreak between alcohol and the illicit drugs. Defining alcohol as a drug would move that firebreak.

But even if the alcohol-as-drug notion should not be incorporated into public education campaigns, that does not imply that it ought not enter into policy thinking. After all, alcohol *is* a drug. That should count for something.

CURRENT PROGRAMS AND POLICIES

American alcohol policy is a patchwork of federal, state, and local laws and of public and private programs. Persons over twenty-one may legally possess alcohol anywhere in the United States, and may buy it, unless they are visibly intoxicated, in all but a few "dry" towns and counties. (In a few more, it may be purchased by the bottle but not by the drink.) Persons under twenty-one may not legally buy it or possess it (religious rituals excepted), and no one (except, in some states, their parents) may legally give it to them. Driving or operating other heavy machinery under the influence, variously defined, is a serious offense. Public drinking and public intoxication are minor offenses. Alcohol may be sold or served only in licensed establishments; the licenses, particularly for service, are scarce and highly prized, and the threat of license revocation is used to enforce compliance with a variety of regulations about hours, quiet conduct, and especially sales to minors. In a few states, the sale of liquor for home consumption ("package goods") is a state monopoly.

Except for distilled spirits advertising, which is banned from television by industry practice, advertising is uncontrolled. It is heavily weighted toward brand-name advertising, which is rich in imagery but virtually free of any information content, rather than retail advertising, that gives consumers information about prices. In addition to print, billboard, and electronic advertising, there is substantial sponsorship of sporting and entertainment events. Packages, but not advertisements, are now required to carry strongly worded, but not necessarily conspicuous, warnings.*

Taxation

Alcohol is taxed by the federal government and the states. Total taxation, including the monopoly profits of state liquor stores, amounts to $10.5 billion per year, one half of one percent of total tax revenues, over and above normal sales and income taxes. This represents an average of about ten cents per "standard reference drink" (a 1.5-ounce shot of whisky, a 6-ounce glass of wine, or a 12-ounce can of beer, in each case between 0.7 and 0.75 ounces of absolute alcohol). Since their high in Korean War days, alcohol taxes have failed to keep pace with inflation. From 1950 to 1988 liquor, beer, and wine taxes fell between 71 and 75 percent in terms of 1988 dollars.[9] That effective tax decrease, plus rising personal incomes, has made alcohol more and more affordable.

But that average hides enormous and only partially rational variation from one form of alcohol to another. Wine pays the lowest tax per unit of alcohol, about six cents per drink on the average, except for champagne, which is considered a luxury. But since wine is taxed by volume and not by alcohol content, the "fortified wines," or "sweet wines," such as sherry and port, which have additional alcohol added after fermentation but are still taxed as wine, pay less than four cents per reference drink. Taking advantage of this tax break, wine producers have developed a special group of potent, inexpensive sweet wines especially for those who want to get as much alcohol per dollar as possible; the familiar brand names here are Ripple and Thunderbird. These products appeal to youngsters, but they are most closely associated with skid-row drunks (thus "wino"). Beer is next, at ten

* The effect of advertising on alcohol consumption is ambiguous. While advertising increases public awareness of name brands, as well as glorifying drinking, some studies conclude that consumption levels are unaffected by alcohol advertising. R. G. Smart, "Does Alcohol Advertising Affect Overall Consumption? A Review of Empirical Studies," *Journal of Studies in Alcohol* (49 [1988]): 314-323.

cents per drink, and distilled spirits (whisky and liqueurs) are highest, at 18 cents. If all taxes had been equalized up to the tax per unit alcohol applied to distilled spirits in 1987, the increase in federal tax revenues from the same sales total would have been $4.6 billion.[10]

The low taxation of wine reflects the political strength of the domestic wine industry, but the argument in its favor has to do with the relative benignity of alcohol consumed in this form. There does seem to be evidence that consumption, except for the wino wines, is less associated with problem drinking than is consumption of alcohol as whisky or beer, though this perhaps reflects the age, social class, and gender of wine drinkers as much as it does any inherent properties of the grape. The cross-cultural evidence seems to support the notion that wine cultures have fewer apparent alcohol problems than beer-and-whisky cultures; the explanation may have something to do with wine's association with drinking at mealtime. A case could be made for leaving ordinary table wine a low-taxed product and reclassifying the fortified wines as "spirits." (There would remain the problem of "wine coolers," mixtures of wine and fruit juice that appeal to adolescents and even preadolescents, especially girls, who tend to find beer distasteful.)

The tax discrimination in favor of beer vis-à-vis whisky can also be analyzed in terms of the relative power of brewers and beer distributors, but it is justified as reflecting the increased danger posed by alcohol in more concentrated form. It is certainly easier, or at least more comfortable, to get splendidly drunk on whisky than on beer. But one must set against that argument the fact that beer is the favored drink (along with wine coolers) of young drinkers. At current beer taxes, beer is priced competitively with name-brand soft drinks; six-packs are available for as little as three dollars. This hardly serves to discourage youthful drinking.[11]

Persuasion

The governmental and private effort to alert the public to the dangers of alcohol is a mass of mush-mouth and mixed messages. Since many school administrators view alcohol as their number-one drug problem—the head of drug programs for one big-city school system told me that he had a wine cooler problem reaching down into the second grade—it tends to get substantial attention in school-based programs. After all, for minors, alcohol is effectively an illicit drug. This presents a problem for those educators who would like to talk to students about responsible drinking rather than only talking about abstinence.

By contrast, media messages focus almost exclusively on drunken driving; naturally, the Media Partnership for a Drug-Free America, which relies on donations of talent from advertising agencies and of space and time from media companies, never mentions drinking. Nor has there been any movement to produce anti-drinking advertisements along the lines of the anti-smoking advertisements that used to appear on television. The absence of such advertisements results partly from the demise of the "Fairness Doctrine,"[12] but the more fundamental reason is that no agency of the U. S. government takes the prevention of drinking as its objective. Unlike the use of illicit drugs or even tobacco, drinking does not have the social status of a Bad Thing.

Drinking by Minors

Ambivalence toward drinking extends even to drinking by minors, particularly boys. Juvenile drunkenness and public disorder are disapproved of and even feared, but many, probably most, parents who are not complete abstainers feel it to be part of their responsibility to introduce their children to a drug that is so intimately connected with American social life. This is referred to as "teaching the kid how to drink" or "how to hold his [less frequently her] liquor." There are strong arguments for this practice, even though many state laws against giving drink to minors do not explicitly exempt parents; the surprise I received at age seven when my father allowed me a sip of his after-dinner liqueur has been a lifetime aid to moderation in drinking.

Even unsupervised juvenile drinking is virtually never treated as a serious offense, either on the part of the minors involved or that of the adults who supply them. Partly as a consequence of this lax enforcement and the attitudes supporting it, juvenile drinking is by many measures completely out of hand. Some 57 percent of all high-school seniors (61 percent of the boys) report themselves as current drinkers. Some 3.7 percent (5.2 percent of the boys) drink daily or almost daily, compared with less than 1 percent for any illicit drug. Perhaps most frighteningly, 32.2 percent (39.1 percent of the boys) have had at least one heavy drinking session (defined as five or more drinks at a sitting) during the past two weeks, and 2.4 percent have had more than five such sessions.[13] While alcohol and driving always constitute a dangerous mix, the combination of alcohol, driving, and youth is particularly explosive: more than eight thousand persons from ages fifteen to nineteen were killed driving automobiles in 1987, making auto accidents the most frequent cause of death in that age group, and it is estimated that 50 percent of those involved drinking.[14] Poor driving judgment is not the only, or even the worst, consequence of underage drinking. Although there are no statistical studies on the links between alcohol and crime or between alcohol and sex among youngsters, anecdote and folk wisdom agree that they are strong.

Given the risks of underage drinking, it might be worth changing the relatively tolerant laws and policies against possession of alcohol by minors and its distribution to them in the direction of the stern treatment now accorded possession and distribution of other drugs. However, the transition problems that would accompany such a change are enormous. The behavior involved, though technically illegal (albeit under state rather than federal law), is now so common that suppressing it with arrests and punishments would exact a terrific toll on both the persons punished and the criminal justice system. Every adult, from an older brother to a skid-row wino who will buy a case of beer for some teenagers for the price of a bottle of Ripple, is a potential point of leakage between permitted and forbidden alcohol use; in the absence of any restriction on the quantity of alcohol any one person may purchase, one adult is able to supply an unlimited number of minors.

At a minimum, any attempt to upgrade enforcement of those laws would need to be attended by a drumroll of publicity to provide a temporary dip in the offense rate, thereby allowing a limited amount of actual punishment to create an adequate level of punishment-per-offense and thus of deterrent risk. But that dip in offense rates would be maintained over time only if the actual cases and punishments were forthcoming. The investigative problems are profound; no one wants undercover agents prowling around schoolyards. It is easier to catch kids drinking than to catch adults giving them liquor, but the problem is how to punish them enough to deter them without interfering with their education and personal development. Some jurisdictions have begun to take action against the driving privileges of underage drinkers; underage drinkers might also be good candidates for "community service" punitive labor.

It is worth repeating that one cause of the teenage drinking problem is the pricing structure created by taxation: too low overall, and dramatically too low for beer and wine coolers, which appear to be the "gateway" alcohol products. Adolescent demand for alcohol is probably more sensitive to price than demand by adults, for two reasons: they have less money, and they are less likely already to be seriously committed to drinking. Raising prices by raising taxes, particularly on the gateway products, would simplify the enforcement problem by reducing the background frequency of sales to minors. That would reduce the level of enforcement required to achieve any given reduction in underage drinking, saving both enforcement resources and the inevitable damage done by apprehension, adjudication, and punishment to minors and those who supply their alcohol.

Treatment

By the standards accepted by researchers and treatment providers, an estimated 17.7 million Americans have drinking problems. How many of these "problem drinkers" agree that they have a problem, and what proportion of those want help in dealing with it, are open questions. Denial is one of the well-known stigmata of addiction, but it does not follow that anyone who denies that he has a drinking problem actually has one. In any population, 10 percent will fall in the top decile of drinkers, and the top decile is likely to drink several times as much as the median. According to the heuristic definition of an alcoholic as "anyone who drinks more than twice as much as I do," the rest of the population is likely to regard the top decile as having a drinking problem.

These quibbles aside, casual observation is sufficient to convince anyone that millions of Americans could benefit from cutting down on their drinking. About eight hundred thousand of them are believed to be reasonably frequent attenders of Alcoholics Anonymous meetings. (For obvious reasons, there are no membership lists.) An unknown, but certainly large, additional number have passed through AA on their way to sobriety but are no longer regular meeting-goers. In addition, 214,000 persons per year pass through residential alcohol treatment programs, and 1.2 million undergo some kind of formal outpatient therapy, at a total cost of $1.71 billion, about half of which comes from public coffers.[15] This excludes those who seek help with their drinking problems from providers of psychological or psychiatric care, clinical social workers, acupuncturists, and so on; it also overlooks the colossal costs of treating alcohol-related disease.[16]

All of the familiar problems in understanding the value of drug treatment programs arise here: some people get better in treatment, some get better without treatment, some do not get better at all, and it's hard to tell why.[17] The private treatment industry is under siege from health insurers and the employers who pay their premiums, many of whom are tightening up on reimbursements. This saves some money and deprives some people of treatment that would have helped them, but no one really knows how much of either, or whether an additional dollar spent on publicly funded alcohol treatment would be a good investment compared with some other way to spend the same dollar.

ALCOHOL PROBLEMS AND THEIR CONTEXTS

Drinking creates different problems in different contexts. Some of those contexts involve organizations and institutions, such as work-places, that have their own alcohol policies, explicitly or implicitly. These private policies may in the aggregate be as important in shaping the alcohol problem as the public policies that influence the conditions under which alcohol is available.

Alcohol as an Individual Problem

Although the damage drinkers do to others deserves serious attention in formulating policy, we should not forget that most of the heaviest losers from drinking are drinkers. Some of this loss is merely the luck of the draw: the person for whom the difference between her normal reaction time and her reaction time after a glass of wine turns a near-miss in crossing the street into a pedestrian fatality or the moderate drinker in whom alcohol happens to trigger throat cancer are simply unlucky. Even with perfect awareness of the risks, these people might reasonably choose not to abstain, in view of the benefits they get from drinking; there are other goals in life besides maximizing one's life expectancy.

But much of the loss to drinkers from drinking is traceable to one or another problem in self-management: either poor management of drinking behavior as a result of ignorance of risk, impulsiveness, temporal myopia, or compulsion and physiological addiction, or poor management of other kinds of behavior as a result of alcohol-induced loss of judgment, coordination, or self-command. Thinking of alcohol abuse in terms of alcoholism, and of alcoholism as a disease, whatever its persuasiveness as a description of reality or its usefulness to those fighting the bottle,[18] may make it harder to persuade drinkers who are not yet problem drinkers to do the work required to stay out of trouble. Good self-management in regard to alcohol extends beyond mere knowledge of the risks of drinking to vigilance about one's own drinking behavior: a combination of monitoring

(How many drinks have I had this week? When was I last drunk? Have the quantities been growing and the intervals shortening? How badly do I need a drink? Have I been needing a drink a lot lately?) and maintaining personal rules, including knowing and respecting one's limit, maxims, such as "Never drink alone" and "Never drink in the morning," and taboos on mixing drinking with other dangerous activities such as driving, boating, and taking other drugs.[19]

Of course, all of these personal rules are more difficult to maintain under the influence of alcohol. That observation alone, without any elaborate theory about a disease called alcoholism whose victims are powerless once they have had a drink, would justify the Alcoholics Anonymous maxim that those who have had drinking problems should never again take the first drink.* Nor is it only drinking that becomes more difficult to manage after a few drinks. It is far easier to remember not to drive while drunk when one is sober than to remember not to drive while drunk when one is drunk.

Part of the behavioral threat that alcohol creates has to do simply with its interference with higher mental functions, including those that contribute to foresight and conscience. Another part has to do with the social beliefs surrounding the drug. Alcohol offers a fine excuse, to oneself and others, for whatever is done under its influence. The widespread belief among Americans that alcohol some-

---

* It may well be true that some people who have been problem drinkers can return to social drinking; it would, indeed, be amazing if problem drinkers were so homogeneous that none of them could ever come to terms with the drug. Thus it is hard at first blush to understand the enormous to-do about a research report that some ex-alcoholics had safely resumed social drinking. See David Armar, J. Michael Polich, and Harriet Stambul, "Alcoholism and Treatment," prepared for the National Institute on Alcohol Abuse and Alcoholism (Santa Monica, Calif.: RAND Corporation, 1976). Though 76 percent of the experimental group had returned to some form of drinking 18 months after alcohol treatment, the researchers show that only 16 percent relapsed to "alcoholic" status. A followup study four years later, J. Michael Polich, David Armar, and Harriet Brailer, "The Cause of Alcoholism: Four Years After Treatment," prepared for National Institute on Alcohol Abuse and Alcoholism (Santa Monica, Calif.: RAND Corporation, 1980): vi, found that 18 percent of the original sample were "drinking without problems." The furious attacks on the researchers involved were hardly justified by whatever methodological errors they may have made, and partially reflect the near-religious fervor that frequently accompanies group self-help. See Chad D. Emrick and Donald W. Stilson, "The RAND Report: Some Comments,"*Journal of Studies on Alcohol* 38 (1 [1977]):152-193; Sheila Blume, "The Relative Effectiveness of Different Treatment Approaches and the Effectiveness of Treatment Versus no Treatment," *Journal of Studies on Alcohol* 36 (1975): 88-108; Press Release, National Council on Alcoholism, New York, 1 July 1976. But given the relative risks involved in either unnecessarily avoiding a drink one could have safely absorbed or falling badly off the wagon, and the difficulty of determining, except by catastrophic failure, whether any particular ex-drinker can maintain self-command after one or two pops, "Never drink again" would seem to be a prudent rule.

how unleashes aggression has some of the characteristics of a self-fulfilling prophecy; experimentally, the belief that one is drinking alcohol when one is not is found to create more aggressive behavior than does actually drinking alcohol when one believes otherwise.[20] It would be helpful to change these beliefs, but the problem with a self-fulfilling prophecy is that it will be fulfilled; drunken Americans are in fact more aggressive drunk than they would be when sober.

Drinking safely therefore requires that one plan while sober to control one's potentially undesirable drunken behavior. One way to do so is by so internalizing certain maxims that one will observe them even when sailing three sheets to the wind. Another is to limit one's ability to do damage once drunk, for example, by giving the car keys to a friend with instructions to use discretion in returning them.[21] On a social level, there might be substantial returns to creating safer environments in which to be drunk and encouraging people who want to drink to use them, or to making the general environment a less hazardous place to be while drunk.[22]

Even at their best, personal rules and safer drinking environments cannot eliminate all, or even most, of the behavioral risks of drinking. Alcohol use is probably inseparable from drunken seduction, drunken victimization, and drunken accidents. Beyond some very modest level, it is certainly inseparable from the risk of organic damage and disease. Those who drink, and those who offer drinks, ought to take those risks into account in deciding how often and how much.

Therein lies another problem with thinking about the alcohol problem primarily in terms of a disease called *alcoholism*. It encourages those who do not think of themselves as alcoholics to underestimate the health and behavioral risks they face when they drink. One of the most striking aspects of drinking practices throughout the Western world is the remarkable casualness with which people offer and accept what is after all a potentially addictive and frequently criminogenic neurotoxin. If the extent of alcohol's behavioral and other risks were better known, some of this casualness might be replaced by caution.

The current alcohol-control regime offers little assistance to those who have decided to quit. Backsliding is as close as the nearest bar or liquor store (in many states, the nearest supermarket), and these are rarely far away. Studies of soldiers who became heroin addicts in Vietnam suggest that those who returned to places where heroin was easily available tended to remain addicts, while those whose homes were far from the heroin markets tended to stay clean.[23] Every American with a drinking problem is in the condition of one of the Vietnam returnees going home to a heroin-infested neighborhood. Drink and drinking cues are all around him.

In effect, we currently treat alcoholism as a problem to be solved by alcoholics, alone or with the aid of professional treatment providers or self-help groups. The alcoholic-beverage industries are not expected to carry any of the burden. Aside from the requirement that they not sell to those already inebriated, bartenders and package-store clerks have no responsibility for preventing alcohol abuse even by customers known to them as abusers. In the struggle within a recovering problem drinker between the drunkard and the sober person, the liquor merchants are allowed to side with the drunkard.

There have been societies whose institutions supported the practice of binding oneself by a vow to do or refrain from something. Vows are still nominally a part of our religious life, but neither our laws nor the rest of our social practices will enforce them. Though vows can be dangerous—Classical literature and Germanic myth are full of examples of the disastrous results of hastily taken vows—they also can be valuable aids to self-mastery.[24] Perhaps someone who wants to quit drinking for good, but is concerned about being able to maintain that resolution, ought to be able to register a decision not to drink and have it enforced by the sellers of alcoholic beverages. If such an opportunity existed, hundreds of thousands, even millions, of Americans might avail themselves of it. But it is hard to see how such a system could be administered—how sellers could be expected to identify those who had sworn off the bottle—without a system of personal licensure for alcohol use.

Alcohol as a Family Problem

Much of the burden of drinking falls on the families of drinkers. Little can be done about the large portion of that burden that is economic—in the form of health-care costs, reduced earnings, and the financial costs of accidents—without changing the broader context of social attitudes and conditions surrounding alcohol use. But some forms of family risk are, or might be, the subjects of specific interventions: fetal damage, neglectful parenting, domestic assault, and the sexual victimization of children.

Reducing the fetal damage done by alcohol poses a variety of conceptual and practical problems: problems that advocates of the legalization of any other drug ought to ponder. That very heavy drinking by a pregnant woman can profoundly damage her child is well established;

Fetal Alcohol Syndrome consists of a clearly distinguishable set of symptoms.[25] More recently, physicians have begun to understand the less-dramatic damage that results from less-intensive alcohol use during pregnancy. That damage, because it is less dramatic, is harder to observe in any individual case, but it emerges in statistical studies of large numbers of newborns.[26] Given that knowledge, what can be done to reduce the damage?

An obvious first step would be to get the word out to pregnant women, not only through communications in the media and at places where alcohol is sold but also by way of physicians and other deliverers of prenatal care and advice. It cannot be assumed that all expectant mothers know, or believe, that otherwise moderate drinking habits may constitute a substantial fetal risk; someone who reads newspapers rather than research journals is far more likely to know about the dangers of cocaine than about those of alcohol.

Of the pregnant women who currently drink and who become aware that they should stop for the baby's sake, most presumably will. Of the rest, some will either not believe the warnings or will decide that the other inconveniences of pregnancy are bad enough without adding to them nine months on the wagon, and others will find that they are unable to stop because of physical addiction to alcohol (fortunately rare in women in their prime child-bearing years) or because of an alcohol habit short of physical dependency. What, if anything, is to be done for and about these women and their children?

Those whose alcohol use is out of control but who are not physically dependent and who want to quit, at least during their pregnancy, would seem to need only an alcohol-free environment. But such an environment is hard to construct in a world where alcohol is an integral part of the social surround. Certainly no woman in a city or town is far from her next drink. One would need a closed, or at least isolated, residential setting. Financing such settings, and managing the resulting dislocation from ordinary family and occupational life, would take some doing. For women whose alcohol problem amounts to an addiction and who require medical supervision during their withdrawal, the problem is worse.

Finally, there are the women who choose to keep drinking. Should they be coerced, as cocaine-using women increasingly are coerced, with threats of prosecution or of presumptive findings of unfitness to raise their babies once born? Should it be a crime for them to drink, or to drink more than some specified amount? Should a bartender, or package-goods clerk, be responsible for enforcing such a law?[27] If so, how are they to know she is pregnant? In the case of cocaine, the drug's illegal status means that its use is banned regardless of gender or fertility. In the case of alcohol, any coercive measures would in effect mean that pregnant women lose some of the rights everyone else has. The general problem of the rights and responsibilities of pregnancy extends far beyond drinking. But it is worth considering that, in many of the subcultures that constitute the American social scene, the loss of one's right to drink would constitute a mild but perceptible social disability rather than merely the deprivation of a pleasure. There is a need to go beyond the designated driver in making nondrinking socially acceptable.

Given what appears to be the great importance of the prenatal environment to health, it seems to me neither irrational nor unjust that pregnancy carry with it both a special claim on social resources and special obligations, without prejudice to women's ability to participate on equal terms in economic and political life. The resonances between the arguments about these matters and the struggles over contraception, abortion, and gender discrimination in the workplace inevitably give any attempt to delineate special privileges and responsibilities for pregnant women an ideological edge. The fact that the world is not neatly divisible into harmful and innocuous activities further complicates the problem; surely pregnant women should not be required to spend nine months doing exactly what the latest research suggests would be ideal for the health of the child. In the end, however, the case for services and the case for coercion are linked; if the entire society has a responsibility to its future citizens that it ought to spend resources—obtained by coercive taxation—to fulfill, surely the mothers of these future citizens also have responsibilities that they can, at least in the extreme, be required as well as exhorted to meet. That the willingness to coerce increases and the willingness to provide services decreases as one moves across the political spectrum from left to right does no credit to the intellectual consistency of either side.*

More or less the same logic applies to infants and children. Their welfare is a social responsibility of great importance, assigned primarily to parents, who can be held accountable for failure to live up to minimal standards. Alcohol use can interfere with the ability and willingness to carry out that responsibility. As in the prenatal

---

* The issue of childhood immunizations, where there are disagreements both about the extent of public funding and about the extent to which the choice about immunization should be made publicly rather than within the family, has a similar logical structure, though it has less political resonance.

situation, the public can intervene both by providing resources to make it more feasible for parents to serve their children's needs and by coercive measures including the removal of children from the care of parents who do not live up to their responsibilities.

The ability of child protective services and family courts to enforce that responsibility is limited both by respect for the family unit and by the lack of adequate alternatives. It is a badly abused child indeed whose lot is improved by the foster care or institutional placements available in most states, and only a high probability that the child will benefit could justify depriving its parents of their rights as natural guardians.

But that threshold is clearly crossed when the child is repeatedly assaulted or sexually abused, and those who deal with such matters all believe that alcohol plays a pervasive role in generating such abuse. Under current laws, the agencies involved have no authority to interfere with the drinking practices of adults as a way of protecting children. That seems unfortunate; if you were a family court judge, would you not want to be able to say to a battering parent, "Turn in your drinking license or lose the child"?

Battered women, like battered children, are frequently the victims of someone else's alcohol use. Also like battered children, they are often dependent, not only psychologically but economically, on their victimizers. They, too, are inadequately served by a process that can address the aftermath of drunkenness but not the drinking itself. If the routine sentence for a first-offense drunken domestic assault were loss of drinking privileges, the notorious unwillingness of the victims to press charges might change.

Alcohol as a Crime Problem

Roughly 40 percent of those now in prison were drinking at the time of their offense; about half of them were only drinking, and the other half were mixing alcohol with one or more other drugs. The rates are a little higher for violent crimes.[28] If drinking leads to stupid crimes and therefore to being caught, these figures may overestimate the role of alcohol in crimes committed against non-intimates. On the other hand, domestic assault and the sexual abuse of children, both alcohol-related crimes, are notoriously underreported and underpunished.

Those disgusted with the use of crime as a symbolic issue in politics and a cover for race-baiting sometimes downplay its importance as a genuine national problem. But it is fact, not campaign rhetoric, that reported rates of violent crime have more than tripled over the past thirty years and the United States has the highest homicide rate among the industrial democracies.[29] While the actual losses from completed crimes in terms of death, injury, and property loss are considerably smaller than the losses from, for example, automobile accidents, they nonetheless amount to an economic value in the tens of billions of dollars annually.[30]

Moreover, it is probable that these victimization losses compose the smaller part of the total social cost of unsophisticated crime. The greater part consists of the direct and indirect costs of crime avoidance, ranging from buying burglar alarms, through staying out of the park after sunset, to moving to the suburbs. Not only do those avoiding crime absorb costs themselves, they also impose them on others. Everyone who stays indoors makes it that much less pleasant and more dangerous for those who still go out; everyone who moves out makes things worse for the neighbors left behind; the crime-driven movement of economic activity out of the central cities reduces job opportunities for those who live there.[31] Less measurably but not necessarily less importantly, the ubiquity of grillworks and shutters and blaring automobile burglar alarms dramatizes and reinforces a fear of victimization that only a population of saints could avoid converting to some extent into a hatred of the victimizers. There is no reason to think that the population of the United States has a lower rate of saintliness than that of other industrialized countries, but the fear of victimization makes a dangerous, even explosive, mixture with underlying tensions along lines of race and social class. For young black men, the experience of being visibly feared by the people they pass on the street is pervasive and psychologically devastating.[32]

All in all, then, if alcohol contributes even 20 percent to the problem of street crime, the control of alcohol-related crime ought to be a major consideration in framing alcohol policy. Here again, the policy of virtually unrestricted availability creates difficulties.

It is a commonplace that some people will do things while drunk that they would never do sober. Insofar as drunken offenses are uncharacteristic—literally, not reflective of character—they partake of the nature of misfortunes, and it is only natural that they should receive less punishment than offenses committed sober. As a matter of law in most states, diminished capacity resulting from voluntary intoxication cannot be offered as a defense or an extenuation, but practice is otherwise.

With respect to reckless driving, we have chosen to reverse this practice, and more than reverse it: the presumption that alcohol leads even otherwise careful drivers to drive recklessly has led us to make drunken driving a crime, even if no actual recklessness is shown. Merely getting behind the wheel while under the influence is taken to reflect a culpable indifference to the safety of others.

But as long as drunkenness itself is not considered culpable—or at least as imposing special responsibilities to take precautions concerning time, place, and circumstance to minimize the risks that one's drunken behavior might pose to others—we must expect our police, prosecutors, and judges, reflecting actual social attitudes rather than statutes, to be less severe with occasional drunken misbehavior than with the same offenses committed sober. That means that drunken assault will continue to have fewer legal consequences than sober assault, thus reinforcing the tendency alcohol has (apparently more as a matter of psychology than of neurophysiology) to release aggression. That being so, those in charge of gatherings where fights are likely to erupt, such as football games, will have to consider whether to restrict the availability of alcohol in order to cut down on the violence. Holding them financially responsible would promote such consideration.

The repeat drunken offender—barroom brawler, drunken domestic assailant, tipsy vandal—poses a different problem. For him (rarely her) the crime is characteristic, even if it is all drunken crime, because the drinking is characteristic. In such cases drunkenness ought to be considered an aggravation of the underlying offense. This would require that prosecutors and judges be able to identify the repeat drunken offender, which in turn would require some form of alcohol testing on arrest.[33]

Part of the sentence for any crime committed under the influence ought to be a period of mandatory abstinence. Outside the world of the small town, in which alcohol sellers and police alike can be expected to know who is and who is not under orders not to drink, such an order will remain largely an empty gesture in the absence of either a personal license that could be revoked or a chemical test for past alcohol use along the lines of urine testing for some of the illicit drugs. (This is a difficult problem technically because alcohol metabolizes primarily to carbon dioxide and water, rather than leaving characteristic metabolites such as ecgonine or the cannabinoids.) However, an abstinence order would at least make the drunken offender vulnerable to additional punishment for subsequent incidents of crime or disorderly behavior. In the case of drinkers with particularly extensive records of serious crime under the influence, there might even be justification for requiring them to take a drug that will cause extreme discomfort if mixed with alcohol. These drugs, of which the best known is disulfiram (Antabuse), are out of clinical favor,[34] but keeping those who commit crimes when they drink from continuing to drink is not entirely a clinical problem.

Some judges routinely require drunken offenders to attend meetings of Alcoholics Anonymous and to come back to court with signed meeting attendance cards, which some meeting clerks are willing to provide.[35]

I confess to a strong prejudice against ordering treatment of any kind as part of a criminal proceeding, partly because I would like to keep the idea of therapy distinct from that of punishment, partly because I would prefer the courts to focus on changes in behavior, such as abstinence, rather than on specific mechanisms for achieving those changes. But someone with a demonstrated inability to behave responsibly may not be the best judge of how to improve. One judge with considerable experience with drunken offenders says, "I tell them to come back in thirty days with thirty signed meeting cards, and they say, 'All right, I'll go to the damned meetings but it's only because you tell me to and I'm not going to pay any attention.' And then they come back thirty days later and they're sober and they're telling their friends to join." If that is true of even 10 percent of offenders, then the disadvantage of forcing the other 90 percent to accept some treatment they do not want may well be overwhelmed by the benefit of helping the minority, and thus the people who would otherwise have been their victims. This is an area in which a small amount of experience is worth a great deal of theory.

While drunken crime is a serious problem, drunken disorderly conduct is not to be ignored. Over the past decade, students of crime have begun to appreciate how much disorder in all its forms contributes to the creation of social settings in which serious victimization is likely to occur and adds to the fear of crime and thus to individually and socially costly crime-avoidance behavior.[36] Disorderly conduct— late-night noise, passing out on doorsteps, abusive language directed at passersby—is also unpleasant even when it does not lead to crime or even provoke fear. In the face of the flood of serious crimes, urban police and courts have no time to deal with such relative trivia: when you're up to your ass in alligators, draining the swamp is not your first priority. Even if officials tried to take disorder seriously, the virtual vacuum in our corrections system between no punishment at all and incarceration would leave them without plausible sentencing options for rowdy kids; if judges had an unlimited supply of sentences to two weekend days picking up trash in the park, they might be able to reduce the volume of a blight less spectacular, but far more common, than serious crime. Perhaps, by providing an early and only moderately painful demonstration that breaking the rules has costs, they might even manage to nip some developing criminal careers in the bud.

Alcohol as a Safety Problem

Crudely speaking, alcohol appears to be responsible for over half of all serious accidents (including accidental fires) or a total of about 47,500 deaths, and upwards of $20 billion in property damage per year to which must be added the health-care costs, pain and suffering, and residual injuries from nonfatal accidents.[37] This is a substantial cost that alcohol imposes on drinkers and that they in turn impose on the rest of us.* The biggest single category of accidents, and the one that has been diminishing the most gradually over the past two decades, is automobile crashes. In 1987 drunken drivers killed 9570 of themselves, 5870 other drivers and passengers, and 1010 pedestrians, accounting for about one-third of all automotive fatalities.[38]

There are five ways to reduce the costs of drunken accidents, other than by diminishing the frequency of drinking and drunkenness through generalized alcohol policies. First, we can redesign equipment and operating circumstances to prevent accidents, even in the face of continued carelessness, and to reduce the severity of the consequences or the accidents that happen anyway: guardrails and airbags will reduce the number of drunken-driving deaths, and flame-retardant fabrics the number killed in fires started by inebriates falling asleep holding lighted cigarettes. Second, we can deter drunken recklessness by punishing those responsible for accidents, for example by surcharges on insurance premiums. Third, we can punish drunkenness itself in situations where it is likely to lead to accidents. Fourth, we can identify people with histories of problem

* When a drug is as widely used as alcohol is, determining how much of any undesirable behavior it causes becomes a little tricky; one has to make allowances for the natural background level. The key concept here is *relative risk*: how much more likely is someone to have an accident after drinking? Mathematically, relative risk is the ratio of the accident rate with the risky conditions to the rate without it. This assumes that drinking and nondrinking drivers are otherwise similar; if not—if, say drinking drivers were younger and younger drivers more likely to crash drunk or sober—the calculation of relative risk must be adjusted accordingly.

drinking or histories of drunken dangerous activity and bar them from operating in dangerous situations at all. Finally, we can test operators for sobriety before allowing them to begin activity on any given occasion.

Much of the credit for the truly astounding society-wide reduction in rates of accidental deaths over the past four decades—especially of nonhighway deaths—must go to redesign efforts.[39] The federal safety-regulation agencies and the tort liability system have been the targets of considerable criticism, much of it justified, and considerable ridicule, much of it earned.[40] Safety has come at considerable, sometimes excessive, cost, in money and inconvenience. But the net result of regulations, damage awards, and increased safety-consciousness in organizations and individuals has been to make the United States a much safer place in general, and for the inebriated in particular.

But such efforts, like all efforts, face a law of diminishing returns, and some risks are simply not reducible in any practical way; no one proposes to equip pedestrians with airbags. At any given level of designed-in safety, the casualty rate is a function of the frequency of careless or reckless behavior, which in turn depends in part on the frequency of intoxicated operation. The more designers have to take drunken clumsiness and stupidity into account as they try to design safety into the environment, the greater the cost and inconvenience their safety measures will create.

Drunken Driving

The spectacular reductions already achieved in workplace and household accident rates leave collisions between motor vehicles and one another, stationary objects, and pedestrians as the largest target for risk-reduction efforts. Drivers, unlike bathtub users or swimmers, are licensed by the state, and their behavior is subject to routine surveillance by the police. Thus public policy toward reducing alcohol-related accidents is largely about drunken driving, or as it is legally called, driving while intoxicated (DWI) or driving under the influence (DUI). Drunken driving poses a number of questions: how to define it, how to detect it, how to prove it, how to punish it.

Alcohol is not the whole of the problem of intoxicated driving; a wide variety of prescription medications and illicit substances can also slow reaction time, impair eye-hand coordination, and cloud judgment. Even at their current rates of consumption, low compared to alcohol, the illicit drugs seem to contribute noticeably to the traffic accident problem, and reducing that contribution has been the subject of a recent burst of research, policy planning, and enforcement activity.[41] How dangerous driving under the influence of any given amount of any given drug actually depends on more than the drug's effects on coordination. There is some evidence that marijuana, for example, tends to lead to slower speeds as well as to less skillful driving. This might mean that stoned driving would lead to many fender-benders and relatively few fatalities, but marijuana looms large in the scattered testing data from drivers in fatal crashes.[42] The control of drugged driving involves a somewhat different set of technical issues from the control of drunken driving because the technologies of detection are different, but the conceptual issues are closely related. Here again, the experience of alcohol provides a warning to those among the advocates of legalizing currently prohibited drugs who are willing to be warned, since an increase in the total consumption of any drug must be expected to lead to an increase in the frequency of driving under its influence.

As recently as fifteen years ago, all of the more-or-less technical problems of drunk-driving control were overwhelmed by a moral one: although driving under the influence was proscribed, it was not very strongly disapproved of, being viewed more as a folly than as a crime. It has taken a vigorous social movement, symbolized and organized by the Mothers Against Drunk Driving (MADD), to overcome some of the ambivalence of legislators, police, prosecutors, judges, and juries in holding otherwise well-behaved citizens criminally liable for having a few drinks and then getting behind the wheel. The normalization of alcohol use itself constituted a substantial part of the reason for that ambivalence. Jurors who have been drunk themselves, have themselves done things under the influence that they would not have done sober, have themselves almost certainly driven after the proverbial "two beers" or even when over the legal limit, are far more likely to think, "There, but for the grace of God..." of a drunk-driving defendant than of a robbery defendant. This encourages jurors to elevate in their minds the occasional fallibility of the breath alcohol test (it may be fooled, for example, by a recent application of an alcohol-based mouthwash) into reasonable doubt that the defendant was in fact intoxicated. Nor is the law enforcement culture an abstemious one; while police assigned to traffic enforcement have come to take drunken driving very seriously indeed, some of their colleagues still regard it as a peccadillo.

The higher average social status of drunken-driving defendants makes them more difficult to process at every stage from arrest through final punishment than typical defendants in other criminal cases: they are more apt than other defendants to have short, or no, criminal histories, to be able to afford private defense counsel, to be able to make bail and thus not have to wait in jail if they demand a trial, to make impressive and believable witnesses, and to share social networks with high police officials, prosecutors, and judges.[43]

Part of the significance of the "designated driver" campaign of recent years—encouraging social groups to decide in advance who is to remain sober to drive home—has been to reduce the costs of not driving drunk, for the designated drivers and for those who no longer need to stagger around at the end of the party begging for a ride home. That movement has also helped overcome the ambivalence about the enforcement of drunken-driving laws. Every person with a designated-driver button and every bar offering free soft drinks to designated drivers helps establish that those who do choose to drive drunk had other choices available.*

With decreasing ambivalence has come a wave of stricter laws, harsher statutory punishments, more vigorous police work, and somewhat greater willingness on the part of judges, jurors, and registry officials to put those punishments into effect. Compared with conditions fifteen years ago, this must be regarded as on balance a move in the right direction. But no more in this area than in other areas of drug abuse control should we expect that an undifferentiated toughness will prove to be the most cost-effective, or the most just, policy.

Defining Drunken Driving

The first issue in drunken-driving policy is what should constitute drunken driving. Alcohol induces a continuum of states from stone-cold sober to passed out on the floor. For any given person under any given set of circumstances (health, sleep status, food content of the stomach, emotional state, setting) a larger dose of alcohol, short of unconsciousness, is likely to generate more risk behind the wheel, but persons and circumstances vary. The choices in defining drunken-driving involve first whether to base the definition on alcohol content alone or to attempt to measure the degree of impairment in driving

---

* In addition, the role of designated driver helps legitimize the otherwise questionable status of a nondrinker among drinkers.

capacity, and then how much alcohol or incapacity to allow before considering the driver under the influence.

Fortunately, the alcohol in the bloodstream is a good measure of the alcohol in the brain, and blood alcohol content (BAC) can be measured cheaply and accurately by analyzing either the blood itself or, less reliably, the breath. Additionally or alternatively, one can attempt to measure intoxication with such simple challenges as walking a straight line or reciting the alphabet backward, or with various mechanical tests. In principle, multiple tests (ideally, a cheap and sensitive screen followed by a highly specific confirmation) should allow a finer discrimination, and a smaller number of false positive and false negative results: persons found to be intoxicated who were in fact able to drive safely and persons found not to be intoxicated who were in fact too drunk to drive. In practice, though, multiplying the number of tests is likely to multiply the opportunities for error, for challenges, and for appeals. It may also allow social discrimination dressed as police, prosecutorial, or judicial discretion to creep even more deeply into a process from which it can never be excluded entirely.

There are three reasons to favor chemical over performance testing. It is mechanically simpler for the person administering the test and thus less liable to errors of operation or subjectivity of judgment. It is, in the case of blood testing, repeatable, since the blood can be stored. Finally, and perhaps most important, it allows the driver to determine fairly accurately in advance whether getting behind the wheel is likely to constitute a crime, simply by calculating the amount of alcohol consumed in proportion to body weight. This reduces the risk that the feeling of "I can handle it" so characteristic of drunkenness will overrule better judgment. In recent years, states have been moving toward what are called "per se" rules, under which a given blood alcohol content itself, without any independent showing of incapacity, constitutes the crime of driving while intoxicated. Depriving some people with high tolerances for alcohol of the right to do legally what they may well be able to do safely does not seem an excessive price to pay for the advantages of such a rule.

This leaves the problem of how much alcohol ought to constitute "under the influence." By comparing the blood alcohol content of a random sample of drivers with that of a sample of the drivers responsible for fatal accidents, one can compute the relative risk of driving after various amounts of drinking. The results are dramatic: not the straight line that they would be if each additional drink added the same additional risk, but a parabola, suggesting that the risks rise faster than the alcohol level. At 0.05 percent blood alcohol by weight, the relative risk is about 1.5: that is to say, it is about as dangerous to drive ten miles at that level (corresponding to three quick drinks for a person weighting 150 pounds) as to drive fifteen miles cold sober. By 0.10 percent BAC, the level that defines legal intoxication in most states, the relative risk is about two. That sounds frightening; someone at that level is twice as dangerous a driver, on average, as a sober person. But the enormous volume of highway carnage reflects the enormous volume of driving more than it does any inherent riskiness of the activity; in fact, the risk of a fatal accident during any one trip is almost vanishingly small—about four fatalities for every hundred million vehicle miles, or less than one chance in two million of having a fatal crash on a ten-mile drive[44]—and doubling that risk leaves it still quite small. Above 0.10 percent, the danger curve rises steeply: at 0.15 percent, the relative risk is about 15; at 0.30 percent, it is somewhere between 50 and 150.[45] That is, someone who has had nine drinks is about ten times as likely to kill himself or someone else as someone who has had three, and someone who has had eighteen drinks is about fifty times as dangerous as someone who has had six.

While it is certainly true that some people are quite vulnerable to the effects of drinking and should not be on the road after even one drink, the absolute rule "Don't drink and drive" is hard to support statistically. The benefits of stricter standards ought to be weighed against their cost, not only to those punished but to the rest of us who rely on the courts to convict and punish wrongdoers and settle our civil disputes. Drunken-driving cases already constitute a financial mainstay of the private defense bar, because so many of the defendants can afford to pay; this makes them a major contributor to the crowding of (particularly urban) court calendars and thus to the delay, error, and injustice, with which they accomplish their mission. Changes in the law that create many additional cases without a corresponding gain in safety should not be made simply because making them makes us feel that we are doing something about drunken driving.

This argument does not by itself establish that higher legal tolerances for alcohol in drivers would be desirable. It is not even clear that the "zero tolerance" rule recently enacted in Sweden is a mistake; simplicity is always a virtue in a law, and it may turn out in practice that fewer people violate a standard that, though stricter and thus more inconvenient to follow, is simpler and therefore less subject to inadvertent violation. Creating a strong taboo against drinking and driving may be valuable even if most of the damage is done by the minority who drive after drinking heavily.

Punishing Drunken Driving

However, since the pattern of relative risks does suggest that drunken driving, like speeding, is in its nature very much a quantitative offense, the penalties imposed, even if not the legal definition of the offense, should rise, and rise rapidly, with the quantity involved.

As with any crime, the punishment also ought to fit the record of the offender. Drunken driving, like burglary, has its habitual offenders, who make up a share of the total problem far out of proportion to their numbers. Some of them are chronic alcohol abusers, for whom treatment referral is an essential supplement to any punishment. Others, even if they get drunk relatively seldom, are mean drunks, and veterans of many alcohol-related crimes, including drunken assaults. In the hands of these habitual alcoholic assailants, an automobile is merely a very heavy weapon, and one unlikely to lead to a felony prosecution unless the victim dies. (Hit-and-run drivers are probably overrepresented in this group.) There are few categories of offenders better worth the expense of a prison cell. The difficulty is in assembling a series of incidents that seem on the surface to be only tangentially related into a pattern of persistent bad behavior.

It would be desirable, then, for prosecutors and judges handling a drunken-driving case to examine the entire criminal history, not merely the record of traffic offenses, in considering a disposition, and similarly for prosecutors and judges handling assaults to pay attention to records of traffic offenses such as DWI and leaving the scene (hit and run). Unfortunately, the rather primitive condition of many state criminal-history systems, added to the pressure for quick dispositions in overcrowded first-level criminal courts, makes this ideal infeasible in many jurisdictions.

The issues of treatment referral and compulsory treatment are much the same in drunken-driving cases as in other cases of alcohol-induced crime. But the superior affluence of many drunken-driving defendants has created a small industry of private, virtually unregulated, "educational" and "treatment" programs to which judges refer defendants as part of their sentence or as a condition of diversion: that is, as part of a punishment-without-trial deal in which the defendant avoids a conviction. In effect, these programs do part of the job of a probation department—administering a mild inconvenience to offenders not worth incarcerating—and pocket what would otherwise be a fine. (A related industry handles middle-class arrestees for possession of illicit drugs.) Despite the ubiquity of these programs there is a lack of careful evaluations of them; the existing studies do not suggest that they are effective.[46] While there might be some benefit in forcing convicted drunk drivers, many of whom have problems controlling their drinking, to spend some time at AA meetings with people trying to get well, compelling them to spend a few hours with one another and a paid lecturer seems less likely to do any good. They could probably do as much useful thinking about the advisability of taking a cab home next time while performing unpaid labor in a "community service" program (to whose financial support they might also be required to contribute by way of a fine) as they can in a formal class.

Oddly, there seems to be no state in which confiscation of the vehicle involved is a routine part of the penalty for drunken driving. Such a penalty might improve compliance with the suspension of driving privileges that does normally accompany a conviction, as well as making a nice parallel with the confiscation of cars used to buy illicit drugs.

License suspension seems straightforward enough: it is useful both in deterring drunken driving among the many and directly preventing it by incapacitating the convicted few. Unfortunately, while a revoked license makes it impossible to obtain insurance or to rent a car, it does not make it physically impossible to drive, and there is evidence that suspensions are imperfectly complied with (though of course even imperfect compliance is much better than nothing).[47] Ensuring that all of those who might lend an offender a car know that he is no longer licensed, and a fortiori proving afterward that whoever actually did so actually knew, is no simple task.

In addition, the centrality of driving in American life makes the inconvenience, social disability, and economic loss imposed on a person who cannot drive substantial, though probably less than the defense lawyer will try to persuade the judge it is. Driving is not a necessity. There do exist car pools to work, public transportation, rides from friends or family members, taxis, bicycles, and even shoe leather; there are millions of Americans never convicted of anything who cannot afford to drive—in part because of insurance premiums inflated by the costs of drunken driving—or cannot drive by reason of disability, and their plight seems to leave the public unmoved. Here again, the fact that the persons involved tend to be nonpoor increases the sympathy felt for them by legislators, judges, and registry officials.*

* A concession to that sympathy less drastic than a complete restoration of driving privileges is a license restricted to daylight hours, or to such specific purposes as commuting to work or shopping for food.

Still, the case for very long suspensions for first-time offenders with relatively low blood-alcohol levels is hard to make even in the abstract; it is still harder to make and maintain as a practical matter in a specific case, even when the behavior involved is more serious and more habitual.

It is at this point that the lack of an alcohol user's license is most to be regretted. That license a judge could suspend, and keep suspended, without a qualm. If its loss could not entirely prevent drinking, it could at least prevent drinking in bars, which would be a good deterrent threat and would cut down on the number of occasions of being drunk away from home. A judge could return a drunken driver's driving license with a much clearer conscience if assured that his drinking license was suspended for a long, long time.

Detecting Drunken Driving

All this discussion of punishment presupposes that police have detected someone in the act of driving while drunk and have accumulated enough evidence to make out at least a prima facie case. The police cannot do so in more than a tiny proportion of the actual instances of drunken driving, simply because they can stop only a tiny proportion of drivers without engaging the entire police force and bringing the highways to a standstill.

Repeating the offense, driving with obvious incompetence or recklessness, and getting into accidents all will tend to increase the drunken driver's risk of eventually being caught, and of course frequent and very dangerous drunken drivers are most worth catching. But even these statistical sources of comfort must be qualified. Just because someone is too drunk to drive safely does not mean that he is incapable of taking steps to prevent being convicted of drunken driving. After an accident, if he and the machine are still capable of operation, he can simply drive home. Leaving the scene of an accident, even an accident in which someone else has been injured or killed, is a traffic violation, while driving under the influence is a crime. That anomaly could and should be fixed with a simple change in the law.

Even if the inebriated motorist is stopped by the police, the game is not over. Since taking a breath or blood sample has the legal character of a "search," the police cannot force the driver to submit to it without first obtaining a search warrant, which requires a process that takes longer than the alcohol stays in the blood. The alert drunk driver therefore refuses the test. In most states, this triggers a (theoretically) automatic license suspension, but it does not constitute evidence of intoxication for the purposes of trial. The jurors will be faced with a sober, respectable-looking citizen testifying to "two beers" and an officer's stereotyped testimony about alcohol on breath, glassy eyes, slurred speech, and so forth, and then asked whether they are sure beyond a reasonable doubt that the defendant was drunk. In effect, refusal of the breath test nullifies the advantages of a per se rule and forces the state to prove intoxication rather than alcohol content.

Some jurisdictions have begun routine videotaping of drivers, either at the roadside or in the police station. This is useful and relatively inexpensive, and may save trial time by persuading the defendant to take a quick plea offer. But since the jury will not consist of experts, and since other conditions, including the terror that an arrest can produce, can cause people to stutter and stumble, justice requires that chemical testing, including a blood test as a backup for the breath test, be available to every defendant who wants it. (Some jurisdictions, for obscure reasons, refuse to provide blood tests.)

Still, neither expert testimony by the police nor a videotape is a perfect substitute for the chemical testing that an experienced drunken driver is likely to know enough to refuse. One way to reduce the incidence of refusal would be to raise the ante, by making loss of the car as well as of the license part of the penalty. As a legal matter, this could be done through a civil forfeiture law parallel to the one controlling the seizure of vehicles used to transport drugs; this requires only "probable cause to believe" that the vehicle was so used, rather than the criminal standard of proof beyond reasonable doubt. (Of course, if forfeiture of the vehicle were also an automatic consequence of a conviction, there would still be no incentive to take the test for those certain that they were over the limit.) Another approach is possible with those already convicted of drunken driving or of leaving the scene: what in California criminal law is called a "search order."[48] This is a judicial order, handed down as part of a criminal sentence or diversion package, making the subject liable for a term of years to particular kinds of searches, relevant to the class of offense of which he has already been found guilty, without a warrant. A five-year search order on a convicted drunk driver, requiring him to submit to any future breath test if stopped behind the wheel, should be able to pass constitutional muster.

The need to improve the chances that a drunken driver will be caught, convicted, and punished in a way that provides protection from him and deterrence for others should not blind us to the problems faced by innocent drunken-driving suspects. The combination of ritual "due process" with inadequate resources and systemic class bias makes American courts bad places for the innocent poor. For someone who does not have the several hundreds of dollars routinely set as bail in drunken-driving cases, the prospect of weeks, even months, in incarceration awaiting trial for an offense for which conviction will not lead to jail may make pleading guilty the only reasonable course, and an overworked public defender or ill-paid court-appointed counsel will not be slow to point that out.

At a minimum, it ought to be possible to offer every person suspected of drunk driving a confirmatory blood test, including a sealed sample that the defendant can have retested independently. If the blood or breath test is below the legal cutoff but police plan to press charges anyway based on field observations, those tests ought to be videotaped. If the police plan to offer their expert testimony as to the driver's inebriated state, a nonpolice expert ought to be available to make his own independent observations, with an occasional sober "ringer" run through the system just to keep the experts on their toes. There is no shortage of guilty drunk-driving defendants; that only increases the obligation to ensure that the innocent ones do not suffer.

Alcohol as a Workplace Problem

Drinking is a problem in the workplace as well as on the highway. Once again, the drinking problem is only part, though the largest part, of a broader problem of impairment by drugs, and here again a discussion of alcohol-control measures is a reminder of the problems that accompany the widespread use of any intoxicant.

Measuring alcohol-related problems in the workplace is much harder than measuring them on the highway. Industrial accidents caused by intoxication can be identified relatively easily, but not those resulting from hangovers. Reduced productivity as a result of alcohol might conceivably be measured on an assembly line, but reduced productivity in the engineering department is another matter. The idea of measuring (as opposed to imagining) the proportion of obviously stupid business decisions to which alcohol is a contributing factor is laughable.

The difficulties involved have not prevented a number of valiant attempts to total up the cost to American businesses of the alcohol use of their employees.[49] These studies find that the bulk of the measurable damage done by all drugs is done by alcohol, and that the total is in the tens of billions of dollars.* Employers suffer not

---

* This tens-of-billions figure is sometimes cited as the cost of "drug use" in industry to support the argument for testing the urine of all employees to detect their use of illicit drugs.

only from reduced productivity and increased accident rates on the job, but from the health-care costs associated with heavy drinking: the cost of treatment for alcohol abuse and the far larger cost of treatment for alcohol-related diseases.

The role of alcohol in generating health-care costs,[50] combined with the rising share of employer-paid health-care premiums in the total cost of labor, has led many companies, particularly large ones, to establish company-wide health promotion, or "wellness," programs, and most of them pay considerable attention to excessive drinking.[51] In addition to spreading the word about the relationships between life-style and health risk, most company programs feature the opportunity for confidential referral to treatment, which may be prompted either by the employee's decision to seek help or his supervisor's observation that the employee has a problem. Many of the Employee Assistance Programs (EAPs) that are now dealing with workers who have tested positive in urine-screening programs for illicit drugs were first established primarily for employees with drinking problems, and problem drinking is twice as prevalent among EAP entrants as all other drug problems combined.[52]

Attempts to prevent employees from developing drinking problems, and to identify and assist those who do, leaves the question of what employers should do about drinking that is not an identifiable part of a "problem" pattern. While it is clear that the costs of alcohol treatment will come only from the chronic heavy drinkers, the other costs of alcohol use are likely to be spread over a much wider population. An accountant who has two glasses of wine with lunch may not be a "problem user" of alcohol, still less a clinical alcoholic, but her drinking may be costing her employer a fortune. The workplace drinking problem is not confined to problem drinking.

In a country where some two-thirds of all adults drink at least occasionally, keeping a workplace "alcohol-free" is a more complicated problem, conceptually as well as practically, than keeping it free of an illicit drug such as cocaine. No large employer is likely to try to tell its employees that they must, as a condition of hiring or of continued employment, never drink, or even that they must never become drunk, in their off-duty hours. Even workers who are subject to emergency summons, such as police and physicians, are not expected to remain cold sober twenty-four hours a day every day of the week. Even the pilots' rule—no alcohol at all within twenty-four hours of work—is far stricter than could be imposed on workers in general. Nor is it obvious that such a rule would lead to sufficient gains in safety or output to make up for the inconvenience to employees and the costs of enforcing compliance. Even for pilots, the pilots' rule is justifiable more as establishing a strong taboo and a bright line than for any likely degradation in performance from a single drink taken the night before a flight.

Rules about drinking immediately before starting or resuming work—specifically, at lunch or dinner breaks—pose a much trickier question, involving both the direct effect of such drinking on performance and the impact of the rules on workers who have drinking problems. Again, there is a trade-off between having an appropriately reasonable and flexible standard and having a bright line; whether one has had a drink at lunch is a matter of easily determined fact, while whether one has become drunk at lunch is a matter of opinion.

It would be fascinating to have a study of the after-lunch alcohol content of the American workforce, and of the variations in productivity, work quality, and safety that accompany variations in drinking short of actual drunkenness. Such a study would be expensive and technically difficult, which is one reason it has never been attempted. Another reason is that it would weaken the identification of the alcohol problem with "alcohol abuse and alcoholism" by paying attention to the costs of nonproblem drinking.

Whatever the rules are about drinking in proximity to work, companies need means of identifying those who violate those rules. There are, in principle, at least six independent sources of such identification for any drug: direct observation of forbidden drug taking, direct observation of the stigmata of intoxication, observation of substandard work by a supervisor or quality-assurance system, chemical intoxication testing, neurological or behavioral intoxication testing, and chemical testing to measure past drug use. Direct observation of drug taking is necessarily a sometime thing, and the unwillingness of many supervisors to confront personnel problems in general and employees' sensitive personal problems in particular, and the failure of companies to generate sufficient incentives for them to do so, tends to make the supervisors weak reeds for drug programs to lean on. Nor are most output-measurement systems adequate to detect variations in performance that may point to drug problems. That leaves the three forms of drug testing: chemical or neurological/behavioral testing for current intoxication, and chemical testing for drug use in the recent past.

Most company drug-testing programs now consist entirely of chemical drug-history testing of urine specimens. These do not detect current intoxication, but only recent use. Nor do they detect alcohol, because alcohol has no distinctive metabolites. The special characteristic, for good and ill, of such historical drug use testing is that it cuts a fairly large swath of time; instead of asking the narrow question, "Is this person under the influence now?" it asks the broader question, "Does this person sometimes use drugs?" Urine testing is a way of identifying possible problem drug users whose use may be influencing their work rather than only those who bring the problems to work with them.

As applied to most of the illicit drugs, urine testing is the only chemical option available; there are no proven breath-testing methods, and taking blood, though it may be justified after an accident, seems too intrusive a procedure for a routine screening. In the case of alcohol, there is the breath test, a fairly reliable though not perfect indicator of the alcohol content of the blood and thus of the degree of current impairment. Unlike a urine test, a breath test measures only drug use unambiguously relevant to work; it is cheap; its results are available at once and can be verified by blood testing; and it involves nothing more humiliating than blowing up a balloon. Yet no company, and no federal agency, routinely and randomly gives its employees (transportation workers aside) breath tests for alcohol. Good arguments can be made to support this pattern—resistance by the workers and their unions would probably be great—but it tears a large hole in the idea of a drug-free workplace. Managing a legal intoxicant is not as easy as some advocates of wholesale drug legalization would like it to be.[53]

The lack of a simple, reliable, universal impairment test is unfortunate. Such a test could be either a performance-based, behavioral test—think of a flight simulator or video game—looking for generalized substandard performance, or a neurological test looking for the specific signs of a nervous system impaired by intoxication. In the latter category, a device called the electronystagmograph, which measures the movements of the tiny muscles that direct the eyeballs, and which purportedly can detect patterns characteristic of particular drugs, has been under development for several years.[54]

Behavioral or performance testing has as advantages its obvious relevance to readiness to work and its ability to detect a wide range of the possible causes of sub-par performance; a simulator can detect the performance degradation resulting from a hangover or an emotional crisis, which a breath tester will miss. Against these are two disadvantages. First, one needs a baseline measurement for each employee against which to detect subnormal performance. Second, some drugs may interfere more with higher mental function than with eye-hand coordination. In relatively easy-to-simulate, safety-related jobs such as operating heavy machinery, performance testing has clear advantages over its alternatives. In other jobs, it could be a useful, relatively nonintrusive, and cheap screening device, to be backed up with chemical testing as appropriate.

CHANGING PERSUASION PROGRAMS

The current legal status of alcohol puts several limits on the capacity of any practicable set of public and private programs to reduce the damage it does. With the single exception of the rules about sales to minors—which are virtually unenforceable as long as adults have unlimited access to cheap drink—the regulations governing the sale of alcohol are so loose as to be scarcely worth the effort to violate them or enforce them. Ordering chronic problem drinkers to practice abstinence or moderation will remain ineffective as long as every bar and package store may lawfully provide them with the means to violate that order. Presumably, the path toward recovery could be smoothed with somewhat more money for professional assistance,[55] but individual and group self-help will remain the primary means of helping people with drinking problems.

The major opportunities within existing laws appear to be in the area of persuasion. Less-tolerant attitudes and more accurate beliefs might substantially reduce the extent of alcohol-related damage. If drinking, or at least excessive drinking, were as widely feared and disapproved of as cigarette smoking, let alone the use of illicit drugs, the alcohol problem would shrink dramatically, because both individual behavior and the limits of politically and organizationally feasible policies would change.

Efforts to persuade people to do less inappropriate or excessive drinking can take three forms: targeted communications in schools or other settings where the audience can be known in detail and messages tailored to fit; efforts aimed at changing the opinions and communications skills of authority figures such as parents, teachers, health-care providers, athletic coaches, and clergy, who in turn can reach various potential problem drinkers; and messages delivered through the mass media.

But changing or intensifying governmental or private anti-alcohol messages is only one approach to changing attitudes about drinking. It is also possible to reduce or restrict the volume of pro-alcohol messages conveyed in advertising and other marketing efforts. True, research on advertising has failed to establish links between commercial messages and attitudes toward classes of products (as opposed to individual brands), but it seems implausible that the sheer weight of pro-drinking propaganda has no aggregate effect. There are three questions to ask about restrictions on advertising: Do they constitute undesirable restraints on freedom of speech? Do they damage consumers by reducing the flow of information? Can they be designed to prevent evasion and circumvention through marketing efforts other than advertising?

The question of restrictions on speech and press freedoms has both legal and policy aspects. The Supreme Court affords "commercial speech" somewhat less-extensive First Amendment protection than noncommercial speech,[56] and the examples of the securities industry, whose advertising is rigidly restricted by the Securities and Exchange Commission,[57] and the pharmaceutical industry, which is under less restrictive but still pervasive regulation by the Food and Drug Administration,[58] suggest that the regulators of regulated industries can control marketing efforts as well as other business decisions. This reflects a reasonable policy judgment: that the freedom that protects political or artistic expression ought not to apply fully to commercial representations, particularly those characterized by imbalance in knowledge and potential discordance of interests between sellers and buyers. Insofar as the alcohol industries could conceal their product advertising under the cloak of political discourse—urging, for example, that their products not be severely taxed or restricted on the grounds that using them in moderation is healthy—they would necessarily remain untouched, but this need not completely cripple the project of reducing the volume of pro-drinking messages received by potential drinkers, especially teenagers.

The concern that controls on advertisers will interfere with the supply of competitive information to consumers is not insuperable. Under the current, largely unregulated system, price and availability information is carried almost entirely by retail advertisements rather than by brand advertisements. There seems little reason to interfere with this part of the information flow. The brands, by contrast, run advertisements that are largely content-free, consisting primarily of attempts to associate a particular brand with success, pleasure, and sexual attractiveness. It is hard to see what valuable information consumers would lose if such ads were forbidden.

Restricting brand advertising would, however, make it difficult to establish new brands in the market, particularly since package goods are notoriously an area in which consumers treat price as a proxy for quality.* Deprived by this peculiarity of their product of the chance to break into the market with low prices, developers of new alcohol products would find an advertising ban, or restriction to informational ads only, a substantial barrier to entry. This would raise the entry-inducing prices in alcoholic-beverage markets—the price, that is, at which new firms would find it worthwhile to enter the market—and thus allow owners of existing brands to raise their prices with less fear of competition.

If we cared only about preventing alcohol abuse, a little additional room for distillers, brewers, and vintners to price-gouge would not count as a disadvantage. The transfer of wealth from drinkers to workers and shareholders in the alcohol industry makes no difference to the drug-policy problem involved, as long as the higher profit margins do not generate additional marketing activity (which under a policy of advertising restriction could not happen). From the standpoint of drug-abuse control, higher profits are just like higher taxes; both are additional deterrents to use. It is not even quite self-evident that the net effect on the distribution of income would be perverse: whether or not it is depends on the relative economic positions of drinkers of brand-name alcoholic beverages on the one hand and of shareholders (largely the holders of life insurance policies and the beneficiaries of pension funds) and employees of alcohol-producing companies, on the other, and on how the increased producers' surplus would be shared between capital and labor.

Still, any public policy that creates economic rents by restricting competition does not deserve approval on that account alone, and one would much rather see the increased prices paid by consumers flow toward public treasuries than toward producers. But it seems unlikely that the sums at stake are significant enough to make the restriction of competition a major disadvantage of limitations on alcohol advertising.

The problem of evasion is more complicated. There are many ways of reminding consumers of brand identities other than buying newspaper, magazine, or billboard space or television or radio time. The sponsorship of entertainment or sports events, or of teams, is already a major form of alcohol-marketing expenditure: when the corporate name is also a brand name, the distinction between corporate-image advertising and product marketing blurs substantially. However, even

---

* Doing so may even be rational from the buyer's perspective for the substantial proportion of alcohol given as gifts or used in conspicuously generous hospitality. An expensive brand may be a better gift than a cheaper but better-tasting brand.

if such evasion took place on so massive a scale that the weight of brand messages did not diminish, their content would change in a desirable direction. After all, it is not the brand-identification part of the advertising message that ought to worry us; it is the attempt to glamorize drinking, to insinuate that drinking confers social status and sexual attractiveness on the drinker and is a part of conviviality and celebration. Those messages are far better conveyed by direct product advertising, or by the even more insidious practice of paying for "product placement" in the story lines of movies, than by the simple association of a brand or corporate name with a tournament or concert. Advertising that merely moves consumers around among brands is socially harmless.

Product advertisements could also be curtailed without being eliminated. For example, content could be expressly regulated, as by forbidding association with sports or messages designed to appeal to minors. The European Community is now negotiating the details of such a regime, but putting such a scheme into practice within the institutional environment of the United States would probably require the creation of a national alcohol regulatory agency to make and enforce the rules.

Advertisers also could be required to incorporate various kinds of warnings prominently into their messages. Unfortunately, the experience of tobacco is not encouraging on this score: the advocates of warnings have concentrated their political efforts on securing strong wording, while the advertisers have concentrated theirs on not requiring prominent display, with the result that the health warnings on cigarette advertisements are barely noticeable even to those who are looking for them. As with the other form of content regulation, the administrative problems are daunting, though not necessarily insuperable; by 1992, one-third of the surface area of a Canadian cigarette package will consist of health warnings.[59] Instead of detailed requirements about wordings, typefaces, and placements, it might make more sense to define a performance requirement in terms of retention by a sample panel of viewers, to be verified by the same research methods that advertising agencies routinely use in pre-testing their commercials. (The same procedures might be used to decide about whether a particular ad appeals to minors or violates some other control-based regulation.)

Finally, advertising efforts could be taxed to support government-produced negative advertising. ("Equal time" or "fairness" requirements amount to almost, but not quite, the same thing.) This would reduce the volume of advertising by increasing its cost and help finance the anti-alcohol advertising effort as well. Paid time or space has two great advantages over donated time or space: the government gets more influence about where and when the messages appear, and the implicit threat now wielded by advertisers to pull their ads in retaliation for unfavorable editorial content is somewhat offset.

The experience with tobacco suggests that a small amount of negative advertising, all of it concentrated on suppressing overall demand, can counterbalance a large amount of positive advertising, much of which is intended to attack or protect brand market shares.[60] This, and the avoidance of any free-speech controversy, strongly suggests that a tax on positive advertising to support negative advertising, even at a ratio as small as one to four or five (or, operationally equivalent but politically less plausible, an equivalent appropriation of general-revenue funds) would outperform an advertising ban. Unfortunately, the idea of an advertising ban sounds simple and morally straightforward—why should companies be allowed to merchandise morbidity?—and therefore appeals to the somewhat puritanical and controlling mood of the anti-drinking (and anti-smoking) forces. It thus diverts their attention from the probably superior alternative.

If mass-media prevention efforts are to center on negative advertising rather than on the restriction of positive advertising, it is important to consider the content of those negative advertisements. What are we trying to prevent?

In the case of smoking, the very high rate of progression from experimentation to compulsive use clearly indicates abstinence as the primary goal of prevention efforts. But the case of alcohol is much less clear. Not only would alcohol abstinence be hard to achieve in the face of overwhelming numbers, it is not even obviously desirable. Persuading most of the fifty million Americans who now drink small quantities at irregular intervals to quit entirely would produce only the slightest of reductions in measurable drinking-related harm. There would be far more benefit in persuading even a few of those who now drink heavily and steadily, or drink in binges, or drink and drive, or drink while pregnant, or drink and assault their intimates, to moderate their habits and restrict their drinking to appropriate times and places. Better to convince people who sometimes get drunk that drunkenness is unattractive than to convince people who sometimes have a drink that drinking is evil, particularly if moderate drinkers provide a model of control for others to follow.

But it should be one of the goals of the official and unofficial persuasion effort to counter the glamorization of drinking in the industry's marketing efforts. Negative advertising could dramatize the unattractive and dangerous aspects of drunken behavior, and the unfavorable comment it draws from those one would like to impress or attract. In doing so, it could play off the established vocabulary of positive drinking images in alcohol advertising, for example by showing an elegantly dressed man with a drink in his hand confidently approaching a desirable woman but stumbling, spilling his drink, or slurring his words, and consequently being rejected. To be avoided is the explicit message "Just say no to alcohol."

There may be more occasion with alcohol than with any other drug, licit or illicit, to stress the delivery of pure information about specific risks in both mass-media and more targeted communications. Because virtually everyone knows someone who drinks and suffers no noticeable health damage, alcohol is widely perceived as safe unless one is an "alcoholic." By now, everyone knows that drunken driving is dangerous, but the risks of other kinds of accidents, and the health damage associated with drinking, especially the risks of even occasional drinking during pregnancy, could use much more exposure. These messages can be carried in the story lines of entertainment programs as well as in explicit anti-alcohol advertisements.*

The role of alcohol in routine social interaction means that the social pressure to drink tends to be greater than the social pressure to use any other drug. This circumstance enhances the value of teaching refusal skills, and not only to schoolchildren. How many salesmen (and women) have fallen into problem drinking because they did not know how politely to refuse a customer's suggestion to have another round?

CHANGING THE LAWS

It would be pleasant to imagine that more vigorous and better-designed persuasion efforts, along with enforcement initiatives directed at underage drinking and drinking by those who repeatedly commit crimes or make hazards or nuisances of themselves under the influence, could over time reduce alcohol-related problems to tolerable size. But that would almost certainly reflect undue optimism. The association of drinking with aggression and with irresponsible behavior are quite deeply rooted in many American subcultures.

* Recent efforts in this direction by the Center for Health Communication at the Harvard School of Public Health have attracted a substantial amount of cooperation from the producers of television programming. It might even be worth spending some money on what might be thought of as "negative product placement" in films.

While that association endures, alcohol will continue to be a major behavioral risk. Even if it were changed, alcohol would remain a significant health risk. Both forms of risk will continue to be greatly exacerbated by the tendency of some proportion of drinkers to lose control of their drinking and to fall into compulsive patterns of steady heavy drinking or episodic bingeing. Even the relatively uncontroversial goal of keeping alcohol out of the hands of minors is largely unattainable as long as the drug remains relatively cheaply and unrestrictedly available to adults.

Therefore, it is likely that very large reductions in the total damage drinking does to drinkers and others will require changes in the total quantity of alcohol consumed—especially, but not exclusively, the quantity consumed by heavy drinkers—which in turn would require a major change in the conditions of its availability.

Prohibition

If the legalization of alcohol has been a failure—if regulations and customs have not sufficed to keep the personal and social costs of alcohol abuse within acceptable limits—why not reverse it? Political feasibility aside, there are two good reasons not to reenact Prohibition. First, the enforcement problem would be overwhelming. While it is true that production and distribution of alcohol is more difficult to conceal than that of the currently illicit drugs—both because the commodity itself is relatively bulky, and because so much drinking now takes place in fixed establishments, which by their nature would be vulnerable to enforcement—the size of the preexisting consumer base would create massive difficulties. While American law enforcement is certainly more honest and competent now than it was during the 1920s, Americans are much richer and probably somewhat less law-abiding than they were the last time the government tried to keep them away from their liquor.

Contrary to the established mythos, the "noble experiment" was not a complete failure. There is evidence that, poorly enforced and flagrantly disregarded as it was, Prohibition produced a substantial net improvement in the nation's health, particularly in its early days before the bootlegging system and the attendant machinery of corruption had become well established.[61] However, its side effects in the form of illicit-market corruption and violence were large and long-lasting, and there is every reason to believe that they might be worse the second time around.

Even if a new Prohibition could be made to succeed—that is, to reduce the level of problem drinking substantially at acceptable costs in poisoning, violence, and law enforcement resources—it might still not be justified in pure cost-benefit terms. The (possible) reduction in total alcohol-related harm to drinkers and others would have to be great enough to counterbalance the (certain) reduction in alcohol-related benefits: the consumers' surplus from drinking (the difference between what noncompulsive drinkers actually pay for alcoholic beverages and what they would be willing to pay) plus the producers' surplus from alcoholic beverage production and distribution (the difference between what labor and capital earn in that business and what they could earn in their next-best opportunity). Prohibition would deprive those who complied with it of the pleasures and comforts associated with drinking. Those pleasures and comforts are far less spectacular than the harm alcohol does in the form of damaged newborns, battered spouses, highway carnage, and lifetimes of fighting the bottle, but they are far more widespread. The obvious objection to a new prohibition is that it is not possible to wish alcohol out of existence; less obviously, it is not at all certain that the wish would be a wise one even if it were granted. "Life is too short," says the bumper sticker, "to drink bad wine." *A fortiori*, it is much too short to drink no wine at all if you are among those to whom wine gives pleasure.

The ideal, then, would be to find a set of alcohol laws that preserved the pleasures of controlled drinking for those who enjoy them while substantially reducing the frequency of excessive drinking and of drunken misconduct. Taxes and regulations both have contributions to make.

Taxation

At a minimum, alcohol taxation should be high enough to cover the costs that the average drink imposes on those who do not drink it; otherwise, the price system will send the wrong signals to consumers choosing between alcoholic beverages and other commodities. A tax assessed on that principle would include, at least: the costs of health care for drinking-induced disease paid by public or private insurance or contributed by health-care providers, the losses of the non-drinking victims of alcohol-induced accidents (not merely lost wages and medical bills, but a sum representing their pain and loss of enjoyment of life); and the costs of alcohol-induced sub-par job performance over and above those reflected in lower wages for drinkers (the burden of which will be divided, in a way depending on the workings of the markets involved, among shareholders, fellow employees, and consumers). A recent reckoning of such a "Pigouvian" tax on alcohol found the total to be 48 cents per ounce (34 cents per drink), more than three times the current average.[62]

But even that reckoning was incomplete. Among the clearly "external" costs, it omitted the value of alcohol-related crimes and public nuisances. If one attributes to drinking a few thousand murders and some tens of thousands of less-successful assaults per year, the cost of crime alone could quickly mount into the tens of billions of dollars annually, adding about 30 cents to the cost of the average drink.* The nuisance value of public drunkenness should also be added in; there is no easy way to measure it, but there is reason to believe that disorder is, in the aggregate, as socially costly as crime, and the proportional contribution of drinking must be at least as great.[63]

The published calculation of the economically optimal alcohol tax also omitted any costs borne by the families of drinkers, but not by the drinkers themselves. A list of such costs would include reduced spending on children because of their providers' reduced income, the

* If one treats being murdered as one variety of low-probability accidental death, the economic cost of a murder is what all of the potential victims would have been willing to pay to reduce their risk in the proportion that one additional murder increased it. Studies of industrial accidents suggest a small-risk willingness-to-pay for avoided sudden death of a few million dollars per incident. W. Kip Viscusi, *Risk by Choice: Regulating Health and Safety in the Workplace* (Cambridge, Mass.: Harvard University Press, 1983). Also see Ron Howard, "On Making Life and Death Decisions," in *Societal Risk Assessment: How Safe is Safe Enough?*, Richard C. Schwing and Walter A. Albers, eds. (New York: Plenum Press, 1980), which reaches a quite similar figure using a completely independent methodology: a calculation of how a rational risk taker would trade off the risk of death against disposable income. Four thousand murders (about 20 percent of the total, reflecting the observation that about 20 percent of violent felons in prison had been drinking heavily, but using no other drug, at the time of the crime) times $3 million is $12 billion. This $12 billion, divided by 105 billion drinks per year, yields an additional external cost per drink due to drinking-related murders alone of about 11 cents. It seems plausible that other crimes and the cost of crime avoidance would at least triple that figure. While it is probably true that murder victims as a class are probably poorer than industrial workers, and therefore willing to pay less to reduce risks to their lives, it is also true that the average murder probably generates more fear than the average industrial accident; the willingness to pay to avoid anxiety must be added to the willingness to pay to avoid risk. There are no market data from which one could estimate victims' willingness to pay to avoid rape or aggravated assault, but even tens of thousands of dollars per incident (would you pay $50 for a taxi if the walking involved a one-in-one-thousand chance of being raped?) times hundreds of thousands of incidents yields an additional total cost in the billions of dollars. To this one should add the other costs of crime in the form of avoidance behavior.

burden on families of dealing with relatives with drinking problems, the long-term ill effects of having had a heavy-drinking parent, the grief suffered by survivors, and criminal victimization in the form of domestic violence. Insofar as these costs and risks are perfectly foreseen by self-controlled drinkers who fully empathize with the sufferings and joys of their families, it is methodologically reasonable to exclude them from the Pigouvian tax calculation, because to that extent they are already fully reflected in consumer decision making about drinking and there is no need to reflect them twice through taxation. But if some drinkers, particularly high-cost drinkers, fail to foresee costs, do not have their drinking fully under voluntary rational control, or take their families' welfare into account only partially or not at all—this last at least must surely be true of domestic assailants—then the 48 cent number further underestimates the appropriate tax on a drink.

To the extent that some drinkers are misinformed about the risks of drinking or have difficulties with self-command or the deferral of gratification, their drinking behavior will not adequately reflect the costs of their drinking even to themselves. Whether the unconsidered costs of drinking to drinkers ought to be added into the tax calculation depends in part on how paternalistic one wants governments to be with respect to drug-taking behavior. Putting a number on this "excess internal" (as opposed to "external") cost per drink would be extraordinarily difficult, involving both an estimate of the total costs and survey information about what consumers think those costs are.

In any case, it is hard to see how the average total external cost, including the costs borne by families, could be reckoned at less than a dollar a drink, a figure that approximates the total after-excise-tax revenues of the alcoholic beverage industries. That is to say, the costs that alcohol imposes on nondrinkers after it is sold are in the same range as the total costs of producing and selling it.

Even more than most, this average covers an enormous range of variation, but the tax system may not be the best way to discourage those users of alcohol with especially large external costs. Discriminations among different forms of alcohol, beyond the adjustment in per-volume rates necessary to account for differences in alcohol content, are not as straightforward as they may seem. Whiskey may well do the most damage per dose in immediate terms, but it is the least likely to be the vehicle of initiation for the young. What is the social cost of a wine cooler sipped by a ten-year-old taking his first steps toward a lifetime problem with alcohol and other intoxicants?

(There may be a better case for some discrimination in favor of table wine, narrowly defined.)

A dollar-a-drink tax would raise some tens of billions of dollars in revenue; exactly how much depends on the short- and long-run price elasticities of demand for alcohol. Lower-income groups would almost certainly pay more of that sum than they would if an equivalent sum were raised by a surcharge on federal taxes generally. (Only "almost certainly" because their demand for alcohol may be substantially more price elastic than that of richer people.) Such a tax would therefore tend to move the federal tax system toward regressivity, though not very far in that direction since tens of billions are a small proportion of one trillion, which is roughly the annual federal tax take. My preference, based on the common-sense notion that the poorer one is, the more it hurts to part with a dollar, is for a more progressive tax system. But this is no insuperable objection to higher alcohol taxes; one could simply use the additional revenues to replace some still more regressive tax, such as the payroll tax on earnings below the median wage. (As a formal matter, this would probably mean an expansion of the Earned Income Tax Credit.)

Since a small proportion of the external costs of drinking come out of public budgets, the revenues from a dollar-a-drink alcohol tax would dwarf any plausible set of alcohol prevention or treatment programs. The purpose of the tax would not be to pay for programs but to discourage drinking, particularly by heavy drinkers and the young.

The effectiveness of such a tax in reducing alcohol consumption is not easy to predict. It would depend on the price behavior of the industry, the sensitivity of various kinds of drinkers to large changes in price—hard to estimate from observations that cover only small changes—and the second-order effects of higher prices and changed behavior on attitudes and customs. For example, one could imagine a perverse effect: higher prices might help further identify alcohol with luxury, thus making its use more attractive. But given what is known about the impact of interstate price variations on youthful drinking, one would expect a decrease in drinking prevalence among the young of at least 25 percent.[64]

Higher taxes would have some disadvantages. Some drinkers would substitute illicit drugs such as marijuana or diverted tranquilizers, or even gasoline and solvents, for alcohol. The demand for untaxed "moonshine" products would rise somewhat, leading to more black-market crime and more damage from adulterated drink. The skid-row drunk who drinks less in the face of higher taxes winds up better off, and so do the neighbors; the skid-row drunk who switches to wood alcohol or Sterno may wind up blind, or dead. By the same token, the poor heavy drinker who refuses to cut back on drinking when the tax rises will wind up just as drunk, but poorer and probably more of a social problem. However, substitution and moonshining were apparently quite minor problems during the early 1950s, when alcohol taxes were several times as high as they are now in purchasing-power terms and even higher than that compared with average wages. It therefore seems that legality, assured purity, brand names, and the convenience of purchase in bars and liquor stores give taxed products such an enormous market edge over untaxed products that the magnitude of these undesired side effects would be small compared to the benefits of putting a large dent in teenage drinking.

Why, then, stop at a dollar a drink? Presumably, the extent of the drinking problem will continue to fall as prices rise, almost without limit. But so will the lost consumers' surplus, the reduction in the pleasures and other benefits of drinking suffered by those nonproblem drinkers who cut back or abstain entirely in the face of higher prices. In addition, while the black-market problem may start small relative to the total problem, it will inevitably grow as taxes rise. In the extreme, high taxation is virtually equivalent to prohibition, and it has the same disadvantages.

Personal Licensure

Taxation and prohibition are alike in being "wholesale" policies that make no distinctions among drinkers or occasions. They are thus necessarily directed at average conditions. But drinkers and occasions are both so heterogeneous that such blanket policies must necessarily deviate greatly from the ideal. A tax far too high for a single glass of wine taken at dinner at home by someone who has had no other drink that week is far too low for the first of ten beers taken in a bar by someone with a history of drunken brawling.

While persons with histories of problem drinking can be forbidden to drink, or forbidden to drink in specific settings, enforcing such individual prohibitions is difficult for the authorities unless they can enlist the aid of retail alcohol dealers. Insofar as problem drinkers are persons who have difficulty managing their own drinking behavior, they may find it easier to observe such individual prohibitions than to follow a course of abstinence or moderation without such an order. Prohibiting a compulsive drinker from drinking, while every bar and liquor store will freely sell him drink, is not much better than ordering someone with a balance problem to walk a tightrope every day but not, under penalty of the law, to fall off. Others, perfectly capable of complying with orders not to drink, simply will not comply if violation is made sufficiently easy.

This analysis points us toward some form of personal drinking license. It could be a "positive" license, obtainable only on application and examination, but a "negative" license, automatically granted to each adult but subject to revocation for misbehavior or to voluntary surrender, might work almost as well, at much lower administrative cost and personal inconvenience. The physical license could be a separate document or merely a marking on a driver's permit. (The latter, though more convenient, would raise the problem of managing stigma.) Having to show the license in order to buy a drink might seem an imposition, but it would be no more inconvenient than the "carding" that young-looking drinkers must now endure; in fact, its universal application would make it less demeaning. Private hosts would no doubt be less compliant than licensed sellers, though as a matter of law they would presumably be responsible for ascertaining that their guests were licensed to drink, as they now are for ascertaining that their guests are of drinking age.

Like any regulation, personal licensure would be imperfectly observed. There would be counterfeiting and leakage, just as there now is in getting drink to minors. While those phenomena would tend to reduce the value of the system, they would not eliminate it unless violations were very widespread indeed. Regulators could exact fairly strict compliance from licensed sellers, as they do now by sending investigators around to pose as unlicensed buyers and then using their disciplinary powers to punish carelessness or deliberate evasion of the law. In addition, regulators would have for the first time a punitive threat—suspension or revocation of the drinking license— to hold out against noncommercial points of leakage, in the form of licensed drinkers who distributed drink to minors or unlicensed adults. For that reason, and because much adult problem drinking takes place in bars, it would be reasonable to expect a higher level of effective compliance with a universal drinking-license system than with the current age restriction.

Compliance with a personal license system could be further increased, and additional benefits obtained, by adding a quantity limit—in effect, a monthly drinking quota—to the personal license. Such a limit, even if set quite high (say, at four reference drinks per

day, or roughly seven fifths of whisky per month), would limit the
drinking of the heaviest chronic drinkers and quantity of drink that
could leak from any one licensed drinker to minors or to those whose
licenses had been suspended. As an administrative and information-
processing matter, this would be not much more complicated than
paying by credit card. Private entertaining would pose a problem;
perhaps special exemptions could be allowed for such social rituals
as weddings, with hosts otherwise using their own quotas or asking
their guests to bring their own bottles. It would not, after all, be
an entirely bad idea to make guests and hosts alike more conscious
about the quantities of alcohol they offer and take. But as a first step
one probably ought to be satisfied with licensure and let the quantity
limit go.

Even without a quantity limit, a personal drinking license system
would carry some administrative overhead in the form of investigators and hearing officers, but the actual costs would be negligible
compared with either the total money paid for drink or the avoided
social costs of inappropriate drinking. If the drinking license were integrated with the driving license, the data-processing system of state
motor vehicle registries could be made to do double duty; given
the share of highway-safety problems traceable to alcohol, this could
hardly be thought of as a diversion of registry resources from their
primary objective.

In addition to its incapacitative effect in denying drink to those
who have shown themselves incapable of handling it, a personal
drinking license system would also have a deterrent effect against
drinking-related misbehavior. Deprivation of one's drinking license,
particularly since it could be done administratively rather than as
the result of a criminal conviction, might be a more powerful deterrent to drunken driving, drunken assault, and drunken disorder
than the threat of jail. While a drunken driver can reasonably plead
economic necessity in his appeal for the return of his driving license,
there would be much less to say in favor of returning his drinking
license.

A danger of a personal license system, especially if the authorities
were overenthusiastic about revoking drinkers' licenses, would be
the development of unlicensed bars and liquor stores to serve unlicensed drinkers. These, like the "after-hours clubs" that now help
drinkers defy closing-hour laws, could easily become centers of violence, disorder, and illicit commerce of all kinds. But a small amount
of enforcement effort, along with the development of a tracking
system for wholesale alcoholic beverage sales, like the one now used

for wholesale sales of controlled pharmaceuticals, should suffice to prevent the birth of a new generation of speakeasies.[65]

The combination of high taxation and personal licensure would probably suffice to greatly reduce the extent of alcohol-related harm without significantly interfering with moderate social drinking. Insofar as personal licensure reduced the average social cost of a drink, the optimal tax would be lower with licensure than without it; in effect, nonproblem drinkers would not have to pay for the damage done by and to as many problem drinkers. It would, I submit, be the appropriate middle course between an unworkable prohibition and an experiment in legalization that has proven insupportably costly.

9

Marijuana

Smoke pot!
The thinking man's cigarette!
—Dave Van Ronk, c. 1962

Why do you think they call it dope?
—Anti-drug advertisement, c. 1968

Marijuana is the most widely used illicit drug. More Americans are current users of marijuana than of all other illicit drugs combined.[1] Thus laws aimed at "drug users" generically, and framed with heroin addicts or crackheads in mind, in fact apply primarily to marijuana smokers. In dollar terms, marijuana probably constitutes the third largest of the illicit drug markets, after cocaine and heroin.[2] As measured by arrests, marijuana attracts a substantial share of total drug enforcement attention.[3]

Yet marijuana does not loom large among American drug problems in terms of observable and measurable harm done to users or to others. Marijuana dealers are not shooting up the cities, marijuana babies are not populating the neonatal intensive care wards, marijuana addicts are not stealing to pay for their drug habits, marijuana use and associated sexual activity are not spreading syphilis and AIDS, victims of marijuana are not clamoring for admission to treatment or flocking into self-help groups.[4] Aside from the almost self-evident proposition that smoking anything is probably bad for the lungs, the quarter century since large numbers of Americans began to use marijuana has produced remarkably little laboratory or epidemiological evidence of serious health damage done by the drug.[5]

Still, marijuana is a powerful intoxicant, and it can generate a powerful bad habit. Crude and necessarily imprecise calculation suggests that, as measured by hours spent in a state of diminished self-command, marijuana contributes about as much to the total intoxication burden on the American mind as alcohol, and far more than cocaine.* In addition, marijuana intoxication is qualitatively different from intoxication with the widely used depressants and stimulants, including alcohol and cocaine, in that it involves more complicated and profound subjective effects, in some ways similar to those of the psychedelics.[6]

To decide how big a problem this is requires judgments of both fact and value. As a matter of fact, how much damage does marijuana intoxication do, in the form of misbehavior, of lost productive hours, or of subtle psychological damage from spending time out of one's natural mind? Is being intoxicated a personal habit and social custom that tends to grow over time? If so, marijuana intoxication may build demand for intoxication of other, more dangerous, kinds. (Alternatively, if some people have a desire to be intoxicated that can be satisfied in a number of different ways, marijuana may substitute for other substances.)[7] As a question of value, how much does

---

* There are two major problems in making such estimates (aside from the poor quality of the underlying data): heterogeneity among users in their susceptibility to intoxication—heavy users, who account for a large fraction of total consumption, are likely to have some tolerance to their drug and thus to get less intoxication per physical unit consumed than the median user—and the spacing of consumption over time. Someone who gets roaring drunk on five drinks in a row may be able to absorb those same five drinks over three hours and never be visibly the worse for liquor. Probably a much larger proportion of alcohol than of marijuana is consumed without the intention or effect of intoxication. Crudely, though, 4000 metric tons of marijuana equals 4 billion grams equals about 8 billion cigarettes. Assuming an average THC content of 5 percent, one cigarette will generate about four hours of intoxication (two each for two users). This yields about 30 billion hours under the influence. That must be too high, because twenty million mostly casual users can't average 1500 hours per year (almost five hours per day) under the influence; the explanation must be in tolerance among heavy users.

In the case of alcohol, the total estimated consumption is roughly 105 billion drinks; if three drinks equals one hour drunk we have 35 billion hours drunk, which again must be reduced for tolerance among heavy drinkers and additionally for non-intoxicating drinking. Obviously, the error bands around the assumptions are too wide to allow any precise conclusions; all the calculation establishes is that the orders of magnitude are roughly the same.

The figure of cocaine is an order of magnitude smaller. Two hundred metric tons, two hundred grams of cocaine, if all converted into crack, would yield about four billion rocks. Even assuming a consumption rate of only one rock per hour, that gives only 4 billion hours under the influence of cocaine. The powder form (except in the relatively rare practice of injection) is probably less efficient in producing intoxicated hours.

or should it bother you that you or your kin, friends, neighbors, or fellow citizens choose to spend time in altered states? Is all intoxication by its nature excessive, or is it a problem only to the extent that it occurs too frequently or under the wrong circumstances? How much, if anything, is it worth to have someone spend an hour drunk on beer rather than high on pot?

In several important ways, marijuana and nicotine are opposites. Nicotine has been tolerated, despite its high rate of compulsive use and the enormous health damage it does, because it is not an intoxicant and thus poses little cultural threat. Marijuana, by contrast, is forbidden, despite its limited potential to create measurable health damage and its lower rate of compulsive use, because it produces an "altered state of consciousness." As a stereotype, marijuana intoxication is physically passive, intellectually dizzy, emotionally volatile, and hypersensitive to touch, smell, taste, music, and humor. All this is threatening to the stereotype of the American, particularly the male. John Wayne can drink, even be drunk, even be mean drunk. John Wayne can't get stoned.

Smoking is an issue because of its side effects. If nicotine could be made safe to physical health and delivered in a way that did not pollute the indoor air, it would not be a matter of public debate. Marijuana is an issue because of its intended effects. Even if marijuana were shown to be innocuous physically, the question would remain: how much do we as a society disapprove of marijuana intoxication?

THE MARIJUANA USE PROBLEM

As noted, it is possible to view marijuana intoxication as a bad thing in and of itself. But putting that concern aside for the moment, we can ask how much measurable damage the drug does to its users and those around them in the form of misbehavior under the influence, health damage, entrapment in long-term heavy use of the drug, or "graduation" to more dangerous drugs.

The research results on the adverse behavioral and health consequences of casual marijuana use are unimpressive, given the commitment of research funds to the effort to discover dangers and the effort by official and unofficial drug education agencies to publicize what negative findings there are and to be as silent as possible about findings not helpful to the cause. For example, a recent finding that adolescents with controlled moderate patterns of marijuana use were less likely to display symptoms of maladjustment than either heavy users or nonusers was subjected to considerable criticism, some of it explicitly directed at the possibility that publication of the results would interfere with drug education efforts.[8]

Those who wish to believe, or to convince others, that marijuana use is likely to be very damaging to health confront an overwhelming piece of negative evidence: millions of persons who started smoking marijuana as college students in the late 1960s, some of whom have been taking the drug more or less regularly ever since, have suffered neither obvious immediate damage nor dramatic aftereffects. Nor have papers begun to appear in the epidemiology journals, finding that, for example, men who arrived in college in 1966 to 1970 have higher morbidity or mortality for their age than men who arrived in college in 1961 to 1965. In the absence of careful panel studies, such negative evidence could not possibly establish that marijuana use is "safe," which in any case it probably is not. But if occasional marijuana smoking over 20 years carried substantial health risks, the evidence should have started to come in by now.*

But, it is argued, the marijuana that college kids smoked in the sixties was far less potent than the marijuana available today. The ratio of potency has been estimated to be as high as ten to one.[9] This assertion is a mixture of underlying truth, conceptual error, and simple mismeasurement.

The potency of a given sample of marijuana is determined by four factors: the genetic composition of the plant from which it was taken; the parts of the plant from which the material comes, whether the potent flowering tops of the plant or the less potent leaves; growing technique, in particular the use of the "sinsemilla" process of growing unpollinated, and therefore, especially potent, female plants; and the age of the material and the manner in which it has been stored (since marijuana stored at room temperature loses potency over periods measured in months).[10] In much of the United States, a variety of the marijuana plant, *Cannabis sativa,* from which hemp used to be made, grows wild. This variety, sometimes known as "ditch-weed," is only very mildly psychoactive; its concentration of THC, the main psychoactive agent in marijuana, tends to be below 1 percent by weight. In the sixties and early seventies, it appears that most of the domestically produced marijuana sold in the United States was

---

* Perhaps the greatest residual worry is the effect of young adult marijuana use on the aging process.

ditchweed, and it still makes up a substantial fraction of the marijuana eradicated with great fanfare by federal and state authorities. Even back then, there was some domestic production of more potent varieties, "commercial grade" marijuana with THC concentrations in the flowering tops of a few percent and a small amount of sinsemilla yielding flowering tops with several percent THC. But the vast bulk of the U.S. market was supplied from foreign sources: imports were mostly commercial grade, with some sinsemilla.

It is probable that over time the average potency of cultivated marijuana, domestic and imported, commercial grade and sinsemilla, has increased, as a result of active plant-breeding measures, the development of a market in higher-potency marijuana seeds, and perhaps more attention to growing conditions. It may also be true that an increasing proportion of the material sold is flowering tops rather than leaves. It is certain that the sinsemilla technique has become more widely practiced in the United States, and that domestically produced, highly cultivated marijuana has enjoyed a rising market share for at least the past decade, largely thanks to the success of interdiction efforts, which have acted as a protective tariff for the domestic marijuana industry.

Thus the potency of the average smoked material has almost certainly been rising, though in the absence of a systematic effort to collect samples from retail buyers there is no precise estimate of how much. There appears to be some material on the market with THC content above 10 percent.[11] Whether rising potency leads to increased intoxication is an open question; some reports suggest that marijuana users learn to "titrate" their dosages, as coffee drinkers and tobacco smokers appear to do. If intoxication does not increase with potency because smokers puff less or hold the smoke less deeply in their lungs, then high-potency marijuana is actually less dangerous than low-potency marijuana because there will be less lung damage if the same amount of active agent is delivered in a smaller cloud of smoke.

But the strong claim for vastly increased potency—which would justify the further claim that the risks of marijuana use today are not comparable to the risks of marijuana use 15 or 20 years ago— appears to rest on a simple measurement error. The samples of early 1970s marijuana that have been reported as containing only 0.5 percent THC have ratios of concentrations of THC and its breakdown products that suggest that much of the THC originally present has decomposed.[12] Contemporary measurements from a laboratory that sold drug-testing services to drug buyers found no sample with less than 2 percent THC.* There is thus little or no reason to believe that the consequences of smoking marijuana in 1991 will be drastically different from those of smoking marijuana in 1971.

Progression to Very Heavy Marijuana Use

At any given time, a significant proportion of those who use marijuana at all regularly use it very heavily. Of a total user population that now seems to number about 20 million, it seems probable that as many as two or three million smoke several "joints" per day.[13]

Although the phenomenon of tolerance implies that several joints per day represent much less intoxication for chronic heavy smokers than they would for those without such experience, these heavy daily smokers are people with serious drug habits, whose ability to work, learn, or make responsible decisions in their own behalf is seriously compromised by marijuana. But as Peter Reuter has pointed out, the startling fact about heavy marijuana use is that it tends to be a quite transient state for any one individual.[14] If the surveys are to be believed, only a small proportion of those who were heavy daily marijuana users at some time in the past are still in that state today; the number who are no longer daily users is much larger than the number who have gone through any formal drug treatment program.

Presumably, the long-term effects of a period of months spent in a cannabis-induced haze are not good, but the extensive drug-abuse literature is devoid of any studies showing past heavy marijuana use to be a risk factor for any undesired condition. Thus, while the risk of progression from casual to heavy marijuana use is not small, its major cost may well be the lost earning, learning, personal, and career development opportunities represented by the months of very heavy use. Having said all this, it is important to recall that for at least a small proportion of heavy marijuana smokers the condition is not transient, and that a small proportion of a few million people is not a small number of significantly disrupted lives. "I'm like all those politicians," a professional colleague once said to me. "I only smoked

---

* John P. Morgan, "American Marijuana Potency: Data Versus Conventional Wisdom" (New York: Department of Pharmacology, City University of New York Medical School, 1990). It should be noted, however, that customers for such services were probably more sophisticated than the general run of marijuana buyers and therefore were probably getting less than their share of a low-potency product.

marijuana one time, and I deeply regret it. The one time was from 1963 to 1969."

Marijuana and Other Drugs: Gateway or Substitute?

Even if marijuana use were entirely benign in itself, it would still represent a problem if it tended to lead to the use of other, more dangerous substances. This is the "gateway" hypothesis. Since marijuana is far more widely used than any other illicit drug, even a weak gateway effect could represent substantial social harm. In my view, this effect ought to be the primary area of concern about marijuana for those who do not regard occasional intoxication as a bad thing in itself and who are either unconvinced of or unperturbed by the lasting attitudinal changes to which marijuana smoking may lead. If marijuana smoking generated an additional one-in-ten, or even one-in-twenty, risk of experimentation with cocaine smoking or opiate injection—additional, that is, over the risks faced by an otherwise similar person who had somehow been prevented from smoking marijuana—that would be enough to justify substantial efforts to control marijuana use.

Marijuana could act as a gateway in several ways. On an individual level, the experience of strong intoxication with subjective enhancement of sensation and a certain kind of thinking—an experience reportedly quite different from that of alcohol intoxication—might generate curiosity about experiencing, and self-assurance about trying, more exotic drugs. The marijuana experience might suggest otherwise unthought of possibilities to be achieved by drug taking, or it could become decreasingly satisfying over time (as a result of pharmacological tolerance or simple boredom with "the same old thing") and lead to the use of other drugs to recapture the pleasure of the early experience.* Other drugs might also be used not instead of marijuana but in combination with it.

On a social level, groups of marijuana users might become fertile culture media for the growth of other drug markets, and the spread of the custom of (nonalcoholic) intoxication might reduce the overall social resistance to new drug "epidemics." Trends in musical composition and the visual arts congenial to altered states of consciousness, fostered by the presence of a body of marijuana users, might provide

* Psychiatrist and drug treatment researcher Herbert Kleber argues that this effect is important: "Marijuana gets boring. People want to try something else."

further encouragement to more dangerous forms of drug experimentation. A similar phenomenon might involve the development of drug paraphernalia shops, drug-taking hobbyist magazines, and the like.

In fact, these subjective experiences and cultural phenomena have already been observed over the quarter century since marijuana emerged as a mass-market drug. It seems beyond doubt that marijuana has played a catalytic role in the transition to the use of other drugs—catalytic in the precise sense of providing a pathway requiring the overcoming of a smaller potential-energy barrier—at least for some users and groups.

While the existence of gateway effects is almost beyond debate, the extent to which the ill effects that flow from the use of other drugs could be reduced by programs to reduce the prevalence and frequency of marijuana use has not been measured, for all the reasons that complicated social processes with long time delays are always difficult to measure. Nor would even an accurate measurement be the end of the story.

The gateway hypothesis is not the only plausible relationship between marijuana use and the use of other drugs. Marijuana might also be—almost certainly is—a substitute for other intoxicants, licit and illicit, for some persons and under some circumstances. For anyone who enjoys being intoxicated, but only on a limited number of occasions, and who has taken to heart warnings about mixing drugs, any two intoxicants will substitute for one another as competing ways of satisfying the demand for mood alteration. To the extent that such substitution occurs, a social cost of making marijuana more expensive or harder to come by is increased use of other drugs: alcohol, tranquilizers, inhalants, hallucinogens, and opiates.

Substitution is always a potential problem for efforts to control drug abuse; it is almost certainly true, for example, that scarcer heroin means more heavy drinking. But marijuana's relatively low incidence of observable damage means that any substitution is likely to involve a drug with more ill effects for users and those around them. Particularly for adolescents, the substitution of alcohol intoxication for marijuana intoxication would probably increase health risks, accident risks, and the frequency of assaultive crime. (The observation that much drinking does not lead to intoxication does not imply that drinking as a substitute for marijuana smoking will not lead to intoxication.)

Thus we would very much like to know the net result of two opposite sets of effects: gateway phenomena and other forms of complementarity between marijuana and other drugs, and substitution phenomena.* There are sprinklings of evidence on this point.

On an individual level, the literature on drug use careers suggests complementarity over time between virtually any pair of substances, licit or illicit. Early or heavy use of a more widely used drug "predicts," in the statistical sense of that term, use of any less widely used drug. For example, adolescent tobacco smoking predicts adolescent marijuana smoking. By the same token, marijuana smoking predicts the use of other illicit drugs; the overwhelming majority of those who begin to use any other illicit substance have already tried marijuana.[15]

But that does not imply a causal connection either between tobacco and marijuana or between marijuana and cocaine or the opiates; there are too many other differences between users of tobacco or marijuana and the non-users. Use of one drug may be a marker, rather than a cause, of being "at risk" for progression to another. The importance of this confounding phenomenon can be investigated by studying the personal and demographic characteristics of the two populations to see how much of a difference remains after statistical adjustments are made to separate out the effects of race, class, gender, neighborhood, school performance, and measurable personality characteristics. But such "statistical controls" are only partly adequate; of two otherwise-matched youngsters, the one who chooses to smoke marijuana probably differs from the one who chooses not to smoke marijuana, in ways that help explain why the former is more likely than the latter to try cocaine.

The most careful study to date along these lines, conducted during the 1970s, explored the marijuana-heroin link among the largely minority-group adolescent population of Manhattan.[16] Its findings confirmed the expected relationship, but with an unexpected twist. Heavy marijuana smokers were indeed at elevated risk of becoming heroin users, but the mechanism did not seem to involve the drug experience itself. Rather, heavy marijuana use appeared to generate involvement in drug selling, either as a way of paying for the marijuana consumed or simply by association with drug sellers, and drug selling in turn gave adolescents access to heroin and to the money to buy it. This suggests that marijuana was a gateway for

---

* Economists call two goods *complements* for one another if an increase in the supply of one leads to an increase in the demand for the other; personal computers and laser printers are complements, so as either one gets cheaper or better consumers are likely to use more of the other. Two goods are called *substitutes* for one another if an increase in the supply of one causes a decrease in the demand for the other; personal computers and typewriters are substitutes.

these adolescents only because it was illicit. By extension, one might speculate that making marijuana licitly available would tend to increase the consumption of marijuana while decreasing that of other illicit drugs, if its effect were to sever the link between marijuana use and drug dealing.

This finding raises an important point: the effect of marijuana consumption on the consumption of other drugs is not simply a characteristic of the drug; it also reflects the policies surrounding its sale and use. The effect of a change in marijuana policy on the use of alcohol or cocaine may easily be more important than its effect on the use of marijuana. It is easy to imagine two proposed policies, each of which would reduce the use of marijuana, but in such different ways that one would increase the use of cocaine while the other would decrease it.

In principle, one could try to answer some of the policy questions with true field experiments. One could use the tax laws to raise the price, and thus reduce the consumption, of tobacco in one of two otherwise similar states and observe the effect on the relative proportions of adolescents in the two states who eventually try marijuana or who become long-term heavy marijuana users. One could, perhaps, increase marijuana prices or search times by increasing enforcement in one state or city but not another and observe what happens to cocaine usage. But those experiments are far easier to imagine than to conduct. Although Justice Brandeis called the states "laboratories of democracy," the states do not (and should not) tend to regard themselves as primarily experimental enterprises. Persuading them to change their tobacco taxes or drug enforcement policies in the cause of science, even policy-relevant science, is likely to be difficult, at least. Even if such experiments were possible, the interpretation of the results would not be straightforward, partly because no two cities or states are ever truly matched and partly because the world will be changing in the interim. We would be interested, after all, not in the transient effects of a one-time local change but in the long-term effects, after everything had settled down, of lasting changes across the country.

Another approach to exploring the question of whether marijuana use, on balance, increases or decreases the use of other drugs would be to study aggregate consumption of, say, alcohol or cocaine over periods of varying marijuana availability, as measured by price or search time. If marijuana and alcohol are substitutes, periods of high marijuana prices or marijuana shortages should coincide with periods of heavy alcohol use. If the drugs are complements, high marijuana prices should tend to depress contemporaneous alcohol use. If marijuana intoxication tends to build a taste for intoxication in general, a taste that alcohol can help satisfy, alcohol use should go up in periods following times of ready marijuana availability, and fall after periods of marijuana scarcity.

Such "natural" experiments do exist. In the late 1980s, for example, a variety of factors, primarily federal enforcement efforts, apparently led to substantial increases in marijuana prices and at least temporary shortages of the drug in some places. This may help provide an active test of the competing hypotheses about marijuana and other drugs; in particular, it would be worth investigating the connection, if any, between conditions in the marijuana market and anecdotal reports of a resurgence in the use of psychedelics, particularly LSD, MDMA, and various psychoactive mushrooms (but not, it seems, PCP).[17]

Because it can handle the interrelationships of multiple factors, econometrics, the unloved child of a liaison between economics and statistics, can serve as an imperfect substitute for true controlled experimentation when the universe refuses to hold still at the social scientist's command. John DiNardo and others at the RAND Corporation have begun to use econometric techniques to explore the relationships of complementarity and substitution between marijuana and alcohol. They report that marijuana and alcohol appear to be substitutes for one another among college students; reduced alcohol availability seems to generate increased marijuana use.[18] The imperfections in the data—price, availability, and consumption must all be estimated from survey results—and the complexity of the relationships among various periods of time (what econometricians call the *lag structure*) reduces the confidence one can have in the results of such explorations. Still, the results to date are noteworthy, and it would be interesting to repeat the investigation using cocaine (and perhaps the hallucinogens) as dependent variables. Karyn Model of the Harvard economics department has taken a different approach, using the legal penalties for marijuana use as the explanatory variable; she finds that decriminalization tends to increase the frequency of marijuana-related visits to hospital emergency rooms, but to decrease the frequency of emergency-room incidents involving other drugs.[19]

For the present, given the variety of possible effects and the paucity of data and careful investigations to date, the only reasonable position is agnosticism. There is no obvious reason to believe that either the substitution effects or the complementarity effects dominate the relationship between marijuana and other drugs or even that the net effect on alcohol has the same sign as the net effect on cocaine. The preliminary RAND finding of substitution between marijuana and alcohol seems plausible enough: both are cheap intoxicants. For the other illicit drugs, the balance between the two effects is likely to be closer; which set of influences dominates may depend on the details of the policies being followed. For example, a rise in marijuana use that accompanied decriminalization (leaving the supply of the drug in the black market) should have a greater tendency to increase the use of other illicit drugs than the same increase in marijuana use brought about by a partial legalization (creating a licit supply to compete with the illicit one); a partial legalization would reduce the opportunities in the marijuana-dealing trade and the contact between marijuana users and dealers in other psychoactives.

If there were any strong interest in making marijuana policy choices on the basis of likely actual results rather than as a part of a cultural struggle, advocates of tightening marijuana controls and advocates of loosening them would be debating over the details of gateway and substitution phenomena, and drug researchers would be vigorously sifting through the data in search of testable hypotheses. That "gateway drug" remains little more than a magical incantation, a quarter of a century into our national experience with the mass consumption of marijuana, suggests how little interest there is in formulating reasoned policy about America's most widely used illicit drug.

Marijuana as a Medicine

Before discussing the possibility of changes in the marijuana laws, we should dispose of a side issue: the question whether marijuana should once again be used as a medicine.

Marijuana, after having been an accepted pharmaceutical drug until medical as well as recreational uses were banned by the Marijuana Tax Act of 1937, had no role in treatment for the next three decades. Then anecdotes and some published research began to show that it helped relieve the nausea and vomiting that often accompany chemotherapy for cancer, discomforts that can be so severe as to lead patients to forgo potentially life-saving treatment.[20] There are many anti-emetic drugs on the market, but they are ineffective, or have serious side effects, in some chemotherapy patients. Consequently, many oncologists recommended marijuana to some patients despite its illegality; 44 percent of clinical oncologists responding to an anonymous survey acknowledged having done so in at least one case.[21] THC, the chief psychoactive ingredient of marijuana, has been approved in pill form as an anti-nausea medicine and appetite enhancer, but marijuana remains banned, despite evidence that it helps some patients not helped by THC.[22]

Whatever medical benefits marijuana proves to have must be weighed against the risks and costs of its approval when viewed from the perspective of drug abuse control. Those risks and costs come in two forms: the risk that the material will leak from licit to illicit channels, as the tranquilizers do, and increase the supply for recreational use; and the risk that medical approval will increase demand, either by improving the drug's public image or by creating a new user base among patients and their friends, as the medical use of morphine is said to have helped generate the opiate addiction problem of the late nineteenth century.

It is hard to take the supply-side risk very seriously in light of the thousands of tons of existing illicit supply. No doubt, some of the licit supply would leak from patients to their friends. But even insofar as this leakage represented an increment to total nonmedical use rather than a simple substitution of sources, the change in total consumption would surely be trivial. If it were proposed to approve marijuana for vague psychological conditions such as anxiety or stress, there would be some reason to worry about the development of drug-retailing operations under medical cover, after the fashion of the "stress clinics" that used to write tranquilizer prescriptions for a fee. Its approval for use in connection with a limited list of physical conditions—cancer, AIDS, multiple sclerosis, glaucoma—should pose no such danger.*

The fact that all of the currently proposed medical uses of marijuana take advantage of various side effects rather than the psychological effect that its nonmedical users seek would also help to reduce the impact of medical approval on attitudes about nonmedical use. Cocaine is a Schedule II rather than a Schedule I drug, but that does not appear to have prevented its developing the evil reputation it deserves in its role as a self-prescribed stimulant. It should be possible to maintain the same distinction about marijuana.

* Because of a quirk in the drug-approval process, once a drug is licensed for one use, physicians have great discretion to prescribe it for other uses. It might be necessary to create special regulations limiting the approval of marijuana to physical indications only, in order to prevent abuses.

Indeed, the appearance that the authorities are suppressing a valuable medicine to maintain the ideology of the war on drugs serves to discredit the whole effort. The prohibition of marijuana for recreational use has a number of inescapable costs, but keeping it out of the pharmacopoeia is not one of them. It is possible and desirable, both conceptually and practically, to separate the question of medical marijuana from that of recreational marijuana. If that separation were made, marijuana would probably be approved for some medical uses.

MARIJUANA LAWS

The current laws with respect to marijuana are simple: trafficking and possession for use are prohibited. These laws create the usual list of prohibition-related harms in the form of black-market transactions, additional drug damage because of adulterated goods and consumer uncertainty about potency, damage done to otherwise law-abiding consumers by defining their purchases as criminal acts, and strain on the law-enforcement system. But marijuana is unusual among illicit drugs in two important ways: its per-dose price is low,[23] and its user base is very large and relatively undeviant.[24]

The low price per dose means that retail marijuana dealing is not a very lucrative business compared with cocaine or heroin dealing. The total sums involved are comparable, but many more persons are involved in selling marijuana than is true of any other drug, and their earnings are correspondingly smaller.[25] In addition, since marijuana buyers tend to buy large numbers of doses per transaction (an ounce of ordinary marijuana or a quarter ounce of the highly cultivated and potent varieties, which now seem to be the standard transaction units, represent approximately fifty doses each), marijuana is rarely traded in the sort of bustling street markets that create the occasion for disorder and violence in the heroin and cocaine trades; users who buy infrequently are willing to wait, or search a little longer to enjoy the benefits of more discreet transactions.

The low price also reduces the importance of the illicit marijuana market as a generator of economic crime by users, though as noted there is some evidence of poor adolescents turning to dealing (primarily marijuana dealing) to keep themselves supplied with the drug.[26] While marijuana continues to account for a large number of possession arrests and for a substantial proportion of the federal drug enforcement effort and the drug-dealer population of the federal prisons,[27] it appears to represent only a modest share of felony case loads and prison populations at the local and state levels, where most of the drug-enforcement action is and where the strain on court and prison capacities is felt most keenly. Thus marijuana prohibition is not an important source of the spectacular side effects of using the criminal law as a means of drug abuse control that have caused even some law enforcement officials to think seriously about the legalization of cocaine.

On the other hand, a large number of Americans who rarely if ever do anything else that might get them arrested, including having in their possession any other controlled substance, do buy and use marijuana fairly regularly. While their individual risk of arrest on any one occasion is modest, the aggregate numbers are quite impressive: there are approximately 350,000 arrests for marijuana possession in the United States every year.[28] For most of the persons arrested, particularly in urban areas, the arrest will be more or less the end of the matter. They will be quickly released on bail or their own recognizance (if indeed they are physically arrested rather than being issued a summons to appear in court), and their cases will be "diverted" before trial or they will be allowed to plead guilty to a misdemeanor. In either case the punishment is apt to be unsupervised probation and an order to undergo some form of drug "education" similar to the "schools" that drunken drivers are forced to attend.[29] If they comply, their criminal records can be "sealed" or "expunged," after which they will have no recorded criminal history and may properly answer no to the question "Have you ever been arrested?" on a job or school application. The most punishing part of the process, aside from fear and humiliation, may be the cost of hiring a lawyer.

But for others, particularly in rural areas and in the South, an arrest for simple possession of marijuana will lead to a criminal conviction and even some incarceration. (The state of criminal justice records and statistics does not allow any estimate of just how frequent this outcome actually is.) Those who buy in street markets may be regarded as justly punished for their contribution to the neighborhood devastation those markets create. For others, the justification for incarceration is harder to find.

Since arrest is the most immediate and frequent part of the punishment process for all crimes, it is important that arrest should retain its social meaning both as involving some substantial risk of further punishment (to maintain its deterrent value) and as resulting from the doing of some substantial harm (to maintain its moral force). The fact that simple possession of marijuana is the third most common cause of arrest[30] puts strains on both of those symbolic links. This contribution to the devaluation of arrest as a sanction ought to be counted as a sizable cost of the current marijuana laws.

Decriminalization

Concern about the effects of marijuana-possession arrests on arrestees and on the criminal justice machinery provides the logical foundation for the movement for the decriminalization of marijuana. As used in this debate, *decriminalization* means leaving production and distribution of the drug entirely illegal, but removing criminal penalties—that is, the threat of arrest and trial, though not necessarily the threat of monetary penalty—for possession for personal use. (This was exactly the situation of alcohol under the Volstead Act.)

During the 1970s, decriminalization appeared to be the wave of the future. Eleven states enacted some version of decriminalization.[31] Although as a technical legal matter, this did not make it lawful to possess marijuana in those states—the federal prohibition remained in full force—as a practical matter marijuana users in those states were, and remain, almost completely immune from arrest and trial. If decriminalization has served to increase marijuana consumption in those states, that effect has been statistically invisible on both of the major national drug-use surveys.[32] Nor do the statistics on drug use among arrestees show any increase in the use of marijuana (or anything else) among offenders in states where its possession is decriminalized compared to those where it remains a crime under state law.*

As a possible policy, decriminalization is in some ways a compromise between maintaining prohibition and full legalization. It eliminates some of the least attractive features of the current regime, including the rather unpleasant irony that, while marijuana laws are primarily designed to protect drug users from themselves, arrest and criminal justice processing is for many users the most substantial risk of using marijuana. While loosening the drug laws has not in recent years been a politically serious idea, decriminalization had a great

---

* But see Karyn Model's research suggesting a small increase in marijuana-related emergency-room visits after decriminalization. Karyn E. Model, "The Effect of Marijuana Decriminalization on Hospital Emergency Room Drug Episodes: 1975–1987" (Cambridge, Mass.: Harvard University Department of Economics, 1991) (unpublished).

vogue in the early 1970s and attracted some highly respectable support, including that of a presidential commission and a study panel
of the National Academy of Sciences.* Not only was the policy attractive enough to pass through eleven state legislatures in one form or
another when liberalizing drug laws was in fashion, it has managed
to survive the toughening eighties virtually unscathed. The lack of
evidence that decriminalization at the state level had any impact on
consumption or on any measured drug problem seems to have been
a factor.

But decriminalization is not a free lunch. From the point of view
of a user or potential user, the risk of arrest is part of the price of
drug use. That current measurement techniques cannot detect the
difference between states with formal decriminalization and other
states may say more about the imprecision of the measurements,
and the variations in actual enforcement practice among states where
laws against marijuana possession remain on the books, than they do
about the deterrent effect of the threat of arrest. In addition, since
the federal law against possession remains in place even if largely
unenforced, we have no experience with removing the moral and
social force of the law itself—as opposed to the risk of arrest—as a
factor in discouraging marijuana use or at least keeping it discreet.

Whatever additional demand a full-scale national decriminalization of marijuana possession might generate would be supplied, as
the current demand is, entirely by the black market. Thus decriminalization is likely to prove to be the worst of all possible policies
when it comes to the drug-dealing aspect of the marijuana problem.
Adding more demand to a multibillion-dollar illicit industry will
have disadvantages: more untaxed income, more economic activity
outside legal control, and probably more corruption and violence.
Before rushing to conclude that decriminalization is a good idea,
one should weigh these costs against its benefits. Better measurements of the actual effects of decriminalization where it has taken

* It should be noted that both reports were disavowed even before they were issued:
the Shafer Commission's by President Richard Nixon (*Marijuana: Signal of Misunderstanding,* First Report of the National Commission on Marijuana and Drug Abuse
[Washington, D.C.: 1972]) and the NAS panel's (*Analysis of Marijuana Policy,* Commission for Behavioral and Social Sciences [Washington, D.C.: National Academy of
Science Press, 1982]) by the President of the National Academy. See foreword from
Frank Press in *Analysis of Marijuana Policy.* This foreword reportedly was written as a
result of a threat by the Director of the National Institute on Drug Abuse that NAS
would see no more federal drug-research money if the report were issued without
such a disclaimer.

place on the state level—effects on consumption, attitudes, criminal justice expenditures, and damage to defendants' futures—would help.

Legalization

The full legalization of marijuana, on something like the current alcohol model, would have effects so different from those of mere decriminalization that the two policies should not be discussed, as they often are, as more and less or thorough-going versions of essentially the same policy. Legalization would represent a much more profound change, for good and for ill.

The most prominent of the benefits of full legalization would arise from the virtual abolition of the black market, with its associated violence and corruption and the opportunity it creates for some users to pay for their own heavy marijuana consumption by engaging in marijuana dealing. This in turn might be expected to eliminate a large share of marijuana's gateway effect: the part that works through entry into drug dealing.

Legalization would also help dissociate marijuana from the other currently illicit drugs. This, too, might be expected to weaken the link between marijuana use and progression to more dangerous substances, for it would mean that the bright line that divides the legal from the illegal would stand between the millions who now use marijuana, but no other illicit drug, and further experimentation. Warnings in the classroom and the mass media about the great dangers of using any illegal substance might be more persuasive if they did not include a substance as widely used as cannabis.*

The legalization of marijuana use might also lead to a lower rate of damage per use incident as a result of changes in the norms and

---

* As a purely tactical political matter, public tolerance for strong measures against drug users in general might increase if marijuana users were not included. Roger Conner of the American Alliance for Rights and Responsibilities has suggested that repeal of the marijuana laws might do for the "war on drugs" what repeal of the draft did for military adventure: make it more palatable politically by taking the burden off those who might be the relatives of Members of Congress. Whether this should be counted as a benefit or a drawback of marijuana legalization depends on one's view of the specific measures that might be in question. As a matter of sound policy, there are certainly programs one might wish to pursue with respect to crack smokers that make no sense as applied to marijuana users, but some of the programs that might become politically and operationally feasible if the total number of illicit drug users was suddenly reduced to a few million might be very bad ones.

customs surrounding marijuana smoking: away from profound intoxication and poly-drug consumption, and toward use at carefully
controlled times and places.[33]

At a minimum, one should expect the licit marijuana companies
or state authorities to be as smarmily in favor of "moderation" and
"responsibility" as the liquor industry is today, and though the source
is suspect, it is hard to imagine that some of the message does not,
and would not, get through. On the other hand, while current marijuana laws do nothing to encourage moderation as such, they do a
great deal to encourage discretion about times and places of use, and
that may be effectively very much the same thing. It is possible that
smokers of legal marijuana would be less wary about letting their
intoxication be seen, and therefore more apt to make nuisances of
themselves, than today's smokers of illegal marijuana.

The savings in federal and local law enforcement expenditures
would be substantial. To be sure, taxes and regulation would have to
be enforced. There would have to be officials to subdue moonshining
and to effectuate rules about times and places of sale, and to enforce
the ban on distribution to minors. But the post-legalization enforcement effort would resemble the current activity of the Bureau of Alcohol, Tobacco, and Firearms and of state-level Alcoholic Beverages
Control Commissions rather than that of the Drug Enforcement Administration. Current spending on marijuana enforcement amounts
to a few (probably less than five) billion dollars per year;[34] the total
post-legalization enforcement budget would be a small fraction of
that sum.

Perhaps more important, hundreds of thousands of otherwise law-
abiding citizens each year would avoid arrest, and additional millions
would be freed from the fear of arrest. The benefits to them are
obvious and direct; the benefits to the rest of us—their increased
reluctance to break other laws and to risk arrest on other grounds—
are more speculative, but not necessarily smaller. A combination of
factors has created a massive imbalance between the range of conduct
currently forbidden by our criminal laws and the resources available
to enforce those laws and to punish those who flout them. As a
result, law-breaking has become undesirably cheap both practically
and psychologically. Even those of us who believe that the primary
response to that problem ought to be providing increased resources
must acknowledge that forbidding a smaller set of activities would
also help. This is not a dispositive argument with respect to any
particular vice now forbidden, any more than a budget deficit is a
dispositive argument with respect to any particular public program.

But it is an argument nonetheless, and one that those who put a premium on crime control as a goal of public policy ought to take more seriously than most of them seem to do.

In addition, a legal trade in marijuana would be subject to taxation: not only ordinary taxes on sales and incomes but also, presumably, specific excises of the kind imposed on other "vices" and "luxuries." While the yield of a new tax on salt or stereo equipment is not a net social benefit, but only a transfer from consumers and producers of these goods to the beneficiaries of the programs those revenues support, the yield of a new tax on a previously prohibited commodity such as marijuana is pure gain. The taxpayers, consumers of the newly legalized good, prefer having it legally available and taxed to not having it legally available. The revenues from marijuana taxes would thus be virtually found money since they would represent no additional burden on consumers as compared to the current situation. Drug dealers would be the only identifiable losers. If taxes were set to keep the price of licit marijuana near current black-market levels, revenues would be several billions of dollars per year: not a large sum compared with the size of the economy (between five and six trillion dollars per year) or to total government revenues and expenditures (roughly one-third of that), but not negligible considered as an expenditure for the purpose of controlling the abuse of marijuana.

If one thinks of current enforcement expenditures plus forgone revenues as the fiscal costs of prohibition, the question becomes whether those several billions of dollars could be better spent. This suggests a thought experiment. If we were to spend an additional $10 billion on drug abuse control—on enforcement directed at the remaining illicit drugs and violations of regulatory laws concerning marijuana, on persuasion, on treatment, and on the control of problem drug users—would the benefits of that spending be enough to counterbalance, or more than counterbalance, the ill effects of marijuana legalization? Not that such a spending increase would be probable, or necessarily desirable; perhaps the money could be better spent on other programs or used to finance reductions in other taxes or to shrink the deficit in the federal budget. Thinking about other drug-related uses of the money is a heuristic device to help us judge whether the benefits of keeping marijuana illegal are worth the $10 billion or so in direct spending and lost revenue they cost.

If one were designing a legal regime for marijuana along the lines of the current regime governing alcohol, the arguments for high taxes would be very strong. The advantages of high taxation are increased revenues per unit consumed; decreased consumption, particularly among the poor and those very heavy users for whom the price of marijuana is an important budget item; and reduced incentives for leakage to those, especially minors, not permitted to buy the drug legally. The disadvantages are lost revenues from lower sales, representing lower total consumption and greater clandestine untaxed production on the pattern of moonshine whisky; increased consumption of substitutes such as alcohol and the hallucinogens; and, in the likely event that the price elasticity of demand near current price levels is relatively inelastic, increased total expenditures by users, leaving them with less money for their other purposes. This last effect is most worrisome if heavy users tend to be poorer than average, because the human importance of the expenditures forgone to pay for higher-priced marijuana is likely to be greater the smaller the budgets of the households paying the tax.

Even at current illicit prices, the money price of marijuana intoxication—roughly a dollar per hour for those who have not built up a tolerance for the drug through chronic heavy use—is low enough, compared with the prices of other intoxicants or other forms of entertainment, that there seems to be little reason to allow it to fall even lower as a result of legalization. Commodities that are cheap compared with their substitutes tend to be in inelastic demand, so higher taxes would lead to sharply higher revenues and only limited amounts of increased consumption of other drugs. (By the same token, of course, inelastic demand puts a limit on the power of taxation as a means of controlling consumption and consumption-related damage.)

Licit marijuana of known provenance, potency, and freedom from adulteration would have a competitive advantage over black-market marijuana as long as the prices were comparable, so there would be little need to undercut current illicit prices as part of the anti-moonshining effort that would be a necessary feature of a post-legalization world. The other likely form of illicit activity, the redistribution of the drug from adults permitted to buy to minors forbidden to buy, would be easier to control the higher the tax was set, since the earnings available to resellers and thus their incentive to engage in resale would depend on the difference between the price faced on the remaining black market and the (licit) price of marijuana purchased for resale.

The major disadvantage of a high marijuana tax would be the financial drain on poor individuals and families who were heavy marijuana users. This is a special case of the general argument that vice taxes are regressive. But it is precisely among the poor that the price elasticity of demand is likely to be highest, and the value of reducing consumption greatest. Indeed, one of the potential benefits of legalization would be lower consumption by some current heavy users. Such a reduction would result from eliminating both the effective volume discount now available to those who buy marijuana in bulk for their own use (and thus skip one or two steep black-market markups) and the ability of some heavy users to finance their marijuana consumption by selling to friends and strangers. There is little evidence that, under current conditions, marijuana expenditures cause any significant number of users to go without necessities or turn to crimes other than marijuana dealing to pay for their drug. Although it is conceivable that legalization with a high tax might change that picture, there is no real reason to believe that the compulsion to smoke marijuana could exert such power over any noticeable number of the drug's devotees.

Thus it seems that, if we were to legalize marijuana, we should do so with taxes calculated to maintain its price near the current black-market price. Presumably, any legal regime would continue to ban distribution to minors (except perhaps by their parents) as is now the case with alcohol, thus reversing the current situation in which marijuana is more easily available to high school and college students than to any other segment of the population. We would be left with a noticeably smaller illicit drug market—marijuana now accounts for perhaps a quarter of total black-market revenues—a correspondingly smaller law enforcement effort, a much smaller population of frequent lawbreakers, a reduced linkage between marijuana use and the use of other dangerous drugs, and several billions of dollars in additional annual public revenue.

On the other hand, making marijuana an item of licit commerce, no longer subject to the strictures of the law but subject to the full marketing ingenuity of the consumer-goods industry, would surely generate an increase in the number of users, particularly over the long run as the change in the laws began to influence attitudes. Each new user would be at some risk of progressing to heavy, chronic use, and probably at some elevated risk (though presumably lower risk than someone who begins to use illegal marijuana today) of progressing to the use of more dangerous, still illicit drugs. The serious question is not whether an increase in consumption would occur, but how large it would be and how much of it would reflect new heavy use. The other unknown is the net effect on the use of other drugs that would accompany the whole complex of social changes surrounding legalization, including the indirect effects of legitimizing a nonalcohol intoxicant.

As is true of almost any legalization proposal, the new policy would count as a major success if the increase in consumption proved to be small, because the individual and social damage associated with any given level of consumption would decrease. Even a substantial rise in the number of users might not reflect a disaster if, on balance, marijuana smoking turned out to be a substitute for drinking. If, on the other hand, the number of users were to triple, and the proportion of total users who became heavy users or went on to use more dangerous drugs remained the same, even the substantial advantages of legalization would begin to look rather small compared with its cost in increased drug abuse.

In particular, the glib assertion of some advocates of legalization that distribution to minors would remain as illegal as it is under current laws cannot be taken at face value. The examples of alcohol and tobacco are before us as reminders of the difficulty of enforcing such laws when every adult is a potential source of leakage. It is possible, though by no means established, that making marijuana use another badge of adulthood would increase its attractiveness to adolescents. Were it not for the fact that the current prohibition also signally fails to deny access to marijuana to minors—more than four in five high school seniors still report it to be easily available[35]—increased access by minors might count as an insuperable disadvantage of legalization.

Nor does a system like the current alcohol-control regime hold out much hope for exerting control over very heavy chronic users, simply because it provides no way to identify them for control. Although the current marijuana regime does very badly on this score, since in effect heavy users get marijuana at a deep discount, in a post-legalization regime we would have to expect the legal distribution system, whether public or private, to serve, and to derive a substantial share of its revenues from, people with out-of-control marijuana problems, just as the alcohol industry does with the population of chronic drunks. We would also have to expect the licit marijuana industry, whether public or private, to resist control measures, though probably not as effectively as the alcohol industry has done.

Considered as a policy proposal, marijuana legalization has one very serious drawback: virtual irreversibility if it goes badly wrong. A tripling of marijuana use does not seem a likely result of legalization on the alcohol model, but it is surely not an impossible one.

Imagine for a moment that marijuana became legal, and that aggregate consumption and the number of compulsive users rose to three times their current levels without any corresponding decrease in drinking. In that circumstance, the fact that the revenues of the marijuana tax (or the profits of the state marijuana agencies) were much higher than anticipated would be cold comfort indeed, and we would have good cause to regret the decision to legalize.

But that regret would not necessarily be sufficient reason to reverse the decision. Reprohibiting marijuana after legalization had tripled the market would mean starting with black-market demand, and thus potential enforcement problems, three times as large as today's. Some of the market that legalization had called forth would dissolve with reprohibition, but only some: the rest would remain as a potentially long-term headache. As Pandora could have warned Humpty-Dumpty, not all processes are reversible.

Faced with this objection, some advocates of legalization have proposed "experimental" approaches to the matter.[36] But it is hard to imagine an experiment sufficiently large-scale and long-lasting to provide convincing answers and yet sufficiently modest to be shut down easily if it starts to get out of hand. It is equally hard to think of research that could be done under current conditions and that would allow a much more confident prediction about the results of legalization. The experiences of other countries are of limited value because, for good and ill, the United States is very much *sui generis*. We probably know about as much relevant to the legalization decision today as we will five or twenty years from now.

In principle, some of the costs now associated with marijuana prohibition could be greatly reduced without changing the drug's legal status. An informal policy of not arresting marijuana users has many of the advantages of formal decriminalization. Enforcement resources can be shifted away from investigating and prosecuting marijuana dealing, just as they have been shifted away from investigating and prosecuting bookmaking, even if the current laws remain unchanged. Employers and probation departments that administer drug tests could omit marijuana, as the District of Columbia Pretrial Services Agency currently does. Anti-drug messages in the mass-media and the classroom could be modulated to acknowledge the difference in risk level between marijuana and crack. Such a policy of continued prohibition plus salutary neglect has a great deal to be said for it, compared with either formal legalization or a vigorously enforced prohibition.

But, even assuming that such a policy is desirable, there is some question about how far it is practical. The strong emotional charge that now attaches to the label *drug* (meaning *illicit drug*) discourages attempts at careful differentiation. That marijuana is by far the most widely used of the currently illicit drugs makes matters harder; how long can people be expected to maintain a strong stand against "drugs" and at the same time not act strongly with respect to the one "drug" they are most likely to encounter?

Maintaining marijuana in the same legal status as cocaine, heroin, and the amphetamines poses a choice between two undesirable alternatives: to apply to marijuana policies that actually make sense only for those more dangerous drugs, or to restrict policies regarding cocaine and the others to those that would make sense for marijuana as well. The stronger these tendencies, the stronger the case for giving marijuana a new legal status.

An Optimal Marijuana Control Regime

But there is no need to choose between keeping marijuana in the illegal status it now has and making it as freely available as alcohol now is; we can look for a third option. In my view, no intoxicant, including alcohol, ought to be available under a regime as loose as the current alcohol-control regime. Such a system has three great flaws: it fails to provide an enforceable ban on distribution to minors; it makes abusable drugs available to those with established patterns of abuse; and it provides inadequate disincentive for obnoxious, reckless, or criminal behavior under the influence.

A personal license to use marijuana with a quantity limit could help remedy those three failures without imposing unworkable administrative burdens or greatly expanding the market for illicitly produced marijuana. The problem of operating a control system is simplified by several facts about marijuana: it is compact and easily storable, the currently conventional purchase quantities represent many dosage units, and there is in the United States no institution for marijuana smoking comparable to the bar, crack house, opium den, or Amsterdam "coffee shop." Thus the number of transactions per user per year would be relatively small, and there would be no need to consummate them quickly, since in general consumers could order new supplies before their current supply had run out.

The simplest system incorporating a personal license and a quantity limit could be operated by the newly legalized marijuana industry or a state-owned marijuana-sales system on the model of the "state stores" that currently sell liquor in states where package goods are a public monopoly. Any would-be user, on presentation of her driver's license (or equivalent non-driver's identification issued by the motor vehicle registry) at any retail outlet, would be entered on the list of licensed users and given a number identical to her driver's license number. To buy marijuana, she would have to call a retail outlet twenty-four hours in advance, giving the retailer enough time to verify her licensed status with the agency or firm operating the central list. That central agency would also record the quantity ordered and audit the quantities purchased by retail vendors against their recorded retail purchase orders. Any of the national credit-card companies would be a natural supplier of list-maintenance and quantity-tracking services; that would leave the public authorities only the task of monitoring the integrity of the service.

The customer could either pick up the marijuana or have it delivered to the address on her license. Purchases over the allowed quantity would simply be refused. Any user who was convicted of a crime connected with her marijuana use, including driving under the influence, or made a public nuisance of herself, or distributed the drug to minors or other unlicensed persons, would face the loss of her license, and users who found their consumption getting the better of them could surrender their licenses voluntarily. Employers could require employees in some job categories not to be licensed users: the job market might work adequately to prevent abuse of this system, or the "sensitive" jobs might be defined by law. It is possible that underwriters of some forms of insurance would want to surcharge licensed marijuana users.

Such a system could be tightened in any of several fashions. Would-be users might be required to pass a test, to undergo some form of education and training, or both. Retail outlets could be abolished entirely and all transactions done by mail order. The reader's ingenuity will probably suggest more such extensions, but it would be futile to speculate about them in advance of experience. Perfect compliance is neither possible nor essential. Such a system can earn its keep by reducing the rates of leakage, misconduct, and heavy chronic use; any attempt to eliminate those problems entirely will produce a system that falls to the ground under its own weight.

The choice of quantity limits under such a system poses a complicated problem. Such limits have two distinct objectives: to prevent large-scale reselling to ineligible buyers and to restrict the drug consumption of the heaviest users, because high volume suggests both problem use and such frequent intoxication that the drug, rather than the user, may be said to be making the purchase decisions.

For the prevention of resale, even a quantity limit quite generous by personal-consumption standards will do the job, which is to keep a single adult from supplying an entire high school. The prevention of abuse is more difficult. The lower the limit, the greater the proportion of demand rechanneled into the illicit market, an especially undesirable result because that market will also be supplying minors. As with alcohol, very heavy users account for such a large proportion of total consumption that even a limit high enough not to constrain the vast majority of users will still leave a significant fraction of the volume licit outside the system.

Compared with the looseness of the current alcohol-control system, a system of revocable personal licenses, especially with quantity limits, seems Big-Brotherish; any mention of computerized lists is sure to raise hackles. But compared to prohibition, it represents a considerable liberalization, while creating much less serious threats than virtually unrestricted commerce.

Such a move by the United States would have implications for the international drug-control regime. The Single Convention on Narcotic Drugs does not provide for any form of nonmedical availability for the drugs to which it applies, including marijuana. Some foreign governments would presumably react with outrage if the United States were to adopt a different approach; others might be relieved, at least in private. How serious a consideration this should be depends on one's view of the value of the international drug-control regime and on how easily the resulting damage could be repaired.

One other alternative to prohibition or free commerce deserves to be mentioned, if only for its great administrative simplicity. In 1975, Alaska's supreme court found that the prosecution of an adult for possession, of a "personal use" amount of marijuana for use at home violated the state's constitutional right of privacy.*

The effect of the ruling was to legalize the growing of marijuana for personal use at home since the purchase and sale of the substance remained a crime. This ruling could not, of course, repeal the federal laws that make such activity a felony, and the evidence of its actual effects is both sparse and mixed, but as a possible nationally legislated policy it has some charms. By restricting growing to the home, it delegates authority over the marijuana use of minors to their parents. By permitting production for personal use (probably no more demanding technically than other kinds of gardening), it removes marijuana both from the criminal justice system and from

---

* *Ravin v. State*, 537 P.2d 494 (1975). Laws against buying, selling, possession, or use outside the home, use while driving, and possession by minors remained in force. A referendum to reverse that ruling passed in 1990 by 55 percent of the vote to 45 percent, leaving the courts to decide whether such a referendum can modify a constitutional interpretation.

commerce, eliminating the criminal trafficker and the brand manager alike.

Neither a personal license and quantity limit nor the Alaskan system would provide a risk-free path to legalization. Some possibility of a great surge in use, including heavy use and use by minors, would remain. In particular, slow cultural change in undesirable directions cannot be ruled out in advance; who could have guessed that television would prove addictive in ways that movies and radio were not? If some quick or slow disaster were to come to pass, going back to prohibition in the face of increased demand for the newly reprohibited good would remain problematic. Still, it seems more likely than not that some form of restricted licit availability represents our least-bad alternative for dealing with the most widely used illicit drug.*

CHANGING PROGRAMS
UNDER CURRENT LAW

All this talk of changing the laws, however valid on its own terms, is for the moment, and for immediate practical purposes, merely idle chat. No such change is on the horizon, because there is very little popular support for it.[37] In terms of actually doing anything soon, it

---

* In a previous volume, I concluded, after rehearsing much the same list of arguments presented here, that the legal availability of marijuana was not a good idea. Since I regarded the matter as a close question then, and still do so, this change of stance is perhaps less dramatic than meets the eye, but I have quite clearly crossed the line from "no" to "yes."

The primary reason for this shift is my belief that regulation by revocable user permits and quantity limits can retain many of the advantages of prohibition while eliminating none of its major disadvantages. Faced with only the choice between legalization on the alcohol model and the current prohibition, I would be much less eager to recommend a change.

In addition, I have become more concerned about the effect of marijuana prohibition on attempts to control other currently illicit drugs, particularly educational and user-responsibility efforts directed generically at "drugs." In a world with only marijuana, I might still prefer to keep it illicit; in a world with cocaine and heroin, it seems more prudent to draw a bright line with them on one side and marijuana on the other. Moreover, the accumulating, though still fragmentary, evidence that marijuana tends to substitute for alcohol and other drugs tends to make the prospect of increased marijuana use as a consequence of its licit availability somewhat less daunting.

I should acknowledge that my colleague Mark Moore, who is fully conversant with this reasoning, remains unpersuaded. He is concerned that any alteration of the current legal boundaries would tend to sow confusion among the millions who have been mobilized with such great effort to oppose drug abuse in all its (illicit) forms. His is the Burkean view: "If it is not necessary to change, it is necessary not to change."

is more important to consider what changes in programs, within the ambit of existing laws, might improve matters.

Singling Out Marijuana

One key to improving programs related to marijuana is to recognize its somewhat anomalous place among the controlled substances. While marijuana maintains its current prohibited status, it is difficult to separate it from the other illicit drugs in the design of ancillary policies, such as those involving workplace testing and testing for offenders. But in some cases the costs of those policies will be unnecessarily large if marijuana is included. Since marijuana is cheap and does not as a rule generate aggression, forcing marijuana-using offenders to abstain from the drug may not reduce their criminal activity. Sending a parolee back to prison to finish a life sentence because he tested positive for marijuana is surely an overreaction.

Since marijuana remains detectable in the urine for many days after use and since heavy or frequent marijuana users compose only a small proportion of all users, there is less reason to think that a positive marijuana test marks an undesirable employee than would be the case for a test showing cocaine, amphetamine, or opiate use. The fact that marijuana is cheap means that a marijuana-using employee will not represent the sort of financial risk posed by a cocaine user.* The fact that employment-related testing threatens the jobs of millions of persons who are not manifestly bad workers fuels much of the opposition to employee testing.

These problems constitute part of the argument for changing the legal status of marijuana. But the connection between legal status and inclusion in testing programs, though natural, is not inevitable. The District of Columbia's program of urine testing for persons released on bail simply does not include marijuana. That example may deserve emulation. Whether any given testing program should include marijuana ought to be decided on the merits, with reference to the purposes for which it is established, and not simply as a "drug-free" reflex reaction.

---

* It may be the case that a preemployment marijuana screen will help weed out potential problem employees; the evidence is mixed. See Craig Zwerling, James Ryan, and Endel Orav, "The Efficacy of Pre-employment Drug Screening for Marijuana and Cocaine in Predicting Employment Outcome," *Journal of the American Medical Association* 264 (20 [28 November 1990]): 2639–2644.

Persuasion

Marijuana is in some ways the most attractive target among the illicit drugs for demand reduction through persuasion. Because marijuana is far more widely used, and therefore far less exotic, than cocaine, heroin, or the psychedelics, there is correspondingly less danger that discussing its risks in school will create a curiosity and an awareness of possibilities that would otherwise have been absent. By the same token, the target efficiency of the messages—the probability that any given recipient would have seriously considered using the drug now or in the future—is higher for marijuana than for any other illicit substance. These might seem to be good reasons to stress marijuana in anti-drug messages.

For the same reason, however, generic anti-drug messages, or even messages about responsible decision making and self-control in the abstract, will influence more potential marijuana users than potential users of other drugs. The anti-marijuana cause thus gets a disproportionate share of the benefits of virtually any persuasion campaign, and focusing messages explicitly on marijuana carries some special disadvantages. The whole campaign may lose credibility if the audience has personal or vicarious experience of apparently harmless marijuana use, and there is a risk of exacerbating the gateway effect by giving marijuana users the implicit message that they have already lost their personal battle against drug abuse.

The statistical correlation between tobacco use and marijuana experimentation among adolescents has not attracted the policy attention or the close causal analysis that has been devoted to the link between marijuana and other drugs, but it is quite strong and suggestive. One or two careful long-term intervention studies, examining, for example, the effects on high-school marijuana use of grade-school anti-tobacco propaganda, might point the way to a valuable national strategy for reducing marijuana demand among teenagers. The recent drastic increase in cigarette taxes in California should provide a natural experiment on the effect of tobacco prices on marijuana consumption (what economists call the cross-elasticity of demand).

Treatment

The treatment of problem marijuana use has never received much attention or public funding, and for good reasons. While the number of chronic heavy marijuana users seems to be large absolutely, though not as a proportion of all marijuana users, few of them seem to be crying out for help, and still fewer make themselves such nuisances that treatment, beyond "drug education," is imposed on them by judges or probation officers. Unassisted quitting is and will remain the primary mode of "treatment," followed by group self-help.

There does appear to be a considerable demand from parents for help in controlling their children's marijuana use, and a substantial private supply of residential clinics and schools. As usual in the drug-treatment field, little is known about costs, benefits, and side effects. There is evidence that some programs dealing with juvenile marijuana users offer "therapy" that may be more drastic than the consequences of smoking too much pot really justify, as is probably true of parental reactions to many other kinds of teenage rebelliousness.[38] Ordinarily, we rely on parents to ensure that the measures applied to their children are proportionate to their problems. One danger of sending out increasingly strong anti-drug messages in the mass media and within the network of parental anti-drug groups is that parents may be led to overreact and turn to cures that are worse than the disease.

Enforcement

It is not now possible to make recommendations about marijuana enforcement on the basis of any very firm knowledge of the current level and direction of activity, since agency budgets and activity reports are neither reported by drug nor centrally collated. But it appears that marijuana attracts a share of enforcement efforts more consistent with the size of the market—in users and dollars—than with its contribution to measurable drug-related damage or the value of enforcement in reducing such damage. The case for redirecting enforcement resources away from marijuana and toward other drugs—heroin most of all—remains strong.[39]

The Federal supply control effect consists primarily of pressure on foreign governments to eradicate marijuana in the field, domestic efforts to do the same (which are largely justified by the need to set a good example for foreign source countries), and interdiction (anti-smuggling) efforts. Somewhat to my surprise, over the past decade these efforts seem to have succeeded in substantially increasing the price of marijuana, even correcting for inflation and changes in potency, and created some spot shortages.* But even very large relative price increases have left marijuana quite cheap compared with other means of intoxication, and there is little evidence that high prices are driving users from the market. Nor have such measures as emergency-room reports of marijuana-related overdoses shown any consistent pattern of decline.[40] The major effect of higher prices has probably been to enrich domestic marijuana growers.

At the same time, the shape of the domestic marijuana industry has been changing. More vigorous enforcement efforts appear to be driving some of the tie-dye and sandals crowd out of marijuana growing, while higher prices and the enforcement-generated premium on tightly organized conspiracy attract a rougher element to the trade. The geographic shift from Northern California to the mountains of Kentucky as the center of the growing industry corresponds to a shift from people whose cultural roots are in the sixties to people whose cultural roots are in moonshining, with its traditions of violence and corruption as ways of dealing with enforcement pressure.[41] This raises a serious threat that domestic marijuana production will be a source of revenues for organized crime (in the ethnically neutral sense of that phrase). In the absence of any compensating gain on the consumption side, this does not seem to be a risk worth taking.

An ideal domestic marijuana enforcement program would concentrate on precisely the sort of organization that has been the unintended beneficiary of marijuana enforcement policy since 1981. Mounting such an effort would involve concentrating on individuals and groups selected in advance for their contribution to violence and corruption, rather than looking for targets of enforcement op-

---

* There appear to be two explanations for the surprising (to me) increase in marijuana price. First, the effort itself, particularly the effort against smuggling, appears to have enjoyed a much larger resource increase than I had conceived of in my earlier calculations. Second, domestic supply has responded relatively slowly to the increase in the demand for home-grown product fostered by reduced imports, with the result that domestic growers appear to be enjoying price increases greater than would be required to compensate them for the increased costs and risks imposed on them by increased domestic eradication and enforcement. In the absence of a cartel, one would expect this to be a transient phenomenon; thus the price of domestically produced marijuana should tend to fall, and the frequency of spot shortages to diminish, over time. Imports of hashish, a concentrated cannabis product whose high ratio of value to bulk makes it more worth smuggling through tight border controls than marijuana, may also contribute to a gradual loosening of supply conditions. It also appears that marijuana demand has been falling since the late 1970s, for reasons seemingly independent of changes in enforcement activity. As argued in Chapter 5, on markets, the long-run impact of falling demand in drug markets is likely to be rising prices, because of the increased impact of any given level of enforcement activity on a smaller industry.

portunity. That, in turn, would require investigative and prospective institutions with strong institutional memory and great patience: institutions more like those used with success against the various Mafia families than those that normally carry out drug law enforcement.

Aside from such an attack on marijuana-related organized crime, it is hard to see the benefits from anything more than minimal, semi-symbolic efforts to squeeze marijuana production and distribution. A policy of informal grudging toleration, like that currently applied to the still-illegal forms of gambling, would seem to be in order.

Such a policy should not be confused with the more-or-less official, ungrudging toleration extended to cannabis sales in the Netherlands, particularly Amsterdam. There flagrant retail traffic in "coffee shops" is ostentatiously ignored by the police, pursuant to written, publicized policies.[42] Even taking at face value reports by Dutch officials that there has been no increase in marijuana use in the wake of this policy, it would be too optimistic to expect that the same results would follow if such a policy were put into effect in the United States. Short of the Dutch approach, however, one could have a policy designed to force growers, sellers, and users to keep their heads down, thus maintaining most of the benefits of prohibition, without attempting to use the machinery of law enforcement to raise price, increase search time, and suppress demand. That is, in effect, the policy of many big-city police departments; unless the neighbors are complaining, they simply refuse to bother with routine small-scale marijuana cases.

On this point, there exists a strong tension between practical politics and the policy analyst's idea of good sense. Many middle-class parents are far more worried about the prospect that their children will get involved with marijuana than with the state of the crack trade in some psychologically and socially distant ghetto neighborhood. Police and prosecutors outside the metropolitan centers want to do their part (and to be seen doing their part) in the war on drugs. For them, retail and small-scale wholesale marijuana-dealing cases are quite attractive. But from the perspective of those without the taste for cultural holy war, the practical rewards of additional marijuana enforcement simply do not cover its costs.

10

Cocaine

*Cocaine is God's way of telling you you have too
much money.*
— George Carlin

Cocaine is a powerful, short-acting central nervous system stimulant. By blocking the reabsorption of the neurotransmitter chemical
dopamine into the neurons that release it, it causes a temporary ac-
celeration of perception and thought. No one knows how much of
the attraction of cocaine as a recreational drug derives from the resulting feeling of increased power, and how much from the drug's
direct effects on the brain's pleasure centers.[1] In any case, cocaine
is powerfully reinforcing in many animal species and humans; that
is, a subject who finds that a given behavior will lead to a dose of
cocaine tends to increase the frequency of that behavior.[2] Tolerance
builds quickly within a use session, more slowly over repeated use.[3]

Unlike the purely spurious sensation of brilliance that fools some
users of other drugs, particularly alcohol—a sensation that derives
almost entirely from the suppression of the drugtaker's higher brain
functions and thus of his critical faculties—the temporary quickening
of thought that cocaine produces is at least partly genuine. (The same
is true of the other stimulants, such as amphetamine and caffeine.) So
is the increased stamina and lengthened wakefulness that result if the
drug is repeatedly taken at short intervals.[4] Thus the early results of
cocaine use on the job are likely to be positive; the managing partner
of a large professional services firm told me that he had learned
to regard an unexplained burst of increased productivity among a
group of his junior professional staff as a warning sign that they had
discovered cocaine.

But if the intellectual stimulation of cocaine is not like the gold
of faerie, which proves on inspection by morning light to have been

nothing but straw all along, it resembles other magical gifts in coming at a price. The artificial speeding up of the nervous system produces by homeostatic reaction an inevitable slowing down, and the stimulation of the pleasure centers seems to generate a reaction syndrome in which pleasure is not experienced at all: anhedonia.[5] Cocaine use can also induce anxiety. This effect can range from a generalized edginess like the effect of too much coffee to a stimulant psychosis like that typical of amphetamine injectors.[6]

The period of depressed cognitive and sensory activity that follows the end of a cocaine-use session—the "crash"—can be extremely unpleasant, particularly by contrast with the preceding period of stimulation.[7] The crash can be postponed by the simple expedient of taking more cocaine, but only at the price of increasing the severity of the crash when it finally comes. This gives rise to the typical "binge" pattern of cocaine abuse: a series of episodes of very heavy use (that can last, thanks to cocaine's tendency to prolong wakefulness, for dozens of hours) separated by periods of non-use.[8] Compulsive cocaine use is thus unlike the typical pattern of compulsive heroin use, which consists of a more or less consistent daily dosage without which the user begins to experience withdrawal symptoms. One could think of cocaine as producing an acute addiction—localized to the individual use session—as opposed to the chronic addiction of the opiates.

For some of the heaviest users, those in whom cocaine has destroyed the capacity to experience ordinary pleasure, the binges themselves seem to be periodic; craving for the drug builds with the time since the last binge.[9] These "coke heads" may fairly be said to be hooked in the same sense that heroin addicts are hooked. No one knows what proportion of all heavy cocaine users experience this pattern; reinforcement would also explain why, once her last crash has worn off, a cocaine user might go searching for the drug again. The situation seems to be more complicated than a simple craving for stimulation; physicians who try to help compulsive cocaine users break the cycle of compulsive use prescribe antidepressants rather than stimulants.

DIMENSIONS OF THE COCAINE PROBLEM

The User Population

As always with illicit drug consumption, accurate numbers are elusive and precise ones completely unavailable. Approximately twenty million Americans appear to have at least sampled cocaine in some form since it regained popularity in the 1970s.[10] Several million still use it at least occasionally,[11] and between two and three million do so weekly or more; most of the latter are probably in some degree of trouble with the drug.[12]

The total number of cocaine users grew by a factor of twenty or more in the period between 1975 and 1985, and has since fallen significantly.[13] (The actual decrease has almost certainly not been as large as the 74 percent drop reflected in the survey figures, because some users who have not stopped using the drug have surely stopped talking about it to interviewers conducting surveys for the government.) By contrast, the number of heavy users (once a week or more often), and presumably of compulsive users, continued to grow through the 1980s, though it had probably stopped growing by 1990.[14] The evidence suggests that use has stabilized, or even begun to decline, in those areas where consumption grew first, and that it is still growing in areas where the phenomenon started later. Use and heavy use are still distributed widely across ethnic gaps and social classes, but use among whites and among the affluent has been shrinking quickly while use among African-Americans and Hispanics and among the poor has been shrinking much more slowly.[15]

In the cities where samples of male arrestees have been tested for recent drug use, the measured rates of cocaine use range from a low of below one-fifth (Indianapolis and Omaha) to a high of almost two-thirds (Manhattan); in the median city, 44 percent tested positive for cocaine. Rates among female arrestees were even higher.[16] Those numbers have leveled off and begun to drop in the cities where the crack epidemic hit earliest but have continued to rise elsewhere.[17]

How much of the crime that led to those arrests is "cocaine-related" is completely unclear; arrestee characteristics may reflect the social customs among the class of young men who dominate the arrestee population as much as they do the determinants of criminal behavior. Police assertions about the drug-relatedness of crime seem to be largely ritual gestures, rarely based on any solid evidence.[18] Unsurprisingly, however, studies of heavy cocaine users in poor neighborhoods suggest that they commit many income-producing crimes, including cocaine dealing.[19] Until money begins to grow on the trees of the mean streets, this will necessarily be true of any expensive drug habit.

The number of reported deaths caused by cocaine soared through the 1980s, to a total of more than 3000 medical-examiner "mentions" in 1989.* The pattern of cocaine injuries as measured by emergency room mentions was similar. The death and injury figures appear to have peaked in late 1988 and early 1989, with deaths leveling off and injuries dropping sharply, though at levels far above those of any other illicit drug and even higher than the ever-present "alcohol-in-combination."†

The fact that the problem grew even as the number of users shrank demonstrates the inadequacy of policies directed only at reducing the total user number. The important policy goals have to do with reducing the important kinds of harm: crime, violence, and neighborhood disruption tied to dealing; crime associated with heavy use; diversion of law enforcement resources from preventing and punishing predatory crime to preventing and punishing cocaine dealing; health damage and death to users; and damage to children exposed to cocaine in the womb or neglected by parents more interested in drug taking than in child-raising. All of these are likely to vary more or less directly with the number of heavy users; they have little to do with the number of casual users, and even less to do with the number of casual users who are employed and respectable, and thus easy targets for workplace drug testing and other "user accountability" measures.

Casual users are important in three ways: as potential problem users, as participants in indiscreet markets and thus contributors to trafficking violence and neighborhood disruption, and as sources of money to support the illicit industry. The first is the strongest reason to worry about the number of casual users. Cutting down on the number of initiations among current non-users and working to increase the rate of quits among current casual users may contribute substantially to reducing the number of heavy users in the future. The second is significant, but involves only a fraction of the casual users, those who buy in street markets or drug houses rather than from dealers who sell in bars or their own living rooms or who make

---

* A medical examiner "mention" means that cocaine was detected while doing an autopsy of someone who died not by violence and not of a disease for which he was under treatment; multiple drugs may be "mentioned" on a single case. While drug poisoning need not be the primary cause of death, these medical examiner mentions are plausibly thought of as fatal overdoses. See National Institute on Drug Abuse, *Annual Data 1988, Data from the Drug Abuse Warning Network*, Series 1, No. 8 (Rockville, Md.: Department of Health and Human Services, 1988): iv.

† Alcohol alone is not counted, partly because the sheer volume would be overwhelming and partly because the DAWN system that counts drug-related injuries and deaths is maintained by the National Institute on Drug Abuse rather than the National Institute on Alcohol Abuse and Alcoholism.

deliveries directly to their customers; it is probably best addressed by user-focused enforcement efforts, preferably ones such as vehicle forfeiture, that do not require arrest and criminal processing. The third is simply an illusion, which can be dispelled by a little arithmetic: if there were four million casual users (more than twice the household survey estimate), and each of them bought $1000 worth of cocaine per year (a generous definition of "casual"), then their total contribution to the cocaine economy would be $4 billion, or only about one-fifth of the total: not a small number absolutely, but hardly the mainstay of the black market.[20]

There have been reports of open cocaine dealing in poor rural areas, the dealers being attracted in part by the paucity of law enforcement resources in counties where twenty small towns may be served by three half-time deputy sheriffs. This is potentially a frightening development because neither the populations nor the public agencies of such areas are prepared to deal with it. Unfortunately, except for surveys, all of the existing systems for collecting drug-related data are concentrated in cities, the perennial centers of illicit drug dealing and consumption and still the centers of the cocaine trade, so there is no easy way to track a rural epidemic if one starts.

Health Damage to Users

More than three thousand persons per year die in the United States from pharmacological action of cocaine (frequently in combination with other drugs).[21] This is a large number of overdoses, each representing a premature death and grief for the victim's intimates, but it is not a large share of the accidental-death toll, and still less of the overall mortality figures.[22] By itself, it hardly constitutes a social crisis.

That figure certainly undercounts the total number of deaths attributable to cocaine taking, because it excludes those who die as a result of the chronic effects of cocaine use in the form of heart disease, stroke, and so on.* There is no published estimate of non-acute pharmacological cocaine deaths, but it is probably substantial, perhaps larger than the count of direct overdose deaths. Nor has anyone calculated the future deaths attributable to current organic damage.

---

* A comparable count of nicotine victims would find none at all, since nicotine as used in cigarettes, cigars, pipes, and chewing tobacco simply does not generate fatal overdoses.

But even if these chronic-disease deaths were added in, the figure would surely not approach the totals for alcohol (approximately 60,000, not counting accidents and homicides) or tobacco (approximately 400,000).[23] Overweight, excessive meat consumption, lack of exercise, and the failure to wear seatbelts all contribute more preventable deaths to the American mortality tables than does cocaine taking. If we are looking for good reasons to treat our current cocaine problem as a national crisis, we must look beyond the health of the current population of cocaine users.

Damage *in Utero*

Not all of those whose health is damaged by cocaine take it by choice. A substantial proportion of heavy cocaine users are women.[24] Cocaine users tend to be in their prime childbearing years, and increasingly they are poor. Women are less likely than men to sell drugs or steal to support drug habits, and are correspondingly more likely to engage in prostitution or exchange sex directly for drugs.* As a consequence, a substantial number of babies are being exposed to cocaine in the womb.

Cocaine is not the only drug that poses a threat to fetal health. Big-city hospitals have been dealing for years with children born addicted to heroin. Heavy drinking by pregnant women can give rise to Fetal Alcohol Syndrome, which leads to well-marked physical and developmental abnormalities.[25] Even more moderate drinking is now suspected of taking a heavy toll on the fetus.[26] Nicotine, too, seems to do significant damage, in part by reducing birth weight.[27]

But cocaine is special in several ways. While some young people are binge drinkers, heavy, chronic drinking of the kind that generates Fetal Alcohol Syndrome tends to take years to develop. By contrast, heavy compulsive cocaine use develops rapidly and is concentrated among the young.[28] In addition, since alcohol is one of the drugs taken by heavy cocaine users to blunt the unpleasantness of the "crash" and allow them to get some sleep, children born to cocaine-using mothers may have been exposed to large amounts of both drugs.

---

* There appears to be a syphilis epidemic related to crack-house sex. See Peter Kerr, "Syphilis Cases Surge with Uses of Crack, Raising AIDS Fears," *New York Times*, 29 June 1988; Robert T. Rolfs, et al., "Risk Factors for Syphilis: Cocaine Use and Prostitution," *American Journal of Public Health* 80 (7 [July 1990]): 853.

The problems of the cocaine babies do not end at birth. One reported characteristic of the victims of fetal cocaine syndrome is extraordinary crankiness with a nerve-wracking, screechy cry; cocaine babies tend to be less rewarding to care for than others. Add a difficult baby to a mother who has a competing interest in her crack pipe, and the result can be neglect amounting to abandonment. In some instances, a crack-using mother simply walks away from the hospital leaving her newborn behind; these are the "boarder babies."[29]

Expert opinions differ about how significant a role cocaine plays in producing damaged and neglected children. Some studies have found a clear correlation between a mother's cocaine use immediately before delivery and the health status of her child. Other studies, more carefully controlled for other factors, have found no such correlation.[30] Field reports are frightening: some family-court judges and child-welfare officials say that they are swamped with cocaine-related cases, and school officials now facing the first wave of cocaine babies find them a particular problem.[31] It would take very clever researchers considerable money and time to determine just how bad the problem really is using the careful techniques of medical research. A cruder but still useful estimate could be made much more quickly and cheaply by systematically asking the clinicians and officials who actually see the babies. For now, all that can be said with certainty is that a large but unknown number of children are suffering a substantial but unmeasured amount of damage. They, and the rest of us, will be bearing its consequences for the next several decades.

Violence and Disorder

It is not the health of users or their children that has made cocaine a front-burner issue, but the violence and disorder that surround cocaine dealing. In the 1970s, the fearsome stereotype associated with the drug problem was the junkie: the heroin-using mugger or burglar with needle tracks on his arms and larceny in his heart. In the 1980s, it became the crack dealer with his beeper, his hundred-dollar sneakers, his assault rifle, and his willingness to use it on rivals and random passersby. As city after city set new homicide records in the later 1980s, the drive-by shooting replaced the street mugging as the definitive drug-related horror.

No one actually knows how many cocaine-related shootings there have been. The rise in homicides has been less spectacular than the press has made it out to be, though it is indeed disturbing that the number of homicides has been rising in a period when the number of males in their prime crime-committing years (ages 18 to 30) has been shrinking due to the "baby bust." The "cause" of an unsolved homicide is much easier to assert than it is to determine.[32] While homicides themselves are well counted, incidents of gunfire, which can frighten a neighborhood out of its wits without actually drawing blood, are not. It is almost certain that the frequency of such incidents has increased, but no one knows by how much.

Even the concept of "drug-relatedness" turns out to be slippery on analysis. If one drug dealer shoots another in a turf war or a dispute about money, the case is clear. So too if the victim is a bystander caught in the cross-fire of such a dispute. But what if two cocaine dealers, whose profession has given them money and motive to buy heavy weapons, shoot it out in a dispute over an insult or a woman? Is that shooting "drug-related"? The cocaine trade has greatly contributed to the arms race among young men in tough neighborhoods, and that contribution may be the greatest harm cocaine has done.

Against the background of gunfire, all of the conditions incident to cocaine dealing—the crowded streets, the lookouts, the cars idling while their drivers haggle over cocaine, the fortified drug houses, even the police raids—become sources of terror to the neighbors. The terror probably does more damage than the actual violence. For every one shot, tens of thousands are scared.

Even those who are relatively unafraid may feel themselves unwelcome visitors on the streets where they live. Virtually every story of successful police and community action against neighborhood markets—and those stories are legion—ends with the observation "People started to sit on their own doorsteps for the first time in two years."

The Burden on Law Enforcement

Cocaine puts additional burdens on already overloaded urban law enforcement agencies: police, courts, prosecutors, and corrections. Because cocaine dealing is so financially rewarding and because it demands no special skills, and perhaps because as a transactional crime it doesn't seem as obviously wrong as theft, it appears to have attracted a large number of people into habitual offending. Even at the end of the 1980s, when as much as half of local law enforcement was devoted to suppressing cocaine dealing in some cities, kids were still waiting in line for their shot at the money cocaine dealing offered.[33] In the meantime, the threshold of seriousness required in order to attract police attention to other forms of crime and disorder had steadily risen because of a sheer lack of resources. In New York City, for example, the theft of an automobile radio, involving a property loss of hundreds of dollars and serious annoyance to the victim, does not even rate an investigation.

Given the apparent rapid decline in the number of new users and particularly new heavy users, it is a fair guess that we have seen the worst of the cocaine epidemic, at least in the cities that were the first to experience major cocaine problems. Crack initiations may well have peaked as early as 1988, as a result of a combination of bad publicity about the drug in the media and bad word-of-mouth generated by the growing number of obvious "burn-out" cases. Availability continued to expand, and prices continued to drop or remain stable at low levels, until the beginning of 1990; thus it is hard to claim that the rising level of enforcement activity succeeded in putting a limit on the market. This does not, of course, mean that enforcement had no effect, still less that cocaine prohibition was a failure. Illicit cocaine, at its cheapest, costs about twenty times as much as the legal version of the same drug. Except for the small proportion of the population that dealt cocaine, had close friends or family in the trade, or lived in neighborhoods with active open markets or notorious crack houses, access to the drug remained problematic, inconvenient, and risky: not enough so to defeat a serious, determined attempt to find crack, but enough to discourage some of the merely curious. If crack use had spread as quickly through the population as did diet soft drinks or VCRs, there would have been substantially more compulsive users by the time the drug's bad reputation became well entrenched.

Having seen the worst is not the same as having the end in sight. After all, the worst of the heroin epidemic was over by 1972 or 1973; the peak of heroin initiations probably came a year or two earlier. Yet the heroin problem—largely in the persons of those who acquired heroin habits between 1967 and 1973— is still with us, because the habit proved quite persistent and because law enforcement failed to close down the retail markets. Since the cocaine market today appears to involve more than twice as many compulsive users as the heroin market at its peak, cocaine has the potential to be a long-term national headache.

How bad a cocaine consumption problem we will have a decade or two hence depends largely on the extent to which open crack dealing continues to spread to those cities where it is still a minor phenomenon and to rural areas, how quickly the recruitment of new users falls off in established markets, and how persistent heavy co-caine use proves to be among the current population of compulsive users. How bad a cocaine control problem we have—how much vi-olence cocaine dealers generate and how much of our scarce law enforcement capacity we will then be devoting to suppressing the market—depends on consumption levels and on the patterns of re-tail dealing. Public policies can influence those levels and patterns, and analysis can aid in designing those policies. But before asking where to go from here, we should consider how we got where we are.

THE COCAINE SURPRISE

In 1968, cocaine was a footnote, a formerly popular drug,[34] a minor adjunct to the heroin market. Its stereotypical user was a middle-aged participant in the jazz/ blues culture, and it was typically taken by injection. Its legal classification as a narcotic, nonsensical from a pharmacological viewpoint because cocaine stimulates the central nervous system while the true narcotics (opiates and opioids) depress it, reflected cocaine's social status as a "hard" drug. The practice of injection—common among poor users as an efficient and therefore economical way of using cocaine—served as a formidable barrier to the expansion of the market.

In 1978, cocaine was something between a curiosity and a men-ace, the smallest but fastest growing of the three major illicit drug markets. It was a fad among the wealthy, almost all of whom took it by insufflation (snorting), and few of whom suffered any obvious damage except to their bank accounts.[35] Cocaine snorting could be a ferociously expensive habit, at $25 for less than half an hour of a rather subtle stimulation (so subtle, in fact, that experienced users proved unable under laboratory conditions to distinguish between cocaine and its equally nose-numbing but nonpsychoactive chemical relative procaine).[36] But the textbooks and the users agreed that co-caine was not addictive, it was almost invisible in reports of deaths and injuries, and it seemed to be unconnected with property or vio-lent crime except among high-level dealers.[37]

By 1988, cocaine had become the drug problem par excellence, with a retail market nearly equal to those for heroin and marijuana combined. When U.S. voters in that year listed "drugs" as the most pressing national problem, cocaine was the drug they had in mind. It was the leading cause of sudden death among the illicit drugs,[38] and the spread of retail dealing from city to city left a trail of violence in its wake. The cocaine-using "crack-head" had replaced the heroin-using "junkie" as the popular image of the menacing drug addict. What happened? How did a minor drug become so major, a seemingly benign drug so horrible?

In a word, crack happened. The rise of crack illustrates how a combination of pharmacological, sociological, and economic changes can transform the usage pattern and social impact of a drug.

While virtually everyone by now has heard of crack, only a minority actually knows what it is. The popular press has defined crack in the public mind as a cocaine derivative, more powerful, more addictive, and cheaper than cocaine itself. That definition is a mixture of fact, fantasy, and confusion. Crack is in fact something much simpler: cocaine sold in smokable form.

Because smoking any drug delivers its molecules to the brain very quickly—within a few seconds—and virtually all at once, its effects are more immediate and more dramatic than if the same quantity of the same drug is snorted.[39] The very rapid increase in drug concentration in the brain can generate the same sort of euphoric "rush" produced by injection (but rarely by snorting or swallowing).[40] A small dose can provide a brief but profound drug experience.

Cocaine smoking combines the dangerous features of snorting and those of injection (except for potential exposure to AIDS through needle sharing) in a particularly insidious way. Smoking provides a rush without either the social stigma or the unpleasantness of using a needle. Smoking is a fairly cheap habit to start, because the initial dose is small. But it is an expensive one to continue; for some users the only way to maintain the high, and stave off the extremely unpleasant "crash" that is much more marked among smokers than among sniffers, is to keep smoking.

Smoking cocaine does not invariably lead to compulsive use. Nor is intranasal use of powder cocaine without risk of habituation. But compulsive use is far more common among cocaine smokers than among cocaine snorters, and some drug users who have succeeded in maintaining controlled use patterns with other drugs, including cocaine in powder form, find crack to be uniquely compelling. As people who start with snorting small amounts of cocaine powder escalate their use, they are likely to shift to a different mode of administration: smoking or, more rarely, injection. In addition, those who begin their cocaine use by smoking are likely to be younger, poorer, and socially more marginal than those who begin by snorting it, and thus to have fewer internal and external props for maintaining controlled use.

The rise of crack was simply the rise of cocaine smoking. It was accompanied by two other changes: the spread of cocaine use from affluent "thirtysomethings" down the age and socioeconomic ladders, and the collapse of cocaine prices. The three changes were interrelated in complicated ways.

Cocaine smoking preceded crack. During the late 1970s, affluent users of powder cocaine (cocaine hydrochloride), which cannot be smoked, discovered that they could convert it into anhydrous cocaine base (freebase), which can be. The process took no special skill, but required a substantial quantity of cocaine. It was also time-consuming and, as Richard Pryor notoriously demonstrated, dangerous.

Sometime in the early 1980s, cocaine dealers invented a different process for making smokable cocaine, one that did not involve the use of the ether that made freebasing so dangerous. (The resulting impurities cause the mixture to crackle when it is heated; folk etymology offers this as the derivation of "crack.") Then some underground marketing wizard had the idea of packaging smokable cocaine in individual dosage units, about one-twentieth of a gram, much smaller than the standard retail quantity for powder cocaine; thus the crack vial was born. The new packaging brought cocaine within the price range of millions of people who did not have $100 for a gram of powder. It also vastly simplified the handling problems associated with selling something very valuable and very easily spilled. (Once the crack-making process had been discovered, cocaine smoking spread rapidly even in markets, such as Chicago's, where for one reason or another dealers continued to sell primarily cocaine powder.)

At the same time, the market for cocaine was undergoing an upheaval. The explosion of powder cocaine use during the late 1970s, fueled by a growing number of users and by the progression of some of those who had started use in the mid-1970s to heavier and heavier use as they built up cocaine tolerance and lost control of their habits, was an enormous bonanza for established cocaine smugglers and for established dealers at every level. With tried-and-true business relationships and operational practices, their enforcement risks were relatively low, but the market price was determined by the costs of new entrants who faced much higher risks and costs. In a growing market, there were enough customers to go around; prices remained high (about $55,000 per kilogram at wholesale, about $100 for a gram of 12.5 percent pure cocaine at retail).[41] Enforcement efforts expanded, but much more slowly than the volume of sales; consequently, enforcement risk per transaction fell as the market grew. Cocaine dealers were quite literally making out like bandits.

Since the Controlled Substances Act did not repeal the laws of
supply and demand, this bonanza could not last forever. Big profits
continued to attract new entrants faster than old ones left because
of imprisonment, death, or (infrequently) the satiation of greed. Existing dealing organizations and less formal "connections" expanded
their transaction volumes. Eventually the quantity that cocaine dealers were willing to offer at the existing price outstripped the quantity
consumers wanted at that price, and the price began to fall sharply,
to about $30,000 per kilogram by 1983.*

Falling prices brought crack within the reach of more and more
people and allowed existing crack users to smoke much larger quantities before running out of money. The resulting increase in physical volume put more downward pressure on price by even further
swamping still-limited enforcement resources. Quantities are even
harder to estimate than prices, but it would be difficult to find an
expert who believes that U.S. residents used as much as ten tons of
cocaine in 1978 or as little as two hundred tons in 1988. Growing
volumes and shrinking enforcement risks drove prices even lower,
until, by the late 1980s, large shipments of cocaine in Miami sold
for as little as $10,000 per kilogram. In the retail market for pow-
der cocaine, these wholesale price decreases were passed through
primarily as purity increases. Eventually, some retail dealers stopped
the practice of dilution altogether and sold virtually pure cocaine at
retail, still for about $100 per gram. Crack sold for about the same
price per milligram of actual cocaine: in the most active markets,
$5 became the standard price for a 50 milligram (one-twentieth of
a gram) rock.[42] Crack was never cheaper than cocaine, since crack
is cocaine. But as crack spread, the price of cocaine in both forms
fell.

During the 1970s, retail dealing in powder cocaine tended to be
discreet. The drug was traded hand-to-hand in living rooms and bars
rather than on street corners or from holes in the walls of abandoned
buildings. No one (except an occasional wholesaler) got shot, and the
neighbors rarely complained.

The crack market stands to this carriage-trade drug dealing as Mc-
Donald's stands to Lutèce. The volumes were enormously larger; the
buyers, more anonymous to the sellers, poorer, and younger. There
developed street-corner markets similar to, but larger than, those in

---

* Such price collapses are not restricted to illicit markets. A similar phenomenon
hit the hand-held calculator market in the early 1970s; the price of a four-function
calculator fell from about $100 to less than $20 within a year, as all the new factories
built to take advantage of the opportunity to sell $4 worth of components for $100
came on line at once.

which heroin had long been bought and sold. In addition, there were "crack houses," either institutions modeled on opium dens, where crack was both sold and consumed, or simply fixed-locations, sometimes fortified against thieves and the police, where the drug was sold for consumption elsewhere.

The amounts of money available to those willing to get involved in retail dealing, though smaller than street mythology made them out to be,[43] were substantial enough, particularly for those with little legitimate opportunity, but also for others.[44] The RAND Corporation's study of the cocaine market in Washington, D.C., estimated average hourly earnings of about $30 in cash, not counting the value of drugs consumed by the dealers from their own inventories.[45]

No other form of low-skill illicit enterprise could match retail cocaine dealing as a source of steady earnings, and the enforcement risk per dollar earned remained substantially below that for such alternative ventures as burglary. The RAND study found that, at current arrest rates, one-third of all the young African-American men in Washington would be arrested for cocaine dealing by the time they reached the age of thirty, suggesting that the proportion of those actually involved in the trade was even larger. It also found that most of the dealers were not in fact unemployed—not even marginally employed at minimum-wage jobs—but rather were using cocaine dealing to supplement legitimate earnings of about eight dollars per hour.[46] It appeared that most would have been willing to deal more (and possibly work less at their straight jobs) but for lack of customers.[47]

Neither the RAND study nor other research into street-level cocaine dealing confirms the stereotype of the retail dealer as a user who begins to deal as a way of paying for his own habit. Rather, the relationship between dealing and use appears to run in the opposite direction: adolescents attracted to cocaine dealing by money sometimes begin to use cocaine because it is easily available to them and because they can now afford it.

This progression from dealing to use, though common enough to count among the gravest risks of becoming a retail crack dealer, is far from universal. Cocaine dealers have two powerful incentives for abstaining from their own product. They see in their customers good arguments for saying no to cocaine, and they are also aware of the risks to their drug-dealing careers and their physical safety posed by using the drugs they are supposed to be selling, if using makes them unable to pay what they owe their suppliers. At least one street cocaine-dealing group, the Chambers Brothers organization (believed at its height to have been the largest in Detroit), was reportedly running a drug-free workplace. Low-level dealers were not allowed to be users; the organization had learned from experience that even a crack dealer's earnings were insufficient to support a crack habit.[48]

Unlike the discreet powder dealers, crack sellers in open street markets or fixed-location crack houses were vulnerable, and thus attractive, targets for violence from thieves, dissatisfied customers, unpaid suppliers, and competitors. That made it advisable for them to arm themselves, which further increased the chances that any dispute within the trade would be settled by gunplay. There followed, in city after city, a kind of arms race as street crack dealers strove to keep up with one another's level of weaponry, and as young men inclined to violence anyway—in some cases members of preexisting street youth gangs—found that their work as crack dealers could finance their gun hobbies as well as their drug habits. Once the weapons were present, they were likely to be used not only in connection with the drug trade but also to resolve the kinds of disputes for which earlier generations of street toughs had armed themselves with knives, zip guns, and "Saturday night specials." As the firepower of the weapons rose, so did the lethality of the disputes. City after city established new records for homicide.

Now the neighbors did complain, loudly, bitterly, and insistently. Sometimes they did not stop with complaining. A group of Detroiters burned a crack house in their neighborhood to the ground (and were acquitted of arson by a sympathetic jury).[49] Eventually, and in most cases reluctantly and against their better professional judgment, police executives responded to public demand and mounted more and more vigorous retail-level enforcement efforts. By that time, the markets were so huge and blatant that they yielded bumper crops of prosecutable arrests.[50] In city after city, cocaine sales cases went from fewer than 10 percent of felony prosecutions in the early 1980s to half or more by 1988.

One result of increasing enforcement pressure was to concentrate crack retailing, which had been quite widespread, into those areas where enforcement risks were lowest: high-crime, largely minority population, inner-city neighborhoods. The stream of automobiles with white drivers and suburban registrations that flowed through those neighborhoods, each pausing only long enough for their occupants to make a purchase, demonstrates that crack dealing is far more concentrated geographically than crack consumption. In economic terms, cocaine is almost certainly a net export for inner-city neighborhoods; that is, sales to suburbanites probably exceed the total cost of the drugs at wholesale. But for Harlem and East Los

Angeles, as for Colombia, the social costs far outweigh the economic benefits.[51]

In the meantime, casualties among the users soared, growing even faster than consumption itself. The low rates of observed damage among powder cocaine users in the 1970s reflected several temporary conditions. A drug with a growing market has mostly new users, who have not had time to get themselves into real trouble; the early affluent users tended to have networks of social support (and alternative means of recreation) to help them control their own drug habits or to keep the consequences of uncontrolled habits private. In addition, snorting is less likely to get out of control than smoking.[52]

Even as total cocaine consumption soared during the late 1980s, the composition of the market was changing. The total number of cocaine users almost certainly declined, with the number of poor users increasing and the number of nonpoor users falling sharply.[53] The quantity consumed per user also rose, as compulsive binge users came to constitute a larger and larger proportion of the total user population.[54] The shrinkage in the number of users reflected a general trend toward health-conscious behavior among the well-to-do, particularly those in their thirties; negative publicity about the drug in the mass media, which enjoy far more credibility among the well-off than among the very poor; and a backlash from bad personal experiences or the bad experiences of friends among the groups' that had been using cocaine the longest time. At the same time, the increasing concentration of dealing, and thus of easy opportunities for purchase, in poor neighborhoods, tended to increase the proportion of users who were poor. The process of lowering the social status of cocaine use, once started, had its own momentum. As cocaine became associated with unwed teenage mothers rather than with rock stars and yuppie greed-heads, it grew less fashionable. (There's no accounting for taste.)

It is very unlikely that cocaine would have maintained the benign reputation it enjoyed in the mid-1970s even if smoking had never been invented. The longer a person has been using cocaine, the more likely she is to have lost control of her use of it and the greater the chance that the ill effects of long-term heavy use will have begun to show. Thus the mere fact that the average cocaine user in 1975 had a use history measured in months while the average cocaine user in 1990 had a use history measured in years would have given the drug a less savory reputation in 1990 than it had in 1975. As David Musto has pointed out, the past 15 years have

largely recapitulated the cocaine experience of the late nineteenth
century, with early favorable experiences being overwhelmed by later
unfavorable ones.[55]

But the invention first of freebase and then of crack both expanded
the market and greatly magnified the associated problems. It is easy
now to see that more vigorous programs aimed at controlling cocaine
abuse in the 1970s might have prevented much misery later, but
it was not easy to see that at the time. Insofar as crack changed
the situation, its invention was as close to a genuinely unpredictable
event as a major social development is likely to be. As Prometheus
no doubt remarked to his brother, hindsight is always 20/20.

That, in a nutshell, is the cocaine problem we now have and how
we came to have it. The problem will not go away; we cannot unin-
vent crack or undo the fact that millions of Americans have tried it
and liked it. Can we find our way to a less bad problem?

CHANGING THE LAWS

One way to trade our current cocaine problem in for a new one
would be to change the laws. The recent flare-up of discussion about
drug legalization has been fueled largely by discontent with the cocaine situation and, in particular, with the violence related to cocaine
dealing and the burden that cocaine-dealing cases now put on police,
courts, and corrections systems.

Cocaine is a Schedule II drug under the Controlled Substances
Act.[56] It is prohibited in all except specific medical uses—as local
anesthetic in oral and ophthalmic surgery—in which its psychoactive
properties play no part.

Changing the cocaine laws would mean making cocaine licitly available to some (nonmedical) users, under some restrictions, at some
price. The challenge facing advocates of such change is to find a
combination of taxes and regulations that, with appropriately designed programs, would produce a less noxious set of problems than
the one we now suffer.

Before considering a general legalization, let us consider smaller
steps. One group for whom cocaine might be legalized comprises
those who are currently buying it illegally. Insofar as prohibition
aims to prevent initiation, this is a group for whom prohibition has
failed. Assuming that they will continue to use the drug, it would
probably be better for them and for everyone else if they had a
legal supply, most of all because their money would cease to support

black-market operations. It would then be possible to concentrate enforcement efforts on the task of preventing sales to new users.

An obvious objection to such a plan is that it would decrease the quit rate among current users, not all of whom will maintain their habits if they are forced to get all of their supplies from the black market. Even if illegality failed to prevent initiation, it can still be an aid to desistance. Against the benefits of improving the welfare and social functioning of those who would have remained users anyway, one would have to set the costs of inducing some to remain trapped in cocaine use who would otherwise have escaped from it.

The apparent tendency of the quantity of cocaine consumed to grow over time, particularly if the supply is convenient and consistent, would also pose a problem for a licit supply system. A system of licit distribution of alcohol (or marijuana) can treat excessive and compulsive use as an aberration, though even for alcohol the question of whether to allow someone to drink himself to death ought to be a troubling one. In the case of cocaine, and especially crack, that question is apt to arise frequently. Since licit availability would remove one barrier to chronic intensive use—the risk and inconvenience of obtaining supplies—the risk of escalation might well be greater within a licit-distribution system than in the current illicit market.

A policy of legal distribution to established users would also have the disadvantage of making the status "cocaine user" a legally privileged one. Doing so would pose moral (and political) problems. It would also create a perverse incentive for current non-users: one's first few, illegally obtained doses would include as a bonus a ticket to further licit use and the prospect of being able to make money by reselling legally obtained cocaine to newer users on the remaining black market. The legal distribution system would need to specify an operational definition of "current user," which might be of the form "five binges in the past month" or "weekly use for the past year." (Should we accept the user's own say-so or demand physical evidence?) There would also need to be sanctions for resale and perhaps limits on the quantity any one user could purchase.

One way to limit entry to the licit, registered-user market would be to force users to go through a humiliating ritual of identifying themselves as drug addicts, filling out forms, answering intimate questions, taking drugs on schedule and under supervision, and submitting to attempts to change their life-style. Perhaps we could find another stimulant less pleasurable than cocaine but similar enough to cocaine to serve as a partial substitute, and hand that out instead of cocaine itself, requiring oral administration or snorting rather than allowing injection or smoking. That is, we could make licit cocaine distribution resemble licit opioid distribution in methadone clinics. But there is no reason to think that any substantial proportion of today's problem cocaine users would enter such a system unless co-erced either directly by a judge's order or indirectly by a drying-up of the illicit market.

If cocaine were to be legalized for current users on a commer-cial rather than a therapeutic model, it would be necessary to decide about price, about whether to limit the quantity available for pur-chase by each registered user, and about whether to sell crack as well as cocaine powder.·

At first glance, the decision about crack seems the most funda-mental: smoking cocaine in the form of crack appears to be far more likely to lead to heavy, chronic, compulsive use than snorting it in the form of cocaine hydrochloride powder. Thus the prospects for main-taining reasonable levels of health and social functioning among the customers of a registered-user system would appear to be far better if they were supplied only with cocaine powder. Against that advan-tage, one would have to set the prospect that many potential regis-tered users who were crack users would be unwilling to switch to the less exciting practice of snorting and therefore remain outside the system. Worse, some might seek crack-like "rushes" by injecting the powder. Others would register themselves and then trade powder for crack on the black market.

In fact, however, the entire question—and any program of mak-ing powder, but not crack, licitly available—falls to earth with the simple observation that cocaine powder can be converted into crack with minimal labor, using only reagents and utensils available in the typical kitchen. Since the invention of smokable cocaine cannot be unmade, we must make policy based on the assumption that crack will be as available as powder is.

How to set prices and quantity limits—the former determined by taxation, the latter by regulation—are interrelated questions, with a tangle of mostly unpalatable answers. The goals of diverting trade from the black market, reducing income-producing criminal activity by cocaine buyers, preventing damage to licit-market customers, and avoiding resale to new users are not all served by the same choices and therefore cannot all be served at once.

Consider first the combination of high price and high, or no, quan-tity limits. A reasonable upper bound on price might be the black-market price, currently about $100 per pure gram, or $5 per rock.

At higher prices, there would presumably be some demand from users who valued the convenience, legality, and quality assurance provided by the licit and regulated market, but the bulk of the existing black-market problem would remain. If quantities were unlimited at that price, consumption by current users, and thus the money they spend for cocaine, would probably increase as a result of the decrease in search time. Those who currently sell sexual services or steal to pay for their cocaine would tend to commit more of those income-producing crimes. In addition, those who now support their cocaine habits by selling cocaine would, to the extent that the program succeeded in shrinking the market, find their source of illicit income reduced. Some would cut back their consumption, some would turn to other forms of crime, and some would do a little of each. Thus a high-price, high-quantity legalization strategy would likely increase the frequency of income-producing predatory crime and of prostitution, even as it reduced the violence linked with cocaine dealing. In effect, the tax collector would replace the crack dealer as the ultimate recipient of the proceeds of theft and commercial sex, and those proceeds would probably rise.

One means of escape from this problem would be to impose a fairly restrictive quantity limit. A quarter-gram per week would not support chronic binge use; the maximum legal habit would be not much more expensive than heavy cigarette smoking. Such a limit would probably cover the current cocaine consumption of three-quarters or more of America's cocaine users.[57]

Such a high-price, low-quantity registered-user program could serve the demands of occasional, truly recreational cocaine users with relative safety in terms of overdose risk and without providing any substantial supply for resale or impetus to criminal activity. Although nothing in the regulatory system would prevent some of those users from supplementing their licit supply on the illicit market and thus markedly elevating their risks, nothing but the current enforcement system prevents those same persons from buying large quantities on today's black market.

What a high-price, low-quantity regime would not do is eliminate the black market. Even if every current adult black-market user relied on the licit system for all consumption up to the legal limit, licit sales would replace less than one-fifth of the total current volume of black-market sales, simply because very heavy users account for the vast bulk of the total quantity consumed. Most of the costs of the black market—nuisance, disruption, adulteration, and violence—would remain.

Low-price regimes would create a different set of problems. Pharmaceutical-grade cocaine used as an anesthetic now sells on the tiny licit market for about five dollars per gram, equivalent to twenty-five cents for a standard rock of crack. This figure presumably represents the lower bound of plausible prices, since there is no apparent reason for the government to subsidize cocaine distribution.

At that price and without quantity limits, the proportion of the cocaine-using population that went on to frequent binge use would probably be much higher than it is now, since low price and easy availability would eliminate two of the major barriers to binge use: running out of money and running out of cocaine. The effects on users' health and on the incidence of psychotic reactions from very heavy use would presumably be substantial. In addition, registration as a user would be a virtual license to print money, since registered users could take unlimited advantage of the gap between the licit price and the black-market price by becoming suppliers to new users, who would then swell the ranks of registered users, and so on. Thus the goal of satisfying the demand of current users without creating many new ones would not be achieved.

A combination of a low price and a strict quantity limit would fail to eliminate the black-market for the same reasons that a high price and a low quantity limit would; too much of the demand by heavy users would be left for the criminals to fill. In addition, it would make the status of registered user economically valuable, since the gap between the licit price and the black-market price would amount to some hundreds of dollars per year.

Thus high prices would generate user crime, while low ones would generate consumption increases. Loose quantity limits or none would open the floodgates of resale into the new-user market by allowing any registered user to supply a large number of new users, while strict quantity limits would create demand among registered users for black-market supplemental supplies, either resold or illicitly produced.

If the whole idea of supplying cocaine to persons with established cocaine habits seems unworkable—and by now it should—note that it differs from other plans of legalization only in its attempt to preserve some barrier between the entire population and cocaine use. All of the problems of pricing, quantity limitation, and form limitation would remain if cocaine purchases were legalized for all adults rather than only for current users.

Only the problem of resale to new users would tend to evaporate, since the licit system would sell to new users directly (except for minors, who would be supplied with cocaine illicitly but undetectably by adults, as is now the case with alcohol). Against that advantage would loom the disadvantage of opening the supply of the drug to everyone, not only those with the determination to make enough illicit purchases to establish a habit. The tendency to progress to problem use would probably be lower among these additional users, given their less urgent desire to try the drug in the first place, than among those who are prepared to break the law to get it. But there is no reason to think that the rate of progression to compulsive use would be zero, and no assurance that it would be lower than the rate of experimentation-to-abuse progression now experienced in the black market; the lower search times created by licit supply would tend to increase that rate. If the licit supply had a strict quantity limit, the effect would be to prepare new customers for the remaining illicit market, which would serve both minors and those adults who wanted to buy more than the licit amount.

It is possible to assume the whole problem away with loose talk about the "total failure" of cocaine prohibition and the current availability of the drug to "anyone who wants it." If it were really true that no one who does not now use cocaine would use it if it were legal and that no one who now uses it sparingly would then use it lavishly, then legalization would transparently be a bargain, sacrificing a merely nominal prohibition in return for the abolition of a large and violent black market, the conversion of tens of billions of dollars of criminal earnings into tax revenues, and the freeing of large amounts of law enforcement capacity for use against predatory crime.

But if we abandon that utterly implausible assumption, legalization looks like a bad deal. Even the various attempts to qualify legalization or otherwise fancy it up—issuing personal use licenses, restricting licit distribution to places where the black market now flourishes,[58] and so on—cannot escape the fundamental problem that, particularly in the presence of crack, freely available cocaine is likely to give rise to self-destructive habits for an unacceptably large proportion of users.

Even assuming a preference for legalization in principle, it is difficult to design a regulatory regime for cocaine that would leave a smaller cocaine problem than exists under prohibition. The tendency of the desire for cocaine to "grow by what it feeds on" makes it perhaps the least attractive candidate for legalization among all the currently illicit drugs.

CHANGING PROGRAMS

Though participants on both sides of the legalization debate sometimes speak and write as if the future of the cocaine problem would
be determined almost entirely by the laws, enormous changes are
also possible in programs: programs to persuade actual and potential
users to change their behavior, programs offering help to and imposing control on problem users, and programs to enforce the laws we
now have. This is fortunate, since the laws are in fact unlikely to be
changed and the current combination of laws and programs leaves
us with substantial drug abuse costs and very large control costs.

Persuasion

Of the three varieties of programs, persuasion offers the least
prospect of great improvement, if only because so much of the job
of persuasion is already done. Over the past decade, public attitudes
have shifted massively against cocaine and cocaine users.[59] The shift
partly reflects personal and vicarious experience with the drug, but
media and classroom campaigns can claim part of the credit. Changing attitudes have led to changed behavior: the number of current
cocaine users was almost certainly lower in 1990 than it had been a
decade before. (Only "almost" because the surveys on which user estimates are based tend to underrepresent the groups whose cocaine
use has been growing while everyone else's has been shrinking and
because increasingly negative attitudes are apt to cause a decline in
self-reported use on an official survey whether or not actual use is
decreasing.)

The remaining user population, especially for crack, and the
groups most at risk for starting cocaine use now, are likely to be those
most difficult to reach by persuasion. They are the same group of
socially displaced late adolescents and young adults whose alcohol
and tobacco use has fallen least. Anyone who pays attention to the
national media or to in-school messages and is willing to sacrifice
immediate pleasure to preserve her own health and social functioning is surely aware by now that cocaine use, and cocaine smoking
most of all, is a high-risk activity. However, by one calculation, almost three in four of the weekly or more-than-weekly cocaine users
are arrested in the course of a year for something other than possessing cocaine.[60] That population is not likely to respond very much
to additional warnings.

Help and Control for Problem Users

There may be much more to gain from programs aimed at current heavy users, who account for the vast bulk of the cocaine consumed and who constitute a substantial proportion of the dealers. The decline in the number of new heavy users increases the value of raising the rate at which current heavy users quit, because any given increase in quitting has a greater effect on the size of the population of heavy users.

Calls for the development of some drug that will act for cocaine as methadone acts for heroin—reducing the compulsion by substitution—seem to reflect a misunderstanding of the nature of the compulsion involved. Some treatment programs in England are giving controlled doses of cocaine, and even smokable cocaine, to some users in an attempt to normalize their lives. The operators of those programs report having had some success, though, as is true for many treatment programs, these claims have not been subjected to outside evaluation. The claims themselves generate considerable puzzlement among orthodox pharmacologists, since successful stimulant maintenance would be a genuinely new phenomenon, and a hard one to understand in light of the tendency of the desire for stimulants to be kindled rather than satiated by taking them.

Be that as it may, there is no reason to believe that developing new drugs is an important piece of the solution. The world is already well supplied with both short-acting stimulants, including cocaine itself, and long-acting ones such as the amphetamines. Inventing new stimulants is less important than determining whether stimulant maintenance can be made a workable treatment strategy.

It might be possible to develop a cocaine antagonist: a drug that, if taken, blocks the effects of cocaine by binding inactively to the cocaine receptor sites on nerve cells. The problem, as with the antagonist developed long ago for the opiates, would be how to get cocaine users to take it and keep taking it.

The only kind of new cocaine substitute worth developing would be a powerful stimulant of which each successive dose gives less pleasure and more unpleasant side effects (as tends to be true, for example, of caffeine). The methoxylated amphetamines, such as MDMA (better known by its street name, "Ecstasy"), are reported to have this tendency,[61] and there is even a tiny amount of evidence that some crack users ease off their crack use after an MDMA experience,[62] but the same build-up of unpleasant side effects that prevents their long-term abuse makes them unsuitable as long-term substitutes. If these drugs have promise in the treatment of cocaine use, it is probably as adjuncts to psychotherapy rather than as maintenance vehicles.[63]

But while maintenance on a substitute seems an unlikely modality of cocaine treatment, there may still be a role for drugs in cocaine detoxification. Some heavy crack users report an inability to experience normal pleasure when they are not using the drug; damage to the dopamine system is a plausible explanation for this phenomenon. Insofar as the problem is transient, and insofar as anhedonia keeps users trapped in a binge cycle, finding drugs or other aids to getting through post-cessation depression is an important goal for treatment. There are reports that some drugs have proven valuable in this regard.[64] (It is worth noting, however, that one of these, buprenorphine, is itself a potential drug of abuse: indeed, it is the primary injected nonmedical drug in Scotland.)[65]

But it remains unclear how many current heavy cocaine users want help in quitting, how many of them need to break an addictive cycle as a preliminary to longer-term treatment, or what proportion of them are likely to succeed in staying away from cocaine if they are successfully detoxified. In this respect, cocaine may be like heroin: detoxification is the easy part of quitting.* Nor can anyone estimate convincingly how much the availability of treatment matters to the overall rate of successful cocaine quitting among various parts of the heavy-user population. Given the methodological and ethical difficulties in conducting treatment experiments, the state of knowledge is unlikely to improve much over the next few years except in the very unlikely event that someone makes a breakthrough discovery whose results are obvious on inspection.

This lack of knowledge greatly complicates the problem of deciding what to do. No one even knows how much money is now spent on publicly funded cocaine treatment, but the total is certainly less than $2 billion per year, probably less than $1 billion. The least that can be said, therefore, is that even if those funds are not well spent, there is little to be saved by cutting back. Given the magnitude of the problem posed by heavy cocaine users, particularly those who are poor and therefore potential clients of publicly funded programs, the poten-

---

* Some of the laboratory animal studies are mildly encouraging on this point. While animals that have been addicted to heroin and are then cut off from their supply will continue for many months to repeat, albeit less and less frequently, the behavior that used to win them heroin, cocaine-using animals display no such lasting craving. T. Thompson and R. Pickens, "Stimulant Self-Administration by Animals: Some Comparisons with Opiate Self-Administration," *Federation Proceedings* 29: 6-12. Lewis S. Seiden and Linda A. Dykstra, *Psychopharmacology* (New York: Van Nostrand Reinhold, 1977), 372.

tial payoffs to even moderately successful treatment are great enough to create a strong argument for increasing funding by a substantial percentage. The losses we are now suffering from uncontrolled cocaine use dwarf the potential losses from spending more money on treatment programs that may not work. But this argument provides little guidance about how to spend whatever additional money becomes available. There is no reason to think that leaving the choice either to the market of treatment providers and potential clients or the bureaucracy of state substance abuse agencies will produce an optimal result. In the meantime, in the absence of any disciplined, rational way to answer questions about how much of what kind of cocaine treatment to offer and how to divide new resources between increasing the number of treatment slots and increasing the resource commitment per slot, it is hard to say whether the political process is doing well or badly in that regard.

It is easier to say which potential clients ought to have priority for treatment attention. Cocaine-using offenders, pregnant women, and mothers of small children are particularly expensive groups to leave untreated. They all have or can be given particularly strong motivation to quit: offenders in the form of post-conviction abstinence orders with sanctions for backsliding, pregnant women and mothers in the shape of maternal concern for their babies and the threat of fitness hearings. Given how expensive and difficult it is for the state to replace even low-quality parental care, threats directed at mothers will necessarily contain a large measure of bluff. But it is worth remembering that, despite the rhetoric of the child custody system, the welfare of the child immediately in question is not in fact the only social value at stake. There is also value in deterring women who intend to have more children from continuing to binge on cocaine and women who intend to continue to binge on cocaine from having more children.

ENFORCEMENT

The bulk of the current governmental effort to control cocaine abuse takes the form of law enforcement. Cocaine dealing now absorbs a substantial share of the attention of big-city police enforcement agencies and of court time and prison and jail space.

The cost of continuing our current cocaine enforcement effort, or still more of expanding it, is the crime of other kinds that could have been prevented with the same resources. That is a very heavy cost, and it has prompted some debate about less costly ways to control the problem: legalization and regulation, increased prevention efforts, increased treatment efforts. There has been less debate about alternative law enforcement strategies.

The federal cocaine enforcement effort takes two largely unrelated forms: interdiction efforts, aimed at making it difficult to smuggle cocaine into the United States from the regions in northern South America where it is grown and processed, and investigations of high-level domestic distribution. In addition, there is a substantial diplomatic effort, backed with a small amount of money, to encourage law enforcement in the source countries, especially Colombia.[66]

A simple cost model of the cocaine industry suggests that events in source countries are unlikely to be important in determining prices and quantities at retail in the United States, because the price at export is so tiny a fraction of the price to the end user. By the same token, source-country efforts appear to be incapable of causing physical shortages, since traffickers can develop new growing, processing, and exporting routines. Border efforts seem doomed to futility by the capacity of traffickers to respond to increased enforcement against one route or mode of smuggling by substituting a different one.[67]

Experience at the end of the 1980s illustrates the ability of the illicit marketers to adapt to changing conditions. In the late 1980s, a variety of high-tech efforts to track and intercept smuggling ships and airplanes virtually eliminated smuggling by dedicated vessels, the simplest mode and thus the most attractive to new, small, and unsophisticated organizations. This probably had little effect on the two largest confederations of processing and exporting organizations, the ones centered on the Colombian cities of Medellín and Cali. Their primary smuggling mode involves concealing cocaine in containers full of legitimate cargo, a mode untouched by aerostat balloons and E2C surveillance planes and virtually unstoppable by any plausible amount of customs inspection. The likely result of increased interdiction thus would have been to eliminate the smaller rivals of the cartels and allow them to increase their share of the market.

However, at the same time, the Medellín group virtually declared war on the rest of Colombian society, launching a series of terrorist attacks aimed primarily at judges, politicians, and journalists and demanding the end of the extradition of cocaine dealers to the United States. The government struck back, and the Medellín group soon found itself on the run, with vastly reduced capacity to export cocaine. As a result, the Cali group found itself in an enviable position: both its largest rival and its smaller competitors were, in different ways, severely curtailed in their capacity to export. Cali enjoyed the position in the cocaine market that Saudi Arabia had in the oil market in the 1970s: it could determine prices by limiting production.

The result was a wholesale price increase of about 50 percent, even as the price of unprocessed coca leaf fell. Some combination of that increase and the rising costs imposed on retail dealing by local law enforcement succeeded in pushing retail prices up. (Much of the retail price increase was manifested in decreases in street purity rather than increases in the price of a vial.) As might have been expected, the higher prices did not last. While smuggling in containers requires more sophistication and organization than smuggling in rented airplanes, at the higher prices there were great rewards for whoever established a container-smuggling enterprise. In addition, there were probably strains within the Cali group, as there are within any cartel, both over pricing strategy and over who got to sell how much. Furthermore, Colombia is not the only place from which cocaine is shipped to the United States; Peru, Brazil, and Guatemala all offer possibilities, and here again higher prices increased the incentive to find new trade routes. As a result, prices fell back to their previous levels within a year of their quick run-up.

As this is written, the new government of Colombia seems to have negotiated a peace treaty with some of the major trafficking groups. The reported terms involve a pledge by Colombia not to implement its extradition treaty with the United States in cases involving cocaine dealers, in return for the dealers' ending their terrorist war against Colombian politicians, journalists, and ordinary citizens. At first blush, such a deal seems to be disadvantageous to the United States, and consequently U.S. embassy officials have been making discouraging public noises.[68]

No doubt, a reduction in Colombian-U.S. cooperation in cocaine enforcement would lead to somewhat larger supplies of Colombian cocaine to the United States and thus presumably somewhat lower prices, particularly if the Medellín group were free to resume business. But even from a purely U.S. perspective, it is not clear that the benefits of higher cocaine prices are enough to outweigh the damage to the stability of the Colombian government at a time when South America remains poised between dictatorship and democracy, given Colombia's status as the country with the longest record of continuously democratic rule on the continent. If a continued war between the government and the traffickers could substantially reduce supplies to the U.S. market, there might be an argument, from a strictly North American viewpoint, for opposing a deal. That, however, seems an unduly optimistic reading of the likely course of events. To sacrifice a chance for civic peace in Colombia only to see cocaine prices continue to fall would be an obviously bad choice, and such a result seems more than possible.

Even those who believe that border efforts in general are largely doomed to futility have to give them some of the credit for the temporary lull in cocaine imports. It appears that the combination of Coast Guard and Customs Service efforts with some military help have succeeded, at least for a while, in getting "over the hump"; the chance of interception was so high for a while that many fewer shipments were being attempted, and total seizures actually fell. Border control moved from interdiction to deterrence, with consequent savings in the costs of processing cases. There is something to be said for a strategy that costs only money and makes sparing use of precious prison capacity. But once air and sea smuggling has been deterred, little can be gained from additional border-control efforts.

The prospects for improving matters with more high-level domestic enforcement are also dim. The quantities of money involved are simply too large to make deterrence workable: no matter how long the sentence, someone will risk it for tens of millions of dollars. The arithmetic of trying to force up prices in a market as big as the cocaine market by imposing costs on major distribution organizations is very discouraging; the Federal Bureau of Prisons just does not have enough cells.[69] The greatest possible benefit of high-level domestic cocaine enforcement efforts is not the costs they can impose on the distribution industry or the throughput capacity they can destroy, but the elimination of those organizations most prone to use violence and corruption as ways of doing business and the creation of incentives for the others to trade as peacefully as possible.

If source-country and border control are near the limits of their effectiveness and high-level domestic enforcement lacks the capacity to shrink the market, what is left is enforcement directed at the buyers and sellers in retail markets. Discreet sellers and their customers are so hard to catch, and their numbers are so large, that keeping cocaine away from those truly determined to have it may not be a feasible objective in some areas. But it is still possible to force flagrant markets underground by eliminating street bazaars and drug houses. Longer search times, along with fewer cues to stimulate demand, will reduce consumption somewhat. More important, it will give a little relief to the neighbors by reducing open disorder and some of the incentive and occasion for gunplay.

Retail cocaine enforcement is already the single largest activity of some local law enforcement agencies. It is necessarily profligate of punishment resources because the incentives for retail dealers to stay in the business are so great. Unfortunately, legislatures around the country have added a layer of unnecessary profligacy in the form of very long mandatory minimum sentences. A deterrence-based punishment strategy should consist of many relatively short sentences and a few long ones for those who use violence, employ children, or otherwise create extraordinary problems over and above their participation in the cocaine trade.

It is also essential to learn how to punish cocaine dealers without paying for their room and board. The very fact that a large proportion of the young, poor population is now selling cocaine suggests that the group of dealers extends beyond the group of extreme deviants. If some of them are capable of controlling their own behavior under appropriate coercive incentives, then locking them up is not the only way to be safe from them. They are good candidates for punitive labor, home confinement or curfews, and mandatory drug abstinence backed by drug testing. Prisons should be used for short sentences for all convicted dealers, to remind them that we mean business, for long sentences for the violent, and as a back-up threat for those who will not comply with the terms of alternative sentences. Making nonprison punishments work is the most important challenge facing the criminal justice system generally; the problem of punishing retail cocaine dealers may finally make it a politically salient issue.

Given adequate punishment capacity and the will to use it, flagrant drug dealing cannot continue to exist. The very openness that makes it a nightmare for the neighbors and a lure to new or recovering users makes it fatally vulnerable to enforcement as long as there is something to do with those who are caught. Where the police are ready to take information and act on it, citizens have proven to be more than willing to provide it.

There are also ways of attacking the trade without arresting dealers, either by closing down locations—boarding up drug houses under nuisance laws or for code violations, seizing property under forfeiture laws or encouraging evictions by landlords or housing authorities—or by inconveniencing or deterring the customers. Enforcement strategies directed at users have the great advantage that many users are easily deterred. Moreover, deterring some users does not generate opportunities for others, as deterring some dealers does. But such strategies also have the great disadvantage that there are many more users than dealers, and it is thus impractical to process any substantial proportion of them through the criminal process of arrest, arraignment, trial, and punishment. The key to deterring users is the development of cheap, credible threats of low-intensity punishment, enough to scare buyers away but not so drastic as to lead them to exercise their expensive (to the government) due-process rights. (Part of that development ought to be—but there is reason to fear it will not be—the creation of review mechanisms to protect the wrongly accused.)

The buyers most worth deterring—those who sell drugs or steal to support their habits—can be deterred from buying by imposing mandatory abstinence and drug testing as part of their sentences once they are caught. Deterring other buyers requires more creativity.

Inkster, Michigan, a poor suburb of Detroit that is the unwilling home to an active street crack market, has begun to experiment with a number of such techniques. At one point, a traffic checkpoint was established at the two street entrances to a major drug market area in the middle of a low-rise housing project. Drivers were stopped and asked for their license, registration, and proof of insurance and waved through if their papers were in order. This simple expedient, involving no arrests (except for two drivers with outstanding warrants), succeeded in drying up the market while the checklane was present.* Recently, the police have started selling fake "crack" to drive-through buyers and then seizing their cars under state forfeiture statutes, again without making physical arrests. The prosecutor's office plans to drop charges and return the vehicles for a negotiated fine of $750.

The current cocaine enforcement effort is ferociously expensive, but it is hard to see how conditions could be improved by easing up; the costs of flagrant dealing are just too high. Neither more enforcement nor less enforcement is as useful as smarter enforcement, designed to deter the most destructive behavior and to take advantage of the vulnerabilities of the market.

---

* A lawsuit forced the discontinuation of the checklane during several months of litigation. The eventual result was a ruling favorable to the town.

11

Tobacco

Thank you for not asking me not to smoke.
—Bumper sticker

Though rivers of ink have been spilled in the battle over tobacco smoking since King James I denounced it in 1607, the tobacco problem is fairly simple in outline: far simpler than the problems of other psychoactive drugs. Many people find the drug nicotine a source of pleasure and comfort. Almost as many find it the basis of a powerful and hard-to-break habit. When taken by smoking, tobacco, particularly in the form of cigarettes, poses grave risks to its users' health, primarily in the form of increased risks of long-delayed chronic diseases of the heart and lung.

Nicotine in tobacco is a health problem, complicated by an addiction problem.[1] This leaves a long list of what nicotine is not. It is not an intoxicant, a behavioral risk (except of addiction), or a source, imagined or real, of great powers or insights. No one commits a crime in a nicotine-induced fury, or wrecks a car in a nicotine-induced daze. No one shows up at work unfit for duty, or at school unable to learn, high on tobacco. While users of many other drugs have lives so entwined with, and determined by, their drug habits that the drug use pattern becomes a social identity—thus we describe a person simply as an alcoholic, a heroin addict, a crack-head—no one, not even among those who die of the effects of long-term smoking, bears "tobacco smoker" as a primary social label.

Except for its chemical basis and its high rate of addiction, smoking resembles other bad health habits—overeating, say, or leading a sedentary life—more closely than it does drug abuse. In particular, the absence of an intoxicated state implies that the overwhelming bulk of the damage done by smoking is done to the smokers themselves.

Others suffer too, of course. Some of the economic cost is spread to nonsmokers through the health-care system. Employers and fellow employees share some of the burden of absenteeism due to smoking-related health problems.[2] Some of the ill health and discomfort falls on children whose mothers smoked during pregnancy and on the "passive smokers" who share indoor air with smokers at home, at work, at public gatherings, and in elevators, buses, and airplanes. Smoking, particularly in combination with drinking, also creates a fire hazard, and consequently imposes losses, risk-reduction costs, and increased fire insurance premiums on smokers and nonsmokers alike. Smokers' families bear some of the economic and psychological costs of smoking-related costs and disease. But if all the damage tobacco does to those who never use it were somehow magically to disappear, that would leave the bulk of the tobacco problem intact. The underlying issue in tobacco policy is what to do about the damage that tobacco users do to themselves. Protecting nonsmokers from smokers is a simple and only moderately important problem compared to protecting the 65-year-olds of half a century hence from the 15-year-olds who are currently in charge of their bodies.

PROTECTING OTHERS

Although the problem of protecting nonsmokers from smokers is dwarfed, in complexity and importance, by that of protecting smokers from themselves, it is not itself a small problem. There is less room for fundamental dispute about protecting nonsmokers from smokers than about protecting smokers from themselves because the issue of paternalism does not arise. The only question is how aggressive it is necessary and appropriate to be in requiring smokers to keep the costs of their habit to themselves.

What does create a largely unnecessary complexity and passion around the issue of protecting nonsmokers is its connection with the problem of protecting smokers. The ideological interests on the anti-smoking side and the economic interests on the pro-smoking side both understand that the debate about protecting nonsmokers is part of the maneuvering around the deeper issue.

Sidestream Smoke

The most obvious and frequently annoying imposition by smokers on the health and comfort of nonsmokers takes the form of exhaled and sidestream smoke. Of the five major health risk factors in cigarette smoke—hot gases, tars, carbon monoxide, particulates, and nicotine—second-hand smoke contains all but the first. The particulates cause the least profound health damage (the tars are the worst carcinogens, nicotine in combination with carbon monoxide the major source of cardiovascular risk) but the most annoyance; they are responsible for the unpleasant, lingering odor smoking leaves behind and much of the upper-respiratory distress, such as coughing and sneezing, it engenders.

Cigarette smoking, alone among drug habits, is nearly inseparable from this sort of immediate damage to others, partly because nicotine users deliver their drug to themselves in clouds of smoke and partly because a moderate smoker spends many more minutes of her day smoking than a heavy drinker spends drinking. To be a cigarette smoker is to need a cigarette frequently; one can be a secret five-drinks-a-day drinker, but hardly a secret pack-a-day smoker. Even someone violently allergic to the smell of beer would not be nearly as inconvenienced by a coworker's drinking as by that same coworker's smoking, because almost no one works with a beer at his desk. Moreover, drinking at work obviously interferes with work, while smoking at work does not, and may actually assist work in the short run. Thus the very facts that make tobacco only a mild threat to personal and social functioning—that it is not an intoxicant and that it can be easily integrated into normal activities—make it an environmental hazard.

It is now well demonstrated that heavy and consistent exposure to second-hand smoke can have effects similar to those of being a moderate smoker oneself, though only in instances where the quarters are close, the air circulation is limited, and the exposure lasts for hours per day, day after day: smoking by family members, roommates, and coworkers creates measurable health risks, while smoking by fellow passengers on airplanes imposes primarily discomfort and annoyance. The total damage to the health of nonsmokers due to passive smoking is a small fraction of the burden on smokers themselves, but it is not trivial in absolute terms; the annual death toll from passive smoking is almost certainly in the thousands, and may be in the tens of thousands.[3]

Even though smokers threaten their own health far more than the health of others, policymakers should give extra weight to the external costs because they are not voluntarily accepted, just as mountain climbers are allowed to take risks to their own lives that it would be criminal to impose on others. But the intensity of the campaign to restrict smoking is not fully explicable even in these terms. Other forms of indoor air pollution are also involuntarily imposed on workers, customers, and passengers, and second-hand smoke is a noticeable but not always a leading contributor to the indoor air pollution problem.[4] Rules against smoking at work are not the only measures, or necessarily the most effective measures for the cost and inconvenience involved, to improve the quality of the air breathed by employees, and they derive much of their popularity from the climate of opinion created by the larger anti-smoking movement.

The clearest evidence that hostility toward the practice of smoking outweighs concern for indoor air quality came when airlines took advantage of the federally mandated nonsmoking policy to reduce the rate of air circulation in flight, thus saving the fuel cost of heating the frigid air at 35,000 feet to breathable temperatures but leaving no net improvement in the quality of cabin air. There were no cries of outrage from the supporters of the smoking ban and in particular no effort to force the airlines to pass the benefits of the ban along to their customers and employees in the form of better air quality.* Part of this passivity is probably attributable to the fact that a smoking ban is simple, while air-circulation rules or air-quality standards are complex, but part of it surely reflects the dominance of anti-smoking interests in the political coalition involved.

The connection between the passive-smoking issue and the larger issues of smoking policy is not purely ideological. Requiring smokers to, as one defiant long-term smoker put it, "sit in the back of the bus" by imposing policies that demean and inconvenience them is one way to prevent smoking initiations and promote smoking cessations, just as arresting marijuana users and denying them driver's licenses is one way to prevent marijuana initiations and promote marijuana cessations. No-smoking rules are one contributor to the progressive

---

* The airline smoking ban did have some clear benefits for cabin crews and perhaps some very frequent flyers, who were otherwise being exposed to dangerous levels of nicotine, coal tars, and other pollutants specific to tobacco smoke, and to those passengers who find the smell of burning tobacco offensive. But the benefits that should have accrued in the form of less carbon monoxide and fewer particulates were almost completely eliminated by the reduction in air turnover. See Niren L. Nagda, Roy C. Fortmann, Michael D. Koontz, Scott R. Baker, and Michael E. Ginevan, *Airliner Cabin Environment: Containment Measurements, Health Risks, and Mitigation Options* (Washington, D.C.: U.S. Department of Transportation, 1989), especially Chapters 4 and 5.

denormalization of tobacco use in American life. By reducing the number of new smokers and increasing the number of ex-smokers, anti-smoker policies do more than promote health among those who stop or do not start; they also change the balance of numbers between those who see themselves as benefiting from, and those who see themselves losing by, anti-smoking policies of all kinds, including higher tobacco taxes. The fewer people who smoke (and the more people who have recently quit), the greater the political power of the anti-smoking lobby.*

Like all anti-user policies, no-smoking rules have benefits (assuming that smoking is, on balance, bad for smokers) for those whom it causes to quit or not start and costs for those who insist on continuing. To force a nicotine addict to go "cold turkey" for the length of an airplane ride or the gap between the mid-morning coffee break and lunch is to impose a noticeable discomfort, as one can verify by watching the smokers light up in the arrival lounges at airports. The hostility of anti-smoking groups to such less environmentally obnoxious nicotine-delivery systems as "smokeless tobacco" (chewing tobacco and snuff) and the nicotine-loaded crack pipe test-marketed by R. J. Reynolds (now RJR/Nabisco) under the brand name Premier reflects their lack of interest in minimizing that discomfort.

The issue of smoking in the workplace is greatly complicated morally, but greatly simplified managerially, by the fact that the prevalence of smoking is now inversely related to social class. The nonsmoking members of a firm's committee on smoking policy are likely to be not only more numerous but also, on average, better-paid, better-educated, more highly placed within the organization, and more articulate than the smokers. In a typical hospital, for example, few of the physicians smoke, but many of the nurses and very many of the orderlies do.[5] While it is easy to dismiss labor-union opposition to bans on workplace smoking as the product of tobacco-company prompting and another reflection of the unions' apparent eagerness to be against whatever the rest of the country has decided to be for, that opposition also reflects the tensions between a working class in which smoking is still accepted and a management class in which it is increasingly seen as something between a peculiarity and an aberration. The class bias involved is even clearer when policies forbid smoking "except in private offices." In a university, for ex-

---

* This dynamic is a general one, applicable to all drug policies, and helps explain David Musto's paradox that the intensity of any anti-drug effort always peaks *after* the epidemic it is intended to control.

ample, such a rule means that professors may smoke at their desks but secretaries may not. At Harvard, it is reported that compliance within a department with the university-wide smoking ban depends largely on whether or not the department chair smokes.

This class division also has a racial tinge; African-Americans and Latinos are now heavier smokers than the rest of the population[6] and thus more heavily burdened by rules against smoking at work. The cigarette manufacturers have not been slow to take advantage of this ideological vulnerability on the anti-smoking side, and minority-rights advocacy organizations are divided about whether to oppose policies that seem to reduce employment opportunities for members of racial and ethnic minorities or to concentrate on reducing minority-group smoking as a way to improve minority-group health. Minority-oriented publications, which derive a large proportion of their revenues from cigarette advertising, have been particularly ambivalent.[7] So have a variety of important cultural organizations in minority communities for whom tobacco companies have been a generous source of contributions.

As long as smoking is a common practice, it will continue to annoy nonsmokers. It is not even clear that the degree of annoyance, as opposed to the actual health damage, tends to decrease along with the number of smokers, because nonsmokers seem to become more sensitive to cigarette smoke the less they encounter it. While the glee with which the anti-smoking forces rush to impose periodic abstinence on nicotine addicts is unseemly, and the race and social-class structure of the issue ought to give us pause, the desire of nonsmokers for clean(er) indoor air has a strong claim to precedence over the desire of smokers to continue to puff in public; it is the smokers, after all, who are the (largely involuntary and even unwitting) aggressors.[8] The notion being promoted by Philip Morris that "common courtesy" can be made to resolve the conflict of interest between smokers and nonsmokers in workplaces, restaurants, and airplanes is simply not true.

But while smoking remains legal and relatively common, there would seem to be an argument for treating nicotine addiction as one of those personal disabilities that employers and places of public resort ought to have to make reasonable efforts to accommodate; not as much so as a fully involuntary and irreversible condition such as blindness or paraplegia, but more so than a mere preference such as not wearing a necktie. As between the interests of smokers and nonsmokers, a simple benefit-cost test among alternative policies is not fully appropriate, because it is easier not to smoke than it is not to cough. But as between inconvenience to smokers and the expense of achieving the same improvement in air quality in some other way (for example, by increased circulation and filtration), the cost-benefit test should apply. If, in effect, the smokers would be willing to pay for the new (possibly very expensive) ventilation system, it should be provided, and the cost of making such accommodations ought to be factored into the decision about the appropriate level of tobacco taxation.

This treatment of a personal habit as deserving at least some minimal deference from others departs from the purely libertarian view that anyone ought to be allowed to do anything that damages no one else, but strictly at his own expense and risk. There is something to be said for that libertarian ideal: it minimizes our reasons and excuses for meddling in one another's behavior. But its application may require more hardheartedness than we can actually muster.

A special class of instances where employers are forced to accommodate their smoking employees arises in the area of employee health and safety regulation and liability. There is persuasive evidence that nonsmokers can tolerate very high levels of coal dust and asbestos, for example; the overwhelming bulk of lung disease incurred by coal miners and asbestos-exposed workers occurred among smokers (a larger proportion of the working population then than now).[9] Retrospectively, the case for insisting that the asbestos manufacturers and coal-mine operators pay compensation seems strong; they knew, or should have known, far more about the risks than the miners or the cigarette companies could. But prospectively, it is much less clear that all factories and mines should have to be designed to be safe for cigarette smokers if the costs of making them safe for only nonsmokers would be much smaller. A legal right to smoke need not imply a right to be protected by others from the consequences of smoking, though the structure of laws and regulations about workplace health and safety implies that it probably will.

There is no comfortable solution to this set of problems. Maintaining a mixed society of smokers and nonsmokers is surely not impossible, but it would be much easier to manage an undivided house, "all one thing, or all the other."

Prenatal Exposure

While prenatal exposure to nicotine does not appear to produce the spectacular ill effects of heavy prenatal cocaine or alcohol use, as a statistical matter the children of women who smoke during pregnancy are noticeably worse off. In particular, their average gestational age at birth and their birthweight are both lower, and prematurity and lower birthweight are correlated with other measures of poor birth outcomes.[10] Whether the total fetal damage done by tobacco is more or less than the total fetal damage done by cocaine is a nearly unanswerable question; the effects per exposed infant are almost certainly smaller, but the number of exposed infants is certainly several times as large.*

The factor that makes prenatal smoking exposure a particularly difficult problem is the high rate of compulsive use among nicotine users. Giving up smoking tends to be much more difficult than most of the other behavioral changes that obstetricians routinely urge on expectant mothers. This is true not only for women who are physically dependent on nicotine and those who have developed reinforcement-based compulsions, but also for those who have learned to use smoking as a device for stress management and find it difficult to let go of that device during a stressful period.

This is not to say that even heavily committed smokers cannot and do not quit when they get pregnant, at least for the duration. They do quit, in large numbers; pregnancy is one of the leading motivations for successful quitting among young women, and some who have failed in repeated tries to quit for their own health succeed when the health of their child is at stake.[11] Unsurprisingly, compliance with this and other prenatal care advice is more consistent among higher-status, better-educated, wealthier women, partly but not entirely because of the superior availability and quality of prenatal health services.

Some women from all walks of life, and more poor and ill-educated women, cannot or will not—in any case do not—give up smoking when they learn that they are pregnant. This will presumably be true as long as women smoke, though a combination of anti-smoking messages specifically targeted at pregnant women (presumably through their health-care providers) and messages specifically about smoking and pregnancy spread through the media and the schools probably has made a difference, and might make more of a difference if more were done. But it would be too optimistic to expect that all or virtually all pregnant women will be able to give up a habit that so many have failed to give up after repeated attempts. No one, as far

* About 2500 infant deaths in 1984 were attributable to maternal smoking. See Centers for Disease Control, "Smoking-Attributable Mortality and Years of Potential Life Lost–United States, 1984," *Morbidity and Mortality Weekly Report* 36 (42 [30 October 1987]): 693–697.

as I know, has suggested that smoking during pregnancy be made against the law, or that mothers who smoke should consequently be considered unfit (although the evidence that infants who grow up around tobacco smoke suffer from it is now quite clear[12]). Thus we must accept that some degree of fetal damage is inseparable from the social custom of smoking, and reckon that factor into our overall consideration of tobacco policy.

Safety

Not surprisingly, smoking can cause fires. Both cigarettes and matches create fire hazards, indoors and outdoors, and an estimated 7 percent of home fires start from cigarettes. A typical accident pattern involves a smoker—frequently one who has been drinking—falling asleep holding a burning cigarette. The 230,000 smoking-generated indoor fires lead to more than 1500 deaths and create more than $4 billion in property damage annually. Smoking also plays an important role in outdoor fires.[13]

Changes in the design of cigarettes could reduce the total fire damage and thus the need for fire precautions. Cigarettes without special chemical additives would go out if not puffed on. Manufacturers add flame-maintaining chemicals as a convenience to smokers, who can lay a cigarette aside in an ashtray and then resume smoking it; a cigarette relit after having gone out reportedly has an unpleasant taste. It seems unlikely that the aggregate benefit to smokers from this convenience is anywhere near as large as the aggregate damage to fire victims and those who pay for fire precautions, but in a competitive market manufacturers necessarily give precedence to the convenience of their customers.

This is a classic case for safety regulation of consumer products for the protection of third parties. That no such regulation exists anywhere in the world illustrates the importance of how an issue is framed: allowing additives is a major issue for cigarette manufacturers, while both anti-smoking and consumer products safety advocates feel they have bigger fish to fry.*

---

* It may also be that consumer advocates, caught in an adversarial rule-making process with fabric manufacturers over flame-resistance standards, felt they would lose ground tactically if they acknowledged the contributory role of smoking. Their position was partially analogous to that of plaintiffs' lawyers in the asbestos liability cases confronted with evidence that it was the combination of asbestos exposure and smoking, rather than the asbestos alone, that did the bulk of the damage.

Cost Sharing Through Risk-Spreading Institutions

Many social arrangements for the spreading of risk—such as group health insurance, life insurance, disability insurance, workers' compensation, progressive income taxation, and employer-paid sick leave—have the unintended effect of spreading some of the costs of smokers' ill health and early death to nonsmokers. This is in addition to what might be thought of as "natural" risk-spreading and cost sharing through the institutions of family, friendship, and neighborhood, and informal risk-spreading through charitable contributions and the receipt of charitable services. Not only a smoker's employer, fellow employees, spouse, parents, and children but also his fellow taxpayers, the members of his church, the persons who benefit from his United Way contribution, and the parents of his children's college classmates have a direct financial interest in the ill health and early death his smoking may engender.

Where risks are spread and costs shared through insurance contracts, it might seem that the ordinary practices of underwriting and risk evaluation would appropriately surcharge smokers and give rebates to nonsmokers. But, custom aside, there are two good reasons why this happens only occasionally, partially, and imperfectly. The first is the simple problem of verification; if there is a nonsmoker's discount, how is the insurer to tell? A cotinine test can measure recent nicotine use, but these tests are neither cheap nor routine.[14] Most insurers are content to accept the word of the insured, which limits the size of the discounts and surcharges.

Even if insurers could measure smoking in the immediate past, or exact a binding promise not to smoke in the future, there would remain the impact of past smoking. An ex-smoker is a better health risk than a current smoker, but not nearly as good a risk as someone who has never habitually smoked.[15] Any underwriting scheme that pays attention only to the future and the immediate past cannot appropriately assign the expected value cost of past smoking to the smoker, and there is no practical way to verify an individual's self-report of his smoking behavior even so much as months into the past.

Since much risk-sharing, including most health insurance, is through employment, and since smokers also have a higher rate of absenteeism than nonsmokers, employers do have incentives to pay attention to the smoking behavior of their employees.[16] Many employers encourage quitting as part of their health-promotion programs, and many now pay for commercial assistance for those who want to quit but doubt their ability to do so on their own.

In principle, an employer might go further and either attempt to screen out smokers as part of the hiring process or require current employees not to smoke as a condition of retaining their jobs. In Massachusetts, where under state law all heart disease suffered by police and firefighters is assumed to be job-related and thus creates a financial liability for the locality that employs them, the localities lobbied successfully for a law to require that employees in these categories not smoke. From a purely financial viewpoint, this seems to make at least as much sense as requirements that potential and current employees abstain from the use of illicit drugs, but such employer intrusion into behavior away from the worksite is naturally resented. The growing ethnic and class disparities in smoking rates make such policies all the more problematical. Verification is less worrisome; a person employed full-time who never smokes at work is probably not a very heavy smoker.

Not all of the external financial impact of smoking is negative; some portion of smokers' losses are nonsmokers' gains. Pension programs, including Social Security as well as private pension plans, and medical care for the elderly, including Medicare and company-paid plans for retirees, pay the most to those who live the longest. Other pensioners and taxpayers thus benefit from the untimely demise of smokers. Since most of the excess deaths linked to smoking occur after the end of a normal working career, smokers as a group contribute almost as much as nonsmokers do to these two large risk-spreading systems—where the risk being shared is that of outliving one's savings—but collect far less. Much of the purely financial cost of smoking carried by persons and institutions outside the family of the smoker is compensated for by smokers' statistical failure to collect their pensions, and the rest seems to be more than covered by existing taxes.[17]

Contagion and Imitation

If we assume or conclude that smoking is, on balance, bad for smokers, then we have to contend with another form of harm that smokers may do to nonsmokers and to one another: the harm of encouraging them to smoke or not to quit. The number of smokers in the immediate environment is clearly one determinant of the probability that a given individual will start smoking or continue to smoke.[18]

An adolescent with many smoking friends will, on average, receive more suggestions to start and more offers of a first cigarette than she would if few of her friends smoked. She will also feel less uncomfortably conspicuous as a smoker and perhaps more uncomfortably conspicuous as a nonsmoker. If her parents smoke, she has a convenient source of supply, independent of the law that forbids her to purchase tobacco. (This is true to a lesser extent even if it is only her friends' parents who smoke.) If she sees adults, particularly respected adults, smoking, that will help create positive associations in her mind. If, as an adult, all of her friends prefer the smoking sections of restaurants and she joins a bowling league or book group where smoking is the norm, that will help maintain her habit. If all her coworkers smoke, her workplace will be less apt to adopt rules about smoking on the job that make life inconvenient for smokers. The more smokers who live in her town, the smaller the chance that it will adopt a tough anti-smoking ordinance, and the less eager her congresswoman will be to vote for higher tobacco taxes.

That a practice is "contagious" in this way from person to person and from social groups to the individuals who compose them is not, in itself, an argument for controlling it. But once we have reason to believe that a practice is harmful, and especially if it is habit-forming as well, contagion effects become additional reasons to work toward reducing its prevalence.

IS SMOKING BAD FOR SMOKERS?

Now that smoking is generally accepted as the largest single cause of preventable deaths in the United States, it seems almost frivolous to ask whether smoking is bad for smokers.[19] But one ought to be cautious about deciding that a practice (seemingly) voluntarily begun and voluntarily continued or resumed by individuals who in other contexts seem competent to take care of themselves is nevertheless a mistake.

If it is a mistake, good explanations for why people make it are at hand: peer pressure on vulnerable adolescents; advertising and other marketing efforts that create psychological associations between smoking and such desired personal qualities as maturity, sophistication, manliness, independence, prosperity, athletic prowess, and sexual attractiveness; ignorance of the full extent of the risks; temporal myopia with respect to a practice that gives immediate pleasure and whose costs are long deferred; and the effects of a strongly reinforcing and often-repeated behavior such as taking a puff on a cigarette. But explaining why a choice might be made even if it were mistaken is not the same as proving that it is in fact a mistake. Reports of the pleasures and other benefits of smoking are remarkably fervent and widespread.

The Benefits and Costs of Smoking

Depending on how it is smoked, a cigarette can be a stimulant or a relaxant, and it appears that smokers learn to adjust their puffing practices to achieve the effect they want in any given situation.[20] As with any drug taken in through the lungs, the effect is nearly immediate. The absence of any intoxication makes smoking consistent with many forms of work and play where alcohol would be inappropriate or even dangerous. Many smokers believe that nicotine helps them concentrate on mentally demanding tasks, and this claim does not appear to be merely illusory; again unlike alcohol, nicotine does not suppress the critical faculties.* It is also largely free of the tendency, common to stimulants ranging from caffeine to cocaine, to cause jangled nerves.

We all know by now that tobacco is, statistically, a killer. Roughly speaking, a lifelong smoking habit doubles one's chance of dying at any given age.[21] (Most of the life-years lost to tobacco are after age 65 simply because mortality rates increase with age.) In addition, those smokers who eventually die of something else still suffer from various kinds of ill health. These range from the foul morning-after taste of "smoker's mouth" through the chronic throat irritation that manifests itself as "smoker's hack," the decreased lung function that interferes with vigorous physical activity, the substantially increased rates of respiratory infection and thus of absenteeism from work, up to the horrors of emphysema and chronic obstructive pulmonary disease (COPD).[22]

---

* As John Pinney of the Corporate Health Policies Group and Jack Henningfield of the Addiction Research Center have pointed out, most of the laboratory evidence of the benefits of smoking comes from studies of experienced smokers. Whether the practice of smoking genuinely improves concentration or relieves stress when compared to a natural baseline, or only relieves the inattention and stress characteristic of nicotine addicts deprived of their drug, is therefore somewhat obscure. But see Daniel Krogh, *Smoking: The Artificial Passion* (New York: W. H. Freeman, 1991).

Thus if smoking were merely a fashion rather than the vehicle for a drug with many attractive characteristics, any reasonable person would drop it like a hot potato. On the other hand, if cigarettes were merely a way of absorbing a mildly and usefully mood-altering drug, nicotine, and did no substantial damage to health, there would be no obvious reason—aside from the expense, the safety hazard, the stench of stale smoke in clothing and furniture, or an aversion on general principles to being influenced by or dependent on a drug—not to smoke.

Such an aversion would be a little more than a mere prejudice. Unwanted homeostatic effects—rebound in the short run, dependency in the longer run—are to be expected from the use of any psychoactive, and nicotine is no exception. The basic phenomenon of tolerance—that of getting a smaller and smaller mood alteration from a given dose—is sufficiently widespread among tobacco users to have formed the basis for one of the best-remembered of all cigarette advertising campaigns: "Smoking more now, but enjoying it less?" Nor can one safely choose to smoke until the pleasure runs out. Many have walked down the path of nicotine tolerance to the point where the pleasure has virtually disappeared and then discovered that they could not easily desist. A combination of straightforward chemical dependency, marked by active discomfort if use of nicotine is discontinued, and bad habit—that is, compulsion based on behavioral reinforcement (sometimes confusingly called "psychological dependency" or "psychological addiction")—keeps them trapped in a behavior pattern they no longer want.

Still, despite all of the costs of smoking, including the very high risk of becoming a compulsive user, it is not self-evident that being able to be either more alert or more relaxed on demand, and to experience oral gratification with no calories and no cholesterol, does not represent an adequately counterbalancing benefit, at least for some smokers. Portable, nonfattening sources of instant comfort are hard to find.

To decide rationally whether to smoke or not, an individual would have to add up the value of its pleasures and comforts, and of any assistance it might give to his work performance, and balance that value against its costs and risks. This would pose no simple problem, since the various outcome dimensions—minutes of relaxation, projects completed, dollar expense, statistical life-years lost—are not easily commensurable. (Dollars are a convenient common measure, but the question of what someone would be willing to pay to avoid, say, a one-in-five chance of contracting COPD, is not easily answerable, even by the person involved.) Still, the calculation can in principle be made for any one person.*

Calculating an average answer valid for a large group of diverse persons is by no means so obviously feasible. Nor is the average the only important question. Assume for the moment that smoking is irrational for smokers as a group: that confronted with an explicit choice between having both its benefits and its costs and having neither, someone representing the interests of smokers as the smokers value them would regard the costs as larger. There might still be a substantial number of persons who, because they derive larger-than-average personal benefits from smoking or face smaller-than-average risks, would reasonably prefer smoking to nonsmoking.

This point would not be worth belaboring if so much of the current discussion about smoking did not assume away its benefits, leaping from the fact that it has heavy costs to the conclusion that it ought to be reduced or abolished. This seems to me just as unreasonable as the cigarette industry's rhetoric about "those who choose to smoke."

Smoking and Regret

In this context, the people whose opinions about smoking are most worth having are the smokers themselves. They have experienced

* As a sample of how part of such a calculation could be made, consider the effect of smoking on premature mortality. Roughly speaking, each pack of cigarettes over a 50-year pack-a-day smoking career reduces one's life expectancy by an average of about an hour and a half: about three expected life-years lost, divided by about twenty thousand packs. (The average is the value to use here because smoking is habitual for most smokers; smoking the ten-thousandth pack is a predictable consequence of smoking the tenth.) This is equivalent in life-expectancy terms to a three-part-per-million risk of immediate death. Two different approaches to calculating the value of such a risk—the empirical method of Moore and Viscusi and the theoretical calculation of Howard—agree that a three-part-per-million risk has a cash value for a representative individual of somewhere between $6 and $15 [See Ron Howard, "On Making Life and Death Decisions," in *Societal Risk Assessment: How Safe is Safe Enough?* Richard Schwing and Walter A. Albers, eds. (New York: Plenum Press, 1980). Also, Michael J. Moore and W. Kip Viscusi, "Doubling the Estimated Value of Life: Results Using New Occupational Fatality Data," *Journal of Policy Analysis and Management*, 7 (3 [Spring, 1988]): 476–490]. Then one way of posing the question of whether the benefits of smoking outweigh its mortality risks would be the following: "Assume that cigarettes did not exist, but another product existed with the same benefits and no mortality risk. How much would you be willing to pay for that product?" Unless the answer is at least $6 per pack more than the cash price of a pack of cigarettes, then it is reasonable to say that the benefits of smoking are less than the monetary equivalent of mortality risk alone to that smoker. Therefore, he ought to prefer—would prefer if he thought about it and could make a free choice (free, that is, from the force of dependency, habit, and social pressure)—not to smoke.

the pleasures of smoking and some of its pains, both personally and as portrayed in the barrage of quit-smoking messages directed at them in recent years. Their opinions will not necessarily be decisive, because it is almost as easy to explain away their self-reported views on smoking as to explain away their behavior. On the one hand, the powerful force of cognitive dissonance leads those who continue to smoke to regard the habit as relatively harmless; otherwise, they would have to acknowledge that something they do many times every day is irrational and that they are too weak to control their own behavior. On the other hand, everyone now knows that respectable and scientifically based opinion is anti-smoking; to categorize oneself as a willing smoker rather than a victim of an addiction acquired as a youthful indiscretion is thus to defy a widespread norm. Moreover, the social inconvenience and disability now imposed on smokers are so considerable that even someone who thought the habit worth its natural price might find the sum of the natural and artificial prices excessive. In particular, any nicotine addict who works in a nonsmoking building or takes frequent long flights on nonsmoking airplanes is exposed to repeated involuntary partial withdrawals, which are certainly helpful to those in the same office or airplane and may be good for the smoker's moral fiber but which are, in any case, a large and artificial cost of maintaining the habit.

Still, the opinion of the smokers is worth having, and it is overwhelmingly negative: 80 percent of all current smokers would like to quit,[23] 66 percent have tried to quit and failed (most of them more than once),[24] and 80 percent wish they had never started.[25] In addition, 43 million persons have gone from being regular smokers to being nonsmokers,[26] most of them with considerable discomfort and inconvenience. Thus regret about smoking is nearly coextensive with smoking itself.

The decision to continue smoking need not contradict the expression of regret about having started, for the same reasons that more people hate where they live than move. Quitting, like moving, has its own disadvantages, and it may be perfectly rational to accept the costs and risks of being a smoker rather than undergo the struggle to become a former smoker. Even for those who decide to quit, the decision is not self-executing; some people continue to smoke although they would prefer not to. If smoking were only harmful, rather than being harmful and hard to quit, it would create a much less convoluted problem. Current smoking makes future nonsmoking costly and difficult; that characteristic distinguishes smoking from many other forms of unhealthy behavior.

Smoking and Adolescence

More evidence that smoking is not freely and rationally chosen behavior comes in the observation that, although many adults continue
to smoke and many former smokers relapse (significantly, former
smokers rarely say they have "decided" or "chosen" to go back to
smoking) very few adults take up smoking for the first time.[27] This is
hard to reconcile with the theory that smoking is a rational choice for
those who engage in it; if it were, one would expect that some of them
would recommend it to some of their friends, and that some of their
friends would then start. It appears that starting to smoke appeals
almost entirely to adolescents, and that maturity and more direct experience with smoking's pleasures and pains lead most smokers to
decide that nonsmoking is preferable.

This distinguishes anti-smoking policies from such clearly paternalistic policies as requiring motorcycle riders to wear helmets.
Rather than forcing competent adults to do as well-intentioned
strangers want them to do, anti-smoking policy is largely about forcing adolescents to behave as the adults they will become will later wish
they had behaved and creating social conditions more conducive to
those adults' being able to act as they wish they could force themselves to act.[28]

The goal of preventing adolescents from taking up smoking is not
the subject of much debate, though current laws and programs are
not doing a very impressive job. The argument is about the vigor with
which laws and programs should press adult smokers to quit. Even
though most smokers will tell an interviewer that they would like
to quit and have tried to quit, such policies as discriminatory taxes
on smoking beyond the level required to compensate for harm to
nonsmokers can be justified only on a quasi-paternalist theory. Strong
libertarians can therefore oppose such measures without denying any
of the factual premises asserted by the anti-smokers.

But the distinction between protecting adolescents and imposing
choices on adults is sharper in theory than in practice. As with any
drug, the extent to which we can protect kids from themselves is
limited by the free availability of tobacco to adults, since each adult
is a potential point of leakage across the age barrier. The ban on
adolescent smoking, like any age discrimination that is not virtually
self-enforcing, may actually increase the attractiveness of smoking
to some adolescents by making it a badge of adulthood, although
this effect will tend to diminish as fewer and fewer adults actually
smoke.

The analysis of smoking initiation as one aspect of adolescent experimentation with drugs directs our attention toward another possible form of smoking-related harm: the role of cigarette smoking as a "gateway" drug habit and a model of drug-taking behavior. Tobacco smoking could lead to other kinds of drug taking in any of several ways: by introducing adolescents to the practice of using nonfood substances deliberately to alter mood; by spreading the skills and equipment (matches, lighters, rolling papers, pipes) that can be used to take a wide variety of drugs;* and by providing countermessages and counterexamples to the anti-drug persuasion campaign. Some of these effects depend on adolescents' own smoking, others only on the existence of smoking as a legitimate social practice openly engaged in by adults.

On an individual level, the association between adolescent tobacco smoking and adolescent marijuana smoking is very strong. Some 94 percent of all high school seniors who smoke more than a pack a day and 75 percent of those who have used cigarettes at least three times have tried marijuana. By contrast, only 20 percent of those who have never used the legal weed have tried the illegal one. The pattern for current marijuana use is the same; 59 percent of the more-than-a-pack-a-day smokers and 35 percent of experimenters have smoked marijuana in the last month, compared with 7 percent of the nonsmokers.[29] Without carefully adjusting for demographic background and personality characteristics, it is impossible to tell how much of this relationship is cause-and-effect and how much is just the clustering of rebellious behaviors among rebellious kids. Still, the gross relationship is strong enough to deserve some serious follow-up research (for example, looking for changes in the frequency of adolescent marijuana initiation in states where cigarette taxes have been sharply increased, using states without such increases as the control group). Official and unofficial drug warriors, including the anti-marijuana "parents' movement," have not paid much attention to the possibility that tobacco is a gateway; this reflects once again the heavy cultural and ideological burden carried by the drug policy debate.

TOWARD A (LARGELY) SMOKE-FREE SOCIETY

The costs of smoking, at least in the form of cigarettes, look so large when viewed from the outside that it would be surprising if a large

---

* It is striking that the widespread laws against the sale of drug paraphernalia never include what are still called (and taxed as) "cigarette rolling papers," even though most of them are actually used to roll marijuana joints. These provide the most unhealthful, as well as the most easily concealable, way of smoking marijuana.

number of people, with experience of its effects and knowledge of its costs, preferred to continue. Survey evidence suggests that they do not and that few adult nonsmokers freely choose to start.

Thus if tobacco were a newly developed drug it is hard to see why it would be permitted by a society trying to help its members promote their own welfare. Millions of people have tried it, and most have found it to be a behavioral trap, a mistake easy to make and hard to undo. In the absence of any way to identify in advance a subclass of potential smokers for whom the practice will produce benefits that will (in their own scheme of evaluation) outweigh its harms, it would be reasonable to have as a social objective, if not a "smoke-free society," at least a world in which smoking is so rare as to be negligible. This objective could be chosen without any reference to the "immorality" of smoking or the "degradation" it inflicts on its addicts, simply as a matter of creating policies that enable as many persons as possible to have what they actually want.

This argument will not convince the hardy libertarian or the stubborn economist of the Chicago school, for both of whom the actual decisions of smokers, day after day, to spend their own money and risk their own health for the pleasures of smoking are sufficient demonstration that they choose to smoke and that interfering with that choice will unjustifiably restrict liberty and inefficiently reduce consumers' surplus. As long as one considers only the damage smoking does to nonsmokers and ignores the damage it does to smokers, there is simply not enough justification for attempting to abolish it.

Even if we were all to agree that a world of no, or very little, cigarette smoking would be a socially desirable outcome, we still face the problem of managing the transition from here to there. What changes in programs or laws could accomplish that transition with the least pain?

PROGRAMS WITHIN EXISTING LAW

In terms of immediate political feasibility, neither prohibition nor virtually prohibitory taxation is on the list of possible policies. How much can be done within existing laws to cut down on smoking and its attendant harms?

The damage tobacco does to smokers and to nonsmokers can be reduced in three ways: by reducing the proportion of adolescents who start to smoke, by increasing the rate at which current smokers quit, and by encouraging people who do use nicotine to do so at times and places, or in forms, less inconvenient to others and less harmful to themselves. Of these three approaches, the first two are consistent with the objective of a smoke-free world. The third is not; making smoking safer will tend to reduce the pressure to stop it entirely, both for individuals and for the whole society. Thus tobacco policies, like policies about other drugs, are subject to a tension between "Just say no" and "harm minimization."

Safer Forms of Nicotine Use

Cigarette smoking is now the dominant form of nicotine use. It is also probably the form most dangerous to smokers and obnoxious to others. Nicotine however administered puts stress on the heart and the rest of the circulatory system by repeatedly constricting the arteries. If it is taken in tobacco, there is added the risk of cancer from carcinogenic compounds. If it is smoked, rather than chewed or taken as snuff, there is further added the burden on the heart of carbon monoxide, and all the damage done to the throat and lungs by hot gases and particulates, plus fire hazard and the imposition of sidestream smoke on nonsmokers.

Of all the forms of smoking, cigarettes are the worst. Cigarette smokers are much more likely than cigar or pipe smokers to inhale their smoke.[30] Not only does inhaling vastly increase the respiratory damage involved, it transforms the drug experience in a way analogous to the switch from snorting cocaine to smoking crack. If the smoke is not inhaled, nicotine is absorbed by the capillaries in the mouth and the nose, and makes its way relatively slowly through the veins to the heart, the lungs, and finally the brain. Inhalation provides a shortcut, taking the drug directly to the lungs.

The composition of American-made mass-market cigarettes may create risks even beyond those inherent in cigarette smoking. Manufacturers, in their search for cigarettes that taste "smooth," that continue to burn if put down for several seconds, and that cost as little as possible to make, treat their tobacco and their paper with a variety of additives, whose nature is kept as proprietary information. The Consumer Product Safety Commission is explicitly forbidden by law to regulate tobacco or tobacco products.[31] The FDA has opted not to assert jurisdiction over cigarettes except in situations where the manufacturer has claimed health benefits for users.[32] Otherwise, cigarettes might not be available at all, since any cigarette that contains tobacco is certain to be carcinogenic and unsafe in its intended use. But the fierce competition to produce cigarettes low in tar and nicotine indicates the existence of a strong demand among cigarette smokers for "safer" cigarettes. A simple labeling requirement with respect to additives might save some lives, both by guiding smokers toward brands with fewer noxious chemicals and by creating competitive pressure to remove additives from existing brands.

Cigarette manufacturers have already produced cigarettes much lower in tar and nicotine than any available a generation ago, but it is not clear that the result has been an improvement in smokers' health. Nicotine, after all, is why people smoke in the first place. The less nicotine in a cigarette, the more effort smokers are likely to make to absorb it all. Those who switch to low-tar, low-nicotine brands tend to smoke their cigarettes farther down, draw the smoke in more deeply and hold it longer, and otherwise defeat their own purpose in buying a "low" brand.[33]

There might be some benefit in creating a product high in nicotine but low in tar. Why no tobacco company has ever done so is unclear; there may be technical difficulties in developing tobacco strains with the appropriate mix of chemicals, but it should be possible to add nicotine to low-tar, low-nicotine leaf. Insofar as a high-nicotine cigarette reduced the number of cigarettes smoked and the intensity with which they were smoked, it would tend to reduce smokers' exposure to hot gases, carbon monoxide, and particulates as well as to coal tars. It is possible that only a few smokers understand, or are willing to acknowledge, their dependency on nicotine, and that a high-nicotine product would therefore not appeal to the safety conscious. Such a brand would also probably enjoy fewer sales per smoker than existing low-tar, low-nicotine brands.

RJR/Nabisco took the concept of separating tar from nicotine to its logical extreme with a smokeless product called Premier, a device with only a trace of tobacco, designed purely and simply to deliver nicotine vapor. It therefore resembled the nicotine gum sold by prescription as an aid to quitting smoking. But anti-smoking activists were not at all grateful that RJR had joined the ranks of the producers of cigarette substitutes. Lawsuits were threatened on the ingenious theory that since Premier was not a cigarette but a nicotine-delivery device, it should be subject (as cigarettes are not) to approval by the Food and Drug Administration. That lawsuit and others were made moot by the fact that the test-marketing of the device went so badly that RJR was forced to abandon, at least temporarily, a product that reportedly cost hundreds of millions of dollars to develop.[34]

Nicotine-delivery systems—gum, Premier, the nicotine-laced skin patches now under development—are to smoking as methadone is to heroin. The health of current smokers and the convenience of those around them would be well served by switching them to some other way of getting nicotine, but not as well as by getting them off nicotine entirely. The question is how many of those who switch from smoking to something else will go on to quit altogether, how many will remain addicted to nicotine in some other form, and how many of that latter group could have gone all the way if gum or whatever had not been there as a convenient stopping place. To avoid attracting nonsmokers, the gum was designed to be so foul-tasting that few can endure using it for very long, but there are exceptions: I know one person who, years after quitting smoking, is a two-pack-a-day chewer. Cigarette substitutes can also substitute for smoking cessation by providing a bridge across required nonsmoking times at work or in airplanes.

The most frightening possibility is that nonsmoking alternatives, including chewing tobacco, snuff, and nicotine delivery devices such as Premier, might serve, particularly for adolescents, as a road into cigarette use rather than a road out. (That is the only serious argument for keeping nicotine gum a prescription item.)

More knowledge of who tries which alternative nicotine-delivery systems, and with what results, would be helpful in framing policies, though in the case of new systems the relevant data would be hard to gather before the decisions are made. It would also be helpful to know something about the quantitative risks of long-term nicotine use in other forms compared with long-term cigarette smoking. If a nicotine-delivery device like Premier were 90 percent as harmful as smoking, there would be a strong case against permitting it; if it were only 10 percent as harmful, the apparent balance of advantage would swing the other way. But there seems to be little hope for such thoughtful consideration of the issue amid the maelstrom of the smoking debate.

Persuasion

The statistics concerning the decline of smoking in the United States have become so familiar that they have lost some of their power to impress, but they are by rights impressive enough. In 1965, 30 percent of those who had ever been smokers had quit and 50 percent of adult males smoked; by 1990, nearly 50 percent of those who had ever been smokers had quit and only 28 percent of men were smoking.[35] Those who now smoke are more likely than before to do so with a consideration for the sensibilities of nonsmokers that sometimes amounts almost to furtiveness. Smoking (unlike drinking) is socially established as a Bad Thing.

This massive change in attitudes and behavior over barely a generation is largely a testimony to the power of persuasion. Recent increases in cigarette taxes and tightening of public and private regulations regarding smoking have followed the trends in attitudes and behavior more than they have shaped them.

Only some of that persuasion effort has been governmental. Certainly the Surgeon General's report in 1964 may fairly be regarded as the start of the anti-smoking movement as a serious force. The anti-smoking advertisements that, in the name of "fairness," television and radio stations were required to run until they were forced to stop cigarette advertising, also had an impact. (The ban on advertising was apparently much less important.[36]) Anti-smoking messages presented in classrooms have had a double effect: building up anti-smoking sentiment among young potential smokers and prompting children to put pressure on their parents to quit. By contrast, no one has succeeded in detecting the impact of the stereotyped health warnings printed in small type on labels and in advertisements, though the original formula is sufficiently well known to count as a familiar quotation.

Another large component of the persuasion effort has come from not-for-profit advocacy groups. Here the key to large-scale efforts seems to have been the enlistment in the anti-smoking cause of the sponsors of health-related charitable efforts—the American Heart Association, the American Lung Association, and, above all, the American Cancer Society. These groups had the credibility and the organizational infrastructure to promote such private persuasion efforts as the Great American Smokeout and to lobby effectively for public efforts, including anti-smoking curricula in schools.

Unwittingly and unwillingly, the cigarette manufacturers themselves may have contributed a third, powerful set of anti-smoking messages. Almost as soon as nicotine and tar were identified as the primary health-damaging substances in tobacco smoke, the companies started to market lower-tar, lower-nicotine brands. The Federal Trade Commission stepped in to regulate their claims, eventually devising its own (not necessarily very accurate) measurement system for the effective tar and nicotine content of rival brands. Then started the "tar wars," with massive advertising campaigns trumpeting the FTC milligram scores as if they were the horsepower of rival automobiles. As Thomas Schelling has pointed out, these claims, which implied that cigarettes, or at least two of their ingredients, constituted a health hazard, were driven home to the population with a weight of advertising far beyond the dreams of the anti-smoking groups. Coming from the manufacturers, they seemed to concede the main point of the opponents of smoking.[37]

The anti-smoking persuasion effort has been a dramatic success. But that success has not been uniform. The weight of social disapproval long kept smoking among women and the young well below the levels typical of adult males. The expense of habitual tobacco use tended to keep smoking by the poor below the level typical of the affluent. But those gaps have been shrinking.

By the time the anti-smoking movement arrived, the gender gap had been narrowing for most of this century, corresponding to increasing equality between the sexes on other fronts. (This observation forms the basis of the famous advertising campaign for Virginia Slims.) Though men and women alike started to reduce their smoking activity after 1966, women quit at a lower rate. Smoking by women over the age of 20 reached a high of 32 percent in 1966 and since then has declined about 6 percentage points. Men's smoking, by comparison, which reached a peak of 51 percent in 1966, has suffered an almost 20 percentage-point drop.[38] Some time in the next few years, the rates will probably equalize.

There has also been gender equalization among adolescents. While smoking among 15- to 16-year-old boys peaked in 1970 at 20 percent and fell to 14 percent by 1979, smoking among girls of the same age continued to rise until 1974, also peaking at 20 percent before declining to 12 percent in 1979. Overall prevalence among adolescents has stabilized. In 1990, 29 percent of high school seniors said they had smoked at least some in the prior month, the same proportion as observed in 1981.[39] The daily smoking rate fell by only one percentage point over the same interval, to 19 percent.[40] It says something about the inefficacy of laws that are not enforced that smoking may soon be as common among adolescents, to whom it is prohibited, as among adults, to whom it is permitted.

The class and ethnic gap has closed not because poor and minority women and children are smoking more, but because affluent adult men—the people who compose what Schelling has called "the necktie-wearing class"—are smoking much less. Smoking among the poor has not been falling nearly as fast, although price now forms more of a barrier than it once did to smoking by the poor; the 1991 average pack price of $2.15 represents 31 minutes of labor at the minimum wage, compared with only 18 minutes in 1954. Families in the bottom fifth of the income distribution now spend on average slightly more dollars (a much larger proportion of their income) on tobacco than families in the top fifth.[41] Part of the explanation surely is that tobacco companies have begun to focus their marketing efforts on the poor and ethnic minorities, for example by using urban billboard advertising.

The poor and ethnic minorities have not been as quick as the rest of the population to respond to good advice about a wide range of health-related behaviors. This may reflect both the fact that the messages are written largely by the white middle class and thus appeal primarily to that same group, and the broader phenomenon that effective action to safeguard the far future becomes more common as one moves up the income scale.[42]

We seem to be near the limit of what can be done by providing information. Future campaigns should probably concentrate on breaking the connection that brand advertising tries to establish between smoking and success, smoking and sophistication, and smoking and sexiness with counter-ads explicitly aimed at deglamorizing smoking.

Given the finding that experimentation with cigarettes is far more widespread among adolescents than is settling down to a lifetime of smoking, more attention should probably be paid to what the old drug-prevention literature calls "secondary prevention": that is, preventing the transition from experimentation to regular use.[43] If it is true that many adolescent smokers are confident that they can smoke for a while and not become addicted, two distinct responses are needed: one to nonsmokers, emphasizing the high risk of becoming captives, and one to new smokers suggesting that there will never be an easier time to quit, or challenging them to prove that they are not addicts by quitting now.

An approach to prevention that may deserve more attention is getting messages to adolescents through their personal authority figures. Pediatricians could do more than they now routinely do if they were adequately indoctrinated about the importance of smoking prevention, trained to deliver anti-smoking messages, and reimbursed by third-party payers (or given credit by employers such as health maintenance organizations) for doing so. Less formally, coaches, recreational supervisors, clergy, and other adults in a position to offer authoritative advice could be encouraged to weigh in on the anti-smoking side and given some training in doing so. Gynecologists and other reproductive-health workers have special opportunities in dealing with young women, telling them both about the harmful interactions between smoking and oral contraceptives and about the risks smoking adds to gestation. Since most of these messages, in general, are delivered in one-on-one situations, they could be shaped to the recipients far more accurately than can classroom or mass-media messages. Since smoking among minors is much more widespread and effectively much less illegal than is the use of any of the strictly illicit drugs, anti-smoking counsel from any of these sources is much more likely to be needed than anti-drug counsel in general, and the preliminary question about current smoking behavior is apt to seem much less threatening and intrusive than a parallel question about use of illicit drugs.

Marketing Restrictions and Labeling Requirements

The proposal to further restrict cigarette advertising and other marketing is a hardy perennial, despite the contentious debate over whether such bans make a difference one way or the other.[44] (The ability and willingness of tobacco companies to use the withdrawal of their advertising dollars to punish magazines and newspapers for their editorial content may be a better reason to support a ban on media advertising.) Increased negative advertising—which could be supported by a tax on tobacco products or even on tobacco-related marketing expenditures—would probably be more effective. At a minimum, there is an argument for allowing continued price advertising as a consumer-protection measure.

Labeling requirements to date seem to have been largely ineffective, in part because of the tiny print in which the warnings are given. It will be interesting to see what effect the more prominent warnings now being required in Canada have on opinions, although, since they will coincide with another round of sharply increased taxes, there will be almost no way to relate them directly to changes in smoking behavior. In any case, since the basic anti-smoking facts are now widely known, it seems too optimistic to pin any great hopes for further smoking reductions on more prominent warnings, unless they said something like "Warning: Smoking is Now Completely Unfashionable, Makes You Look Like a Nerd, and Drastically Reduces Your Sexual Attractiveness."

Enforcing Age Restrictions

Smoking by adolescents is of particular social concern for the usual reasons: kids are more prone than adults to making short-sighted decisions, the biological consequences of smoking are likely to be more profound during a period of growth, and early initiation of the use of one drug is a predictor both of going on to chronic heavy use of that drug and of beginning the use of any other drug.

These general concerns are heightened in the instance of smoking by three observations. First, virtually all the people who will ever start smoking have done so by their nineteenth birthday,[45] so adolescence is a crucial moment for prevention efforts. Second, rates of smoking among adolescents, especially poor adolescents, have not been falling as sharply as rates among adults. Third, over a wide range of cancers and carcinogenic substances, the probability of contracting the disease is a power function (with an exponent of approximately four) of the period of exposure.[46] By this rule, delaying the onset of smoking from age 13 to age 18 would be expected to reduce the probability of developing cancer by age 65 by more than one-third. (In addition, there are more life-years to be lost by dying younger.)

All of this makes the relatively modest success to date in reducing the rates of adolescent smoking initiation a great disappointment. Aside from presenting more anti-smoking messages in schools, what can be done about it without changing the legal status of smoking for adults?

Higher taxes would help. Adolescent demand for cigarettes is more sensitive to price than adult demand, both because kids have less money to spend and because they are less likely already to be compulsive smokers.[47]

More direct, but perhaps less helpful, would be legal and regulatory changes to reduce the leakage of cigarettes across the age barrier. Unlike the case of alcohol, the largest current source of tobacco for kids appears to be retailers rather than adult friends, parents, or siblings. Some 90 percent of teenagers say they buy their own cigarettes, 5 percent from vending machines; fewer than one-fifth say they get them from parents or friends.[48] Partly because the laws are not enforced, and partly because, unlike liquor sellers, they have no licenses to lose, vendors who sell to minors currently have little to fear, and violations are therefore widespread; one study in Massachusetts found that 73 percent of the vendors who knew that selling to minors was illegal were still willing to sell cigarettes to an 11-year-old girl.[49]

Turning cigarette selling into a licensed activity, as liquor selling now is, could make a difference. Even under the current system, the money to be made selling cigarettes to minors is not so great that increased investigative activity, backed by stiff fines, could not significantly reduce the number of retailers willing to break the law.

Cigarette vending machines are a great convenience for young smokers who prefer to avoid possibly inquisitive salesclerks. Lately there has been a movement to restrict those machines to places not open to minors. To the extent that retail sales have been brought under control or that some kids are afraid or ashamed to try to purchase from a human being, restrictions on vending machines might make some difference. New York City recently banned cigarette vending machines from most public places.[50] It would be interesting to study how this affects smoking rates among teens in the city, but unwise to be very optimistic.

As always, however, commercial sale is the easiest part of the problem to control. Even if efforts to prevent it were successful, any child with parents, older friends, or siblings who smoke would still have easy access to cigarettes. Few, if any, of these routes present plausible targets for public intervention as long as adults remain free to buy cigarettes in unlimited quantities. Sending underage "mystery buyers" to a limited number of retail outlets is one thing; introducing undercover agents on high school playgrounds to catch seniors who supply sophomores is quite another. Are parents who fail to lock up the cigarette supply to be regarded as abusive or neglectful?

It is far easier to observe adolescents smoking cigarettes than buying them, if only because smoking takes longer and produces a pungent odor. This may be a case for a small dose of "user accountability." Given the frequency of adolescent experimentation with smoking—an experimentation that frequently ends quickly and with little or no damage done—any approach to punishing adolescents for cigarette use would have to involve relatively mild sanctions: easy to assess, easy to inflict, and not very damaging to the adolescent's future. Arrest would never be appropriate. Forty hours of "community service" involuntary labor—which might even be performed at school in the mornings or afternoons—plus subjection to a barrage of antismoking propaganda, and perhaps occasional saliva testing for cotinine, ought to be a more than ample punishment. (Fines are easier to collect, but their disparate impact on different income classes would present a major equity problem.) Since these would be entirely juvenile court proceedings, the creation of an adult criminal history would not be at issue.

The purpose of such a law would not be to catch and punish a large number of offenders, but to restrict the circumstances in which minors can comfortably smoke. Even so, it may seem shocking to consider introducing the apparatus of the criminal law into the problem of limiting smoking by adolescents. But in some states it is already a criminal offense for a minor to attempt to purchase cigarettes. A law against actual smoking by minors differs only in that it may be enforceable.

Treatment

A substantial set of enterprises—some voluntary, some commercial—engage in helping people quit smoking, as individuals or in groups. It is hard, for the usual reasons, to gauge the actual helpfulness of the various quit-smoking approaches, ranging from simple group self-help to such arcana as acupuncture, hypnosis, and aversion therapy. Without some way of randomly assigning potential quitters to treatment and control groups, it will always be difficult to judge "what works," even on average, and the differences in response from one individual to another are sure to be large and hard to predict.

The three most striking statistics on quitting smoking are that nine out of ten successful quitters quit without professional help, that those who do receive such help are less likely than average to finally succeed (presumably having been the harder cases to start with), and that the best single predictor of eventual success is the number of attempts to quit. These are all discouraging findings for the treatment industry.[51]

On the other hand, the cash value to employers of having their employees quit is large enough that some companies routinely pay for quit-smoking programs; even a small additional probability of success may be worth paying for. Since which company chooses which quit-smoking program is more or less random with respect to the composition of the employee groups, these company-sponsored programs may provide fertile ground for research on their comparative effectiveness.

Most smoking treatment is drug-free, but nicotine gum provides a form of drug-assisted withdrawal or, in some cases, even long-term maintenance. As noted, the most that can now be said about gum and potential new alternative nicotine-delivery systems is that they will be better than smoking for those who would have continued but not as good as quitting for those who would eventually have quit.

Even relatively high-cost help in quitting is justified in the case of pregnant women, because quick results are valuable in that situation and a strategy of waiting until the smoker is "ready to quit" is unattractive. Other than that, no one has even proposed public funding for nicotine treatment, but there is no reason to rule out the possibility that someone will develop a method so cheap and effective, at least for some population subgroups, as to be deserving of public provision to the medically indigent. There might also be a public role in measuring and certifying the effectiveness of commercially offered programs to help overcome the lack of reliable consumer information that is one barrier to the development of a vigorous nicotine-treatment industry.

Since most quitting will continue to be self-initiated and unassisted, maintaining a steady and well-targeted stream of messages encouraging quitting is as important to smoking treatment as to smoking prevention. Here again, more attention could usefully be paid to getting authority figures and opinion leaders, including but not limited to physicians, to deliver the right messages.

Liability Litigation

A number of lawsuits are now pending in which smokers dying of tobacco-related diseases, or the estates of smokers who have died of such diseases, are asking that the cigarette manufacturers be held liable. In effect, the companies are accused of acting negligently in distributing a product they knew to be harmful. The defense in these cases offers two seemingly contradictory theories: that cigarettes are not really harmful (or at least cannot be shown conclusively to have caused the disease in question) and that everyone, including the smoker, knew how harmful they were and that the smoker therefore "voluntarily assumed" the risk involved. In particular, for any smoking since the time when health warnings were required on the packages, the industry has argued—largely successfully so far—that the warning put smokers on notice of the hazards they were incurring. To this the plaintiffs' attorneys respond that smoking is an addiction, and that people who became addicted before the risks were generally known (but after they were known, or should have been known, to the manufacturers) were unable to stop smoking even once they knew it was harmful.[52]

Aside from the legal and moral issues in these cases we can ask what the consequences would be if the companies were to start losing such lawsuits, particularly with respect to those who started smoking after the warnings came into use. Presumably, the companies would have to factor the cost of future lawsuits into their current product prices. In effect, some of the health-care cost and mortality risk of smoking would be collected from all smokers by the companies and paid out to the big losers in the smoking lottery (with, if similar mass litigation is any guide, between one-third and two-thirds of the total going to the lawyers for the two sides). But not all of the additional cost would be imposed on smokers; in an oligopoly market, some of it would come out of the profits of the manufacturers and thus eventually out of the pockets of their current stockholders and perhaps their current executives.

As a moral judgment, one could argue the cigarette manufacturers did far more conscious and egregious damage to smokers than, for example, asbestos manufacturers did to asbestos-exposed workers. As a matter of public policy, however, any desired combination of discouragement of future smoking and compensation to the victims of past smoking could be accomplished more equitably and efficiently by imposing a tax and paying out benefits on some schedule than by the necessarily capricious and costly process of litigation.

Ending Tobacco Subsidies

No discussion of tobacco-related programs would be complete without a mention of the tobacco subsidy program administered by the U.S. Department of Agriculture. This program provides price supports, linked to production restrictions, for domestic tobacco growers. This is a famous example of governmental cross-purposes: the Agriculture Department is subsidizing what the Surgeon General is trying to suppress.

A little economic analysis suffices to reveal that the notorious inconsistency between anti-smoking policies and tobacco price supports is symbolic rather than real. The effect of a price-support system is to reduce supply, thus increasing the price of the crop to its buyers: in this case, primarily cigarette manufacturers. The effect of this tiny cost increase, about 0.2 percent of the total retail value of American-made cigarettes* is presumably an equally tiny price increase (the

---

* This estimate is based on the 1989 tobacco mix and the 1990 prices for flue-cured and burley tobacco (Maryland tobacco, also in the mix, is not price supported). There are 0.71 pounds of flue-cured, at a price of $1.67 per pound, and 0.53 pounds of burley tobacco, at a price of $1.75 per pound in 1000 cigarettes. Thus, there is $1.18 of flue-cured plus $.93 worth of burley ($2.11 total) in 1000 cigarettes (or 50 packs). This translates to approximately 4.2 cents of price-supported tobacco per pack. About 10 percent of this cost is the effect of the price support. Ten percent of 4.2 cents is approximately less than half a cent, and a retail pack of cigarettes sells for $2.15 at retail. See Economic Research Service, *Tobacco Situation* (Washington, D.C.: Economic Research Service, U.S. Department of Agriculture, 1990).

workings of markets, like the cigarette market, characterized by "monopolistic competition" among brands commanding strong loyalties, are obscure, but higher raw-materials prices should not generate *lower* retail prices).

From the anti-smoking viewpoint, tobacco price supports are a tiny step in the right direction economically and a means of dividing tobacco farmers from the pro-smoking coalition politically. Like other agricultural price supports, they may lead to inefficient pricing, but they no more promote smoking than milk price supports promote milk drinking. Only an anti-smoking rage so great that it extends to blaming tobacco farmers for not growing a less noxious crop could justify opposing the tobacco-support program on smoking-policy grounds.

Export Restriction

The much more serious conflict is between anti-smoking policy and international trade policy. U.S. cigarette manufacturers, resigned to a shrinking domestic market, are eager to build their brand identities and market shares abroad, particularly in developing countries, where smoking remains fashionable and consumers are less likely to have been warned of its health risks.[53] Some countries have policies and practices designed to protect their own domestic cigarette manufacturers from foreign (particularly U.S. and British) competition. Others have general bans on cigarette advertising, which makes it difficult for any new competitor to gain market share. The Office of the U.S. Trade Representative, under pressure from Senator Jesse Helms of tobacco-producing North Carolina, reportedly put immense pressure on some nations, including threats of retaliation against South Korean and Thai textile exports to the United States if restrictions on cigarette advertising were not lifted. To some extent, that pressure has been effective.[54]

Even if the actual contributions of U.S. tobacco companies' marketing efforts to the cigarette problem in the developing world were less significant than they appear to be, our position in this matter is at best undignified and not entirely consistent with our views of what developing-country governments should be doing to help with the parts of the worldwide drug problem in which they are the exporters and we the importers. The parallel with the Opium Wars is not precise—after all, none of the countries in question bans, or has proposed to ban, tobacco—but it is too close for moral comfort.

Taxation

The theory of excise taxation as a regulatory mechanism is straightforward. If the price of some commodity does not include all of the
costs of its production and use, consumers will respond to that false
signal by overconsuming it. A tax equal to the unpriced costs will
then improve matters by giving consumers appropriate incentives.
The classic case for such a tax arises when the production or consumption of the good causes environmental harm; an appropriate
severance tax would force coal consumers to pay for the damage to
the hillside where it is mined and the pollution of the air where it
is burned as well as for the labor of the miners and the cost of the
mining machinery.

From this perspective, determining an appropriate excise tax entails measuring the social costs not included in the market price. If
these "external costs" vary widely from one unit of the commodity to another, it will be hard to find the "right" level; any uniform
tax will be too high for low-cost uses but too low for high-cost uses.
In this respect, cigarette taxation is simpler than alcohol taxation,
because cigarette smoking is far less heterogeneous than drinking;
one cigarette resembles another, in terms of its social cost, far more
closely than one drink resembles another. There are no spectacular costs in the form of crime or accident to be allocated. Instead
of a division into problem and nonproblem users or use occasions,
we have a relatively uniform toll, cigarette by cigarette, taken on
smokers' health. This uniformity of social cost makes the calculation of an appropriate tax level less problematic for tobacco than for
alcohol.

But the fact that most of the costs of a cigarette that are not included in the price are borne by the smoker himself and his family
creates a great conceptual complexity. The costs of additional fire
precaution and excess health-insurance claims are external: they are
borne by neither the buyer nor the seller of cigarettes, and their being imposed on unwilling third parties forms the justification for
a discriminatory excise. But the costs to the smoker are already
"internalized," at least insofar as he knows what they are and has
weighed them in making his purchase decision. Similarly, if his domestic sidestream smoke or his smoking-related ill-health imposes
economic or psychological costs on his family, we ordinarily expect
him to take account of such costs himself (perhaps with some prompting from them). It is not in most circumstances the role of the state
to protect family members from one another's bad habits.

A careful calculation of the strictly external costs of smoking—those costs borne neither by smokers nor by their families—concludes that the U.S. average tax level in 1989 (federal plus state) of 37 cents per pack almost exactly matched the rate that would be justified on a strictly Pigouvian external-cost calculation. Once one subtracts out the savings to pension plans from smokers' shorter lifespans, the net external cost of the average pack of cigarettes is 38 cents.[55] This calculation counted measurable harms only; strictly speaking, one should add in the value of the discomfort not amounting to disease suffered by nonsmokers sharing public places with smokers, the value of cigarette-scorched furniture and rugs, and so on, but these adjustments would not greatly affect the total. A much higher estimate of deaths from passive smoking, however, could greatly increase it; each 1000 additional annual deaths would raise the estimate of the optimal tax by about 10 cents.*

On the other hand, an external cost calculation assumes away the costs to smokers and their families. The ordinary assumption that such costs are already accounted for does not seem justified in this instance, given the youth of those who start to smoke and the difficulty of breaking the cigarette habit. If we added to the tax what we might think of as the "excess internal costs" of smoking—the costs that smokers and their intimates will eventually bear above and beyond the money price—the appropriate level would rise by more than an order of magnitude. Unless smokers value their lives much less than the rest of us value ours, the mortality risk alone is worth close to ten dollars per pack: far more than most smokers would be willing to pay in cash.

Economists are always uncomfortable with the proposition that some group of people systematically acts irrationally. The doctrine of "revealed preference"—which holds that the way people actually behave is the best guide to what they actually want—is a useful methodological principle, and it is important to remind ourselves that what looks irrational from the outside may just be maximization according to a set of preferences we do not share.[56] But when one form of behavior seems to reveal a set of preferences completely inconsis-

---

* $3 million per lost life multiplied by 1000 additional deaths per year equals $3 billion per year. $3 billion per year divided by 27 billion packs of cigarettes sold per year equals 11 cents per pack. [See again Ron Howard, "On Making Life and Death Decisions," in *Societal Risk Assessment: How Safe is Safe Enough?* Richard Schwing and Walter A. Albers, eds. (New York: Plenum Press, 1980). Also, Michael J. Moore and W. Kip Viscusi, "Doubling the Estimated Value of Life: Results Using New Occupational Fatality Data," *Journal of Policy Analysis and Management* 7 (3 [Spring, 1988]): 476–490.]

tent with the preferences the same persons act on in other contexts, then one may doubt that the behavior in question is under conscious rational control. In the case of smoking, that doubt is amplified by smokers' unsuccessful attempts to quit and their willingness to pay for help in quitting. Add to this the pharmacological and behavioral roots of nicotine dependency and compulsive smoking, and the case against taking smokers' behavior as a guide to their welfare seems very strong.

After all, virtually no one chooses to become a pack-a-day cigarette smoker after a careful review of the pros and cons. Smoking is almost always started in adolescence, and therefore by people with less impulse control than they will develop later and very little sense of their own mortality. Most probably plan to smoke for a while and then quit before getting hooked. None has personal experience with the difficulty of quitting. The families that will be most directly damaged by smoking—future spouses and children—are still hypothetical. The assumption that people who start smoking are acting as rational stewards of their own welfare is more than heroic, it is above and beyond the call of duty.

Thus the optimum cigarette tax for new smokers will reflect not only external costs but the smokers' own (future) desire not to be nicotine addicts, with the attendant health damage and mortality risk, and their (future) families' interests as well. That tax would be several dollars per pack: a virtual prohibition for new smokers, since few of them would be willing to pay it. There probably would be a substantial demand at that price from existing smokers, though it too could be expected to decrease over time.

Taxes of several dollars per pack would create a potentially profitable business in contraband, untaxed cigarettes; much smaller differentials between New York and the tobacco-producing states of the Southeast were enough to generate a substantial smuggling business 15 years ago.[57] But that business worked by selling untaxed cigarettes to normal retail outlets for resale; the final customers bought the same brand, in the same package, from the same stores, that they were used to. Brand loyalty is a powerful force among smokers, and if the tax were collected at the point of manufacture, as alcohol taxes are, the remaining problem of strictly illicit "moonshine" production would probably be minor. Smuggling from Mexico, both by consumers and by black-market operators, would be a problem for the United States, as smuggling from the United States has been for Canada.[58]

Thus, if there were no current smokers, a very high, virtually prohibitory, tax on cigarettes would be justified. In fact, however, current smokers number in the tens of millions. For some of them, a very high tax on cigarettes would literally be a life saver. For many who have been trying to quit, a dramatically higher price would provide the needed additional impetus; for some who have not tried, the higher price would be a reason to quit. Demand for help in quitting smoking would rise, and the substitutes for cigarettes, ranging from nicotine gum to cigars, would become more popular.

Even so, it is probable that only a minority of today's heavy smokers would quickly succeed in quitting. The rest would find themselves with the suddenly huge financial cost of smoking—at $5 a pack in taxes, a pack-a-day habit would cost nearly $2000 per year—added to all of its other disadvantages. They and their families would simply wind up poorer, without being better off in any other way. A few might even turn to crime to support their nicotine habits, or switch from nicotine to some more dangerous drug.

Determining the optimal price of tobacco is like determining the optimal price of heroin: the best result, if it were attainable, would be a very high price (in money or inconvenience) for new users, in order to keep them away, and a lower price for those current users who cannot be induced to quit, in order to keep them from being impoverished by their habits.[59] With tobacco as with heroin, even existing users do not have completely inelastic demand; the higher the price they face, the higher the quitting rate. The pain from higher taxes thus tends to shrink, and their benefits to grow, over time. But, as destructive as smoking is, it hardly seems worth creating widespread impoverishment and even criminal behavior in order to reduce its frequency.

The desirable degree of price discrimination between new smokers and current smokers cannot be achieved by a uniform tax, and non-uniform taxes are too complicated to be administratively feasible. Therefore, taxation alone cannot do all the work of anti-smoking policy; we also need to reduce the supply to new smokers. Thus the need for more effective age restrictions.

All cigarette taxes effectively redistribute income from smokers to nonsmokers. Since smokers tend to be poorer than nonsmokers, this redistribution is regressive. While higher prices would change the economic profile of the smoking population by putting more pressure to quit on the poor than on the rich, the immediate effect would still be to make the overall distribution of income more un-equal. Near current levels of taxation, this effect is so small as to be negligible: cigarette excises now constitute only about 1 percent of total governmental revenues in the United States, so they have almost no impact on the overall progressivity or regressivity of the tax structure.[60] Moreover, given the market structure of the cigarette industry, much of the additional revenue would come out of the profits of the manufacturers of the dominant brands, which have already been able to set prices well above production and marketing costs as a way of milking the brand loyalty of their customers. Thus the regressive tax on smoking would be partly balanced by a progressive tax on the capital of cigarette manufacturers.

With tax increases into the dollars-per-pack range now being explored by Canada the worry about unwanted distributional side effects becomes more serious. The shift of the tax burden from the rich to the poor could be balanced out by reducing other regressive taxes, such as the payroll tax for Social Security, or by applying them to programs whose benefits fall heavily on the lower end of the income distribution. It is harder to avoid impoverishing those who are unable to quit smoking without undoing the incentive to quit. If one thinks of heavy taxation as an alternative to tort litigation, some of the revenues could be devoted to death benefits for the surviving family members of the victims of smoking-related disease, but the administrative problems would be great.

Unless one restricts the term *drug* to intoxicants, the level of tobacco taxation is one of the most important drug-policy issues. As between current American levels of cigarette taxation and much higher levels—say, a dollar per pack—the weight of the argument in favor of the higher tax seems decisive, both to discourage smoking by new smokers and to encourage current smokers to quit. A tax increase from current levels to a dollar a pack would increase retail prices by about 25 percent. If the long-run price elasticity of demand for tobacco were even negative 0.4—reflecting less sensitivity of consumption to price than most estimates—the result would eventually be a 10 percent decrease in smoking that would save 40,000 lives per year.*

* It should be noted that some experts, including Thomas Schelling, believe that the figure of −0.4 is excessively optimistic for a product without close substitutes. It is to be hoped that the substantial recent excise tax increases in Canada and California will allow refinement of these estimates. For current estimates, see Congressional Budget Office, *Federal Taxation of Tobacco, Alcoholic Beverages and Motor Fuels* (Washington, D.C.: Government Printing Office, 1990), 71; Eugene Lewit, Douglas Coate, and Michael Grossman, "The Effects of Government Regulation on Teenage Smoking," *Journal of Law and Economics* 24 (3 [December 1981]); Eugene Lewit and Douglas Coate, "The Potential for Using Excise Taxes to Reduce Smoking," *Journal of Health and Economics* 1(2 [August 1982]); and Michael Grossman, "Health Benefits of Increases in Alcohol and Cigarette Taxes," Working Paper No. 3082 (Cambridge, Mass.: National Bureau of Economic Research, August 1989).

Increasing tobacco taxation thus offers the single greatest opportunity for reducing the toll drug taking takes on American life. There
is no comparable opportunity for improving health through changes
in policy regarding any of the currently illicit drugs. Nor would all
this life-saving come at great cost: a tobacco tax increase would have
none of the unwanted side effects or budget impacts of increasing
drug law enforcement. If the apparent gateway effect from cigarette
smoking to marijuana smoking is not a mere statistical artifact, higher
tobacco taxes might even contribute something to the control of the
illicit-drug problem.

Considering truly drastic tax increases—up to or beyond Canadian
levels—would require more complicated calculations and judgments
about how many poor current smokers would be unable to quit (or
switch to another form of nicotine use) and thus wind up poorer but
still hooked. But U.S. citizens and policymakers have no practical
need to engage in that argument now. For the present, it is enough
to ask why so many drug warriors turn pacifist when the battle is
about cigarette taxes.

PROHIBITION: SHOULD
NICOTINE BE ON SCHEDULE I?

If smoking is a bad habit even as evaluated by most smokers, why
not go all the way and prohibit it entirely? Failure to do so will leave
us with a cigarette problem into the indefinite future, because the
highest tax we will be willing to impose on current smokers will not
be sufficient to prevent hundreds of thousands of adolescents from
joining the ranks of nicotine addicts every year. No plausible combination of persuasion and enforcement would change that fact.

There are three major objections to prohibiting tobacco: the losses
experienced by those adults who, with their eyes open, would be
willing to accept tobacco's risks to experience its pleasures; the problem of managing the existing base of addicted users; and the likely
emergence of an illicit market. The major objection to continuing to
allow tobacco, aside from leakage to new adolescent smokers, is the
increased difficulty of quitting and the additional risk of relapse created by the ready availability of cigarettes for purchase on impulse.

Is it possible to design a practicable tobacco-control policy that
meets all of these objections? We are looking for a regime that
provides tobacco on demand and without excessive expense or inconvenience to adults with a settled desire to smoke, while effectively

denying tobacco to children and to those whose desire is a passing impulse: a regime that controls children's smoking and helps, but does not force, adults to control their own. Keeping tobacco away from kids depends on enforcing the laws about sales directly to them and limiting the quantity adults may purchase, to restrict leakage; adults can be protected from their own impulsiveness about tobacco by requiring that tobacco purchases be arranged in advance.

To prohibit tobacco immediately and totally would be an act of pointless cruelty and folly. Even if it were true that quitting at some time would be in the interest of every single current smoker, that would still not imply that they should all be required to quit at once. Nor does the proposition that smokers would on average be better off if they had never started imply that current smokers would all benefit from quitting. Some people may differ from the average, and in any case the combination of withdrawal distress and the residual damage from smoking implies that the costs of becoming an ex-smoker are larger, and its benefits smaller, than those of remaining a nonsmoker. To impose a cold-turkey withdrawal on millions of victims of a legally acquired habit would be unfair even if it were workable.

And it might well not be workable. Prohibition would virtually eliminate public smoking and push many current smokers to quit, but many would not, and some could not, quit, although the difficulty of concealing one's smoking would probably reduce the number of cigarettes per smoker. A market of tens of millions of already committed smokers, with habits totaling tens of billions of dollars per year at current licit-market prices, would be the greatest gift to illicit enterprise since the Volstead Act. Given the potential size of the market and the opportunities to smuggle in prepackaged goods from countries where tobacco remained legal, unless we mounted a massive enforcement effort we would have to expect high volumes and therefore relatively low prices: surely higher than today's licit-market prices, but perhaps not even as high as could be achieved by taxation which left tobacco legal. Once a substantial black market had been created, it would be extraordinarily difficult to uproot (except by re-legalization) and would serve new smokers as readily as existing ones.

Thus the observation that we would be better off without a licit tobacco industry does not mean that we can proceed at once to abolish the one we have. The transition from a smoking to a nonsmoking world must be managed without putting so much pressure on current smokers that any substantial number of them turn to illicit sources of supply.

New smokers, by contrast, are likely to be much easier to influence. Without the peculiarly inelastic demand characteristic of the addicts of relatively inexpensive drugs, their willingness to pay for nicotine is likely to be quite limited. Recent and continuing increases in Canadian tobacco taxes—by the time this volume is in print, a pack of cigarettes will cost between five and six Canadian dollars—will provide a natural experiment on the effects of very large price changes, but those effects are certain to be greater for new smokers than for current ones. For some, higher prices will create an inducement to smoke, by associating smoking with affluence, but this effect can hardly outweigh the more direct effect of high prices.

Justice and the practicalities of enforcement alike, then, point toward phasing in tobacco prohibition, in effect creating a maintenance program for existing cigarette addicts. The mechanics of such a program would not be simple, but they could be relatively straightforward. Each current smoker (over the age of, say, sixteen) could register himself as such, and be able to buy a quantity he set for himself (up to some limit, perhaps two packs a day) from the mail-order supplier of his choice. One's registration as a smoker and one's chosen quota would be available to health and life insurance companies for purposes of underwriting. After a year, the rolls would be closed, except to new immigrants. Thus when the last of today's 16-year-olds died, tobacco smoking would no longer be legal.

Sellers would be required to verify that the user was within quota by checking with, and updating, a central register; identity could be verified by a document and by a personal identification number like that used in automated teller machines. There is no reason for the government to operate any of this machinery; sellers could establish one system or a set of competing systems, each registered buyer signing up with one. Competition would encourage sellers to help solve problems created by missed deliveries, cigarettes stolen in transit, and sudden out-of-town trips. Regulators could audit the sellers to ensure their compliance.

Leakage would be a problem, but could probably be kept from getting out of hand. Some people who do not smoke would register in order to be able to sell on the black market, and some who do smoke would attempt to register multiple times. But the immediate inducements to do so would be quite limited. At first, the only potential customers for smuggled or diverted cigarettes would be younger adolescents, adults unwilling to register, and a small number of more-than-two-pack-a-day smokers. Few of these customers would be willing to pay as much as 10 dollars a pack. The potential arbitrage profit—the difference between the black-market price and the taxed licit-market price times the monthly quota—might be a few hundred dollars a month: by no means a small sum, but not a living wage for a potential criminal. Relatively modest enforcement efforts should suffice to make entry into the private resale market sufficiently risky to scare off most potential resellers, even if the only penalties imposed were substantial fines and loss of cigarette-buying privileges.

A little auditing and occasional undercover efforts by enforcement officials (or volunteers from the anti-smoking movement), backed by the threat of license revocation, could keep the licensed sellers reasonably honest. Since two packs a day would satisfy all but the heaviest smokers, adults would create no substantial demand for black-market tobacco. Adolescents, unable to buy their own from stores or vending machines, could steal them, get them from their parents, or buy them on the black market, but it seems unlikely that many adolescents would pay black-market prices for enough cigarettes to get themselves trapped in either a psychological compulsion to smoke or a physical dependency on nicotine.

Later on, the black-market price might rise, as the adolescents who managed to get themselves hooked despite the law acquired adult incomes and thus a greater willingness to pay to maintain their habit. But with the smoking rolls closed, additional demand could not call forth additional diverted supply, except from those who quit smoking themselves. The opportunity to smuggle such a bulky drug to supply such a limited black market would not be very tempting to international drug dealers, though some smuggling would surely take place.

When the last registered smoker died, he would leave behind a very small number of unregistered smokers. Immigrants and foreign visitors would constitute a residual problem; perhaps we could allow them to bring along a three-month supply but no more, or create a "grandfather" clause for those who entered the country already addicted.

There are strong arguments against extending a ban on cigarettes to the other forms of tobacco use. None of them has the full range of noxious properties associated with cigarettes: widespread current social acceptance and promotion leading to a high rate of experimentation, extraordinarily high rate of "capture" from experimentation to compulsive use, great difficulty in cessation, carcinogenesis, throat damage, heart damage, lung damage, sidestream smoke, and fires.

The most impressive piece of evidence for a smoking ban is that an overwhelming majority of cigarette smokers wish they were non-smokers. There is no comparable evidence that most of the people who smoke pipes or cigars wish that they did not or regret that they started. (Most chewers of nicotine gum presumably wish they could quit, but virtually all of them were smokers first.) Thus, a ban on cigarette smoking, rather than restricting individual liberty, can reasonably be seen as helping individuals do as they actually want to do rather than as their transient adolescent impulses and compulsive behavior patterns lead them to do. The same claim could not be so plausibly made about a ban on cigar smoking.

If cigarettes were illegal but something else involving nicotine were legal, smokers and cigarette companies alike would have incentives to find the closest legal substitute. For example, there are already very small cigars that are almost cigarettes. However, a high per-unit tax on cigars could discourage chain-smoking without substantially inconveniencing those who like an occasional cigar after dinner or at a card game.

As long as cigarettes are legal, smokers will continue to inconvenience nonsmokers, because the combination of compulsive use with sidestream smoke makes some involuntary smoking almost inevitable. This is much less true of the other ways of taking nicotine, which either are not as likely to lead to compulsive use (cigars, pipes) or do not intrude on others (chewing tobacco, snuff, nicotine gum).

It is possible that manufacturers or consumers will succeed in inventing a new form of nicotine use as dangerous as cigarette smoking. Premier, or something like it, may be a case in point. But we can cross that bridge if we come to it. There would be one great advantage in banning all smoking: it would reduce the number of legitimate reasons for possessing pipes, rolling papers, cigarette lighters, and other means of smoking any drug, not just tobacco, and thus perhaps make paraphernalia laws a serious discouragement, rather than just a nuisance, for those who want to smoke marijuana, cocaine, methamphetamine, heroin, and so on. But it is hard to see that this advantage would justify the prohibition of what for many are important and relatively harmless pleasures.

Whether legal or not, pipe smoking and the nonincendiary forms of tobacco use, which require less capital equipment on the production side, would probably linger longer than cigarette smoking. In any case, nicotine in its most destructive and socially pervasive form would be largely a thing of the past. That would be an accomplishment worth celebrating.

12

Heroin

Before the emergence of crack, heroin represented, in the public mind and in the plans of officials, the drug problem at its most horrible. The addicted, unemployed, malnourished, exposed, infected, criminally active junkie defined for citizens and policymakers the sort of person all drug policies were designed to prevent our neighbors and our kids from becoming, for their sake and ours. The prohibition of other, demonstrably less harmful drugs was justified on the grounds that their use might lead to heroin. Heroin was, in John Kaplan's words, "the hardest drug."[1] Since the advent of crack, heroin has become yesterday's news. But it deserves our attention for several reasons.

First, the continuing social costs of heroin use and heroin dealing are very large, and there are ways of reducing them. Heroin is a significant contributor to crime and the second most important vector of HIV, the virus of AIDS.

Second, the case of heroin illustrates a central paradox of the logic of drug prohibition: when we use the criminal law and law enforcement for the protection of public health and morals, the result is often an increase in predatory crime over the level that would otherwise have obtained. Insofar as successful enforcement of heroin laws—especially cases against importers and high-level dealers—leads to higher heroin prices, the result may well be more crime by heroin users who need more money to support their habits. By contrast, treatment services, which are considered part of health care, clearly reduce crime. Thus the "hard line" on drug policy will lead to more crime, though less drug abuse, while the "softer" options will be more effective in controlling crime but arguably less effective in controlling drug abuse by preventing the formation of new heroin habits.

Third, if the crack problem fades away, with a sharp decrease in the number of new users and a slow attrition of the existing population of heavy users, it may come to resemble the heroin problem of the 1980s, which consisted primarily of the continuing toll taken by a strongly habituating drug on a concentrated population of very dysfunctional heavy users, and by them on the rest of us. We can thus learn from heroin something about the shape and management of the aftermath of the great crack epidemic.

Fourth, it is possible that the 1990s will witness a major upsurge in the use of heroin, most likely starting with a wave of new users who start by snorting or smoking the drug rather than injecting it. Preventing a new heroin epidemic should rank as a major drug-policy objective, and as yet not enough concentrated thought and action are being devoted to that task.

HEROIN AND THE LOGIC
OF DRUG ABUSE CONTROL

Depending on one's point of view, heroin is either the great success or the great catastrophe of prohibitionist drug policy. A fiercely attractive and destructive drug that was sweeping through the American population in the late 1960s and early 1970s has been contained within a small, aging, and probably shrinking group of users.[2] At a guess—and no more than a guess is available—the current population of heavy, long-term, regular heroin users is somewhere between half a million and three-quarters of a million, with an additional number, perhaps even an equal number, of occasional, controlled users, or "chippers."

Current recruitment into hard-core heroin use appears to be sufficient only to replace those lost to death—about 3 percent per year—or desistance—unknown, but also likely to be in the range of a few percent per year.* This suggests new heroin addicts number in the tens of thousands per year. The number of new users, like the total number of users, represents a tiny proportion of the population, even of the population groups one might define as "high risk." But the small group of heavy heroin users is miserably off, responsible for much crime, and includes the second largest group of persons with AIDS.

* Phillip Cooley and Elsa Liner, "Heroin Prevalence Estimation," Paper prepared for NIDA (Research Triangle Park, N.C.: Research Triangle Institute, 1990).

If heroin had been legalized two decades ago, it would be much more widely used, but the average member of that larger population would be better off and less likely to commit crimes. Scores of thousands of heroin users would never have been infected with HIV. The spread of that virus from heroin users to their sexual partners, and the consequent birth of HIV-infected infants, would be a footnote to the AIDS problem rather than a focus of concern.

No practical purpose would be served at this moment in history by re-arguing the question of heroin's legal status. Perhaps, if the AIDS epidemic had been foreknown, a convincing argument could have been made that the increase in heroin addiction as a result of one or another form of legal availability would have been more than compensated for by the reduction in HIV transmission. But the epidemic spread so quickly through the heroin-injecting population that it is hard to see when that decision could have been made with information in hand, even if it had somehow been politically feasible.

It is, however, worth taking some time to examine the logical structure of the effects of heroin prohibition, both because that structure has something to teach us about the design and execution of heroin-control programs and because some of the same logic applies to other drugs.[3] In this connection, and not as a practical policy proposal, it makes sense to imagine what the problem of heroin would look like if there were no special laws governing its purchase or use.[4] It would not resemble our current problem very much.

THE HEROIN PROBLEM UNDER LEGALITY

Heroin in a world without drug laws would be a very cheap, potent central nervous system depressant providing a highly euphoric intoxication and sometimes an extremely pleasurable, though brief, period of onset: the "rush." It would be taken in a variety of ways: by swallowing, snorting, and smoking as well as the injection that is now the predominant form of heroin use in the United States. (Smoking— "chasing the dragon"—has always been the dominant form of heroin taking in East Asia, but it has, at least until now, only been significant in the United States among Chinese immigrants near the turn of the last century and soldiers in Vietnam.)

The pleasures of legal heroin, like those of any opiate, would be subject to a rapidly built-up tolerance, and most of those who used it day after day for a period of weeks would find themselves physically dependent on it, subject to highly unpleasant withdrawal symptoms if they tried to quit. The combination of physical dependency and behavioral reinforcement would put those who experimented with heroin at substantial risk of becoming compulsive users, and the habit, once established, would prove extremely persistent; even those who succeeded in "kicking" the physical dependency would remain at risk of relapse and subject to cravings for periods of months, even years, after quitting.[5]

Physically, the heroin habit would be only moderately harmful. Its chronic heavy use, unlike cocaine, alcohol, or nicotine, is not directly life-threatening. A user of legal heroin who managed to maintain reasonable eating habits and a sanitary pattern of drug use would live to more or less a normal life span, though subject to constipation and, if male, diminished sexual drive. Heavy heroin users would tend to be somewhat impoverished by unemployment or underemployment because of drug-induced incapacity or unwillingness to work, though some, like some heavy drinkers, would continue to lead more or less normal work lives. Many of them would be somewhat careless in their hygiene. These two facts would put heroin users at higher-than-average risk for all the diseases associated with being poor, malnourished even if not undernourished, and exposed to cold and dirt. But they would be spared the poverty that comes from an artificially expensive drug habit and most of them could avoid the ill health that afflicts those who commit predatory crimes, sell their sexual services, and repeatedly spend time behind bars.

In a world of cheap heroin, there would be no need to share doses, and in a world without paraphernalia laws, there would be no reason to share needles. Thus even those who took their heroin by needle would be at much less risk of spreading the viruses of AIDS and hepatitis B than those who do so today.

Socially, economically, and emotionally, the habit would not be so benign. Heroin use, except among those who managed to avoid addiction and restrict it to occasional off-duty hours, would tend to interfere with work and family life, and heavy users would tend to find nondrug pleasures decreasingly attractive and the voice of duty decreasingly commanding.[6]

Some proportion of all heroin users would be heavy, regular users, and a substantial proportion of heavy, regular heroin users would lead lives without much dignity, (nondrug) satisfaction, or social usefulness. Most would probably regret the decision to start and make at least occasional attempts to quit, if only because their tolerance to the drug made taking it less and less satisfying and not taking it more and more uncomfortable. Heroin users would make less than their share of contributions to common resources and more than their share of demands on them.*

They would not, however, be the kind of problem heroin users found in the United States today. The drug itself would be too cheap to generate much crime to buy it, although heroin addicts without independent wealth might find themselves turning to crime as the most attractive way to obtain money without working regular hours. The effects of the drug in producing passivity and physical immobility would tend to preclude much drug-induced assault, or even much intoxicated driving or handling of heavy machinery, though the disorder incident to public intoxication would be a problem and their defenselessness would make heroin inebriates attractive targets for crime.†

Here, then, is the paradox. Police and prosecutors see their function as punishing lawbreakers and reducing crime. But heroin prohibition is an attempt, not to control crime, but to prevent drug abuse. Prohibition causes crime by users and dealers. Thus heroin prohibition and its enforcement use criminal justice mechanisms to serve a public-health goal, at substantial cost to criminal justice objectives. To make good choices in regard to heroin programs requires understanding that paradox and accommodating that understanding into policy planning. This avoids the trap of thinking that all heroin law enforcement is crime reducing because law enforcement agencies pursue it, while the process of helping and controlling problem users—"treatment"—is primarily a health program because its rhetoric is the rhetoric of therapy.

Heavy users of legal heroin would therefore be much better off personally and much less of a problem to others than heavy users of illegal heroin, but much worse off personally and more of a problem socially than moderate users or non-users. The big question is how many heavy users there would be (and how many fewer, or conceivably more, heavy, chronic drinkers).

---

* The nineteenth-century literature on opium and opiate use, starting with Thomas de Quincey's *Confessions of an English Opium-Eater*, supports this account. De Quincey's book was written before there were drug laws, and does not make cheerful reading. Heroin is simply the opiate experience at its most extreme.

† These effects would be somewhat moderated if there were "heroin dens" that encouraged their customers to remain on the premises while under the influence, but drug-induced poverty might keep many heroin addicts from being able to afford to use such a facility unless it were publicly subsidized, just as skid-row winos do very little of their drinking in bars.

Aside from actually performing the experiment of making heroin freely available, there is no way to estimate what proportion of all heroin users would be chronic, heavy users. Heroin's combination of strong reinforcement with rapid build-up of tolerance and a high liability to physical dependence suggests that its "capture ratio" would be higher than those of the current mass-market intoxicants: alcohol, marijuana, and cocaine. Heavy users might constitute a smaller proportion of all users than they do under illegality, because heroin users would have better opportunities to maintain the external ties and personal strengths that tend to support occasional rather than constant use.* On the other hand, ready availability and low price would probably work against moderation by making it easier and cheaper to go through one's first "run" of steady, heavy use and perhaps by making it harder to avoid the cues and circumstances that can trigger relapse.

The total number of users, by contrast, would almost certainly be higher under complete legal availability than under prohibition. Not only would starting be easier, cheaper, and less risky, but the very improvement in the welfare and behavior of the average heroin user that made legal availability an attractive option would also present a reduced deterrent to becoming an addict. This reduced deterrent would operate both through rational calculation and through a reduction in the irrational horror that now attends the words *heroin* and *junkie*.

One of the major barriers to the spread of heroin use has been the fact that it is taken by injection. For many persons, the very sight of a needle and syringe poses a nearly insuperable barrier to voluntarily taking any drug by injection. Even for those without any irrational fear of needles, the risk of topical infection from any lapse in needle hygiene makes injection an unattractive mode of drug taking, even leaving aside the role of shared needles in spreading various deadly viruses. In addition, injection has been the form of nonmedical drug taking most associated with poverty and degradation, and is therefore unfashionable.

If heroin taking meant only heroin injection, it would be possible to imagine that even legal heroin would remain the habit of a tiny proportion of the population. However, injection is not the only way

* Despite its mythos, heroin is not always a drug of addiction, and even under illicit conditions a substantial proportion, perhaps even the majority, of heroin users are "chippers" or "weekenders." See Leon Gibson Hunt and Carl D. Chambers, *The Heroin Epidemics: A Study of Heroin Use in the US: 1965–1975* (New York: Spectrum Publications, 1976).

to take a drug, nor even the one that gives the greatest effect. It is merely the most sparing in its consumption of the drug; snorting or smoking wastes about half, and swallowing is even less efficient. Under illicit conditions, U.S. heroin users inject the drug because they are poor and it is expensive. Licit heroin could easily spread as a snorted or smoked drug.

In a debate over the legalization of heroin conducted in 1980, neither the AIDS problem nor the potential spread of smokable heroin would have played much of a role: AIDS, because its spread via shared needles was still unsuspected; smokable heroin because before the advent of crack the market potential of smokable forms of powerful drugs had not been established. This illustrates a central frustration of drug-policy analysis: the greatest benefit or cost of a policy may turn out to be its contribution to preventing or promoting a largely unforeseeable disaster. At least it illustrates the value of policies that will, if they fail, "fail safe." (Alas, it is hard to get much credit for what has *not* happened.)

The case for heroin prohibition is simply that a number, probably a large number, of persons who now lead reasonably satisfying, dignified, and useful lives would, if heroin were legal, find themselves leading, and regretting, lives with a narrowed range of satisfactions, impaired dignity and self-command, and reduced usefulness to their families, friends, neighbors, coworkers, and fellow citizens. To prevent this we pay a price in the form of increased misery for those who become heavy heroin users despite prohibition, and increased external costs: the spread of disease, user crime, black-market crime, neighborhood disruption from open dealing, and the expenditure of law enforcement resources that could instead be used to suppress predatory crime.

PROGRAMS UNDER CURRENT LAWS

Assuming that heroin continues to be prohibited, the practical problem facing us is managing the programs directed at it. Three objectives stand out among the many that such programs might serve: protecting potential heroin addicts from developing bad habits centered on the drug, controlling predatory crime, and containing the spread of diseases—AIDS most of all, but also hepatitis B—among heroin users by shared injection equipment and from them to their sexual partners. In addition, there is reason to fear that heroin may be ready to break out of its long quiescence and begin a new wave of epidemic spread. Preventing a new heroin epidemic counts as a fourth goal of heroin policy.

Heroin Programs and Drug Abuse Control

If the great value of the policy of prohibition that underlies the rest of our approach to heroin is that it reduces the number of persons caught in bad heroin habits, and if it is those heavy users who support the black market, commit heroin-related crime, and spread the AIDS virus, our inquiry into heroin programs should start by examining them from the perspective of their role in drug abuse control. Persuasion, help, and control of problem users, and law enforcement all have something to contribute here, and none of them is now being employed to its best effect.

General anti–drug-abuse messages are of limited value in preventing heroin addiction, because those at greatest risk of trying heroin and of becoming addicted are least likely to pay attention to messages from schools or the mass media. Specifically anti-heroin messages are problematical because only a tiny fraction of any identified population is likely to start heroin in the absence of persuasion efforts. Thus if anti-heroin messages have any inadvertent "advertising" effect, which is almost inevitable if they mention the drug at all, the number of new users inadvertently attracted could easily overwhelm the number of new users deterred.

Consequently, anti-heroin messages need to be targeted even more carefully than other anti-drug messages. Current heavy users are apt to be enormously resistant to messages; the prospects of telling them something they do not already know are dim. To the extent that recently recruited heroin users can be identified, however, either among health-care recipients or law enforcement subjects, they could be made the targets of what are sometimes called "secondary prevention" efforts: messages, and offers of help, designed to prevent progression to heavy use rather than initiation of use.

Similar efforts could be directed at those cocaine smokers who are not also heroin users. They may be at risk of starting heroin use either in conjunction with cocaine, as a way of easing the crash, or as a substitute (in the economic rather than the pharmacological sense) when crack burn-out hits. If empirical investigation bears out this hypothesis, it would be worth designing some anti-heroin messages to be used with cocaine smokers.

The heroin treatment system nationally is still recovering from two great shocks: the emergence of AIDS as a source of increased willingness to seek treatment among heroin addicts (and an intensification of the life-or-death character of success or failure in heroin treatment) and the supplantation of heroin by cocaine, and in particular crack, as the widely acknowledged number-one drug problem. At the same time that increased demand for heroin treatment, especially in the form of methadone maintenance, outstripped the capacity of heroin treatment programs, the programs also faced persistent questions from those in charge of allocating treatment resources about why the ratio of treatment slots to estimated total problem users should be so much higher for heroin than for cocaine. Opening new methadone programs in the age of crack seemed a little like digging trenches in the age of the tank.

Unhappily, heroin declined only as compared to cocaine. There was no decrease in the number of heroin users. Thus the falling market share of heroin among illicit drugs did not mean decreasing need for heroin treatment. Moreover, the advocates of providing more heroin treatment have what the advocates of providing more cocaine treatment lack: a program, methadone maintenance, that retains a large proportion of those who enter it and produces marked improvements in the welfare and behavior of a large proportion of those who remain in it. In addition, the benefits of moving from less resource-intensive to more resource-intensive forms of heroin treatment are more straightforward than the benefits of increasing expenditures per slot in cocaine treatment. The more resources a methadone program has, the better able it is to establish and maintain authoritative expectations about the behavior of its clients. A methadone maintenance program, precisely because it gives away drugs, is in a position to drive a fairly hard bargain with its clients, for their own long-term benefit and for the benefit of their families and neighbors. That potential is lost if the ratio of clients to staff is so large that the staff can no longer effectively monitor and cajole.[7]

Methadone programs also have been under pressure from those who prefer drug abstinence as the only worthwhile goal of treatment and drug-free therapy as the means. This pressure is partly the result of the excessive promises made by some early enthusiasts for methadone, who touted it as an aid to detoxification and a way-station to being off drugs entirely. Instead, it turns out that most persons who become addicted to heroin become no less addicted to methadone. Some ex-addicts who enter twelve-step programs after years on methadone reportedly are quite bitter about the experience, regarding methadone as a detour on the way to recovery.

There is little doubt that, in terms of dignity, autonomy, quality of life, or social functioning, successful drug abstinence is preferable to successful methadone maintenance. But there is equally little doubt that successful methadone maintenance is, on those same criteria, preferable to unsuccessful drug abstinence or that methadone has a far higher success rate, across a far wider range of clients, than any drug-free therapy, simply because more of its clients stay with the program.

Aside from the advantages of not having to buy at black-market prices, substituting methadone for heroin has some pharmacological benefits. Methadone is an addictive narcotic, but it is not simply "legal heroin." In addition to being longer-acting and thus more consistent with holding a steady job, it appears to be substantially easier to sustain at a constant dose, as opposed to the rollercoaster pattern typical of heroin.[8]

For those who enter the treatment system from the criminal justice process, having been convicted of some serious crime, a sufficiently coercive drug-free program might work better than methadone. But all of the (admittedly scanty) evidence suggests that efforts to compel voluntary treatment entrants who want methadone to accept abstinence instead are likely to fail, often catastrophically.*

Heroin law enforcement, considered as a means of drug abuse control, has the same two intermediate objectives as enforcement directed at any other drug: decreasing the effective availability of the drug (that is, increasing the distribution of search times for the various categories of current and potential users) and increasing its effective (purity-adjusted) money price. On the one hand, since the heroin market has a smaller number of users and a smaller aggregate dollar volume than the cocaine market, it would seem that making progress on either search time or price would be easier for heroin

---

* Of seventeen Swedish heroin addicts randomly selected for drug-free therapy rather than methadone, seven were dead and four in prison after 7 years. Of those randomly assigned to methadone, none were dead and none in prison. The fact that the study was done by the operator of a methadone program should generate some skepticism about this finding, but the burden of offering new evidence would now seem to be on the advocates of drug-free programs. Lief Gronbladh and Lars Gunne, "The Swedish Methadone Maintenance Program," in G. Serban, ed. *The Social and Medical Aspects of Drug Abuse* (Jamaica, N.Y.: Spectrum, 1984), 205–213.

than for cocaine. On the other, existing heroin markets tend to be long-established, and the regular users tend to have long experience in buying and a great resistance to change; these factors work against the heroin enforcement effort. A heroin seller who deals only with buyers whom he has known by sight for years is largely invulnerable to most routine enforcement activity. Inner-city street heroin markets are far less dependent than the comparable crack markets on flocks of casual users from the suburbs who can be scared away by the threat of having their automobiles confiscated or their pictures printed in the local newspaper.

But even long-established street markets can be disrupted with sufficient police presence, as the example of Operation Pressure Point on New York's Lower East Side demonstrates.[9] Moreover, even today not all retail heroin markets are of long standing, and the newer ones may be relatively easy to uproot. The example of Lynn, Massachusetts, where a small police task force was able to break the back of a small but flourishing open heroin market, is still worth imitating where the conditions are right.[10] Shutting down all of the open heroin dealing in a city may well have more value as long-term drug abuse control than shutting down a fifth of the open crack dealing while putting minimal pressure on the rest, and any city with an open heroin market ought to consider whether to reallocate to heroin enforcement some of the police resources now directed at cocaine dealing.

Much the same analysis applies to high-level enforcement efforts that can increase the price of heroin. "Quality" cases against heroin dealers are harder to make, because a smaller market generates fewer major deals. But the value of a given level of aggregate enforcement pressure on the market may well be higher; since heroin users in the aggregate have less money to spend on their drug than cocaine users in the aggregate, the number of cell-years of total punishment required to dent the large-scale heroin market should be smaller than the number required to dent the large-scale cocaine market. Prosecutors making plea bargains or sentencing recommendations, judges handing out prison time, and legislators and sentencing commissions adjusting the statutes and guidelines governing who does how much time should consider the possible value of reallocating some prison cells from cocaine dealers to heroin dealers.

The prospects for improving the domestic heroin abuse problem through source control and interdiction are even more dismal than the prospects for cocaine. Poppy production is far more dispersed around the world than coca production; the Burma-Thailand-Laos "Golden Triangle," the Afghanistan-Pakistan-Iran "Golden Crescent," Mexico, Lebanon, and, recently, Colombia all grow poppies for the illicit market. Since U.S. heroin consumption represents only a tiny fraction of world opium demand, changes in poppy production in either direction would probably leave prices and volumes in the U.S. domestic market largely unaffected. Heroin is not smuggled in boats or airplanes dedicated to illicit traffic, but is carried on (or in) the persons of passengers or concealed in containers of legitimate cargo. The small bulk of heroin imports—several tons per year, less than one-twentieth of the flow of cocaine—makes the smuggling problem relatively easy for the traffickers and almost impossible for the Customs Service. Heroin, even more than cocaine, insofar as it can be addressed by drug law enforcement, must be addressed by domestic drug law enforcement.

Heroin Programs and Crime Control

Heroin is a very expensive drug; a quick calculation from imperfect data suggests that the average heroin addict uses more than $10,000 worth per year.* Most heavy heroin users would have only modest legitimate economic opportunities even if their drug habits did not stand in the way of their maintaining steady employment. While wages, gifts from families and friends, and payments from public income-maintenance programs of various kinds all contribute money to the heroin economy, many heroin addicts commit income-producing crimes—heroin dealing, theft, and prostitution—and use some of the money so obtained to buy heroin.[11]

---

* Five metric tons, the estimated total consumption in the United States, equals five billion milligrams. At the estimated street price of $1.73 per pure milligram, that amount of heroin would represent a total retail value of $8.7 billion. Occasional users cannot account for any noticeable fraction of this: half a million weekend users, even at $50 per weekend every weekend, would spend only $2600 × 500,000 = $1.3 billion, leaving $7.4 billion to spread among the estimated half-million heavy regular users, or almost $15,000 per addict per year. Given the imprecision of the estimates, "more than $10,000" is about as much as can be said with any confidence. Those heroin users who are also dealers get their own supplies at below retail prices; however, unlike the market for cocaine in powder form, the heroin market has very few, if any, users who can afford to buy in truly wholesale lots for their own and their friends' consumption. See National Narcotics Intelligence Consumers Committee, *The NNICC Report 1989: The Supply of Illicit Drugs to the United States* (June 1990): 28–54; Peter Reuter, "The (Continued) Vitality of Mythical Numbers," *The Public Interest* 75 (1984): 135–147.

Heroin addicts responding to a survey of prison inmates reported having committed substantially more crimes in their last year free on the street than their non-heroin-using cellmates, and heroin users are substantially overrepresented among high-rate dangerous offenders.[12] More than 20 percent of all nondrug felony arrestees in cities such as New York and Chicago have used heroin in the two or three days before their arrest.[13] Recent cocaine use is more than twice as common among arrestees;[14] but cocaine has perhaps four times as many heavy regular users.

As with any drug, it would be a mistake to attribute to heroin all the crime committed by heroin users. Most of them had begun to commit crime for money before they began to use heroin, and their income from illicit sources does not fall to zero when they abstain from heroin.[15] But the connection between heroin and crime is more than accidental; when property criminals begin to use heroin, they step up their rates of criminal activity, their periods of heavy heroin use tend to coincide with their periods of frequent crime, and their rates of crime commission drop by about two-thirds during periods of heroin abstinence.[16]

Reducing heroin use by current heavy heroin users thus tends to reduce the frequency of theft and other income-producing crimes. Increasing the availability of methadone maintenance will therefore likely reduce crime, especially if the methadone programs are either sufficiently strict to act as effective controls on their clients' behavior or sufficiently generous with the methadone to give them little incentive to try to supplement their incomes in order to supplement their doses. In some low-dosage, low-control methadone programs, more than a third of the clients reportedly use cocaine; this compromises the programs' value in reducing crime.[17] More opportunities for supervised (not necessarily physician-supervised) detoxification would also help reduce crime, even if most of their participants eventually returned to heroin use. There is clearly unmet latent demand for detox services; where there is more capacity than active demand, "peer outreach" efforts staffed by ex-addicts can be effective recruiting tools.[18]

Voluntary participation in treatment is not, however, the only approach. Heroin addicts are so few, compared with heavy crack users and relative to the amount of crime they account for, that it is possible and worthwhile to spend public resources to manage their behavior in detail. Arrest is a relatively frequent incident in the life of a heroin addict; results of urine tests of arrestees suggest that the number of heroin-positive arrestees each year is close to the number of heroin addicts.* Thus it would be possible, by instituting a program of drug testing for arrestees, to identify by name a large proportion of all the heroin addicts in the United States, without making any elaborate outreach effort. As a literally captive audience, they could be given written material to peruse or videos to watch while held in jails or lockups. These materials should stress not the disadvantages of heroin use (with which addicts are presumably familiar) but the availability of help in quitting. Those who test positive for heroin or refuse to be tested, and are eventually convicted or plead guilty, should be helped and pressured to quit both while in custody and after release.

This help and pressure could take several forms. Compulsory residential drug treatment can, if managed properly, reduce both heroin use and crime by its clients once they regain their freedom, when compared with an otherwise similar group not forced into treatment.[19] Prison inmates who participate in a therapeutic community attached to a prison have measurably lower rates of subsequent criminal activity than other inmates.[20] Mandatory abstinence monitored by urine testing and backed by sanctions for noncompliance can greatly reduce heroin use among probationers, even in the absence of formal treatment, and the results of doing so jurisdiction-wide can be seen in aggregate rates of property crimes such as burglary.[21]

None of these programs are cheap. Residential drug-free programs in secure settings cost about $20,000 per participant per year.[22] A

---

* Again, any such calculation must start with the mythical half-million heroin addicts. In all, there are about 14 million arrests in the United States each year, representing about 10.8 million different persons. The average person arrested in any year is arrested about 1.3 times, implying that the number of different persons arrested is the number of arrests divided by 1.3. A. Blumstein, J. Cohen, and P. Hsieh, *The Duration of Adult Criminal Careers*, Report to the National Institute of Justice (1982), and M. A. Greene and S. Stollmack, "Estimating the Number of Criminals," *Models in Quantitative Criminology* (New York: Academic Press, 1981). In the twenty-one cities covered by the Drug Use Forecasting (urine-testing) program in 1989, 10.65 percent of the arrestees tested positive for heroin. Those cities, which include all of the large cities with active heroin markets, accounted for approximately 3.5 million arrests that year, suggesting that heroin-positive arrests in those cities alone would have totaled 373,000 incidents and 287,000 different persons. This does not count suburbs, rural areas, or those cities (primarily smaller ones) not covered by DUF. A variety of methodological problems are inherent in making this sort of estimate: DUF is not a random sample of persons arrested; heroin addicts may have a higher rate of arrests per arrestee than other arrestees; not all urine-positives are addicts. But one arrest per addict per year seems at least as likely to be too low an estimate as too high. Federal Bureau of Investigations, *Uniform Crime Reports of the United States* (Washington, D.C.: Department of Justice, 1988); Drug Use Forecasting Annual Report, "Drugs and Crime—1989," *Research in Action Series* (Washington, D.C.: National Institute of Justice, 1989).

therapeutic community will add about $2000 to $3000 to the cost of ordinary imprisonment.[23] Random weekly urine testing costs about $1500 per participant,[24] to which must be added the expense of sanctions for those who fail to comply. But even the largest of these sums is small when compared to the cost of the crimes committed by the average uncontrolled heroin addict free on the street.[25]

Since one of the crimes committed by heroin users is selling heroin, helping and forcing them to reduce their heroin use will also help reduce the number of active heroin sellers, and thus the heroin use of addicts and chippers alike, current users as well as new ones. This simple analysis shows the inadequacy of the division of programs into "demand control" and "supply control" or into "therapy" and "coercion." If one assumes that using less heroin is healthy, these coercive programs are undeniably therapeutic. Reducing spending on heroin by user/dealers—a classic "demand-side" approach—can reduce the supply of heroin at retail.

There is also crime-control value in some traditional "supply control" law enforcement efforts. High-level enforcement to raise prices probably does not reduce crime in the short run, because the relatively inelastic demand of heroin addicts can translate higher prices into greater spending on heroin and thus more property crime.[26] But in the longer run, as higher prices cause lower initiation and relapse rates and greater quit rates, enforcement to increase prices may in fact be crime-reducing. Preventing the slow price decrease of the past decade, or even more the sort of dramatic price collapse that accompanied the cocaine epidemic, is worth doing for crime control as well as other reasons. We are still paying for the low price of heroin in the late 1960s and early 1970s.

But the most important enforcement contribution to reduced heroin-related crime would be a decrease in the overall availability of heroin as measured by the search times facing current users and potential new users. While changes in price have ambiguous effects on income-producing crime, an increase in search time clearly tends to reduce crime by users, because it reduces the quantity purchased without increasing the (money) price paid.* Moreover, the disorder generated by open retail drug dealing, and the violence that follows that disorder, will also tend to diminish. Street-level drug crackdowns

---

* The resulting reduction in the total value of the heroin market may also tend to reduce violent crime by and against heroin dealers, but this effect will be offset at least to some extent by an increase in enforcement-related violence and in violent income-producing crime, such as robbery, committed by those displaced from work in the heroin trade.

in Lynn, Massachusetts, and on the Lower East Side of Manhattan produced substantial reductions in violent and property crimes.[27]

Heroin Programs and AIDS Control

The sharing of needles and syringes for the injection of illicit drugs— primarily heroin, though increasingly cocaine as well—is the second- leading cause of HIV infection among those currently diagnosed with AIDS in the United States.[28] Heroin is also indirectly responsi- ble for most of the HIV transmission through heterosexual activity; the overwhelming majority of women with AIDS, and of the mothers of babies born HIV-infected, were either infected by needle sharing or had sexual partners who were intravenous drug injectors.[29] About one-quarter of all U.S. heroin addicts are HIV-positive; that propor- tion varies enormously from city to city.[30]

Over the past several years, the rate of new HIV infection among currently uninfected heroin users seems to have fallen, in part be- cause the population of the most susceptible individuals and the areas (above all New York) with the most dangerous injection and sharing practices were virtually saturated by 1987, and in part because of the spread of knowledge of risks and precautions.[31] The growth of a black market in new injection equipment may also have helped.[32]

Nothing about the pharmacology of heroin necessarily connects it with infection. Injection as such is not risky, only injection with equipment that has been used by someone else and not sterilized in the meantime. Legal heroin, sold in nonreusable syringes, would not be a vector of HIV, or of the less deadly but more widespread hepatitis B virus, which also spreads from one heroin user to another. At the moment, though, the practical question is how best to limit the transmission of HIV in connection with the use of illegal heroin, and increasingly with the use of cocaine as the practice of injection becomes more common among cocaine users.

Every time someone not yet infected uses a needle previously used by someone else, there is some chance of infection. That chance is directly proportional to the probability that a previous user was infected. It also, presumably, varies with the details of the injection procedures used: drawing blood up into the syringe clearly increases the risks for subsequent users.

Conceptually, there are four ways to reduce the spread of HIV by shared needles: reducing the frequency of injection; reducing

the proportion of injections that involve shared equipment; changing injection practices, for example, by increasing the frequency of
sterilization (a relatively simple process that can be performed with
household bleach, or even boiling water); or reducing the rate at
which infected and uninfected users use the same equipment (for
example, by reducing the number of different needle-sharing partners the average injector has).[33]

This last point may require some elaboration. The number of
needle-sharing partners has the same significance for HIV infection
among intravenous drug users as the number of sexual partners has
for its sexual spread. If a given person has only one or a few partners, and if, by chance, none of them is infected, that person will be
entirely safe from the virus, no matter what they do together or how
often. The larger the group of partners, the higher the probability
that at least one of them is infected.*

The number of heroin injections might shrink if the price of heroin
fell sharply, as it surely would if enforcement were greatly relaxed,
even without formal legalization. Heroin is injected primarily because it is expensive. Injection is the most efficient means of getting
molecules of a drug to the brain of a user; almost none of the drug
is wasted. In Vietnam, where heroin was cheap and pure, American
soldiers smoked it rather than injecting it.[34] But even putting aside
the other disadvantages of making heroin cheaper, it is not certain
that lower prices would lead to less injection. Alternatively, lower
prices might engender many more heroin users. In that case, even if
injectors were a smaller proportion of all users, they might be more
numerous in absolute terms.

The number of heroin injections could also be lowered by reducing the prevalence of heroin use, by making the drug more expensive and harder to find, by persuading new users not to start, or
by persuading, helping, or coercing current users to quit. All of the
programs discussed above under the heading "Drug Abuse Control"
are relevant here, including law enforcement.

For some reason, the relevance of law enforcement has not been
evident to many of those concerned with AIDS as a public-health

---

* To be precise, the cumulative risk of infection over a long series of risky acts performed with a single partner drawn at random from a population with an infection
prevalence of p grows asymptotically toward p. The cumulative risk over the same series of acts with different partners drawn at random from the same population grows
asymptotically toward 1 (representing certainty). See Mark A. R. Kleiman, "AIDS,
Vice, and Public Policy," *Law and Contemporary Problems* 51(-1[Winter 1988]): 316–321.
Any turnover among needle-sharing groups dramatically reduces the protective value
of small group size.

problem. While public-health experts agree that we can and should reduce smoking-related lung cancer by making tobacco more expensive and reducing the marketing efforts devoted to it, the seemingly analogous proposition that we can and should reduce heroin-related HIV-infection by making heroin more expensive and reducing the number of sellers is not as widely appreciated, and drug law enforcement has not been high on the priority list of AIDS advocacy groups.

The police, for their part, have been anything but eager to identify themselves with the cause of HIV-infection control. There is no evidence that the rise of AIDS led police to reallocate resources to heroin enforcement; as the cocaine trade grew, so too did cocaine's share of local enforcement attention. Nor have police departments made concerted attacks on the "shooting galleries" where constantly shifting groups of heroin users gather to inject themselves, frequently with shared needles. The galleries were arguably benign institutions in the pre-AIDS era; they kept heroin users relatively safe from exposure or robbery, and reduced the public nuisance of having addicts nodding off on street corners and park benches. But they served the role in the spread of HIV by injection that the bathhouses served in the spread of HIV via homosexual contact: places where multiple risky acts, involving many partners per participant, took place. The reason for the apparent police indifference to the AIDS epidemic is simply that the police do not regard public health, and least of all the health of chronic lawbreakers, as part of their official concern. As one high-ranking big-city narcotics officer said in an off-the-record conversation, "As far as most cops are concerned, the faster all the junkies die, the better." Thus an important social objective is not pursued because the use of coercive means for compassionate ends does not appeal to either the preachers of compassion or the wielders of coercion.

For similar reasons, the enormous potential of police lockups and jails as sites for distributing information about safe needle practices and as recruitment centers for treatment has gone largely unutilized. Prisons are far more likely to counsel their guards about the risk of being bitten (actually minimal if not zero) than to teach their inmates about how to remain HIV-free on the outside.[35]

The treatment system, by contrast, is alive to its role in AIDS control. Counseling about how to avoid infection is now routine practice in virtually all heroin treatment programs. But even the treatment providers do not seem to have thought through how their policies affect the course of the epidemic. In particular, they have overlooked the effects of the rate of contact between infected and uninfected heroin users. Where slots are scarce—that is, where there are waiting lists for treatment—the value of a slot in controlling the spread of the virus would be increased by giving treatment priority to infected users in areas of low HIV prevalence, to prevent them from spreading the virus to others, and giving priority to uninfected users in areas of high HIV prevalence, to prevent them from being infected themselves.[36] But no treatment program in a high-prevalence city has adopted a policy of giving preference to HIV-negatives; the most likely reason, beyond simple inertia, is the inconsistency between the ethic of therapy and the mode of thinking involved in establishing policies of this kind.

The laws against the possession and sale of heroin are not the only ones that complicate the problem of controlling the HIV epidemic. Injection equipment is also subject to legal control. In twelve states, including most of those with major heroin problems, possession of syringes and needles without a prescription is legally equivalent to possession of controlled substances.[37] Injection equipment is also covered by the drug paraphernalia laws in almost all states and by the federal paraphernalia law enacted in 1986.[38]

These laws have not made injection equipment impossible to obtain. Needles "leak" from licit to illicit uses, primarily via theft. They also leak, like firearms, from states with weaker controls to states with stronger controls. One solution to the leakage problem would be to make the needle-syringe units used in hospitals nonreusable (as opposed to "disposable," which is an economic rather than a technical characteristic). There is at least one design currently proposed for a needle-and-syringe combination in which the plunger can only be retracted once, but the prospects of regulatory change to force the redesign of so basic a piece of medical equipment do not seem bright. Even if the scheme were technically and organizationally workable, it is not clear that a reduction in the supply of injection equipment would reduce, rather than increase, the frequency of needle sharing.

Even in states with tight control and large numbers of users, such as New York, a black-market needle-syringe unit sells for a few dollars, a tiny fraction of the value of the heroin that will pass through it before it is broken, lost, or confiscated, or simply becomes too dull to use. (Heroin users also create their own injection equipment, by sharpening eyedroppers for example, but these makeshifts are less satisfactory than the real thing.)

Heroin users share needles for several reasons. Some are simply too careless of their health, or too greedy for heroin, to want to spend even part of the price of a dose on injection equipment when they can borrow their friends'. Some fear arrest for possession of "works" or have recently had their equipment confiscated by the police. Some have injected themselves so often that all of the veins they can see are too scarred to be comfortable injection sites; they often frequent shooting galleries to use the services of "hit men," who provide injection services for a fee and as a rule use their own "works" on many clients in succession. Sharing "works" can also be part of sharing a dose, for users without enough ready cash to buy a whole bag. Finally, needle sharing can be the heroin addict's version of "passing the bottle" as practiced by skid-row winos and English gentlemen alike: a ritual of good fellowship around a shared drug experience.*

Even when the only diseases in question were hepatitis B and topical infections around injection sites, it was far from clear that the ban on "works" produced benefits sufficient to balance its unwanted side effects. It is certainly conceivable that there are some potential heroin users, not deterred by the other pains and risks of heroin use, for whom the unavailability of sharp, sterile injection equipment is enough to prevent their becoming heroin users or progressing from experimental use to addiction, but it is hard to believe that there are very many. It is more plausible that some current users of other drugs in less hazardous fashions might switch to injection if needles were easy to come by, but even this notion is based on speculation and anecdote rather than on anything resembling hard evidence. The link between injection and risk is now so well fixed in the public mind that the number of initiations to injection is likely to remain low, regardless of needle-supply conditions.[39]

Surely, then, if there were no controls on "works" now in place, this would be no time to enact them. As a political matter, however, it is also not a very opportune time to repeal the existing controls. The furious political battles about needle exchange make it clear that needle legalization is not in the cards.[40]

The simplest step toward encouraging heroin users to maintain their own, unshared, personal needle and syringe would be to stop arresting them for possession of "works." This would require no legislation; a policy decision, even an informal one, by police departments would suffice. Convincing police, both management and rank-and-file,

---

* Don Des Jarlais of Narcotic and Drug Research, Incorporated, the leading researcher on the link between AIDS and heroin, believes that since addicts became aware of AIDS, scarcity of needles has become the dominant reason for sharing.

of the desirability of such a policy would not be simple or easy, but it might be possible.

Another step requiring no new legislation would be the promotion of sterilization, particularly sterilization by means of bleach. In some cities, AIDS outreach workers have handed out very small bottles of bleach with needle-permeable rubber tops, allowing injectors to sterilize by simply plunging the needle through the top into the bleach and pumping it a few times. Sterilization is clearly second-best to the avoidance of sharing altogether, if only because having one's own "works" is simpler. The great advantage of sterilization campaigns over needle-distribution programs is that they do not disseminate the means of heroin use. The practical difference may not be very great—if the risk of AIDS is a deterrent to heroin use or an incentive to quit, relieving that risk by encouraging sterilization promotes heroin use, just as reflective clothing promotes bicycle riding—but the symbolic difference is all-important, and not only to the full-time drug warriors. The most fervent opponents of needle-exchange programs include recovering heroin addicts and the political leaders of minority, particularly African-American, neighborhoods.[41]

Even putting the symbolic issues aside, the operational logic of needle exchange is not entirely clear. In their need to distinguish themselves from the politically impossible proposal of open needle distribution, the designers of needle-exchange programs (some legally sanctioned, some operating in frank defiance of the law) have put themselves on the horns of a practical dilemma. The relevant characteristic of a needle is not whether it is new or old but whether it is shared or unshared. Insofar as the reason for needle sharing is a shortage of needles, only an increase in the supply of needles will help. Thus it is not obvious to what problem a simple one-for-one, new-lamps-for-old needle exchange is the solution. Some programs compromise by handing out one or even several "free" needles to new participants, requiring only that they be brought back in return for new ones, but reported return rates are always well under 100 percent.[42]

The great benefit of needle-exchange programs is that they can use the availability of new needles (sharp and therefore more comfortable to use) as a means of drawing heroin users into AIDS-prevention counseling and perhaps into treatment. The clean, new "works" then serve as a continuing reminder of the importance of not sharing.

Therefore, needle exchange should be seen not as a solution in itself but as one among several alternative means of marketing AIDS-prevention messages and services to heroin users. Whether, so conceived, they are worth their enormous political cost is an open question. No one can doubt the courage or the dedication of those who have risked jail to do something they thought would save lives, but one can doubt the efficiency of their actions. The future course of HIV infection among heroin users probably depends less on the fate of needle-distribution programs than on the overall vigor of outreach efforts.

Keeping heroin users from being infected is only one aspect of the task of controlling heroin-related AIDS. The other is keeping infected users from transmitting the virus to their sexual partners. Although it once appeared that prostitution by female heroin users might be a significant route of spread of the virus to non-heroin-using men and thus to the other sexual partners of those men, this threat has faded. For whatever reason—the lesser frequency of genital skin lesions among men seems the most likely—female-to-male HIV transmission is not nearly as common in the United States as in Africa.[43] The two groups most at risk of HIV infection as a result of someone else's heroin use are women whose (male) lovers are heroin users and their children.[44]

There are two ways to approach this problem: by communicating with male heroin users, encouraging them to know their HIV status, to share that knowledge with their sexual partners, and to use barrier methods of contraception; and by communicating directly with the women at risk. The men are easier to locate and, in most relationships, probably in a better position to influence what actually happens; the women have a much stronger incentive to do something, because it is their lives that are at stake. Both sorts of efforts should be made, but it would be rash to expect that either will have great success.

PREVENTING THE NEXT HEROIN EPIDEMIC

As the cocaine tide reaches full flood and begins to ebb, the natural question is "What's next?" One possible answer is *ice,* the pure dextrorotatory isomer of methamphetamine, which can be smoked like crack with, reportedly, a less euphoric but longer-lasting high.[45] But aside from offering more hours of drug experience per dollar, ice seems to have few advantages over crack, and the crack experience has probably decreased the potential market for another smokable stimulant.

A second possibility is some drug with more or less "psychedelic" properties: perhaps psylocybin, the active ingredient of hallucinogenic mushrooms; or LSD, now being more widely used than in the recent past and in doses much lower than those used in the 1960s; or MDMA ("ecstasy") or another of the methoxylated amphetamines, which blend the effects of stimulants and psychedelics; or some unknown designer drug now being developed. But despite some evidence of renewed interest in "consciousness expansion" through chemistry, flashbacks from the national "bad trip" of the flower-child era will probably limit the mass interest in this family of drugs for some time to come.[46]

A third possible answer, of course, is "nothing." It may be that the national appetite for drug novelty has been sated for a long while and that the next great drug wave will not come until the generation that remembers crack has passed from the scene. This is the prediction of historian David Musto, based on his reading of the history of the first cocaine epidemic around the turn of the twentieth century.[47]

But there are reasons to think that heroin is about to make a big comeback. The number of large heroin seizures at the border has risen sharply, and the recent seizure of more than a ton in San Francisco set an all-time record. In part because of the diversion of drug enforcement resources to cocaine, heroin now costs less (in inflation-adjusted dollars per purity-adjusted gram) than at any other time since the great heroin epidemic of 1967 to 1973.*

The primary effect of that price decrease so far has probably been to allow current heroin addicts to increase their doses. Larger doses may make it harder for them to quit; otherwise they do little harm. According to anecdotal reports, some ex-addicts are now being drawn back in to the market by falling prices, and some heroin treatment programs are beginning to see more clients with recently acquired habits.[48]

But the truly frightening reports are that heroin is beginning to be used in forms other than injection, primarily snorting. This reflects both the fear of AIDS and the declining retail price that is

---

* For many years, the retail price of heroin held steady at between $2.00 and $2.50 per pure milligram, which meant in effect that the real price was falling at the rate of inflation. In 1990, the national average price was estimated at $1.78, with the price in New York as low as $1.03. This does not mean that bags of heroin are cheaper (though there are some reports of discounting) but that their heroin content is greater; national average purity rose from about 5 percent in 1980 to more than 18.2 percent in 1990. National Narcotics Intelligence Consumers Committee, *The NNICC Report: 1990* (Washington, D.C.: Drug Enforcement Agency, 1991), 13.

expressed as increasing purity. At its previous high price, heroin was simply too expensive for most of its users to take in any form but the super-efficient needle. The falling price brings snorting and smoking within reach of a wider audience, including many who, for fear of AIDS, stigma, or sharp objects, do not want to use any drug intravenously. The fact that most heroin snorters and smokers have been doing so for a relatively short time, and thus are less likely to have reached the stage of compulsive use characteristic of long-term heroin injectors, helps spread the belief that nonintravenous heroin use is "not addictive."*

The fear of the needle has been one layer of protection between the United States and a new heroin epidemic. A second is simply the word *heroin*. Not only do people fear the drug, they also do not want to think of themselves, or have others think of them, as heroin addicts. The next sign that a heroin wave may be upon us would be the introduction of a new term for the drug in a new form, as far from *heroin* as *ice* is from *crank* (the slang term for methamphetamine). A packaging innovation like the crack vial could also make a difference.

To date, none of the national monitoring systems shows evidence of a new wave of heroin use. That is reassuring as far as it goes. But if the price keeps falling and the purity keeps rising, the threat of growing use will intensify. Heroin does not now have the enormous retail distribution system that has built up around cocaine and crack, but the diminution of demand for crack will leave a large number of unemployed or underemployed drug dealers ready to respond to new demand if it arises.

The preoccupation of policymakers, experts, and citizens with heroin and marijuana prevented the rapid redeployment of drug law enforcement resources to meet what can now be seen in retrospect as the last clear chance to prevent the cocaine epidemic in the late 1970s and early 1980s. It would be tragic to repeat that mistake, in reverse, with what may be the heroin epidemic of the mid-1990s. In drug policy as elsewhere, preventing disasters is much easier than cleaning up after them.

---

* I have been predicting the rise of heroin smoking for several years now, on the theory that lower prices would make it possible and the crack experience would alert dealers and users alike to the opportunities offered by the pipe. This prediction seems now to have been wrong; drug enforcement agents report that supplies of heroin in smokable form are available in some cities but find few takers. The most likely explanation is that crack and crack users have given the pipe as bad a reputation as the needle.

V

RECAPITULATION AND CONCLUSION

13

Against Excess: Drug Policy in Moderation

Passion has helped us,
but can do so no more.
It will in future be our enemy.
Reason, cold, calculating,
unimpassioned reason,
must furnish all the material
for our future support and defense.   —Lincoln

You pays your money,
and you takes your choice.   —Punch

A number of chemicals can alter mood, perception, cognition, and behavior in ways other than simply providing nutrition. Among them are caffeine, nicotine, alcohol, diazepam (Valium), marijuana, amphetamine, cocaine, heroin, MDMA, and LSD. These are called psychoactive drugs, or sometimes simply drugs. Some of these chemicals often produce a marked intoxicated state, with thoughts, moods, and behavior alien to ordinary life. Others, such as nicotine and caffeine, do not.

Some people like or want (or have learned to like, or think they want) various of the effects these drugs produce or are thought to produce: relief of discomfort; energy or concentration; relaxation and increased capacity for sociability; inspiration; and pleasure. Some find intoxication pleasurable, or desire it as a good excuse for behavior they desire to engage in but do not want to acknowledge, to themselves or to others, as fully their own.

The use of any of these chemicals, particularly to the point of intoxication, carries with it dangers: direct health damage or lasting psychological change from the drugs themselves; the bad results of intoxicated behavior; and the possibility of progressing to compulsive use, either in binges or as a steady habit. That is, drug users can lose control of themselves, by doing things in the drugged state they would not otherwise do and later regret or by losing control of their drug use.

Drugs can also make people less reliably able to fulfill the threefold role that a social system founded on principles of freedom must assign to its adult members: to be the stewards of their own welfare; to carry out their voluntarily assumed responsibilities as, for example, parents, neighbors, and coworkers; and to control their actions within limits set by civility and the rights of others.

The fact that some people can use a drug responsibly and even beneficially does not imply that it is safe. We all know people who drink and take no harm from it, and we all know people whose lives have been wrecked by alcohol. By the same token, the fact that some users of a given drug are badly off and dangerous does not mean that all users of that drug will be that way. The question is one of probabilities and populations at risk; a drug with "only" a one-in-six chance of turning an experimental user into a compulsive user is a very dangerous drug if millions do the experiment.

Since many people are less self-controlled in response to drugs than they are in response to other consumer goods, it makes sense to have a different set of policies about buying and selling drugs than about buying and selling office supplies. Drug policies can be divided into laws and programs. Laws can include taxes, regulations, and prohibitions. Programs are aimed at enforcing the laws; at persuading actual and potential users of drugs in general or of some particular drug to abstain, use in moderation, or use under controlled circumstances; or at helping and controlling those whose drug use has become a problem to themselves or others.

Policies have unwanted side effects. Taxes create moonshining, regulation creates evasion and corruption, prohibition creates black markets, programs cost money and often create perverse incentives. Since all drugs are dangerous and all policies are costly, we ought to consider, for each drug and for all of them together, what set of policies would create the least onerous overall problem, adding together the damage done by drug abuse and the damage done by attempts to control it.

Under current policies, some drugs are virtually in free commerce, including caffeine, nicotine, and alcohol. Others—the "controlled substances," including marijuana, heroin, and cocaine—are strictly forbidden or restricted to medically supervised therapeutic uses. It would be surprising if there were no drug too dangerous for free commerce but not so dangerous as to warrant a complete ban on nonmedical use. If there are such substances, either among the currently permitted or among the currently prohibited, the appropriate policy toward them might be one of grudging toleration: discriminatory taxation, a conditional and revocable license for personal use, vigorous enforcement of bans on sale to minors, limitations on marketing, negative advertising, and so on.

Even if some drugs deserve a grudging toleration, for others there may be no feasible set of laws and programs that will outperform a simple prohibition: a control regime strong enough for alcohol may well be strong enough for marijuana as well, but not for either cocaine or nicotine in the form of cigarettes.

Among the programs, a few stand out as worth expanding: education and training in moderation and self-command, short-term interventions to funnel problem drug users into long-term group self-help efforts, helping and forcing user/offenders to quit, and breaking up flagrant drug markets with as few arrests and trials as possible. Programs, like laws, should be judged by their results, not by the warm feelings they give those who design them and carry them out.

If we treat drug policy as a social problem to wrestle with seriously rather than as the occasion for a cultural holy war, we can reduce the damage done by drugs and by drug control efforts. The politics of the crusade against the currently illicit drugs often clashes with the practicalities of drug abuse control. Creating a measured fear of drugs—leading people to understand that drug use is risky and encouraging them to disdain a life spent under the influence—is an important technique of drug-control policy. But intolerance is always a danger in a puritanical republic, and the logic of "us against them" forces us to ignore the most widespread problems. Many of the loudest advocates of a war on drug sellers and users exclude alcohol and tobacco from their account, despite the enormous health cost of tobacco and the widespread crime and disorder associated with drunkenness.

There is no way to remove the ideological struggle over the morality of seeking "altered states" from the drug debate. But it is the real, observable damage done by drugs to users and others that has made the drug problem a prominent public issue. Although the antiprohibition forces have seized on "harm reduction" as a slogan, they have no monopoly on giving the reduction of drug-related harm priority over more abstract goals of drug policy.

The more important the problem, the less adequate a response based on values and symbols alone. We need policies that express both disapproval and compassion, and the debate about what we disapprove of and whom we have compassion for is worth conducting. In the end, though, good intentions are not enough. We need good policies.

The polarization of the drug issue on such axes as prohibition versus legalization or treatment versus enforcement represents more than a contest between conflicting practical views about the likely results of alternative policies; the struggle engages deeply held beliefs about human nature and the human good. But more attention to practical detail would improve the discussion.

Making drug policy has something in common with taking drugs: both are activities prone to excess, and the key to avoiding problems with either one is knowing when to stop (which sometimes means knowing not to start). The problem is to replace excess with moderation, in a double sense: a policy to encourage moderation in use, and moderation in the making and implementation of policy. This would mean abandoning unattainable goals, policies without reasonable connections with their nominal objectives, and, above all, laws and programs made and executed in anger. Drugs can madden their opponents as well as their users, and a drug-crazed drug warrior can be as great a public menace as a drug-crazed addict.

Public policy toward drugs involves so many unknown, almost unknowable facts and so many complicated issues of value that any certainty about which of two alternative policies is the better is likely to be misplaced. This book has reached many conclusions and argued for many recommendations, but most of them could prove to be wrong under plausible factual circumstances or as measured against defensible sets of values. Even the underlying belief that careful reasoning will produce better policies than enthusiasm and emotion is not invariably true; fanaticism can work wonders, and sometimes, if only by accident, it is deployed in good causes. But neither individuals nor nations can remain in a passionate frenzy forever; eventually we must learn to discuss our drug policies without raising our voices.[1]

No doubt, anyone who has read this far has disagreed with more than one of the opinions offered. That is as it should be. This book was designed to enable those of its readers who prefer to act on their considered judgments rather than on their emotions and their prejudices to do so in the drug policy arena. That their judgments should be the same as mine was no part of my purpose.

Notes

PREFACE AND WARNING

1. *The Prince*, Ch. 14.
2. For discussions of the experiences of other countries, see Mathea Falco and Peter Reuter, eds., *Drug Problems and Drug Policies: An International Perspective* (forthcoming).
3. See, among many examples, Michael Montagne, "Drug-Taking and Artistic Creativity," *Social Pharmacology* 1 (4 [1987]): 339–356; Alexander Shulgin and Ann Shulgin, *PIHKAL: A Chemical Love Story* (Berkeley, Calif.: Transform Press, 1991); Harold A. Robinson, ed., *The Use of LSD in Psychotherapy and Alcoholism* (New York: Bobbs-Merrill, 1967); Walter Hanston Clark, *Chemical Ecstasy: Psychedelic Drugs and Religion* (New York: Sheed and Ward, 1969). For a beautifully written nontechnical introduction see Adam Smith [George J.W. Goodman], *Powers of Mind* (NewYork: Random House, 1975), 26–57, 297–323.
4. See Conelieu E. Guigea, "The Nootropic Concept and its Prospective Implications," *Drug Development Research* 2 (1982): 441–446; and Bruno J. Nielaus, "Chemistry and Pharmacology of Nootropics," *Drug Development Research* 2 (1982): 463–474.
5. C. Lowman, et al., "Alcohol Use Among Black Senior High School Students," *Alcohol Health and Research World* 7 (1983): 37–46.
6. Andrea N. Kopstein and Patrice T. Roth, *Drug Abuse Among Race/Ethnic Minorities* (Rockville, Md.: National Institute on Drug Abuse, 1990), 9, 13.

INTRODUCTION
HOW TO STOP LOSING THE WAR ON DRUGS

1. See Ethan A. Nadelmann, "The Case for Legalization," *The Public Interest* (Summer 1988); James Ostroski, "Thinking About Drug Legalization," *Policy Analysis* (Washington, D.C.: CATO Institute, 1989); Richard Lawrence Miller, *The Case for Legalizing Drugs* (New York: Praeger, 1991); Jeffrey A. Miron, "Drug Legalization and the Consumption of Drugs: An Economist's Perspective," in *Searching for Alternatives,* Melvyn Krauss and Edward Lazear, eds. (Palo Alto, Calif.: Hoover Institute Press, forthcoming).

2. National Institute on Alcohol Abuse and Alcoholism, *Sixth Special Report to the U.S. Congress on Alcohol and Health* (Rockville, Md.: Department of Health and Human Services, 1987), 6; National Institute on Drug Abuse, *Data from the Drug Abuse Warning Network, 1988* (Rockville, Md.: Department of Health and Human Services, 1988), Series I, No. 8: 52.

3. Office of Smoking and Health, *Smoking and Health; A National Status Report* (Rockville, Md.: U.S. Department of Health and Human Services, 1987). Office of Smoking and Health, *Nicotine Addiction: The Health Consequences of Smoking* (Rockville, Md.: Office of Smoking and Health, 1988).

4. The classical statement of the case for this rule is John Stuart Mill's *On Liberty.* Among contemporary thinkers in this tradition, Milton Friedman, Robert Nozick, and Thomas Szasz have all argued for state noninterference in drug taking. Joel Feinberg, *The Moral Limits of the Criminal Law* Vol. 1, *Harm to Others,* 1984; Vol. 2, *Offense to Others,* 1985; Vol. 3, *Harm to Self,* 1986 (Oxford: Oxford University Press) is an attempt to qualify and modify Mill's view while maintaining its flavor.

5. Thomas Szasz, *Ceremonial Chemistry: The Ritual Persecution of Drugs, Addicts, and Pushers* (Holmes Beach, Fla.: Learning Publications, 1985).

6. Office on Smoking and Health, *Smoking and Health; A National Status Report.* Office on Smoking and Health, *Nicotine Addiction: The Health Consequences of Smoking.*

7. F. L. Iber, *Alcohol and Drug Abuse as Encountered in Office Practice* (Boca Raton, Fla.: CRC, 1991), 107.

8. Office on Smoking and Health, *Reducing the Health Consequences of Smoking: 25 Years of Progress, A Report of the Surgeon General* (Washington, D.C.: Department of Health and Human Services, 1989): vi, 285.

9. Lloyd D. Johnston, Patrick O'Malley, and Jerald G. Bachman, *Illicit Drug Use, Smoking and Drinking by America's High School Students, College Students, and Young Adults: 1975–87* (Rockville, Md.; National Institute on Drug Abuse, 1989), Tables 37 and 38, pp. 252–253.

10. William Bennett, Director, Office of National Drug Control Policy, speech at the Institute of Politics, Kennedy School of Government, Harvard University, 11 December 1989.

11. Robert L. DuPont, "Never Trust Anyone Under 40: What Employers Should Know About Drugs in the Workplace," *Policy Review* 48 (Spring 1984): 52.

12. Lincoln called the contemporary temperance movement "A living, breathing, active and powerful chieftain, going forth conquering and to conquer." Presumably he expected most of his listeners to miss the allusion to *Revelations* 6:2. See Temperance Address, delivered before the Springfield Washington Temperance Society (22 February 1845) in Roy P. Basler, ed., *Collected Works 1* (New Brunswick: Rutgers University Press, 1953), 271–279.

13. *Criminal Justice Report for the District of Columbia* (Washington, D.C.: Office of Criminal Justice Plans and Analysis, 1990), 16.

1
THINKING ABOUT DRUG POLICY

1. Don Marquis, "Certain Maxims of Archy," in *Archy and Mehitabel* (Garden City, N.Y.: Doubleday, Inc., 1931).

2. Denise B. Kandel and Kazuo Yamaguchi, "Developmental Patterns of the Use of Legal, Illegal, and Medically Prescribed Psychotropic Drugs from Adolescence to Young Adulthood," in *Etiology of Drug Abuse: Implications for Prevention,* National Institute on Drug Abuse Research Monograph 56, Coryl LaRue Jones and Robert J. Battjes, eds. (Rockville, Md.: Department of Health and Human Services, 1987).

3. Temperance address delivered to the Springfield Washington Temperance Society (22 February 1845) in Roy P. Basler, ed., *Collected Works 1* (New Brunswick: Rutgers University Press, 1953), 271–279. Robert L. DuPont, *Getting Tough on Gateway Drugs: A Guide for the Family* (Washington, D.C.: American Psychiatric Press, Inc., 1984).

4. Robert J. Battjes and Roy W. Pickens, eds., *Needle Sharing Among Intravenous Drug Users: National and International Perspectives,* NIDA Research Mongraph 80 (Rockville, Md.: NIDA, 1988); Donald Des Jarlais and Saul Friedman, "HIV Infection Among Intravenous Drug Users: Epidemiology and Risk Reduction," *AIDS: International Bimonthly Journal* 1 (1987): 67–76. But note that HIV prevalence among heroin users is as high in some European cities where needles are freely sold in drug stores as it is where needles are contraband. See Table 1 in R. Friedman and D. C. Des Jarlais, "HIV Among Drug Injectors: The Epidemic and The Response," *AIDS Care* 3 (3 [forthcoming, 1991]).

5. In Washington, D.C., the average income per crime for personal robbery was between $129 and $215; for burglary of a residence between $115 and $344; and for personal larceny with contact (purse-snatching and pickpocketing) between $49 and $82. Incomes in other cities are probably similar. See Peter Reuter, Robert MacCoun, and Patrick Murphy,

Money from Crime: A Study of the Economics of Drug Dealing in Washington, D.C., R-3894-RF (Washington, D.C.: RAND Corporation, 1990), 155–156. An earlier study reported an *average* annual income for burglary of $760, for robbery of $625, and for mugging of $745 (1979–1980 figures). See W. Kip Viscusi, "The Risks and Rewards of Criminal Activity: A Comprehensive Test of Criminal Deterrence," *Journal of Labor Economics* 4 (3, pt. 1 [1986]): 333.

6. On average, for each burglary committed, burglars serve an average of about nine days behind bars; for robbery, the figure is about sixty days. See Mark A. R. Kleiman, Kerry Smith, Richard Rogers, and David Cavanagh, "Imprisonment to Offense Ratios," Bureau of Justice Statistics Discussion Paper (15 November 1988).

7. In Washington, median weekly incomes reached as high as $700 for crack dealers. Peter Reuter, et al., *Money from Crime: A Study of the Economics of Drug Dealing in Washington, D.C.*, p. 59.

8. Dean Gerstein, "Alcohol Use and Consequences," in *Alcohol and Public Policy: Beyond the Shadow of Prohibition,* Mark H. Moore and Dean R. Gerstein, eds. (Washington, D.C.: National Academy Press, 1981).

9. Moore and Gerstein, *Alcohol and Public Policy: Beyond the Shadow of Prohibition,* pp. 274–276. NIDA, *Alcohol and Health: Sixth Annual Report to the U.S. Congress* (Rockville, Md.: Department of Health and Human Services, 1987), Table 4, p. 6.

10. Bureau of the Census, *Vital Statistics of the United States 1939* part 1 (Washington, D.C.: GPO, 1941), 26; Bureau of the Census, *Mortality Statistics 1929* (Washington, D.C.: GPO, 1936), 100. Note that changes in the reporting area between 1929 and 1939 may account in part for the absolute numerical increase. However, the incidence of cirrhosis also increased, from 7.2 per 100,000 in 1929 to 8.3 per 100,000 in 1939.

11. Cocaine involvement in sudden death was reported by medical examiners in 3308 deaths in 1988. Not all of these were *caused* by cocaine alone, but on the other hand the count did not include, for example, excess heart-attack deaths brought on by chronic cocaine use or excess infant mortality from fetal cocaine syndrome. National Institute on Drug Abuse, *Annual Data 1988, Data from the Drug Abuse Warning Network,* U.S. Department of Health and Human Services, Series 1, Number 8 (1989): 62.

12. M. Davis, "Alcoholic Liver Injury," *Proceedings of the Nutrition Society* 47 (2 [July 1988]): 115–20.

13. *Goodman and Gilman's The Pharmacological Basis of Therapeutics,* Alfred Goodman Gilman, Louis S. Goodman, and Alfred Goodman, eds., 6th ed. (New York: Macmillian, 1980), 499–500, 512.

14. N. Sacks, J. R. Hutcheson, Jr., J. M. Watts, and R. E. Webb, "Case Report: the Effects of Tetrahydrocannabinol on Food Intake During Chemotherapy," *Journal of the American College of Nutrition* 9 (6 [December 1990]): 63–65. N. Lane, F. E. Smith, R. A. Sullivan, and T. F. Plasse, "Dronabinol and Prochlorperazine Alone and in Combination as Antiemetic Agents

for Cancer Chemotherapy," *American Journal of Clinical Oncology* 13 (6 [December, 1990]): 480–484. M. McCabe, F. P. Smith, J. S. Macdonald, P. V. Woolley, D. Goldberg, and P. S. Schein, "Efficacy of Tetrahydrocannabinol in Patients' Refractory to Standard Antiemetic Therapy," *Investigational New Drugs* 6 (3 [September 1988]): 243–246.

15. *Goodman and Gilman's, pp. 444–447.*

16. John L. Eadie, "Benzodiazepine Abuse and Misuse: New York State's Response," paper presented at the American Medical Association's National Symposium on Medicine and Public Policy, 13 December 1988. When drug enforcement agencies seize illicit laboratories, the product involved is rarely diazepam.

17. Mark A. R. Kleiman, *Marijuana: Costs of Abuse, Costs of Control* (New York: Greenwood, 1989), p. 24, applies this argument to Federal marijuana enforcement efforts. Kleiman, "Drug Enforcement and Organized Crime," in *The Politics and Economics of Organized Crime*, Herbert Alexander and Gerald Caiden, eds. (Lexington, Mass.: Lexington Books, 1985), makes the argument about drug enforcement more generally.

18. Peter Reuter and Mark A. R. Kleiman, "Risks and Prices: An Economic Analysis of Drug Enforcement," in *Criminal Justice: An Annual Review of Research* Vol. 7, Michael Tonry and Norval Morris, eds. (Chicago: University of Chicago Press, 1986).

19. Peter Reuter, "Quality Illusions and Paradoxes of Drug Interdiction: Federal Interdiction into Vice Policy," *Law and Contemporary Problems* 51 (1 [Winter 1988]): 233–252.

20. Office of National Drug Control Policy, *National Drug Control Strategy #1* (Washington, D.C.: GPO, 1989).

21. Mark H. Moore, *Buy and Bust: The Effective Regulation of an Illicit Market in Heroin* (Lexington, Mass.: Lexington Books, 1977), 7, 8.

22. George F. Brown and Lester Silverman, "Retail Price of Heroin: Estimation and Applications," *Journal of the American Statistical Association* 69 (347 [September 1974]); Kleiman, *Marijuana: Costs of Abuse, Costs of Control*, Ch. 2.

23. Mark Moore has been making this point since the 1970s.

24. Victor H. Fuchs, *The Health Economy* (Cambridge, Mass.: Harvard University Press, 1986), 243–257.

25. J. Michael Polich, *Strategies for Controlling Adolescent Drug Use* (Santa Monica, Calif.: RAND Corp, 1984). Nancy S. Tobler, "Meta-Analysis of 143 Adolescent Drug Prevention Programs: Quantitative Outcome and Results of Program Participants Compared to a Control or Comparison Group," *Journal of Drug Issues* (Fall 1986): 537–567.

26. Mary Ann Pentz, James H. Dwyer, David P. MacKinnon, Brian R. Flay, Willam B. Hansen, Eric Yu I. Wang, and C. Anderson Johnson, "A Multicommunity Trial for Primary Prevention of Adolescent Drug Abuse," *Journal of the American Medical Association* 261 (22 [9 June 1989]): 3259–3266. Gina Kolata,

"Community Program Succeeds in Drug Fight," *New York Times* (11 June 1989): 33.

27. D. D. Simpson and S. B. Sells, "Effectiveness of Treatment for Drug Abuse," *Advances in Alcohol and Substance Abuse* 2 (1982): 7–29.

28. Harry Wexler, Gregory Falkin, and Douglas Lipton, "Outcome Evaluation for Prison Therapeutic Community for Substance Abuse Treatment," *Criminal Justice and Behavior* 17 (March 1990): 71–92.

2
DRUG ABUSE AND OTHER BAD HABITS

1. See Peter K. Levison, Dean R. Gerstein, and Deborah R. Maloff, eds., *Commonalties in Substance Abuse and Habitual Behavior* (Lexington, Mass.: D. C. Heath and Company, 1983).

2. Thomas Hobbes, *Leviathan* (Harmondsworth, England: Penguin Books, 1968), Ch. 14, 192. Cf. Aristotle, *Nicomachean Ethics,* 1.1 1094a.

3. John Stuart Mill, *On Liberty,* David Spitz, ed. (New York: W. W. Norton, 1975), 10–11, 53–54.

4. *Black's Law Dictionary,* 5th ed. (St. Paul, Minn.: 1979), 412. This maxim gives rise to the doctrine of "assumption of risk."

5. See, for example, Francis Bator, "The Simple Analytics of Welfare Maximization," *American Economic Review* 47 (March 1957): 22–59.

6. See Charles L. Schultze, *The Public Use of Private Interest* (Washington, D.C.: Brookings Institution, 1977), 14–15.

7. Michael O'Hare, "A Typology of Governmental Action," *Journal of Policy Analysis and Management* 8 (4 [1989]): 610–672.

8. See George Ainslie, "Specious Reward: A Behavioral Theory of Impulsiveess and Impulse Control," *Psychological Bulletin* 82 (July 1975): 463–496.

9. See Thomas C. Schelling, "The Intimate Contest for Self-Command," and "Law, Ethics, and the Contest for Self-Command," in *Choice and Consequence*, Thomas Schelling, ed. (Cambridge, Mass.: Harvard University Press, 1984), 57–82, 83–112.

10. See Jon Elster, *Ulysses and the Sirens: Studies in Rationality and Irrationality* (Cambridge: Cambridge University Press, 1979), esp. Section II.

11. See, for example, Dan J. Lettieri, Mollie Sayers, and Helen Wallenstein Penson, eds., *Theories on Drug Abuse: Selected Contemporary Perspectives,* National Institute on Drug Abuse Research Monograph 30 (Washington, D.C.: GPO, 1980).

12. For alcohol, see O. A. Parsons and W. R. Leber, "The Relationship Between Cognitive Dysfunction and Brain Damage in Alcoholics: Causal or Epiphenomenal?" *Alcoholism: Clinical and Experimental Research* 5 (2 [1981]): 326–343. For opiates, see C. A. Dackis and M. S. Gold, "Depression in Opiate Addicts," in *Substance Abuse and Psychotherapy,* S. Mirin, ed. (Washington, D.C.: American

Psychiatric Press, 1984), 20–39. For barbiturates, see *Sedative/Hypnotic Drugs: Risks and Benefits* (Washington, D.C.: National Institute on Drug Abuse, 1977).

13. L. Hollister, "Effects of Hallucinogens in Humans," in *Neurochemical, Behavioral and Clinical Perspectives*, B. Jacobs, ed. (New York: Raven, 1984).

14. Robin Room and Gary Collins, "Introduction," in *Alcohol and Disinhibition: The Nature and Meaning of the Link*, Room and Collins, eds., Research Monograph No. 12, National Institute on Alcohol Abuse and Alcoholism (Washington, D.C.: Department of Health and Human Services, 1983). But see the skeptical discussion in Jeffrey Fagan, "Intoxication and Aggression," in *Drugs and Crime* Vol. 13, Michael Tonry and James Q. Wilson, eds. (Chicago: University of Chicago Press, 1990), 290–293.

15. For the behavioral definition of addiction, see Donald R. Wesson and David E. Smith, "Cocaine: Treatment Perspectives," in *Cocaine Use in America: Epidemiologic and Clinical Perspectives*, Nicholas J. Kozel and Edgar H. Adams, eds., National Institute on Drug Abuse Research Monograph 61 (Washington, D.C.: GPO, 1985), 193–203.

16. A. Wikler, *Opiod Dependance: Mechanisms and Treatment* (New York: Plenum, 1980). Stanton Peele, *The Meaning of Addiction* (Lexington, Mass.: Lexington Books, 1985).

17. G. F. Koob and F. G. Bloom, "Cellular and Molecular Mechanisms of Drug Dependence," *Science* 242 (4879 [1988]): 715–723.

18. M. S. Gold and N. S. Miller, DSM III-R (Revised) "Substance Disorders Reviewed," in *Drugs of Abuse*, A. J. Giannini and A. E. Slaby, eds. (Oradell, N.J.: Medical Economics, 1989), 340–342. L. Shuster, "Genetics of Responses to Drugs of Abuse," *International Journal of Addictions* 25 (1a [1991]): 57–79.

19. For barbiturates and alcohol, see D. A. Gross and D. J. Rotondo, "Neuropsychiatric Examination of the Substance Abuser," in *Drugs of Abuse*, A. J. Giannini and A. E. Slaby, eds. (Oradell, N.J.: Medical Economics, 1989), 293. For tranquilizers, see R. Fontaine, G. Chouinard, and L. Annable, "Rebound Anxiety in Anxious Patients after Abrupt Withdrawal of Benzodiazepine Treatment," *American Journal of Psychiatry* 141 (1984): 848; J. Holden, "Benzodiazepine Dependence," *Practioner* 233 (8 November 1989): 1478–1480, 1483. For nicotine, see J. K. Bobo, "Nicotine Dependence and Alcoholism Epidemiology and Treatment," *Journal of Psychoactive Drugs* 21 (3 [July–September 1989]): 323–329.

20. M. S. Gold and H. D. Kleber, "A Rationale For Opiate Withdrawal Symptomatology," *Drug and Alcohol Dependency* 4 (1979): 419.

21. L. R. Goldfrank, N. E. Flomenbaum, N. A. Lewin, R. S. Weisman, and M. A. Howland, *Goldfrank's Toxicologic Emergencies* (Norwalk, Conn.: Appleton and Lange, 1986), 537.

22. L. Shuster, "Genetics of Responses to Drugs of Abuse," pp. 57–79. D. A. Gross and D. J. Rotondo, "Neuropsychiatric Examination of the Substance Abuser," p. 293.

23. This thought experiment is adapted from Schelling's case of a torture victim who has to go through intense pain for five minutes every day, after which he can press a button to make it stop. If he once goes half an hour without pushing the button, he will never have to suffer it again. See Schelling, "The Intimate Contest for Self-Command," in Schelling, *Choice and Consequence*, p. 67. Withdrawal can present a comparable situation, though the discomfort is more closely analogous to a bad spell of disease than to torture.

24. Thomas De Quincey, *Confessions of an English Opium-Eater* (New York: New American Library, 1966).

25. F. H. Gawin, "Cocaine Addiction: Psychology and Neurophysiology," *Science* 251 (5001 [29 March 1991]): 1580–1586.

26. Ibid, p. 1581.

27. M. S. Gold, A. Washton, and C. A. Dackis, eds., *Cocaine Abuse: Neurochemistry, Phenomenology, Treatments*, NIDA Research Monograph No. 61 (Washington, D.C.: GPO, 1985). Also T. Di Paolo, C. Roillard, M. Morisette, D. Levesque, and P. J. Bredard, "Endocrine and Neurochemical Actions of Cocaine," *Canadian Journal of Physiology and Pharmacology* 67 (9 [September 1989]): 1177–1181.

28. Gawin, "Cocaine Addiction: Psychology and Neurophysiology," pp. 1581–1582.

29. See Lewis S. Seiden and Linda A. Dykstra, *Psychopharmacology* (New York: Van Nostrand Reinhold, 1977), Ch. 11.

30. J. H. Jaffe, N. G. Cascella, K. M. Kumor, and M. A. Sherer, "Cocaine-Induced Cocaine Craving," *Psychopharmacology* 97 (1989): 59–64.

31. Patricia G. Erickson and Bruce K. Alexander, "Cocaine and Addictive Liability," *Social Pharmacology* 3 (3 [1989]): 249–270.

32. M. Douglas Anglin and George Speckart, "Narcotics and Crime: A Multi-sample Multi-method Analysis," *Criminology* 26 (2 [May 1988]): 197–233.

33. Patrick Biernacki, *Pathways from Heroin Addiction: Recovery without Treatment* (Philadelphia: Temple University Press, 1986); Norman Zinberg, "Heroin Use in Vietnam and the United States," *Archives of General Psychiatry* 26 (1972): 486–488; L. N. Robins, J. E. Hesselbrock, and E. Wish, "Vietnam Veterans Three Years after Vietnam: How Our Study Changed Our View of Heroin," in *Yearbook of Substance Use and Abuse*, L. Bull and C. Winick, eds. (New York: Human Sciences Press, 1980). Also F. L. Iber, *Alcohol and Drug Abuse as Encountered in Office Practice* (Boca Raton, Fla.: CRC, 1991), 196.; Richard Brotman and Alfred M. Freedman, *Continuities and Discontinuities in the Process of Patient Care for Narcotic Addicts* (New York: New York Medical College, 1965), 73.

34. For an attempt to model addictive behavior as a form of utility maximization, see Gary S. Becker and Kevin M. Murphy, "A Theory of Rational Addiction," *Journal of Political Economy* 96 (4 [1988]): 680–685.

35. V. P. Dole and M. E. Nyswander, "Methadone Maintenance Treatment: A Ten-Year Perspective," *Journal of the American Medical Association* 235 (19 [1976]): 2117–2119.

36. K. Blum and M. C. Trachtenberg, "Alcoholism: Scientific Basis of a Neuropsychogenic Disease," *International Journal of Addictions* 23 (8 [August 1988]): 781–796.

37. Frank Gawin and Everett Ellinwood, "Cocaine and other Stimulants: Actions, Abuse, and Treatment," *New England Journal of Medicine* 318 (18 [May 5, 1988]): 1173–1183; M. S. Gold, A. Washton, and C. A. Dackis, "Cocaine Abuse: Neurochemistry, Phenomenology, Treatments," in *Cocaine Use in America: Epidemiologic and Clinical Perspectives*, ed. Nicholas J. Kozel and Edgar H. Adams, NIDA Research Monograph 61 (Rockville, Md.: NIDA, July 1985); Travis Thompson and Chris E. Johanson, eds., *Behavioral Pharmacology of Human Drug Dependence*, NIDA Research Monograph 37 (Rockville, Md.: NIDA, July 1981).

38. Office on Smoking and Health, *Nicotine Addiction: The Health Consequences of Smoking* (Rockville, Md.: Dept. of Health and Human Services, 1988).

39. See John Kaplan, *The Hardest Drug: Heroin and Public Policy* (Chicago: University of Chicago Press, 1983), 19; Norman Zinberg, *Drug, Set, and Setting: The Basis for Controlled Intoxicant Use* (New Haven: Yale University Press, 1984), 133. See also Nelson H. Donegan, Judith Rodin, Charles P. O'Brien, and Richard L. Solomon, "A Learning-Theory Approach to Commonalties," in *Commonalties in Substance Abuse and Habitual Behavior,* Peter K. Levison, Dean R. Gerstein, and Deborah R. Maloff, eds. (Lexington, Mass.: D. C. Heath and Company, 1983), 122–123. One study noted that out of 100 hospital patients surveyed who had received morphine on a regular basis, only one reported any craving when treatment with the drug stopped. Other studies involving the substitution of placebos for drugs report similar results. See Stanton Peele, *The Meaning of Addiction: Compulsive Experience and its Interpretation* (Lexington, Mass.: Lexington Books, 1985), 17, 24–25.

40. Jerome Jaffe, "Misinformation: Euphoria and Addiction," in *Advances in Pain Research and Therapy* Vol. 2, C. S. Hill and W. S. Fields, eds. (New York: Raven Press, 1989). More recent anecdotes indicate that patients are refusing pain medication because of their desire to "say no to drugs."

41. Thompson and Johnson, *Behavioral Pharmacology of Human Drug Dependence*. Office on Smoking and Health, *Smoking and Health: A National Status Report* (Rockville, Md.: U.S. Dept. of Health and Human Services, 1987). Office on Smoking and Health, *Nicotine Addiction: The Health Consequences of Smoking*.

42. William Bennett, speech at the Institute of Politics, Kennedy School of Government, Harvard University, 11 December 1989.

43. C. van Dyke and R. Byck, "Cocaine," *Scientific American* 246 (March, 1982): 128–134.

44. See, for example, comments by Sen. Daniel Patrick Moynihan, in *Congressional Record* (12 July 1990): S-9604.
45. Edith Stokey and Richard Zeckhauser, *A Primer For Policy Analysis* (New York: Norton, 1978), 159–176.
46. Robert H. Strotz, "Myopia and Inconsistency in Dynamic Utility Maximization," *Review of Economic Studies* (1955–56): 165–180.
47. See, for example, Howard Raiffa, *Decision Analysis: Introductory Lectures on Choices Under Uncertainty* (New York: Random House, 1968).
48. Daniel Kahneman, Paul Slovic, and Amos Tversky, eds., *Judgment under Uncertainty: Heuristics and Biases* (Cambridge: Cambridge University Press, 1982); Richard J. Herrnstein and Drazen Prelec, "Melioration: A Theory of Distributed Choice," Working Paper (Cambridge, Mass.: Division of Research, Harvard Business School) 89-030.
49. It has been suggested that this old expression derives from a colonial Massachusetts statute regulating wife beating and should be abandoned as a relic of a sexist past. The derivation seems farfetched. More plausibly, the phrase originally referred to carpenters' use of the last thumb joint as an approximation for an inch measure, and then entered the vocabulary of schoolmasters, meaning first a computational algorithm, then by extension a heuristic approximation.
50. S. H. Huse, J. Deese, and H. Egeth, *The Psychology of Learning,* 4th Edition (New York: McGraw-Hill, 1975), 134–164.
51. Ibid.
52. Jack E. Henningfield, "Nicotine Dependence: Interface Between Tobacco and Tobacco-Related Disease," *Chest* 93 (February 1988 Supplement): 37S–55S.
53. Gawin, "Cocaine: Psychology and Neurophysiology," pp. 1580–1586.
54. James G. March and Herbert A. Simon, *Organizations* (New York: John Wiley and Sons, 1963), 138–139.
55. Ibid., pp. 169–171.
56. Norbert Wiener, *The Human Use of Human Beings: Cybernetics and Society* (New York: Da Capo Press, 1988). See also John D. Steinbruner, *The Cybernetic Theory of Decision: New Dimensions of Political Analysis* (Princeton: Princeton University Press, 1974).
57. Thompson and Johnson, *Behavioral Pharmacology of Human Drug Dependence.* Travis Thomson and Charles R. Schuster, *Behavioral Pharmacology* (Englewood Cliffs, N.J.: Prentice-Hall, Inc., 1968).
58. John L. Falk, Peter B. Dews, and Charles R. Schuster, "Commonalities in the Environmental Control of Behavior," in *Commonalities of Substance Abuse and Habitual Behavior,* Levinson, Gerstein, and Maloff, eds., p. 50.
59. C. P. O'Brien, J. W. Ternes, J. Grabowski, and R. Ehrman, eds., "Classically Conditioned Phenomena in Human Opiate Addiction," in *Behavioral Pharmacology of Human Drug Dependence,* Travis Thompson and Chris E. Johanson, eds., NIDA Research Monograph No. 37 (Washington, D.C.: GPO, 1978), 221–235.
60. C. P. O'Brien, "Experimental Analysis of Conditioning Factors in Human Narcotic Addiction," *Pharmacological Reviews* 27 (4 [December

1975]): 533; C. W. Schindler, J. L. Katz, and S. R. Goldberg, "The Use of Second-Order Schedules to Study the Influences of Environmental Stimuli on Drug-Seeking Behavior," in *Learning Factors in Substance Abuse*, Barbara Ray, ed., NIDA Monograph 84 (Rockville, Md.: National Institute on Drug Abuse: 1988).

61. Gordon Black, personal communication, based on Partnership Attitude Tracking Survey. By contrast, a prospective-sample study showed much lower rates of progression to heavy use among a group of cocaine users, with only 5 to 10 percent of first-time users becoming weekly users and only 10 to 25 percent of weekly users becoming compulsive users. See Patricia G. Erickson and Bruce K. Alexander, "Cocaine and Addictive Liability," *Social Pharmacology* 3 (1989): 249–270.

62. The classical description of this effect is in Thorstein Veblen, *The Theory of the Leisure Class* (New York: A. M. Kelly, 1899). For a more recent popular description with examples see Vance Packard, *The Status Seekers; An Exploration of Class Behavior in America and the Hidden Barriers that Affect You, Your Community, Your Future* (New York: D. McKay Co., 1959). For the general logic of such "signaling" behavior, see A. Michael Spence, *Market Signaling: Informational Transfer in Hiring and Related Screening Processes* (Cambridge, Mass.: Harvard University Press, 1974).

63. James Anthony, "The Epidemiologic Study of Drug Addiction and Related Syndromes," in *Handbook of Drug and Alcohol Addiction*, N. S. Miller, ed. (New York: Marcel Dekker, 1990).

64. For a general theory of the cycle of drug use, see David Musto, *The American Disease: Origins of Narcotic Control* (New York: Oxford University Press, 1987). For heroin, see Leon Gibson Hunt and Carl D. Chambers, *The Heroin Epidemics: A Study of Heroin Use in the United States: 1965–1975* (New York: Spectrum, 1976). For cocaine, see Mark A. R. Kleiman, "The Changing Face of Cocaine," Working Paper 87-01-07 (Cambridge, Mass: Program in Criminal Justice Policy and Management, Kennedy School of Government, Harvard University, 1987).

65. Here again I part company from Feinberg, who says of a drug user who acts with knowledge of the medical literature, "If, given all that, he is still willing to take a chance, we have to admit that he knows what he is doing." Joel Feinberg, *The Moral Limits of the Criminal Law* Vol. 3 *Harm to Self* (Oxford: Oxford University Press, 1986), 161.

3
THE OTHER VICTIMS OF DRUG ABUSE

1. This idea is developed at length in James Q. Wilson and Richard J. Herrnstein, *Crime and Human Nature* (New York: Simon and Schuster, 1985).

2. See James B. Bakalar and Lester Grinspoon, *Cocaine: A Drug and Its Social Evolution* (New York: Basic Books, 1985), 143–145. Lester Grinspoon

and Peter Hedbloom, *The Speed Culture: Amphetamine Use and Abuse in America* (Cambridge, Mass.: Harvard University Press, 1975).

3. See Edward Preble, et al., *Taking Care of Business: The Economics of Crime by Heroin Abusers* (Lexington, Mass.: Lexington Books, 1985).

4. See Leon Festinger, *A Theory of Cognitive Dissonance* (Evanston, Ill.: Row, Peterson and Co., 1957). Leon Festinger, *Conflict, Decision, and Dissonance* (Stanford, Calif.: Stanford University Press, 1964).

5. Wilson and Herrnstein, *Crime and Human Nature,* p. 356.

6. Consider, for example, the social costs of a decline in the willingness to donate blood. See Richard M. Titmuss, *The Gift Relationship: From Human Blood to Social Policy* (London: Allen & Unwin, 1970). See also Mark H. Moore, "On the Office of the Taxpayer and the Social Process of Taxpaying," *Income Tax Compliance: A Report of the ABA Section of Taxation Invitational Conference on Income Tax Compliance* (American Bar Association, 1983).

7. See Joel Feinberg, *The Moral Limits of the Criminal Law* (Oxford: Oxford University Press, 1985). Feinberg asserts flatly that "offense" (a category in which Feinberg includes nuisance) "is surely a less serious thing than harm" (which he defines as "setbacks to interest"). Vol. 2, *Offense to Others,* p. 2; Vol. 1, *Harm to Others,* pp. 31–36. This seems too strong. If persons are willing to pay money to avoid nuisances, then the damage done them by the nuisance must be larger (in their estimation) than the damage done by the loss of the money involved. But Feinberg acknowledges that the loss of a wager can set back one's "pecuniary interest" (p. 35). Thus if taking away someone's money is "harm," then inflicting a nuisance that he would pay to avoid must also be "harm," and the relative magnitudes involved depend entirely on the situation and not whether the victim confronts a crime such as theft or a mere nuisance such as inebriates sleeping on his doorstep.

8. For the relationship between crowding and the importance of external costs, see William J. Baumol, "Macroeconomics of Unbalanced Growth: The Anatomy of Urban Crisis," *American Economic Review* 57 (June 1967): 415–426.

9. D. Rush and K. R. Callahan, "Exposure to Passive Cigarette Smoking and Child Development: A Critical Review," in *Prenatal Abuse of Licit and Illicit Drugs,* Donald E. Hutchings, ed., Vol. 562 of the *Annals of the New York Academy of Sciences* (New York: New York Academy of Sciences, 1989); D. M. Fergusson, L. J. Harwood, F. T. Shannon, and B. Taylor, "Parental Smoking and Lower Respiratory Illness in the First Three Years of Life," *Journal of Epidemiology and Community Health* 35 (1981): 180–184; L. Garfinkel, "Time Trends in Lung Cancer Mortality Among Non-Smokers and a Note on Passive Smoking," *Journal of the National Cancer Institute,* 66 (6 [June 1981]): 1061–1066; A. L. Wright, C. Holberg, F. D. Martinez, and L. D. Taussig, "Relationship of Parental Smoking to Wheezing and

Non-wheezing Lower Respiratory Tract Illness in Infancy," Group Health Medical Associates, *Journal of Pediatrics* 118 (2 [February 1991]): 207–214; A. M. Ugnat, Y. Mao, A. B. Miller, and D. T. Wigle, "Effects of Residential Exposure to Environmental Tobacco Smoke on Canadian Children," *Canadian Journal of Public Health* 81 (5 [September-October 1990]): 345–349.

10. A. H. Wu-Williams and J. M. Samet, "Environmental Tobacco Smoke: Exposure-Response Relationship in Epidemiologic Studies," *Risk Analysis* 10 (1 [March 1990]): 39–48.

11. K. R. Warren and R. J. Bast, "Alcohol-related Birth Defects: An Update," *Public Health Reports* (Hyattsville) 103 (6 [November-December 1988]): 638–643.

12. See "My Baby... Strong and Healthy: Preventing Alcohol-Related Birth Defects," *Alcohol Health and Research World* 10 (1 [Fall 1985]), National Institute on Alcohol Abuse and Alcoholism; Anastasia Toufexis, "Innocent Victims," *Time* (13 May 1991); "Effects of Fetal Exposure to Cocaine and Heroin," *American Family Physician* 41 (5 [May 1990]); Office of Smoking and Health, *Health Consequences of Smoking for Women: A Report of the Surgeon General* (Washington, D.C.: U.S. Department of Health and Human Services, 1980); Committee to Study Prevention of Low Birthweight, *Preventing Low Birthweight* (Washington, D.C.: National Academy Press, 1985); K. Prager, H. Malin, C. Graves, et al., "Maternal Smoking and Drinking Behavior During Pregnancy," in *Health, United States* (Washington, D.C.: National Center for Health Statistics, 1983); Barbara A. Ray and Monique C. Brande, eds., *Women and Drugs: A New Era for Research*, NIDA Research Monograph 65 (Rockville, Md.: NIDA, 1986); NIDA, *National Household Survey on Drug Abuse: Population Estimates* (Rockville, Md.: NIDA, 1989).

13. Lois A. Fingerhut, Joel C. Kleinman, and Juliette S. Kendride, "Smoking Before, During, and After Pregnancy," *The American Journal of Public Health* 80 (5 [May 1990]): 541–545.

14. J. Gittler and M. McPherson, "Prenatal Substance Abuse," *Children Today* 19 (4 [July-August 1990]): 3–8.

15. W. Q. Sturner, K. G. Sweeney, R. T. Callery, and N. R. Haley, "Cocaine Babies: The Scourge of the '90s," *Journal of Forensic Sciences* 36 (1 [January 1991]): 34–39.

16. This ingenious approach was suggested by Stephen Goldsmith when he was the prosecutor for Marion County (Indianapolis), Indiana.

17. See, for example, the Illinois Juvenile Court Act, Ill. Rev. Stat., Ch. 37, Para. 802-3, section 2-3(1)(c) (1989). Other states, including Indiana, Nevada, Oklahoma, Minnesota, Florida, and Utah have passed similar laws, which consider maternal drug use during pregnancy as evidence of child abuse. See Kary Moss, "Recent Development: Substance Abuse During Pregnancy," *Harvard Women's Law Journal* 13 (Spring 1990): 278, 293.

18. Joseph B. Trester, "Plan Lets Addicted Mothers Take Their Newborns Home," *New York Times* (14 September 1991): p.1, c.5.

19. See Aaron Wildavsky, *Searching for Safety* (New Brunswick: Transaction Books, 1988).

20. See, for example, Robert Duncan Luce and Howard Raiffa, *Games and Decisions: Introduction and Critical Survey* (New York: John Wiley, 1957).

21. See J. D. Hammond and Arnold F. Shapiro, "AIDS and the Limits of Insurability," *Milbank Quarterly* 64, suppl. 1 (1986): 143–167.

22. See George A. Akerlof, "The Market for Lemons: Quality Uncertainty and the Market Mechanism," *Quarterly Journal of Economics* 84 (August 1970): 488–500. In addition, well-meaning legislators often try to forbid insurance premium discrimination by risk groups on the grounds of fairness. See Deborah A. Stone, "AIDS and the Moral Economy of Insurance," *The American Prospect* I (1 [Spring 1990]), for an argument against allowing insurers to charge higher life insurance premiums to those already infected with the AIDS virus. Attempts to write or enforce insurance contracts that would not cover, for example, losses related to drug use, would meet similar political and practical barriers.

23. Richard Zeckhauser, "Risk Spreading and Distribution," in *Redistribution through Public Choice,* Harold M. Hochman and George E. Peterson, eds. (New York: Columbia University Press, 1974), 206–228.

24. See Franklin Zimring, *The Changing Legal World of Adolescence* (New York: Free Press, 1982), 139–140.

25. Denise Kandel, Orta Simcha-Fagan, and Mark Davies, "Risk Factors for Delinquency and Illicit Drug Use From Adolescence to Young Adulthood," *Journal of Drug Issues* 16 (1 [Winter 1986]); D. H. Huizinga and D. S. Elliott, *A Longitudinal Study of Delinquency and Drug Use in a National Sample of Youth: An Assessment of Causal Order,* The National Youth Survey Project Report No. 16 (Boulder, Colo.: Behavioral Research Institute, 1981); D. Kandel and J. A. Logan, "Patterns of Drug Use from Adolescence to Early Adulthood—I. Periods of Risk for Initiation, Stabilization and Decline in Drug Use from Adolescence to Early Adulthood," *American Journal of Public Health* 71: 660–666; Nicholas J. Kozel and Edgar H. Adams, "Epidemiology of Drug Abuse: An Overview," *Science* 234 (21 November 1986): 970–974; Patrick H. Hughes and Gail A. Crawford, "A Contagious Disease Model for Researching and Intervening in Heroin Epidemics," *Archives of General Psychiatry* 27 (August 1972): 149–155.

26. J. H. Donnelly and J. M. Ivancevich, "A Methodology for Identifying Innovator Characteristics of New Brand Purchasers," *Journal of Marketing Research* 11 (August 1974): 331–334; J. Jacoby, "Personality and Innovation Proneness," *Journal of Marketing Research* 8 (May 1971): 244–247; J. W. Loy, Jr., "Social Psychological Characteristics of Innovators," *American Sociological Review* 34 (1 [February 1969]): 73–81; S. A. Baumgarten, "The Innovative Communicator in the Diffusion Process," *Journal of Marketing Research* 12 (February 1975): 12–18.

27. See the penetrating analysis of this approach in Dean R. Gerstein, "Alcohol Use and Consequences," in *Alcohol and Public Policy: Beyond the Shadow of Prohibition,* Mark H. Moore and Dean R. Gerstein, eds. (Washington, D.C.: National Academy Press, 1982), 188–195.

28. I owe this point to Mark Moore.

29. See Mark Moore, "Criminogenic Substances," in *Crime and Public Policy,* James Q. Wilson, ed. (San Francisco: ICS Press, 1983).

30. There is no consistently published time series on cocaine consumption, but few who follow such matters believe that the United States consumed as much as 20 tons of cocaine in 1979 or as little as 200 tons in 1989. Rates of predatory crime change more slowly; a tripling over a decade counts as a great crime wave. (Between 1965 and 1975, robberies and burglaries reported to the police did not quite triple.) See Katherine M. Jamieson and Timothy J. Flanagan, eds., *Sourcebook of Criminal Justice Statistics, 1988* (Washington, D.C.: Department of Justice, 1989), Table 3.115, p. 427. On the dynamics of criminal predation, see Phillip Cook, "The Demand and Supply of Criminal Opportunity," in *Crime and Justice: An Annual Review of Research,* Norval Morris and Michael Tonry, eds. (Chicago: University of Chicago Press, 1986). For the comparable dynamics of drug dealing, see Jonathan Caulkins, *The Distribution and Consumption of Illicit Drugs* (Cambridge, Mass.: Massachusetts Institute of Technology, unpublished doctoral dissertation, 1990), Ch. 7.

31. Paul J. Goldstein, "The Drug/ Violence Nexus: A Tripartite Conceptual Framework," *Journal of Drug Issues* (Fall 1985); P. A. Adler, *Wheeling and Dealing: An Ethnography of an Upper Level Dealing and Smuggling Community* (New York: Columbia University Press, 1985).

32. Mark A. R. Kleiman, "Drug Enforcement and Organized Crime," in *The Politics and Economics of Organized Crime,* Herbert Alexander and Gerald Caiden, eds. (Lexington, Mass.: Lexington Books, 1985).

33. George Kelling and James Q. Wilson, "Broken Windows: The Police and Neighborhood Safety," *Atlantic Monthly* (March 1982); George Kelling and James Wilson, "Making Neighborhoods Safe," *Atlantic Monthly* (February 1989); Wesley Skogan, *Disorder and Decline: Crime and the Spiral of Decay in American Neighborhoods* (New York: Free Press, 1990).

34. Sevgi O. Aral and King K. Holmes, "Epidemiology of Sexually Transmitted Diseases," in *Sexually Transmitted Diseases,* K. K. Holmes, et al., eds. (New York: McGraw-Hill, 1990). For a discussion of drug-related prostitution, see Dana E. Hunt, "Drugs and Consensual Crimes," *Drugs and Crime* Vol. 13, Michael Tonry and James Q. Wilson, eds. (Chicago: University of Chicago Press, 1990), 192–196. Peter Kerr, "Syphilis Cases Surge with Use of Crack, Raising AIDS Fears," *New York Times* (29 June 1988): p. B1, c. 2.

35. Robert J. Battjes and Roy W. Pickens, eds., *Needle Sharing Among Intravenous Drug Users: National and International Perspectives,* NIDA Research Monograph 80 (Rockville, Md.: NIDA, 1988).

36. Donald Des Jarlais and Saul Friedman, "HIV Infection Among Intravenous Drug Users: Epidemiology and Risk Reduction," *AIDS: International Bimonthly Journal* 1 (1987): 67–76.

37. See Mark A. R. Kleiman and Richard A. Mockler, "AIDS and Heroin: Strategies for Control" (Washington, D.C.: The Urban Institute, 1988). Enforcement might also increase infection rates if it led to higher prices and led users to share injection equipment as a way of sharing doses.

4
LAWS

1. Ps. 104:15.

2. The annual prevalence of inhalant use among high school seniors has more than doubled since 1976, to almost 7 percent. Lloyd D. Johnston, Jerald G. Bachman, and Patrick M. O'Malley, *Monitoring the Future: 1990* (Ann Arbor, Mich.: Institute for Social Research), Table 2 (preliminary data).

3. On adulterated drugs, see Margaret Kreig, *Black Market Medicine* (Englewood Cliffs, N.J.: Prentice-Hall, Inc., 1967) and Edward Brecher, *Licit and Illicit Drugs: The Consumers Report Guide to Narcotics* (Boston: Little, Brown, 1972).

4. John P. Morgan, "Prohibition Was—and Is—Bad For the Nation's Health," paper presented at the Hoover Institution Conference on U.S. Drug Policy, November 1990.

5. Norman Zinberg makes this point specifically about drug laws in *Drug, Set and Setting: The Basis for Controlled Intoxicant Use* (New Haven: Yale University Press, 1984). Joel Feinberg makes the argument in more general terms in *The Moral Limits of the Criminal Law* Vol. 3, *Harm To Self* (Oxford: Oxford University Press, 1986), 24.

6. Measuring price elasticity is complicated. See Philip J. Cook and George Tauchen, "The Effect of Liquor Taxes on Heavy Drinking," *Bell Journal of Economics* 13 (1982): 379–390; Henry Saffer and Michael Grossman, "Beer Taxes, The Legal Drinking Age, and Youth Motor Vehicle Fatalities," *Journal of Legal Studies* 16 (June 1987): 351–374; Gary S. Becker, Michael Grossman, and Kevin Murphy, "An Empirical Analysis of Cigarette Addiction," Working Paper No. 3322 (Cambridge, Mass.: National Bureau of Economic Research, 1990); George F. Brown and Lester Silverman, "Retail Price of Heroin: Estimation and Applications," *Journal of the American Statistical Association* 69 (347 [September 1974]). See the discussion of demand curves for drugs in David Boyum, *Reflections on Economic Theory and Drug Enforcement*, Ph.D. dissertation (Cambridge Mass.: Harvard University, forthcoming), Ch. 4.

7. Douglas R. Bohi and Mary Beth Zimmerman, "An Update on Econometric Studies of Energy Demand Behavior," *Annual Review of Energy*

9 (Palo Alto, Calif.: Annual Reviews, Inc., 1984); Carol A. Dahl, "Gasoline Demand Survey," *The Energy Journal* 7 (1 [January 1986]): 67–82; see *Federal Taxation of Tobacco, Alcoholic Beverages, and Motor Fuels,* Congressional Budget Office (Washington, D.C.: GPO, 1990), 74.

8. This principle was first worked out by A. C. Pigou, and economists call such levies "Pigouvian taxes." A. C. Pigou, *Wealth and Welfare* (London: Macmillan, 1912). See also R. H. Coase, "The Problem of Social Cost," *Journal of Law and Economics* (October 1960): 1–44, and William J. Baumol and Wallace E. Oates, *The Theory of Environmental Policy,* 2nd ed. (Cambridge: Cambridge University Press, 1988). For a very clear exposition of the application of such taxes to environmental management, see Larry E. Ruff, "The Economic Common Sense of Pollution," *The Public Interest* 19 (Spring 1970): 69–85. Lester Grinspoon has introduced Pigouvian taxation into the debate on drug regulation in "A Proposal for Regulation and Taxation of Drugs," *Nova Law Review* 11 (3 [Spring 1987]): 927–930. For an attempt to compute Pigouvian taxes for alcohol and tobacco see Willard G. Manning, Emmett B. Keeler, Joseph P. Newhouse, Elizabeth M. Sloss, and Jeffrey Wasserman, "The Taxes of Sin: Do Smokers and Drinkers Pay Their Way?" *Journal of the American Medical Association* 261 (11 [17 March 1989]): 1604–1609.

9. For a sample calculation see W. G. Manning, et al., "The Taxes of Sin: Do Smokers and Drinkers Pay Their Way?"

10. The 1937 Marijuana Tax Act was a prohibition in intention and in effect, although in legal form it was merely a very high tax.

11. Mary Williams Walsh, "Smoke Schemes: Some Would Rather Risk Arrest Than Pay Canada's Super Tax on Cigarettes; They Smuggle in Cheaper U.S. Tobacco in Kayaks, Frozen Turkeys, Car Seats..." *Los Angeles Times* (9 September 1991): p.1, c.2. Mary Williams Walsh, "Market Scene: U.S. Prices Are Definitely Right For Canadian Shoppers," *Los Angeles Times* (18 June 1991): p.2, c.1.

12. Marsha Rosenbaum, Jeanette Irwin, and Sheigla Murphy, "De Facto Destabilization as Policy: The Impact of Short-Term Methadone Maintenance," *Contemporary Drug Problems* 15 (4 [Winter 1988]): 491–517.

13. Congressional Budget Office, *Federal Taxation,* Tables 9, 10, pp.77–79.

14. U.S. Bureau of the Census, *Statistical Abstract of the United States: 1989* (Washington, D.C.: GPO, 1989), 268.

15. The *Value-Line Investment Survey* declares, "Cigarettes are probably the most profitable consumer product in the world...[whose manufacturers] enjoy incredible price flexibility." *The Value-Line Investment Survey Part 3: Ratings and Reports* (30 December 1988): 324–334.

16. Congressional Budget Office, *Federal Taxation,* pp. 81–86.

17. Thorstein Veblen, *The Theory of the Leisure Class* (New York: A. M. Kelly, 1899); John Kenneth Galbraith, *The Affluent Society* (Boston: Houghton Mifflin, 1958); Herbert Gintis, "Neoclassical Welfare Economics and

Individual Development," *Occasional Papers of the Union for Radical Political Economics* 3 (July 1970).

18. For an argument that advertising of rival cigarettes' claims to lower tar and nicotine helped decisively in spreading the message about the health hazards of tobacco, see Thomas C. Schelling, "Whose Business is Good Behavior?" in *American Society: Public and Private Responsibilities*, Winthrop Knowlton and Richard Zeckhauser, eds. (Cambridge, Mass.: Ballanger Publishing, 1986), 169–170; also see Schelling, "Addictive Drugs: The Cigarette Experience," unpublished manuscript, 1991. But note that these were not required warnings but competitive claims.

19. L. Schneider, B. Klein, and K. M. Murphy, "Government Regulation of Cigarette Health Information," *Journal of Law and Economics* 24 (December 1981): 575–612; Kenneth E. Warner, "Clearing the Airways: The Cigarette Ad-Ban Revisited," *Policy Analysis* 5 (4 [Fall 1979]): 435–450; J. L. Hamilton, "The Demand for Cigarette Advertising: The Health Scare and the Cigarette Advertising Ban," *Review of Economics and Statistics* 54 (November 1972): 401–411; Kenneth Warner, *Selling Smoke: Cigarette Advertising and Public Health* (Washington, D.C.: American Public Health Association, 1986). See Gideon Doron, *The Smoking Paradox: Public Regulation in the Cigarette Industry* (Cambridge, Mass.: Abt Books, 1979).

20. Joe Tye, "Buying Silence: Self-Censorship of Smoking and Health in National Newsweeklies," *Tobacco and Youth Reporter* 4 (1 [Spring 1989]).

21. See the issue of *Newsweek* for 6 June 1983.

22. See Gideon Doron, *The Smoking Paradox: Public Regulation in the Cigarette Industry* (Cambridge, Mass.: Abt Books, 1979), esp. 49–79.

23. Nason W. Russ and E. Scott Geller, "Training Bar Personnel to Prevent Drunken Driving: A Field Evaluation," *American Journal of Public Health* 77 (8 [August 1987]).

24. Jerome Jaffe, "Misinformation: Euphoria and Addiction," in *Advances in Pain Research and Therapy* Vol. 2, C. S. Hill and W. S. Fields, eds. (New York: Raven Press, 1989). John P. Morgan and David L. Pleet, "Opiophobia in the United States: The Undertreatment of Severe Pain," in *Society and Medication: Conflicting Signals for Prescribers and Patients*, John P. Morgan and Doreen V. Kagan, eds. (Lexington, Mass.: Lexington Books, 1983).

25. See, for example, Bruce Eisner, *Ecstasy: The MDMA Story* (Berkeley: Romin Publishing, Inc., 1989).

26. John P. Morgan and Doreen V. Kagan, eds., *Society and Medication: Conflicting Signals for Prescribers and Patients* (Lexington, Mass.: Lexington Books, 1983).

27. "Benzodiazepines: Prescribing Declines Under Triplicate Program," *Epidemiology Notes* 4 (12 [December 1989]).

28. Everett H. Ellinwood, "The Epidemiology of Stimulant Abuse," in *Drug Use: Epidemiology and Sociological Approaches*, Eric Josephson and Eleanor Carroll, eds. (Washington, D.C.: Hemisphere, 1974), 303–333.

29. D. E. Smith and D. R. Wesson, "Legitimate and Illegitimate Distribution of Amphetamines and Barbiturates," *Journal of Psychedelic Drugs* 5 (1972): 177–181; R. C. Smith, "Traffic in Amphetamines: Patterns of Illegal Manufacture and Distribution," *Journal of Psychedelic Drugs* 2 (1969): 20–24.

30. Eight of the twenty drugs most frequently mentioned in the Drug Abuse Warning Network (DAWN) emergency room system in 1988 were prescription drugs of abuse. More than 10 percent of all DAWN mentions were for tranquilizers. National Institute on Drug Abuse, *Annual Data: Data From The Drug Abuse Warning Network, Series I* (Rockville, Md.: Department of Health and Human Services, 1988), No. 8, Table 2.06A, p. 26.

31. Institute of Medicine, *Treating Drug Problems Vol. 1,* Dean Gerstein and Henrick Harwood, eds. (Washington, D.C.: National Academy of Science Press, 1990), 174–176; R. Resnick, "Methadone Detoxification from Illicit Opiates and Methadone Maintenance," *Research on the Treatment of Narcotic Addiction: State of the Art,* NIDA Treatment Research Monograph (Rockville, Md.: NIDA, 1983), 160–178; S. G. Cole, et al. "Inpatient vs. Outpatient Treatment of Alcohol and Drug Abusers," *American Journal of Drug and Alcohol Abuse* 8 (3 [1981]): 329–345; D. Novick, et al. "Medical Maintenance: A New Model for Continuing Treatment of Socially Rehabilitated Methadone Maintenance Patients," in *Problems of Drug Dependence 1988,* NIDA Research Monograph 90 (Rockville, Md.: Department of Health and Human Services, 1988), 168–176; Bill Landis, "Hooked: The Madness in Methadone Maintenance," *The Village Voice* (5 April 1989); J. C. Ball and A. Ross, *The Effectiveness of Methadone Maintenance Treatment* (New York: Springer-Verlag, 1991), 239–241.

32. M. Douglas Anglin and George Speckart, "Narcotics Use and Crime: A Multi-sample Multi-method Analysis," *Criminology* 26 (2 [May 1988]): 197–233; Bruce Johnson, "Once an Addict, Seldom an Addict," *Contemporary Drug Problems* 7 (1 [Spring 1978]): 48–49. See the discussion in John Kaplan, *The Hardest Drug: Heroin and Public Policy* (Chicago: University of Chicago Press, 1983), 34–38.

33. See Arnold Trebach, *The Heroin Solution* (New Haven: Yale University Press, 1982).

34. V. Dole and M. Nyswander, "Methadone Treatment for Diacetylmorphine (Heroin) Addiction," *Journal of the American Medical Association,* 193 (1985): 646.

35. James A. Inciardi, *Methadone Diversion: Experiences and Issues* (Rockville, Md.: National Institute on Drug Abuse, 1977). Edward Preble and Thomas Miller, "Methadone, Wine and Welfare," in *Street Ethnography: Selected Studies of Crime and Drug Use in Natural Settings,* Robert S. Weppner, ed. (Beverly Hills, Calif.: Sage Publications, 1977), 236.

36. Office of Smoking and Health, *Reducing the Health Consequences of Smoking: 25 Years of Progress. A Report to the Surgeon General* (CDC) 89-8411

(Washington, D.C.: Department of Health and Human Services, 1989), 304.

37. Preliminary data from Johnston, O'Malley, and Bachman, *Monitoring the Future 1990*, Table 9.

38. Joseph R. DiFranza and Joe B. Tye, "Who Profits From Tobacco Sales to Children?" *Journal of the American Medical Association* 263 (20 [23/30 May 1990]). D. G. Altman, V. Foster, L. Rasenick-Douss, and J. B. Tye, "Reducing the Illegal Sale of Cigarettes to Minors," *Journal of the American Medical Association* 261 (1989): 80–83. K. C. Hoppock and T. P. Houston, "Availability of Tobacco Products To Minors," *Journal of Family Practice* 30 (1990): 174–176.

39. For the general problem of the leakage privileges from adults to minors, see Franklin Zimring, *The Changing Legal World of Adolescence* (New York: Free Press, 1982).

40. A steady 80 to 90 percent of high school seniors report that marijuana is easy to get. Lloyd D. Johnston, et al. *Drug Use, Smoking: National Survey Results from High School, College, and Young Adult Populations, 1975–1987* (Washington, D.C.: National Institute on Drug Abuse, 1989): 163–164.

41. See Richard Wilmot and Timothy M. Ryan, "The Drug License," in *Drug Policy 1989–1990: A Reformer's Catalogue,* Arnold S. Trebach and Kevin B. Zeese, eds. (Washington, D.C.: Drug Policy Foundation, 1989).

42. Unfortunately, such a system would be likely to selectively discourage the most moderate drug users, for whom the price per drink of a drinker's license might easily seem excessive. Given the sort of quantity-limit system discussed below, this problem could be finessed by allowing users to choose a minimal-quantity license (two drinks per week, for example).

43. Mark A. R. Kleiman and Aaron Saiger, "Drug Legalization: The Importance of Asking the Right Question," *Hofstra Law Review* 18 (2 [Spring 1991]).

44. This argument is most concisely made in Brecher, *Licit and Illicit Drugs: The Consumers Report Guide to Narcotics,* pp. 215–216. See also John P. Morgan, "Prohibition Was—and Is—Bad for the Nation's Health."

45. Jeffrey Miron and Jeffrey Zwiebel, *Alcohol Consumption During Prohibition* (Cambridge, Mass.: National Bureau of Economic Research, March 1991). Mark Moore and Daniel Gerstein, eds., *Alcohol and Public Policy: Beyond the Shadow of Prohibition* (Washington, D.C.: National Academy Press, 1981).

46. Morgan, "Prohibition Was—and Is—Bad for the Nation's Health," makes a polemical but carefully reasoned attempt to arrive at such a judgment.

47. See Mark Thornton, "Alcohol Prohibition was a Failure," *Policy Analysis* (157 [17 July 1991]), and the critique of Thornton by Patrick Burns, *Alcohol Prohibition and the Misuse of History* (Washington, D.C.: American Alliance for Rights and Responsibilities, 1991).

48. *Marijuana: A Signal of Misunderstanding,* First Report of the National Commission on Marijuana and Drug Abuse (Washington, D.C.:

GPO, 1972); Commission for Behavioral and Social Sciences, *Analysis of Marijuana Policy* (Washington, D.C.: National Academy Press, 1982).

49. See Mark A. R. Kleiman, *Marijuana: Costs of Abuse, Costs of Control* (New York: Greenwood Press, 1989), 163–178.

5
THE MARKETS FOR ILLICIT DRUGS

1. Mark H. Moore, "Supply Reduction and Drug Law Enforcement," in *Drugs and Crime*, Michael Tonry and James Q. Wilson, eds. (Chicago: University of Chicago Press, 1990), 109–158.

2. A tobacco cigarette costs about a dime (of which about two cents is tax). A teabag can be had for less than a nickel. The marijuana in a 0.4 gram joint now sells for $2 to $4. For an estimate of the price of a marijuana cigarette in 1985, see Mark A. R. Kleiman, *Marijuana: Costs of Abuse, Costs of Control* (New York: Greenwood Press, 1989), 43; for the increase in retail marijuana prices since then, see the NNICC reports for 1987 (p. 9) and 1990 (p. 30). National Narcotics Intelligence Consumers Committee, *The NNICC Report: The Supply of Illicit Drugs to the United States* (Washington, D.C.: Drug Enforcement Administration, 1988, 1991).

3. In September 1989, the New York State Division of Substance Abuse Services reported that the illicit "street" price of diazepam (Valium) was between $4.50 and $6.00, compared to a pharmacy price of approximately 20 cents. New York State Department of Health, *Epidemiology Notes* 5 (1 [January 1990]): 8.

4. Convention on Psychotropic Substances, signed at Vienna, Austria (21 Feb. 1971); Controlled Substances Act, 21 U.S.C. Sections 801 *et seq.*

5. See Paul Aaron and David Musto, "Temperance and Prohibition in America: A Historical Overview," in *Alcohol and Public Policy: Beyond the Shadow of the Prohibition*, Mark H. Moore and Dean Gerstein, eds. (Washington, D.C.: National Academy Press, 1981), 164–165; but compare John P. Morgan, "Prohibition Was—and Is—Bad for the Nation's Health," paper presented at the Hoover Institute Conference on U.S. Drug Policy (November 1990).

6. Zachary Tumin, "Summary of the Proceedings: Findings and Discoveries of the Harvard University Executive Session for State and Local Prosecutors, 1986–1990" (Cambridge, Mass.: Program in Criminal Justice Policy and Management, Kennedy School of Government, Harvard University, 1990), 11–14. Mark H. Moore and Mark A. R. Kleiman, "The Police and Drugs," *Perspectives on Policing* (11 [September 1989]).

7. Mark H. Moore, "Criminogenic Commodities," in *Crime and Public Policy*, James Q. Wilson, ed. (San Francisco: ICS Press, 1983); George Kelling

and James Q. Wilson, "Broken Windows: The Police and Neighborhood Safety," *The Atlantic Monthly* (March 1982).

8. George F. Brown and Lester Silverman, "Retail Price of Heroin: Estimations and Applications," *Journal of the American Statistical Association* 69 (347 [September 1974]).

9. For 1982, Abt Associates estimated that the retail value of the markets for heroin, cocaine, and marijuana totaled $22 billion, the prostitution market $11.6 billion, and the illicit gambling markets $2.4 billion. Abt Associates, *Unreported Taxable Income for Selected Illegal Activities* (Cambridge, Mass.: Abt Associates, 1984), Table 2.20, p. 62; Table 4.9, p. 145; Table 3.16, p. 108; see also U.S. Internal Revenue Service, *Income Tax Compliance Research: Estimates for 1973–1981* (Washington, D.C.: GPO, 1983), 39.

10. Peter Reuter and Mark A. R. Kleiman, "Risks and Prices: An Economic Analysis of Drug Enforcement," in *Crime and Justice: An Annual Review of Research* Vol. 7, Norval Morris and Michael Tonry, eds. (Chicago: University of Chicago Press, 1986), pp. 301–306.

11. Peter Reuter, Robert MacCoun, and Patrick Murphy, "Money from Crime: A Study of the Economics of Drug Dealing in Washington, D.C.," R-3894-RF (Washington, D.C.: RAND Corporation, 1990).

12. National Narcotics Intelligence Consumers Committee. *The NNICC Report 1982* (Washington, D.C.: Drug Enforcement Administration, 1982), 45.

13. Drug Enforcement Administration, "From the Source to the Street," *Intelligence Trends* (Washington, D.C.: Dept. of Justice, 1990) Vol. 17, No. 1.

14. NNICC, 1980, p. 49; NNICC, 1984, p. 24; NNICC, 1988, p. 32; NNICC, 1990, p. 1. These numbers are of uncertain origin and should not be relied on too greatly.

15. Paul Goldstein, Douglas S. Lipton, Edward Preble, Ira Sobel, Tom Miller, William Abbott, William Paige, and Franklin Soto, "The Marketing of Street Heroin in New York City," *Journal of Drug Issues* (Summer 1984): 553–566.

16. In the film *Atlantic City*.

17. Oliver E. Williamson, *Markets and Hierarchies: Analysis and Antitrust Implications* (New York: The Free Press, 1975) points out that such effects are also significant in many legitimate markets. For the reasons given in the text, they are more significant in illicit drug transactions.

18. Joe Davidson, "How a 24-Year-Old Reigned as Local Hero Until His Drug Arrest," *Wall Street Journal* (13 November 1989).

19. Robert Stutman told me this when he was Special Agent in charge of the Drug Enforcement Administration, New York Field Office. I have not been able to confirm it from a published source, but it is widely believed among law enforcement agencies.

20. See Mark A. R. Kleiman, "Compliance and Enforcement in a Binary-Choice Framework," in *Modelling Drug Markets* (Cambridge Mass.: Program in Criminal Justice Policy and Management, Kennedy School of Government, Harvard University, 1991). Reuter and Kleiman, "Risks and Prices."

21. Mark H. Moore, "Policies to Achieve Discrimination in the Effective Price of Heroin," *American Economic Review* 63 (May 1973): 270–279.

22. This was once cited to me as an old police adage. I have been unable to trace its origin, and few of the police officers I have met had in fact heard it.

23. For heroin, see Bruce Johnson, Paul Goldstein, Edward Preble, James Schmeidler, Douglas Lipton, Barry Spunt, and Thomas Miller, *Taking Care of Business* (Lexington, Mass.: D. C. Heath and Co., 1985), Table B-2, p. 225; heavy heroin users bought the drug on two-thirds of the days on which they used it. Some of the other use-days presumably involved drugs received not for money but by theft, trade, or gift; see Table B-5. This leaves very little room for inventory holding. Bruce Johnson of Narcotic and Drug Research, Inc., who has been interviewing drug users about their economic behavior, confirms that this is still true among heroin users and even more so for crack users.

24. Bruce Johnson reports that the consignment-sale system is no longer in use for crack dealing in New York, largely for this reason.

25. Mark H. Moore, *Buy and Bust: The Effective Regulation of an Illicit Market in Heroin* (Lexington, Mass.: Lexington Books, 1977), 96–105; Reuter and Kleiman, "Risks and Prices," pp. 292–295; Drug Enforcement Administration, "From the Source to the Street," *Intelligence Trends* (Washington, D.C.: Department of Justice 1987), Vol. 14, No. 3: 2–3, 6–7.

26. See *Principals and Agents: The Structure of Business*, Richard J. Zeckhauser and John W. Pratt, eds. (Boston: Harvard Business School Press, 1985).

27. Thomas Hobbes, *Leviathan*, Ch. 13.

28. Peter Reuter, *Disorganized Crime: The Economics of the Visible Hand* (Cambridge, Mass.: MIT Press, 1983).

29. See Barbara A. Ray, *Learning Factors in Substance Abuse*, NIDA Research Monograph 84 (Rockville, Md.: National Institute on Drug Abuse, 1988). Harriet de Wit, "Reinforcing and Subjective Effects of Diazepam in Non-Drug-Using Volunteers," *Pharmacology, Biochemistry, and Behavior* 33 (1989): 205–213.

30. D. H. Huizinga and D. S. Elliott, "A Longitudinal Study of Delinquency and Drug Use in a National Sample of Youth: An Assessment of Causal Order," *The National Youth Survey Project*, Report No. 16 (Boulder, Colo.: Behavioral Research Institute, 1981). Denise Kandel, Orta Simcha-Fagan, and Mark Davies, "Risk Factors for Delinquency and Illicit Drug Use From Adolescence to Young Adulthood," *Journal of Drug Issues* 16 (1 [Winter 1986]).

31. Kenneth E. Warner, "Smoking and Health Implications of a Change in the Federal Cigarette Excise Tax," *Journal of the American Medical Association* 255 (1986): 1028–1032.

32. Moore, *Buy and Bust*, p. 8; Richard Brotman and Alfred M. Freedman, *Continuities and Discontinuities in the Process of Patient Care for Narcotics Addicts* (New York: New York Medical College, 1965), 73. M. Douglas Anglin and George Speckart, "Narcotics Use and Crime: A Multi-sample Multi-method Analysis," *Criminology* 26 (2 [May 1988]): 197–233; John Kaplan, *The Hardest Drug: Heroin and Public Policy* (Chicago: University of Chicago Press, 1983). Bruce Johnson, "Once an Addict, Seldom an Addict," *Contemporary Drug Problems* 7 (1 [Spring 1978]): 197–233. F. L. Iber, *Alcohol and Drug Abuse as Encountered in Office Practice* (Boca Raton, Fla.: CRC, 1991).

33. Mark H. Moore, "An Analytic View of Drug Control Policies," Working Paper (Cambridge, Mass.: Program in Criminal Justice, Kennedy School of Government, Harvard University, 1990).

34. Gary S. Becker, Michael Grossman, and Kevin M. Murphy, "Rational Addiction and the Effect of Price on Consumption," AEA Papers and Proceedings, *American Economic Review* 81 (2 [May 1991]): 237–241.

35. Gary S. Becker and Kevin M. Murphy, "A Theory of Rational Addiction," *Journal of Political Economy* 96 (4 [1988]).

36. See Karyn Model, "The Effect of Marijuana Decriminalization on Hospital Emergency Room Drug Episodes: 1975–1978" (Cambridge, Mass.: Department of Economics, Harvard University, 1991).

37. Reuter and Kleiman, "Risks and Prices."

38. Kleiman, *Marijuana*, pp. 77–82; John DiNardo, "Are Marijuana and Alcohol Substitutes? The Effect of State Drinking Age Laws on the Marijuana Consumption of High School Seniors" (Santa Monica, Calif.: RAND Corporation, 1991) (unpublished).

39. Gerald Godshaw, Ross Koppel, and Russell Pancoast, *Anti-Drug Law Enforcement Efforts and Their Impact*, prepared by Wharton Econometrics (Bala Cynwyd, Penn.) for the U.S. Customs Service, Department of the Treasury (Washington, D.C.: GPO, 1987). Peter Reuter, "Quantity Illusions and Paradoxes of Drug Interdiction: Federal Intervention into Vice Policy," *Law and Contemporary Problems* (Winter, 1988).

40. Peter Reuter, Gordon Crawford, and Jonathan Cave, *Sealing the Borders: The Effects of Increased Military Participation in Drug Interdiction* (Santa Monica, Calif.: RAND Corporation, 1988). Peter Reuter, "Quantity Illusions and Paradoxes of Drug Interdiction: Federal Intervention into Vice Policy."

41. Drug Enforcement Administration, "From the Source to the Street."

42. William Rhoads and Douglas McDonald, "What America's Users Spend on Illegal Drugs" (Washington, D.C.: Office of National Drug Control Policy, June 1991).

43. Ibid.

44. Donald Putnam Henry, "The Effects of Interdiction on Drug Exports," in *Sealing the Borders*, Reuter, et al., Appendix A, pp. 133–141.

45. Jonathan P. Caulkins, *Distribution and Consumption of Illicit Drugs: Some Mathematical Models and Their Policy Implications*, Ph.D. dissertation (Cambridge, Mass.: Massachusetts Institute of Technology, 1990), pp. 105–117.

46. Caulkins, *Distribution and Consumption of Illicit Drugs*; Kleiman, "Overview," in *Modelling Drug Markets*, Ch. 3. David Boyum has developed an alternative model with similar implications. See David Boyum, *Reflections on Economic Theory and Drug Enforcement*, Ph.D. dissertation (Cambridge, Mass.: Harvard University, forthcoming 1991), Ch 2.

47. Kleiman, "Compliance and Enforcement in a Binary-Choice Framework."

48. Mark A. R. Kleiman, "The Changing Face of Cocaine," Working Paper 87-01-07 (Cambridge, Mass.: Program in Criminal Justice Policy and Management, Kennedy School of Government, Harvard University, January 1987). See also Kleiman, *Marijuana*, Ch. 4.

49. George Stigler and Gary Becker, "De Gustibus non est Disputandum," *American Economic Review* 67 (March 1977): 76–90.

50. Mark Moore, "Policies to Achieve Discrimination in the Effective Price of Heroin"; Kleiman and Smith, "State and Local Drug Enforcement: In Search of a Strategy" (Cambridge, Mass.: BOTEC Analysis Corporation); "Drug Abuse in Jackson County, Missouri: Problem Assessment and Recommendations" (Cambridge: BOTEC Analysis Corporation, 1990). Patrick Burns and Roger Conner, *The Winnable War: A Community Guide to Eradicating Street Drug Markets* (Washington, D.C.: American Alliance for Rights and Responsibilities, 1991).

51. Lynn Zimmer, "Operation Pressure Point: The Disruption of Street-Level Drug Trade in New York's Lower East Side" (New York: New York University School of Law, Center for Research in Crime and Justice, 1987). Mark A. R. Kleiman, "Crackdowns: The Effects of Intensive Enforcement of Retail Heroin Dealing," in *Street Level Enforcement: Examining the Issues*, Marcia R. Chaiken, ed. *Issues and Practices in Criminal Justice* (Washington, D.C.: National Institute of Justice, 1988).

52. Moore, "Policies to Achieve Discrimination in the Effective Price of Heroin"; Kleiman, "Crackdowns"; Kleiman and Smith, "State and Local Drug Enforcement"; BOTEC Analysis Corporation, "Drug Abuse in Jackson County."

53. Kleiman, "Crackdowns"; Kleiman and Smith, "State and Local Drug Enforcement"; BOTEC Analysis Corporation, "Drug Abuse in Jackson County"; Caulkins, *Distribution and Consumption of Illicit Drugs*, Ch. 4; Kleiman, "Compliance and Enforcement in a Binary-Choice Framework."

54. Mark A. R. Kleiman and Rebecca M. Young, "The Factors of Production in Retail Drug Dealing," in *Modelling Drug Markets*.
55. Patrick Burns and Roger Conner, *The Winnable War.*
56. On the system-jamming potential of retail drug cases, see Aric Press, "Piecing Together the System: The Response to Crack" (New York: New York Bar Association, 1987). For alternative approaches, see BOTEC Analysis Corporation, "Drug Abuse in Jackson County."

6
ENFORCEMENT

1. Mark H. Moore, *Buy and Bust: The Effective Regulation of an Illicit Market in Heroin* (Lexington, Mass.: Lexington Books, 1977).
2. This point is argued in Mark A. R. Kleiman, *Marijuana: Costs of Abuse, Costs of Control* (New York: Greenwood Press, 1989).
3. Bureau of International Narcotics Matters, *International Narcotics Control Strategy Report—March 1991* (Washington, D.C.: Department of State, March 1991), 13–20, 43–44. See also Bureau of Public Affairs, *International Drug Problems and U.S. Foreign Policy* (Washington, D.C.: State Department, 1988), 9–10.
4. Ethan A. Nadelmann, "The International Drug Problem and U.S. Government Policies," Working Paper, Program in Criminal Justice Policy and Management, Kennedy School of Government, Harvard University, 1987, 32–39; Bradley Graham, "Drug Raids Raise Doubts in Bolivia: Role of U.S. Troops Triggers Concerns," *Washington Post* (21 July 1986): 1.
5. See "U.S.-Mexico Opium, Poppy and Marijuana Aerial Eradication Program: Statement of Joseph Kelly," General Accounting Office, 1987. Testimony to Select Committee on Narcotic Abuse and Control, House of Representatives.
6. Guy Gugliotta and Jeff Leen, *Kings of Cocaine: Inside the Medellín Cartel* (New York: Simon and Schuster, 1989); William Long, "Colombia's Censorship by Terror: Drug Cartels Assassinate Journalists," *Los Angeles Times* (7 July 1990); James Brooks, "Drug Traffickers in Colombia Start a Counterattack: Declare 'Absolute War': Political Offices are Bombed—Violence, Centered in Cartel Base, Medellín," *New York Times* (25 August 1989); Jill Smolowe, "The Drug Thugs: Narcotic Traffickers Are Muscling In on Legitimate Governments," *Time* (7 March 1988): 28–37.
7. Peter Reuter, "Eternal Hope: America's International Drug Control Efforts," *The Public Interest* (Spring 1985).
8. Michael Wires, "Influx of Cocaine in U.S. Has Slowed, Drug Officials Say: Colombia Assault Cited," *New York Times* (9 September 1989). See

National Narcotics Intelligence Consumers Committee, *The NNICC Report 1990: The Supply of Illicit Drugs to the United States* (Washington, D.C.: Drug Enforcement Agency, 1991), 1.

9. National Narcotics Intelligence Consumers Committee, *The NNICC Report 1990*, pp. 7–8; Bureau of International Narcotics Matters, *International Narcotics Control Strategy Report 1991* (Washington, D.C.: U.S. Department of State, 1991), 95–103.

10. Kleiman, *Marijuana*, p. 73.

11. Gerald Godshaw, Ross Koppel, and Russel Pancoast, *Anti-Drug Law Enforcement Efforts and Their Impact*, prepared for U.S. Customs Service, Department of the Treasury (Washington, D.C.: GPO, 1987) gives mathematical form to the argument for the interdiction efforts. Peter Reuter, "Quantity Illusions and Paradoxes of Drug Interdiction: Federal Intervention into Vice Policy," *Law and Contemporary Problems* (Winter 1988) offers a critique.

12. Reuter, "Quantity Illusions and Paradoxes of Drug Interdiction."

13. Donald Putnam Henry, "The Effects of Interdiction on Drug Exports," in Reuter, et al., *Sealing the Borders: The Effects of Increased Military Participation in Drug Interdiction* (Santa Monica, Calif.: The RAND Corp., 1988): Appendix A, 133–141.

14. Drug Enforcement Administration, "From the Source to the Street," *Intelligence Trends* (Washington, D.C.: DEA, 1990), Vol. 17, No. 1.

15. Godshaw, Koppel, and Pancoast, *Anti-Drug Law Enforcement Efforts and Their Impact*.

16. Bureau of Justice Statistics, *Sourcebook of Criminal Justice Statistics—1989* (Washington, D.C.: Department of Justice, 1990), 584, Table 6.45.

17. Ibid., Tables 6.45, 6.58 (p. 601), 6.51 (p. 591).

18. Mark A. R. Kleiman and Kerry D. Smith, "State and Local Drug Enforcement: In Search of a Strategy," in *Crime and Justice: An Annual Review of Research*, Vol. 7, Norval Morris and Michael Tonry, eds. (Chicago: University of Chicago Press, 1986); Peter K. Manning, *The Narcs' Game: Organizational and Informational Limits on Drug Law Enforcement* (Cambridge, Mass.: MIT Press, 1980).

19. Drug Enforcement Agency, "From the Source to the Street: Current Prices for Cannabis, Cocaine, and Heroin," in *Intelligence Trends* (Washington, D.C.: Department of Justice, 1987), Vol. 14, No. 3; Moore, *Buy and Bust*, Table 2-17, pp. 108–109. Peter Reuter and Mark A. R. Kleiman, "Risks and Prices: An Economic Analysis of Drug Enforcement," in *Crime and Justice: An Annual Review of Research*, Norval Morris and Michael Tonry, eds. (Chicago: University of Chicago Press, 1986).

20. Jonathan P. Caulkins, *The Distribution and Consumption of Illicit Drugs; Mathematical Models and Their Policy Implications*, Ph.D. dissertation (Cambridge, Mass.: Massachusetts Institute of Technology, May 1990), Ch. 3.

21. Ibid.

22. Mark A. R. Kleiman, *Marijuana,* Ch. 4. Kleiman, "Overview," in *Modelling Drug Markets* (Cambridge, Mass.: Program in Criminal Justice Policy Management, Kennedy School of Government, Harvard University, 1991).

23. See Aric Press, "Piecing Together New York's Criminal Justice System: The Response to Crack" (New York: New York Bar Association, 1987).

24. Thomas Schelling, "What is the Business of Organized Crime?" in Schelling, *Choice and Consequence* (Cambridge, Mass.: Harvard University Press, 1984), 194.

25. Office of National Drug Control Policy, *What America's Users Spend on Illegal Drugs* (Washington, D.C.: Office of National Drug Control Policy, 1991), 40.

26. 31 C.F.R. Sections 103.11, 103.21, 103.22, and 103.26 govern the reporting of cash transactions of over $10,000.00; 31 U.S.C. Sections 5322 *et seq.* prohibit the structuring of financial transactions to evade the reporting requirements.

27. See, for instance, 21 U.S.C. SS841(b)(1)(A), (B).

28. 21 U.S.C. Section 848.

29. 21 U.S.C. Section 841(b)(1)(A)(ii).

30. See Linda Greenhouse, "Mandatory Life Term is Upheld in Drug Cases," *New York Times* (28 June 1991): A12, c. 5.

31. Kleiman and Smith, "State and Local Drug Enforcement," p. 98.

32. See for example, Mark A. R. Kleiman, Mary Ellen Lawrence, and Aaron Saiger, "A Drug Enforcement Program for Santa Cruz County" (Cambridge, Mass.: BOTEC Analysis Corporation, 1987), and BOTEC Analysis Corporation, "Drug Abuse in Jackson County, Missouri: Problem Assessment and Recommendations" (Cambridge, Mass.: BOTEC Analysis Corporation, 1990).

33. For a list of practical suggestions, see Patrick Burns and Roger Connor, *The Winnable War: A Community Guide to Eradicating Street Drug Markets* (Washington, D.C.: American Alliance for Rights and Responsibilities, 1991). For applications to a specific market, see BOTEC Analysis Corporation, "Drug Abuse in Jackson County, Missouri." For a theoretical exploration, see Mark A. R. Kleiman and Rebecca Young, "Factors of Production in Retail Drug Dealing," in *Modelling Drug Markets.*

34. See Lewis H. Spence, "Low Income Public Housing: 'Safe Havens?'" Working Paper (Cambridge, Mass.: Program in Criminal Justice Policy and Management, Kennedy School of Government, Harvard University, January 1989).

35. Saul N. Weingart, Francis X. Hartmann, Rebecca M. Young, and David Osborne of Harvard University have assembled substantial information, as yet unpublished, about such volunteer efforts.

36. Malcolm Sparrow, Mark H. Moore, and David Kennedy, *Beyond 911: A New Era for Policing* (New York: Basic Books, 1990); Herman Goldstein, *Problem-Oriented Policing* (Philadelphia: Temple University Press, 1990);

George L. Kelling, "Police and Communities: The Quiet Revolution," *Perspectives on Policing* 1 (National Institute of Justice, June 1988); Malcolm K. Sparrow, "Implementing Community Policing," *Perspectives on Policing* 9 (National Institute of Justice, November 1988); Lee P. Brown, "Community Policing: A Practical Guide for Police Officials," *Perspectives on Policing* 12 (National Institute of Justice, September 1989).

37. David M. Kennedy, "Closing the Market: Controlling the Drug Trade in Tampa, Florida" (Washington, D.C.: National Institute of Justice, forthcoming).

38. This tactic is now being tried in Inkster, Michigan, by the Wayne County Sheriff's Department.

39. Joan Petersilia, "When Probation Becomes More Dreaded Than Prison," *Federal Probation* 54 (1 [1990]), and Joan Petersilia and Susan Turner, *Intensive Supervision for High-Risk Probationers* (Santa Monica, Calif.: RAND Corporation, 1990).

40. See Fred Martens, "Narcotics Enforcement: What Are the Goals and Do They Conflict?" Paper prepared for the Organized Crime Narcotic Enforcement Symposium, Villanova University, 1988.

41. Thomas Schelling, "What is the Business of Organized Crime?"; James B. Buchanan, "A Defense of Organized Crime," in *The Economics of Crime and Punishment,* Simon Rottenberg, ed. (Washington, D.C.: American Enterprise Institute, 1973).

42. Peter Reuter, "The Value of a Bad Reputation: Cartels, Criminals, and Barriers to Entry" (Santa Monica, Calif.: RAND Corporation, 1982).

43. Jonathan Cave and Peter Reuter, *The Interdictor's Lot: A Dynamic Model of the Market for Drug Smuggling Services* (Santa Monica, Calif.: RAND Corporation, 1988).

44. For examples of this argument, see Anthony Bouza, "Evaluating Street-Level Drug Enforcement," in *Street-Level Drug Enforcement: Examining the Issues,* Marcia R. Chaiken, ed. (Washington, D.C.: National Institute of Justice, 1988); Michael Tonry, "Public Prosecution and Hydro-Engineering," *Minnesota Law Review* 75 (3 [February 1991]): 971–992. For a careful analysis, see Robert Barr and Ken Pease, "Crime Placement, Displacement, and Deflection," in *Crime and Justice: An Annual Review of Research* Vol. 12, Michael Tonry and Norval Morris, eds. (Chicago: University of Chicago Press, 1990).

45. Peter Reuter, Robert MacCoun, and Patrick Murphy, *Money from Crime: A Study of the Economics of Drug Dealing in Washington, D.C.* (Santa Monica, Calif.: RAND Corporation, 1990), 156.

46. Mark A. R. Kleiman, Kerry D. Smith, Richard A. Rogers, and David P. Cavanagh, "Imprisonment-To-Offense Ratios." Discussion paper prepared for Bureau of Justice Statistics (November 15, 1988).

47. See James Q. Wilson and Richard J. Herrnstein, *Crime and Human Nature* (New York: Simon and Schuster, 1985), 148–172.

48. Bureau of Justice Statistics, *Sourcebook of Criminal Justice Statistics—1988* (Washington, D.C.: Department of Justice, 1989), 489–493.
49. Jan M. Chaiken and Marcia R. Chaiken, *Varieties of Criminal Behavior* (Santa Monica, Calif.: RAND Corporation, 1982); P. Greenwood and A. Abrahamse, "Selective Incapacitation," Report R-2815-NIJ (Santa Monica, Calif.: RAND Corporation, 1982).
50. On this point, see Phillip J. Cook, "The Demand and Supply of Criminal Opportunities," in *Crime and Justice: An Annual Review of Research*, Norval Morris and Michael Tonry, eds. (Chicago: University of Chicago Press, 1986).
51. These are my calculations based on figures given in Reuter, MacCoun, and Murphy, *Money from Crime*. All of these are averages and may not represent the career of any given dealer.
52. Ibid., p. 58.
53. Ibid., pp. 62–66.
54. For an explanation of why dealers' wages do not fall to "clear" the labor market, see Caulkins, *The Distribution and Consumption of Illicit Drugs*, Ch. 3, pp. 92–94.
55. Office of Criminal Justice Plans and Analysis, *Criminal Justice Report for the District of Columbia* (Washington, D.C.: Department of Justice, 1990), 16.
56. Ibid. In the District of Columbia drug dealing cases made up fewer than half of all arrests in 1990, for the first time in five years.
57. Bureau of Justice Statistics, *Sourcebook of Criminal Justice Statistics—1988* (Washington, D.C.: Department of Justice, 1989), 2.
58. Office of Management and Budget, *Budget of the U.S. Government, FY 1989;* Bureau of the Census, *Statistical Abstract of the U.S.—1989* (Washington, D.C.: Department of Commerce, 1989); *Economic Report of the President: 1990* (Washington, D.C.: GPO, 1990); Office of Research and Demonstrations, *Health Care Financing Review* II (2 [Winter 1990]): 17.
59. For the general argument, see Donald Black, *The Behavior of Law* (Orlando, Fla.: Academic Press, 1976), and Donald Black, *Sociological Justice* (New York: Oxford University Press, 1989). For an application to race in the United States, see Randall Kennedy, "McCleskey v. Kemp: Race, Capital Punishment and the Supreme Court," *Harvard Law Review* 101 (7 [May 1988]): 1388–1443.
60. See James K. Stewart, "The Urban Strangler: How Crime Causes Poverty in the Inner City," *Policy Review* 37 (Summer 1986): 6–10.
61. Andrew Hacker, "Black Crime, White Racism," *New York Review of Books* 35 (3 [March, 1988]).
62. *Serrano vs. Priest*—96 Cal. Rptr. 601 (1971).
63. Bureau of Justice Statistics, *Sourcebook of Criminal Justice Statistics—1989* (Washington, D.C.: Department of Justice), Table 2.27, pp. 146–147; Table 2.31, pp. 152–153.
64. Bureau of Justice Statistics, *Sourcebook of Criminal Justice Statistics—1988*, p. 2.

65. See M. Douglas Anglin and George Speckart, "Narcotics Use and Crime: A Multi-sample Multi-method Analysis," *Criminology* 26 (2 [May 1988]): 197–233.

66. George F. Brown and Lester P. Silverman, "The Retail Price of Heroin: Estimation and Applications," *Journal of the American Statistical Association* 69 (September 1974): 595–606.

67. For the general analysis of the problem, see Thomas C. Schelling, "What is the Business of Organized Crime?" For an application to local drug dealing, see Fred Martens, "Narcotics Enforcement: What Are the Goals and Do They Conflict?" Paper prepared for the Organized Crime Narcotic Enforcement Symposium, Villanova University, 1988; Kleiman, *Marijuana,* p. 24, makes the same argument about Federal marijuana enforcement. See also Mark A. R. Kleiman, "Drug Enforcement and Organized Crime," in *The Politics and Economics of Organized Crime,* Herbert Alexander and Gerald Caiden, eds. (Lexington, Mass.: Lexington Books, 1985).

68. See Larry Sherman, "Police Crackdowns and Residual Deterrence," in *Crime and Justice: A Review of Research* Vol. 12, Michael Tonry and Norval Morris, eds. (Chicago: University of Chicago Press, 1990); H. Lawrence Ross, "Law, Science and Accidents: The British Road Safety Act of 1967," *Journal of Legal Studies* 2 (1 [1973]): 1–78.

69. For a discussion of crime control, see James Q. Wilson and Richard J. Herrnstein, *Crime and Human Nature* (New York: Simon and Schuster, 1985), 397–401.

70. Median times-to-deposition for felonies run more than 100 days in most U.S. jurisdictions, *Sourcebook of Criminal Justice Statistics—1989,* Table 5.39, p. 518.

7
PERSUASION, HELP, AND CONTROL

1. See, for instance, Mary Ann Pentz, James H. Dwyer, David P. MacKinnon, Brian R. Flay, William B. Hansen, Eric Yu I. Wang, and C. Anderson Johnson, "A Multicommunity Trial for Primary Prevention of Adolescent Drug Abuse," *Journal of the American Medical Association* 261 (22 [June 9, 1989]): 3259–3266.

2. Mark A. R. Kleiman and Kerry D. Smith, "State and Local Drug Enforcement: In Search of a Strategy," in *Crime and Justice: An Annual Review of Research*, Norval Morris and Michael Tonry, eds. (Chicago: University of Chicago Press, 1986).

3. J. Michael Polich, et al., *Strategies for Controlling Adolescent Drug Abuse* (Santa Monica, Calif.: The RAND Corporation, 1984).

4. Francis X. Hartmann and Saul N. Weingart, "Strategies for Demand Side: Prevention, Early Intervention and Treatment" (Report to Ford Foundation, Working Paper 87-01-02, 1987).

5. Louise Potvin, François Champagne, and Claire Laberge-Nodeau, "Mandatory Driver Training and Road Safety: The Quebec Experience," *American Journal of Public Health* 78 (9 [September 1988]): 1206.

6. Opponents of sex education have made similar arguments, but in that case any claims of a "curiosity effect" would be very weak indeed; adolescents are already curious about sex.

7. This is based on unpublished data from studies conducted by the Gordon S. Black Corporation for the Media Partnership for a Drug-Free America.

8. Oscar Wilde, *The Artist as Critic: Critical Writings of Oscar Wilde*, Richard Ellman, ed. (London: Allen, 1970).

9. Joseph Treaster, "Stepping Up the Drug Fight, From Toys to TV Shows: Marketing of Anti-Drug Messages," *New York Times* (16 March 1991): 7, c. 1.

10. J. K. Ockene, "Physician-delivered Interventions for Smoking Cessation: Strategies for Increasing Effectiveness," *Preventive Medicine* 16 (1987): 723–737.

11. Lloyd D. Johnston, Patrick M. O'Malley, and Jerald G. Bachman, *Drug Use, Drinking, and Smoking: National Survey Results from High School, College, and Young Adult Populations: 1975–1988* (Rockville, Md.: Department of Health and Human Services, 1989), 30–46, 255, 267–271. National Institute on Drug Abuse, *National Household Survey on Drug Abuse: Population Estimates 1988* (Rockville, Md.: Department of Health and Human Services, 1989), 23–35.

12. I owe these observations to the Reverend Dr. David Weeks of the North Conway Institute in Boston.

13. Philip Dormer Stanhope, Lord Chesterfield, *Letters to his Son* (London: Folio Society, 1973).

14. Norman E. Zinberg, *Drug, Set, and Setting: the Basis for Controlled Intoxicant Use* (New Haven: Yale University Press, 1984).

15. J. Michael Polich, et al., *Strategies for Preventing Adolescent Drug Use* (Santa Monica, Calif.: The RAND Corporation, 1983), 146–147.

16. Jonathan Shedler and Jack Block, "Adolescent Drug Use and Psychological Health," *American Psychologist* 45 (5 [May 1990]): 612–630. For a discussion of the longer-term effects of adolescent drug use, see Michael D. Newcomb and Peter M. Bentler, *Consequences of Adolescent Drug Use: Impact on Young Adults* (Newbury Park, Calif.: Sage Publications, 1988).

17. On the market significance of casual users, see, for example, the calculations in Mark A. R. Kleiman, *Marijuana: Costs of Abuse, Costs of Control* (New York: Greenwood Press, 1989), 34–39.

18. According to the *National Household Survey*, more than 70 million Americans reported using an illicit drug at some time. National Institute on Drug Abuse, *National Household Survey on Drug Abuse: Population Estimates, 1988* (Rockville, Md.: U.S. Department of Health and Human Services, 1989), 17, Table 2-A. The Institute of Medicine study panel found

that 2.2 million people were clearly and 3.1 million were probably in need of drug treatment. Institute of Medicine, *Treating Drug Problems* Vol. 1 (Washington, D.C.: National Academy Press, 1990), 97, 101.

19. J. Michael Polich, et al., *Strategies for Preventing Adolescent Drug Use.*

20. Mark H. Moore, "Policy Towards Heroin Use in New York City," Ph.D. dissertation (Cambridge, Mass.: Kennedy School of Government, Harvard University, 1973). See also Mark H. Moore, *Buy and Bust: The Effective Regulation of an Illicit Market in Heroin* (Lexington, Mass.: Lexington Books, 1977); Mark H. Moore and Dean R. Gerstein, *Alcohol and Public Policy: Beyond the Shadow of the Prohibition* (Washington, D.C.: National Academy Press, 1981).

21. This argument is made in Norman Zinberg, *Drug, Set, and Setting: The Basis for Controlled Intoxicant Use* (New Haven: Yale University Press, 1984). Examples of drug education materials written from this viewpoint include Andrew Weil and Winifred Rosen, *Chocolate to Morphine: Understanding Mind-Active Drugs* (Boston: Houghton Mifflin, 1983), and Edward Brecher, *Licit and Illicit Drugs: The Consumers Union Report on Narcotics* (Boston: Little, Brown, 1972).

22. Bureau of Justice Assistance, "An Invitation to Project DARE: Drug Abuse Resistance Education" (Washington, D.C.: Department of Justice 1988); William DeJong, "Project DARE: Teaching Kids to Say 'No' to Drugs and Alcohol," Report prepared for National Institute of Justice (Washington, D.C.: Department of Justice, March 1986).

23. Phyllis L. Ellickson and Robert M. Bell, "Drug Prevention in Junior High: A Multi-Site Longitudinal Test," *Science* 24 (March 1990): 1299–1305.

24. Mary Ann Pentz, James H. Dwyer, David P. MacKinnon, Brian R. Flay, William B. Hansen, Eric Yu I. Wang, and C. Anderson Johnson, "A Multicommunity Trial for Primary Prevention of Adolescent Drug Abuse," *Journal of the American Medical Association* 261 (22 [June 9, 1989]): 3259–3266.

25. Evaluation and Training Institute (ETI), "DARE Longitudinal Evaluation Annual Report, 1987–88" (Los Angeles, Calif.: Evaluation and Training Institute, 1988).

26. Brian Flay and S. Sobel, "The Role of Mass Media in Preventing Adolescent Substance Abuse," in *Preventing Adolescent Drug Abuse: Intervention Strategies*, T. J. Glynn, C. G. Lyekefeld, and J. P. Ludford, eds. NIDA Research Monograph 47 (Rockville, Md.: National Institute of Drug Abuse, 1983).

27. Gideon Doron, *The Smoking Paradox: Public Regulation in the Cigarette Industry* (Cambridge, Mass.: Abt Books, 1979).

28. The evaluation was performed by Gordon S. Black Corporation. See its "Partnership Attitude Tracking Study: A Summary of the Fourth Year Results" (Rochester, N.Y.: Gordon Black Corporation, 1991). The results are summarized in Partnership for a Drug-Free America *Newsletter* 4 (3 [Fall 1990]).

29. See Ethan Nadelmann, "The Case for Legalization," *The Public Interest* 92 (3 [Summer 1988]): 3–32.

30. For a critique of this concept, see Herbert Fingarette, *Heavy Drinking: The Myth of Alcoholism as a Disease* (Berkeley: University of California Press, 1988).

31. Institute of Medicine, *Treating Drug Problems: Vol. 1* (Washington, D.C.: National Academy of Sciences Press, 1990).

32. Much of the discussion here relies on the review article by M. Douglas Anglin and Yih-Ing Hser, "Treatment of Drug Abuse," in *Drugs and Crime* Vol. 13, Michael Tonry and James Q. Wilson, eds. (Chicago: University of Chicago Press, 1990).

33. National Institute on Alcohol Abuse and Alcoholism, *Alcohol and Health 7th Special Report to the U.S. Congress* (Washington, D.C.: Department of Health and Human Services, 1990), 266.

34. National Institute on Drug Abuse, *National Household Survey on Drug Abuse: Main Findings 1985* (Rockville, Md.: U.S. Department of Health and Human Services, 1988), 16; Lloyd D. Johnston, Patrick M. O'Malley, and Jerald G. Bachman, *Drug Use, Drinking, and Smoking: National Survey Results from High School, College, and Young Adult Populations: 1975–1988* (Rockville, Md.: National Institute on Drug Abuse, 1989), 215, 216.

35. M. Fiore, et al. "Smoking Cessation: Data from the 1986 Adult Use of Tobacco Survey," in *Smoking and Health 1987: Proceedings of the 6th World Conference on Smoking and Health*, Tokyo, 9–12 November 1987 (New York: Excepta Media, 1988); J. L. Schwartz, *Review and Evaluation of Smoking Cessation Methods: U.S. and Canada, 1928–1985* (Rockville, Md.: National Institute of Health, 1987).

36. Institute of Medicine, *Treating Drug Problems: Vol. 1*, pp. 170–174; Richard Rawson, "Cut the Crack: Policy Makers' Guide to Cocaine Treatment," *Policy Review* (Winter 1990): 17.

37. Institute of Medicine, *Treating Drug Problems: Vol. 1*, p. 135.

38. Ibid.

39. Herbert D. Kleber, "Treatment of Narcotics Addicts," *Psychiatric Medicine* 3 (4 [1987]): 389–418; National Institute on Drug Abuse, "Effectiveness of Drug Abuse Treatment Programs" (Rockville, Md.: National Institute on Drug Abuse, 1981).

40. Robert Willar, "A Drug to Fight Cocaine," *Science* (March 1986): 42.

41. The current clinical practice is to use the benzodiazepine family of minor tranquilizers instead. National Institute on Alcohol Abuse and Alcoholism, *Alcohol and Health 7th Special Report to the U.S. Congress* (Washington, D.C.: Department of Health and Human Services, January 1990), 266.

42. Institute of Medicine, *Treating Drug Problems: Vol. 1*, pp. 174–176.

43. Ibid., p. 176.

44. The data are extremely imperfect. For heroin, see D. S. Lipton and M. J. Maranda, "Detoxification from Heroin Dependency: An Overview of Methods and Effectiveness," *Advances in Alcohol and Substance Abuse*

2 (1): 31–55. For alcohol, see Donald Cahalan, *Understanding America's Drinking Problem* (San Francisco: Jossey-Bass, 1987), 136.

45. Cost figure derived from Institute of Medicine, *Treating Drug Problems: Vol. 1,* pp. 290, 291.

46. J. O. Prochasta and C. C. Diclemente, "Stages and Processes of Self-Change of Smoking: Towards an Integrative Model of Change," *Journal of Consulting and Clinical Psychology* 51 (3 [1983]). Office of Smoking and Health, *Nicotine Addiction: The Health Consequences of Smoking* (Rockville, Md.: Department of Health and Human Services, 1988).

47. J. Jackson and L. Rotkiewicz, "A Coupon Program: AIDS Education and Treatment," Presented at the Third International Conference on AIDS (Washington, D.C.: June 1987).

48. Institute of Medicine, *Treating Drug Problems: Vol. 1,* p. 16.

49. Ibid., pp. 154–167; "Understanding Drug Treatment" (Office of National Drug Control White paper, June 1990).

50. Institute of Medicine, *Treating Drug Problems: Vol. 1,* p. 167.

51. On the total institutions generally, see Erving Goffman, *Asylums: Essays on the Social Situation of Mental Patients and Other Inmates* (Chicago: University of Chicago Press, 1970). On therapeutic communities, see Sethard Fisher, *Residential Treatment of Felon Drug Addicts: State Agents as Therapists* (New York: P. Lang, 1987); Robert Weppner, *The Untherapeutic Community: Organized Behavior in a Failed Addiction Treatment Program* (Lincoln: University of Nebraska Press, 1983); B. Sugarman, "Structure, Variations and Context: A Sociologized View of the Therapeutic Community," and G. De Leon, "The Therapeutic Community for Substance Abuse: Perspective and Approach," both in *Therapeutic Communities for Addictions*, G. De Leon and J. T. Ziegerfuss, Jr., eds. (Springfield, Illinois: Charles C. Thomas, 1986).

52. Peter Cerlson, "The Oxford House Experiment," *Washington Post Magazine* (12 November 1989): 15.

53. For evidence of the limited effectiveness of such programs, see Sung-Yeon Kang, "Outcomes for Cocaine Abusers After Once a Week Psychosocial Therapy," *American Journal of Psychiatry* 148 (May 1991): 630–635.

54. Institute of Medicine, *Treating Drug Problems: Vol. 1,* p. 169.

55. Barry Spunt, Dana E. Hunt, Douglas S. Lipton, and Douglas Goldsmith, "Methadone Diversion: A New Look," *Journal of Drug Issues* 16 (1986): 569–583.

56. General Accounting Office, "Methadone Maintenance: Some Treatment Programs Are Not Effective; Greater Federal Oversight Needed" (Report to the Chairman, Select Committee on Narcotics Abuse and Control, March 1990), 17–20.

57. Institute of Medicine, *Treating Drug Problems: Vol. 1,* Ch. 5.

58. M. D. Anglin, W. H. McGlothlin, G. R. Speckart, and T. M. Ryan, "Shutting Off Methadone: The Closure of the San Diego Methadone Maintenance Program" (Final Report, National Institute on Drug Abuse, 1982).

59. Bruce Johnson, "Once an Addict, Seldom an Addict," *Contemporary Drug Problems* 7 (1 [Spring 1978]): 48–49.

60. Office of National Drug Control Policy, *National Drug Control Strategy* (Washington, D.C.: GPO, 1990); Institute of Medicine, *Treating Drug Problems: Vol. 1*, pp. 211–219.

61. General Accounting Office, "Substance Abuse Treatment: Medicaid Allows Some Services but Generally Limits Coverage" (Report to Congressional Requesters, June 1991), 3–4.

62. M. A. Morrisey and G. A. Jensen, "Employer-Sponsored Insurance Coverage for Alcoholism and Drug Abuse Treatments," *Journal of Studies on Alcohol* 49 (1988): 456–461. United States Bureau of the Census, *Statistical Abstract of the United States* (Washington, D.C.: Department of Commerce, 1989), 90–93.

63. Machiavelli, *The Prince*, Ch. 17.

64. A. T. McLellan, G. E. Woody, L. Luborsky, and L. Goehl, "Is the Counselor an 'Active Ingredient' In Substance Abuse Rehabilitation?" *Journal of Nervous Mental Disorders* 176 (1988): 423–430.

65. General Accounting Office, "Methadone Maintenance: Some Treatment Programs Are Not Effective; Greater Federal Oversight Needed." Report to Select Committee on Narcotics Abuse and Control (Washington, D.C.: March, 1990), 17–20.

66. *Treatment is the Answer: A White Paper on the Cost Effectiveness of Alcoholism and Drug Dependency Treatment* (Washington, D.C.: National Association of Addiction Treatment Providers, March 1991).

67. For a description of the "two-tiered" treatment system, see Institute of Medicine, *Treating Drug Problems: Vol. 1,* pp. 200–219.

68. This is a frequent refrain of the IOM study panel, Institute of Medicine, *Treating Drug Problems: Vol. 1,* pp. 132–199.

69. Ibid., pp. 250–252.

70. Harry K. Wexler, Douglas S. Lipton, and Bruce D. Johnson, "A Criminal Justice System Strategy for Treating Cocaine-Heroin Abusing Offenders in Custody," *Issues and Practices in Criminal Justice* (Washington, D.C.: National Institute of Justice, March 1988).

71. The literature on "selective incapacitation" is extensive and rather polemical. See Peter W. Greenwood and Allan Abrahamse, *Selective Incapacitation* (Santa Monica, Calif.: RAND Corporation, 1982), and critiques in Cohen, Spelman, Moore, et al., *Dangerous Offenders: Elusive Targets of Justice* (Cambridge, Mass.: Harvard University Press, 1984).

72. Eric Wish, K. A. Klumpp, A. H. Moorer, and E. Brady, *An Analysis of Drugs and Crime Among Arrestees in the District of Columbia* (Springfield, Va.: National Technology Information Service, 1980).

73. Joan Petersilia, *Expanding Options for Criminal Sentencing* (Santa Monica, Calif.: RAND Corporation, 1987).

74. Mark A. R. Kleiman, Denise Kulawik, and Sarah Chayes, *Program Evaluation: Santa Cruz Regional Street Drug Reduction Program* (Cambridge, Mass.: BOTEC Analysis Corporation, 1990).

75. M. Douglas Anglin, "A Social Analysis of Compulsory Treatment for Opiate Dependence,"*Journal of Drug Issues* 18 (4 [Fall 1988]).
76. Harry K. Wexler, G. P. Faulkin, and D. S. Lipton, *A Model Prison Rehabilitation Program: An Evaluation of the Stay'n Out Therapeutic Community* (New York: Narcotic and Drug Research Inc., 1988).
77. Ibid.

8
ALCOHOL

1. Lawrence Jolidad, "Sands Dry, Troops Dry, Crime Blotter Dry," *USA Today* (11 December 1990), 5A.
2. *Current Population Reports: Population Estimates and Projections* (Washington, D.C.: Department of Commerce, 1990).
3. A "standard reference drink" consists of a 1 ½-ounce shot of whiskey, a 12-ounce can of beer, or a 6-ounce glass of wine; in each case this amounts to between 0.7 and 0.75 ounces of absolute alcohol. In 1988, Americans consumed 10.3 billion six-packs of beer, or about 60 billion cans; 1.9 billion bottles of whiskey, or about 33 billion shots; and 2.8 billion bottles of wine, or about 12 billion glasses. See Congressional Budget Office, *Federal Taxation of Tobacco, Alcoholic Beverages, and Motor Fuels* (Washington, D.C.: Congress of the United States, 1990), table A-8, p. 110. For spending on alcohol, see Jobson Publishing, *Jobson's 1991 Handbook Advance* (New York: Jobson Publishing Corporation, 1991). For spending on illicit drugs, see Office of National Drug Control Policy, "What America's Users Spend on Illegal Drugs," Technical Paper (Washington, D.C.: June 1991).
4. N. S. Miller and M. S. Gold, *Alcohol* (New York: Plenum Press, 1991), 13.
5. Ibid., pp. 11–22. J. D. Miller et al., *National Survey on Drug Abuse: Main Findings* (Rockville, Md.: NIDA, 1985).
6. David J. Pittman and Charles R. Snyder, eds., *Society, Culture, and Drinking Patterns* (New York: John Wiley, 1962).
7. Ibid.
8. William Bennett, remarks at the John F. Kennedy School of Government, Harvard University, 11 December 1989.
9. For changes in constant dollar tax rates, see Congressional Budget Office, *Federal Taxation of Tobacco, Alcoholic Beverages, and Motor Fuels* (Washington, D.C.: Congress of the United States, 1990), 11–12; tax rates per drink calculated based on Tables A-3, p.104; A-8, p.110; A-10, p.112, adjusted for changes in federal alcohol taxation enacted in 1990.
10. Ibid., Tables A-5, p.106 and A-8, p.110.
11. Indeed, some reports conclude that tax policy can be a particularly potent public policy tool in controlling youthful drinking, even more effective than a change in minimum age drinking laws. See Henry

Saffer and Michael Grossman, "Beer Taxes, the Legal Drinking Age, and Youth Motor Vehicle Fatalities," *Journal of Legal Studies* (June 1987).

12. The Fairness Doctrine was a policy of the Federal Communications Commission that required FCC licensees that broadcast political messages to give equal time to opposing views. It abandoned that policy in 1985.

13. Preliminary data from Lloyd D. Johnston, Jerald G. Bachman, and Patrick M. O'Malley, *Monitoring the Future 1990* (Ann Arbor, Mich.: Institute for Social Research, 1991), Table 9.

14. National Highway Traffic Safety Administration, *Drunk Driving Facts* (Washington, D.C.: National Center for Statistics and Analysis, August 1988).

15. National Institute on Drug Abuse and National Institute on Alcohol Abuse and Alcoholism, *Highlights from the 1987 National Drug and Alcoholism Treatment Unit Survey* (Rockville, Md.: NIDA/NIAAA, 1989). Of the money spent on alcohol treatment, 34.6 percent is paid by private health insurance, 13.8 percent by treatment clients or their families, 8.5 percent by public medical insurance (Medicaid for the poor, Medicare for the disabled and elderly, and the services of the Veterans Administration), and 37.7 percent through publicly funded alcohol treatment programs.

16. Institute of Medicine, *Broadening the Base of Treatment for Alcohol Problems* (Washington, D.C.: National Academy Press, 1990), 99–101; D. A. Regier, I. D. Goldberg, and C. A. Taube, "The de facto U.S. Mental Health Services System: A Public Health Perspective," *Archives of General Psychiatry* 35 (1978): 685–693; Henrick Harwood, et al., *Social and Economic Costs of Alcohol Abuse and Alcoholism* (Research Triangle Park, N.C.: Research Triangle Institute, 1985).

17. Harwood, *Social and Economic Costs of Alcohol Abuse and Alcoholism*.

18. For a critique, see Herbert Fingarette, *Heavy Drinking: The Myth of Alcoholism as a Disease* (Berkeley: University of California Press, 1988).

19. For a general discussion of self-management in regard to drug taking, see Norman E. Zinberg, *Drug, Set, and Setting: The Basis for Controlled Intoxicant Use* (New Haven: Yale University Press, 1984).

20. Brad J. Bushman and Harris Cooper, "Effects of Alcohol on Human Aggression: An Integrative Research Review," *Psychological Bulletin* 107 (3 [1990]): 341–354; G. A. Marlatt and D. J. Rohsenow, "Cognitive Processes in Alcohol Use: Expectancy and the Balanced Placebo Design," in *Advances in Substance Abuse: Behavioral and Biological Research*, N. K. Mello, ed. (Greenwich, Conn.: JAI Press, 1980); A. R. Lang, D. J. Goecher, V. G. Adesso, and G. A. Marlatt, "Effects of Alcohol on Aggression in Male Social Drinkers," *Journal of Abnormal Psychology* 84 (1975): 508–518; J. G. Hull and C. F. Bond, "Social and Behavioral Consequences of Alcohol Consumption Expectancy: A Meta-Analysis," *Psychological Bulletin* 99 (1982): 347–360.

21. For a general discussion of problems of this sort, see Thomas C. Schelling, "The Intimate Contest for Self-Command" in *Choice and Consequence*, Thomas Schelling, ed. (Cambridge, Mass.: Harvard University Press, 1984).

22. This is a theme of Mark H. Moore and Dean R. Gerstein, eds., *Alcohol and Public Policy: Beyond the Shadow of Prohibition* (Washington, D.C.: National Academy Press, 1981).

23. Lee N. Robins, *The Vietnam Drug User Returns,* Special Action Office for Drug Abuse Prevention Monograph, Series A, No. 2 (May 1974).

24. On vows, see Thomas C. Schelling, "Law, Ethics and the Exercise of Self-Command," in *Choice and Consequence,* pp. 99–100.

25. E. L. Abel, *Fetal Alcohol Syndrome and Fetal Alcohol Effects* (New York: Plenum, 1984).

26. R. E. Little, R. L. Asler, P. D. Sampson, and J. H. Renwick, "Fetal Growth and Moderate Drinking in Early Pregnancy," *American Journal of Epidemiology* 123 (1986): 270–278; A. P. Streissguth, H. M. Barr, et al., "Attention, Distraction and Reaction Time at Age 7 Years and Prenatal Alcohol Exposure," *Neurobehavioral Toxicology and Teratology* 8 (1986): 717–725; Daniel Coleman, "Lasting Costs for Children are Found From a Few Early Drinks," *New York Times* (16 February 1989).

27. Robb London, "Two Waiters Lose Jobs for Liquor Warning to Women," *New York Times* (10 March 1991): 5, c. 3.

28. Christopher A. Innes, "State Prison Inmate Survey, 1986: Drug Use and Crime," Bureau of Justice Statistics (Washington, D.C.: Department of Justice, 1988).

29. Timothy J. Flanagan and Katherine Maguire, eds., *Sourcebook of Criminal Justice Statistics 1989* (Washington, D.C.: Department of Justice); Lois Fingerhut and Joel Kleinman, "International and Interstate Comparison of Homicide Among Young Males," *Journal of the American Medical Association* 263 (27 June 1990): 3292–3295.

30. For some calculations, see David Cavanagh and Mark A. R. Kleiman, "A Cost-Benefit Analysis of Prison Cell Construction and Alternative Sanctions." Report prepared for National Institute of Justice (Cambridge, Mass.: BOTEC Analysis Corporation, 1990).

31. For a sketch of this argument, see James K. Stewart, "The Urban Strangler: How Crime Causes Poverty in the Inner City," *Policy Review* 37 (Summer 1986): 6–10.

32. Ron Ferguson and Mary Jackson, "Nurturing Environments, African-American Males, and Drugs," Working Paper (Malcolm Weiner Center for Social Policy, Kennedy School of Government, Harvard University, November 1990).

33. For the general problem of dealing with repeat offenders, see Mark H. Moore et al., *Dangerous Offenders: The Elusive Target of Justice* (Cambridge, Mass.: Harvard University Press, 1984). See also Peter W. Greenwood and Allan Abrahamse, *Selective Incapacitation* (Santa Monica, Calif.:

RAND Corporation, 1982), and the voluminous critical literature it has attracted.

34. Institute of Medicine, *Broadening the Base of Treatment for Alcohol Problems*, p. 75; B. I. Liskow and D. W. Goodwin, "Pharmacological Treatment of Alcohol Intoxication, Withdrawal, and Dependence: A Critical Review, *Journal of Studies on Alcohol* 48 (1987): 356–370; J. H. Jaffe and D. A. Circulo, "Drugs Used in the Treatment of Alcoholism" in *The Diagnosis and Treatment of Alcoholism*, J. H. Mendelson and N. K. Mello, eds. (New York: McGraw-Hill, 1985), 355–389.

35. Other clerks regard compulsion as being in conflict with the spirit of the fellowship; in addition, there has been at least one constitutional challenge to such a judicially imposed condition of sentence on the basis that AA is quasi-religious in nature. See *Youle* v. *Edgar,* 172 Ill. App. 3d 498, 526 N.E. 894, 899 (Ill. App. 4 Dist. 1988). The *Youle* court rejected the challenge, noting that the driver was free to select any ongoing support program in AA's stead.

36. James Q. Wilson and George Kelling, "Making Neighborhoods Safe: Sometimes 'Fixing Broken Windows' Does More To Reduce Crime Than Conventional 'Incident-Oriented' Policing," *Atlantic Monthly* (February 1989).

37. See *Seventh Special Report to the U.S. Congress on Alcohol and Health* (Rockville, Md.: U.S. Department of Health and Human Services, 1990), 165–168 for a discussion.

38. National Highway Traffic Safety Administration, "National Center for Statistics and Analysis—1987 Fatality Facts" (Washington, D.C.: Department of Transportation, 1988).

39. Fatal accidents occurring in the workplace have fallen by two-thirds since the 1930s, while the home accident death rate per 100,000 has dropped from 21.2 in 1948 to 8.6 in 1985. *Economic Report of the President: January 1987* (Washington, D.C.: GPO, 1987): 179–181.

40. Aaron Wildavsky, *Searching for Safety* (New Brunswick, N.J.: Transaction Books, 1988).

41. A. C. Stein, R. W. Allen, M. L. Cook, and R. L. Karl, "A Simulator Study of Combined Effects of Alcohol and Marijuana on Driving Behavior—Phase II," National Highway Traffic Safety Administration Report No. DOT HS 806-405 (Washington, D.C.: U.S. Department of Transportation, February 1983).

42. A. C. Stein, et al., "Use of Controlled Substances and Highway Safety," A Report to Congress, March 1988, National Highway Traffic and Safety Administration; S. M. Owens, et al., "Use of Marijuana, Ethanol and Other Drugs Among Drivers Killed in Single Vehicle Crashes," *Journal of Forensic Sciences* 28 (2 [1983]): 372–379.

43. For an analysis of the effects of social status on arrest, trial, and punishment, see Donald Black, *The Behavior of Law* (Orlando, Fla: Academic

Press, 1976), and *Sociological Justice* (New York: Oxford University Press, 1989).

44. Approximately 1.5 trillion vehicle passenger miles were driven in 1987. Bureau of the Census, *Statistical Abstract of the United States* (Washington, D.C.: Department of Commerce, 1989), Table 1000, p. 589.

45. Alan C. Donelson, "The Alcohol-Crash Problem," in *Social Control of the Drinking Driver,* Michael Laurence, John Snortum, and Franklin Zimring, eds. (Chicago: University of Chicago Press, 1988).

46. Institute of Medicine, *Broadening the Base of Treatment for Alcohol Problems,* p. 493; Appendix B, p. 535.

47. National Institute on Alcohol Abuse and Alcoholism, *Alcohol and Health* (Washington, D.C.: Department of Health and Human Services, January 1990), 248–249.

48. California Penal Code Sections 1203, *et seq.*

49. Henrick Harwood et al., "Economic Costs to Society of Alcohol and Drug Abuse and Mental Illness: 1980" (Research Triangle Park, N.C.: Research Triangle Institute, 1984); "Alcohol & Drugs in the Workplace: Costs, Controls, and Controversies," Bureau of National Affairs Special Report, 1986. A. Cruze, H. Harwood, P. Kristiansen, J. Collins, and D. Jones, "Economic Costs of Alcohol and Drug Abuse and Mental Illness—1977" (Research Triangle Park, N.C. Research Triangle Institute, 1981).

50. For estimates of the prevalence of alcohol problems among patients needing various kinds of medical care, see Institute of Medicine, *Broadening the Base of Treatment For Alcohol Problems,* pp. 229–230.

51. Bureau of Labor Statistics, *Employee Benefits in Medium and Large Firms 1987,* Bulletin 2287 (Washington, D.C.: GPO, 1987).

52. P. Roman, "Employee Alcoholism Programs in Major Corporations in 1979: Scope, Change, and Receptivity," in *Prevention, Intervention and Treatment: Concerns and Models,* J. deLuca, ed. (Washington, D.C.: GPO, 1982), and P. Roman and T. Blum, "The Core Technology of Employee Assistance," *The ALMACAN* 15 (3).

53. For a general discussion of legal issues on both licit and illicit drugs in the workplace, see Daniel D. Polsby "Employer Drug Testing: Where Things Stand Now; Where They're Going; Where They Ought to Go" (unpublished); *Alcohol and Drugs in the Workplace: Costs, Controls, and Controversies,* BNA Special Report (Washington, D.C.: The Bureau of National Affairs, 1986).

54. "Science Watch: Drivers' Brain Waves Tested for Use of Specific Drugs," *New York Times* (25 June 1985), p. C4.

55. Institute of Medicine, *Broadening the Base of Treatment for Alcohol Problems.*

56. See *Zauderer* v. *Office of Disciplinary Counsel of the Supreme Court of Ohio,* 471 U.S. 635, 637, 105 S.Ct. 2265, 2274 (1985); *Bolger v. Youngs Drug Products Corp.,* 463 U.S. 60, 103 S.Ct. 2875 (1983).

57. 17 C.F.R. Section 230.135(a).

58. 21 U.S.C. Section 352(n).

59. D'Arcy Jenish, "Warning Smokers: Messages on Packs Will Be More Visible," *Macleans* 103 (6 [5 Febuary 1990]): 51.

60. See Gideon Doron, *The Smoking Paradox: Public Regulation in the Cigarette Industry* (Cambridge, Mass.: Abt Books, 1979).

61. See Mark H. Moore and Dean R. Gerstein, eds., *Alcohol and Public Policy: Beyond the Shadow of Prohibition* (Washington, D.C.: National Academy Press, 1981). For a contrary view, stressing the devastating effects of adulterated alcohol products, see John Morgan, "Prohibition Was—and Is—Bad for the Nation's Health." Paper submitted to the Hoover Institute Conference on U.S. Drug Policy, Stanford, Calif., 15 November 1990.

62. Willard Manning, Joseph Newhouse, et al., "The Taxes of Sin: Do Smokers and Drinkers Pay Their Way?" *Journal of the American Medical Association* 261 (11 [1989]). Manning, et al. report an average 1989 tax level of 23 cents per ounce (17 cents per standard reference drink), but this appears to be a computational error.

63. See James Q. Wilson and George Kelling, "Broken Windows: The Police and Neighborhood Safety," *Atlantic* (March 1982); Wesley Skogan, *Disorder and Decline: Crime and the Spiral of Decay in American Neighborhoods* (New York: Free Press, 1990).

64. Phillip Cook and George Tauchen, "The Effect of Liquor Taxes on Heavy Drinking," *Bell Journal of Economics* 13 (1982).

65. Lowry E. Heussler brought the importance of this potential problem to my attention.

9
MARIJUANA

1. National Institute on Drug Abuse, *Drug Abuse and Drug Abuse Research, The Third Triennial Report to Congress from the Secretary of the Department of Health and Human Services* (Washington, D.C.: Department of Health and Human Services, 1991), Table 4, p. 19. Total self-reported "current" (last-month) use of any illicit drug was 7.3 percent. Current use of marijuana was 5.9 percent; of cocaine (including crack), 1.5 percent; of other stimulants, sedatives, tranquilizers, and analgesics, 1.7 percent; of hallucinogens, 0.4 percent (heroin use is too rare to be measured by such surveys). Thus, users of all drugs except marijuana totaled no more than 3.6 percent of the respondents; allowance should also be made for overlap.

2. William Rhoads and Douglas McDonald, "What America's Users Spend on Illegal Drugs" (Washington, D.C.: Office of National Drug Control Policy, June 1991).

3. Marijuana charges accounted for 34 percent of all drug arrests in 1988. Bureau of Justice Statistics, *Sourcebook of Criminal Statistics—1989* (Washington, D.C.: Department of Justice, 1990), Table 4.32, 456–457.

4. Marijuana clients represent less than one-sixth of publicly supported drug treatment admissions. National Association of State Alcohol and Drug Abuse Directors, "An Analysis of State Alcohol and Drug Abuse Profile Data" (Washington, D.C.: 1991).

5. Leo Hollister, "Health Aspects of Cannabis," *Pharmacological Reviews* 38 (1 [1986]): 17 summarizes health-related studies to date. "Chronic use of marijuana may stunt the emotional growth of youngsters. Evidence for an amotivational syndrome is largely based on clinical reports; whether marijuana use is a cause or effect is uncertain. A marijuana psychosis, long rumored, has been difficult to prove . . . brain damage has not been proved. Physical dependence is rarely encountered in the usual patterns of social use, despite some degree of tolerance that may develop. The endocrine effects of the drug might be expected to delay puberty in prepubescent boys, but actual instances have been rare. As with any material that is smoked, chronic smoking of marijuana will produce bronchitis; emphysema or lung cancer have not yet been documented. Cardiovascular effects of the drug are harmful to those with preexisting heart disease; fortunately the number of users with such conditions is minimal. Fears that the drug might accumulate in the body to the point of toxicity have been groundless. . . . The drug is probably harmful when taken during pregnancy, but the risk is uncertain. . . . No clinical consequences have been noted from the effects of the drug on immune response, chromosomes, or cell metabolism." See also Institute of Medicine, *Marijuana and Health* (Washington, D.C.: National Academy Press, 1982), and National Institute on Drug Abuse, *Correlates and Consequences of Marijuana Use* (Rockville, Md.: Department of Health and Human Services, 1984).

6. See William Novak, *High Culture* (New York: Alfred A. Knopf, 1980).

7. For a strongly made argument that there is an underlying demand for mood alteration, see Ronald Siegel, *Intoxication: Life in Pursuit of Artificial Paradise* (New York: Dutton, 1989).

8. Jonathan Shedler and Jack Block, "Adolescent Drug Use and Psychological Health: A Longitudinal Inquiry," *American Psychologist* 45 (5 [May 1990]): 612–619.

9. This statistic has received great attention in anti-drug advertisements and speeches.

10. John P. Morgan, "American Marijuana Potency: Data Versus Conventional Wisdom" (New York: Department of Pharmacology, City University of New York Medical School, 1990).

11. National Narcotics Intelligence Consumers Committee, *The NNICC Report 1990: The Supply of Illicit Drugs to the United States* (Washington, D.C.: Drug Enforcement Agency, 1990), 29.

12. John P. Morgan, "American Marijuana Potency."
13. The National Household Survey projects a total of 20.5 million Americans as having used marijuana in the past year, 10.2 million as "current users" who have taken the drug within the past month, 5.5 million as using once or more per week, and 3.3 million as "daily" users (defined as having used the drug on twenty or more days in the month before the survey). See National Institute on Drug Abuse, *National Household Survey on Drug Abuse: Population Estimates 1990* (Washington, D.C.: Department of Health and Human Services, 1991). All of these numbers are almost certainly underestimates, since the survey excludes several populations whose rates of marijuana use may be higher than average: prisoners, the homeless, students living in dormitories and under the age of fifteen, and, significantly, the 20 percent of those selected to be surveyed who cannot be found or who refuse the questionnaire. Among the users in these omitted populations, the frequency of heavy use is probably greater than it is among respondents who reported use.
14. Reuter bases his conclusion on the "Monitoring the Future" studies by Lloyd Johnston and his colleagues. Four out of five high school seniors who report having been daily marijuana smokers at some time report that they are not currently daily smokers. See Lloyd D. Johnston, Patrick O'Malley, and Jerald G. Bachman, *Illicit Drug Use, Smoking and Drinking by America's High School Students, College Students, and Young Adults: 1975–87* (Rockville, Md.: National Institute on Drug Abuse, 1989), 289–294.
15. For a brief summary of this literature, see J. Michael Polich, et al., *Strategies for Controlling Adolescent Drug Use* (Santa Monica, Calif.: RAND Corporation, 1984), 124.
16. Richard R. Clayton and Harwin L. Voss, *Young Men and Drugs in Manhattan: A Causal Analysis,* NIDA Research Monograph No. 39 (Rockville, Md.: Alcohol, Drug Abuse and Mental Health Administration, 1981).
17. See, for example, Laura Blumenfeld, "The Acid Kids," *The Washington Post* (18 August 1991): F1.
18. John DiNardo, "Are Marijuana and Alcohol Substitutes? The Effect of State Drinking Age Laws on the Marijuana Consumption of High School Seniors" (Santa Monica, Calif.: RAND Corporation, 1991).
19. Karyn Model, "The Effect of Marijuana Decriminalization on Hospital Emergency Room Drug Episodes: 1975–1987" (Cambridge, Mass.: Harvard University Department of Economics, 1991) (unpublished).
20. D. Beaconsfield, J. Ginsburg, and R. Rainsbury, "Therapeutic Potential of Marijuana," *New England Journal of Medicine* 289 (1973): 1315.
21. Richard E. Doblin and Mark A. R. Kleiman, "Marijuana as Antiemetic Medicine: A Survey of Oncologists' Experiences and Attitudes," *Journal of Clinical Oncology* 9 (7 [July 1991]): 1314–1319. See "Cross-Eyed and Painless," *The Economist* (6 July 1991): 89; Brian Hecht, "Out of Joint: The Case for Medical Marijuana," *The New Republic* (15–22 July 1991): 7–10.

22. V. Vinciguerra, M. S. W. Moore-Terry, and E. Brennan, "Inhalation Marijuana as an Antiemetic for Cancer Chemotherapy," *New York State Journal of Medicine* 88 (1988): 525–527; A. Chang, D. Shiling, R. Stillman, et al., "Delta-9-Tetrahydrocannabinol as an Antiemetic in Cancer Patients Receiving High-Dose Methotrexate," *Annals of Internal Medicine* 91 (1979): 819–824. For a useful if one-sided account of the regulatory and legal battle over medical marijuana, see R. C. Randall, ed., *Marijuana, Medicine, and the Law* Vols. 1–3, (Washington, D.C.: Galen Press, 1988, 1989, 1990).

23. It is impossible to be precise about the price per dose of marijuana because of the variation in prices, potencies, and users. But for the majority of users who smoke marijuana only occasionally and therefore have not developed much tolerance, the cost of an intoxicated hour, even after the price increases of the past few years, is likely to be no more than a dollar. For example, at the relatively high price of $10 per gram (nearly $300 per ounce) the marijuana in a typical 0.4 gram cigarette would cost $4. If two persons sharing such a dose remained intoxicated for two hours each, they would be paying $1 per person-hour for the experience. For marijuana retail prices, see the 1990 NNICC report, p. 30. For the size of a joint, see Peter Reuter, "La Signification Economique des Marches Illegaux aux Etats-Unis: Le Cas de Marijuana," in *Les Economies Non Officielles*, Edith Archambault and Xavier Greffe, eds. (Paris: 1984), 92.

24. *The National Household Survey Population Estimates 1990*, p. 23, reports that 66 million Americans, almost 40 percent of the population, have tried marijuana.

25. Kleiman, *Marijuana*, Table 5.2, pp. 82–85.

26. Richard R. Clayton and Harwin L. Voss, *Young Men and Drugs in Manhattan: A Causal Analysis.*

27. Bureau of Justice Statistics, "Federal Offenses and Offenders: Drug Law Violators, 1980–1986," *Special Report* (Washington, D.C.: Department of Justice, 1988), 4–5; Bureau of Justice Statistics, *Sourcebook of Criminal Justice Statistics—1989* (Washington, D.C.: U.S. Department of Justice, 1990), 500.

28. Federal Bureau of Investigation, *Crime in the United States 1988* (Washington, D.C.: Department of Justice, 1989), 167–168, reports 326,922 marijuana possession arrests for 1988.

29. In Massachusetts, for example, where marijuana has not been decriminalized, the statutory maximum penalty for first-time possession of less than one gram of marijuana is six months "continued without a finding" (in effect, unsupervised probation). Massachusetts General Laws, Chapter 94C, Section 34.

30. Federal Bureau of Investigation, *Crime in the United States: 1988*, pp. 171–172.

31. Alaska, Maine, Minnesota, Mississippi, Nebraska, Oregon, California, New York, North Carolina, Ohio, and Colorado. See Eric W. Single, "Impact of Marijuana Decriminalization: An Update," *Journal of Public Health Policy* 10 (4 [Winter 1989]).

32. Ibid.

33. This is the general argument of Norman E. Zinberg, *Drug, Set, and Setting: The Basis for Controlled Intoxicant Use* (New Haven: Yale University Press, 1984).

34. No one has done a precise estimate for total national expenditures on marijuana enforcement. At the federal level, the 1986 budget appeared to be around $800 million; see Kleiman, *Marijuana: Costs of Abuse, Costs of Control,* pp. 74–77. The figure has certainly grown considerably since then with the growth of the Federal enforcement effort overall. To this one must add the state and local effort.

35. National Institute on Drug Abuse, *Illicit Drug Use, Smoking, and Drinking by America's High School Students, College Students, and Young Adults, 1975–87* (Washington, D.C.: Department of Health and Human Services, 1988), 153–154.

36. Daniel E. Koshland Jr., "The War? Program? or Experiment? on Drugs," editorial, *Science* 245 (22 September 1989).

37. Sixteen percent of Americans favor the legalization of marijuana use, while 81 percent do not think marijuana use should be made legal. Bureau of Justice Statistics, *Sourcebook of Criminal Justice Statistics—1989,* Table 2.83, pp. 198–199. There might be more support for legalization of marijuana if its advocates avoided the trap of debating the legalization of "drugs," in the abstract, but probably only a little more, at least for now.

38. Programs operated by Straight, Inc., have repeatedly run into trouble with regulators. See Deneen Brown and Dan Beyers, "Straight Answer Elusive: Debate on Tactics Trails Drug Program to Md.," *The Washington Post* (8 August 1991): C1. For a horror story, see Arnold S. Trebach, *The Great Drug War* (New York: Macmillan, 1987), 25–63.

39. My previous volume, *Marijuana: Costs of Abuse, Costs of Control* (New York: Greenwood Press, 1989), treats this set of problems in depth. Specialists in search of a more detailed discussion of these points are invited to join the select company of those who have read it. See in particular Chapters 1, 2, 5 through 9, and 12.

40. U.S. Department of Health and Human Services, Public Health Service, Alcohol, Drug Abuse, and Mental Health Administration, National Institute on Drug Abuse, *Data from the Drug Abuse Warning Network,* Series 1, No. 8, 1988.

41. Ralph Weishheit, "Cash Crop: A Study of Illicit Marijuana Growers," Final Report to the National Institute of Justice (September 1990).

42. See "War by Other Means...," *The Economist* (10 February 1990): 50.

10
COCAINE

1. Frank Gawin, "Cocaine Addiction: Psychology and Neurophysiology," *Science* 251 (500 [29 March 1991]): 1580–1586. M. W. Fischman, "The Behavioral Pharmacology of Cocaine in Humans," in *Cocaine: Pharmacology, Effects, and Treatment of Abuse,* John Grabowski, ed. (Rockville, Md.: National Institute on Drug Abuse, 1984), 72–91.
2. J. H. Jaffe, N. G. Cascella, K. M. Kumor, and M. A. Sherer, "Cocaine-induced Cocaine Craving," *Psychopharmacology* 97 (1989): 59–64; M. W. Fischman, "The Behavioral Pharmacology of Cocaine in Humans."
3. Frank Gawin, "Cocaine Addiction."
4. M. W. Fischman, "The Behavioral Pharmacology of Cocaine in Humans," p. 42.
5. Frank Gawin, "Cocaine Addiction."
6. Ibid.
7. R. B. Resnick and E. Schuyten-Resnick, "Clinical Aspects of Cocaine: Assessment of Cocaine Abuse in Man," in *Cocaine: Chemical, Biological, Clinical, Social, and Treatment Aspects,* S. J. Mule, ed. (Cleveland: CRC, 1976), 219–228. This report, consistent with anecdotal accounts, has been hard to replicate. See Fischman, "The Behavioral Pharmacology of Cocaine in Humans," p. 78.
8. Frank Gawin, "Cocaine Addiction," p. 1581.
9. Frank Gawin and Everett Ellinwood, "Cocaine and Other Stimulants: Actions, Abuse and Treatment," *New England Journal of Medicine* 318 (18 [5 May 1988]): 1173–1183; Frank Gawin and Herbert Kleber, "Cocaine Abuse in a Treatment Population: Patterns and Diagnostic Distinctions," in *Cocaine Use in America: Epidemiologic and Clinical Perspectives,* Nicholas J. Kozel and Edgar H. Adams, eds., National Institute on Drug Abuse Research Monograph 61 (Washington, D.C.: National Institute of Drug Abuse, 1985), 182–193.
10. The National Household Survey reports that 22.7 million people have tried cocaine, and 6.2 million have used it within the past year. NIDA, *National Household Survey on Drug Abuse: 1990* (Rockville, Md.: Department of Health and Human Services), 29.
11. NIDA, *National Household Survey on Drug Abuse: 1990*, p. 29.
12. For the derivation of this estimate of weekly use, see U.S. Senate, Committee on the Judiciary, "Hard-Core Cocaine Addicts: Measuring—and Fighting—the Epidemic," Staff Report, 10 May 1990; and U.S. Senate, Committee on the Judiciary, "Drug Use in America: Is the Epidemic Really Over?" Staff Report, 19 December 1990. This estimate became the center of a political firestorm because it seemed to contradict claims that the war on drugs was at last being won. Both the Director of the Office of National Drug Control Policy (the "Drug Czar") and the Secretary of

Health and Human Services denounced the Senate report as politically motivated. That rather comic-opera controversy left its numerical calculations largely undisturbed, and unfortunately passage of time has left them largely unimproved on as well. See William Rhoads and Douglas McDonald, "What America's Users Spend on Illegal Drugs" (Washington, D.C.: Office of National Drug Control Policy, June 1991). The lack of anything resembling a comprehensive data collection and analysis effort to support drug abuse control programs is a low-level scandal. For an illustration and analysis of the problem, see Peter Reuter, "The (Continuing) Vitality of Mythical Numbers," *The Public Interest*, and its predecessor, Max Singer, "Addict Crime: The Vitality of Mythical Numbers," *The Public Interest* 23 (Spring 1971). See also Mark Kleiman, "Data and Analysis Requirements," in *America's Habit: Drug Abuse, Drug Trafficking, and Organized Crime: Report to the President and the Attorney General,* President's Commission on Organized Crime, 1985. Institute of Medicine, *Treating Drug Problems Vol. 1,* Dean Gerstein and Henrick Harwood, eds. (Washington, D.C.: National Academy of Science Press, 1990), 76–88. A fairly comprehensive but practicable set of reforms is recommended in Peter Reuter and John Haaga, eds., "Improving Data for Federal Drug Policy Decisions," *A RAND Note* (Washington, D.C.: Office of National Drug Control Policy, 1991).

13. NIDA, *National Household Survey on Drug Abuse: 1990.*
14. Office of National Drug Control Policy, *National Drug Control Strategy, 1991* (Washington, D.C.: The White House, 1991), Introduction, "Drugs and Crime in America." See also the reports from the Drug Use Forecasting studies published as "DUF Annual Reports" in the National Institute of Justice *Research in Action* series (Washington, D.C.: Department of Justice).
15. Michael Isikoff, "'Two-Tier' Drug Culture Seen Emerging: Studies Show Cocaine Use Declining Among Middle Class, Concentrating Among Urban Poor," *Washington Post* (3 January 1989): A.3.
16. National Institute of Justice, *1989 DUF Annual Report.*
17. In New York and Washington, male arrestees testing positive for recent cocaine use has dropped noticeably; in New York, from a 1988 average of 74 percent to a second quarter 1990 report of 58 percent, and in Washington, from a 1988 peak near 70 percent to a second quarter 1990 result of 46 percent. Meanwhile, though, cities such as St. Louis (38 percent in 1988 to 48 percent in second quarter 1990) and Houston (49 percent to 62 percent) have been seeing increasing percentages of cocaine-using male arrestees throughout the past two years. (*DUF reports*).
18. Paul Goldstein, "Drugs and Violent Crime," in *Pathways to Criminal Violence,* Neil A. Weiner and Marvin E. Wolfgang, eds. (Beverly Hills, Calif.: Sage Publications, 1989), 16–48.
19. David Hunt, "Drugs and Consensual Crimes: Drug Dealing and Prostitution," and J. M. Chaiken and Marcia Chaiken, "Drugs and Predatory

Crime," both in *Drugs and Crime* Vol. 13, Michael Tonry and James Q. Wilson, eds. (Chicago: The University of Chicago Press, 1990).

20. NIDA, *National Household Survey on Drug Abuse: Population Estimates 1988* (Rockville, Md.: U.S. Dept. of Health and Human Services, 1989). "What America's Users Spend on Illegal Drugs," Office of National Drug Control Policy (Technical Paper, June 1991).

21. NIDA, *Data from the Drug Abuse Warning Network,* Series 1, No. 8 (Rockville, Md.: Department of Health and Human Services, 1988), pt. iv.

22. Total accidental deaths were 114,600 in 1970, 105,700 in 1980, and 93,500 in 1987. Bureau of the Census, *Statistical Abstract of the United States, 1990* (Washington, D.C.: U.S. Department of Commerce, 1990), 79.

23. For alcohol, see National Institute on Alcohol Abuse and Alcoholism, *Sixth Special Report to the U.S. Congress on Alcohol and Health* (Rockville, Md.: Department of Health and Human Services, 1987), Table Y, p. 6. For tobacco, see Office on Smoking and Health, *Reducing the Health Consequences of Smoking: 25 Years of Progress* (Rockville, Md.: Department of Health and Human Services, 1989), 161.

24. NIDA, *Annual Data 1988: Data from the Drug Abuse Warning Network* (DAWN), 30.

25. E. L. Abel, *Fetal Alcohol Syndrome and Fetal Alcohol Effects* (New York: Plenum, 1984).

26. C. B. Ernhart, A. W. Wolf, P. L. Linn, R. J. Sokol, M. J. Kennard, and H. F. Filipovich, "Alcohol Related Birth Defects: Syndromal Anomalies, Intrauterine Growth Retardation, and Neonatal Behavioral Assessment," *Alcoholism: Clinical and Experimental Research* 9 (1985): 447–453. R. E. Little, et al., "Fetal Growth and Moderate Drinking in Early Pregnancy," *American Journal of Epidemiology* 123 (1986): 270–278; A. P. Streissguth, et al., "Attention, Distraction and Reaction Time at Age 7 Years and Prenatal Alcohol Exposure," *Neurobehavioral Toxicology and Teratology* 8 (1986): 717–725.

27. Committee to Study the Prevention of Low Birthweight, *Preventing Low Birthweight* (Washington, D.C.: National Academy Press, 1985); Office on Smoking and Health, *Health Consequences of Smoking for Women: A Report of the Surgeon General* (Washington, D.C.: Department of Health and Human Services, 1980).

28. Persons under 30 accounted for more than half of DAWN emergency room mentions of cocaine. NIDA, *Annual Data, 1988*: Data from the Drug Abuse Warning Network, 36.

29. T. T. Chiu, A. J. Vaughn, and R. P. Carzoli, "Hospital Costs of Cocaine-Exposed Infants," *Journal of the Florida Medical Association* 77 (10): 897–900. James Willwerthy, "Should We Take Away Their Kids?" *Time* (13 May 1991): 62.

30. See Gideon Koren, Heather Shear, Karen Graham, and Tom Einarson, "Bias Against the Null Hypothesis: The Reproductive Hazards of Cocaine," *The Lancet*, 2 (8677 [16 December 1989]): 1440–1442. If, as appears to be the case, cocaine use early in pregnancy does most of the damage, studies focused on use immediately before birth (the easiest characteristic to measure and the ones used in most of the current studies) will miss most of what is going on. Barry Zuckerman, et al., "Effects of Maternal Marijuana and Cocaine Use on Fetal Growth," *New England Journal of Medicine* 320 (12 [1989]): 762–769.

31. Anastasia Toufexis, "Innocent Victims," *Time* (13 May 1991). Peter Kerr, "Babies of Crack Users Fill Hospital Nurseries," *New York Times* (25 August 1986): B.1.

32. Paul Goldstein, "Drugs and Violent Crime."

33. Peter Reuter, Robert MacCoun, and Patrick Murphy, *Money from Crime: A Study of the Economics of Drug Dealing in Washington, D.C.* (Santa Monica, Calif.: RAND Corporation, June 1990).

34. For an account of cocaine's earlier popularity see David Musto "America's First Cocaine Epidemic," *The Wilson Quarterly* 13 (3 [Summer 1989]).

35. Lester Grinspoon and James Bakalar, *Cocaine: A Drug and Its Social Evolution* (New York: Basic Books, 1985).

36. Craig Van Dyke and Robert Byck, "Cocaine," *Scientific American* (March 1982): 128; Jerome Jaffe, "Drug Addiction and Drug Abuse," in *Pharmacological Basis of Therapeutics*, Alfred Goodman Gilman, Louis Goodman, and Alfred Goodman, eds. (New York: Macmillan, 1980); L. Rivier and J. G. Bruhn, eds., *Coca and Cocaine—1981: A Special Issue, Journal of Ethnopharmacology* 3 (2, 3 [March/ May 1981]).

37. Grinspoon and Bakalar, *Cocaine*.

38. *DAWN, Annual Data,* 1988 Series 1, Number 8, p. 53.

39. M. W. Fischman, "The Behavioral Pharmacology of Cocaine in Humans," p. 74.

40. Ibid.

41. National Narcotics Intelligence Consumers Committee, *Narcotics Intelligence Estimate: The Supply of Drugs to the U.S. Illicit Market from Foreign and Domestic Sources in 1980* (Washington, D.C.: Drug Enforcement Administration, 1981), 49. (This series later changed its title to *The NNICC Report.*)

42. Terry M. Williams, *The Cocaine Kids: Inside Story of a Teenage Drug Ring* (Reading, Mass.: Addison-Wesley Publications, 1989), 56.

43. Gina Kolata, "Selling Crack: The Myth of Wealth," *New York Times* (26 November 1989).

44. See T. Williams, *The Cocaine Kids*, pp. 124–125; one of the dealers described, in the Washington Heights section of Manhattan, quits the cocaine trade to go back to college.

45. Peter Reuter, et al., *Money from Crime: A Study of the Economics of Drug Dealing in Washington, D.C.* (Santa Monica, Calif.: RAND Corporation, 1990).

46. Peter Reuter, et al., *Money from Crime*, pp. 62–66.

47. Peter Reuter, et al., *Money from Crime*, pp. 76–77.

48. Isabel Wilkerson, "Detroit Crack Empire Showed All Earmarks of Big Business," *New York Times* (18 December 1988). Williams, *The Cocaine Kids*, pp. 47–48, describes a selling group that allowed its members to snort cocaine but not to smoke it.

49. Isabel Wilkerson, "'Crack House' Fire: Justice or Vigilantism?" *New York Times* (22 October 1988): A1.

50. In 1980 there were 22,655 arrests for heroin and cocaine combined, in 1989, 260,085. In that period heroin arrests grew only slightly. Federal Bureau of Investigation, *Crime in the United States, 1980, 1989* (Washington, D.C.: Dept. of Justice, GPO, 1980), 189–191 and *1990*, 171–172. (These are the Uniform Crime Reports.)

51. For a description of the social impact of cocaine dealing in one poor neighborhood, see William Finnegan, "A Reporter at Large: Out There," *The New Yorker* (10 September 1990).

52. See Ronald K. Siegel, "Cocaine Smoking," *Journal of Psychoactive Drugs* 14 (4 [1982]): 277–359. Patricia G. Erickson and Bruce K. Alexander, "Cocaine and Addictive Liability," *Social Pharmacology* 3 (3 [1989]): 249–270.

53. Michael Isikoff, "'Two-Tier' Drug Culture Seen Emerging," *The Washington Post* (3 January 1989): A3. The drop in middle-class use is reflected in NIDA, *1990 National Household Survey*, p. 29.

54. U.S. Senate, Committee on the Judiciary, "Hard-Core Cocaine Addicts: Measuring—and Fighting—the Epidemic," Staff Report, 10 May 1990.

55. David Musto, "Lessons of the First Cocaine Epidemic," *Wall Street Journal* (11 June 1986).

56. 21 U.S.C. Section 812(c). According to the Controlled Substances Act, a Schedule II drug is one that "has a high potential for abuse," has a "currently accepted medical use in treatment or with severe restrictions," and whose "abuse may lead to severe psychological or physical dependence." 21 U.S.C. Section 812 (b).

57. This assumes about two million heavy users out of about eight million total users, both considerably higher than the estimates from the National Household Survey. (See *1991 National Drug Control Strategy*, p. 11, and the Judiciary Committee report on "Hard-Core Cocaine Addicts.")

58. Ethan Nadelmann made the suggestion of legalizing cocaine sales only where they are already rampant in a forum at the Harvard School of Public Health in March 1989.

59. Lloyd D. Johnston, Patrick M. O'Malley and Jerald G. Bachman, *Monitoring the Future, 1990* (Ann Arbor, Mich.: Institute for Social Research, 1991), Tables 12 and 13 (preliminary data).

60. U.S. Senate, Committee on the Judiciary, "Hard-Core Cocaine Addicts."

61. See Jerome Beck, Marsha Rosenbaum, Deborah Harlow, Douglas McDonnell, Pat Morgan, and Lynn Watson, "Exploring Ecstasy: A Description

of MDMA Users" (Rockville, MD: National Institute on Drug Abuse, 1989); Jerome Beck, *MDMA Controversy: Contexts of Use and Social Control* (Ph.D. dissertation, University of California, Berkeley, 1990).

62. Jerome Beck, *MDMA Controversy: Contexts of Use and Social Control.*

63. Deborah Harlow's still unpublished reports on interviews with therapists who have employed MDMA in this way are intriguing. Concerns about the reported neurotoxic effects of MDMA on laboratory animals have, to date, prevented clinical research.

64. Institute of Medicine, *Treating Drug Problems: Vol. 1* (Washington, D.C.: National Academy of Sciences Press, 1990), 175; Frank Gawin, et al., "Desipramine Facilitation Decanoate: A Preliminary Report," *Archives of General Psychiatry* 46 (1989): 322–325; F. S. Tennant and A. A. Sagherian, "Double-blind Comparison of Amantadine and Bromocriptine for Ambulatory Withdrawal from Cocaine Dependence," *Archives of Internal Medicine* 147 (1987): 109–112; C. Dackis, et al., "Single Dose Bromocriptine Reverses Cocaine Craving," *Psychiatry Research* 20 (1987): 261–264.

65. Gerry V. Stimson, "The Social and Historical Context of Drug Policy in the United Kingdom," presented at "American and European Drug Policies: Comparative Perspectives," RAND Conference, 6–7 May 1991, Washington, D.C.

66. See Office of National Drug Control Policy, *National Drug Control Strategy, 1991.*

67. Jonathan Cave and Peter Reuter, *The Interdictors' Lot: A Dynamic Model of the Market for Drug Smuggling Services* (Santa Monica, Calif.: The RAND Corporation, 1988); Peter Reuter, Gordon Crawford, and Jonathan Cave, *Sealing the Borders: The Effects of Increased Military Participation in Drug Interdiction* (Santa Monica, Calif.: RAND Corporation, 1988), Ch. 6, 7.

68. Douglas Farah, "With Ties Strained, Colombians Warn U.S. of Threat to Anti-Drug Efforts," *Washington Post* (27 June 1991): A30.

69. See the calculations in Peter Reuter and Mark Kleiman, "Risks and Prices: An Economic Analysis of Drug Enforcement," in *Crime and Justice: An Annual Review of Research* Vol. 7, Norval Morris and Michael Tonry, eds., (Chicago: University of Chicago Press, 1986), and in Chapter 6 of this volume.

11
TOBACCO

1. Jack E. Henningfield and R. Neweth-Coslett, "Nicotine Dependence: Interface Between Tobacco and Tobacco-Related Disease," *Chest* 93 (February 1988 Supplement): 37S–55S.

2. Katherine R. Parkes, "Relative Weight, Smoking and Mental Health as Predictors of Sickness and Absence from Work," *Journal of Applied*

Psychology, 72 (2 [May 1987]); Robert L. Bertera, "The Effects of Workplace Health Promotion on Absenteeism and Employment Costs in a Large Industrial Population," *The American Journal of Public Health* 80 (9 [September 1990]).

3. For the higher estimates, see Stanton Glantz, "Passive Smoking and Heart Disease: Epidemiology, Physiology and Biochemistry," *Circulation* 83 (1 [January 1991]). Smoking-attributable deaths are now estimated at 434,000 per year. *Mortality and Morbidity Weekly Report* 40 (4 [1 February 1991]). The lower estimate is reported in *The Health Consequences of Involuntary Smoking: A Report of the Surgeon General* (Washington, D.C.: Department of Health and Human Services, 1986).

4. For a variety of analyses of the unjustly neglected problem of indoor air pollution, see the "Workshop on Indoor Air Quality" published in *Risk Analysis: An International Journal* 10 (15 [March 1990]).

5. F. A. Stillman, et al., "End Smoking at the Johns Hopkins Institutions: An Evaluation of Smoking Prevalence and Indoor Air Pollution," *JAMA* 264 (12 [September 1990]): 1564–1569. The authors found that in 1989, 5 percent of MDs and 17 percent of RNs at Johns Hopkins smoked. In an earlier study R. Brackbill, T. Frazier, and S. Shilling, "Smoking Characteristics of U.S. Workers, 1978–90," *American Journal of Industrial Medicine* 13 (1 [1988]): 43–58, found that in 1978 17 percent of MDs and 30 percent of RNs smoked.

6. Jerald Bachman, et al., "Racial/Ethnic Differences in Smoking, Drinking, and Illicit Drug Use Among American High School Seniors, 1976–1989," *American Journal of Public Health* 81 (3 [March 1991]): 372–378. See also, Luis G. Escobedo, Robert F. Anda, Perry F. Smith, Patrick L. Remington, and Eric E. Mast, "Sociodemographic Characteristics of Cigarette Smoking Initiation in the United States," *Journal of the American Medical Association* 264 (12 [26 September 1990]): 1550–1555.

7. Alyson Pytte, "Tobacco's Clout Stays Strong Through Dollars, Jobs, Ads," and "Will Marlboro Man Go Tombstone?" *Congressional Quarterly Weekly Reports* 48 (20 [19 May 1990]).

8. Robert E. Goodin, *No Smoking* (Chicago and London: University of Chicago Press, 1989).

9. Stephen K. Hall, "Pulmonary Health Risk: Abnormalities in Workers Handling Asbestos Products," *Journal of Environmental Health* 52 (3 [November–December 1989]): 165–168.

10. Committee to Study the Prevention of Low Birthweight, *Preventing Low Birthweight* (Washington, D.C.: National Academy Press, 1985); Office on Smoking and Health, "Health Consequences of Smoking for Women: A Report of the Surgeon General" (Washington, D.C.: Public Health Service, Department of Health and Human Services, 1980).

11. Lois A. Fingerhut, Joel C. Kleinman, and Juliette S. Kendride, "Smoking Before, During and After Pregnancy," *The American Journal of Public Health* 80 (5 [May 1990]): 541–545.

12. Office on Smoking and Health, *The Health Consequences of Involuntary Smoking: A Report of the Surgeon General* (Washington, D.C.: Department of Health and Human Services, 1986), 38–59.

13. Statistics on the proportion of residential and nonresidential fires are generated by the National Fire Protection Association survey and the U.S. Fire Administration's National Fire Incident Reporting system. Other figures from Alison Miller, "U.S. Smoking Material Fire Problem Through 1988," unpublished manuscript (Quincy, Mass.: National Fire Protection Association, 1990).

14. Smith Kline Laboratories quotes urine cotinine tests at about $100 each.

15. Office on Smoking and Health, *Reducing the Health Consequences of Smoking: 25 Years of Progress. A Report of the Surgeon General* (Washington, D.C.: Department of Health and Human Services, 1989), 141–152.

16. Parkes, "Relative Weight, Smoking, and Mental Health as Predictors of Sickness and Absence from Work"; Bertera, "The Effects of Workplace Health Promotion on Absenteeism and Employment Costs in a Large Industrial Population."

17. Willard G. Manning, Emmett B. Keeler, Joseph P. Newhouse, Elizabeth M. Sloss, and Jeffrey Wasserman, "The Taxes of Sin: Do Smokers and Drinkers Pay Their Way?" *Journal of the American Medical Association* 261 (11 [17 March 1989]): 1604–1609. Note that this calculation is very sensitive to assumptions about mortality from passive smoking.

18. See, for example, C. S. Crow, "Smoking Areas on School Grounds: Are We Encouraging Teenagers to Smoke?" *Journal of Adolescent Health Care* 5 (1984): 117–119.

19. Office on Smoking and Health, *Reducing the Health Consequences of Smoking,* pt. iv.

20. Ovid F. Pomerleau and Cynthia S. Pomerleau, "Neuroregulators and the Reinforcement of Smoking: Towards a Biobehavioral Explanation," *Neuroscience and Biobehavioral Review* 8 (4 [1984]): 503–513. Some researchers also believe that smokers may be self-medicating depression. See Richard Glass, "Blue Mood, Blackened Lungs: Depression and Smoking," *Journal of the American Medical Association* 264 (12 [26 September 1990]): 1583–1584.

21. Office on Smoking and Health, *Reducing the Health Consequences of Smoking,* pp. 141–152.

22. Ibid., pp. 33–116.

23. Ibid., p. vi.

24. Ibid., p. 285.

25. George Gallup, Jr. and Frank Newport, "Many Americans Favor Restrictions on Smoking in Public Places," *The Gallup Poll Monthly* (July 1990): 19–27.

26. Office on Smoking and Health, *Reducing the Health Consequences of Smoking,* p. 285.

27. Ninety percent of smokers began smoking before the age of 20. See Office on Smoking and Health, *Reducing the Health Consequences of Smoking,* p. 299. Kandel and Logan found that almost all first use of cigarettes took place before age 19. Denise B. Kandel and J. A. Logan, "Patterns of Drug Use From Adolescence to Young Adulthood: Periods of Risk for Initiation, Continued Use and Discontinuation," *American Journal of Public Health* 74 (7 [1984]): 660–666.

28. See the analysis in Robert E. Goodin, *No Smoking* (Chicago and London: University of Chicago Press, 1989). For the problem of apparent conflicts of interest within a single personality, see Thomas C. Schelling, "The Intimate Contest for Self-Command," in *Choice and Consequence,* Thomas Schelling, ed. (Cambridge, Mass.: Harvard University Press, 1984).

29. Lloyd D. Johnston, Patrick M. O'Malley, and Jerald G. Bachman, *National Trends in Drug Use and Related Factors Among American High School Students and Young Adults, 1975–1986,* (Washington, D.C.: Department of Health and Human Services, National Institute on Drug Abuse, 1987), 252–254.

30. Office on Smoking and Health, *Reducing the Health Consequences of Smoking,* p. 50.

31. 15 U.S.C. Section 2052(a)(1)(B).

32. *Action on Smoking and Health v. Harris,* 655 F.2d 236 (D.C. Cir. 1980) (rejecting anti-smoking group's challenge to FDA's determination not to assert jurisdiction over cigarettes); *United States v. 354 Cartons *** Trim Reducing-Aid Cigarettes,* 178 F. Supp. 847 (D.N.J. 1959) (FDA enforcement action against cigarette manufacturer claiming weight-loss benefits for cigarette smokers); *United States v. 46 Cartons *** Fairfax Cigarettes,* 133 F. Supp. 43 (D.N.J. 1957) (FDA seizure of cigarettes whose manufacturer claimed they prevented respiratory disease).

33. L. T. Kozlowski, *Tar and Nicotine Ratings May be Hazardous to Your Health: Information for Smokers Who Are Not Yet Ready to Stop* (Toronto: Alcoholism and Drug Addiction Research Foundation, 1982). L. T. Kozlowski, R. C. Frecker, and M. A. Pope, "The Misuse of 'Less Hazardous' Cigarettes and its Detection: Hole Blocking of Ventilated Filters," *American Journal of Public Health* 79 (1982): 1202–1203.

34. Betsy Moms and Peter Waldman, "The Death of Premier," *Wall Street Journal* (10 March 1989); Malcolm Gladwell, "Smokeless Cigarette Sales Halted: Testing of Markets Yields Weak Response," *Washington Post* (1 March 1989).

35. "Smoking," in *The Gallup Report: Political, Social and Economic Trends,* Report No. 286 (July 1989); "Smokers Who Successfully Quit," Washington Health Section, *Washington Post* (19 February 1991): WH5. Office on Smoking and Health, *Reducing the Health Consequences of Smoking: 25 Years of Progress, A Report of the Surgeon General* (Prepublication version, 11 January 1989), 269, 286.

36. Gideon Doron, *The Smoking Paradox: Regulation in the Cigarette Industry* (Cambridge, Mass.: Abt Books, 1979).

37. Thomas C. Schelling, "Whose Business is Good Behavior?" in *American Society: Public and Private Responsibilities*, Winthrop Knowlton and Richard Zeckhauser, eds. (Cambridge, Mass.: Ballanger Publishing, 1986), 169–170.

38. Office on Smoking and Health, *Reducing the Health Consequences of Smoking*, pp. 269, 286.

39. Ibid., pp. 304–311.

40. Lloyd D. Johnston, Patrick M. O'Malley, and Jerald G. Bachman, *Monitoring the Future: 16th Annual Survey of American High School Seniors* (Ann Arbor, Mich.: Institute for Social Research, 1991), Table 4.

41. Congressional Budget Office, *Federal Taxation of Tobacco, Alcoholic Beverages and Motor Fuels* (Washington, D.C.: GPO, 1990), Table 2, p. 28.

42. Victor R. Fuchs, *The Health Economy* (Cambridge, Mass: Harvard University Press, 1986), 243–257.

43. Paul D. Cleary, Jan L. Hitchcock, Norbert Semmer, Laura J. Flinchbaugh, and John M. Pinney, "Adolescent Smoking: Research and Health Policy," *The Milbank Quarterly* 66 (1 [1988]): 137–171.

44. For an excellent and highly readable account of these arguments see Kenneth E. Warner, *Selling Smoke: Cigarette Advertising and Public Health* (Washington, D.C.: American Public Health Association, 1986).

45. See note 27 above.

46. Bruce Ames, Renae Mogaw, and Lois Swirsky Gold, "Ranking Possible Carcinogenic Hazards," *Science* 286 (17 April 1987): 271–280.

47. Kenneth E. Warner, "Smoking and Health Implications of a Change in the Federal Cigarette Excise Tax," *Journal of the American Medical Association* 255 (8 [1986]): 1028.

48. J. D. Forster, K. Kunt-Inge, and R. W. Jeffrey, "Sources of Cigarettes for Tenth Graders in Two Minnesota Cities," *Health Education Research* 4 (1989): 45–50.

49. Joseph DiFranza, et al., "Legislative Efforts to Protect Children from Tobacco," *Journal of the American Medical Association* 257 (24 [24 June 1987]): 3387–3389.

50. "State Panel Seeks Ban on Cigarette Machines," *New York Times* (26 September 1990): B4 (L), and "Steps, and A Misstep, Against Smoking," *New York Times* (22 October 1990): A18.

51. Michael Fiore, Thomas Novatny, John Pierce, Gary Giovino, Evridiki Hatziandreu, Polly Newcomb, Tanya Surawicz, and Ronald Davis, "Methods Used to Quit Smoking in the United States," *Journal of the American Medical Association* 263 (20 [23/30 May 1990]): 2760–2765. See also Stanley Schachter, "Nicotine Regulation in Heavy and Light Smokers," *Journal of Experimental Psychology: General* 106 (1977): 5–12; Sheldon Cohen, et al., "Debunking Myths About Self-Quitting," *The American Psychologist*

44 (11): 1355–1365; and Stanley Schachter, "A Reply to Cohen, et al.," *The American Psychologist* 45 (12 [December 1990]): 1389.

52. The lead case in this area is *Cipollone v. Liggett Group,* 693 F. Supp. 208 (D.N.J. 1988), *aff'd in part, rev'd in part,* 893 F. 2d 541 (3d Cir. 1989), *cert. granted,* 111 S. Ct. 1386 (1991). For commentary see "After Cipollone: How Wide Will the Floodgate Open?" (case note by Douglas N. Jacobson), 38 Am. U.L. Rev. 1021–1059 (Spring 1989); "The Effect of Cipollone: Has the Tobacco Industry Lost its Shield?" (case note by Michael J. Hannon III), 23 Georgia L. Rev. 783–786 (Spring 1989).

53. "More Cigarette Exports Seen: High Asian Demand Forecast," *New York Times* (31 March 1988): D5, and "Cigarette Export Boom," *New York Times* (22 June 1988): 52.

54. Alyson Pytte, "Tobacco's Clout Stays Strong Through Dollars, Jobs, Ads," *Congressional Quarterly Weekly Reports* 48 (20 [19 May 1990]); Helen White, "Thailand, Bowing to Foreign Pressure, Will End its Ban on Cigarette Imports," *Wall Street Journal* (12 October 1990); Clyde Farnsworth, "U.S. Policy on Tobacco Export is Criticized," *New York Times* (20 July 1989); Colman McCarthy, "Exporters of Cancer: U.S. Tobacco Companies Force Far East Governments to Accept American Cigarettes" *Washington Post* (1 July 1989).

55. Willard G. Manning, Emmett B. Keeler, Joseph P. Newhouse, Elizabeth M. Sloss, and Jeffrey Wasserman, "The Taxes of Sin: Do Smokers and Drinkers Pay Their Way?" *Journal of the American Medical Association* 261 (11 [17 March 1989]): 1604–1609.

56. George Stigler and Gary Becker, "De Gustibus non est Disputandum," *American Economic Review* 67 (March 1977): 76–90.

57. "The Profits in Bootleg Cigarettes," *Business Week* (7 April 1975): 69.

58. Mary Williams Walsh, "Smoke Schemes: Some Would Rather Risk Arrest Than Pay Canada's Super Tax on Cigarettes; They Smuggle in Cheaper U.S. Tobacco in Kayaks, Frozen Turkeys, Car Seats . . . ," *Los Angeles Times* (9 September 1991): 1.

59. See the classic paper by Mark Moore, "Policies to Achieve Discrimination on the Effective Price of Heroin," *American Economic Review* 63 (2 [May 1973]).

60. U.S. Bureau of the Census, *Statistical Abstract of the United States: 1989* (Washington, D.C.: GPO, 1989), 268.

12
HEROIN

1. Much of this chapter is a reworking and compression of material in John Kaplan, *The Hardest Drug: Heroin and Public Policy* (Chicago: University of Chicago Press, 1983), which remains "must" reading.

2. James Q. Wilson cites the instance of heroin as a case in point against the legalization of cocaine. See James Q. Wilson, "Against the Legalization of Drugs," *Commentary* 89 (2 [February 1990]): 21–29.

3. The strategy of examining drug policy by starting with the counterfactual world of free availability I owe to Mark H. Moore. See Mark H. Moore, "An Analytic View of Drug Control Policies," Working Paper 90-01-19 (Cambridge, Mass.: Program in Criminal Justice, Kennedy School of Government, Harvard University, 1990).

4. See Kaplan, *The Hardest Drug: Heroin and Public Policy*, Chapter 3, "Free Availability."

5. F. L. Iber, *Alcohol and Drug Abuse as Encountered in Office Practice* (Boca Raton, Fla.: CRC, 1991): 137–138.

6. C. Winick, "The Life Cycle of the Narcotic Addict and of Addiction," *Bulletin of Narcotics* 26 (1 [1964]). C. P. O'Brien, G. E. Woody, and A. T. McLellan, "Long-term Consequences of Opiate Dependence," *New England Journal of Medicine* 304 (1981): 1098.

7. For illustrations of the potential problems, see General Accounting Office, "Drug Abuse: Research on Treatment May Not Address Current Needs," Report to the Chairman, Select Committee on Narcotics Abuse and Control, House of Representatives (September 1990).

8. For the last point I am indebted to psychiatrist Robert Millman of the Cornell University/New York Hospital Medical Center.

9. L. Zimmer, "Operation Pressure Point: The Disruption of Street-Level Drug Trade on New York's Lower East Side," Occasional paper (New York: New York University School of Law, Center for Research in Crime and Justice, 1987).

10. See Mark A. R. Kleiman, "Crackdowns: The Effects of Intensive Enforcement on Retail Heroin Dealing, in *Street Level Drug Enforcement: Examining the Issues*, Marcia R. Chaiken, ed. (Washington, D.C.: National Institute of Justice, 1988).

11. The classic study here is Bruce D. Johnson, Paul Goldstein, Edward Preble, et al., *Taking Care of Business: The Economics of Crime by Heroin Abusers* (Lexington, Mass.: Lexington Books, 1985).

12. Jan M. Chaiken and Marcia R. Chaiken, *Varieties of Criminal Behavior* (Santa Monica, Calif.: RAND Corporation, 1982). Even more startling estimates are reported from a sample of heroin addicts known to the Baltimore police. John C. Ball, David N. Nurco, E. G. Friedman, and L. Rosen, "Criminality of Heroin Addicts: When Addicted and When Off Opiates," in *The Drugs-Crime Connection*, J. A. Inciardi, ed. (Beverly Hills, Calif.: Sage, 1981).

13. "Arrestee Drug Use," *Drug Use Forecasting, Research in Action Series* (Washington, D.C.: National Institute of Justice, January–March 1990).

14. Ibid.

15. See Jan M. Chaiken and Marcia R. Chaiken, "Drugs and Predatory Crime," in *Drugs and Crime*, Michael Tonry and James Q. Wilson, eds. (Chicago: University of Chicago Press, 1990).

16. M. Douglas Anglin and George Speckart, "Narcotics Use, Property Crime, and Dealing: Structural Dynamics Across the Addiction Career," *Journal of Quantitative Criminology* 2 (4 [1986]); John C. Ball, et al., "Criminality of Heroin Addicts When Addicted and When Off Opiates," Prepared for National Institute on Drug Abuse (9 October 1980); James A. Inciardi, "Heroin Use and Street Crime," *Crime and Delinquency* 25 (3 [July 1979]): 335–346; Robert Gandossy, et al., *Drug Use: A Survey and Analysis of the Literature* (Washington, D.C.: National Institute of Justice, 1980), 82–87; Bruce Johnson, Paul Goldstein, Edward Preble, et al., *Taking Care of Business: The Economics of Crime by Heroin Abusers* (Lexington, Mass.: Lexington Books, 1985).

17. General Accounting Office, "Methadone Maintenance: Some Treatment Programs Are Not Effective; Greater Federal Oversight Needed" (Report to the Chairman, Select Committee on Narcotics Abuse and Control, March 1990); Dana Hunt, Barry Spunt, et al., "The Costly Bonus: Cocaine-Related Crime Among Methadone Treatment Clients," *Advances in Alcohol and Substance Abuse* 6 (2 [1987]).

18. J. Jackson and L. Rotkiewicz, "A Coupon Program: AIDS Education and Drug Treatment," Paper presented at the Third International Conference on AIDS, Washington, D.C., June 1987.

19. M. Douglas Anglin, "A Social Policy Analysis of Compulsory Treatment for Opiate Dependence," *Journal of Drug Issues* 18 (4 [Fall 1988]).

20. Harry K. Wexler, Douglas S. Lipton, and K. Forester, "Outcome Evaluation of a Prison Therapeutic Community for Substance Abuse Treatment," *Criminal Justice Behavior* 17 (1 [March 1990]): 71–92.

21. Mark A. R. Kleiman, Denise Kulawik, and Sarah Chayes, "Program Evaluation: Santa Cruz Regional Street Drug Reduction Program" (Cambridge, Mass.: BOTEC Analysis Corporation, 1990).

22. Institute of Medicine, *Treating Drug Problems: Vol. I*, Dean Gerstein and Henrick Harwood, eds. (Washington, D.C.: National Academy Press, 1990), 189.

23. Harry Wexler, Douglas Lipton, and Bruce Johnson, "A Criminal Justice System Strategy for Treating Cocaine–Heroin Abusing Offenders in Custody," *Issues and Practices in Criminal Justice* (Washington, D.C.: National Institute of Justice, March 1988).

24. Metwest Labs, Tarzana, California, personal communication.

25. Mark A. R. Kleiman and David P. Cavanagh, "A Cost Benefit Analysis of Prison Cell Construction and Alternative Sanctions," Report prepared for the National Institute of Justice (Cambridge, Mass.: BOTEC Analysis Corporation, 1990); Chaiken and Chaiken, *Varieties of Criminal Behavior*.

26. For some slight evidence of this effect, see George F. Brown and Lester P. Silverman, "Retail Price of Heroin: Estimation and Applications," *Journal of the American Statistical Association* 69 (347 [September 1974]): 595–606.

27. Mark A. R. Kleiman and Kerry D. Smith, "State and Local Drug Enforcement: In Search of a Strategy." Arnold Barnett, "Drug Crackdowns

and Crime Rates: A Comment on the Kleiman Report," in *Street Level Drug Enforcement: Examining the Issues*, Marcia R. Chaiken, ed. (Washington, D.C.: National Institute of Justice, 1988), points out that crime rates in Lynn returned to previous levels after three years. This appears to have resulted from the dispersion of the task force and the rise of a crack market in Lynn. Still, three years of substantial crime reductions in a city of 81,000 seems a more than adequate return on the investment of six officers for eighteen months.

28. Charles F. Turner, Heather G. Miller, and Lincoln E. Moses, *AIDS: Sexual Behavior and Intravenous Drug Use* (Washington, D.C.: National Academy Press, 1989); 16.

29. Ibid.

30. Ibid., Table 3-3: 227; Table 3-6: 238. See R. Friedman and D. C. Des Jarlais, "HIV Among Drug Injectors: The Epidemic and the Response," *AIDS Care* 3 (3 [forthcoming]).

31. Turner, Miller, and Moses, *AIDS: Sexual Behavior and Intravenous Drug Use*, pp. 203, 209.

32. This is the opinion of Don Des Jarlais.

33. For a slightly mathematical treatment, see Mark A. R. Kleiman, "AIDS, Vice, and Public Policy," Working Paper 87-04-02 (Cambridge, Mass.: Program in Criminal Justice Policy and Management, Kennedy School of Government, Harvard University, 1987).

34. Lee Robins, John Helzer, and Darlee Davis, "Narcotic Use in Southeast Asia: An Interview Study of 898 Vietnam Returnees," *Archives of General Psychiatry* 32 (8 [August 1975]): 955–961.

35. Theodore Hammett, "AIDS in Correctional Facilities: Issues and Options, Third Edition" (Washington, D.C.: National Institute of Justice, 1988), especially Appendix D; Theodore Hammett, Dana Hunt, and Saira Moini, "U.S. Criminal Justice and Correctional Agencies Response to AIDS: Perceived Roles and New Opportunities," Sixth International Conference on AIDS, San Francisco, June 1990; Saira Moini and Theodore Hammett, "1989 Update: AIDS in Correctional Facilities," *Issues and Practices* (Washington, D.C.: National Institute of Justice, May 1990).

36. This argument is made in detail in Mark A. R. Kleiman and Richard A. Mockler, "AIDS and Heroin: Strategies for Control" (Washington, D.C.: Urban Institute, 1988).

37. California, Connecticut, Delaware, Illinois, Maine, Massachusetts, New Hampshire, New Jersey, New York, Pennsylvania, Rhode Island, and the District of Columbia. *1987–1988 Survey of Pharmacy Law* (Chicago, Ill.: National Association of Boards of Pharmacy, 1987).

38. Kerry Murphy Healey, "State and Local Experience With Drug Paraphernalia Laws," *Issues and Practices* (Washington, D.C.: National Institute of Justice, February 1988).

39. Having proposed a repeal of the ban on injection equipment very early in the heroin-related HIV epidemic, I succeeded in talking myself out

of the idea on the grounds that more works would mean more injection, particularly injection with drugs other than heroin. In principle, the result might have been more rather than less HIV infection if some people had started to inject because needles were available and then become less careless about needle hygiene with the progress of addiction. But as increased demand has created additional supplies of black-market "works" over the past several years, there has been no outbreak of, for example, diazepam (Valium) injection.

40. William Booth, "Sullivan Opposes Needle Exchange Programs," *Washington Post* (20 July 1989): A3.

41. Michael Mamott, "New York's Blacks and Hispanics Angered by Needle Exchange Program," *New York Times* (7 November 1988); Todd Pardum, "Dinkins Decides to Cancel Needle-Exchange Program," *New York Times* (14 February 1990).

42. Gerry Stimpson, et al., "Preventing the Spread of HIV in Injecting Drug Users—The Experience of Syringe-Exchange Schemes in England and Scotland," in *Problems of Drug Dependence—1988*, NIDA Research Monograph 90 (Rockville, Md.: National Institute on Drug Abuse, 1988), 302–311; J. A. R. Van der Hoek, H. J. A. van Haastrecht, and R. A. Coutinho, "Risk Reduction Among Intravenous Drug Users in Amsterdam Under the Influence of AIDS," *American Journal of Public Health* 79 (10 [1989]): 355–357; Dr. Harold Ginzburg, "Needle Exchange Programs: A Medical or a Policy Dilemma?" *American Journal of Public Health* 79 (10 [1989]).

43. N. S. Padian, S. L. Chiboski, and N. P. Jewell, "Female-to-Male Transmission of Human Immunodeficiency Virus," *Journal of the American Medical Association* 266 (12 [25 September 1991]): 1664–1667. Peter Piot, et al., "Heterosexual Transmission of HIV," in *The Heterosexual Transmission of AIDS in Africa*, Dieter Koch-Weser and Hannelore Vanderschmidt, eds. (Cambridge, Mass.: Abt Books, 1988): 106–110.

44. Donald Des Jarlais and Saul Friedman, "HIV Infection Among Intravenous Drug Users: Epidemiology and Risk Reduction," *AIDS: International Bimonthly Journal* 1 (1987): 67–76; Theodore Hammett, et al., "Stemming the Spread of HIV Infection Among IV Drug Users, Their Sexual Partners, and Children: Issues and Opportunities for Criminal Justice Agencies," *Crime and Delinquency* 37 (1 [January 1991]): 101–124.

45. Drug Enforcement Administration, "A Special Report on "Ice" (D-Methamphetamine Hydrochloride)", in *Proceedings of the Community Epidemiology Work Group* (Washington, D.C: Department of Health and Human Services, 1989); Michael Saiger, "The Ice Age," *Rolling Stone* (8 February 1990): 55; National Institute on Drug Abuse, *Trends and Patterns of Methamphetamine Abuse in the U.S.* (Rockville, Md: Department of Health and Human Services, 1988); "The Fire of 'Ice'," *Newsweek* (27 November 1989): 37. The etymology of the term *ice* is unknown; it may be a shortening of *isomer*.

46. For a fascinating account of that era, see Jay Stephens, *Storming Heaven: LSD and the American Dream* (New York: Atlantic Monthly Press, 1987).

On MDMA, see Jerome Beck, Marsha Rosenbaum, Deborah Harlow, Douglas McDonnell, Pat Morgan, and Lynn Watson, "Exploring Ecstasy: A Description of MDMA Users" (Final Report, National Institute on Drug Abuse, 1989); Jerome Beck, "MDMA Controversy: Contexts of Use and Social Control," (Ph.D. dissertation, Berkeley: University of California, 1990); and P. J. O'Rourke, "Tune In, Turn On, Get to Work Late on Monday," *Rolling Stone* (December 1985), 463–464. For anecdotal evidence of rising LSD use, see Laura Blumenfeld, "The Acid Kids," *Washington Post* (18 August 1991): F1, F4. Lloyd D. Johnston, Patrick O'Malley, and Jerald G. Bachman, "Monitoring the Future: A Continuing Study of the Lifestyles and Values of Youth" (Ann Arbor, Mich.: Institute of Social Research 1991): 3.

47. David Musto, "Lessons of the First Cocaine Epidemic," *Wall Street Journal* (11 June 1986).

48. Arthur Y. Webb, Paul C. Puccio, and Ronald S. Simeone, "Current Drug Use Trends in New York City" (New York: New York State Division of Substance Abuse Services, 1991), 5–8.

13
AGAINST EXCESS: DRUG POLICY IN MODERATION

1. George Orwell makes a powerful argument about the political inadequacy of instrumental reasoning in "Wells, Hitler, and the World State," 1941, in *Collected Essays* (London: Secker and Warburg, 1961): 160–167.

Subject Index

Name Index